THE
COLLEGE
PRESS
NIV
COMMENTARY

GENESIS
VOLUME 2

THE COLLEGE PRESS NIV COMMENTARY

GENESIS
VOLUME 2

PAUL KISSLING

Old Testament Series Co-Editors:

Terry Briley, Ph.D.
Lipscomb University

Paul Kissling, Ph.D.
TCMI Institute

college
press
Joplin, Missouri

ISBN: 978-0-89900-034-3 (paperback)
ISBN: 978-0-89900-876-9 (hardback)

A WORD
FROM THE PUBLISHER

Years ago a movement was begun with the dream of uniting all Christians on the basis of a common purpose (world evangelism) under a common authority (the Word of God). The College Press NIV Commentary Series is a serious effort to join the scholarship of two branches of this unity movement so as to speak with one voice concerning the Word of God. Our desire is to provide a resource for your study of the Old Testament that will benefit you whether you are preparing a Bible School lesson, a sermon, a college course, or your own personal devotions. Today as we survey the wreckage of a broken world, we must turn again to the Lord and his Word, unite under his banner and communicate the life-giving message to those who are in desperate need. This is our purpose.

ABBREVIATIONS

AB . . . . *Anchor Bible*
ABD . . . . *Anchor Bible Dictionary*
ANE . . . . *Ancient Near East*
ANET . . . . . . *Ancient Near Eastern Texts relating to the Old Testament*
Ant. . . . . *Antiquities*
BA . . . . *Biblical Archaeologist*
BDB . . . . *Brown, F., S.R. Driver, and C.A. Briggs, A Hebrew and English Lexicon of the Old Testament*
BHS . . . . *Biblia Hebraica Stuttgartensia*
BTB . . . . *Biblical Theology Bulletin*
CD . . . . *Cairo manuscripts of the Damascus Document*
COS . . . . *The Context of Scripture*
DCH . . . . *Dictionary of Classical Hebrew*
DNTB . . . . . . *Dictionary of New Testament Background*
DOTP . . . . . . *Dictionary of the Old Testament: Pentateuch*
EBC . . . . *Expositor's Bible Commentary*
EDB . . . . *Eerdmans Dictionary of the Bible*
ESV . . . . *English Standard Version*
FOTL . . . . . . *Forms of Old Testament Literature*
GKC . . . . *Gesenius' Hebrew Grammar*
HALOT . . . . . *The Hebrew and Aramaic Lexicon of the Old Testament*
IVPBBCOT . . *InterVarsity Press Bible Background Commentary: Old Testament*
JAOS . . . . *Journal of the American Oriental Society*
JNES . . . . *Journal of Near Eastern Studies*
JPSTC . . . . . . *Jewish Publication Society Torah Commentary*
JPSV . . . . *Jewish Publication Society Version*
JSOT . . . . *Journal for the Study of the Old Testament*
JSOTSupp . . . *Journal for the Study of the Old Testament Supplement Series*
JTS . . . . *Journal of Theological Studies*

KB . . . . *Ludwig Koehler and Walter Baumgartner, HALOT, Study Edition*
MT . . . . *Masoretic Text*
NAC . . . . *New American Commentary*
NASB . . . . *New American Standard Bible*
NIB . . . . *New Interpreter's Bible*
NICOT . . . . . *New International Commentary on the Old Testament*
NIDOTTE . . . *New International Dictionary of Old Testament Theology and Exegesis*
NIVAC . . . . . . *New International Version Application Commentary*
NRSV . . . . . . *New Revised Standard Version*
OBT . . . . *Overtures to Biblical Theology*
OTL . . . . *Old Testament Library*
SBL . . . . *Society of Biblical Literature*
SP . . . . *Samaritan Pentateuch*
TB . . . . *Theologische Bücherei*
TDOT . . . . . . *Theological Dictionary of the Old Testament*
TLOT . . . . . . *Theological Lexicon of the Old Testament*
TOTC . . . . . . *Tyndale Old Testament Commentaries*
UF . . . . *Ugarit-Forschungen*
VT . . . . *Vetus Testamentum*
WBC . . . . *Word Biblical Commentary*
ZAW . . . . *Zeitschrift für die alttestamentliche Wissenschaft*

Simplified Guide to Hebrew Writing

Heb. letter	Translit.	Pronunciation guide
א	’	Has no sound of its own; like smooth breathing mark in Greek
ב	b	Pronounced like English B *or* V
ג	g	Pronounced like English G
ד	d	Pronounced like English D
ה	h	Pronounced like English H, silent at the end of words in the combination āh
ו	w	As a consonant, pronounced like English V or German W
ו	û	Represents a vowel sound, pronounced like English long OO
ו	ô	Represents a vowel sound, pronounced like English long O
ז	z	Pronounced like English Z
ח	ḥ	Pronounced like German and Scottish CH and Greek χ (chi)
ט	ṭ	Pronounced like English T
י	y	Pronounced like English Y
כ/ך	k	Pronounced like English K
ל	l	Pronounced like English L
מ/ם	m	Pronounced like English M
נ/ן	n	Pronounced like English N
ס	s	Pronounced like English S
ע	‘	Stop in breath deep in throat before pronouncing the vowel
פ/ף	p/ph	Pronounced like English P *or* F
צ/ץ	ṣ	Pronounced like English TS/TZ
ק	q	Pronounced very much like כ (k)
ר	r	Pronounced like English R
שׂ	ś	Pronounced like English S, much the same as ס
שׁ	š	Pronounced like English SH
ת	t/th	Pronounced like English T *or* TH

Note that different forms of some letters appear at the end of the word (written right to left), as in כָּפַף (*kāphaph*, "bend") and מֶלֶך (*melek*, "king").

Vowels in Hebrew (except where the ו is used to represent a vowel sound), are represented by "vowel points" added to the consonant. For example: הַ (*ha*, "the"). The letter *yod* (י, y) also becomes a *part of* certain vowel sounds, as in the conjunction כִּי (*kî*, "that"). Originally, Hebrew was written as "unpointed" text, with just the consonants. For convenience, the different vowel points are shown below on the letter Aleph (א).

אָ	ā	Pronounced not like long A in English, but like the broad A or AH sound
אַ	a	The Hebrew short A sound, but more closely resembles the broad A (pronounced for a shorter period of time) than the English short A
אֶ	e	Pronounced like English short E

א	ē	Pronounced like English long A, or Greek η (eta)
א	i	Pronounced like English short I
א	î	The same vowel point is sometimes pronounced like אִ (see below)
א	o	This vowel point sometimes represents the short O sound
א	ō	Pronounced like English long O
א	u	The vowel point ֻ sometimes represents a shorter U sound and
א	ū	is sometimes pronounced like the וּ (û, see above)
אֵ	ê	Pronounced much the same as א
אֵ	ê	Pronounced much the same as א
אִ	î	Pronounced like long I in many languages, or English long E
אְ	ǝ	An unstressed vowel sound, like the first E in the word "severe"
אֳ, אֲ, אֱ	ŏ, ă, ĕ	Shortened, unstressed forms of the vowels א, א, and א, pronounced very similarly to א

ACKNOWLEDGMENTS

Contemporary commentators on Genesis stand on the shoulders of those who have preceded them and taught them. That is certainly the case with this commentary. I have benefited immensely from my own teachers of Genesis, in particular Gordon Wenham and John Sailhamer. I have also been greatly aided by a long list of earlier commentators whose work has stimulated my own. I am grateful. I am surprised to find that I come to the end of writing nearly 1,000 pages on Genesis with the feeling that I have only just begun to plumb its depth. My appreciation for Genesis began many years ago as a new Christian when I memorized the text in the King James Version for a quiz competition called Bible Bowl. Many local church people and College and Seminary students have endured my obsession with Genesis for more than 25 years now and have sharpened my thinking. I have many fond memories of engaging students from around the world with this crucial portion of God's word. The sacrifices which others have made so that I could be free to research and write have been generous and considerable. I am grateful to the staff and administration of TCMI Institute in Heiligenkreuz, Austria, for providing me the time and resources to write. My office in the basement along the Sattelbach with its calming current and playful trout have made the task of writing easier. Three friends spent considerable time during their summer vacations to give me helpful feedback. My thanks to John Nugent, Gary Hall, and Laurence Turner. Undoubtedly only my own stubbornness has prevented me from adopting all of your thoughtful suggestions. Most of all I owe debts which I cannot pay to my wife Cathy for her encouragement and for making life a wonderful adventure. This volume is dedicated to her and to our first grandchild, David Michael Kissling, born February 23, 2008, in Toledo, Ohio.

PREFACE

THE AUTHOR OF THIS COMMENTARY

No scholar or any other interpreter approaches the Bible without presuppositions which to one degree or another have the potential to bias his or her reading. In our postmodern age with its hermeneutic of suspicion, one way to mitigate this problem is to forthrightly acknowledge one's potential biases. You should know who I am before you hear what I have to say about the book of Genesis. I write unashamedly as an evangelical Christian who accepts the entire trustworthiness of Scripture. Although I do not think that this set of convictions commits me to a particular way of reading Genesis, it does affect the way I quite intentionally interpret Genesis within the textual, historical, and theological contexts of the entire Old and New Testaments. I quite intentionally read Genesis as the foundational part of the macronarrative of the Bible and seek for readings that make sense of that macronarrative. I am also a Caucasian male born in America's upper midwest, but have spent a significant part of my adult life teaching and at times living in Western Europe. In recent years I have spent a considerable amount of my life offering graduate theological education to church leaders from the former Soviet bloc of countries. As I have had the privilege of teaching these men and women I have been struck by how their experience parallels the experience of dispersed Jewish people who came to accept the Pentateuch as Scripture and the experience of the earliest Christians.

THE AUDIENCES OF THIS COMMENTARY

In line with the aims of this series of commentaries I have tried to write at a level an adult Bible school teacher could understand. Some of the earliest memories of my father are watching him get up early on Sunday morning, taking out the old Bible Study Textbook series commentaries, usually along with William Barclay's Daily Study Bible if he was working on the New Testament, and preparing a Sunday school lesson with great care. I have been told by numerous people that he was a good teacher. In the main text of the commentary I have tried to write for someone like him. A first-generation Christian, he loved the Bible and especially appreciated the insights of careful scholars when they wrote accessibly. He knew no Greek or Hebrew, but nevertheless wanted to know as much as he could about the original language.

In the footnotes of the commentary I have a different audience in mind. Seminary students, ministers, and pastors who once studied Hebrew, and even professors will find more specific information on the details of the original language as well as pointers to the broader scholarly discussion about Genesis. The Hebrew words given in the text follow the convention of the series. Many of these Hebrew words are either relatively well-known or their pronunciation is significant for appreciating the text's nuances. For any words needing more technical explanation or discussion, I have left the information in the footnotes. I hope that the Hebrew and the footnotes will not discourage readers without the requisite background to appreciate them. The text can safely be read without the Hebrew or the footnotes.

A NOTE ON THE NIV

Anyone reading this commentary will notice that I sometimes disagree with the most popular translation of the Bible in the American church today, the New International Version. Although this text is printed in the commentary, the basis for my comments is the Hebrew text. The NIV is popular because it reads well while still retaining an essentially literal approach to translation. It thus lies somewhere between a more literalistic translation like the New American Standard and a paraphrase like the New Living Translation. Unfortunately at times the noble desire to provide a translation that reads well results in missing subtle clues to the perspective of the Hebrew narrator of Genesis. In particular the repetitive nature of Hebrew narration is received as cumbersome and boring to contemporary readers. The natural reaction to this perceived repetitiveness is to use variation to create interest. But this sometimes results in obscuring the point which such repetition makes.

I fear that having come to the end of this two-volume commentary that some readers will infer that I regard the NIV as an untrustworthy translation. I do not. While at times it reflects the reformed theology of many evangelical Bible scholars, the NIV is a solid translation which Christians can safely read and find comfort in and motivation for living for Christ. But as a translation for careful study of the text the NIV's periphrastic tendencies sometimes obscure the subtle clues which Hebrew narrative uses to display its viewpoints. Hebrew narrators usually stay in the background and make very few explicit comments on the events and human persons in the narrative. The narrator's perspective must be carefully teased out from the clues given in the narrative. The comments (especially in the footnotes) about this should not be regarded as a general criticism of the NIV.

INTRODUCTION

THE AUTHORSHIP OF GENESIS

It is often asserted in popular-level communications, both written and oral, that Moses wrote the entire Pentateuch, including the book of Genesis. But no statement in the entire Bible makes such a claim. Jesus does say that Moses wrote of him (John 5:46) and the Pentateuch is sometimes called "the law of Moses."[1] Certainly Moses did write some parts of the Pentateuch (Exod 34:27; 17:14; 24:4; Num 33:2; Exod 25:16,21-22; Deut 31:9,24), perhaps substantial portions of it. But the internal evidence of the Pentateuch itself does not suggest that Moses is responsible for writing the entirety of it. There are a series of texts within the Pentateuch itself which have been discussed at least since the early Middle Ages that make the theory of Mosaic authorship of the entire Pentateuch problematic. These texts are known as "Post-Mosaica" — texts which were written after the time of Moses and "A-Mosaica" — texts which may well have been written at the time of Moses but are unlikely to have been written by Moses himself. I have discussed some of these texts in the introduction to the first volume of this two-volume commentary.[2] There is no reason to believe that Moses wrote of himself, "Now the man Moses was very meek, more than all people who were on the face of the earth" (Num 12:3, ESV). Only a presupposition of Mosaic authorship would lead one to conclude that Moses wrote of his own death and burial (Deut 34:5-8) and that "no prophet ever arose like Moses whom the LORD knew face to face" (Deut 34:10).

But if Moses is not responsible for the final form of the Pentateuch, who is? The honest answer is that as regards authorship the Pentateuch and each of its five books are, strictly speaking, anonymous.

---

[1]1 Kgs 2:3; 2 Kgs 14:6; 23:25; 2 Chr 23:18; 30:16; 35:12; Ezra 3:2; 6:18; Neh 8:1; 13:1; Dan 9:11,13; Mal 4:4; Mark 12:26; Luke 2:22; 16:29,31; 24:27,44; John 8:5; Acts 13:39; 15:5,21; 28:23; 1 Cor 9:9; 2 Cor 3:15. None of these texts claim that Moses wrote the entirety of the Pentateuch.

[2]Paul J. Kissling, *Genesis Volume 1,* College Press NIV Commentary Series (Joplin, MO: College Press, 2004), pp. 42-45.

DATE AND HISTORICITY

On the theory that the earliest date for the writing of an historical document is sometime after the last event recorded in it, the book of Genesis must have been written sometime after the rise of a line of kings in the nation of Edom and the rise of the monarchy in Israel (Gen 36:31). If one presumes that Genesis was a part of the Pentateuch from its origins, the earliest date would probably be pushed into the postexilic era when prophecy had come and had either faded or was beginning to fade from the scene.[3]

This does not at all imply that the majority of the Pentateuch is late. A series of indirect indicators suggest that much of Genesis and the Pentateuch is quite early. In my judgment, Hoffmeier's groundbreaking works on the Egyptian background of the Exodus and Wilderness traditions have successfully rebutted so-called "minimalist" approaches to the historicity of Exodus through Numbers. If Israel has spent several centuries in Egypt, much of it as slaves, one would expect there to be numerous cultural effects on Israel. Hoffmeier carefully mines the evidence and finds precisely that to be the case. For example, one would expect that names for Hebrew children would be affected by the Egyptian environment. Hoffmeier[4] discusses eleven names within the Pentateuch and seven names outside it which have certain or likely Egyptian origin. Most of these names occur among the Levites. Hoffmeier plausibly explains the names outside of the Pentateuch as an indication of the conservatism characteristic of clergy which would keep alive ancient names.[5] A detailed study of the Tabernacle reveals numerous connections with Egypt. Hoffmeier gives detailed discussion of the Egyptian background for acacia wood, gold overlay, linen, and dolphin skin leather. He also notes striking Egyptian parallels with the ark of the covenant, the oil-holding cups in the menorah, the bronze altar, incense dishes, the gemstones in the High Priest's breastplate, silver trumpets,

---

[3]Deut 34:10 "No prophet ever arose in Israel like Moses whom the LORD knew face to face" (my translation). This text assumes that a series of prophets have come and perhaps now gone. But none of them was the prophet like Moses which he had predicted would arise in Deuteronomy 18:15-18. Even if one accepts the rendering of the ESV ("And there has not arisen a prophet since in Israel like Moses") the implication seems to be the same. Prophets have arisen, but none of them ever equaled Moses.

[4]James K. Hoffmeier, *Ancient Israel in Sinai* (New York: Oxford University Press, 2005), pp. 223-228.

[5]Ibid., p. 229.

as well as weights and measures.[6] Hoffmeier also gives a careful, balanced discussion of the route of the Exodus,[7] the likely location of the crossing of the Reed Sea,[8] and the approximate location of Sinai. He debunks a current popular theory which would place Sinai in modern Arabia.[9] In each case he demonstrates the historical plausibility of the biblical narrative. Although this evidence does not prove that every word of the Pentateuch comes from the Mosaic period, it does argue strongly for the essential historicity of the Pentateuchal narrative.

The above evidence argues for the general historicity of the narrative structure of Exodus through Deuteronomy. But what of Genesis? Is there evidence which is specifically germane to the first book of the Bible? Once again Hoffmeier does not disappoint. He begins by noting the evidence for Semites in Egypt during the relevant period: "It has been well known for decades, however, that there were Semites in the Delta starting after the collapse of the Old Kingdom (ca. 2190) and reaching a zenith during the Hyksos or Second Intermediate Period (ca. 1700–1550 B.C.) and on into the New Kingdom (1550–1069 B.C.)."[10] The evidence for the enslavement of Semites and their work in the making of bricks for Egyptian construction projects during the period when the Bible claims that Israel was enslaved is even more striking.[11] He follows Kenneth Kitchen's observation that the price for which Joseph was sold into slavery, 20 shekels, indicates the period 2000–1500 B.C. Later in the second millennium (1500–1000) the price was 30 shekels and in the first millennium (1000–0 B.C.) 60 or 70 shekels.[12] Hoffmeier also notes that Joseph's title while serving Potiphar, "overseer of the house" (Gen 39:4) is a literal translation of an Egyptian expression.[13] More significantly Hoffmeier points to three Semites who obtained high office in Egypt, Bay, '3-m-mi-t-w, and the more recently uncovered name, Aper-el. The last of these men has many parallels to Joseph, including group burial, a similar sort of status in the government of Egypt and a wife with an Egyptian name.[14] Hoffmeier also notes that Joseph dies at the ideal age in Egypt, 110 years.

---

[6]Ibid., pp. 209-221.

[7]James K. Hoffmeier, *Israel in Egypt: The Evidence for the Authenticity of the Exodus Tradition* (Oxford: Oxford University Press, 1996), chs. 7, 8.

[8]Ibid., ch. 9. Also Hoffmeier, *Ancient Israel*, ch. 5.

[9]Hoffmeier, *Ancient Israel*, ch. 6.

[10]Hoffmeier, *Israel in Egypt*, p. 53.

[11]Note figures 8, 9, 11, and 12 and Hoffmeier's (*Israel in Egypt*) discussion in chs. 3, 4, and 5.

[12]Ibid., pp. 83-84.

[13]Ibid., p. 84.

[14]Ibid., pp. 93-95.

Although this evidence is indirect and suggestive rather than direct and definitive, it does argue that the author of Genesis or the sources used had a remarkable knowledge of Egypt in the period suggested by the book. A plausible case for historicity has been made. Those who would deny general historicity must now account for the evidence which Hoffmeier has so carefully assembled.[15]

Another indirect indication of the antiquity of the Patriarchal narratives or the sources behind them is the obvious differences between the Torah given to Israel at Mount Sinai (Exodus and Leviticus) and Mount Nebo (Deuteronomy) and the actual practices of the Patriarchs. If the Patriarchal narratives were created after the giving of the Torah one would expect that the forefathers of the nation would be depicted as being strictly obedient to that Torah. After all an author would not presume that the contemporary Israel would obey the law when the nation's spiritual forbearers disregarded it. The tendency would be to hide any violations of the law for fear that the contemporary audience would use this as justification for their own disobedience. They might say, "If father Abraham did that (or did not do this), why shouldn't I?" The reality is that the author of Genesis made no attempt to conform the actions of the patriarchs to the Torah which was later revealed at Sinai and after.[16] Jacob violates Israel's incest laws by marrying two sisters (Gen 29:21-30; Lev 18:9,11,18; 20:7). Judah and Simeon marry Canaanite women, something strictly prohibited in the law (Exod 34:16; Deut 7:3). Isaac and Jacob "violate" the later law by giving or intending to give a larger share to junior sons (Deut 21:15-17). The patriarchs erect pillars, pour libations over them, and plant trees which had the purpose of marking religious sites, all in "violation" of the later law (Deut 12:2-3). Longman helpfully concludes:

> This list presents just a sample of serious incongruities between the picture of the patriarchs in Genesis and later beliefs, and we must ask: how likely is it that much later writers, writing purely out of their imagination, would paint a picture of their founding fathers that included such things. It is far more likely that this picture is as

[15]Hoffmeier's books were published by a secular publisher with a high reputation in the academic community (Oxford University Press). His work is an example to other evangelicals of what is required if one wants to make apologetic arguments that are convincing to those not already convinced of the historicity of the Bible on theological grounds.

[16]See the discussion in Iain Provan, V. Philips Long, and Tremper Longman III, *A Biblical History of Israel* (Louisville, KY: Westminster John Knox, 2003), pp. 115-116.

it is because the authors of Genesis had already inherited a firm patriarchal tradition that they had to accommodate, whatever their larger religious and social aims in telling their story.[17]

The case for general historicity must not, however, be used to claim more than is warranted. Genesis is not an attempt to write a history book in a modern sense. Genesis 11:27–50:26 is theological literature which draws lessons from events in the lives of the Patriarchs for Israel and through Israel for Christians of every age. There is no attempt to give a comprehensive biography of Abraham or Jacob. Only those events which have significance for the wider instructional purposes of the Pentateuch are included. Long stretches of time are routinely passed over without comment. What did Abraham do up until the age of 75 when he moved to Canaan? We are not told. What happened during the thirteen years between the move to Canaan and the birth of Ishmael? We know of only a few events. What happened between the birth of Ishmael and the birth of Isaac? We know next to nothing. The hero of the narrative is God, not Abraham, Isaac, Jacob, or Joseph. The narrative is held together by the promises of God, not by the actions of the patriarchs. The theme which drives the plot of the Pentateuch drives the plot of Genesis, the partial fulfillment and partial nonfulfillment of the promises of God to the Patriarchs.[18]

THE AUDIENCES OF GENESIS

A book should ordinarily be read from front to back, not from back to front. It was certainly designed to be read that way. If we want to listen to the message of the book and not impose our own meaning on it, we should read it as it was intended to be read. This basic principle has several implications. One is that we should seek to understand a book in the order in which it is written. We should give a fair hearing to the reading which a first-time reader would be expected to discover.[19] For a book as familiar as Genesis, where we already know the story, or think we do, this can be a challenge. A second implication is that we seek to understand the book on its own terms and strive to genuinely seek the

---

[17]Ibid., p. 116.

[18]On this see David J.A. Clines, *The Theme of the Pentateuch*, JSOTSupp 10 (Sheffield: JSOT, 1978), p. 29.

[19]For the insights which such first-time reading provides see Laurence Turner's seminal work, *Announcements of Plot in Genesis*, JSOTSupp 96 (Sheffield: JSOT, 1990).

meaning intended for the original readers. This again presents challenges for the reader of Genesis. To begin with we are not entirely sure exactly when the book was written. Even if we could establish with confidence a date soon after the entrance into the land for the great majority of the book, we still would have the issue of the final updating and canonical editing. Who is the audience intended for this updating and editing? Because of this uncertainty I have chosen to systematically ask the question of what the probable meaning of Genesis would be for both the original and canonical audiences.

The original readers of Genesis are the nation of Israel relatively soon after they have entered the land of Canaan. They have been deeply impacted in negative ways by the experience of slavery in Egypt. One need only be reminded of the golden calf incident to recognize this. Only weeks from the plagues and the crossing of the Reed Sea, the nation all too easily reverts to the forms of worship and conceptions of God which they had acquired in Egypt. But there is a deeper problem. They are confronted by Canaanite culture and its alluring fertility religions. The LORD had warned Israel of these twin dangers in Leviticus 18:3: "You must not do as they do in Egypt, where you used to live, and you must not do as they do in the land of Canaan, where I am bringing you. Do not follow their practices" (NIV). Genesis is written in light of this situation even though it records events in the lives of the Patriarchs who did not themselves face it in the same way. What happened at Sodom in an isolated way in the time of Abraham was common in the land of Canaan to which Israel had recently come. The Torah is a sort of instructional manual for Israel as the nation faces the new challenges of living in Canaan after having been slaves in Egypt for several centuries. As part of that Torah the book of Genesis, chapters 12–50 in particular, explains the origin of the nation of Israel and their transformation from a clan of wandering nomads into a great nation ready to take possession of the land which God had promised to them.

The canonical readers were in a very different and yet strikingly similar situation. They too had been enslaved in exile in a powerful empire, Babylon. They too faced the dangers of religious and cultural capitulation to the ways of the nations. They knew of the problem of syncretism. They faced it every day whether they were back in Palestine or still living in the Diaspora. They faced the problem of intermarriage and religious accommodation. But they also knew the lesson of the nation's history. Their unfaithfulness to the Torah throughout their time of independence had eventually brought God's judgment. Their internal divisions, anticipated in the book of Genesis, had resulted in a fractured nation which was scattered and exiled by the great powers of the day, Assyria and Babylon. With the Persians now in control, the remnants of the nation had a new opportunity to return to the land and begin to rebuild the nation. For them the warnings against disobedience to the Torah were very real. The Torah was no longer a book for a faithful minority. It was the law for the entire community. They had publically committed themselves to obeying it in the time of Ezra.

But Genesis is not merely an Old Testament book. The book of Genesis is one book in a multibook collection which we call the Christian Bible. The Bible contains the New Testament and its witness to Jesus Christ as the ultimate fulfillment of God's promises to Abraham (2 Cor 1:20). Genesis is the beginning of the Bible's macronarrative, the overarching narrative which stretches from the creation in Genesis 1 and 2 to the new creation in Revelation 21 and 22. To read Genesis as Christian Scripture requires that we also read Genesis in light of its meaning for Christians who know Jesus Christ to be the ultimate seed of Abraham (Gal 3:16). As in the case of the original and canonical readers, I have tried to systematically ask the question of what the meaning of Genesis might be for Christian readers. But I have done so with a particular qualification in mind. Given the tendency among popular Bible interpreters to over-Christianize the Old Testament without regard for its original context, I have usually limited my interpretations for Christian readers to meanings which flow directly from the original and canonical meanings.

A GUIDE TO READING GENESIS 11:27–50:26

I have described my approach to reading Genesis in the first volume of this two-volume commentary.[20] Here I would merely add a few comments of special relevance to Genesis 11:27–50:26. This section of Genesis differs from chapters 1–11 in two main ways. First it deals with the chosen family, the precursor to the nation of Israel. Second it focuses much more on the lives of individual characters, who come to life on its pages.

The concept of election or "chosenness" refers to God's choice of particular individuals as the human channels of his blessing to the entire world. Often God's choice runs counter to the human choice. Isaac is chosen over Lot and Ishmael; Jacob over Esau; Judah over his older brothers Reuben, Simeon, and Levi. Joseph, the tenth son, is elevated

---

[20]Paul J. Kissling, *Genesis Volume 1*, pp. 18-24. I read Genesis canonically, historically, sensitively, poetically, and theologically.

above his brothers. The chosen nation descends from a series of individuals chosen for other reasons than their order of birth or expected social status. Israel is a chosen nation descended from the unlikely and improbable choices that God made of individuals. This theme of God's surprising choices binds the narratives of Genesis together and hints at the humility that the chosen nation Israel must have toward their own election. Moses later warned the nation of taking pride in their election, "[It is] not because of your righteousness or the uprightness of your heart that you are going in to possess this land. . . . Know, therefore, that the LORD your God is not giving you this good land to possess because of your righteousness, for you are a stubborn people" (Deut 9:5,6 ESV).

But Genesis 11:27–50:26 is even more notable for the striking portraits of individuals who emerge. Unlike the earlier section of Genesis where human characters are little more than types, in this section of Genesis we have full-fledged characters such as Abraham and Sarah, Isaac and Rebekah, Jacob, Joseph, and Judah. With full-fledged characters comes the complexity and ambiguity of such characters. The traditional approach to the characters of Genesis has been to make heroes out of those characters which seem to be on God's side and villains out of those who are not. But this hardly does justice to the complexity of such characters as Jacob and Esau, for example. A test case for this tendency to make heroes is the claim that Abraham makes that Sarah is actually his half sister (Gen 20:12). The narrator makes no such statement. The narrator merely records Abraham as saying it. Further, when the narrator provides Abraham's genealogy, he or she does not mention this (Gen 11:27-30). Further, when Abram suggested that Sarai portray herself as his sister the first time, there is no indication that it was even a half-truth (Gen 12:13). Abraham only comes up with this explanation when confronted by Abimelech about his lie. While the narrator does not explicitly rule out the possibility that Abraham and Sarah were actually half brother and sister, there seems little reason to believe this other than a preconception that Abraham is a godly man who would not lie! This assumption overrides the evidence, and Abraham is assumed to be telling the truth even though it seems more likely that he is making up another lie to cover the first lie! The characters in Genesis are not portrayed as good Christian people! They were not Christians, and their narrative portrayals are not simplistic. The lessons we learn from them come as much from their weaknesses and mistakes as they do from their moral examples. Is Esau the nonchosen that much worse, morally speaking, than Jacob the chosen? Not in the text of Genesis. Is Ishmael morally deficient in comparison with Isaac? That would be difficult to prove from the text of Genesis. If there is a hero in the narrative of Genesis, it is the God who persists in relationship with chosen people who are far from examples of faith or moral rectitude. The characters of Genesis are not white-hatted heroes riding white horses or black-hatted villains riding black ones. The message of Genesis is elsewhere than in simplistic moralizing.

THE STRUCTURE OF GENESIS 11:27–50:26

Although modern scholars can and have speculated about the structure of Genesis, it is safest to use the structural markers given explicitly by the author. The phrase, "[these are] the generations of" (וְאֵלֶּה תּוֹלְדֹת, wᵊ'ēlleh tôlᵊdōth), is the most obvious structural marker in the book and (with the possible exception of 2:4a) is used as an introductory formula. Generally speaking there is alternation between narrative material and name list or genealogical material. This yields the following structure for the book:[21]

1:1–2:4	Prologue (Narrative)
2:4–4:26	History of the Heavens and the Earth (Narrative with Genealogy)
5:1–6:8	Family History of Adam (Genealogy)
6:9–9:29	Family History of Noah (Narrative)
10:1–11:9	Family History of Noah's Sons (Genealogy with Narrative)
11:10-26	Family History of Shem (Genealogy)
11:27–25:11	Family History of Terah (Narrative)
25:12-18	Family History of Ishmael (Genealogy)
25:19–35:29	Family History of Isaac (Narrative)
36:1–37:1	Family History of Esau (Genealogy)
37:2–50:26	Family History of Jacob (Narrative)

Notice the following:

1) Terah's family history is dominated by Abraham; Isaac's by Jacob; and Jacob's by Joseph. Why? Terah sets out for the land of Promise but never gets there, so the significant role that he could have played in the outworking of God's promise was given to his son who did have the faith to go to the Promised Land. Perhaps Isaac's role is taken by Jacob because he too is resistant to the promise to a degree

---

[21]I have adapted this section from my *Genesis Volume 1*, pp. 30-31.

(e.g., the attempt to bless Esau when he knew God had other plans). Perhaps Jacob's part is taken by Joseph because he was already the focus of the previous section and because the narrative is not just about Joseph, but about Jacob's sons, and therefore it would be inappropriate to call it the family history of Joseph. I will argue in the commentary that, although the section seems to be dominated by the figure of Joseph, in fact something more subtle is happening. Judah's status rises throughout the narrative until he equals, and in some senses even surpasses, Joseph. The narrative is not about Joseph at all but about how Judah rises to eclipse even Joseph.

2) Notice that offshoots of the promise are written out by genealogies rather than narratives (Ishmael, Esau, Noah's sons). For the author of Genesis these nonchosen relatives of Israel are, nevertheless, still under God's blessing.

3) Notice the alternation between genealogy with a few narrative comments and straight narrative with occasional genealogical information. Why? Certainly the "major" characters in the story are given narratives and the relatively speaking "minor" ones are given genealogies, but is there more? Perhaps the genealogies catch the narrative up, so to speak? They also by contrast give emphasis to the nonchosen sons of the Patriarchs (Ishmael, Esau) and Noah (Ham).

4) Genesis 36:1,9 repeats the phrase, "these are the generations of." Esau is thus given a sort of double genealogy. This seems to be part of a significant theme in Genesis 11:27–50:26 concerning the importance of the nonchosen branches of the family of Abraham.

5) The genealogies are obviously crucial to the structuring of the book, and we should expect to find good reasons for their existence other than an antiquarian interest on the part of the author of Genesis.

6) The genealogies are written in light of the circumstances of Israel within the Promised Land. The origins of Israel's neighbors and enemies is explained, and this points forward to the later discussion in Numbers and Deuteronomy about "banned" and nonbanned peoples.

THE THEOLOGY OF GENESIS 11:27–50:26

Genesis 11:27–50:26 is not theology per se. It is narrative. Deriving theology from narrative can be a tricky business. What is merely descriptive? What is intended to be read prescriptively? How does one know the difference? While one must proceed cautiously, Genesis screams to be read theologically. In this section I will briefly introduce the central implications of Genesis 11:27–50:26 about God, humanity, and creation.

GOD IN GENESIS 11:27–50:26

In this section of Genesis we see the creator God of Genesis 1:1–11:26 turn into a God who chooses a single family and focuses his attention on them. The God of creation and world history becomes an electing God. This indicates a shift in strategy by God in light of the persistent rebellion of humanity culminating in the episode at Babel in Genesis 11:1-9. God's purposes in creating humanity in the first place are to find fulfillment through his chosen people, the descendants of Abraham, Isaac, and Jacob. While God has not given up on his concern for the world, his universal blessing at creation (Gen 1:26-28) is now to be channeled primarily through a single human family.

God's universal judgment also changes. After the Flood God had promised to never again allow the evil in the human family to result in the wholesale destruction of creation through a de-creating flood (Gen 8:21-22). But since evil in the human family was not stopped by the flood (Gen 6:5; 8:21) what could God do? He does not give up on justice, for this is against his very nature. God could no more become unjust and ignore the injustices of the human family than he could give up on his love and faithfulness. Instead God chooses to intervene with his purgative justice before the evil of violence has had a chance to spread to the rest of the human family. Just as the surgeon cuts away the cancer, so God in his judgment removes the cancerous evil of violence before it has a chance to spread to the rest of the creation as happened prior to the flood. The chief example of this change of strategy is the destruction of Sodom and Gomorrah in Genesis 19. The numerous echoes of the Flood narrative in Genesis 19 demonstrate that for the author of Genesis the behavior of the residents of Sodom and its environs is strikingly similar to the universal behavior which brought God's judgment on the generation of the flood. The violence, particularly sexual violence, which brought on the flood calls forth God's judgment on Sodom. The destruction of creation, both human and nonhuman, is thus localized.

But it is not only God's judgment which is localized after the flood. God also comes to "localize" his relationship with the human family. Up until the Babel episode God had chosen to work through all humankind without distinction. There is no sense of election of a chosen people prior to Genesis 11. In lieu of the Babel episode we see a shift in God's strategy. The builders of Babel seek to make a name for themselves and explicitly reject God's commission to spread out and fill the earth so that they could rule as God's representatives over creation. In light of that rejection of God's creation commission God decides to choose a particular family and use them as the channels of his blessing to all the rest of humankind. At first it seems that Terah, Abram's father will be that chosen person. But when Terah decides to stop halfway to the Promised Land in Haran, God calls his son, Abram to leave his father's house and go all the way to Canaan. Genesis 11:27–50:26 tells the story of God's relationship to a particular elect family. Its plot is driven by the twists and turns of human interference in the working out of God's plan. But God is a God who persists with his chosen people despite their tendency to take matters into their own hands and complicate the fulfillment of the promises to Abram in Genesis 12. Sometimes he works overtly; at other times his work is behind the scenes in what theologians often term providence. All along he grants the chosen family remarkable freedom, for good and for ill, to participate with him in faith in the outworking of his purpose to bless all the families of the earth through Abraham's descendants.

God is also a God who chooses to work through the unexpected and the unlikely. We see this in the pattern of choosing the younger son, not the firstborn. Isaac the younger, not Ishmael the firstborn, will be Abraham's heir. Jacob, not his older brother Esau, will inherit the promises. Equally surprising is the case of Judah. With three older brothers who disqualify themselves, it is left to Judah, the fourth son, to receive the mantle of leadership from his father. What is even more surprising, however, is that Judah is given this honor despite Jacob's obvious favoritism for his son Joseph. Judah, not Joseph, is given the highest place within the family that turns into the twelve-tribe nation of Israel.

In Genesis 11:27–50:26 God is also a God who blesses and protects his people. The concept of blessing first occurs in the Bible in the creation commission in Genesis 1. But the concept blossoms and flourishes in the promises of God to the Patriarchs and in his tangible actions of blessing them and protecting them from the harm of their potential enemies. God blesses Abram and Lot with material possessions while they are in Egypt as he does Jacob while in the employ of Laban. He also blesses Esau. He blesses Joseph and all that is placed under his authority in Egypt so that even as a slave he is elevated to second in command under Pharaoh. The LORD blesses Ishmael, Esau, and Jacob with large families, which in time result in entire nations who claim them as their forefathers. Sarah and Rebekah are protected from harm when taken into the harems of foreign kings. God protects Abram in a battle with a coalition of five kings who have taken Lot captive.

In Genesis 11:27–50:26 God is also a God who reveals himself to his chosen people. He speaks to Abram, calling him to participate in God's blessing for the entire world. He explicitly identifies Canaan as the Promised Land (Gen 12:7), even expanding its ideal borders to the Euphrates and the border with Egypt (Gen 15:18-20). He reassures Abram about the number of his descendants (Gen 15:5; 17:2-7) and clarifies that only a son born through his direct action would be Abram's heir (Gen 17:15-19). He ultimately makes an unalterable promise that Abraham would indeed be the channel of his blessing to all the nations of the earth (Gen 22:18). God also reveals himself to Isaac (Gen 26:3-4,24) and to Jacob (Gen 28:13-14; 35:11-12) reaffirming the promise. His final revelation is given to Jacob reassuring him that moving his family to Egypt is part of God's plan to make a great nation out of his descendants (Gen 46:3). Somewhat surprisingly God is silent while the family is in Egypt, working behind the scenes, but not overtly revealing himself. Nevertheless, his providential care of the chosen family is obvious even when it is behind the scenes (Gen 45:5-10; 50:20).

HUMANITY IN GENESIS 11:27–50:26

The strikingly similar divine statements about humanity before and after the flood (6:5; 8:22) make it clear that humanity's sinfulness since being expelled from the garden had become a pattern which was repeated generation after generation. The Babel incident is a sort of last straw for humanity. The question of Genesis 11:27–50:26 is, Will a chosen family do any better? The answer is "no and yes," rather than "yes and no." To begin with the positive, the chosen family is concerned about the promise and works (and schemes) to try to ensure its fulfillment. Even though such scheming is misguided, it does indicate a level of faith and determination that the promises come to fruition. Abraham at first assumes Lot will be his heir. Later he and Sarai scheme to produce a son, Ishmael, through Sarai's handmaiden Hagar. Jacob and Rebekah scheme to swindle Esau out of birthright and blessing. Jacob is willing to wrestle with a divine person who has divine power in order to secure the blessing. Abraham and Isaac are willing to sacrifice their wives to see the promises come to fruition. Whatever weaknesses these actions imply, they also imply a genuine confidence in the reality of God's promises and a commitment to do whatever is necessary to ensure that those promises come true.

But Genesis' dominant message about the elect family is how flawed they are. Were it not for God's commitment to his promises, the patriarchs would have forfeited them on numerous occasions. In a sense Abraham seems to unintentionally endanger the promises whether by risking Sarah's being taken into a foreign king's harem or by offering Lot the rights to the Promised Land. All of the patriarchs complicate the fulfillment of the promise and show striking weaknesses. This all points to the fact that, at some level, the promises belong to God. They are his to make, and they are ultimately his to fulfill. The promises cannot depend upon human faithfulness, even from the chosen family, for their fulfillment. If they are to find fulfillment, it will only be through God's grace and mercy.

What is initially surprising about Genesis' message about humanity is its portrayal of those who are not in the chosen line. Ishmael and Esau, though not chosen, are still blessed. Melchizedek is a priest of God Most High even though he has no direct connection to the chosen family. Abimelech, though a pagan king, is still concerned about righteousness. Tamar, though a Canaanite, is more righteous than Judah, by Judah's own admission. Even the Pharaoh in Joseph's time shows some level of openness to God by accepting God's revelation of the meaning of his troubling dreams. There are many people outside of the chosen line who nevertheless desire to be faithful to God. Of course there are plenty of other humans who display no inclination to be godly and fall under God's judgment. The most obvious example of this is the king of Sodom and the men of Sodom who seek to rape the angelic visitors. In Genesis humanity is full of both weakness and evil, but also at times shows remarkable capacity to respond to God.

CREATION IN GENESIS 11:27–50:26

Following the flood God makes a decision to sever the close relationship between the destiny of the entire earth and his relationship to humanity. He solemnly promises never again to destroy the entire physical system with a flood. The problem for God was that even the flood did not drive evil from the human heart (Gen 8:21). Had he continued to destroy the system every time human evil reared its ugly head, there would be a never-ending cycle of creation, rebellion, and de-creation. Instead when human evil begins to rise to the horrendous level it reached before the flood, God determines to step in with localized judgment to stop that evil from spreading. The narrative of the destruction of Sodom with its numerous echoes of the Flood narrative makes this clear. God still allows humanity enormous freedom, for good and ill. He is patient with human weakness, sin, and wickedness (Gen 15:13-16). But he will not allow the violence and sexual licentiousness of Sodom to spread without judgment. The sulfuric deposits in and around the Dead Sea served as a reminder and a warning to the chosen nation of the consequences of a radical departure from God's will in human society.

But there is another side to the story. The world which God had made was a fruitful world that God had blessed with the capacity to regenerate itself. The earth's fertility as exemplified in the Promised Land was a perpetual sign of God's blessing. God had created a good world which had ample capacity to feed humanity and all of God's creatures. But even that fruitful world displayed the brokenness of the fall. The famines of Genesis remind us that while God created the world with beauty and goodness, human rebellion resulted in a cursed creation. Even the Promised Land experienced the distortions of such a cursed creation from time to time.

GENESIS 11:27–50:26 AND THE REST OF THE BIBLE

Genesis 11:27–50:26 is the continuation of Genesis 1:1–11:26. The book of Genesis is part of the Pentateuch. The Pentateuch is part of the Old Testament. The Old Testament is the first three quarters of the Christian Bible. These simple facts must always be kept in mind when interpreting Genesis 11:27–50:26. The relationship between this section of Genesis and the rest of the Bible is a theological one, but it is theology expressed in narrative. Genesis 11:27–50:26 is a crucial link in the Bible's macronarrative.

THEOLOGICAL RELATIONSHIP WITH GENESIS 1:1–11:26

Genesis 11:27 marks the turning point in the book of Genesis and the turning point in the macronarrative of the Bible. Up until this time God has chosen to work through the entirety of humankind. There is no chosen nation among the nations of the world. In part this is because up until the Babel episode in Genesis 11:1-9[22] there were no nations with differing cultures and languages. But there is another reason. The Babel narrative marks the end of a strategy which God had used up until that time in relating to humanity. From creation to the fall to the flood to the post-Flood expansion of human population, God had worked directly with humanity as a whole. There was no elect or chosen

---

[22]The nations mentioned in Genesis 10 arise after the events at Babel in Genesis 11:1-9. On this chronological disruption see Kissling, *Genesis Volume 1* at Genesis 10.

people. But with the call of Abram the focus of God's work in the world is narrowed to one man and his descendants. God's blessing that was given to all humanity at creation (Gen 1:26-28) will now flow through Abram and his descendants; through Abram's descendants all the families of the earth will be blessed (Gen 12:3). The promise of God is thus not the center of the Bible to which creation is merely the prologue. Instead the promise to Abram is a continuation of God's creational purposes, but with a new strategy. One can speculate on the reasons for a shift in strategy. God's early attempts to deal with humanity as a whole have been repeatedly frustrated by human rebellion. The original human pair rejected the conditions for life lived in the immediate presence of God in Eden. The post-Eden generations degenerated into systemic violence which demanded God's cosmic judgment. The post-Flood generations deliberately rebelled against the Noachic commission to fill the earth and brought judgment yet again. It is only after this third judgment at Babel that the divine strategy changes. God's creational intention to bless humanity as they rule over all the earth is focused to the promises to Abram. He will both receive God's blessing and channel that blessing to the entire human family. He and his descendants will experience the blessings of a Promised Land until such time as God's blessings can spread to the entire earth.[23]

THEOLOGICAL RELATIONSHIP WITH THE PENTATEUCH

Genesis is not a stand-alone book. From our earliest knowledge of it, it is the first and foundational book of the Torah or Pentateuch. All of Genesis is written with the assumption that the exodus has already occurred and that the laws have been revealed to Israel through Moses at Mount Sinai, in the wilderness, and at Mount Nebo. As such Genesis is related narratively and theologically to the rest of the Torah. Genesis is written for the nation of Israel in the Promised Land. The narratives of Genesis 11:27–50:26 are especially relevant for the nation because they describe its creation from the calling of Abram until the family of Jacob moves to Egypt. The name Israel is first of all the name given to Jacob. The "children of Israel" are first mentioned in relation to Jacob in Genesis 32:32. The relationships between the twelve tribes of Israel are founded on the relationships between the twelve sons of Jacob as are the tensions between them.

---

[23]In Hebrew the word for "land" and the word for "earth" are the same (הָאָרֶץ, hā'āreṣ). For the original readers there would be a natural connection between the "land" of Canaan and the entire "earth."

There is no doubt that for the original audience of Genesis the patriarchal era was very different from their own era. Although the patriarchs sometimes obey the law before the law is given, they also sometimes disobey that same law. Abram tithes before he was required to do so, and ensures that his son Isaac does not marry a Canaanite woman. But he also is willing to sacrifice his child to his god and planted a tree as a marker of a place of worship, both things forbidden in the law (Deut 12:2-3; Lev 20:1-5). The patriarchs were not pure monotheists in the modern sense but traveled a path that led to monotheism. The audience is expected to make allowances for the fact that Abraham and his earliest descendants were originally polytheists who came to a more accurate understanding of God over time. What does connect the patriarchs more directly to the rest of the Torah are the promises of God which were originally given to Abraham, Isaac, and Jacob and were beginning to find fulfillment in the generations which departed from Egypt and entered the Promised Land. What Abraham and his descendants did in accepting the importance of the promise and seeking its fulfillment prepared the ground for the nation of Israel to take that promise several steps further.

THEOLOGICAL RELATIONSHIP WITH THE OLD TESTAMENT

While the Pentateuch prepares for the fulfillment of the promises to Abraham, the rest of the Old Testament tells the tragic story of how his descendants nearly saw its fulfillment only to see it lost through persistent disobedience and outright rebellion. They had the land promised to Abraham even in its ideal form only to see foreign armies conquer it all (cp. Gen 15:18-20 and 1 Kgs 4:21). They became a great nation only to be scattered and exiled throughout the ancient Near East by the Assyrians and Babylonians. They had received abundant material blessings only to see those blessings turn to curses. They were attracting the nations to the LORD, only to see the nations mock them derisively as they were humiliated by their enemies (1 Kgs 10:1-13; 24). N.T. Wright perceptively comments: "Israel, the children of Abraham, may be the carriers of the promise, but they turn out to be part of the problem themselves. This unwinds through a massive and epic narrative, from the patriarchs to the exodus, from Moses to David, through the twists and turns of the Israelite monarchy, ending finally with Israel in exile."[24]

---

[24]N.T. Wright, *Evil and the Justice of God* (Downers Grove, IL: InterVarsity, 2006), p. 46.

Genesis 11:27–50:26 details what God promised. The remainder of the Old Testament tells the tragic story of how Israel had it all within their grasp only to see it slip through their fingers and end up a broken and scattered nation. As the Old Testament ends, the promises are still in effect, but their fulfillment is beyond Israel's capacity. Only God can fulfill the promises through a broken and scattered and chastened nation.

THEOLOGICAL RELATIONSHIP WITH THE ENTIRE BIBLE

The rest of the Bible tells the story of how it eventually was left to one truly faithful descendant of Abraham to bring the promises to fulfillment. His name was Joshua; in Greek, Jesus. He descended from the tribe of Judah to take over the leadership of the nation. He is the ultimate "descendant" or "seed" of Abraham (Gal 3:16), and those who belong to him by faith are children of Abraham (Gal 3:6,7), the true circumcision (Rom 2:28-29), and even the true Israel (Gal 6:16). What the nation of Israel could not do because of their persistent unfaithfulness, Jesus, the new Israel incarnate, did. The faith of the patriarchs kept the promises alive. The unfaithfulness of the patriarchs and especially of their descendants made it clear that if God's promises were to come to fruition, it would only be by more direct action of God. He would have to intervene; the descendants of the patriarchs could not be trusted to do it with their own resources. The sinfulness of all humanity was narrated in Genesis 1–11. Genesis 12–50 makes clear that even the chosen family is itself significantly sinful. This prepares the ground for the Bible's great surprise ending. God himself, in his son Jesus the Messiah, the son of David, the son of Abraham, took on flesh and brought the answer "Yes" to all God's promises (1 Cor 1:20).

HISTORICAL-CRITICAL APPROACHES TO GENESIS

It is not the purpose of a commentary like this one to engage with traditional historical-critical approaches to the patriarchal narratives in Genesis. Bible-believing Christians must not, however, put their heads in the sand in regard to the way critical scholarship has interpreted these narratives. Although I will not systematically engage with historical-critical approaches (Source Criticism, Form Criticism, Tradition History, etc.) in the verse-by-verse commentary, I have attempted to do three things. First, in the Introduction to volume 1 I have addressed these approaches in general terms.[25] Second, in this volume I include an excursus on the historical-critical approach to the story of Jacob's dream at Bethel (Gen 28:10-22) as a sort of test case for these sorts of methods. This passage is often used as a prime example of the value of source criticism and the necessity of some such explanation for the writing of the Pentateuch. Genesis 28 will thus receive more sustained and detailed interaction with historical-critical approaches than other texts. Third, I will from time to time use the footnotes in the verse-by-verse commentary to interact with especially noteworthy passages which have traditionally been highlighted by those scholars interpreting Genesis through traditional historical-critical methods.

---

[25]Kissling, *Genesis Volume 1*, pp. 42-51.

INTERPRETIVE OUTLINE OF GENESIS 11:27–50:26

THE STORY OF ABRAHAM AND HIS SONS

I. THE STORY OF TERAH BECOMES ABRAM'S STORY — 11:27–12:9
  A. Terah Travels Halfway to the Promised Land — 11:27-32
  B. Abram Receives God's Promise and Commission — 12:1-3
  C. Abram Responds to God's Promise — 12:4-6
  D. God Identifies the Land of His Promise — 12:7-9

II. THE LOT STRATEGY — 12:10–15:21
  A. The First Challenge to the Promise: A Famine Sends Abram to Egypt — 12:10-20
    1. Abram Leaves the Promised Land — 12:10
    2. Abram's Strategy to Protect Himself Outside of the Promised Land — 12:11-15
    3. Abram Receives Material Blessings in Egypt — 12:16
    4. Egypt Receives God's Curse — 12:17-19
    5. Abram Returns to the Promised Land — 12:20
  B. The Second Challenge to the Promise: Coping with Material Prosperity, the Separation of Abram and Lot — 13:1-18
    1. Abram Returns to the Promised Land a Rich Man — 13:1-4
    2. Riches Obtained in Egypt Lead to Internal Conflict with Lot — 13:5-7
    3. Abram Risks Giving Away the Promised Land to Lot, but Does Not — 13:8-13
    4. The LORD Renews the Land Promise after Lot's Departure — 13:14-18
  C. The Third Challenge to the Promise: The Need to Rescue Lot, the Presumed Heir — 14:1-16
    1. War between Mesopotamia and Transjordan Results in Lot's Being Captured — 14:1-12
      a. Initial Victory of the Mesopotamian Coalition over Transjordan Kings — 14:1-4a
      b. Rebellion and Defeat of Transjordan Kings — 14:4b-11
      c. Lot's Capture — 14:12

37

2. God Protects the Promised Child despite Abraham and Abimelech — 20:3-7
3. Abimelech Confronts Abraham over His Lie — 20:8-13
4. Abimelech Blesses Abraham despite His Lie — 20:14-16
5. Abraham, the Liar, Is Still the Intermediary for the Healing of Abimelech's Nation — 20:17-18

B. The Joke Is on Abraham and Sarah: The Birth of Isaac — 21:1-7

C. The Endgame of the Ishmael Strategy: The Expulsion of Ishmael — 21:8-21

1. Sarah Demands the Expulsion of Ishmael and Hagar — 21:8-11
2. The LORD Promises to Care for Hagar and Ishmael — 21:12-13
3. Abraham Expels Hagar and Ishmael — 21:14
4. The LORD Protects and Provides for Hagar and Ishmael — 21:15-21

D. A Covenant with the People of the Land — 21:22-34

1. Abimelech Recognizes God's Blessing of Abraham — 21:22
2. Abraham Commits to Deal Loyally with Abimelech — 21:23-24
3. Conflict with Covenant Partners — 21:25-26
4. A Ritual to Seal and Remember the Agreement — 21:27-34

E. The Maturing of the Faith(fulness) of Abraham — 22:1-19

1. Divine Testing of Abraham's Faith(fulness) — 22:1-2
2. Abraham's Obedience — 22:3-6a
3. Isaac's Involvement in the Test — 22:6b-8
4. Abraham (and Isaac?) Pass the Test — 22:9-11
5. Isaac Is Spared through the LORD's Provision — 22:12-14
6. The Promise Sealed and Reaffirmed — 22:15-19

F. Potential Marriage Partners for Abraham's Descendants — 22:20-24

G. The Death and Burial of Sarah — 23:1-20

1. Sarah's Death — 23:1-2
2. Abraham Asks Permission to Buy a Grave — 23:3-9
3. Abraham Pays the High Price for the Grave — 23:10-16
4. Abraham Buries Sarah — 23:17-20

H. A Wife for Isaac — 24:1-67

1. Abraham Requires an Oath from His Servant to Find a Wife for Isaac from His Extended Family — 24:1-9
2. The Servant Prays for a Sign of the Chosen Wife — 24:10-14
3. The Prayer Is Answered with Rebekah — 24:15-28
4. Abraham's Servant Explains the Lord's Guidance to Rebekah to Her Family — 24:29-49
5. Laban and Bethuel Confirm the Lord's Guidance — 24:50-51
6. Abraham's Servant Praises the Lord for His Guidance — 24:52

THE NARRATIVE OF JACOB'S SONS

B. Joseph's Brothers Sell Him as a Slave in Egypt — 37:12-36
1. Joseph's Brothers Plot to Kill Him When He Visits Them — 37:12-20
   a. Joseph Sent to Report on the Welfare of His Brothers — 37:12-14a
   b. Joseph Finds His Brothers at Dothan — 37:14b-17
   c. Joseph's Brothers Plot to Kill Him — 37:18-20
2. Reuben Tries to Save Joseph, but Judah Actually Does — 37:21-30,36
   a. Reuben Convinces His Brothers Not to Kill Joseph (Reuben Plans to Rescue Joseph) — 37:21-22
   b. Joseph's Brothers Cast Him into the Cistern — 37:23-24
   c. Judah Convinces His Brothers to Enslave Joseph Rather Than Kill Him — 37:25-28
   d. Reuben Returns to See Joseph Gone — 37:29-30
3. The Brothers Fool Jacob into Assuming That Joseph Is Dead — 37:31-35
4. Joseph Ends Up as Potiphar's Servant — 37:36

II. JUDAH'S STORY BEGINS BADLY — 38:1-30
   A. Judah Abandons Tamar — 38:1-12
1. Judah's Family through Marriage to a Canaanite Woman — 38:1-5
2. Judah's First Two Sons Die under Divine Judgment While Married to Tamar — 38:6-10
3. Judah Fails to Give Shelah to Tamar in Levirate Marriage — 38:11-12
   B. Tamar Tricks Judah into Impregnating Her - 38:13-26
1. Tamar Tricks Judah into Sex with Her — 38:13-18
2. Judah Fails to Find Prostitute to Pay Her and Recover Personal Items — 38:19-23
3. Tamar Discovered to Be Pregnant, and Judah Discovers He Is the Father — 38:24-26
   C. Tamar Bears Two Sons for Judah — 38:27-30

III. JOSEPH ENDS UP AS A SLAVE AND PRISONER IN EGYPT — 39:1-23
   A. Joseph's Initial Elevation in Potiphar's House — 39:1-6a
   B. Joseph Falsely Accused of Adultery by Potiphar's Wife — 39:6b-19
   C. Joseph Imprisoned, but Elevated — 39:20-23

IV. JOSEPH INTERPRETS THE DREAMS OF PHARAOH'S CUP-BEARER AND BAKER — 40:1-23
   A. The Imprisoned Joseph Comes to Know Influential People in the Court of Pharaoh — 40:1-3

BIBLIOGRAPHY

Alexander, T. Desmond. *From Paradise to the Promised Land.* Grand Rapids: Baker Books, 1995.

Alt, Albrecht, *Der Gott der Väter.* Stuttgart: Kohlhammer, 1929.

_____ . "The God of the Fathers." In *Essays on Old Testament History and Religion,* pp. 1-100. Trans. by R.A. Wilson. Garden City, NY: Anchor Books, 1968.

Alter, Robert. *The Art of Biblical Narrative.* New York: Harper Collins, 1981.

_____ . *Genesis.* New York: W.W. Norton, 1996.

Amit, Yairah. *Reading Biblical Narratives: Literary Criticism and the Hebrew Bible.* Trans. by Yael Lotan. Minneapolis: Fortress, 2001.

Anderson, J.N.D. "Law." *New Dictionary of Theology,* pp. 377-378. Downers Grove, IL: InterVarsity, 1988.

Arnold, Bill T., and John H. Choi. *A Guide to Biblical Hebrew Syntax.* Cambridge: Cambridge University Press, 2003.

Ash, P.S. "Borders." *DOTP.* Edited by T. Desmond Alexander and David W. Baker. Downers Grove, IL: InterVarsity, 2003.

Astour, Michael C. "Shaveh, Valley of." *ABD,* 5:1168.

Avalos, Hector. "Blindness." *EDB,* p. 193.

Baer, D.A., and R.P. Gordon. "חֶסֶד." *NIDOTTE,* 2:211-218.

Baker, D.W. "God, Names of." *DOTP,* pp. 359-368.

Baker, D.W., J.K. Hoffmeier, and A.R. Millard, eds. *Faith, Tradition, and History.* Winona Lake, IN: Eisenbrauns, 1994.

Baldwin, Joyce G. *Haggai, Zechariah, Malachi.* TOTC. Downers Grove, IL: InterVarsity, 1972.

_____ . *The Message of Genesis 12–50.* Leicester, Eng.: Inter-Varsity, 1986.

Balentine, Samuel E. *Prayer in the Hebrew Bible: The Drama of Divine-Human Dialogue.* OBT. Philadelphia: Fortress Press, 1993.

Bar-Efrat, Shimon. *Narrative Art in the Bible*. JSOTSupp 70. Sheffield: Almond, 1989.

Benjamin, Don C. "Israel's God: Mother and Midwife." *BTB* 19 (1989): 115-120.

Berlin, Adele. *Poetics and Interpretation of Biblical Narrative*. Sheffield: Almond, 1983.

Blomberg, Craig L. "Matthew." In *Commentary on the New Testament Use of the Old Testament*. Edited by G.K. Beale and D.A. Carson. Grand Rapids: Baker, 2007.

Boyarin, Daniel. *A Radical Jew: Paul and the Politics of Identity*. Berkeley, CA: University of California, 1994.

Brenner, Athalya. *Colour Terms in the Old Testament*. JSOTSupp 21. Sheffield: JSOT Press, 1982.

Brichto, Herbert Chanan. *The Names of God: Poetic Readings in Biblical Beginnings*. New York: Oxford University Press, 1998.

_____ . *Toward a Grammar of Biblical Poetics*. Oxford: Oxford University Press, 1992.

Brodie, Thomas L. *Genesis as Dialogue*. Oxford: Oxford University Press, 2001.

Brown, Walter E. "Potiphar." *EDB*, p. 1072.

Browning, Daniel C. Jr. "Goshen." *EDB*, p. 521.

Bruckner. James K. *Implied Law in the Abraham Narrative: A Literary and Theological Analysis*. JSOTSupp 335. Sheffield: Sheffield Academic, 2001.

Brueggemann, Walter. *Genesis*. Interpretation. Atlanta: John Knox Press, 1982.

_____ . *Theology of the Old Testament: Testimony, Dispute, Advocacy*. Minneapolis: Fortress, 1997.

Buchard, C. "Joseph and Asenath: A New Translation and Introduction." *Old Testament Pseudepigrapha*, pp. 176-241. Volume 2. Edited by James H. Charlesworth. New York: Doubleday, 1985.

Buechner, F. *The Magnificent Defeat*. San Francisco: Harper and Row, 1966.

Buescher, Alan Ray. "Honey." *EDB*, p. 603.

Bulliet, R. *The Camel and the Wheel*. Cambridge, MA: Harvard University Press, 1975.

Burton, Keith A. "Spices." *EDB*, p. 1247.

Buth, Randall. "Methodological Collision between Source Criticism and Discourse Analysis." In *Biblical Hebrew and Discourse Linguistics*. Edited by Robert D. Bergen. Dallas: Summer Institute of Linguistics, 1994.

Byrne, Ryan. "Siddim, Valley of." *EDB*, p. 1218.

Carmichael, C.M. "Some Sayings in Genesis 49." *JBL* 88 (1969): 435-444.

Carr, David M. *Reading the Fractures of Genesis.* Louisville, KY: Westminster John Knox, 1996.

Carroll, Robert P. *Jeremiah.* OTL. Philadelphia: Westminster, 1986.

Carson, Donald A. *Exegetical Fallacies.* Grand Rapids: Baker, 1984.

Cassuto, Umberto. *A Commentary on the Book of Genesis: Part One: From Adam to Noah. Part Two: From Noah to Abraham.* Jerusalem: Magnes Press, 1961, 1964.

Childs, Brevard S. *Biblical Theology of the Old and New Testaments.* Philadelphia: Fortress, 1992.

Chirichigno, Gregory C. *Debt-Slavery in Israel and the Ancient Near East.* JSOTSupp 141. Sheffield: Sheffield Academic, 1993.

Clines, David J.A. *The Theme of the Pentateuch.* JSOTSupp 10. Sheffield: JSOT Press, 1978.

_____ . *What Does Eve Do to Help? And Other Readerly Questions to the Old Testament.* JSOTSupp 94. Sheffield: Sheffield Academic, 1990.

Coats, George W. *Genesis with an Introduction to Narrative Literature.* FOTL. Grand Rapids: Eerdmans, 1983.

Collins, John J. *Introduction to the Hebrew Bible.* Minneapolis: Fortress, 2004.

Crenshaw, James. "Journey into Oblivion: A Structural Analysis of Gn. 22:1-19." *Soundings* 58 (1975): 243-256.

Crüsemann, Frank. "Human Solidarity and Ethnic Identity: Israel's Self-definition in the Genealogical System of Genesis." In *Ethnicity and the Bible*, pp. 57-76. Edited by Mark G. Brett. Leiden: Brill, 2002.

Currid, J.D. "Travel and Transportation." *DOTP*, pp. 870-874.

Dawson, David Allen. *Text-Linguistics and Biblical Hebrew.* JSOTSupp 177. Sheffield: Sheffield Academic, 1994.

de Hoop, Raymond. See Hoop, Raymond de.

Dozeman, Thomas B., and Konrad Schmid. *A Farewell to the Yahwist? The Composition of the Pentateuch in Recent European Interpretation.* Atlanta: Society of Biblical Literature, 2006.

Eichler, Barry. "On Reading Genesis 12:10-20." In *Tehillah le-Moshe: Biblical and Judaic Studies in Honor of Moshe Greenberg*, pp. 23-37. Edited by Mordechai Cogan, Barry L. Eichler, and Jeffrey Tigay. Winona Lake, IN: Eisenbrauns, 1997.

Etheridge, J.W. *The Targums of Onkelos and Jonathon Ben Uzziel on the Pentateuch with the Fragments of the Jerusalem Targum.* New York: KTAV, 1968.

Evans, C.A. "Messianism." *DNTB*, pp. 698-706.

Evans, Craig A., and Stanley Porter, eds. *Dictionary of New Testament Background.* Downers Grove, IL: InterVarsity, 2000.

Fields, Weston W. *Sodom and Gomorrah.* JSOTSupp 231. Sheffield: Sheffield Academic, 1997.

Fishbane, Michael. "Composition and Structure in the Jacob Cycle (Gen 25:19–35:22)." *JTS* 26 (1975): 15-38.

_____. *Text and Texture.* New York: Schocken Books, 1979.

Fokkelman, Jan P. *Narrative Art in Genesis.* Amsterdam: van Gorcum, 1975.

Fox, Everett. *The Five Books of Moses.* Schocken Bible, volume I. New York: Schocken Books, 1995.

Fretheim, Terence E. *Genesis.* NIB 1. Nashville: Abingdon, 1994.

_____. *God and World in the Old Testament: A Relational Theology of Creation.* Nashville: Abingdon, 2005.

Friedman, Richard Elliot. "Torah (Pentateuch)." *ABD*, VI:605-622.

Frishman, Judith, and Lucas Van Rompay, eds. *The Book of Genesis in Jewish and Oriental Christian Interpretation.* Traditio Exegetica Graeca 5. Louvain: Peeters, 1997.

Frymer-Kensky, T. "Patriarchal Family Relationships and Near Eastern Law." *BA* 44 (1981): 209-214.

Geller, Steven. "Struggle at the Jabbok: The Uses of Enigma in a Biblical Narrative." *JNES* 14 (1982): 50-65.

Gemser, B. "Beeber Hajjardeb: In Jordan's Borderland." *VT* 2 (1952): 349-355.

Goldingay, John. "The Significance of Circumcision." *JSOT* 88 (2000): 3-18.

_____. *Theological Diversity and the Authority of the Old Testament.* Grand Rapids: Eerdmans, 1987.

Goodfriend, Elaine Adler. "Prostitution (OT)." *ABD*, V:507-508.

Greenfield, J., "*The Etymology of* אמתחת," *ZAW* 84 (1965): 90-92.

Greidanus, Sidney. *Preaching Christ from Genesis: Foundations for Expository Sermons.* Grand Rapids: Eerdmans, 2007.

Gruber, M. "Hebrew *qĕdēšâh* and Her Canaanite and Akkadian Cognates." *UF* 18 (1986): 133-148.

Hamilton, Victor P. *The Book of Genesis Chapters 1–17.* NICOT. Grand Rapids: Eerdmans, 1990.

_____. *The Book of Genesis Chapters 18–50.* NICOT. Grand Rapids: Eerdmans, 1995.

Hays, Richard B. *The Moral Vision of the New Testament.* San Francisco: HarperCollins, 1996.

Heard, R. Christopher. *Dynamics of Diselection.* SBL Semeia 39. Atlanta: Society of Biblical Literature, 2001.

Hertz, J.H., ed. *The Pentateuch and HafTorahs.* London: Soncino Press, 1956.

Hess, R.S. "The Slaughter of the Animals in Genesis 15:18-21 and Its Ancient Near Eastern Context." In *He Swore an Oath: Biblical Themes from Genesis 12–50*, pp. 55-65. Edited by R.S. Hess, P.E. Satterthwaite, and G.J. Wenham. 2nd edition. Grand Rapids: Baker, 1994.

Hess, Richard S., Gordon J. Wenham, and Philip E. Satterthwaite, eds. *He Swore an Oath. Biblical Themes from Genesis 12–50.* Grand Rapids: Baker, 1994.

Hiebert, Theodore. "Beyond *Heilsgeschichte*." In *Character Ethics and the Old Testament*, pp. 3-10. Edited by M. Daniel Carroll R and Jacqueline E. Lapsley. Louisville, KY: Westminster John Knox, 2007.

Hoffmeier, James K. *Ancient Israel in Sinai.* New York: Oxford University Press, 2005.

_____. *Israel in Egypt: The Evidence for the Authenticity of the Exodus Tradition.* Oxford: Oxford University Press, 1996.

Hooks, Steve M. *Sacred Prostitution in the Bible and the Ancient Near East.* Ph.D. Dissertation. Cincinnati: Hebrew Union College, 1985.

Hoop, Raymond de. *Genesis 49 in Its Literary and Historical Context.* Atlanta: Society of Biblical Literature, 1999.

Hostetter, Edwin C. "Kenaz." *EDB*, p. 763.

Hübner, Ulrich. "Jalam." *ABD*, III:616.

Huehnergard, J. 'Asseverative **la* and Hypothetical **lu/law* in Semitic." *JAOS* 103 (1983): 569-593.

Hunt, J.H. "Dreams." *DOTP*, pp. 197-201.

Ishida, T. "The Structure and Historical Implications of the Lists of Pre-Israelite Nations." *Biblica* 60 (1979): 461-490.

Johnson, P.S. "Life, Disease and Death." *DOTP*, pp. 532-536.

Johnston, Philip S. *Shades of Sheol: Death and Afterlife in the Old Testament.* Downers Grove, IL: InterVarsity, 2002.

Joüon, Paul. *A Grammar of Biblical Hebrew: Part Three: Syntax.* Translated and revised by T. Muraoka. Rome: Editrice Pontificio Istituto Biblico, 1991.

Kaiser, Walter C. *Toward an Old Testament Theology.* Grand Rapids: Zondervan, 1978.

Kaminsky, Joel. *Yet I Loved Jacob: Reclaiming the Biblical Concept of Election.* Nashville: Abingdon, 2007.

Kissling, Paul J. *Genesis Volume 1.* College Press NIV Commentary Series. Joplin, MO: College Press, 2004.

——————. *Reliable Characters in the Primary History.* JSOTSupp 224. Sheffield: Sheffield Academic, 1996.

——————. *A Sketch of Old Testament Theology.* Lansing, MI: GLCC, 1999.

Kitchen, Kenneth A. *On the Reliability of the Old Testament.* Grand Rapids: Eerdmans, 2003.

Knauf, Ernst Axel. "Teman." *ABD*, VI:347-348.

——————. "Yahweh." *VT* 34 (1984): 460-468.

Koch, K. "עָוֹן, ʿāwōn." *TDOT*, X:546-562.

Kotter, Wade D. "Mamre (Place)." *EDB*, pp. 850-851.

Labuschagne, C.J. "The Life Spans of the Patriarchs." *Oudtestamentum Studien* 25 (1989): 121-127.

Levenson, Jon D. *The Death and Resurrection of the Beloved Son: The Transformation of Child Sacrifice in Judaism and Christianity.* New Haven, CT: Yale University Press, 1993.

Liedke, G. "רִיב, rîb to quarrel." *TLOT*, 3:1233. Edited by Ernst Jenni and Claus Westermann. Trans. by Mark E. Biddle. Peabody, MA: Hendrickson, 1997.

Long, V. Philips. *The Art of Biblical History.* Foundations of Contemporary Interpretation 5. Grand Rapids: Zondervan, 1994.

Manns, Frederic, ed. *The Sacrifice of Isaac.* Jerusalem: Franciscan Printing Press, 1995.

Marlowe, W. Creighton. "Nebaioth." *EDB*, p. 952.

Mars, Rick R. "Balm." *EDB*, p. 145.

Matthews, Kenneth A. *Genesis 11:27–50:26*. NAC. Nashville: Broadman, 2005.

Mazow, Laura B. "Rehoboth." *EDB*, pp. 1116-1117.

McConville, Gordon J. "בְּרִית." *NIDOTTE*, pp. 747-755.

McEntire, Mark. *The Blood of Abel: The Violent Plot in the Hebrew Bible*. Macon, GA: Mercer University Press, 1999.

McMillen, S.I., and David E. Stern. *None of These Diseases*. 3rd edition. Grand Rapids: Revell, 2000.

Merrill, Eugene H. *Everlasting Dominion: A Theology of the Old Testament*. Nashville: Broadman & Holman, 2006.

Meyers, Carol, ed. *Women in Scripture: A Dictionary of the Named and Unnamed Women in the Hebrew Bible, the Apocryphal/Deuterocanonical Books, and the New Testament*. Grand Rapids: Eerdmans, 2000.

Milgrom, Jacob. *Numbers*. JPSTC. Philadelphia: Jewish Publication Society, 1990.

Miller, James E. "Sexual Offences in Genesis." *JSOT* 90 (2000): 41-53.

Moberly, R.W.L. *The Bible. Theology, and Faith: A Study of Abraham and Jesus*. Cambridge: Cambridge University Press, 2000.

_____. *Genesis 12–50*. Sheffield: Sheffield Academic, 1995.

_____. *The Old Testament of the Old Testament*. OBT. Minneapolis: Fortress, 1992.

Moran, W.L. "Gen. 39.10 and Its Use in Ezek. 21.32." *Biblica* 39 (1959): 405-425.

Morschauser, Scott. "Hospitality, Hostiles and Hostages: On the Legal Background to Genesis 19:1-9." *JSOT* 27 (2003): 461-485.

Myers, Carol L., and Eric M. Myers. *Haggai, Zechariah 1–8*. AB. Garden City, NY: Doubleday, 1987.

Niccacci, Alviero. *The Syntax of the Verb in Classical Hebrew Prose*. Trans. by W.G.E. Watson. JSOTSupp 86. Sheffield: Sheffield Academic Press, 1990.

Niehoff, M. "Do Biblical Characters Talk to Themselves? Narrative Modes of Representing Inner Speech in Early Biblical Fiction." *JBL* 111 (1992): 577-595.

Noth, Martin. *Die israelitischen Personennamen in Rahmen der gemeinsemitischen Namengebung*. Stuttgart: Kohlhammer, 1928.

Perry, Robin. *Old Testament Story and Christian Ethics: The Rape of Dinah as a Case Study.* Paternoster Biblical Monographs. Milton Keynes: Paternoster, 2004.

Plaut, W. Gunther. "Genesis." In *The Torah: A Modern Commentary.* Edited by Gunther W. Plaut. New York: Union of American Hebrew Congregations, 1981.

Princeton Abridgement of BDB in Gramcord Software.

Pritchard, J.B., ed. *Ancient Near Eastern Texts relating to the Old Testament.* 3rd ed. Princeton, NJ: Princeton, 1969.

Provan, Iain, V. Philips Long, and Tremper Longman III. *A Biblical History of Israel.* Louisville, KY: Westminster John Knox, 2003.

Rad, Gerhard von. *Genesis.* Revised Edition. OTL. Philadelphia: Westminster, 1972.

Rashi. *Commentaries of the Pentateuch.* Trans. by Chaim Pearl. New York: W.W. Norton, 1970.

Rendsberg, Gary A. *The Redaction of Genesis.* Winona Lake, IN: Eisenbrauns, 1986.

Rendtorff, Rolf. *The Canonical Hebrew Bible: A Theology of the Old Testament.* Trans. by David E. Orton. Leiderdorp, NE: Deo, 2005.

Rosenberg, Roy A. "*Besaggam* and *Shiloh.*" *ZAW* 105 (1993): 258-261.

Ross, Allen P. *Creation and Blessing.* Grand Rapids: Baker, 1988.

Ruppert, L. *Die Josephserzählung der Genesis: Ein Beitrag zur Theologie der Pentateuchquellen.* Studien zum Alten und Neuen Testament. München, 1965.

Safren, Jonathan D. "Ahuzzath and the Pact of Beer-Sheba." *ZAW* 101 (1989): 184-198.

Sailhamer, John H. *Genesis.* EBC 2. Grand Rapids: Zondervan, 1990.

—————. *Genesis Unbound.* Sisters, OR: Multnomah Books, 1996.

—————. *The Pentateuch as Narrative.* Library of Biblical Interpretation. Grand Rapids: Zondervan, 1992.

Sarna, Nahum M. *Genesis.* JPSTC. Philadelphia: Jewish Publication Society, 1989.

—————. *Studies in Biblical Interpretation.* Philadelphia: Jewish Publication Society, 2000.

—————. *Understanding Genesis.* New York: Schocken Books, 1966.

Satterthwaite, P.E., and D.W. Baker. "Nations of Canaan." *DOTP,* pp. 596-605.

Schmidt, Brian B. "Molech." *EDB*, pp. 912-914.

Schnittjer, Gary E. *The Torah Story: An Apprenticeship on the Pentateuch.* Grand Rapids: Zondervan, 2006.

Sheridan, Mark, ed. *Genesis 12–50.* Ancient Christian Commentary on Scripture. Downers Grove, IL: InterVarsity, 2002.

Shinan, A., and Y. Zakovitch. *The Story of Judah and Tamar.* Jerusalem: Magnes, 1992.

"Shuah." *EDB*, p. 1216. No author. David Noel Freedman, editor.

Sinclair, Lawrence A. "Philistines." *EDB*, pp. 1050-1051.

Smith-Christopher, Daniel L. "Dreams." *EDB*, pp. 356-357.

Speiser, Ephraim. *Genesis.* AB 1. New York: Doubleday, 1964.

Spina, Frank Anthony. *The Faith of the Outsider: Exclusion and Inclusion in the Biblical Story.* Grand Rapids: Eerdmans, 2005.

Sprinkle, J.M. "Sexuality, Sexual Ethics." *DOTP*, pp. 741-752.

Steck, Odil Hannes. *Old Testament Exegesis: A Guide to the Methodology.* 2nd Edition. Trans. by James D. Nogalski. Atlanta: Scholars Press, 1998.

Sternberg, Meir. *Hebrews between Cultures.* Bloomington, IN: Indiana University Press, 1998.

_____ . *The Poetics of Biblical Narrative.* Bloomington, IN: Indiana University Press, 1985.

Tatum, Lynn. "Negeb." *EDB*, p. 955.

Taylor, Marion Ann, and Heather E. Weir. *Let Her Speak for Herself: Nineteenth-Century Women Writing on Women in Genesis.* Waco, TX: Baylor University Press, 2006.

Tigay, Jeffrey H. *Deuteronomy.* JPSTC. Philadelphia: JPS, 1996.

Tov, Emmanuel. *Textual Criticism of the Hebrew Bible.* Minneapolis: Fortress, 1992.

Turner, Laurence A. *Announcements of Plot in Genesis.* JSOTSupp 96 Sheffield: JSOT, 1990.

_____ . *Genesis.* Readings. Sheffield: Sheffield Academic, 2000.

Vancil, Jack W. "Sheep, Shepherd." *ABD*, V:1188-1189.

van der Toorn, Karel. "Prostitution (Cultic)." *ABD*, V:510-513.

Van Seters, John. *The Pentateuch.* Sheffield: Sheffield Academic, 1991.

Vergote, J. *Joseph en Egypte.* Louvain: Publications universitaires, 1959.

Waltke, Bruce K. *Genesis: A Commentary.* Grand Rapids: Zondervan, 2001.

Waltke, Bruce K., and M. O'Connor. *Introduction to Biblical Hebrew Syntax.* Winona Lake, IN: Eisenbrauns, 1990.

Walton, John. "**6596** *'alūmiym.*" NIDOTTE, 3:417-418.

————. *Genesis.* NIVAC. Grand Rapids: Zondervan, 2001.

Walton, John, Victor H. Matthews, and Mark W. Chavalas, eds. *The IVP Bible Background Commentary: Old Testament.* Downers Grove, IL: InterVarsity, 2000.

Walton, Kevin. *Thou Traveller Unknown: The Presence and Absence of God in the Jacob Narrative.* Paternoster Biblical Monographs. Milton Keynes: Paternoster, 2003.

Wenham, Gordon J. "Bethulah." *VT* 22 (1972): 326-348.

————. *Genesis 1–15.* WBC 1. Waco, TX: Word, 1987.

————. *Genesis 16–50.* WBC 2. Waco, TX: Word, 1994.

————. "The Religion of the Patriarchs." In *Essays on the Patriarchal Narratives.* A.R. Millard and D.J. Wiseman, eds. Leicester: Inter-varsity, 1980.

————. *Story as Torah: Reading Old Testament Narrative Ethically.* London: T & T Clark, 2000.

Westermann, Claus. *Genesis 12–36.* Continental Commentary. Trans. by John J. Scullion. Minneapolis: Fortress Press, 1995.

————. *Genesis 37–50.* Continental Commentary. Trans. by John J. Scullion. Minneapolis: Fortress Press, 1986.

Whybray, R.N. *The Making of the Pentateuch: A Methodological Study.* JSOTSupp 53. Sheffield: JSOT Press, 1987.

Williams, P.J. "The LXX of 1 Chronicles 5:1-2 as an Exposition of Genesis 48–49." *TB* 49 (1998): 368-371.

Williamson, P.R. "Circumcision." *DOTP*, pp. 122-125.

Wilson, Lindsay. *Joseph Wise and Otherwise: The Intersection of Wisdom and Covenant in Genesis 37–50.* Paternoster Biblical Monographs. Milton Keynes: Paternoster, 2004.

Wilson, Robert R. *Genealogy and History in the Biblical World.* New Haven, CT: Yale University Press, 1977.

Wright, N.T. *Evil and the Justice of God.* Downers Grove, IL: Inter-Varsity, 2006.

Yoder, John Howard. "If Abraham Is Our Father." In *The Original Revolution.* Scottdale, PA: Herald Press, 1971.

————. *The Jewish-Christian Schism Revisited.* Edited by Michael G. Cartwright and Peter Ochs. Grand Rapids: Eerdmans, 2003.

Yonge, C.D., trans. *The Works of Philo.* Peabody, MA: Hendrickson, 1993.

Zarins, Juris. "Myrrh." *EDB*, p. 930.

Zlotnick, Helena. *Dinah's Daughters: Gender and Judaism from the Hebrew Bible to Late Antiquity.* Philadelphia: University of Pennsylvania Press, 2002.

Zornberg, Avivah Gottlieb. *Genesis: The Beginning of Desire.* Philadelphia: The Jewish Publication Society, 1995.

Zuckerman, Bruce. *Job the Silent.* New York: Oxford University Press, 1991.

GENESIS 12

THE STORY OF ABRAHAM AND HIS SONS
(11:27–25:18)

This major section of Genesis is introduced as the story of Terah with the words "This is the account of Terah." But after 11:32 Terah is never mentioned again. Instead Abra(ha)m[1] dominates the narrative until his death in Genesis 25:1-11. The immediately following section (Gen 25:12-18) is about Ishmael but is quite brief. Isaac, the heir to the promises of God, never really gets a section of his own since what begins as his section ("This is the account of Abraham's son Isaac" Gen 25:19) is dominated by his sons Jacob and Esau. I have therefore chosen to combine the sections on Abraham and Ishmael into one under the title, "Abraham and His Sons."

The narrative of Abra(ha)m's life begins with his leaving Ur in southern Iraq with his father to go to Canaan. His father Terah only makes it halfway to the Promised Land and takes up permanent residence in Syria. It is only then that Abram receives the LORD's commandment to leave his family behind and the LORD's promises for a future for his descendants that will impact the entire world. Those promises (Gen 12:1-3) form the underlying plot or theme of the rest of Genesis and indeed of the entire Pentateuch. The remainder of the Abrahamic narrative relates how the promise seems to be put at risk by the actions and failures of the very people to whom it was given, only to see God providentially ensure that it remains intact for the next generation. Abra(ha)m endangers the promise by twice surrendering his wife Sarai/h to a foreign king's harem, by taking one of his relatives along when the LORD told him to leave them, by offering the Promised Land to Lot rather than reserving it for his real heir Isaac, by agreeing to and

---

[1]While inelegant, this conglomerated word is designed to remind my readers that the father of the faithful was originally called Abram and only later, at God's command, called Abraham.

participating in his wife's plan to have an heir through surrogacy with a concubine, etc. The plot is carried along by the question, Will God allow Abra(ha)m to defeat his promises by his own planning and scheming? The answer, of course, is "No." The promise is never really in danger because ultimately God is in control. Not even the foolish efforts of the faithful to help him fulfill his promises will stop him.

But the LORD respects Abra(ha)m's freedom and allows him to complicate the fulfillment of the promises. Abraham's story is a story of his growing into the father of the faithful. Only in chapter 22 when Abraham is willing to give back to God the child whom God has provided do we see the full flowering of Abraham's faith(fulness). The story of the development of Abraham's faith is a reminder that faith and faithfulness comes at the end of and as a result of a maturing process. Our faith(fulness) is never sufficient to have any claim on God's mercy. Abram's story reminds Israel and also us that God initiates the relationship with us. Yes, we must respond with faith and obedience. But our faith and our obedience is every bit as imperfect and partial as was Abram's.

I. THE STORY OF TERAH
BECOMES ABRAM'S STORY (11:27–12:9)

The story of Abra(ha)m does not actually begin with him but with his father Terah. The genealogy that finishes off the so-called "Primeval History" in 11:10-26 leads to Terah and his sons, Abram, Nahor, and Haran. The introductory formula,[2] translated "this is the account of" in the NIV, is about Terah, not Abram. But the narrative which follows in 11:27–25:11 is dominated by Abra(ha)m; Terah plays a very marginal role. The question then becomes, "Why is the narrative introduced as though it would be about Terah when in fact it is actually mostly about Abra(ha)m?" This section explains how it is that Terah's story becomes Abram's. Terah, after fathering a family, set out to go to Canaan (11:31). But having traveled approximately halfway there, Terah stops his journey short and takes up permanent residence in Haran. As I will argue below, it is from Haran that the LORD commands Abram to leave his father's house and complete the journey. We as Christians today are the spiritual sons of Abraham because he, unlike his father Terah, in faith and obedience, made it all the way to the Promised Land.

---

[2] וְאֵלֶּה תּוֹלְדֹת, wᵊ'ēlleh tôlᵊdōth. See the discussion in Kissling, *Genesis Volume 1*, pp. 30-32.

A. TERAH TRAVELS HALFWAY TO THE PROMISED LAND
(11:27-32)

11:27 This is the account of Terah. Terah became the father of Abram, Nahor and Haran. And Haran became the father of Lot.

This verse begins with the formulaic introductory marker that the author of Genesis uses throughout the book.[3] Here Terah's sons are apparently listed in the order of their significance for the continuing narrative, not in their birth order.[4] From the ensuing narrative it seems[5] that Haran is older than Abram by 60 years. There is no way to determine the age of Nahor.

11:28 While his father Terah was still alive, Haran died in Ur of the Chaldeans, in the land of his birth.

This verse helps to explain why Abram took Lot with him when he went to Canaan. With no heir of his own due to Sarai's barrenness (v. 30) and his brother Haran dead, Lot is the natural candidate in Ancient Near Eastern culture to become Abram's heir.

11:29 Abram and Nahor both married. The name of Abram's wife was Sarai, and the name of Nahor's wife was Milcah; she was the daughter of Haran, the father of both Milcah and Iscah.

This verse begins with a Hebrew construction (*waw*-consecutive) which typically indicates narrative sequence. In other words the normal way to read this verse would imply that **Abram and Nahor** married after the death of their older brother **Haran**. Assuming that the same person is intended in verses 28 and 29 Haran[6] had three children who are men-

---

[3]Ibid.

[4]On the nature of biblical genealogies see the discussion in Kissling, *Genesis Volume 1*, pp. 247-249.

[5]It is possible that Nahor was the oldest. However, the fact that he married Haran's daughter (11:29) and that Haran died before the move to the city of Haran, argues for Haran being the oldest. What the text does seem to imply is that Abram is 60 years younger than his oldest brother. Terah had sons beginning at age 70 (11:26) and died 135 years later at age 205 (11:32) when Abram was only 75 years old (12:4).

[6]R. Christopher Heard (*Dynamics of Diselection*, SBL Semeia 39 [Atlanta: SBL, 2001], pp. 25-26) warns against assuming that the Haran in verse 29 is the same Haran in verse 28. He suggests that the (for him) oddly redundant phrasing, "the daughter of Haran, the father of both Milcah and Iscah" is designed to suggest that this Haran was a different one from the one in v. 28 who was Lot's father. He notes, however, that this may be because of the different genders of the children mentioned. Abram took responsibility for Lot as his own son but Nahor took Milcah to be his wife. The text does not say what happened to Iscah.

tioned, his son Lot and two daughters **Milcah and Iscah**. Nahor married his older brother's daughter Milcah. **Abram's wife Sarai** is apparently not related to him. Abram later (Gen 20:12) claims that she is in fact his half-sister when under pressure from Abimelech to explain his lying about her being his sister, but the narrator does not endorse this claim.

11:30 Now Sarai was barren; she had no children.

This statement is crucial for the ensuing narrative. Sarai's barrenness and Abram's (and her) attempts to compensate for this fact through some humanly contrived means is what creates tension in the narrative. Abram lies (the first time) about **Sarai** being only his sister evidently because he can see no way that she can be the literal mother of his children. But the readers, both original and canonical, know that she ends up being the mother of the great nation which came from Abraham's seed. This verse anticipates the fact that this comes about only after a divine intervention.

11:31 Terah took his son Abram, his grandson Lot son of Haran, and his daughter-in-law Sarai, the wife of his son Abram, and together they set out from Ur of the Chaldeans to go to Canaan. But when they came to Haran, they settled there.

Abram's brother Nahor evidently came to **Haran** later and not during the initial migration. The initially intended destination was Canaan, but when they had gotten approximately halfway, they stopped and settled permanently at the city of **Haran**.[7] While the introductory formula for the section suggests that this is Terah's section, in fact it comes to be his son Abram's section. Abram goes all the way to the Promised Land, the initial goal of his father Terah's journey **from Ur**. The mention of **Chaldeans** in the description of **Ur** leads the canonical reader to distinguish this Ur in Babylon from another Ur. That Ur was quite near to the northern city of Haran near the source of the Euphrates in modern Syria.

11:32 Terah lived 205 years, and he died in Haran.

According to Genesis 11:26 **Terah** was 70 years old when he became a father. If one assumes that Abram was the first born child (he is listed first), then Abram was 135 when his father Terah **died**. But the other chronological data about Abram make this unlikely. Abram was 75 when he left Haran to move to Canaan (Gen 12:4), 87 when Ishmael was born, 100 at the birth of Isaac, and only 140 when Isaac married Rebekah (Gen 25:20). There is no indication that Abram ever again had any contact with his father after he left for Canaan.

---

[7]In Hebrew the place name Haran (חָרָן, *ḥārān*) is spelled differently than the person's name (הָרָן, *hārān*).

B. ABRAM RECEIVES GOD'S PROMISE AND COMMISSION (12:1-3)

Terah did not go on from Haran to the Promised Land as he orig-inally intended. Consequently it is Abram who receives God's promises. These promises are prefaced with a command to leave his family and adopted homeland and go all the way to a land he had never seen but which the LORD promised to show to him. The fivefold use of the con-cept of blessing in this theologically crucial passage echoes the creation narrative in Genesis 1:26-28 and the re-creation commission to Noah after the flood (Gen 9:1-6). While this might seem to be a minor verbal echo, the theological ramifications are massive. The promise of blessing for Abram is a continuation of the creation commission, which was itself a blessing. That the promised blessing included a land also echoes the creation narrative. In Hebrew the usual word for "land" and the word for "earth" are the same word (אֶרֶץ, *'ereṣ*). The original audience would have seen the connection between a blessing intended for the entire earth (Gen 1:26-28) and a blessing associated with a particular part of that earth, the "land" of Canaan.

The choice of the LORD to focus the accomplishing of his creation-al purposes on a single chosen person and his descendants shows the clear relationship between creation, on the one hand, and such major Old Testament theological categories as covenant, election, and prom-ise on the other. In a sense Abram is the new Adam and the new Noah. He is the chosen person through whom God's desire to bless the entire earth will be channeled.

The tendency of evangelical and many other forms of protestant the-ology[8] to subordinate creation to covenant or minimize the importance of creation in relationship to redemption is challenged by the way the plan of redemption follows necessarily from creation and not vice versa.

12:1 The LORD had said to Abram, "Leave your country, your people and your father's household and go to the land I will show you.

The NIV uses a forced harmonization in translating the *waw*-con-secutive as a past perfect ("had said"). The normal way to read this would be to assume that the LORD called Abram after the death of his father. The NIV's translation assumes that this conversation happened earlier, while Abram was still in Ur of the Chaldeans. While it is true

---

[8]For a helpful critique of this tendency to marginalize creation in historical-crit-ical interpretation of the Old Testament see Theodore Hiebert, "Beyond *Heils-geschichte*," in *Character Ethics and the Old Testament*, ed. by M. Daniel Carroll R. and Jacqueline E. Lapsley (Louisville, KY: Westminster John Knox, 2007), pp. 3-10.

that Genesis 15:7 refers to the LORD "bringing" Abram "out from the Ur of the Chaldeans," that text does not say what the NIV translators assume it says. For another way to understand Genesis 15:7 see the commentary there.

The LORD begins with Abram's responsibility to leave. Those who would interpret this text as an unconditional covenant have difficulty with the LORD beginning his "promise" with a commandment essential for the promise's fulfillment. If Abram does not leave, neither he nor his descendants will ever inherit the Promised Land. While the LORD certainly initiates the relationship, the response of Abram is a necessary condition expected in the LORD's very first word to Abram, "**Leave**."

The word translated "**people**" (מוֹלֶדֶת, *môledeth*) by the NIV is apparently a grouping of people larger than Abram's father's household but smaller than the larger tribal or ethnic group. He must leave his immediate family, his extended family, and even the place where both of them reside if he is to receive the blessings which the LORD is about to promise him. The promise must take priority over everything and everyone else.

The place where Abram will end up is left undefined. The LORD promises to show him it when he leaves. This does not mean that Abram had no idea about where Canaan was. His father had left Ur of the Chaldeans with the intention of going to Canaan. But Abram had never been there, and the exact extent of the boundaries of the land which God was promising him would only be revealed in the future (Gen 12:7).

12:2 "I will make you into a great nation and I will bless you; I will make your name great, and you will be a blessing.

The Hebrew text begins with the word "and" here. By omitting it, as in the NIV, the connection between the commandment in verse 1 and the promise in verse 2 is lost. God's promise is conditioned upon Abram's obedience in leaving his homeland, people, and relatives. While the promise is conditioned upon Abram's faithful obedience, the promise is the LORD's to make and, as we shall see, the LORD's to fulfill. Notice how the divine "I" occurs five times in verses 2 and 3. Abram must remember that the LORD promised to make Abram **into a great nation**. He did not need Abram's help with this, only his obedience in leaving his family behind.

The NIV, like many other translations, translates the last clause of this verse as a simple indicative, "**and you will be a blessing**." But the Hebrew has the imperative,[9] "And be a blessing!" Abram is commanded

---

[9] The qal imperative of הָיָה (*hāyāh*).

by the LORD to be a blessing among the other nations. He is not blessed for his own sake, but in order to bless others. By rewording the imperative into an indicative, translations like the NIV minimize the conditions attached to the promise. While this is helpful in that it emphasizes the important biblical theme of God's grace, it also tips the balance too far away from the responsibility of those chosen by God to use the advantages of being chosen to help others receive that same chosenness.

12:3 I will bless those who bless you, and whoever curses you I will curse; and all peoples on earth will be blessed through you."

This theologically key verse begins with the LORD's promise to treat the nations in the way that they choose to treat Abram's descendants. They are to be the chosen nation, and at a minimum the other nations are expected to leave them alone to fulfill their divinely mandated function.

Why the verbal root for the first occurrence of the word curse (אָרַר, 'ārar) is different from the root of the second occurrence of the word curse (קָלַל, qll) is perplexing. The latter is in the piel. It may be a causative piel meaning to "make contemptible" (in the eyes of others?).[10] Alternatively this may be a case of the use of variation for purely stylistic reasons.

A great debate rages over the translation of the verb "bless" in this text and four others in the patriarchal narratives (18:18; 22:18; 26:4; 28:14). Here the niphal stem, usually the Hebrew passive ("be blessed") is used (also in 18:18 and 28:14) while in the other two cases there is a hithpael, typically the Hebrew reflexive ("bless themselves"). In all five texts God promises to bless the nations because of one of the patriarchs. The NIV translates all five texts as passives, while the NRSV more accurately uses the passive for the niphals (with the reflexive option in the footnote) and the reflexive for the hithpaels. Surprisingly the NASB and the newer ESV translate all five passages as passives. The JPSV has reflexive for all five. I can only wonder at how theological bias has subtle effects on translations. The standard evangelical or conservative translations (NIV, NASB, ESV) tend to be calvinistically oriented, and so, wanting to emphasize the work of God and de-emphasize the response of man, ignore the typical translation of the hithpael as a reflexive ("bless themselves") in Genesis 22:18 and 26:4. The NASB at least provides the more typical rendering in the footnote. The ESV perplexingly provides a footnote of the alternative in 12:3 but does not even mention the issue in the two occurrences of the hithpael. The JPSV is a Jewish

---

[10]Bruce K. Waltke and M. O'Connor, *Biblical Hebrew Syntax* (Winona Lake, IN: Eisenbrauns, 1990), pp. 398-400.

translation and it seems to want to emphasize the response of man and so translates the three niphals (12:3; 18:18; 28:14) along with the two hithpaels as reflexives. Only the NRSV is strictly literal and accurate in both the text and the footnotes. It escapes me why God cannot have said both that the nations would be blessed by Abraham's descendants and that they would bless themselves through Abraham's descendants! Only an imposed theological grid can explain the violation of the literal translation methods of these standard translations in these key texts. This requires one to choose between either God working alone in salvation and spiritual blessing or humanity somehow participating in blessing itself. It cannot be both. Evangelical Christians should contemplate the irony that in this case the purportedly more mainline or "liberal" NRSV is the more strictly accurate translation here.

Tendentious Translations of the Promise to the Patriarchs

Text	NIV	NRSV	NRSV fn	ESV	ESV fn	NASB	NASB fn	JPS
12:3 N	P	P	R	P	R	P		R
18:18 N	P	P	R	P		P		R
22:18 H	P	R		P		P	R	R
26:4 H	P	R		P		P	R	R
28:14 N	P	P	R	P		P		R

N = Niphal   H = Hithpael   fn = footnote   P = Passive   R = Reflexive

C. ABRAM RESPONDS TO GOD'S PROMISE (12:4-6)

The Bible here anticipates what it will soon narrate. On the one hand Abram obeys and leaves his family behind in faith that the LORD would fulfill his promises. On the other hand Abram's obedience is less than complete or perfect. He takes Lot with him along with the servants they had acquired in Haran. In taking Lot Abram was, strictly speaking, disobeying the LORD's command. Abram undoubtedly had good reasons for doing so; reasons which he thought made his taking Lot an act of faith and not an act of disobedience. But his less-than-complete obedience has long-term consequences for the working out of the promises.

12:4 So Abram left, as the LORD had told him; and Lot went with him. Abram was seventy-five years old when he set out from Haran.

Abram obeyed the LORD's command and left. But there is a qualification to this obedience. Abram does respond in obedience, but the exception is permitting a member of his father's household and his people to come along, Lot. I would suggest the translation of "and" as "but" in this passage, i.e., "Abram left as the LORD commanded, but Lot went[11] with him." It should be remembered that at least initially Lot acted to go with Abram. Abram merely allowed it to happen. It is only in verse 5 that Abram is said to have actually taken Lot with him. This seemingly minor disobedience ends up bringing with it disastrous consequences in the long term. It is a reminder that God's people have a long track record of making the fulfillment of God's promises more complicated than need be by incomplete obedience.

12:5 He took his wife Sarai, his nephew Lot, all the possessions they had accumulated and the people they had acquired in Haran, and they set out for the land of Canaan, and they arrived there.

Verse 5 begins with another *waw*-consecutive, the most common way to indicate temporal succession in Hebrew narrative. One might translate it, "Then he took his wife . . ." If the *waw*-consecutive is understood in its common use implying the next thing that happened, it would imply that it was only after leaving that Abram took his wife, nephew, and possessions. This seems unlikely in this context. If the *waw*-consecutive is read as implying logical rather than temporal sequence one might translate, "And so he took his wife, his nephew . . ." In any case Abram takes a family member (Lot) with him in disobedience to the LORD's command.

He also took "**the people**" whom they had acquired while living in Haran. This evidently refers to servants, although the Hebrew is interesting. The word which the NIV renders as "people" is actually the Hebrew word *nephesh* in the singular. It might be translated "the life." The word does occasionally refer to animal life, although in this case it probably refers to the servants obtained in Haran. Abram evidently did well economically during his time in Haran.

12:6 Abram traveled through the land as far as the site of the great tree of Moreh at Shechem. At that time the Canaanites were in the land.

Why are the Canaanites mentioned here? The land of Canaan is mentioned twice in verse 5.[12] Perhaps the point is that while the Canaan-

---

[11]Does the second *waw*-consecutive in verse 4 imply that Abram first went "as the LORD said to him" and then, after obeying completely, allowed Lot to come along? In any case Lot's accompanying of Abram is separated grammatically from Abram's leaving.

[12]The NIV is paraphrastic in verse 5, using "there" for the second mention of Canaan in the Hebrew.

ites were in control of the land, it would take real faith for Abram to believe that God would give him a land they already occupied. In accepting God's promise of the gift of an already occupied land, Abram serves as a model for Israel to trust God's gift of the land. This is so even though they too face an already occupied land.

D. GOD IDENTIFIES THE LAND OF HIS PROMISE (12:7-9)

When the initial promise was given in 12:1-3, the land was left undefined, the LORD promising to show it to Abram. This does not seem to mean that Abram had no idea of where the land was. His father had left Ur to go to Canaan. Abram knew what direction to head toward when he left Haran.

Abram arrives in the Promised Land, stopping in the north near Shechem, in the middle at Bethel, and finally in the south in the Negev. In so doing Abram visits the land in its entirety, in a sense claiming it as the Promised Land.

12:7 The LORD appeared to Abram and said, "To your offspring I will give this land." So he built an altar there to the LORD, who had appeared to him.

Previously the LORD had merely spoken to Abram. Here he "appears" (niphal of הָאָר, *r'h*) to him. Seemingly, this makes the revelation more certain now that he has taken the risk and left. In 12:1 the LORD promised to "show" Abram the land (hiphil of *r'h*). Abram not only "saw" the land, but also "saw" the LORD. This confirms that the land is the correct one, even though it is named after a person and inhabited by his descendants. The LORD promises to give this land specifically to Abram's "offspring" or more literally "seed." One wonders whether Lot could qualify as Abram's seed, given that he is actually only Abram's nephew.[13] Abram, unlike the LORD, apparently regards Lot as his heir and thus would not see the LORD's point. This seems to be the most likely explanation for the ensuing events. Abram protects Lot above even his own wife (Gen 12:10-20); he shows great concern for his welfare, even risking his own safety by fighting a coalition of kings in order to bring him back safely (Gen 14:13-16).

12:8 From there he went on toward the hills east of Bethel and pitched his tent, with Bethel on the west and Ai on the east. There he built an altar to the LORD and called on the name of the LORD.

The second stopping place as Abram travels through the land from north to south is Bethel. The original and canonical audiences would have made the connection between Abram building an altar between Bethel and Ai and the nation's defeat of those cities immediately after

---

[13]Heard, *Dynamics*, p. 27.

the taking of Jericho (Josh 8:1-29). The statement, "And he called on the name of the LORD," echoes Genesis 4:26 when humanity first began to call on the name of the LORD in worship after the expulsion from Eden.

12:9 Then Abram set out and continued toward the Negev.

With this third segment of Abram's initial journey to the Promised Land the entire land has been traversed; the north at Shechem, the center at Bethel, and the south in the Negev. He thus symbolically "takes ownership" of the land the LORD promised to him. This places Abram in the part of the country nearest to Egypt (to which he travels in v. 10) and also in the most desolate region. In the Bible the Negev (derived from a root meaning "to be dry")[14] usually refers to the "Beer-sheba drainage basin."[15] While he dies with only a single grave site purchased at an exorbitant price, the imagined audience knows that they traverse the same land which Abram had earlier traveled, only this time they will actually take possession of it. For the canonical audience this provides reassurance that though they are subservient to an empire, the land remains God's gift.

II. THE LOT STRATEGY (12:10–15:21)

Throughout the narrative Abra(ha)m struggles to come to the point where he leaves the fulfillment of God's promises in God's hands. Up until Isaac's near sacrifice in chapter 22 the narrative is driven by a series of attempts by Abra(ha)m to see to the fulfillment himself. In doing so he unwittingly places the promise in jeopardy. The first of those strategies involves adopting Lot, formally or informally, as his own son and presumptive heir. This creates a series of problems such as risking Sarai's life, offering to give away the rights to the Promised Land, risking the personal safety of Abra(ha)m as he goes into battle against a coalition of kings in order to save Lot, etc. The end result of taking Lot with him is the creation of two long-term enemy nations immediately to Israel's east, the Moabites and the Ammonites.

A. THE FIRST CHALLENGE TO THE PROMISE:
A FAMINE SENDS ABRAM TO EGYPT (12:10-20)

Abram just arrived in the Promised Land and received divine confirmation that it was in fact the very land that would be given to Abram's

---

[14]*HALOT*, "נגב," p. 665.
[15]Lynn Tatum, "Negeb," *EDB*, p. 955.

descendants. The reader is then shocked to learn that a famine drives Abram from the land to danger in Egypt. What sort of Promised Land is it if those to whom it is promised face famines which drive them to leave the land? The original and canonical audiences would see the parallel between Abram's situation and the later situation of the family and then nation of Israel. Another famine drove Israel the person, otherwise known as Jacob, to leave the Promised Land for Egypt (Gen 41:57; 46:1-7).

1. Abram Leaves the Promised Land (12:10)

12:10 Now there was a famine in the land, and Abram went down to Egypt to live there for a while because the famine was severe.
 Already in the Negev, an arid part of the land, Abram faces the first of several challenges to the fulfillment of God's promise when the land is struck by a heavy **famine**. Abram did not go merely to visit **Egypt**, but to "sojourn" (גּוּר, *gûr*) there. The famine was evidently heavy enough that Abram planned to stay for some time, although not permanently. The imagined audience knows from personal experience the dangers which threaten the chosen people in Egypt. It was another famine which resulted in the family of Israel going to live in Egypt in the time of Joseph. For the original audience this text would be history anticipating itself.

2. Abram's Strategy to Protect Himself Outside of the Promised Land (12:11-15)

Abram instinctively knew the dangers a wandering nomad with an extraordinarily beautiful wife would face in Egypt, and he prepares for that danger. Either Abram is a monster who does not take seriously his responsibility as head of the house in a patriarchal social system to protect his wife, or something else is going on in this narrative.[16] Given the

---

[16]Barry Eichler ("On Reading Genesis 12:10-20," *Tehillah le-Moshe: Biblical and Judaic Studies in Honor of Moshe Greenberg*, ed. by Mordechai Cogan, Barry L. Eichler, and Jeffrey Tigay [Winona Lake, IN: Eisenbrauns, 1997], pp. 23-37) argues from biblical and other ANE sources about the social importance of a brother as the protector of an unmarried sister. He cites Genesis 34 (the rape of Dinah) and 2 Samuel 13 (the rape of Tamar), the latter turning to her brother Absalom, not her father David, for help. From this he seems to find a way of absolving Abram of responsibility for lying and of endangering Sarai in this text. The parallels which Eichler cites are read as simplistically and heroically as he reads Genesis 12.

total context, the most likely explanation is that Abram at this point regards Lot as his potential heir since Sarai has long ago been determined to be barren (Gen 11:32). For Abram, Lot is the key to the fulfillment of God's promise. This does not absolve Abram of his lying or his lack of faith in God's protection. Unfortunately he only regards Sarai's safety and well-being as essential when he thinks she is necessary to the fulfillment of the promise of a great nation of descendants. But this does make some sense of why Abram does what he does.

12:11 As he was about to enter Egypt, he said to his wife Sarai, "I know what a beautiful woman you are.

The physical beauty or otherwise of biblical characters is rarely commented upon. When we do receive comment, it is almost always important for the understanding of the plot. Given Sarai's age the reader might be confused at why Pharaoh would want her for his harem. Abram's evaluation of Sarai's beauty, even at age 65, turns out to be accurate as Pharaoh's princes notice and praise Sarai to Pharaoh. Even younger men notice her beauty!

12:12 When the Egyptians see you, they will say, 'This is his wife.' Then they will kill me but will let you live.

While Abram's actions in this narrative are hardly justifiable and sound suspiciously like risking his wife's life in order to protect his own, there is an explanation (partial though it be) which the narrative context supplies. The promise at this point had been made to Abram, not to Sarai and Abram together. As noted above, the apparent motive for taking Lot along was to provide a means for the fulfillment of the promise through Lot since Sarai had long been barren. She was at least 65 years of age at this time and had never had children. Abram did not yet know that the LORD intended to supply an heir through miraculous intervention (Gen 17:16).

12:13 Say you are my sister, so that I will be treated well for your sake and my life will be spared because of you."

Abram sees the material blessings which he will receive (one of the elements of God's promise!) by his scheme. He does not seem to realize that by endangering Sarai he is endangering the mother of the promised "great nation." But the reader knows that he is doing just that. This is the second instance of a pattern in the portrayal of Abra(ha)m in which he persists in endangering the very promise which he so desperately wants to see fulfilled. His and Sarai's scheming do nothing but complicate the fulfillment of the promise with long-term consequences for the nation which descends from them.

12:14 When Abram came to Egypt, the Egyptians saw that she was a very beautiful woman. 12:15 And when Pharaoh's officials saw her, they praised her to Pharaoh, and she was taken into his palace.

As Abram had predicted the Egyptians saw Sarai's great beauty. The point is emphasized even further by the word "very." The "officials" of Pharaoh are actually called "princes" in the Hebrew, a word which rhymes with Sarai's name, which means "princess."[17] The princes saw the 65-year-old princess and praised her to Pharaoh.[18] The result was that Pharaoh took Sarah into his harem. The mother of the promised nation is one of Pharaoh's potential sexual partners.

3. Abram Receives Material Blessings in Egypt (12:16)

Although the text does not in any way praise Abram for his lying or for his attempting to help God out in the fulfillment of his promises, the original and canonical audience will see both God's protection of Abram from harm and his blessing him with the "spoils of Egypt" while he was there.

12:16 He treated Abram well for her sake, and Abram acquired sheep and cattle, male and female donkeys, menservants and maidservants, and camels.

The form of good treatment which Abram had anticipated with his scheme is explained. The inclusion of menservants and maidservants among the list of possessions which Abram was given in Egypt is troublesome to modern readers who are sensitive to the horrors of modern slavery. It is unlikely that the original audience (whether imagined or canonical) would have reacted this way. Slavery was a fact of life in the ancient world and was quite common. While the Old Testament laws attempt to mitigate its effects, they do not prohibit it. But the imagined and canonical audiences would have been sensitive to the hard realities of slavery having recently experienced it in Egypt and in exile. Israel's law did prohibit the enslaving of fellow Israelites except in the exceptional circumstances of debt slavery, something akin to indentured servanthood in more modern times.[19] The irony of Abram obtaining slaves

---

[17]Sarai's name is שָׂרַי (*śāray*) in Hebrew while the Egyptians are termed שָׂרֵי (*śārê*).

[18]The Hebrew word for "praise" here is הָלַל (*hālāl*) from which we derive the word, "hallelujah."

[19]See Gregory C. Chirichigno, *Debt-Slavery in Israel and the Ancient Near East*, JSOTSupp 141 (Sheffield: Sheffield Academic, 1993).

in Egypt where his descendants would later serve for centuries as slaves to the Egyptians would not be lost on the original readers.

The NIV reorders the list of presents. In the Hebrew the order is: sheep, oxen, (male) donkeys, menservants, maid servants, she asses, and camels. Sarna suggests that the male donkeys are separated from the female donkeys because of the experience of ancient ass-herders. Males become uncontrollable when they scent the presence of females and so they are kept separate.[20]

The NIV's "**acquired**" is too strong, implying Abram's activity in obtaining his wealth. The implication seems to be that these things (and persons) were given to Abram as a gift when Sarai was taken into Pharaoh's harem.

The imagined audience would undoubtedly relate the material possessions which Abram gained in Egypt to the "plundering" of the Egyptians in the time of the Exodus (Exod 12:35). Because of God's protective hand, the oppression in Egypt became the very occasion and means for the material blessing of his people.

The mention of camels being acquired by Abram has long been pointed to as a demonstration of the anachronistic nature of the Genesis narratives.[21] The first certain reference to a domesticated camel in the regions immediately adjacent to Palestine is from the eleventh century B.C.[22] But such assumptions must be questioned today. R. Bulliet[23] argues that camels were used in caravans during the third millennium B.C. and by 1000 B.C. were used for military purposes throughout the ancient Near East. Further, these camels were acquired in Egypt. Trade between Egypt and southeastern Arabia, where domesticated camels are first attested, was undoubtedly prolific.

4. Egypt Receives God's Curse (12:17-19)

Here God not only protects Abram from harm, but he also actively curses those who would curse him by taking the mother of the promise

---

[20]Nahum M. Sarna, *Genesis*, JPSTC (Philadelphia: Jewish Publication Society, 1989), p. 96.

[21]This longstanding assertion has recently been repeated by as careful a scholar as John J. Collins (*Introduction to the Hebrew Bible* [Minneapolis: Fortress, 2004], pp. 85-86).

[22]From the time of Assur-bel-kala from Assyria (c. 1074–1057 B.C.). J.D. Currid, "Travel and Transportation," *DOTP*, p. 872.

[23]R. Bulliet, *The Camel and the Wheel* (Cambridge, MA: Harvard University Press, 1975), cited in Currid, "Travel and Transportation," *DOTP*, p. 871.

into Pharaoh's harem. God had promised to curse those who would curse Abram and here we see one example of how that works out in practice.

12:17 But the LORD inflicted serious diseases on Pharaoh and his household because of Abram's wife Sarai.

The word translated "**diseases**" in the NIV (נְגָעִים, *nᵉgāʿîm*) is also used in reference to the final plague in Exodus 11:1. The original audience would undoubtedly see the parallel between the LORD plaguing the Pharaoh in the time of Abram and the LORD plaguing a later Pharaoh at the original Passover with its plague on the firstborn. The same God who had protected Abram later protected Abram's descendants, the nation of Israel.

12:18 So Pharaoh summoned Abram. "What have you done to me?" he said. "Why didn't you tell me she was your wife?

We are not told how Pharaoh came to know that Sarai was Abram's wife, not his sister. Did Sarai tell him? Unlike Abram's expectations Pharaoh does not seek to kill Abram when he discovers this.

12:19 Why did you say, 'She is my sister,' so that I took her to be my wife? Now then, here is your wife. Take her and go!"

Pharaoh's question to Abram is evidently rhetorical since no answer is given or expected. Pharaoh commands Abram to leave just as the Pharaoh of the Exodus commanded the nation to leave many years later (Exod 12:32)

5. Abram Returns to the Promised Land (12:20)

Just as God later brought the nation out of Egypt and (eventually) into the Promised Land, in this passage the forefather of the nation anticipates the later journey out of Egypt and into the Promised Land.

12:20 Then Pharaoh gave orders about Abram to his men, and they sent him on his way, with his wife and everything he had.

Abram is sent away with the many possessions he received as presents when the Egyptians thought Sarai was his sister. His scheme has worked but only because of the LORD's protecting hand. Abram has put the promise at risk from a human point of view, but the LORD has seen to it that even Abram's bumbling, in the end works toward the fulfillment of his purposes.

GENESIS 13

B. THE SECOND CHALLENGE TO THE PROMISE: COPING WITH MATERIAL PROSPERITY, THE SEPARATION OF ABRAM AND LOT (13:1-18)

When Abram and Lot return to the Promised Land they return with significant wealth, much of which was given to them by Pharaoh. That wealth, however, turns out to be a mixed blessing. On the one hand it is a sign of God's protection and blessing. His promises have already begun to be fulfilled. But Abram and Lot and the extended family of wives, children, and servants, are still wandering Bedouin with no claim on the Promised Land. The "sheep and cattle, male and female donkeys, menservants and maidservants, and camels" which Abram has received through his deceitfulness must now have enough pasturage to keep them healthy. But Abram does not own or have permanent rights to a single acre of such pasturage in Canaan. He lives on the margins of society and wanders from place to place trying to find enough unoccupied or lightly guarded land to feed his multitudinous animals. And the decision to allow Lot to come also begins to cost Abram. Suddenly there is division in the family. There are Abram's shepherds and there are Lot's shepherds, and they are at odds with each other. Abram, in what he must have regarded as an act of generosity to keep the peace, offers Lot the choice of pasturage; but in doing so Abram gave Lot the opportunity to choose the Promised Land. The descendants of his nephew Lot, not the descendants of Abram through his wife Sarai are offered the land which God had specifically promised to Abram. The promise of the land is unwittingly put under threat by Abram's offer! But as always throughout this narrative, the LORD is in ultimate control and does not allow even Abram's unwise generosity to get in the way of the fulfillment of the promise. Of course none of this conflict would have arisen if Abram had been strictly obedient when the LORD called upon him to leave his family behind in Haran.

1. Abram Returns to the Promised Land a Rich Man (13:1-4)

13:1 So Abram went up from Egypt to the Negev, with his wife and everything he had, and Lot went with him.

Abram returned to the place ("**the Negev**") from which he left the Promised Land. This verse thus rounds off the previous narrative. It also prepares the reader for the conflict which is about to arise. The Negev was, oddly enough, the semidesert region in the southern portion of ancient Palestine which allowed only for subsistence agriculture or Bedouin shepherding.

The way in which Lot is described as accompanying him reminds the reader of Genesis 12:4, where Lot's company is also described in a separate clause. This is in contrast to Genesis 12:5 where Abram "took" Lot. This may be a subtle indication that Lot is distinct from Abram's own family and that, therefore, the narrator does not give approval for the complications which his presence creates for the working out of the promises of the LORD to Abram.

13:2 Abram had become very wealthy in livestock and in silver and gold.

The wealth in livestock and the need for pasturage becomes a point of contention between Lot and Abram. Ironically the material possessions which Abram had obtained become the source of internal tension within the family. The material possessions prove to be a mixed blessing. The servants which Abram had acquired in Egypt (Gen 12:16) are not mentioned.

13:3 From the Negev he went from place to place until he came to Bethel, to the place between Bethel and Ai where his tent had been earlier 13:4 and where he had first built an altar. There Abram called on the name of the LORD.

The striking repetition between this passage and Genesis 12:8-9 (see chart oposite) seems to indicate a return to a state of normalcy before the decision to move south to the Negev and from there to Egypt. Notice that both passages refer to Bethel, Ai, and the Negev (in reverse order). Both passages mention a tent and an altar built between Bethel and Ai where Abram called on the name of the LORD. The result of this is to demonstrate that Abram has retraced his steps.[1] Bethel and Ai recall the earliest days of Israel's entering the land under Joshua (Josh 7–8). After Jericho the only defeat of Israel occurs at Ai because of Achan's sin of

---

[1]For another, more complex, example of geographical chiastic structure see, Paul J. Kissling, *Reliable Characters in the Primary History*, JSOTSupp 224 (Sheffield: Sheffield Academic, 1996), p. 156.

stealing the plunder for himself and his family. After the resolution of the incident, Ai and Bethel are defeated. Bethel is located in the center of the Promised Land, not on its southern border. Abram has returned to the center of the land with God's material blessings in tow. The implied audience would see that their forefather Abram had first traveled on the way that they were later to travel.

Bethel (12:8)   Bethel (13:3b-4)
  Negev (12:9)   Negev (13:3)
            Egypt (12:10-20)

Geographical Chiastic Structure in Genesis 12–13

Genesis 12:8-9	Genesis 13:3-4
From there he went on toward the hills east of *Bethel* and pitched *his tent*, with *Bethel* on the west and *Ai* on the east. *There* he *built an altar* to the LORD and *called on the name of the* LORD. Then Abram set out and continued toward the *Negev*.	From the *Negev* he went from place to place until he came to *Bethel*, to the place between *Bethel* and *Ai* where *his tent* had been earlier and where he had first *built an altar*. *There* Abram *called on the name of the* LORD.

2. Riches Obtained in Egypt Lead to Internal Conflict with Lot (13:5-7)

13:5 Now Lot, who was moving about with Abram, also had flocks and herds and tents.

Lot is not identified as Abram's presumed heir, but as a relative who was "moving about with Abram." This may be a subtle way for the narrator to distinguish between the real heir and the heir whom Abram presumes he already has. The mention of "tents" seems to clarify that Lot does not directly live with Abram. He has his own place to live no matter what Abram may think about him as a potential heir.

13:6 But the land could not support them while they stayed together, for their possessions were so great that they were not able to stay together.

I wonder if this might echo for the audience the problem that the transjordanian tribes expressed and that resulted in their living on the other side of the Jordan in Numbers 32:1-5. They, like Abram and Lot, came out of Egypt with a great number of cattle (Num 32:1). This seeming blessing resulted in the temptation to live outside of the land on the other side of the Jordan. The canonical audience of course was all too aware of the problem that the descendants of Lot, the Ammonites in particular, created for the nation (Neh 13:1-9; Ezra 9:1).

**13:7 And quarreling arose between Abram's herdsmen and the herds-
men of Lot. The Canaanites and Perizzites were also living in the land
at that time.**

While Genesis 12:6 mentions only the Canaanites living in the land,
this verse adds the Perizzites to the Canaanites. This could imply that the
situation had changed while Abram was in Egypt during the famine. The
Perizzites had moved in, and this had exacerbated the problem of too
many people (with their animals) and too little land. The parallel between
these two rather pedantic seeming comments (12:6 and 13:7) is another
piece of evidence for the chiastic structure of this section. The word
"quarreling" (רִיב, *rîb*) is often used in legal contexts of a lawsuit.[2] Here it
refers to normal quarreling of a serious nature. The permanent inhabitants of the land made scarce the vacant land available for Bedouins.

3. Abram Risks Giving Away the Promised Land to Lot,
but Does Not (13:8-13)

**13:8 So Abram said to Lot, "Let's not have any quarreling between you
and me, or between your herdsmen and mine, for we are brothers.**

Abram takes the initiative in resolving the quarrel. While the argument is actually between their herdsmen, the potential for conflict which
might damage their relationship is there. Abram refers to Lot as his
"brother" although literally he is his nephew and has apparently been
viewed as Abram's heir apparent. The independent wealth of Lot in terms
of flocks and herds (acquired mainly in Egypt in Lot's case perhaps)
means that they now relate to one another in a different way. Abram recognizes this. Lot is no longer Abram's nephew, but his brother.

**13:9 Is not the whole land before you? Let's part company. If you go
to the left, I'll go to the right; if you go to the right, I'll go to the left."**

Abram, in what for him must have been intended as an act of generosity, suggests that they part[3] amicably and gives Lot first choice of
land. It is not entirely clear what Abram refers to as the "whole land."
Is it the land of Palestine? In Hebrew it could mean the entire earth,
although this seems unlikely in this context. Since what Abram suggests
is that they part company, the question arises, has there been a change
in Abram's thinking about Lot, or is it merely a physical separation with-

---

[2] G. Liedke, "רִיב, *rîb* to quarrel," *TLOT*, ed. by Ernst Jenni and Claus Westermann, trans. by Mark E. Biddle (Peabody, MA: Hendrickson, 1997), 3:1233.

[3] The word translated, "part company" (פָּרַד, *pārad*) is used of the separation
of nations in Gen 10:5,32; 25:23.

out permanent implications? The reader, of course, knows that even
though Abram's offer was well-intended, he is once again putting the
promise at risk. If Lot had chosen the land around Bethel within the
Promised Land proper (on the west side of the Jordan) this would create a great difficulty for the fulfillment of the promise. Lot's descendants, the Moabites and the Ammonites, were not to be conquered by
Israel when they finally entered the Promised Land (Deut 2:9,19). Like
Esau's descendants, the Edomites, Israel was to leave them alone. If
Lot's descendants ended up in the Promised Land, how could the
promise of the land be fulfilled? What seems at first to be an act of generosity on Abram's part in fact creates a potential complication for the
fulfillment of the promise of the land.

**13:10 Lot looked up and saw that the whole plain of the Jordan was well
watered, like the garden of the LORD, like the land of Egypt, toward
Zoar. (This was before the LORD destroyed Sodom and Gomorrah.)**

The "plain of the Jordan" is evidently the flat land on the eastern side
of the Jordan. Its suitability for grazing flocks is attested by the later desire
of two-and-a-half tribes to settle there rather than cross over to the
Promised Land proper because they had very large herds and flocks
(Num 32:1). Its lushness is compared to Eden and the land of Egypt which
was situated on the Nile. The freed slaves of Israel knew at first hand the
lushness that the Nile's annual flooding provided the Egyptians. The
author informs the reader that this region was even more well-watered
prior to the destruction of Sodom and Gomorrah by brimstone. The
Moab that the audience was familiar with was quite arid. Prior to the judgment, Lot is attracted by the ease of obtaining water and pastureland for
his burgeoning flocks and herds on the other side of the Jordan.

**13:11a So Lot chose for himself the whole plain of the Jordan and set
out toward the east.**

While Abram unintentionally created a potential problem for the
promise of the land, we see here God working behind the scene in
ensuring that Lot does not choose part of the Promised Land. He chose
what seemed to be the best part for himself, leaving Abram with what
remained. He could not have known the long-term consequences of his
somewhat self-serving decision. He ended up living in Sodom with its
negative effect on his wife, his sons-in-law, and even his daughters and
himself. Moving to the east in the book of Genesis is not a sign of God's
favor, but his judgment. When Adam and Eve leave Eden they travel
east. Cain is banished to wandering in the east. Babel was built in the
east. The non-chosen sons of Abraham and Keturah are sent out to the
east. When the Israelites left the presence of God in the Tabernacle or

Temple they went east. The fact that Lot travels east is a hint to the readers that he is heading into danger away from the LORD's presence.

13:11b The two men parted company: 13:12 Abram lived in the land of Canaan, while Lot lived among the cities of the plain and pitched his tents near Sodom.

Abram remains in the Promised Land of Canaan while the now affluent herdsman Lot moved his tents near to the city of Sodom. He is now in some sense or other a city dweller, albeit one who still lives in tents since he lives "in" or "among" (בְּ, *bᵉ*) the cities of the plain, near Sodom. When next we meet him, he has moved into the city of Sodom (Gen 14:12). Lot's story would remind the original readers (and dare I say us too!) of the real dangers of becoming too comfortable in the midst of pagan culture. The influence is gradual enough as to be unnoticeable. Any rational herdsman looks for pasturage with plentiful water. A successful herdsman finds the convenience of city life preferable to the hassle of Bedouin existence. But the potentially negative influence of a pagan culture on one's family and even one's own relationship with the LORD must always be considered.

13:13 Now the men of Sodom were wicked and were sinning greatly against the LORD.

When Lot pitched his tents near Sodom, he was placing himself and his family in danger. Interestingly it is the *men* of Sodom who are singled out. This may be an omen of what is to come in chapter 19. They are described as the "wicked" and as great "sinners" against the LORD. Judgment is coming and Lot has chosen to move into the vicinity of those who are under the LORD's judgment.

4. The LORD Renews the Land Promise after Lot's Departure (13:14-18)

It is significant that the promise of the land is reiterated to Abram only after the departure of Lot. Before that time Abram had evidently presumed Lot to be his heir, but now that Lot had chosen land in the Transjordan outside of the Promised Land, the LORD makes it clear that the land promise is for Abram's descendants, not for Lot's descendants. This implies that there must be another way for the promise to be fulfilled. While Abram continues to feel responsible for Lot as the events of chapters 14 and 18 demonstrate,[4] here the LORD makes clear that the land promise is not dependent in any way on Lot's presence with Abram.

---

[4]In ch. 14 Abram chases down an army and defeats them in battle in order to

13:14 The LORD said to Abram after Lot had parted from him, "Lift up your eyes from where you are and look north and south, east and west. 13:15 All the land that you see I will give to you and your offspring forever.

After the separation from Lot the LORD reaffirms the promise of the land to Abram. He had just nearly given it away to Lot. By waiting until Lot is gone, the reader sees the LORD hinting to Abram that the separation with Lot should not be something that concerns Abram. It is to Abram and not Lot that the promise has been given. Somewhat perplexingly Abram is promised whatever land he is able to see in every direction. When Lot "lifted up" his "eyes," he saw the whole plain of Jordan. But Abram was not being promised the land which Lot has chosen. Perhaps he could not see as far as Lot! In any case, Lot at first sight seems to have gotten the better land. It was relatively unoccupied and well-watered, perfect for a herdsman. Abram's land was occupied, hilly, and less well-watered. The LORD's promise to Abram of land in Genesis 12:7 was now expanded. Its boundaries would be as far as the eye could see in any direction, and he reveals the permanence of the promise with the word "forever" (עַד־עוֹלָם, 'ad-'ôlām),[5] something not said in Genesis 12:7. Though the English word "forever" when pushed to its mathematical sense is an inappropriate translation, the LORD does promise Abram a lasting inheritance in the land that is left to him. Lot has taken what seems to have been the best portion for himself. The LORD also mentions Abram's offspring. The more literalistic translation for this word is "seed." With Lot now gone it implies that Abram's seed is not to come through Lot and will require that the aged man finally has children.

13:16 I will make your offspring like the dust of the earth, so that if anyone could count the dust, then your offspring could be counted.

The "seed" or "offspring" which the LORD promises Abram will be uncountable. In fact it is only to be counted at the LORD's command and not at human initiative.[6] Just as the dust cannot be counted, so the descendants of Abram will be without number.[7]

---

free Lot who had been taken prisoner. In ch. 18 Abraham bargains with the LORD over the destruction of Sodom at least partly in order to save Lot and his family.

[5]The phrase literally translated means "unto the age" and depending on context does not necessarily imply anything more than a long period of time.

[6]The LORD twice commands the numbering of Israel in the wilderness (Num 1:2,3; 26:2), but when David takes it upon himself to number the fighting men, he receives stern judgment (2 Sam 24:1,2).

[7]Cf. Revelation 7:9 where the great multitude which has come through the great tribulation cannot be counted.

13:17 Go, walk through the length and breadth of the land, for I am giving it to you."

Abram is commanded to walk through the entirety of the land to experience for himself just how great and generous the gift is. The Hebrew verb translated as "walk through" is in the hithpael, an unusual form which occurs in instances of God's special presence. The LORD "walked"[8] in the Garden in the cool of the day (Gen 3:8); Enoch and Noah were said to have walked with God (Gen 5:22,24; 6:8). The LORD's presence in the Tabernacle or Temple is often indicated by reference to his "walking" in the hithpael (1 Sam 2:30,35; 2 Sam 7:6,7; 1 Chr 17:6). Since the land is God's gift, to walk through the length and breadth of it is, in a sense, to experience God's presence and this is hinted at by the use of the hithpael of הָלַךְ (hālak, "walk"). The LORD here clarifies that the promise of the land is for Abram alone,[9] not Lot.

13:18 So Abram moved his tents and went to live near the great trees of Mamre at Hebron, where he built an altar to the LORD.

The LORD had commanded Abram to walk through the length and breadth of the land and we see Abram doing this. The verb translated, "moved his tents" may actually refer to the obtaining of grazing rights[10] which would make moving one's tents feasible. He went to the south near Hebron although this time not as far south as the Negev (Gen 12:9). This second visit to the southern portion of the land is different. Now Abram builds an altar to the LORD as he had done previously at Shechem in the north and Bethel in the middle of the land. Abram has now constructed a series of three altars stretching from the north to the south. The land is marked out for the worship of the LORD even though Abram owned none of it.

Abram came to live near the great trees of Mamre. Mamre was one of three Amorite brothers with whom Abram was in some sort of covenant relationship (Gen 14:13). It may also, as here, refer to the place which is named after him.

---

[8]The hithpael typically is reflexive in Hebrew although it can be "iterative" indicating repeated action; cf. Bill T. Arnold and John H. Choi, *A Guide to Biblical Hebrew Syntax* (Cambridge: Cambridge University Press, 2003), pp. 47-48.

[9]In the Hebrew the "you" is singular.

[10]"I אהל," KB, pp. 18-19.

GENESIS 14

C. THE THIRD CHALLENGE TO THE PROMISE:
THE NEED TO RESCUE LOT, THE PRESUMED HEIR (14:1-16)

The original decision to bring Lot along from Haran led to Abram lying about Sarai in Egypt and having her taken into Pharaoh's harem. Later it led to conflict over rights to pasturage between Abram's and Lot's herdsmen and Abram offering to give the Promised Land away to Lot. In this passage it led to Abram becoming embroiled in an armed conflict between two coalitions of kings. The wandering Bedouin feels that he must take up arms to save his nephew Lot, who was taken captive during the war. In so doing Abram puts the promise at risk yet again. And yet again the LORD protects Abram.

Sarna discusses the unusual features of this passage in comparison with the rest of Genesis.[1] This may imply that it was copied from a source document. While we thus far have no specific extrabiblical confirmation of this event, the general historical situation and the names of the kings from the east and north do have an air of plausibility.

1. War between Mesopotamia and Transjordan Results in Lot's Being Captured (14:1-12)

Initial Victory of the Mesopotamian Coalition over Transjordan Kings (14:1-4a)

14:1 At this time Amraphel king of Shinar, Arioch king of Ellasar, Kedorlaomer king of Elam and Tidal king of Goiim

Amraphel comes from **Shinar**, another name for the area of Babylon, not the city. His name is Semitic. While the land of **Ellasar** is not attested in our extant sources, the name of its king, **Arioch** is attested at Mari and Nuzi in northern Mesopotamia. **Kedorlaomer** means "servant of Lagamar," the name for an Elamite language and deity. **Elam** is another Fertile Crescent nation on the Tigris, south of Assyria. **Tidal,**

---

[1]Sarna, *Genesis*, pp. 101-103.

who bears an early Hittite name ("Tud") is called **"king of Goiim."**
Ordinarily this word means "nations." Kitchen argues that this may be
a Hebrew translation of a known title in Anatolia (roughly modern
Turkey).[2] Traditional historical-critical scholarship has tended to dismiss
this narrative as fictional. However, the evidence of the names of the
kings given is entirely plausible even though the specific events mentioned have not been confirmed in the archeological record.

**14:2 went to war against Bera king of Sodom, Birsha king of Gomor-
rah, Shinab king of Admah, Shemeber king of Zeboiim, and the king
of Bela (that is, Zoar).**

The opponents of the Fertile Crescent powers are Sodom, the new
residence of Lot, and four cities nearby on the east bank of the Dead
Sea. The city of **Bela** was evidently unknown to the original and/or
canonical audience(s) and so its contemporary name, **Zoar**, is given.
This could be another piece of evidence that the author of Genesis is
here copying from a source to which he adds an explanatory note.

**14:3 All these latter kings joined forces in the Valley of Siddim (the
Salt Sea). 14:4a For twelve years they had been subject to Kedorlaomer,**

The place where the king of Sodom and his allies gathered was by
the time of the audience covered by the "salt sea" — evidently a description of what is now called the "Dead Sea," a body of water 400 meters
below sea level and reputedly the lowest place on earth. Consequently
there is no natural outlet for the silt and other impurities which flow
into it from the Jordan rift.

Rebellion and Defeat of Transjordan Kings (14:4b-11)

14:4b but in the thirteenth year they rebelled.

These kings had served the Elamite king Kedorlaomer for a dozen
years before deciding to rebel. At one time it was doubted whether a
king from Elam could have controlled territory so far away from home
base on the Tigris at such an early period. With more data, however,
this skepticism has been shown to be unnecessary.[3]

**14:5 In the fourteenth year, Kedorlaomer and the kings allied with
him went out and defeated the Rephaites in Ashteroth Karnaim, the
Zuzites in Ham, the Emites in Shaveh Kiriathaim 14:6 and the Horites
in the hill country of Seir, as far as El Paran near the desert.**

---

[2]Kenneth A. Kitchen, *On the Reliability of the Old Testament* (Grand Rapids:
Eerdmans, 2003), p. 320.

[3]See the discussion in Kitchen, *Reliability*, pp. 319-323.

An empire means nothing if you cannot put down a rebellion. **Kedorlaomer** gathered his army of allies together and came west to put it down. During the campaign the eastern kings took the opportunity to defeat other kings in the area who were not direct participants in the rebellion. The kingdoms defeated, not much more than local chiefdoms at the time, included the lands later occupied by Moab, Ammon, Edom, and the Amorite kings Sihon and Og. The relative weakness of this area provides an explanation for the ease with which the "dis-elected" descendants and relatives of Abram (Lot and Edom) as well as the transjordanian tribes took control of these areas. The original audience would notice that from the earliest days the Fertile Crescent powers had military designs on Canaan and its environs. Canaan had a strategic location in the ancient world. It was the only land bridge between Mesopotamia and northern Africa and gave ready access for Mesopotamian powers to the Mediterranean Sea.

14:7 Then they turned back and went to En Mishpat (that is, Kadesh), and they conquered the whole territory of the Amalekites, as well as the Amorites who were living in Hazazon Tamar.

The coalition from the Fertile Crescent was not satisfied with small sheikdoms to the east of the Jordan rift. They also conquered peoples to the south of Canaan and west of the Jordan and the Dead Sea. Kadesh is otherwise known as Kadesh Barnea, the oasis south of Judah from which the twelve spies were sent on their mission (Num 13:26). The **Amalekites** were the first nation to attack Israel as they came out of Egypt (Exod 17:8-16). The coalition is portrayed as systematically picking off the neighboring kingdoms of the Sodom and Gomorrah alliance. Likely this would be to feed the troops and to eliminate any potential alliances against them. Of course it was also an opportunity for the Elamite-led coalition to further entrench its control of the areas around Palestine with its lucrative spice trade. Caravans traveling through from Arabia to the Mediterranean and northern Africa could easily be "taxed" as they traveled through Canaan.

14:8 Then the king of Sodom, the king of Gomorrah, the king of Admah, the king of Zeboiim and the king of Bela (that is, Zoar) marched out and drew up their battle lines in the Valley of Siddim 14:9 against Kedorlaomer king of Elam, Tidal king of Goiim, Amraphel king of Shinar and Arioch king of Ellasar—four kings against five.

The battle between the transjordanian kingdoms and the northern coalition finally occurs. Undoubtedly **the king of Sodom** and his allies knew that such a battle was inevitable given their rebellion. They seek the battle in a place of their own choosing. Siddim may be a reference to the southern end of the Dean Sea where bitumen deposits float in the water.[4]

For some reason in verse 9 the order of the kings from the east is changed. Sarna suggests that the original listing was alphabetical.[5] This may be no more than minor variation for purely stylistic reasons; but it could be a way of signaling that Kedorlaomer, who is listed first, had by then become the unquestioned leader of the alliance.

14:10 Now the Valley of Siddim was full of tar pits, and when the kings of Sodom and Gomorrah fled, some of the men fell into them and the rest fled to the hills.

The actual battle is not described. Perhaps it never occurred as the men allied with the king of Sodom simply ran away. The Hebrew seems to suggest that it was **the kings[6] of Sodom and Gomorrah** who fell into the tar pits. Tar and asphalt are found in the southern part of the Dead Sea, floating in the water. The word translated "rest" (niphal participle of שָׁאַר, šā'ar) is one of the words for "remnant" in Hebrew.

14:11 The four kings seized all the goods of Sodom and Gomorrah and all their food; then they went away.

Interestingly only Sodom and Gomorrah, not Admah, Zeboiim, and Bela, are plundered. Perhaps the other towns were too small to be bothered with. The food may have been taken to feed the army on their long return to Mesopotamia. It undoubtedly left the cities in a difficult situation. If the campaign took place in the spring (2 Sam 11:1), the grain which had been stored to last the winter would be gone.

Lot's Capture (14:12)

14:12 They also carried off Abram's nephew Lot and his possessions, since he was living in Sodom.

When last we saw Lot, he was living near Sodom. By this time he has moved into the city. The conveniences and attractions of living in the city that is full of wickedness are not without their consequences. The wealth that Lot has gained as a part of the family of Abram is now taken as spoils by the victorious coalition of kings. The Hebrew syntax of this verse is odd. Literally it reads, "Then they took Lot and his possessions, the son of the brother of Abram. Then they went; now he was living in Sodom." While the sense is clear, it seems as though the possessions of

---

[4]Ryan Byrne, "Siddim, Valley of," *EDB*, p. 1218.

[5]Sarna, *Genesis*, p. 102.

[6]The MT is actually singular, "king" here, while the verb implies a plural subject. The SP, Syriac, and LXX read "king of Sodom *and king of* Gomorrah . . ."

Lot are given emphasis by being brought forward. Lot is once again described as the son of Abram's brother. Perhaps this emphasizes that he is not Abram's son and therefore not his legitimate heir.

2. Abram Fights a Battle to Rescue Lot (14:13-16)

Abram Is Informed of Lot's Capture (14:13)

14:13 One who had escaped came and reported this to Abram the Hebrew. Now Abram was living near the great trees of Mamre the Amorite, a brother of Eshcol and Aner, all of whom were allied with Abram.

Abram is referred to as "the Hebrew," a term that ordinarily is used by foreigners to refer to Israel or by Israelites to distinguish themselves from foreigners.[7] Its usage may be evidence that the author of Genesis is quoting from a non-Israelite source which recorded the events of the battle from a non-Israelite perspective.[8] The great trees of Mamre were near Hebron in the southern part of Canaan. We are told that Abram was in a covenant relationship (בְּרִית, *bᵉrîth*) with three Amorite leaders.

Abram's Defeat of the Mesopotamian Coalition (14:14-15)

14:14 When Abram heard that his relative had been taken captive, he called out the 318 trained men born in his household and went in pursuit as far as Dan.

Lot is referred to as Abram's "brother" (עָח, *'āḥ*). Somewhat surprisingly Abram has **318** experienced[9] servants who had been born in his household who could serve as a small army[10] in an emergency. These servants must have been Abram's while he still lived in Haran prior to the move to Canaan as there is not sufficient time for Egyptian servants to be born and raised in his house to adulthood. This presumes that chapter 14 is in chronological sequence.[11]

---

[7]Princeton Abridgement of BDB, "עִבְרִי" in Gramcord.

[8]Sarna, *Genesis*, pp. 101-103.

[9]The idea of Abram having militarily "trained" men as the NIV suggests seems unlikely. The word's etymology (it is only found here) from חָנַךְ (*ḥānak*) meaning "to dedicate" suggests something nonmilitary.

[10]Walton, et al. (*IVPBBCOT*, p. 46), suggests that this "army would have been a match for any other armed force in the region."

[11]Abram was 75 when he left Haran, and Ishmael, whose birth is recorded in chapter 16, was born when Abram was 87. If the events of ch. 14 occurred before the events of ch. 16, no servant who was born in his household could be any older than 11.

The mention of "**Dan**" is anachronistic since the northern location of Dan did not occur until sometime after the conquest (Josh 19:47; Judg 18:1-31). This is an example of a *post-mosaica*[12] in the Pentateuch, something that Moses could not have written. This instance, however, may be nothing more than a copyist updating a place name whose original name would have been unfamiliar to his audience.

Abram's willingness to take a great risk[13] in militarily challenging an army of four allied kingdoms shows his selfless loyalty to Lot. But once again the reader must ask about the wisdom of allowing Lot to come with him to Canaan in the first place. If Lot had not come with Abram, he would not here be placing the promise at risk by attacking an alliance of foreign conquerors.

14:15 During the night Abram divided his men to attack them and he routed them, pursuing them as far as Hobah, north of Damascus.

While Abram acted boldly, he did not act foolishly. Outnumbered, he attacked by night, after dividing his servants (not "men" as in the NIV) into strategic groups. The strategy was successful. He defeated the enemy and pursued them to Hobah, north of Damascus. The imagined audience would no doubt see that the LORD protected Abram though he was outnumbered and granted him victory just as he did later when he brought Israel out of Egypt and into the Promised Land. The Gideon narrative comes to mind in particular — the LORD saves by a few, not by many.

Locating Hobah has so far proved impossible. But driving a foreign army north of Damascus may hint at the ideal borders of the Promised Land extending to the northern branch of the Euphrates as revealed to Abram in the next chapter (Gen 15:18). While Abram has once again put the promise at risk by taking up arms, the LORD's promised protection from all enemies continues.

The Return of Lot and Booty (14:16)

14:16 He recovered all the goods and brought back his relative Lot and his possessions, together with the women and the other people.

During the battle Abram was able to recover the goods from the kings allied with Sodom along with the women and people (presumably servants) who had been captured. More importantly for Abram, his "brother"[14] Lot was saved.

---

[12]See Kissling, *Genesis 1*, pp. 43-44.

[13]Of course since God is in control, Abram never really risks the promise. He only seems to do so.

[14]The NIV paraphrases as "relative" but this may miss the point. Lot is no longer a potential heir. He is a close relative who lives nearby, but not an heir.

D. THE CONTRASTING REACTIONS OF TWO INHABITANTS TO GOD'S PROTECTION OF ABRAM: MELCHIZEDEK AND THE KING OF SODOM (14:17-24)

In the aftermath of the battle in which the lowly Bedouin Abram had defeated an alliance of kings, Abram meets two different inhabitants of the land, Melchizedek and the unnamed king of Sodom. The two could not be more different. Melchizedek is a priest of El Shaddai, but the king of Sodom rules over a city which is full of men who were very wicked sinners in the LORD's eyes. Because the inhabitants of Canaan end up being like Sodom, God's judgment is to fall on them (Lev 18:22-28). But there are other inhabitants who are genuine worshipers of God, like Melchizedek. The contrasting moral character of these two men and Abram's very different reaction to them reminds us of something. God's choice of Abram does not mean that he is the only one open to the LORD. Melchizedek is perhaps the Bible's first example of the spiritually open and seeking outsider. He is followed by Rahab, Ruth, and the people of Nineveh to name just a few. These faithful outsiders pave the way for the ultimate mission to the nations of Jesus Christ and his followers.

1. Abram Receives Melchizedek's Blessing, and Melchizedek Receives Abram's Tithe (14:17-20)

14:17 After Abram returned from defeating Kedorlaomer and the kings allied with him, the king of Sodom came out to meet him in the Valley of Shaveh (that is, the King's Valley).
The location of the valley of Shaveh is uncertain. It is plausible to assume that it is near Salem (Jerusalem) since both the king of Sodom and the king of Salem appear to meet Abram at the same time. The narrator explains the location of this valley in terms with which his or her readers would be familiar, the so-called "king's valley." Second Samuel 18:18 informs us that David's son Absalom, lacking heirs, erected a monument to himself there. Josephus (*Ant.* 7.10.3 §243) claims that this monument was two stadia (400 yards) from Jerusalem. The word "Shaveh" is derived from the root שָׁוָה (*šāwah*) meaning "to make level or smooth" perhaps implying a plain or level area. Astour argues that the location can be proven definitively as the "little plain formed by the junction of the valleys of Hinnom, Tyropoeon, and Kidron,"[15] south and east of Jerusalem.

---

[15]Michaal C. Astour, "Shaveh, Valley of," *ABD*, 5:1168.

14:18 Then Melchizedek king of Salem brought out bread and wine. He was priest of God Most High,

Abram was presumably returning to his home near Hebron when he passed by Salem, evidently an earlier name for Jerusalem.[16] There he was met by **Melchizedek**, who is both **king of Salem** and **priest of "God Most High"** (אֵל עֶלְיוֹן, 'el 'elyōn). The bread and wine which he brings is evidently part of a fellowship meal in which God Most High will be praised. Melchizedek seems to come from nowhere and leave just as mysteriously. This lack of information led to a history of speculative interpretation. For the original readers it would be striking to find an example of such faithfulness living in the midst of Canaan with its fertility religions and other forms of idolatry. For the canonical audience the merger of royal and priestly functions, perhaps even in a single person,[17] would be reminiscent of the same merger that was happening in the concept of the messiah both within the canonical documents (e.g., Jer 33:15-18; Ps 110:4; Zech 6:9-15[18]) and later on at Qumran.[19]

"God Most High" as a way of referring to God is well-attested in the Old Testament, especially in the Psalms. It can be used alone (Ps 50:14; 77:4; 78:17; 82:6; 87:5; 91:1,9), in synonymous parallelism with both יהוה (YHWH; Ps 18:14; 83:19; 92:1) and אֱלֹהִים ('ĕlōhîm; Ps 46:5; 73:11), and in the phrases "God Most High" (אֱלֹהִים עֶלְיוֹן, 'ĕlōhîm 'elyôn, here and in Ps 57:3; 78:35,56; 107:4) and "LORD Most High" (יהוה עֶלְיוֹן, YHWH 'elyôn; cf. Ps 7:18; 47:3; 97:3). God's revelation was not limited to Abram and his descendants (Amos 9:7), Melchizedek is an example and a reminder to Israel of that fact.

14:19 and he blessed Abram, saying, "Blessed be Abram by God Most High, Creator of heaven and earth.

Melchizedek blesses both Abram and the Most High God who had stood behind Abram in giving the wandering Bedouin victory over an

---

[16]Psalm 76:2 places "Salem" in synonymous parallelism with "Zion" another name for Jerusalem. The Genesis Apocryphon from Qumran and the Aramaic Targums also understood it this way. See Michael C. Astour, "Salem," *ABD*, 5:905, for later attempts to locate it at or near Shechem.

[17]Joyce Baldwin, *Haggai, Zechariah, Malachi*, TOTC (Downers Grove, IL: InterVarsity, 1972), pp. 136-137.

[18]Carol L. Myers and Eric M. Myers, "Haggai, Zechariah 1–8," *AB* (Garden City, NY: Doubleday, 1987), pp. 350-362, reject the theory of a single person in Zechariah 6, but show the interrelatedness of the office of king and priest.

[19]C.A. Evans, "Messianism," *DNTB*, p. 703, discusses "Diarchic Messianism" and cites 1QS 9:11 "until there come the Prophet and the Messiahs of Aaron and Israel" and CD 2:23–13:1; 14:19; 19:10-11; 20:1 as evidence.

alliance of four relatively powerful eastern kings. We are not told how Melchizedek had heard of Abram's victory nor how he came to attribute it to the power of God Most High whom Melchizedek served as priest. God Most High is described as the "maker" (קֹנֵה, *qōnēh*) of heaven and earth. This is not one of the typical Hebrew words for creating or making something. It usually refers to the buying or acquiring of something. Perhaps it is better, in this passage, to think of God as the "owner" of heaven and earth rather than specifically its creator.

14:20 And blessed be God Most High, who delivered your enemies into your hand." Then Abram gave him a tenth of everything.

Melchizedek's blessing is not only for Abram but also for the God who has stood behind him in battle. The word translated "delivered" has a related noun meaning "shield." The LORD had been a shield around him even though he had initiated the rescue operation. The LORD had promised Abram that he would curse those who cursed him (Gen. 12:3). And here we see yet another example of the LORD's faithfulness to that aspect of the promise.

Abram responds to Melchizedek's blessings by giving a tithe of everything acquired in the battle.[20] How did Abram know to tithe since the laws on tithing had not yet been given? This is one of a number of texts in Genesis where God's people who live prior to the giving of the law at Sinai obey it. Whether the readers are to presume that this is done instinctively by some innate sense of what God requires or because of more specific revelation of which we are not informed is beside the point. For the original readers this would indicate that the laws which had been revealed to them at Sinai were not arbitrary rules imposed upon them. Instead they were particular instantiations of more universal principles which godly people had observed from the earliest days. Abram obeyed the tithing law before there was a tithing law. Should not the people of Israel, who had received careful instructions regarding it, do the same?

Some have used texts like this to argue that such matters as tithing and Sabbath observance are actually part of the so-called "natural law" and are therefore binding on all people irrespective of whether they lived under the laws revealed at Sinai. Christians therefore tithe and obey the Sabbath[21] because the foundation of these laws is natural revelation.

---

[20]The tithe was given before the king of Sodom told Abram to return the people in v. 21. This demonstrates that Abram regarded the possessions (including the people) won in battle as his own. The King of Sodom is thus being presumptuous in expecting Abram to give him what Abram already "owned."

[21]Many evangelical Christians would apply the law of tithing to Christians, but

Obedience to them has nothing to do with the fact that the physical nation of Israel was required to observe them. This is, at least, a more sophisticated argument than the selective use of Malachi 3:10 to encourage Christians to tithe, as though we continue under the Mosaic covenant. The reasoning is, however, flawed in my judgment. While Abram and Noah were not under the law, the narratives of their obedience to the law before the law was revealed are part of the Pentateuch. The Pentateuch was written for, and specifically addressed to, the nation of Israel who had recently come out of slavery in Egypt. In the case of the canonical audience the slavery they had come out of had been in Babylon. The purpose of narrating that the forefathers of Israel's faith had obeyed laws prior to the giving of the laws in the wilderness period is to encourage Israel to be faithful to their obligations. Christians are not Israel and therefore not under the laws revealed in Leviticus and Deuteronomy. We do learn, however, something about moral principals from the law. While we are not a nation with borders and a literal Promised Land to defend, Abram's example of tithing shows us that giving back to God from what he has graciously given to us is the normally expected response of a person who understands just who God is. While the percentage of giving required of Christians[22] ought not to be derived from this text,[23] the attitude expressed by Abram in responding to God's gracious protection remains instructive.

2. Abram Rejects the King of Sodom's Possessions (unlike the King of Egypt's) (14:21-24)

In terms of ancient custom, Abram had won both the people and the material goods of Sodom in battle. They belonged to him. So the king of Sodom pretending to "give" Abram the goods is a bit presumptuous. He was in no position to bargain with Abram. But in this passage, Abram refuses to keep what he had gained at great risk to himself. In

---

not the law about the Sabbath which is also, in some texts, a law observed before the covenant with Israel and grounded in the pattern of Creation (Exod 20:6). On Noah's apparent obedience to Sabbath rest during the flood see Gordon J. Wenham, *Genesis 1–15*, WBC (Waco, TX: Word, 1987), p. 177.

[22]For affluent Christians in the west, the idea that giving 10% is some great sacrifice and a badge of spirituality shows a failure to understand the materialism and self-absorption that has affected us all. We in the west have been raised to turn whims, desires, and preferences into "needs."

[23]Passages such as 2 Cor 8:1-15; 9:1-15 seem more appropriate texts for giving guidance to Christians on such matters.

chapter 12 Abram gladly received the gifts of Pharaoh. Here, however, Abram recognizes that he should avoid even the appearance of accepting something from the king of Sodom. Those who were "great sinners, wicked in the LORD's sight" (Gen 13:13) were under God's judgment, and Abram knew that he must avoid any commitment which might place him under obligation to the king of Sodom.

14:21 The king of Sodom said to Abram, "Give me the people and keep the goods for yourself."

Unlike Melchizedek who brought out a meal to celebrate God Most High's deliverance of Abram from his enemies, **the king of Sodom** came out to demand that the people taken captive by the eastern alliance be returned. He is under no illusions as the defeated king that he will receive back his possessions. Interestingly he is in no position to make demands or to offer the goods to Abram. They are Abram's. He has won them in war. This would ordinarily be true of the people also. His rhetoric may be an attempt to take control of a situation over which he really has no control. The king does not specifically ask for the return of the women although this may be implied in the word **"people."** The contrast between Melchizedek and the unnamed king of Sodom is striking. The former comes with gifts expecting nothing in return. The latter is under obligation to Abram and comes with demands. The imagined audience might well see an insight into the inhabitants of Canaan. Some, like Melchizedek and Rahab, are quite open to the LORD; others contemptuous of the things and people of God. Faced with the temptation to assimilate too easily with the people of Canaan, whether in the earliest years after coming into the land or after the return from exile, the audience must remember the remarkable openness to God among some "pagans" even while not being naïve about the danger that assimilation poses with others. The people of God throughout their history have struggled to keep this balance correct.

14:22 But Abram said to the king of Sodom, "I have raised my hand to the LORD, God Most High, Creator of heaven and earth, and have taken an oath 14:23 that I will accept nothing belonging to you, not even a thread or the thong of a sandal, so that you will never be able to say, 'I made Abram rich.' 14:24 I will accept nothing but what my men have eaten and the share that belongs to the men who went with me—to Aner, Eshcol and Mamre. Let them have their share."

Abram responds to the somewhat presumptuous demand of the king of Sodom by informing him (and the readers[24]) that he had taken

---

[24]Has Abram actually taken such an oath and the reader is not informed of it, or is this more rhetorical?

an oath to refuse gaining from the battle through which the LORD had led him. Abram adopts the description of God which Melchizedek had just given him, God Most High, Creator of heaven and earth. He adds (or more likely the narrator) adds the word LORD to the description to ensure that readers understand that the God worshiped and served by Melchizedek is the same God who later brought the nation out of Egypt.[25] Abram decided to keep nothing which he had gained through the battle, not even a thread which belonged to the king of Sodom's coalition. He wanted the LORD to be given the credit for blessing him and not the king of a city whose iniquity was notorious and well-deserved. Abram, of course, cannot volunteer what belongs to others. His "young men" had eaten some of the food recovered and his allies, Aner, Eshcol, and Mamre, had the right to a share of the spoils as victors. By reminding the king of Sodom of this, Abram makes it clear that the spoils are his to take if he so chooses. The king of Sodom no longer owns them and so cannot give them to Abram. But Abram's allies had also taken great risks and they were entitled to their fair share.

---

[25]See the discussion of this point with reference to Genesis 22 in R.W.L. Moberly, *The Bible, Theology, and Faith: A Study of Abraham and Jesus* (Cambridge: Cambridge University Press, 2000), pp. 94-97.

GENESIS 15

E. THE FOURTH CHALLENGE TO THE PROMISE: ABRAM'S UNCERTAINTY LEADS TO THE PROMISE BEING REAFFIRMED (15:1-21)

We do not know exactly when the events recorded in this narrative happened. Apparently Abram had been in the Promised Land for some time. With Lot permanently settled in Sodom and no longer his pre-sumptive heir and Sarai still barren, the issue arises of just how the promises which the LORD had made to Abram when he left Haran were to be fulfilled. In this passage the LORD speaks to Abram to reaffirm the promise only to see Abram express his uncertainty about its fulfillment. Such uncertainty, if not contained, could lead to the promise being nul-lified by Abram's lack of faith. But the LORD responds to that uncer-tainty by clarifying and expanding the promise. Lot will not be his heir. Abram will himself father a son! But the promise of the land will be for Abram's descendants, not Abram. Even his descendants will have to wait until the time comes for God's judgment to fall on the Canaanites.

1. Abram's Uncertainty (15:1-3)

15:1 After this, the word of the LORD came to Abram in a vision: "Do not be afraid, Abram. I am your shield, your very great reward."

After the victory over the eastern coalition and the rescue of Lot, Abram was granted a vision in which the LORD spoke to him. He is told not to fear. He had just taken a great risk by pursuing the four kings. Living in the Promised Land or its environs had proven to be very dan-gerous and threatening. The LORD tells Abram that He is his shield (מָגֵן, *māgēn*) of protection. Abram had just experienced that very facet of God's promise. The word for shield is etymologically related to the verb translated "delivered" in Genesis 14:20 (מִגֵּן, *māgān*). The LORD had shielded Abram when he pursued the kings, and he promises to con-tinue to be his shield.

The second part of the message, however, is harder for Abram to accept. The LORD reassured Abram that he was not only his protector but that he would also give him or be for him a "very great reward." The word translated "reward" usually means wages for work performed, but that seems to stretch the analogy too far in this instance. Abram is not earning anything in his relationship with God. The NRSV suggests translating the nominal clause, "your reward *will be* very great" (italics mine). In other words, it will be worth it in the end for Abram to remain faithful.

15:2 But Abram said, "O Sovereign LORD, what can you give me since I remain childless and the one who will inherit my estate is Eliezer of Damascus?"

Abram interprets the LORD's promise of a very great reward as something that the LORD would give him. Abram uses an unusual designation for God here. The NIV's "Sovereign LORD" shows the Calvinistic tendency of the translation.[1] The NRSV uses "Lord GOD." In each case the presence of the Tetragrammaton[2] is indicated by the use of small capitals. In using this unusual[3] designation for God Abram expresses his confidence in God's gracious power while at the same time asking an honest question. Lot is now obviously permanently gone. Abram is somewhere between 75 and 86 years of age at this point and his wife ten years younger. He has been "stripped"[4] of any hope for descendants. In fact with Lot now gone he has no heir and a servant, **Eliezer**, will inherit the wealth that the LORD had given him. We do not know who Eliezer was, but his hometown, Damascus, may hint that he was only recently brought into Abram's house during the pursuit of the eastern coalition past Damascus. The LORD had promised that a great nation would descend from Abram's seed and so far he had no hope of realizing the promise.

15:3 And Abram said, "You have given me no children; so a servant in my household will be my heir."

With no intervening response from the LORD Abram essentially repeats the concern. This time he says that the LORD had given him no "seed" (זֶרַע, *zera‘*). It is not entirely clear why Abram repeats the same

---

[1]The word "Sovereign" is often a sort of code word for the Calvinistic concept of sovereignty.

[2]The four-consonant word for God in his special relationship with Israel (יהוה) is usually vocalized as Yahweh, although the Jewish scribes who copied the Massoretic text had stopped vocalizing it from an early date.

[3]The phrase occurs in 291 verses in the Hebrew Bible, 210 of those in Ezekiel.

[4]The Hebrew word for "childless" is derived from a root, ערר ('*rr*) meaning "to strip."

complaint. This time, however, the person is not named. He is only described as "a son of my house" meaning evidently someone already in his house as a servant will end up being the heir.

2. Divine Reassurance of an Heir from Abram's Own Body (15:4-6)

15:4 Then the word of the LORD came to him: "This man will not be your heir, but a son coming from your own body will be your heir."

This time the LORD responded to Abram's expression of concern, reassuring him that a servant would not be his heir. Instead a son, yet to be born from Abram's own body would be his heir. While this does not make clear that it is to be a son born from Abram and Sarai, it at least makes it clear that neither Lot nor a servant already within the household would be the heir. Abram is to have a son.

15:5 He took him outside and said, "Look up at the heavens and count the stars—if indeed you can count them." Then he said to him, "So shall your offspring be."

In order to reinforce this point the LORD takes Abram outside at night to look at the stars. There he gives Abram a moment to attempt to count the stars and then tells him the point of the field trip. The numberless stars are to be a continuing metaphor for the numberless descendants of Abram[5] that now joins the previous metaphor of the dust of the earth (Gen 13:16).

15:6 Abram believed the LORD, and he credited it to him as righteousness.

Abram's response, though silent, is significant enough to warrant a narrator's comment. Abram places his confidence[6] in what the LORD has just promised. Alternatively the text could be expressing an ongoing state of trust in the person of the LORD.[7] That trust is then[8] regarded as

---

[5]Gen 26:4; 22:17; Exod 32:13; Deut 1:10; 10:22; 28:62; 1 Chr 27:23; Neh 9:23.

[6]The English word "believed" may cause confusion here as it certainly does in the New Testament when it translates πιστεύω (*pisteuō*) and related words. While the hiphil stem of this verb certainly does mean "trust" in a number of contexts, this trust is never to be separated from a person's actions as though actions which demonstrate trust are easily separated from trust itself. The root meaning of the word is "reliable" or "faithful."

[7]The construction, w^a plus perfect may indicate here a continuing reality rather than a momentary experience. The Hebrew does not use the *waw*-consecutive with imperfect. The relatively common future meaning of this construction does not fit the context. GKC, § 112 ss, p. 339, suggests this as a pos-

equivalent[9] to righteousness. The fact that verse 7 continues on from the previous *waw*-consecutive from verse 5 indicates that this verse is not speaking to the next sequential thing that happened but is temporarily departing from chronological statements to recall something very important about the ongoing relationship of the LORD and Abram. While the Old Testament does not often speak of faith, when it does, it is usually of great significance. Abram's mistakes, and there are plenty of them, are mistakes of one who is trying to be faithful. Throughout the narrative Abram is seeking for the LORD's promises to him to come to fruition. While he should not have taken Lot along, or gone to Egypt, or lied about Sarai being his wife, or offered the Promised Land to Lot, in all of these cases the motivation for his actions was confidence in the LORD and his promises.

The second half of the verse is usually assumed to mean that God credited Abram's faith as righteousness. Since he was not righteous by his own efforts, his trust in the LORD and his promises is a sort of substitute for the righteous character which the LORD required. But the Hebrew is actually ambiguous as to whether the LORD or Abram is the subject of the second half of the sentence. Rendtorff references Medieval Jewish interpretation that it is Abraham who recognizes God's promise as an expression of his righteousness.[10]

---

sibility here ("constant continuance in a past state") as the construction fits into none of the more typical uses of w^a plus perfect.

[8]The *waw*-consecutive form of the verb implies that as a logical or temporal consequence of Abram's confidence in the LORD, the LORD then counted that confidence as righteousness.

[9]The Hebrew verb חשׁב (*ḥāšab*) is used instructively in Leviticus 18:27,30 of the offering which Levites bring from the tithes that have been given to them by other Israelites. These offerings were *regarded as though they were* the product of the Levite's own threshing floor. Abram's confidence in the LORD is regarded as though it was equivalent to his own righteous behavior.

[10]Rolf Rendtorff, *The Canonical Hebrew Bible: A Theology of the Old Testament*, trans. by David E. Orton (Leiderdorp, NE: Deo, 2005), p.27 [on Genesis 15:6]: "the linguistic structure leaves the subject of the second half of this sentence open. According to the traditional interpretation, God counted Abraham's faith as righteousness. But in Medieval Jewish interpretation we already find the view that it is Abraham who recognizes and acknowledges God's promise as an expression of God's righteousness (cf. Gaston, 1980; Mosis, 1989; cf. Oeming, 1983). This finds support in Neh 9."

3. Divine Reassurance of the Eventual Fulfillment
of the Land Promise (15:7-21)

The LORD began this conversation with Abram by promising to be Abram's very great reward, and Abram continued it by asking what it was that the LORD could actually give him that would be a reward for him. While the earlier parts of this chapter deal with the promise of descendants, this section addresses the promise of the land. But God does more than reaffirm the land promise. He expands the borders to the Euphrates in the north and east and to the border with Egypt in the south and west. God also clarifies the timing of the fulfillment of the land promise and the moral conditions under which he can justifiably dispossess the Canaanites of the land they then occupied.

A Ritual to Reaffirm the LORD's Commitment to the Land Promise (15:7-11)

15:7 He also said to him, "I am the LORD, who brought you out of Ur of the Chaldeans to give you this land to take possession of it."

In addition to the promise of innumerable descendants the LORD then[11] renewed the promise of the land. He reminds Abram that he was behind the initial trip of his father Terah who set out from Ur of the Chaldeans in southern Mesopotamia to go to Canaan (Gen 11:27). While it was not until the next generation that anyone actually arrived in Canaan, the LORD was behind even that initial trip. He had brought Abram out of Ur, not just called him from Haran. Most commentators take this act as proof that either this Ur must be the Ur near the northern Euphrates[12] or that Genesis 12:1 must not be in chronological sequence (despite the *waw*-consecutive construction in the Hebrew). The LORD's purpose from the beginning had been, he reminds Abram, to give him possession of the land of Canaan. His tenuous position as a wandering Bedouin notwithstanding, the promise of the land was an essential part of God's purpose in guiding Abram's life. The fact that Lot had left him and that he still owned not even an acre of the land must not be taken to imply that the land promise was no longer relevant.

15:8 But Abram said, "O Sovereign LORD, how can I know that I will gain possession of it?"

Abram again addresses the LORD as "Lord GOD."[13] How can the

---

[11]The *waw*-consecutive indicates narrative sequence here contra the NIV's "also."

[12]And that therefore the defining phrase, "of the Chaldeans" comes from another hand who misunderstood what Ur was being referred to here.

[13]The NIV's "Sovereign LORD" shows its Calvinistic tendency here. The Hebrew reads יְהוָה אֲדֹנָי (*'ǎdōnāy YHWH*).

promise be true when he sees no evidence of it and not even a pattern of evidence that might lead in that direction? The land is full of inhabitants and he is only a herdsman. Abram asks for some sign of reassurance that the promise will in fact come to fruition.

15:9 So the LORD said to him, "Bring me a heifer, a goat and a ram, each three years old, along with a dove and a young pigeon."

The animals that the LORD requests are all legitimate sacrificial animals in the Law.[14] While Abram had not received the Law, he obeys it unwittingly by obeying the LORD's command. The animals were to be of adult age (three years old[15]). The word for "young pigeon" is only found elsewhere in Deuteronomy 32:11 where it refers to a baby eagle.

15:10 Abram brought all these to him, cut them in two and arranged the halves opposite each other; the birds, however, he did not cut in half.

The LORD does not tell Abram how to prepare and arrange the animals, so Abram most likely knows this from his own cultural experience of covenant making. It is commonly understood that the dividing of the animals into halves was part of a covenant formation ceremony. The parties would walk between the animal halves. The logic was that the parties to the covenant placed a curse upon themselves, in effect saying, "If I break my commitment to this covenant may I become like one of these animals." The birds may not have been split because of their size. The primary evidence for this view is ancient Near Eastern parallels and Jeremiah 34:18: "The men who have violated my covenant and have not fulfilled the terms of the covenant they made before me, I will treat like the calf they cut in two and then walked between its pieces." An Old Aramaic Inscription from Sefire translated by Fitzmeyer records a covenant between Bar-ga'yah and Mati'el in which a curse on the latter is given: "[Just as] this calf is cut in two, so may Mati'el be cut in two, and may his nobles be cut in two!"[16] Hess notes a parallel between this text and a land grant treaty from Alalakh in which the suzerain "Abbael swore the oath to Yarimlim and cut the neck of a lamb, [saying] 'If I take back what I have given you [may I be cursed]'").[17]

---

[14]Heifer (Deut 21:3-6); goat (Lev 1:10; 9:3); ram (Lev 5:16); also dove (Lev 1:14).

[15]Alternatively the Hebrew word could refer to three animals each of the heifers, goats, and rams. Cf. Sarna, *Genesis*, p. 115.

[16]*COS*, II:214.

[17]*COS*, II:370. Hess discusses this in more detail in "The Slaughter of the Animals in Genesis 15:18-21 and Its Ancient Near Eastern Context," in *He Swore an Oath: Biblical Themes from Genesis 12–50*, ed. by R.S. Hess, P.E. Satterthwaite, and G.J. Wenham, 2nd ed. (Grand Rapids: Baker, 1994), pp. 55-65.

15:11 Then birds of prey came down on the carcasses, but Abram drove them away.

The birds of prey see the opportunity for an easy meal but Abram knows the solemnity of the moment and drives them off. It may be that there is something more here. Perhaps the birds are symbolic of those forces which threaten the fulfillment of God's covenant promises to Abram. Jeremiah 34:20 refers to those who had "walked between the pieces of the calf," i.e., were partners to the covenant, as having their "bodies become food for the birds of the air." In that passage the birds are symbols for the enemies of the nation who will conquer them if they are disobedient to their covenant with the LORD.[18]

Divine Revelation of a Delay in the Land Promise (15:12-16)

15:12 As the sun was setting, Abram fell into a deep sleep, and a thick and dreadful darkness came over him.

While the word translated "**deep sleep**" can be used literally (1 Sam 26:2; Prov 19:15), it sometimes refers to times of important revelation (Gen 2:24; Job 4:13; 33:15). The next phrase is difficult to know how to translate. Literally it reads, "And behold, terror, great darkness fell upon him." The point of the word "terror" ("**dreadful**" in the NIV) is apparently to indicate the terrorizing fear which comes over human beings when they experience the presence of God.[19] In this case the certainty of the promise, which is the apparent purpose of the ensuing revelation, is reinforced for Abram by the experience of dread at the presence of God, a God so awe-inspiring that to fall into his hands is a fearful thing (Heb 10:31).

15:13 Then the LORD said to him, "Know for certain that your descendants will be strangers in a country not their own, and they will be enslaved and mistreated four hundred years.

In the middle of the frightening phenomena which accompany this theophany the LORD speaks to Abram. He begins with an emphatic construction[20] that emphasizes the certainty of Abram's knowledge of the future because it is based upon the certainty of God's promise. The certain thing about the future, however, is at first not welcome news. Abram's descendants (his "seed") will live as strangers in a land not their

---

[18]Robert P. Carroll, *Jeremiah*, OTL (Philadelphia: Westminster, 1986), p. 650.

[19]Sarna, *Genesis*, p. 115: "Here, as in Job 4:13ff. and 33:15f., the abnormally deep sleep is associated with the dread inspired by the awareness of the Divine Presence (Cf. Dan. 8:18; 10:9)."

[20]An infinitive absolute followed by the imperfect of the same verb is a common way of indicating emphasis in biblical Hebrew.

own and will even be enslaved and mistreated there. Further, this will last four hundred years! Any hopes of a quick fulfillment to the promise are now gone. The original audience would, of course, have known from personal experience what the LORD was revealing to Abram. They and their forefathers and mothers had lived under that slavery in Egypt. The text assures them that even the brutal experience of slavery in Egypt was within God's sovereign control. There was a good reason for it, and the experience was not wasted but formed them into the people that God wanted them to be. The canonical audience had experienced a different and yet all too similar form of slavery in Babylon. They too had been freed from Babylonian and Assyrian captivity. They too had recently entered the land. While knowing that in all things God works for the good of those who love him and are called according to his plan (Rom 8:28) does not take away the pain of life, it does give us a new perspective on that pain. Nothing is wasted in what God intends for us to go through or even allows us to go through, no matter how painful it may be. That was true for Israel, and it remains true for us.

15:14 But I will punish the nation they serve as slaves, and afterward they will come out with great possessions.

The LORD makes it clear to Abram, and the narrator clear to his or her readers, that the LORD did not want Israel to be enslaved. Therefore the nation will be punished for what it will do to Abram's descendants. God had promised to curse those who cursed Abram and his seed. Here he affirms that this promise will retain its validity even after four hundred years as strangers in a strange land. The reference to coming out with "great possessions" is something Abram had already experienced in Egypt and something the original audience had also experienced when they "plundered" the Egyptians by asking for articles of silver and gold and clothing as they or their parents were leaving Egypt (Exod 12:35,36). For the original audience this is a demonstration of God's control of history. He had explained to Abram what was to happen to his descendants long before it happened, and they had themselves experienced the fulfillment of it. When God's people, in any age or situation, read the promises of Scripture and then experience the fulfillment of those promises in their own contemporary situations, their faith is deepened.

15:15 You, however, will go to your fathers in peace and be buried at a good old age.

But God's promises are not just for the future. Abram will receive a down payment in the circumstances of his own life and death. Abram will die in peace. He will not have to keep on fighting wars as he did in chapter 14. And he will live to an even older age. Both of these promises come true for Abram as he never fights another battle and dies some 90 or more years later at the age of 175 (Gen 25:7; cf. 16:3).

15:16 In the fourth generation your descendants will come back here, for the sin of the Amorites has not yet reached its full measure."

The four-hundred-year period of waiting for the promise of the land to be fulfilled mentioned in verse 13 is called the fourth generation. While popular-level sources sometimes speak very confidently of the length of a generation in the Bible,[21] this passage should give us pause. In this passage a generation is one hundred years! The fact is — there is no consistent length for a generation in the Bible.

While Abraham's descendants will have to wait for a long time, this verse explains why that is so. The reason[22] Abram and his descendants must wait is given in verse 16b, usually translated, "For the iniquity of the Amorites is not yet full." This clause has a number of interpretive issues which will be examined below.[23]

One question that arises is why "Amorites" are specifically mentioned. Would not the more typical generic "Canaanites" be more appropriate?[24] Most commentators regard the word Amorites as an imprecise designation for the inhabitants of the land as a whole and thus like the generic use of the word Canaanites.[25] But there may be other reasons. Certainly Israel on the verge of the Promised Land, the implied audience, would have remembered that Sihon and Og, the two transjordanian kings already conquered, were Amorites. Since they had already shown their hostility to Israel, been defeated, and put to the ban by Israel, it makes narrative sense to use the word "Amorite" here. The defeat of the Amorite Kings, Sihon and Og, was used in the Pentateuch as the paradigmatic example to encourage a nation that is reluctant to conquer the land through Yahweh-war west of the Jordan.[26] Another possibility is Jacob's reference in Genesis 48:22 to a battle which he

---

[21]I have often heard 40 years as the figure.

[22]Here כִּי, (ki) is used in the causal sense; cf. *HALOT*, כִּי, p. 470.

[23]For much of what follows see my unpublished paper delivered at the Stone-Campbell Journal Conference, St. Louis, MO, in 2003.

[24]Ironically the nearest mention of Amorites, textually speaking, is in Genesis 14:13 where Mamre the Amorite was an ally of Abram in his defeat of a coalition of kings who had kidnapped Lot. In Abram's time the Amorites are not yet enemies of the people of Abraham.

[25]For the use of "Amorite" and "Canaanite" as interchangeable generics for the original inhabitants of the land see Joshua 7:7,9.

[26]See Deut 3:2; 3:8; 4:46,47; 31:4; Josh 2:10; Judg 11:19-24; Ps 135:11; 136:19.

claims to have waged with the Amorites. It may be that it was specifically Amorites who threatened the Patriarchs with violence.[27]

A second issue is the translation of the Hebrew word עָוֹן (*'āwōn*), which the NIV renders as "sin" but more traditional translations render as "iniquity." While the Hebrew word *'āwōn* can sometimes be translated by "sin,"[28] it is not one of the usual Hebrew words for sin. Typically discussion of meaning refers to sin, guilt caused by sin, and punishment for guilt, with the emphasis being on the later. Koch notes the word "cannot refer to the actual act of transgression itself" but expresses a "dynamic holistic thought" that tries to conceive in a single sweep "the various phases of a misdeed-consequence process (deed-consequence completion)."[29] The word *'āwôn* is the result of *ḥaṭṭā'th* and *peśa'*, two of the more common Hebrew words for "sin," and not sin by itself.

One problem modern readers have with the translations "iniquity," "sin," or even "guilt" is that all of these translations are typically read as being distinct from the consequences of sin, i.e., its punishment. Guilt is often read by the contemporary reader, scholarly or not, as guilt feelings and not the quite tangible burden of guilt which is part and parcel of the consequences of sin.

A classic crux which illustrates the difficulty of the contemporary tendency to gnosticize theological words like *'āwôn* is the statement of Cain, "My iniquity/guilt/punishment is more than I can bear." While it is theoretically possible that Cain is confessing his sin as Sailhamer argues,[30] a careful study of the word and of the context of Cain's statement makes this extremely unlikely. Cain complains that his punishment is too severe in that he would be driven from the soil (the source of his previous livelihood) and from Yahweh's presence and would face life as a fugitive in danger of blood vengeance. The word "punishment" is a far more appropriate translation. The burden which Cain bears is the burden of far more than guilt feelings. His plea is for the mitigation of some of the consequences of his sin, a plea which is answered in part in that he does not end up living as a fugitive but in a city and is protected from

---

[27]Genesis 48:22 has Jacob promising Joseph, "And to you, as one who is over your brothers I give the ridge of land I took from the Amorites with my sword and my bow." The only episode recorded in Genesis that this might apply to is the slaughter of the Shechemites by Jacob's sons, led by Simeon and Levi, after the rape of Leah's daughter with Jacob, Dinah. There could, of course be another episode to which Jacob refers which is not mentioned elsewhere in Genesis.

[28]Although I would recommend avoiding this translation if at all possible.

[29]K. Koch, "עָוֹן, *'āwōn*," *TDOT*, X:559.

[30]Sailhamer, *Genesis*, EBC (Grand Rapids: Zondervan, 1990), p. 65.

human retribution by threat of a sevenfold divine retribution. He is, however, driven from Yahweh's presence and from the soil.

Throughout the Pentateuch and the rest of the Old Testament *'āwôn* depicts sin and its consequences together. Unless there is a carefully prescribed intervention, whoever bears *'āwôn* is already destined to be punished. Certainly the translation "punishment" fits the context in Genesis 15:16. The punishment that is coming on the Amorites is already in existence but will come to fruition with their expulsion from the land. The reason that Abram and his descendants must wait is that Yahweh's punishment of the Amorites is not yet[31] ready to be completed. The expulsion from the land is the final enactment of Yahweh's punishment on the Amorites.

While the phrase "fourth generation" could be merely an indication of time, it may well be that a deeper meaning is intended. In what is perhaps the Old Testament's most succinct statement of the nature of God, the LORD is described as someone who shows steadfast love to thousands [of generations] but who also visits "the iniquity of the fathers on the children to the third and the fourth generation of those who hate me."[32] The use of the phrase "fourth generation" in this paradigmatic text may find an echo in Genesis 15:16. The punishment that God meted out on those who hated him was limited in time to the third and fourth generation.[33] Then the judgment was complete.

Another question is, exactly what is completed[34] in the fourth generation? Is it the sin, which when completed, will result in the judgment of

---

[31]The Hebrew text plays on the double meaning of the word הֵנָּה (*hēnnāh* = "here"), used twice in this verse, i.e., "here" in this land *geographically* and "here" *temporally*, i.e., up to here in time.

[32]Exod 20:5,6. The negative side of this defining description of Yahweh is repeated with variations in Exodus 34:6-7; Numbers 14:18; Nahum 1:3. See Walter Brueggemann, *Theology of the Old Testament: Testimony, Dispute, Advocacy* (Minneapolis: Fortress, 1997), pp. 215-224.

[33]Ancient households were typically made up of three or four generations in a single household. What the head of the household did had consequences not only for himself, but also for the other generations who lived with him. Cf. Jeffrey H. Tigay, *Deuteronomy*, JPSTC (Philadelphia: JPS, 1996), p. 66: "That is, upon grandchildren and great-grandchildren (or upon great- and great-great-grandchildren, if the parents are not counted as the first generation). Living to see three or four generations is as long as one could naturally live. Thus God extends punishment only to descendants the guilty are likely to see in their own lifetimes. This indicates that the suffering of the descendants is intended as a deterrent to, and punishment of, their ancestors, not a transfer of guilt to the descendants in their own right."

[34]The NIV paraphrases here with, "reach its full measure."

the Amorites being expelled so that Israel can possess the land? Or, is it that the process of punishing the Amorites will only be finalized then? Is God waiting for the Amorites to raise their sin to such a level that it calls for divine judgment? Or is the expulsion of the inhabitants of the land the final stage of that judgment? If '*āwôn* means the consequences of sin, and not the sin itself, the latter would seem to be the meaning.

In either case, God's decision to destroy the Canaanites was not an arbitrary decision on God's part. His justice demanded it. But his justice also demanded that he not forgo the requirements of justice for the Canaanites even for the sake of his promise to Abram. Instead Abram and God must wait until justice required the punishment of the Canaanites.

The Lord Makes an Unconditional Land Promise (15:17-21)

15:17 When the sun had set and darkness had fallen, a smoking firepot with a blazing torch appeared and passed between the pieces.

The narrator draws the reader into the action by the way he narrates this event. Literally the Hebrew says, "And behold! A firepot of smoke and a torch of fire which passed between *these* pieces." It is as though the reader is seeing the action herself. The smoke and fire are apparently symbols of the divine presence. As has been often noted, Abram does not pass between the animal pieces; only those things which symbolize God's presence do. This means that only God calls down a curse on himself if he does not fulfill his commitment to the promise. The point is evidently that God is making a promise to Abram. He will do what he has promised. Abram merely serves as witness. Abram does not bind himself to anything. The Lord places the divine life under a self-curse if he should somehow fail to fulfill the promises just made.

Often this event is spoken of as an "unconditional" covenant as though Abram could do nothing to disannul it or for that matter to ensure its fulfillment. Attention is sometimes drawn to supposed parallels between this text and the ancient Near Eastern context where land grant treaties are interpreted as being "unconditional."[35] A suzerain rewards a loyal subject for prior acts of loyalty by granting to him some cities or land as his own, in perpetuity. The vassal does nothing, supposedly, in response to this land grant. It is therefore, in formal terms at least, "unconditional." I find this analogy strained, at best. In a land grant of a powerful suzerain and a weaker vassal one can be certain that

---

[35]E.g., Eugene H. Merrill, *Everlasting Dominion: A Theology of the Old Testament* (Nashville: Broadman & Holman, 2006), pp. 238-240.

the suzerain expects continued loyalty from the vassal and that, unconditional or not, the covenant will be broken if the vassal proves to be unfaithful. The suzerain will bring an army against an unfaithful vassal and take back any land granted to him and more if the vassal does not remain loyal. If there is a parallel between this passage and the so-called "land grant" treaties, it would teach us that it is simply assumed that Abram will remain faithful and that even though the language sounds to us as though it is unconditional, in fact Abram must remain faithful.[36] The fact that only the LORD passes between the halves of the animals does, however, tell the reader that the fulfillment of the promise is God's job, not Abram's. He is expected to remain faithful and obedient and keep trusting, but only God can fulfill a promise hundreds of years after the death of Abram!

15:18 On that day the LORD made a covenant with Abram and said, "To your descendants I give this land, from the river of Egypt to the great river, the Euphrates—15:19 the land of the Kenites, Kenizzites, Kadmonites, 15:20 Hittites, Perizzites, Rephaites, 15:21 Amorites, Canaanites, Girgashites and Jebusites."

In passing through the animal pieces the LORD "made"[37] a covenant with Abram. On the same day as the vision, the LORD spoke to Abram making explicit just what the land promise entailed. The land will not just be Canaan proper, from Dan to Beersheba. In its fullest sense the land will extend from the border with Egypt to the northern end of the Euphrates. The "river of Egypt" is not the Nile, as we might be tempted to think, but a seasonal river, the Wadi el-Arish[38] or perhaps the Wadi Besor, just north of Gaza.[39] This was the traditional border with Egypt in ancient times. Only in the time of Solomon were these borders actually realized (1 Kgs 4:21).

In verses 19-21 a list of ten nations is given. The list that began with just the Canaanites (12:6) and expanded to also include the Perizzites after the return from Egypt (13:7) now includes an additional eight nations. Missing from the common seven nations[40] are the Hivites.

---

[36]This puts the lie to the notion that the grant of the land is truly eternal and that therefore the contemporary state of Israel has a divine right to the land of Palestine which Scripture records.

[37]The Hebrew phrase is literally translated "cut a covenant" and may refer to the cutting up of the animals.

[38]Num 34:5; Josh 15:4 seem to refer to this Wadi.

[39]P.S. Ash, "Borders," *DOTP*, p. 102.

[40]The seven nations most commonly attested in full lists of the inhabitants are: Hittites, Canaanites, Amorites, Perizzites, Hivites, Jebusites, and less frequently

Included are four nations which are unique to this list: Kenites, Kenizzites, Kadmonites, and Rephaites. "Kenites" were itinerant smiths who traveled from place to place selling their valuable services. Caleb the faithful spy or his father was a Kenizzite (Num 32:12; Josh 14:6,14). The Kadmonites are only mentioned here. Literally translated they would be "Easterners." None of these three show up in later lists. This could be explained in a variety of ways. All three were typically located in the southern portion of the land. By the time Israel entered the land, perhaps they were either no longer in existence (the Kadmonites?), had joined the people of Israel (as Caleb of Kenizzite lineage had done), or were no longer a threat to the nation. The destiny of even these peoples who are placed under a prediction of future expulsion is dependent on what happens later.

The term "Rephaites" appears to be a general designation which included the Emim, Anakites, and Zamzummites (Deut 2:10,11,20). Of these only the Anakites were still around in the experience of the original audience by the time Israel came into the Promised Land. The Rephaites controlled the area around the Dead Sea especially the area that was later populated by Moab and Ammon. For the original audience this would seem to suggest that Canaanite nations had a say in their futures in relation to the people of God. Some nations, once under judgment, could be embraced by the people of God, others faded into extinction under God's judgment prior to the time of the Exodus, and some remained to challenge Israel as they entered under Joshua.

Another item of interest in this list is the mention of the Jebusites. Since the Jebusites controlled Jerusalem and its environs, it seems odd at first that the home of Melchizedek, to whom Abram had just recently paid tithes, would also be listed.

Hittites[41] is used to refer to four different ethnic groups in the ancient world. The most famous controlled much of modern Turkey during the second millennium B.C. Their empire fell c. 1200 B.C., but the remnants of that empire continued for some time. In the Pentateuch all those termed Hittites have Semitic names. They are located around Hebron and Beersheba in the southern portion of Palestine. Whether they are related to each other, to groups called Hittite in the north of Palestine, and/or to the Hittites of Anatolia (Turkey) is debated.

Perizzites are not mentioned in the Table of Nations in Genesis 10, unlike the other peoples mentioned. In Genesis they are located in

---

the Girgashites. See P.E. Satterthwaite and D.W. Baker, "Nations of Canaan," *DOTP*, p. 598.

[41]See ibid., p. 602.

north central Palestine near Bethel and Ai (Gen 13:7; 34:30). Some link them to the Hurrians while others suggest that originally the term referred to rural people in contrast to the more urban Canaanites.[42]

Amorites[43] is the general term used to describe all of the inhabitants of the land in verse 16. The term can be used imprecisely at times. Etymologically the term is thought to derive from an Akkadian word *amurru* meaning "west" and referring to peoples living west of Mesopotamia. Amorites lived on both sides of the Jordan, although never spreading all the way to the Mediterranean coast as the Canaanites did (Num 13:29; Josh 5:1).

The designation "Canaanites" can be the most common general designation of ancient inhabitants of Palestine, but can also refer to a specific ethnic group. Canaanites are most often listed first when the inhabitants of Canaan are listed. When Israel first entered the Promised Land as a nation led by Joshua, this ethnic subgroup seems to have lived especially along the Mediterranean Sea (Gen 13:7; 34:30).

The Girgashites descended from Ham's son Canaan (Gen 10:15) and are only mentioned in genealogical lists that do not indicate their location. Some suggest a location in northern Palestine on the basis that this area is not assigned to any other of the peoples mentioned. If, however, the list is arranged from south to north, the Girgashites would be somewhere south of Jerusalem.

Ishida suggests that the list is geographically arranged from south to north and argues that the Kenites, Kenizzites and Kadmonites "represent the foreign elements in the South whose absorption into the tribe of Judah was complete by the time of David."[44]

---

[42]Ibid., p. 603.

[43]For what follows see ibid., pp. 601-602.

[44]T. Ishida, "The Structure and Historical Implications of the Lists of Pre-Israelite Nations," *Biblica* 60 (1979): 484.

GENESIS 16

III. THE HAGAR STRATEGY (16:1–19:38)

A. THE FIFTH CHALLENGE TO THE PROMISE: HELPING GOD OUT WITH HIS PROMISE THROUGH SURROGATE PARENTHOOD (16:1-16)

Abram's confidence in the promise was reinvigorated through God's repetition, clarification, and expansion of it in chapter 15. In chapter 16 we see Abram and Sarai begin to act on this new revelation of the promise. But once again their all-too-human plan only serves to place impediments in front of the promise and its progress. God had just told Abram that a son would be born of his own body. Since he had not specifically mentioned Sarai at this point, she comes up with a plan. In the ancient world in situations in which the matriarch was infertile as Sarai was, a secondary wife could serve as a sort of surrogate mother for her.[1] Any children from such a surrogacy would be viewed as the heirs of the matriarch. While the custom was acceptable by ancient standards and should not be judged dismissively by modern standards, Sarai's scheme only serves to put the promise at risk yet again. Instead of asking the LORD what they should do, Sarai and Abram come up with their own scheme, and like all such humanly contrived schemes, it causes a series of problems for the fulfillment of the promise with long-term negative consequences.

1. Sarai Suggests Surrogacy (16:1-2)

16:1 Now Sarai, Abram's wife, had borne him no children. But she had an Egyptian maidservant named Hagar; 16:2 so she said to Abram, "The LORD has kept me from having children. Go, sleep with my maid-

---

[1] T. Frymer-Kensky, "Patriarchal Family Relationships and Near Eastern Law," *BA* 44 (1981): 209-214.

servant; perhaps I can build a family through her." Abram agreed to what Sarai said.

The reader is reminded of the continuing barrenness of Sarai, here described as Abram's wife.[2] While the LORD had renewed the promise of innumerable descendants for Abram, he had not specifically indicated that Sarai was to be the mother of those descendants. Sarai had an Egyptian maidservant named Hagar. She may well have been among the servants that Abram received as gifts while in Egypt as chapter 13 records. Verse 2 begins with a *waw*-consecutive. The NIV translators take it as a "logical" consecutive ("so") rather than temporal. In Sarai's view the LORD had prevented Sarai from having children. It was not something which had just "happened." She seems to reason in the following way. The LORD had clarified, reaffirmed, and indeed expanded the promise. But the LORD also had prevented her from having children. Since Lot was no longer an option as an heir, the only solution was to follow ancient custom[3] and have Abram take Hagar as a secondary wife (concubine) and have descendants through her. Interestingly it never occurs to her (or to Abram!) that Abram might be the cause of their infertility. Abram obeyed (וַיִּשְׁמַע אַבְרָם לְקוֹל שָׂרָי, *wayyišmaʿ ʾabrām lᵉqôl śārāy*) Sarai's scheme. In doing so he created the possibility and, as it turned out, the actuality, of a series of long-term problems within the family.

2. Surrogacy Seems to Work (16:3-4a)

16:3 So after Abram had been living in Canaan ten years, Sarai his wife took her Egyptian maidservant Hagar and gave her to her husband to be his wife. 16:4 He slept with Hagar, and she conceived.

This verse begins with a *waw*-consecutive. The NIV confuses this by bringing the temporal clause forward into first position for stylistic reasons. The use of the word "so" may indicate that the NIV translators viewed this as logical consequence as much as temporal succession. Why did Abram and Sarai wait for ten years before attempting their scheme? Or is it a wait? They had been living in Canaan for ten years. Had they lost hope? Was the idea something they had soon after the events of chapter 15? There is no *waw*-consecutive (in v. 1) and so the time is somewhat ambiguous. Perhaps we are supposed to experience the ambiguity as readers. After living in Canaan for 10 years Abram is now 85 years old and Sarai is 75.

---

[2] Perhaps to emphasize the point that she was not his sister, despite Abraham's later claim (Gen 20:12).

[3] T. Frymer-Kensky, "Patriarchal Family Relationships," p. 212.

It is interesting and may be significant that Sarai says specifically that Hagar will be Abram's wife. In a parallel situation when Rachel wanted to have a child through Bilhah she made it very clear that any children born would be hers and not Bilhah's (Gen 30:3). But it may well be that there Rachel is portrayed as having learned the lesson from the Hagar situation. Sarai may have caused herself even greater problems by giving Hagar to Abram as his wife and not making it explicitly clear that Hagar was not receiving a status equal to Sarai's.[4] Abram did as Sarai instructed, and it seems to work. Hagar gets pregnant. There is hope for the fulfillment of the promise after all! But like all humanly contrived plans which attempt to fulfill God's promises for him, this one only complicates matters.

3. Problems in the Relationship between Sarai and Hagar (16:4b-6)

16:4b When she knew she was pregnant, she began to despise her mistress.

All human schemes, especially those conceived of as means of helping God to fulfill his promises, have consequences which were not anticipated. Since Hagar was a wife and the only wife that had any chance, humanly speaking, of producing an heir, she began to take advantage of what she thought was an advantageous situation. The first sign was that she began to curse[5] her mistress.

16:5 Then Sarai said to Abram, "You are responsible for the wrong I am suffering. I put my servant in your arms, and now that she knows she is pregnant, she despises me. May the LORD judge between you and me."

Sarai, having experienced the cursing of Hagar, addresses Abram. She begins by saying, "[May] the violence done to me [be] upon you."[6] Sarai then records what has happened from her perspective. Sarai makes clear that Hagar is her own handmaiden ("servant" in NIV), not Abram's wife. Now that she is pregnant, Hagar assumes that she has a

---

[4]Leah, like Sarai but unlike Rachel, gives her handmaid, Zilpah, to Jacob as a wife (Gen 30:9). Once again, however, Leah, as the unfavored wife may not have felt she had any choice in the matter.

[5]While the Hebrew verb translated "despise" in the NIV (קָלַל, *qālal*) can mean to "regard as insignificant," it more often refers to cursing someone. Significantly it is the verb used in the promise to Abram in Genesis 12:3, "Whoever *curses* (*qālal*) you, I will curse."

[6]The NIV is periphrastic at this point.

different status and is free to despise or curse Sarai. Sarai blames Abram for this since Hagar did not have this attitude when she was placed on Abram's bosom (NIV has "arms").[7] Her confidence in the rightness of her complaint is indicated by her asking for the LORD to judge the case.

16:6 "Your servant is in your hands," Abram said. "Do with her whatever you think best." Then Sarai mistreated Hagar; so she fled from her.

Interestingly Abram does not contest what Sarai says. He refers to Hagar as Sarai's handmaiden ("servant" in NIV) not as his own (secondary) wife. Abram gives Sarai the freedom to do to her "what is right in [her] eyes."[8] While this phrase is sometimes used of doing what is right in the eyes of the LORD or of a righteous person acting rightly, it also sometimes has the connotation of giving a person the freedom to do what is evil. Given that permission, Sarai "mistreated" Hagar. The vocabulary is interesting. The word translated "mistreated" (עָנָה, 'ānāh) is used in the piel stem of the Egyptians oppressing the nation of Israel when they were slaves (Exod 1:11-12). The mother of the slaves freed from Egypt oppresses her Egyptian slave! It seems unlikely that the reader is intended to view this positively. The law warned against treating slaves harshly precisely because Israel had been enslaved in Egypt and knew from personal experience the horrors of slavery (Exod 22:20-22). Hagar quite naturally fled from such treatment.

4. Angel's Promise Brings Hagar Back to Sarai and Abram (16:7-14)

16:7 The angel of the LORD found Hagar near a spring in the desert; it was the spring that is beside the road to Shur.

Hagar evidently was headed to Egypt, her homeland, when the angel of the LORD found her. The road of Shur ran south of the parallel road, "the way of the land of the Philistines" through the northern portion of Sinai and ended at Lake Timsah on the eastern border of Egypt. This would have enabled Hagar to avoid the busier coastal road.[9] She was stopped by a spring along the dry, dusty road. The author assumes that the audience is familiar with the road and perhaps even the spring from their time spent in the wilderness.

---

[7]The Hebrew חֵיק (ḥêq) means bosom or chest and implies a more personal relationship than is usually implied by the words "arms" although it can be accurately translated that way.

[8]The NIV paraphrases here.

[9]For a detailed discussion of the location of Shur see Hoffmeier, *Ancient Israel in Sinai*, pp. 159-161.

16:8 And he said, "Hagar, servant of Sarai, where have you come from, and where are you going?"

"I'm running away from my mistress Sarai," she answered.

Interestingly the angel addresses Hagar with her name, perhaps an indication of respect. But he[10] then immediately follows this up with the descriptive phrase, "handmaid of Sarai." The question about her place of origin and her destination is evidently rhetorical. Hagar treats it as such and with disarming candor explains that she is fleeing from Sarai, her "queen."[11]

16:9 Then the angel of the LORD told her, "Go back to your mistress and submit to her."

The verb translated "submit" is the reflexive form of the verb used in verse 6 of Sarai mistreating Hagar. Sarai had tried to force Hagar into submission, but this merely resulted in her taking the planned heir Ishmael away with her back to Egypt. Now the LORD's representative instructs her to voluntarily submit to Sarai's authority.

16:10 The angel added, "I will so increase your descendants that they will be too numerous to count."

The commandment to return to Sarai has a promise added to it. This is not intended as an inducement. The angel nowhere explicitly connects the promise to Hagar's obedience.[12] But it does give Hagar reassurance that in the long run such obedience will matter. The promise given her is a striking echo of the promises given to the Patriarchs. The blessings which Hagar was to receive as the nonchosen mother of Abraham's descendants are no worse than the promises given to the chosen descendants. Hagar's descendants, like those of Sarai, will be too numerous to count. God's blessings are not a zero-sum game. Blessing Sarai's children does not mean that God will not also bless Hagar's! The theme of the blessing of the nonchosen in the Old Testament has been largely ignored in biblical scholarship.[13] While it is true that the Old Testament in general and the book of Genesis in particular focus most attention on the chosen people, those not chosen are not necessarily devoid of God's blessing.

---

[10]Whether angels are masculine or not, this angel is referred to with masculine pronouns.

[11]The Hebrew word translated "mistress" in the NIV (גְּבִירָה, *gᵉbîrāh*) often means "queen" or "queen mother" (1 Kgs 11:17; 15:13; 2 Kgs 10:13; 2 Chr 15:16; Isa 47:5,7; Jer 13:18; 29:2).

[12]In fact the promise is separated grammatically from the command by a *waw*-consecutive. This may be viewed as a logical consecutive.

[13]A welcome exception is R. Christopher Heard, *Dynamics of Diselection: Ambiguity in Genesis 12–36 and Ethnic Boundaries in Post-Exilic Judah.*

16:11 The angel of the LORD also said to her: "You are now with child and you will have a son. You shall name him Ishmael, for the LORD has heard of your misery.

The angel reassures Hagar that the child she is bearing will indeed be born;[14] it will be a son whom she will name Ishmael. The name "Ishmael" means "God hears" not "Yahweh hears." In this case the author of Genesis is speaking from the perspective of a mature Yahwistic faith and has changed an original, "God has heard" to "the LORD has heard."[15] The word translated "misery" in the NIV (עֳנִי, 'ānî) is etymologically related to the verbs "mistreated" and "submit" in verses 6 and 9 respectively. Just as the LORD heard the cries of his people Israel in their slavery in Egypt, the Egyptian slave Hagar's cries are also heard and responded to.

16:12 He will be a wild donkey of a man; his hand will be against everyone and everyone's hand against him, and he will live in hostility toward all his brothers."

Ishmael will be a "wild donkey man." The wild donkey is known for its lust when in heat (Hos 8:9; Jer 2:24) and its wandering homelessly (Job 24:5-8) living by scavenging in the wasteland (Isa 2:14; Job 24:5; 39:5). This may indicate the nomadic existence of Ishmael and his descendants.

The translations, including the NIV, are confusing here. The Hebrew is far more ambiguous and does not necessarily imply hostility between the descendants of Ishmael and the descendants of his brothers. The Hebrew literally reads, "His hand [will be] in [the hand of] all and the hand of all [will be] in his [hand]. And he will dwell before all his brothers." It is the translators who interpret "in" (בְּ, bᵉ) to mean "against" and the phrase "before" (עַל־פְּנֵי, 'al-pᵉnê) to mean "in hostility towards." But these words can just as easily indicate living a life of partnership in the middle of his brothers.[16] One might be forgiven for wondering whether the current conflict between the west and the Islamic world which claims descent from Ishmael has had an unconscious effect on the translational choices of commentators and translation committees.

16:13 She gave this name to the LORD who spoke to her: "You are the God who sees me," for she said, "I have now seen the One who sees me."

---

[14]Contemporary readers should remember just how dangerous pregnancy was in the ancient world for both the mother and children without the wonders of modern medicine.

[15]Gordon J. Wenham, "The Religion of the Patriarchs," in *Essays on the Patriarchal Narratives*, A.R. Millard, and D.J. Wiseman, eds. (Leicester: Intervarsity, 1980), p. 181.

[16]See the careful discussion of the Hebrew in Heard, *Dynamics*, pp. 69-73.

Hagar says, "El Roi" meaning "the God who sees me" or "God who makes an appearance." The narrator, from his later Yahwistic perspective, says that she gave this name to the LORD, not to God. While Hagar did not literally use the name of the LORD, for the narrator "God" and the "LORD" are identical.

The appearance of the angel evidently reassures Hagar that God is watching over her, no matter how difficult the circumstances. By seeing the angel and hearing the LORD's reassuring words Hagar now knows of his concern and care. By seeing God[17] Hagar is able to accept that God always sees her whether or not she has a direct experience of it at the time. Hagar's words actually seem to be a question in the Hebrew. She asks, "Have I not here seen the one who sees after me?"[18] Another possible translation is, "Have I not here seen the back of the one who sees me?" If this is correct, Hagar is reflecting on the fact that she has not had a direct glimpse of God, but, like Moses in Exod. 33:23, only a glimpse of his back.

16:14 That is why the well was called Beer Lahai Roi; it is still there, between Kadesh and Bered.

The name Beer Lahai Roi means "well of the living one who sees me." The narrator then informs the original and/or canonical readers[19] that the well is still around at the time of writing and can be visited between Kadesh Barnea and Bered in the southern desert. Hagar knows that God is alive and sees and cares about what is going on in each person's life.

5. Birth of the Surrogate Son (16:15-16)

16:15 So Hagar bore Abram a son, and Abram gave the name Ishmael to the son she had borne.

While Hagar had been told that she would name her son Ishmael, at least formally Abram did the actual naming. This is used as evidence

---

[17]While the narrator is clear that the person who talks with Hagar is the angel of the LORD, Hagar does not distinguish between seeing the LORD and seeing his angel. The popular-level idea that no one can ever see God under any circumstances has difficulty with texts such as Exodus 24:10.

[18]הֲגַם הֲלֹם רָאִיתִי אַחֲרֵי רֹאִי (hăgam hălōm rā'îthî 'aḥărê rō'î). Wenham, *Genesis 16–50*, p. 2.

[19]It is not possible to know what period of time is being referred to here, but the well would in any case still be in use centuries after the time of Abram. This remarkable fact in an arid land draws the narrator's remark.

that this passage comes from the hypothetical source P where men do the naming, as opposed to J where women do it.[20] But where did Abram get the name from? Clearly from Hagar who had it revealed to her by the angel. More likely the text implies that Abram accepts the verdict about the child which the angel had revealed to Hagar. God had heard, but Ishmael is not to be the promised child.

16:16 Abram was eighty-six years old when Hagar bore him Ishmael.

This is yet another example of the interest of the narrator in the chronology of the Patriarchal period. In traditional source criticism it is argued that only the P source was interested in such matters. In any case the ages are consistent with the narrative no matter what their source. Abram had moved to Canaan at the age of 75. After ten years in Canaan with no heir on the horizon, he accepts participation in Sarai's plan to have her heir through Hagar. Allowing a year for the pregnancy, Abram is now 86.

---

[20]Genesis 4:1 has Eve naming Cain while Genesis 29:32-35 has Leah naming her sons, both P passages supposedly.

GENESIS 17

B. THE PROMISES SYMBOLIZED, REAFFIRMED, AND CLARIFIED (17:1–18:15)

After the birth of Ishmael and his survival to young manhood, Abram and Sarai evidently think that their strategy has worked. Ishmael will be the heir that Sarai could not provide from her own body. In this section the LORD clarifies for both Abram and Sarai that Ishmael is not to be the heir. The "Hagar Strategy" never had the LORD's approval. Instead he promises to provide the impossible, a child born of a barren woman of 90 to a man of 100! The promises are reaffirmed and even expanded (17:4-8,15-21). Abram and Sarai become Abraham (17:5) and Sarah (17:15), indicating their new status. This section begins with a command for Abram to live in fellowship with God and live a blameless life (17:1). This is a precondition for a new phase of the outworking of the promise (17:2). That promise is to be symbolized and carried forward for each generation through the sign of circumcision (17:9-14). Abraham signals his acceptance of this newly expanded promise by obeying the command to circumcise every male member of his household (17:22-27). At a second appearance the LORD accepts Abraham's hospitality and reiterates the promise regarding Sarah (18:1-15).

1. The Promises Symbolized: The Covenant Sign of Circumcision (17:1-14)

In this section the LORD appeared to Abram again, this time to formalize the covenant with the covenant sign of circumcision and clarify and expand the associated promises. Ishmael is now about twelve years old and thus about to enter adulthood. He is to be included in the covenant sign of circumcision as is any other male descendant of Abram. The section begins with a commandment to Abram to live in fellowship with God and live a blameless life (v. 1). This will result in God's promise to "give" Abram a covenant (v. 2) with expanded blessings

(vv. 3-8). Abram's responsibility is to ensure that the covenant sign of circumcision is the permanent identifying sign of all his male descendants (vv. 9-13). Failure to obey the command to circumcise will result in being cut off from Abram's people for breaking the covenant (v. 14).

Israel was not unique among ancient peoples in practicing circumcision. Most of Israel's neighbors practiced a form of it at puberty or as part of a prenuptial ceremony.[1] But for Abram's descendants the ceremony was to be done to all newborn boys of whatever racial background[2] at eight days of age. Circumcision was the sign of inclusion in the covenant, a way of guaranteeing that the covenant would be maintained throughout the generations, and the means of including outsiders who wanted to join the covenant. The person receiving circumcision was expected to accept the responsibilities which membership in the covenant community entailed as well as its privileges.[3] Circumcision was never merely a sign of the covenant. The Torah speaks of circumcision of the heart (Lev 26:41) and lips (Exod 6:12) and of the circumcision of the first harvests of fruit trees when Israel enters the Promised Land (Lev 19:23).

Goldingay suggests that the physical rite had another metaphorical significance which explains why it was only performed on males.[4] Circumcision reminds the male descendants of Abram that the very thing which ensured their biological reproduction and thus the future of the promise of a great nation must be symbolically disciplined. The discipline of male sexual drives was necessary for Israel to avoid the fertility cults of Canaan and for her kings to avoid projecting their power through the symbolic sexual bravado of the harem (Deut 17:17; 1 Kgs 11:1-18).

The LORD Offers to Formalize the Covenant (17:1-2)

17:1 When Abram was ninety-nine years old, the LORD appeared to him and said, "I am God Almighty; walk before me and be blameless.

Thirteen years pass in silence while Abram waited for the fulfillment of the promise. The LORD appears to Abram with time running out on the promise. He is 99 years old and Sarai 89.[5] While the narrator calls him the LORD, he actually introduces himself as God Almighty (אֵל שַׁדַּי, 'ēl šadday). Abram apparently needed to be reminded of God's power since he had been trying to give assistance to the all powerful

---

[1]P.R. Williamson, "Circumcision," *DOTP*, p. 122.
[2]Ibid., p. 123, notes it "was not a sign of racial purity."
[3]Ibid.
[4]J. Goldingay, "The Significance of Circumcision," *JSOT* 88 (2000): 3-18.
[5]Once again the interest in chronology is attributed to the P source.

who had no need of it. Instead of trying to play God, Abram is commanded to "walk" before the LORD. This verb הָלַךְ (*hālak*, "to walk") is
used in the hithpael in instances where the LORD is, or is to be, especially near. The LORD "walked"[6] in the Garden in the cool of the day
(Gen 3:8); Enoch and Noah were said to have walked with God (Gen
5:22,24; 6:8). The LORD's presence in the Tabernacle or Temple is often
indicated by reference to his walking in the hithpael (1 Sam 2:30,35;
2 Sam 7:6-7; 1 Chr 17:6). Here Abram is commanded to "walk before"
the LORD. In Genesis 24:40 the aged Abraham tells his servant that he
has, in fact, been walking before the LORD.

Abram is also commanded to be "blameless" (תָּמִים, *tāmîm*), a word
that does not imply moral perfection but "wholeness" or "soundness."
It is often[7] used of sacrificial animals which are healthy and without
injury or visible blemish.

**17:2 I will confirm my covenant between me and you and will greatly
increase your numbers."**

The NIV omits the word "and" at the beginning of this verse. This
weakens the connection between the command, "walk before the LORD
and be blameless" to the making of the covenant. This may in a subtle
way show the Calvinistic bias which occasionally occurs in the NIV. The
text as it stands makes a connection between God's promise and the
obedience of Abram to the command to "be blameless." The NIV
chooses the word "confirm" for the Hebrew word נָתַן (*nāthan*), usually
translated "give." For some reason the text does not use the more typical phrase "cut" a covenant.[8] It may be that the NIV is right and this narrative is only a confirmation of a previously established covenant. On
the other hand the promised increase in numbers sounds very much
like an element of the original promise (Gen 12:2) and its reaffirmations
(Gen 13:16; 15:5). The idea that a promise of God is in some way
dependent upon Abram's walking in the presence of God and being
blameless creates theological difficulties for many evangelical Christians.
Some fear that this suggests a covenant dependent upon flawed human
beings like Abram for its fulfillment. This seems too tenuous a basis for
a promise which Christians know culminates in the sending of Abram's
seed, Jesus the messiah. But this line of reasoning limits God's power to
fulfill his purpose in spite of human failings. As John the Baptist once

---

[6]The hithpael typically is reflexive in Hebrew although it can be "iterative" indicating repeated action; cf. Arnold and Choi, *Biblical Hebrew Syntax*, pp. 47-48.

[7]Exod 12:5; 29:1; Lev 1:3,10; 3:1,6; 4:3, etc.

[8]כָּרַת (*kārath*) with בְּרִית (*bᵉrîth*) in Hebrew.

remarked, "God is able to raise up out of these stones children to Abraham!" (Matt 3:10b).

Abram Accepts the LORD's Offer (17:3)

17:3 Abram fell facedown, and God said to him,

Abram shows his respect for and gratitude to God by falling upon his face. The command is not seen as burdensome in light of the privilege of a direct appearance of the LORD to him and a reaffirmation of the promise of a great number of descendants. Interestingly, it is God who is said to speak to him, not the LORD, as in verse 1. These sorts of variations are typically interpreted as signs of alternating sources between J and E or P in traditional source criticism. But more recent scholarship has questioned whether variations in divine names are a reliable indicator of sources.[9]

God's Commitment in the Formalized Covenant (17:4-8)

17:4 "As for me, this is my covenant with you: You will be the father of many nations.

Not only will Abram have innumerable descendants; he is now promised that he will be the father of an entire crowd[10] of nations. To have the promise of a great number of descendants is a great act of grace; but to be promised that an entire crowd of nations would be descended from Abram is beyond the mind to conceive. Many entire peoples would look to Abram as their forefather.

17:5 No longer will you be called Abram; your name will be Abraham, for I have made you a father of many nations.

With the expanded promise comes a new name. Abram's name meant "exalted father"; his new name Abraham means "father of a multitude." That this is spoken to Abram when he has no heirs is striking. His name is changed to reflect an expansion of the promise to include a whole crowd full of nations before he has even seen the birth of a single son as a legitimate heir.[11] The use of the past tense[12] ("made you") implies the certainty of the promise in this case. Abraham has already

---

[9]E.g., R.N. Whybray, *The Making of the Pentateuch: A Methodological Study*, JSOTSupp 53 (Sheffield: JSOT Press, 1987), pp. 63-72.

[10]The Hebrew word הֲמוֹן (*hămôn*) is not the ordinary word for "many."

[11]The LORD does not regard Ishmael as a legitimate heir for the purposes of the promise.

[12]Technically there are no tenses in Hebrew. The use here of the perfect without a conjunction is as close as Hebrew gets to a simple past tense.

been made into a father of many nations in God's mind. His name change signifies this.

17:6 I will make you very fruitful; I will make nations of you, and kings will come from you.

The use of the verb "make fruitful" (פָּרָה, *pārāh*) is an echo of the creation account (Gen 1:22,28) and the recommissioning of creation after the flood (Gen 8:17; 9:1,7). The promise to Abraham is God's way of fulfilling his creation commission and intention. The point is emphasized by the word "very."[13] Often in recent theological discussion a great chasm has been made between creation and covenant or creation and election as though these concepts were at odds and impossible to harmonize. Some of this is understandable given Karl Barth's firm stand against Hitler's implicit grounding of Nazism in the creation of race and land. His rejection of that sort of natural theology was courageous and necessary. But the book of Genesis is clear that the promise to Abraham is a new strategy for fulfilling his creation purpose for humanity. Humanity's commission was frustrated by the persistent, stubborn, and continuing refusal to submit to God's intention for creation. In Abraham and his descendants that commission would be fulfilled. God adds that he would "give you to nations, and kings will come out of you." The NIV interprets this as meaning "I will make nations of you." While this is possible and fits the parallel clause, it does require a bit of interpretation. It is striking that Abraham is promised that kings will descend from him given the Old Testament's well-attested reservations about kings that imitate the nations (1 Sam 8:1-22). But the Old Testament is not against the institution as such as the law in Deuteronomy 17:14-20 demonstrates. In fact at a certain point in the nation's history a king was not only permissible but needed (Judg 17:6; 21:25).

17:7 I will establish my covenant as an everlasting covenant between me and you and your descendants after you for the generations to come, to be your God and the God of your descendants after you.

God now speaks of the longevity of the covenant. The word "everlasting" is an interpretation which may create the wrong impression in contemporary western readers. Perhaps "lasting" would be a better translation.[14]

The content of the covenant is that God would be Abraham's God and the God of his descendants throughout the generations. The impli-

---

[13]The Hebrew בִּמְאֹד מְאֹד (*bim'ōd m'ōd*) is emphatic.

[14]The Hebrew word עוֹלָם (*'ōlām*) does not necessarily imply eternity or everlastingness. The Princeton abridgment of BDB has "of long duration" as its first definition for the word.

cation is that Abraham's descendants are to recognize no other God but God. The imagined audience would undoubtedly be reminded of what Christians call the first commandment, "You shall have no other gods before me" (Exod 20:3).

17:8 The whole land of Canaan, where you are now an alien, I will give as an everlasting possession to you and your descendants after you; and I will be their God."

Here God reassures Abraham of the promise of the land given previously in Genesis 12:7; 13:14-15; 15:18. Abraham knew what it meant to live as an alien in a land possessed by others. The imagined and canonical audiences also knew of this from their experiences in Egypt and Babylon respectively. Abraham is promised the entire land of Canaan as an enduring possession.[15]

Notice the repetition of the fact, first affirmed in verse 7, that the God of Abraham's descendants would be God alone and no other god. This seems a rather simple demand in the contemporary world where the viable options for most people are some form of agnosticism or atheism or monotheism. Polytheism is not a great temptation in our scientific age. But for Abraham and for Israel the idea of recognizing only one God and to worship him exclusively was revolutionary.

Abram's Responsibilities in the Formalized Covenant (17:9-14)

17:9 Then God said to Abraham, "As for you, you must keep my covenant, you and your descendants after you for the generations to come.

After making several unilateral promises in verses 4-8, God then turns to Abraham's responsibilities as a covenant partner. Abraham and his descendants must keep watch[16] over the covenant. Both Abraham and his descendants are responsible for doing this within their generations. The Bible knows of no covenants in which one of the partners has nothing to do.

17:10 This is my covenant with you and your descendants after you, the covenant you are to keep: Every male among you shall be circumcised.

---

[15]Once again the NIV translates the Hebrew word עוֹלָם (*'ôlām*) by the English word "everlasting." But once again such a translation can be confusing. Obviously the canonical audience did not experience eternal possession of the entire land of Canaan nor had the nation throughout its history with rare exceptions. The imagined audience also knew of the conditionality of the land promise and the very real danger of exile from it for unfaithfulness (Deut 29; 30).

[16]The Hebrew verb שָׁמַר (*šāmar*) often has connotations of "guard," "protect," "watch over," etc.; cf. "שמר," KB, pp. 1582-1583.

The Hebrew word order places the verb, "to be circumcised" in the first position and the phrase "every male" in the last position. This seems to place emphasis on the action of circumcision rather than on those who will receive it. The covenant is defined as the act of circumcising every male. We tend to view this as merely the sign of the covenant as though the act of circumcision pointed to the relationship rather than forming that relationship. But modern and postmodern distinguishing between the sign and the reality should not be read back into the ancient world. The act itself brought one into the covenant and placed one under its blessings and obligations.[17] This does not preclude it also being a sign; in fact it enhances its sign-making function.

A question we often ask is, Why is circumcision used as the sign? Perhaps the idea is that the male sexual organ represents its function of being the instrument which brings forth children. Since all of Abraham's descendants are to be set apart to the LORD and the LORD's purposes, circumcision is a visual reminder to Abraham's descendants that they all belong to the LORD. This does not preclude the hygienic purposes of circumcision (of which the Israelites were presumably unaware[18]) or the fact that some cultures in the area around Palestine also practiced circumcision.[19] Another possibility was suggested by Philo[20] and later adapted by scholars such as Goldingay[21] that circumcision symbolizes the disciplining of often problematic sexual urges of males within the covenant.

17:11 You are to undergo circumcision, and it will be the sign of the covenant between me and you.

The "you" is plural in both cases implying that the covenant does not apply to Abraham alone, but to all of his male descendants. The act will not only be the covenant (as in v. 10), but will also serve as the sign of the covenant between God and the descendants of Abraham. One of

---

[17]A similar sort of distinction between baptism as the sign of conversion and conversion itself is often asserted, once again in tension with the explicit statements of the New Testament that does not separate the act from the internal attitude of the person submitting to the act. Like circumcision, baptism is both the covenant forming act and the sign of that formation.

[18]Although Philo in the first century A.D. certainly sees such hygienic purposes behind circumcision (*Special Laws 1.4-5*).

[19]According to P.R. Williamson ("Circumcision," *DOTP*, pp. 122-125), circumcision was practiced by most of Israel's neighbors, primarily as a marriage or fertility rite performed at marriage or puberty (123).

[20]Philo, *Special Laws 1.9*.

[21]Goldingay, "Significance of Circumcision."

the distinctive characteristics of Israel's religion in its ancient Near Eastern environment is the way that sex was separated from worship in Israel. The sign of circumcision which may imply the need for the disciplining of sex, reminds outsiders (and insiders tempted to compromise sexually) that Israel's relationship with God is unique.

17:12 For the generations to come every male among you who is eight days old must be circumcised, including those born in your household or bought with money from a foreigner—those who are not your offspring.

Circumcision is the sign and means of inclusion into the covenant promises and obligations for every male descendant of Abraham. It is also the sign and means of admission to that covenant for outsiders. The imagined audience is reminded of the requirement that every male participating in the Passover feast was to be circumcised (Exod 12:44,48). Only those who in circumcision have identified themselves with God's people Israel would escape divine judgment. Unlike in the nations around Israel, circumcision was performed soon after birth as a sign of entrance into the covenant family. The eighth day may reflect high infant mortality rates in the ancient world. Waiting until the eighth day would ensure that the child was strong enough to live and survive the operation.[22]

17:13 Whether born in your household or bought with your money, they must be circumcised. My covenant in your flesh is to be an everlasting covenant.

The repetition of the phrase, "born in your household or bought with your money" emphasizes the importance of every male within the covenant community which will descend from Abraham being circumcised. The emphatic nature of the command is further strengthened by the use in the Hebrew of a special emphatic construction[23] which the NIV renders "must be circumcised." This emphasis may be because obedience to this commandment had been an issue for the imagined audience, whether it be in Moses' own family (Exod 4:24-26) or in the wilderness generation as a whole (Josh 5:2-7).

---

[22]The explanation that this command was given because by the eighth day the blood clotting factors in the blood would be at their peak is not something the original audience would have known about, if in fact it is the case. S.I. McMillen and David E. Stern, *None of these Diseases*, 3rd ed. (Grand Rapids: Revell, 2000), pp. 80-87.

[23]Infinitive absolute followed by the imperfect of the same root and stem, in this case niphal. Cf. Waltke & O'Connor, *Biblical Hebrew Syntax*, pp. 584-588.

In this passage circumcision is once again identified as a covenant and not merely the sign of one (cf. v. 10). This covenant is not to be a temporary agreement that lasts only for Abraham's generation, but a lasting (NIV has "everlasting") one.

17:14 Any uncircumcised male, who has not been circumcised in the flesh, will be cut off from his people; he has broken my covenant."

The importance of the commandment is indicated by the penalty. Refusal to circumcise a covenant member will result in the life[24] of that person being cut off from his people. This text may give the imagined audience[25] vital information necessary for understanding Exodus 4:24-26 where, immediately after calling Moses, "the LORD sought to kill him." The issue there is evidently the refusal of Moses to circumcise his own son because of his wife Zipporah's resistance to the idea. This covenant in chapter 17 can be broken by the refusal of Abraham or his descendants to practice circumcision on all members of the covenant community. Such disobedience breaks or nullifies the treaty and the person cannot remain among the covenant people. The seriousness of the commandment is thus emphasized. Every generation of Abraham's descendants would have a lifelong reminder of the promise of a seed, an innumerable people all descending from Abraham who had no children until age 86!

2. The Promise Reaffirmed and Clarified (17:15-18:15)

Having established the covenant sign, God spoke again[26] to Abraham. This time he reaffirms and clarifies the promise. Sarai, now renamed Sarah, will not be forgotten. Barren though she had been for all of her 89 years, Sarah would herself have a son (17:15-16). Both Abraham (17:17) and later Sarah (18:12) find this promise incredible and struggle to believe it. Abraham first attempts to have Ishmael reinstated as the one through whom the blessing will flow (17:18). God reassures Abraham that Ishmael will indeed be blessed (17:20). But Ishmael will not be the heir which Abraham so desperately sought.

---

[24]The Hebrew has נֶפֶשׁ (*nephes̆*) here, meaning "life." This is not indicated in the NIV. This word is sometimes translated as "soul," but the connotations of that word in English do not apply to the Hebrew word.

[25]Note that the imagined audience reads the Pentateuch as a whole and not just the book of Genesis.

[26]The *waw*-consecutive with which v. 15 begins may imply that this was a later conversation following the one recorded in 17:1-14.

God's Blessings for Sarai in the Formalized Covenant (17:15-16)

17:15 God also said to Abraham, "As for Sarai your wife, you are no longer to call her Sarai; her name will be Sarah.

The promises do not stop with Abraham; Sarai also receives promises. She too will have a change of name indicating a change of identity. Both forms of the name mean "princess" although they are pronounced differently. With the clarification of her necessary role in the working out of the promise which follows, the new name, even if it is only a new pronunciation, indicates her newly revealed significance. God refers to Sarai as Abram's wife, not his half-sister as Abraham claims, once again perhaps anticipating Abraham's lie about this in Genesis 20:12.

17:16 I will bless her and will surely give you a son by her. I will bless her so that she will be the mother of nations; kings of peoples will come from her."

The previous narratives portray Abram and Sarai as operating under the assumption that after so many years it was impossible for Sarai to have children. But God clarifies that she, under her new name Sarah, will also participate in the blessings promised to Abraham. She in fact will herself bear a son by which the promises will find their fulfillment. Not only will she have a son, she will receive such blessing that nations (in the plural) will trace their descent from her. And furthermore, leaders of entire peoples will come from her. The first-time reader sees that the attempts to find an heir in Lot and Ishmael ultimately came from failing to wait for God's timing. Just as Abraham had been promised to have kings for descendants (v. 6) here it is explicitly revealed that those kings would trace their lineage from Sarah. While the kings of Israel and the kings of the nations become a problem in the Old Testament, here the fact that such leaders will descend from Abraham and Sarah is an element of the promise. The problem is thus not kingship *per se*, but the type of king "like the nations" which the nation later adopted as their model for kingship.

The relating of the word "bless" to the fertility of birth echoes the creation narrative (Gen 1:22,28). This is another piece of evidence that, for the author of Genesis, the covenant with Abraham was a new strategy for seeing the fulfillment of God's original purposes in creation.

Abraham's Attempt to Renegotiate (17:17-18)

17:17 Abraham fell facedown; he laughed and said to himself, "Will a son be born to a man a hundred years old? Will Sarah bear a child at the age of ninety?"

Abraham's reaction is to laugh with his face to the ground. He finds the idea of a son being born to a man of one hundred and a woman of ninety ridiculous. This is the first example of the theme of laughter, a concept that forms a *leitmotif* for the ensuing narrative. The Hebrew syntax places emphasis on the word "son" and "a man a hundred years old" by bringing them forward into first and second position in the sentence. Abram does not laugh out loud, but understandably finds the very idea of Sarah and him having a son preposterous. Interestingly though, he uses the name Sarah, not Sarai. He has heard the promise that nations and kings would descend from her barren womb.

17:18 And Abraham said to God, "If only Ishmael might live under your blessing!"

What Abraham actually says to God is implicitly a prayer that Ishmael might be reconsidered as an heir. In a sort of pun, Abraham effectively says, "If only God would hear my prayer regarding 'God will hear' (the meaning of Ishmael's name)." The Hebrew word translated "if only" however, is often used in contexts of an unreal situation which the speaker knows is only "hypothetical" and "contrary to known fact or reasonable expectation."[27] Abraham would like God's decision about Ishmael to be different, but he knows that it will not be. Surprisingly, God does listen to Abraham's plea for Ishmael, although not in the sense intended by Abraham.

God's Clarification and Reaffirmation (17:19)

17:19 Then God said, "Yes, but your wife Sarah will bear you a son, and you will call him Isaac. I will establish my covenant with him as an everlasting covenant for his descendants after him.

God does take up the request for Ishmael with the word "Yes," but this does not change where the heir will come from. In a sort of joke which lets Abraham know that he has heard his laughter, under his breath though it was, God tells Abraham that he will call his son Isaac, meaning "he will laugh." His name will be a lasting reminder to Abraham (and to Sarah) that God is quite capable of accomplishing what men find to be laughably improbable. The covenant will be reaffirmed with "he will laugh" and even with his descendants. Once again the translation "everlasting" may be too strong.[28]

---

[27]J. Huehnergard, "Asseverative *la and Hypothetical *lu/law in Semitic," *JAOS* 103 (1983): 569-593, quoted in Waltke and O'Connor, *Biblical Hebrew Syntax*, pp. 637-638.

[28]The Hebrew phrase עַד־עוֹלָם (*'ad-'ôlām*) literally translated means "unto the age" and depending on context does not necessarily imply anything more than a long period of time.

Ishmael's Secondary Blessing (17:20)

17:20 And as for Ishmael, I have heard you: I will surely bless him; I will make him fruitful and will greatly increase his numbers. He will be the father of twelve rulers, and I will make him into a great nation.

Once again we have a wordplay. Abraham had asked implicitly that God would hear his prayer for his son whose name means, "God will hear." Taking up the pun God says explicitly, "With regard to God Will Hear (Ishmael), I have heard you." Abraham had asked for Ishmael to live under God's blessing without much confidence. God assures him that he will receive God's blessing. The echoing yet again of the creation commission to be fruitful and multiply and of the Abrahamic promises is striking. The blessing of fertility will be his (Gen 1:28), and Ishmael, like Abraham and Sarah, will father rulers.[29] That they will number twelve shows the parallel nature of the promise to Ishmael and Israel which was composed of 12 tribes. The promise that Ishmael will be made into a "great nation" is an obvious echo of the initial promise to Abram in Genesis 12:2.[30] The theological point seems to be that though Ishmael is not chosen for the role of heir to the Abrahamic promises, he is still under God's blessing. The election (choice) of Isaac and his son Jacob (Israel) does not preclude God from choosing and blessing others. Israel is not the only great nation that descended from Abraham and the original readers would have noticed this. God's grace overflows the boundaries of the covenant community and reminds Israel of the ultimate universal purpose of its election.

Isaac's Primary Blessing (17:21)

17:21 But my covenant I will establish with Isaac, whom Sarah will bear to you by this time next year."

While Ishmael will receive blessings reminiscent of the promise, the promise itself and the covenant underlying it will find its primary fulfillment in Isaac, the promised son. In this verse the promise of verse 19 is further specified. Isaac will be born within a year! The word for "time" (מוֹעֵד, *môʿēd*) in the NIV is used of special occasions such as festivals and other liturgical services at the Tabernacle or Temple. The imagined audience would see the birth of Isaac as an event of momentous importance, on a par with the feast of Passover or Tabernacles. The time for

---

[29]The Hebrew for "rulers" (נְשִׂיאִם, *nᵉśîʾim*) is not the same word as that translated "kings" in the promises to Abraham and Sarah (vv. 6,16), but the concept is similar.

[30]The verbs differ in the two promises: עָשָׂה (*ʿāśāh*) is used in Genesis 12:2 while נָתַן (*nāthan*) is used here, although the distinction is not very great.

the beginning of the fulfillment of the promise of a great nation descending from Abraham has now come.

Abraham's Obedience to the Formalized Covenant (17:22-27)

17:22 When he had finished speaking with Abraham, God went up from him.

Enough has been said. Now it is up to Abraham to obey. God removes himself from the special direct contact which he has been having with Abraham.[31]

17:23 On that very day Abraham took his son Ishmael and all those born in his household or bought with his money, every male in his household, and circumcised them, as God told him.

Abraham's obedience is shown by the fact that the circumcision which God had commanded was performed that very day.[32] The text carefully delineates the strict obedience of Abraham to God's commandment. He circumcised all those born in his house or bought with his money as God had commanded in verse 13. Ishmael is in particular singled out. He too is a member of the covenant family and its promised blessings. Abraham's obedience is highlighted by the phrase "as God told him."

17:24 Abraham was ninety-nine years old when he was circumcised, 17:25 and his son Ishmael was thirteen; 17:26 Abraham and his son Ishmael were both circumcised on that same day. 17:27 And every male in Abraham's household, including those born in his household or bought from a foreigner, was circumcised with him.

The point of Abraham's strict obedience to God's command is reinforced by giving the ages of Abraham and Ishmael at their circumcisions. This is further underscored with the repetition of the phrase "that very day" from verse 23.[33] The repetition in this passage of "every male in Abraham's household," "born in his household," and "bought" gives emphasis.[34] Abraham's faith in God's promises, now clarified to include a named son from Sarah, is demonstrated by his willing obedience.

---

[31]This may be the significance of the terminology "went up" (עָלָה, *'ālāh*).

[32]The Hebrew draws the reader into the story by saying "this day" as though the readers were participating in the events of that day. The phrase "bone of this day" (בְּעֶצֶם הַיּוֹם הַזֶּה, *bᵉ'eṣem hayyôm hazzeh*) means "this very day" (cf. Gen 7:13; Exod 12:17,41,51 of Passover; Lev 23:14,21,28,29,30; Deut 32:48; Josh 5:11; 10:27; Ezek 2:3; 24:2; 40:1.

[33]By paraphrasing to "that same day" the NIV loses the connection with verse 23.

[34]The chiastic repetition of verses 23-27 emphasizes both the quick and willing obedience of Abraham and the importance of the event.

GENESIS 18

2. The Promise Reaffirmed and Clarified
(17:15–18:15, continued)

The LORD Appears Again to Abraham and Sarah (18:1)

18:1 The LORD appeared to Abraham near the great trees of Mamre while he was sitting at the entrance to his tent in the heat of the day.

This section records yet another[1] appearance of God[2] to Abraham. The appearance occurs at the "oaks" (NIV "great trees") of Mamre,[3] the last place in which Abraham is said to have lived (Gen 14:13). The phrase "heat of the day" means something like noontime. The Old Testament contains no precise segmenting of time into hours. This may be mentioned because typically people would not be out and about during this time, and it surprised Abraham to see the three men.[4]

Abraham's Elaborate Welcome of His Divine Guests (18:2-8)

18:2 Abraham looked up and saw three men standing nearby. When he saw them, he hurried from the entrance of his tent to meet them and bowed low to the ground.

Abraham saw three men standing "upon him" (NIV has "nearby"). They must not have been immediately in front of him since he "ran" (NIV has "hurried") to meet them. By running during the heat of the day Abraham shows the importance with which he regards his guests. He shows his respect by bowing himself to the ground.[5]

---

[1]The *waw*-consecutive which begins this verse in the Hebrew implies temporal succession here.

[2]In this case, unlike ch. 17, the deity is referred to as the "LORD" (יהוה, *yahweh*), the covenant name for Israel's God, not the more generic "God" (אלהים, *'ĕlōhîm*).

[3]Although the identification is uncertain, Mamre is commonly assumed to be Haram Ramet el-Kahlil two miles north of Hebron; cf. Wade D. Kotter, "Mamre (Place)," *EDB*, pp. 850-851. In Genesis 23:19 Mamre is identified with Hebron as the location of the Cave of Machpelah.

[4]Sarna, *Genesis*, p. 128.

[5]The NIV's "low" is not in the Hebrew text.

18:3 He said, "If I have found favor in your eyes, my lord, do not pass your servant by.

While Abraham has seen three men, he addresses only one. The language which Abraham uses does not necessarily mean that he recognizes immediately that this is an appearance of God. The use of "my lord" and "your servant" may be nothing more than the ordinary politeness of ancient Near Eastern culture.

18:4 Let a little water be brought, and then you may all wash your feet and rest under this tree. 18:5 Let me get you something to eat, so you can be refreshed and then go on your way—now that you have come to your servant." "Very well," they answered, "do as you say."

While Abraham had only spoken with one of the men, he offers the hospitality of water and rest and food to all three. The "you" and "your" are plural in the Hebrew. The offer of hospitality may be simply an indication of Abraham's character. But there may be other reasons. Perhaps Abraham thinks he might get the opportunity to interact with these divine visitors if he can get them to stay with him until their needs are met. They agree to accept his hospitality because they have other reasons to talk with Abraham.

18:6 So Abraham hurried into the tent to Sarah. "Quick," he said, "get three seahs of fine flour and knead it and bake some bread."

Once again we see Abraham rushing. He hurries and he asks Sarah to hurry.[6] Just as at the Passover, there is no time to wait for the bread to rise. It must be made quickly. The imagined audience, Israel recently freed from Egypt, would undoubtedly recall the "hurry" that is a part of the original Passover. The unleavened bread which was produced in such circumstances had an ongoing symbolic value for the community. At any moment the LORD might reveal himself and call upon us to act. We must therefore be ever ready to respond. The amount of flour is extraordinarily large and shows the generosity of Abraham. The fact that "fine flour" rather than ordinary flour is used also indicates this.

18:7 Then he ran to the herd and selected a choice, tender calf and gave it to a servant, who hurried to prepare it.

Again Abraham runs, this time to select a choice calf for his visitor. The "young man"[7] in Abraham's household also hurries in preparing it. The entire household is involved in the hospitality for these important guests.

---

[6]In the Hebrew the word "hurried" and the word "quick" are the same verb (מָהַר, *māhar*).

[7]The NIV's "servant" is a paraphrase.

18:8 He then brought some curds and milk and the calf that had been prepared, and set these before them. While they ate, he stood near them under a tree.

Why are we informed that Abraham stood near them "under a tree"? Actually the Hebrew says, "the" tree.[8] Although hurriedly prepared, the meal was sumptuous. Abraham is portrayed as inviting his guests to eat meat and milk together, something the later tradition forbade.

The Promise regarding Sarah Repeated and Specified (18:9-10)

18:9 "Where is your wife Sarah?" they asked him. "There, in the tent," he said.

Notice that the visitors refer to Abram's wife as "Sarah" not as "Sarai." This is clear evidence that the visitors are divine representatives and are there to further elaborate on the promises given to Abraham and Sarah in chapter 17.

18:10 Then the LORD said, "I will surely return to you about this time next year, and Sarah your wife will have a son." Now Sarah was listening at the entrance to the tent, which was behind him.

For the first time the visitor is identified as the divine being, "the LORD." He promised that within a year Sarah would have a son of her own. Sarah thinks she is secretly overhearing the conversation. The Hebrew is ambiguous as to whether the entrance to the tent was behind the LORD (so NIV) or the LORD was behind the entrance to the tent. In the first case the LORD knows of Sarah listening in on the conversation by divine knowledge. If the other meaning is assumed, the LORD was actually behind Sarah and was able to see her by normal means.

Sarah's Failure to Trust the Repeated Promise (18:11-15)

18:11 Abraham and Sarah were already old and well advanced in years, and Sarah was past the age of childbearing.

The reader is reminded of the age and physical condition of Abraham and Sarah so as to explain Sarah's reaction. She is not only barren, but has also gone through her menses. From a human point of view there is no hope for her to have a son with Abraham, the promises of God in chapter 17 notwithstanding.

18:12 So Sarah laughed to herself as she thought, "After I am worn out and my master is old, will I now have this pleasure?"

Sarah's response on hearing the conversation taking place outside the tent is to "laugh to herself." The NIV seems to assume that we have

---

[8]The tree was evidently famous to the original audience.

Sarah's thoughts expressed here, but the usual meaning of the Hebrew word refers to what Sarah actually said (לֵאמֹר, lē'mōr). Sarah's laughter receives condemnation (18:13-14) while Abraham's did not in 17:17 even though the reasoning seems remarkably similar.

Sarah expresses doubt that at Abraham's age and in her physical condition they could have such pleasure. The word translated "pleasure" in the NIV literally means "lust" (עֶדְנָה, 'ednāh).[9] One wonders whether this is not a delicate way of implying that Abraham and Sarah had given up sleeping together after their hopes of having a child together had been dashed.

Genesis 17:17	Genesis 18:12
Abraham fell facedown; he laughed and said to himself, "Will a son be born to a man a hundred years old? Will Sarah bear a child at the age of ninety?"	So Sarah laughed to herself saying, "After I am worn out and my master is old, will I now have this pleasure?"

Why is Abraham never condemned for his laughter while Sarah is? The most likely explanation once again comes from careful narrative analysis. Abraham laughed and spoke inwardly. Sarah laughed inwardly and then spoke. Abraham laughed when he first heard of the idea of him at 100 and Sarah at 90 having a child together. There the LORD gave further explanation which was apparently accepted by Abraham since he obeyed the command to circumcise himself and the male members of the family. But he does not laugh in 18:10 when the time of the birth is clarified as being within the next year. Sarah laughs at something the LORD had already promised previously.

Sarah refers to Abraham as her "Lord" (אָדוֹן, 'ādôn). The NIV's "master" tends to suggest a master and slave relationship, something this word does not connote in Hebrew when referring to a relationship between a husband and wife. First Peter 3:6 is probably referring to this passage when it notes that Sarah showed her obedience to and respect for Abraham by calling him "Lord" (κύριος, kurios).

18:13 Then the LORD said to Abraham, "Why did Sarah laugh and say, 'Will I really have a child, now that I am old'"

Interestingly the LORD addresses Abraham about Sarah's laughter and not Sarah herself. This may be because the promise of a son from Sarah was addressed to Abraham in chapter 17, and it would presum-

---

[9] Cf. "עֶדְנָה, 'ednāh," KB, p. 793.

ably be his responsibility to accurately convey the LORD's words to his wife.[10] Has Abraham not communicated the promise to Sarah? The fact that the LORD knows that Sarah had laughed indicates one of two things. He may have overheard it by normal means. If not, it shows his divine knowledge.

18:14 Is anything too hard for the LORD? I will return to you at the appointed time next year and Sarah will have a son."

The LORD asks a theological question. Literally the question is, "Is anything too wonderful[11] for the LORD [to be able to do]?" The Hebrew word translated "appointed time" in the NIV (מוֹעֵד, *mô'ēd*) often refers to the meeting which takes place between God and Israel at the Tabernacle and to the feasts where Israel is to gather to meet with God. The miracle which is to take place, takes place at a time appointed by the LORD just as he does things in Israel at such appointed times.

18:15 Sarah was afraid, so she lied and said, "I did not laugh." But he said, "Yes, you did laugh."

Evidently Sarah overheard the conversation. The problem was not with Abraham's communication of the promise but in Sarah's difficulty in believing it. Apparently out of fear of embarrassment or judgment Sarah lied, evidently thinking that no one could possibly have heard her internal laughter. The LORD then pointed out that he knew what only a divine person could know, Sarah's internal speech. Perhaps this was the LORD's way of showing Sarah his divine characteristics as a sort of sign that he was well able to bring about the miraculous birth he had promised.

C. THE ENDGAME ON THE LOT STRATEGY: THE HARD LESSON OF THE LONG-TERM RESULTS OF TRYING TO FULFILL GOD'S PROMISES FOR HIM (18:16–19:38)

In this section, which is dominated by the LORD's destruction of Sodom and Gomorrah, we see the long-term consequences of Abram's decision to allow Lot to go with him when he left his father's household behind in chapter 12. The narrative begins with the LORD deciding to inform Abraham of his intention to judge Sodom and Gomorrah

---

[10]The parallel with the Garden of Eden narrative is noteworthy and may be deliberate. Just as Adam was addressed first since he alone had received the commandment not to eat of the tree, here Abraham is addressed in a similar situation.

[11]The Hebrew verb is פָּלָא (*pālā'*).

(18:16-19) should their wickedness prove to be as great as had been rumored (18:20). Abraham then negotiates to save the entirety of Sodom and Gomorrah for the sake of the few righteous who might be there (18:22-33). The angels then test the people of Sodom by visiting them as strangers. They confirm the Sodomites' wickedness when the inhabitants threaten to homosexually rape the visitors (19:1-11). The angels save Lot and those family members who were willing to leave, along with the village of Zoar (19:12-22), before the destruction falls on all those who remain (19:23-29). Lot ends up living in a cave near Zoar with his two daughters and bearing two sons through them, Moab and Ben-Ammi. They were the ancestors of the nations of Moab and Ammon, later transjordanian rivals of the descendants of Abraham. In the final analysis, the decision to bring Lot along resulted in two rival nations whose relations with Abraham's descendants were testy at best.

The Sodom and Gomorrah narrative is notable for the many ways in which it echoes the flood narrative and is echoed in the awful story in Judges 19–21. God had promised that he would never again send a universal flood to undo creation in order to contain the human propensity for evil (Gen 8:21-22). But what will the righteous judge of all the earth do with a society which displays the same sort of evil as the pre-Flood generations? The Sodom and Gomorrah narrative provides the answer. The LORD will bring individual, isolated judgment in such cases to contain the evil before it spreads to the entire cosmos as it did before the flood.

1. Bargaining over Sodom (18:16-33)

In this section the LORD discusses with the two men with him, and apparently in Abraham's presence, his intention to include Abraham in the decision whether to destroy Sodom or not (18:16-21). After the men have gone on to Sodom, the LORD remains behind with Abraham to discuss the decision (18:22-33). Abraham may well be concerned about Lot and his family who are living there. In any case, Abraham bargains for the saving of the entire city on behalf of the small minority of righteous people there. Finding initial agreement that the entire city would be spared for the sake of fifty righteous people, Abraham bargains down to a mere ten righteous people. Evidently beyond this, Abraham, even with his personal concern for Lot and family, does not want to go. The first scene explains to the two men why Abraham should be included in the decision-making process. All nations will be blessed through him (18:18), and the LORD is contemplating the destruction of one of those nations.[12] Surely, the LORD reasons, Abraham should be included in such a decision.

The LORD Includes Abraham in the Specific Working Out of the Promise (18:16-21)

18:16 When the men got up to leave, they looked down toward Sodom, and Abraham walked along with them to see them on their way.

With the promise confirmed and Sarah rebuked for her lack of faith, it was time for the men to leave. From the elevation of the central hill country at Mamre at approximately 3,000 feet above sea level, the three divine visitors looked down onto the city of Sodom on the other side of the Dead Sea some 1300 feet below sea level. Lot, Abraham's nephew and once his presumptive heir, lived there. The men knew its time for judgment had arrived. The only task remaining was to see if anyone in Sodom could be spared. Abraham had accompanied them to the place where they looked down upon Sodom.

18:17 Then the LORD said, "Shall I hide from Abraham what I am about to do?

The LORD presumably spoke to the two other men who were with him. We discover later that they were angels. The LORD asks a rhetorical question. He has no intention of hiding his intentions from Abraham but encourages his involvement and intercession, much as he later does with Moses (Numbers 14:11-12; Exod 32:9-10). The question may be a way of involving the angels who are with him in the divine-human relationship. Alternatively this speech could be regarded as a rare example of the LORD's internal speech or thoughts.

18:18 Abraham will surely become a great and powerful nation, and all nations on earth will be blessed through him.

The LORD reminds the angels (or himself!) of Abraham's destiny. The promise to make of him a great nation is assured. It will surely happen.[13] His descendants will become a great and numerous[14] nation and the ultimate purpose of the promise is recalled. All nations on earth will be blessed through Abraham. Whether this is divine internal speech or speech to the angels, the promise, with its universal purpose, is affirmed yet again (Gen 12:3).

---

[12]The Hebrew גּוֹי (gôy) must not be misinterpreted as referring to the modern concept of a nation state such as England or Austria. It can refer to tribal groups which are relatively small in number.

[13]The NIV captures the emphatic Hebrew construction (qal infinitive absolute followed by a verb of the same root in the imperfect) with the word "surely."

[14]The Hebrew עָצוּם ('āṣûm) has the connotation of powerful in number.

18:19 For I have chosen him, so that he will direct his children and his household after him to keep the way of the LORD by doing what is right and just, so that the LORD will bring about for Abraham what he has promised him."

The Hebrew text reads, "For I knew him" rather than "have chosen." The verb used (יָדַע, *yāda‘*) sometimes has the connotation of personal, intimate knowledge. The LORD's knowledge of Abraham and his coming to know the LORD in response had a purpose. Abraham would "charge" his sons and his house coming after him. The result of Abraham's charge would be that his descendants would keep the way of the LORD by[15] doing righteousness and justice. The end result of Abraham's descendants practicing righteousness and justice is the fulfillment of the promise to Abraham. The LORD chose Abraham for this purpose, but the fulfillment of the promise is dependent upon the obedience of his descendants. This places a great obligation upon the original readers who are Abraham's descendants. The canonical readers realize the difficulty. The descendants of Abraham have not consistently practiced righteousness and justice. It will take a new work of God among the descendants of Abraham in order for them to fulfill their obligations and see the blessing of God flow through them to all the nations of the world. A Christian reader, of course, knows that only one truly faithful descendant of Abraham ever arose, Jesus the Messiah. Only he truly kept the way of the LORD by doing what was right and just.

18:20 Then the LORD said, "The outcry against Sodom and Gomorrah is so great and their sin so grievous 18:21 that I will go down and see if what they have done is as bad as the outcry that has reached me. If not, I will know."

The words, "The LORD said" evidently means that these words were spoken out loud so that Abraham could hear them. Literalistically the LORD's words in verse 20 could be rendered, "O the outcry of Sodom and Gomorrah! For it is great. And their sins! For they are very heavy!" The word translated "outcry" (צְעָקָה, *s*ᵉ*‘āqāh*)[16] is also used in Exodus 3:7,9 of the "outcry" of the Hebrew slaves against their masters. This may hint at the fact of the oppression of the weak and vulnerable in Sodom and Gomorrah.

The words, "I will go down" are reminiscent[17] of the Babel narrative's "Let us go down" and suggest that judgment is coming as it did there.

---

[15]The Hebrew לְ (*l*ᵉ) with the infinitive often explains the circumstances of a preceding action and is thus translated "by." See Waltke and O'Connor, *Biblical Hebrew Syntax*, 36.2.3e.

[16]My thanks to Gary Hall for reminding me of this connection.

[17]In both cases the verb יָרַד (*yārad*) is used.

Obviously the LORD who can hear Sarah's interior speech does not need to be informed at a literal level as to what the people of Sodom and Gomorrah are up to. He is visiting it with the idea of bringing judgment. "If not" suggests that even at this late date the residents of Sodom have the opportunity of avoiding judgment through repentance.

Abraham Negotiates with the LORD over the Judgment on Sodom (18:22-33)

18:22 The men turned away and went toward Sodom, but Abraham remained standing before the LORD.

The men with the LORD understand the LORD's words as an implicit directive to travel to Sodom and give its citizens one last chance to avoid judgment. Abraham, however, did not give up and return home. He remained standing with[18] the LORD in order to intercede for the city where his nephew lived.

18:23 Then Abraham approached him and said: "Will you sweep away the righteous with the wicked?

While Abraham had been standing "before" the LORD, he approaches even nearer. Abraham uses language which is similar to the language God had used in verse 19 to describe what he wanted to see in the descendants of Abraham in order for the universal part of the promise to be fulfilled. The LORD wanted Abraham's descendants to "do righteousness" (לַעֲשׂוֹת צְדָקָה, la'ăśôth ṣᵉdāqāh, v. 19). Would he then allow those who are "righteous" (צַדִּיק, ṣaddîq) to suffer the punishment of the wicked? Abraham may be thinking of his nephew Lot. Surely a God of justice would differentiate in his just judgment between the wicked and those who are righteous like Lot.

18:24 What if there are fifty righteous people in the city? Will you really sweep it away and not spare the place for the sake of the fifty righteous people in it?

Abraham tentatively[19] suggests the possibility of fifty righteous people living in Sodom. Surely the LORD would not sweep away the entire city if there are fifty righteous who will die with the wicked!

---

[18]The original wording of this verse was "but Yahweh still stood before Abraham." Cf. Rendtorff, *Canonical Hebrew Bible*, p. 28: "[A]ccording to tradition, the 'men of the great synagogue'; (cf. Aboth 1:1) took offence at the šekînāh (the 'indwelling' of God on earth) standing before Abraham, because 'stand before' can also mean 'serve' (e.g., 1 Kgs 17:1). So they changed the text to, 'but Abraham still stood before Yhwh;' the change has been preserved as a *tiqqûn sofᵉrîm*, an 'alteration of the scribes (cf. Biblia Hebraica)."

[19]The Hebrew particle אוּלַי ('ûlay, "perhaps") usually expresses a hope, but also a fear or doubt about the truth of what has been suggested. BDB cites Genesis 27:12; Job 1:5 as examples of this latter usage.

18:25 Far be it from you to do such a thing—to kill the righteous with the wicked, treating the righteous and the wicked alike. Far be it from you! Will not the Judge of all the earth do right?"

Abraham appeals to the LORD's character. The LORD expected righteousness and justice of the descendants of Abraham (Gen 18:19). Surely the God of such a people would act with righteousness and justice himself. Abraham emphasizes the point by twice using the phrase, "far be it from you." Abraham's intercession is the beginning of a pattern in the Pentateuch. The chosen leader intercedes with God on the basis of his character and reputation among other nations about what overly strict judgment might seem to imply about his character (Exod 32:11-14; Num 14:13-19). In Hebrew there is wordplay between the word translated "judge" (הַשֹּׁפֵט, *hăšōphēṭ*) and the word translated "right" (מִשְׁפָּט, *mišpāṭ*). One might say, "the giver of justice must be just."

18:26 The LORD said, "If I find fifty righteous people in the city of Sodom, I will spare the whole place for their sake."

Like Moses' intercession, with which the audience was familiar, the LORD listens to Abraham's plea and graciously promises to spare the entire city for the sake of fifty righteous people.

18:27 Then Abraham spoke up again: "Now that I have been so bold as to speak to the Lord, though I am nothing but dust and ashes, 18:28 what if the number of the righteous is five less than fifty? Will you destroy the whole city because of five people?" "If I find forty-five there," he said, "I will not destroy it."

Abraham becomes extremely polite and conscious of with whom he speaks. The Hebrew might be rendered, "Behold, please, I have undertaken to speak with my sovereign and I [am merely] dust and ashes!" In other words, Abraham acknowledges that he has no right to speak to his Lord as a creature made of nothing more than dust and ashes.[20] The fact that he only reduces the number by five this time is another indication of his reticent politeness. Once again Abraham suggests the possibility, not the probability of there being 45 righteous. Abraham shows no confidence that this might be the case. The LORD quickly assented to Abraham's plea once again. The irony is that people who recognize that they have no right to demand anything of God because they are so conscious of their own frailty are the very ones whose intercessions are often accepted by God.

18:29 Once again he spoke to him, "What if only forty are found there?" He said, "For the sake of forty, I will not do it."

---

[20]For a similar use of "dust and ashes," see Job 42:6.

Having succeeded twice, Abraham again lowers the number, this time to forty. Once again he expresses it as an unlikely possibility. The LORD assents quickly yet again.

18:30 Then he said, "May the Lord not be angry, but let me speak. What if only thirty can be found there?" He answered, "I will not do it if I find thirty there."

Again Abraham treads carefully, not wanting to raise the LORD's anger. This time he jumps further, reducing the number by ten to thirty. Yet again the word "perhaps" (*'ûlay*) occurs as in the three previous intercessions, indicating the unlikelihood of the LORD actually finding that many righteous people in Sodom. Once again the LORD accepts Abraham's intercession.

18:31 Abraham said, "Now that I have been so bold as to speak to the Lord, what if only twenty can be found there?" He said, "For the sake of twenty, I will not destroy it."

Abraham repeats the humble introduction with which he began verse 27, the first reduction in number. Abraham is conscious of his real position with God and recognizes that he has no right to be so bold. This time the number is reduced for the second time by another ten people to twenty. The LORD's acceptance is again portrayed in a straightforward manner.

18:32 Then he said, "May the Lord not be angry, but let me speak just once more. What if only ten can be found there?" He answered, "For the sake of ten, I will not destroy it."

Here the introduction from verse 30 is repeated, but this time Abraham realizes he has reached the end of the process. He adds "just once more." One reason that Abraham and Moses are successful intercessors with the LORD is that they knew when to quit. They somehow have a sense of what is, and is not, appropriate in the circumstances. Prayer is most effective when those who pray are concerned with discerning what the LORD is up to in a specific situation.

18:33 When the LORD had finished speaking with Abraham, he left, and Abraham returned home.

Interestingly the narrator says that the LORD finished speaking with Abraham and not the other way around. While Abraham is functioning as an intercessor, he is invited to that role by the LORD. But the LORD is actually in charge of the conversation even though Abraham does most of the talking. Abraham returned to "his place" which the NIV interprets as his home. Perhaps something more specific is being hinted at here. The place at which Abraham started in this narrative was the

entrance to his tent near the great trees at Mamre. The phrase,
"entrance of the tent" (פֶּתַח־הָאֹהֶל, *pethaḥ-hā'ōhel*) is almost always used
of the Tabernacle where sacrifices are offered and revelations take
place.[21]

---

[21]Cf. Exod 29:4,11,32,42; 33:8; 38:8,30; 40:12; Lev 1:3,5; 3:2; 4:4,7,18, etc.
Exceptions are Exodus 33:10; Numbers 11:10; 16:27.

GENESIS 19

2. The Destruction of Sodom and Gomorrah (19:1-29)

The story of the divine judgment on Sodom and Gomorrah and its environs echoes the story of the Flood[1] in many striking ways. In both cases there is a cataclysmic divine judgment on the entire environment. In both cases all humanity is destroyed with the exception of a small remnant who are faithful and who trust the warnings of judgment and obey divine commands to avoid the judgment. In both cases the sinfulness of humanity reoccurs after the judgment. In both cases the godly leader gets drunk and in both cases the child or children of that godly leader use the drunkenness to engage in some sort of horrible activity with sexual connotations. In both cases God "remembered" a faithful person and brought them out of the judgment (8:1; 19:29).

The purpose of these echoes is to signal a shift in the LORD's strategy when human evil becomes so pervasive as to call for cataclysmic judgment. Leading up to the Flood human evil in the form of (sexual) violence had reached such a level that the LORD decided to wipe the slate clean and begin creation anew. Since the Flood did not eradicate the human tendency toward evil,[2] God promised to use a different strategy in the future. He promised to never again destroy the world by a flood because of human evil. In the Sodom narrative the connection between human morality and the physical environment is still retained. What human beings do and do not do affects the physical environment. But something has changed. The LORD no longer gives human evil a chance to grow out of control. The destruction of Sodom and Gomorrah implies that in the future the LORD will be more proactive in stamping out certain forms of systemic evil before it is allowed to spread throughout the creation.[3]

---

[1]There are also many striking echoes with the awful story of the men of Gibeah in Judges 19–21, but for different reasons.

[2]See the very similar evaluations of what had become of humanity both before and after the Flood in Genesis 6:5 and 8:21-22.

[3]John Nugent reminded me of the parallel between this situation and God's

Lot's Reception of the Messengers (19:1-3)

19:1 The two angels arrived at Sodom in the evening, and Lot was sitting in the gateway of the city. When he saw them, he got up to meet them and bowed down with his face to the ground.

The parallels between this verse and Genesis 18:1-2 where Abraham sees the three men while seated at the gate of the tent are remarkable and unlikely to be accidental.

18:1-2	19:1
The LORD appeared to Abraham near the great trees of Mamre while he was sitting at the entrance to his tent in the heat of the day. ²Abraham looked up and saw three men standing nearby. When he saw them, he hurried from the entrance of his tent to meet them and bowed low to the ground.	The two angels arrived at Sodom in the evening, and Lot was sitting in the gateway of the city. When he saw them, he got up to meet them and bowed down with his face to the ground.

Both passages mention the time of day, that the human protagonist was sitting at the entrance, that the protagonist "saw" the divine figures, that he went to meet them, and that he bowed down. The differences are also striking and are put into clearer view by the similarities. The divine figures include the LORD in Abraham's case, while in Lot's it is only angels.[4] The "heat of the day" allows for significant interaction to take place between the divine figures and Abraham. The fact that the angels arrive at Sodom in the evening means that the townspeople will be out and there is urgency for them to come under the protection of Lot's roof. Abraham is said merely to "bow himself" while Lot's "nostrils" (אַפַּיִם, *'apayim*) are said to have touched the ground.

19:2 "My lords," he said, "please turn aside to your servant's house. You can wash your feet and spend the night and then go on your way early in the morning." "No," they answered, "we will spend the night in the square."

---

statement to Abram in Genesis 15:16. God told Abram that he was waiting for the iniquity of the Amorites to become full before he would give the Promised Land to Abram's descendants. God's proactivity does not mean that he will not be patient, just that he will not allow such iniquity as was present at Sodom and later in Canaan to spread to the entire creation.

[4]The Hebrew word for "angels" (הַמַּלְאָכִים, *hammal'ākîm*) as well as the NT Greek word (ἄγγελοι, *angeloi*), means "messengers" who may or may not be spiritual creatures.

Once again we see the parallels between this account and the account in chapter 18.

18:3-5	19:2
He said, "If I have found favor in your eyes, my lord, do not pass your servant by. ⁴Let a little water be brought, and then you may all wash your feet and rest under this tree. ⁵Let me get you something to eat, so you can be refreshed and then go on your way—now that you have come to your servant."	"My lords," he said, "please turn aside to your servant's house. You can wash your feet and spend the night and then go on your way early in the morning."

The similarities and differences between these passages are striking. In both the protagonist refers to himself as "your servant" and the men as "lord" (אֲדֹנָי, ʾǎdōnay); in both, washing the feet and resting (and later something to eat) are offered as signs of hospitality; in both, reference is made to the divine figures going on their way after they have received the hospitality offered. But Abraham speaks to a single individual who turns out to be the LORD himself; Lot invites the men into his house while Abraham suggests that they rest under the tree; Abraham asks for the privilege of extending hospitality on the basis of his relationship to the LORD, while Lot merely wants to protect them from the townsmen. In fact Lot wants them to leave early in the morning, perhaps out of fear of what might happen should they remain.

19:3 But he insisted so strongly that they did go with him and entered his house. He prepared a meal for them, baking bread without yeast, and they ate.

Again we see the similarities and differences with the account in chapter 18. Abraham is extremely polite and feels honored to be visited by three divine figures. Lot is afraid for their safety, and so he insists strongly that they come under the protection of his roof. This seems to suggest that Lot, unlike Abraham, does not fully appreciate who the men are who have come to Sodom. Both Abraham and Lot prepare a meal that includes unleavened bread.⁵ Lot is said to provide a "feast" (מִשְׁתֶּה, mišteh) for his guest while the details of Abraham's meal are given. In Lot's case the "hurry" of unleavened bread is necessitated by the late hour; in Abraham's case by his desire to not keep his guests waiting. The original and canonical audience would undoubtedly see an allusion to the Passover narrative in which God's people are saved from

---

⁵In the case of Abraham this is an inference from the word "quick."

an announced cataclysmic judgment by holding a feast which includes unleavened bread.

Interestingly the comparisons between Lot's hospitality and Abraham's shows that Lot was an even more welcoming host.[6] Lot offered up his two daughters to save angels, while Abraham twice offered up his wife to save himself. This contrast and parallel is significant. Although Rashi claimed that Abraham was the better host, Safran argues that Lot offered a meal at an inconvenient, late time, offered a banquet – more than Abraham offered – cooked the meal himself (19:3b), showed even greater respect,[7] and even offered to let them spend the night.[8]

The Men of Sodom Attempt to Rape the Messengers (19:4-11)

19:4 Before they had gone to bed, all the men from every part of the city of Sodom—both young and old—surrounded the house.

The narrator is at pains to emphasize the comprehensiveness of the crowd which surrounded the house. It included men both "young and old, all the people to the last [man]."[9] If all of the city's men were there, it could hardly be the case that there were righteous men who had stayed home. The fact that they surrounded the house is a hint of the ominous intentions of the crowd.

19:5 They called to Lot, "Where are the men who came to you tonight? Bring them out to us so that we can have sex with them."

The crowd wants Lot to bring the two "men," who unbeknownst to the crowd are actually angels, out to them. Literally the Hebrew indicates their purpose as coming to "know" them. The NRSV retains this literal translation. The NIV, quite correctly, indicates the real point of the euphemistic language. They do not want to merely meet them, but to have intimate, carnal knowledge of them. In other words they want to homosexually rape them. One wonders whether the NRSV is trying to be politically correct[10] or merely following its traditional practice of as literal as possible translation in the King James tradition.

---

[6]This was first suggested to me by Safran in a paper at the International SBL Meeting in Vienna, 2007.

[7]He "bowed low with his face to the ground" 19:1b // 18:2.

[8]In Abraham's case this was not necessary since the men came in the middle of the day.

[9]The NIV is periphrastic here. The NRSV is more literal.

[10]By translating the verb "know" literally the NRSV leaves the contemporary reader in doubt that sex is what is intended. The ancient reader would have been in no doubt about this. This text is used to condemn contemporary homosexuality. What it condemns is homosexual rape. This (mis)use of the text may explain NRSV's rendering.

This text has been the object of great interest in recent days in light of the discussion of the rights of homosexual and lesbian citizens in modern western societies. But this text should not be used to stereotype all homosexuals as violent rapists like the men of Sodom. While the Bible seems to regard homosexual practice as sinful along with all other types of sex outside of heterosexual covenantal marriage,[11] the condemnation of the men of Sodom is for the violent homosexual rape of visitors.

The intended sexual violence of the men of Sodom is one of a number of intertextual echoes between the Flood narrative and this one. Violence, and sexual violence in particular, was a precursor to God's decision to send the flood.[12] What had happened, prior to the Flood, on a worldwide scale has arisen again in a certain locality. This time the LORD will not allow it to spread throughout the world bringing with it a necessary universal judgment like the Flood. It will be stopped in its tracks.

19:6 Lot went outside to meet them and shut the door behind him 19:7 and said, "No, my friends. Don't do this wicked thing. 19:8 Look, I have two daughters who have never slept with a man. Let me bring them out to you, and you can do what you like with them. But don't do anything to these men, for they have come under the protection of my roof."

Lot, seeking to protect his guests, goes out to the crowd, rather than letting them come in. He apparently still does not recognize that his guests are angels and in no real danger. He shuts the door behind him protectively. The Hebrew brings up the parallel with Abraham in chapter 18 yet again. Literally it reads, "And Lot went out of the entrance *to them*, and the door, he shut behind him." The unnecessary use of the word "entrance" recalls Abraham coming from the entrance of his tent to meet the three men. Lot addresses them as "brothers" (NIV has "friends"). He tells them not to do the "evil"[13] thing they intend. This shows the error in trying to argue that the knowledge which the crowd seeks is merely personal acquaintance and not sexual.[14]

While modern readers are horrified at Lot's suggested solution to the situation, this may have been mitigated to a degree in the ancient

---

[11]See the helpful discussion in Richard B. Hays, *The Moral Vision of the New Testament* (San Francisco: HarperCollins, 1996), pp. 379-406.

[12]See the discussion in Kissling, *Genesis Volume 1*, pp. 261-264.

[13]The NIV's periphrastic "wicked" causes confusion with the "wicked" mentioned in Abraham's intercession with God in chapter 18 where רָשָׁע (rāšā') is used, not רַע (rā'a') as here.

[14]Contra Scott Morschauser, "'Hospitality,' Hostiles and Hostages: On the Legal Background to Genesis 19:1-9," *JSOT* 27 (2003): 461-485.

world where the obligations of the host were taken much more seriously than they are in contemporary western cultures. The author and readers of Genesis lived in a culture more influenced by conventions of
shame and honor than by guilt. In such a culture it was less shameful to
offer one's daughters than to violate the duty to protect one's guests.[15]

This in no way justifies Lot's suggested solution which displays a
form of male chauvinism that is to be condemned. Lot is willing to sacrifice the virginity of his two daughters in order to spare his guests being
subject to the mob's violence. Interestingly the crowd wants to "know"
the two angels, and Lot offers, in desperation, his two daughters to them
instead, who have never "known" a man.[16] Lot offers the crowd the freedom to do with his daughters what is "right in your eyes."[17] When people in the Bible do what is right in their own eyes, they invariably do
what is wrong.[18] The two men have come under the "shadow of Lot's
roof beams" (literal Hebrew) and he has a sacred duty to protect them.[19]
It is possible that, given the same-gender nature of the crowd's lust, Lot
realizes that they will not in fact be interested in his offer of sexual relations with his daughters. In any case, Lot is in desperate circumstances.
But there is no justifying his suggesting the sacrificing of his presumably
innocent daughters out of some sense of duty to strangers.[20]

**19:9 "Get out of our way," they replied. And they said, "This fellow
came here as an alien, and now he wants to play the judge! We'll treat
you worse than them." They kept bringing pressure on Lot and moved
forward to break down the door.**

Morschauser has argued that Lot's original location at the city gate,
where the courts of ancient Israelite cities were held, and the use of the
word "judge" indicates that Lot has taken the two men under his legal
protection. He offered his daughters as hostages to assure that his
guests do nothing mischievous. For Morschauser the intended crime is

---

[15]My thanks to Gary Hall for reminding me of this.

[16]The NIV's paraphrase, "slept with" misses the wordplay in the Hebrew.

[17]The NIV once again paraphrases, and thus loses the connection with other
examples where people do what is right in their own eyes (Judg 17:6; 21:25).

[18]The so-called "appendix" in the book of Judges (chs. 17–21) graphically por-
trays this (17:6; 21:25).

[19]This obligation is given emphasis in the Hebrew text by the use of an emphatic construction (כִּי־עַל־כֵּן, kî-'al-kēn) rather than simply the word "for" (כִּי, kî).

[20]While Lot's adult-male guests as strangers are vulnerable, his daughters are
presumably even more vulnerable. Sometimes a sacred duty becomes a sacred
cow that distorts moral reasoning.

not sexual, but legal. The mob refuses to follow normal legal proce-dures in the treatment of strangers. This seems unconvincing at best. In any case the mob gathered around Lot's house refuses to listen to him and commands him to stand back. Apparently others in the crowd bring up the fact that Lot is no citizen of Sodom, only a temporary resident.[21] As an alien he has no right to play the judge in condemning their action as evil. The talk among the people in the crowd then turns and address-es Lot with the threat to do more evil to him than they intended to do to the two men. Their use of the word "evil"[22] and the complaint about Lot the foreigner setting himself up as judge of their actions shows their disregard for Lot and all "aliens" in the land. The crowd begins to surge forward, driving Lot back toward the door, fully intending to break it down and take the guests by force. The original and canonical readers would remember that their ancestors had lived as aliens in Egypt. The law consequently expected Israel to accept and protect aliens.[23]

19:10 But the men inside reached out and pulled Lot back into the house and shut the door.

The men quickly pulled Lot back into the house and out of danger, shutting[24] the door behind him in order to protect him from the mob. What they saw confirmed what they had feared. The city was beyond repentance.

19:11 Then they struck the men who were at the door of the house, young and old, with blindness so that they could not find the door.

The two men now show their divine powers by blinding the mob. This is not the ordinary word for blindness[25] and may imply the tempo-rary blindness from a flash of light. The blindness struck young and old alike, just as the spiritual blindness that brought it on them. The Hebrew read literalistically says, "they were weary from [not being able] to find the door." The pathetic searching of the crowd for the door with its access to the men even after they had been blinded is a sad com-mentary on how human passions can irrationally rule us.

---

[21]NIV: "alien" Hebrew: גֵּר (gēr).

[22]The NIV has "worse" but this loses the wordplay with verse 7 where Lot describes their intended action as "evil."

[23]Exod 22:21; 23:9; Lev 19:33; Deut 24:21-22.

[24]It is possible that there is an intended wordplay between the word for "alien" (gēr) and the word for shutting the door (סָגַר, sāgar).

[25]The word used, סַנְוֵרִים (sanwērîm) is only found elsewhere in 2 Kings 6:18 where the Arameans are smitten with temporary blindness. The more common word is עִוֵּר ('iwwēr).

The Messengers Save the Righteous and the Willing in Sodom (19:12-17)

19:12 The two men said to Lot, "Do you have anyone else here—sons-in-law, sons or daughters, or anyone else in the city who belongs to you? Get them out of here, 19:13 because we are going to destroy this place. The outcry to the LORD against its people is so great that he has sent us to destroy it."

While we only hear of Lot's wife, his two daughters, and two fiancés or sons-in-law, the angel's question raises the possibility of there being other members of the family. In fact the two men refer to Lot's sons as well as his daughters who are presumably different from the two he offered the mob. There is also the possibility that some of Lot's servants had taken up residence in Sodom ("anyone else in the city who belongs to you"). The angels warn Lot they are going to destroy Sodom and its environs. The "outcry" of the people of Sodom is so great in the LORD's presence that he has sent the angels to destroy it.[26] What the LORD had heard has been amply confirmed by the way his messengers had been threatened. The time for judgment has come and Lot must hurry to save as many as possible while there is time.

19:14 So Lot went out and spoke to his sons-in-law, who were pledged to marry his daughters. He said, "Hurry and get out of this place, because the LORD is about to destroy the city!" But his sons-in-law thought he was joking.

The Hebrew is not clear as to whether Lot's "sons-in-law" were already married to his daughters or merely pledged to be married.[27] If they were already married, one wonders whether they had been present in the crowd. Since Lot claims that the two daughters in the house are virgins, one also wonders whether they might be married to other unmentioned daughters of Lot. If they were actually married, it seems odd that Lot did not directly address his married daughters. In any case, his sons-in-law, whether actual or hypothetical, thought that he was making a joke. The word "joking" is the same word, although in a different stem, as the word translated "laughing" in chapters 17 and 18. There it referred to the incredible promise of God to give Abraham and Sarah a baby to be named "He will laugh." Here the laughter is more cynical and refers not

---

[26]Both the NIV and NRSV assume that the outcry is against the people of Sodom from (presumably) those who are being harmed by them. The Hebrew does not contain anything that would be translated "against its people." The Hebrew merely refers to "their outcry" being before the face of the LORD.

[27]The Hebrew participle לֹקְחֵי (*lōqḥê*), literally, "the takers of" his daughters, could imply that they had already taken them in marriage or that they had merely pledged to do so.

just to the difficulty human beings have in believing God's promises, but to the mocking refusal to even consider that God may be involved in the governance and punishment of the world. This "laughter" is more akin to the mocking which Ishmael later directs at the infant Isaac (Gen 21:9). Considering a warning of divine judgment a joke is a sign of the depravity of Sodom, even among those who would marry Lot's daughters. Clearly the negative influence of Sodom on Lot and his family was more significant than Lot's positive influence on the Sodomites.

19:15 With the coming of dawn, the angels urged Lot, saying, "Hurry! Take your wife and your two daughters who are here, or you will be swept away when the city is punished."

Lot had evidently gone to speak with his "sons-in-law" during the night since in the morning the angels led them out of the city. The men are here identified as angels yet again. Perhaps this reflects the fact that Lot now realizes who they are. The angels tell Lot to "arise,"[28] take his wife and two daughters and leave. They warn Lot that the alternative is to be swept away in the "iniquity" of the city. The word translated in the NIV as "punished" is actually the same noun found in Genesis 15:16 where the "iniquity" of the Amorites is said to not yet be completed. The word refers to the sin and its consequent punishment.[29] Here, as in 15:16, the focus is on the punishment. The angels pressed Lot to act and act quickly if they were to avoid the punishment soon to come on Sodom.

19:16 When he hesitated, the men grasped his hand and the hands of his wife and of his two daughters and led them safely out of the city, for the Lord was merciful to them. 19:17 As soon as they had brought them out, one of them said, "Flee for your lives! Don't look back, and don't stop anywhere in the plain! Flee to the mountains or you will be swept away!"

Lot's hesitation is interesting. Has Sodom had its effects on him? Psalm 119:60 reminds us that we should not hesitate (the same Hebrew verb) to obey the Lord's commands. But the Lord is merciful even with the hesitant. The two angels each grabbed two hands to lead the four members of Lot's family out of the city. The unnecessary mention of each member of the family shows the Lord's concern for each person who has any openness at all to the Lord. As they are coming out of the city, the angels give Lot a warning which was intended for the entire family.[30] Twice Lot is told to "flee," and he is specifically told not to look

---

[28]The NIV's "Hurry!" is paraphrastic.

[29]K. Koch, "עָוֹן," *TDOT*, X:546-562.

[30]The NIV emphasizes the applicability of the commands to Lot's wife and children by translating the second person singulars of the Hebrew as plurals.

back or stop in the plain. This helps to explain what later happens to
Lot's wife.

Lot Negotiates the Sparing of Zoar (19:18-22)

**19:18 But Lot said to them, "No, my lords, please! 19:19 Your servant
has found favor in your eyes, and you have shown great kindness to
me in sparing my life. But I can't flee to the mountains; this disaster
will overtake me, and I'll die.**

Lot addresses the angels as "my lords" an expression which in
Hebrew (אֲדֹנָי, *'ădōnay*) can refer to God or other divine beings, or to
exalted human figures. He begins with an expression of deference and
gratitude. He is their servant and they have shown great steadfast love[31]
to him by sparing his life.[32] He begs that he not be sent to the mountains. Lot claims that he is not able (יָכֹל, *yākōl*) to flee to the mountains.
Lot could be indicating his advanced age here. The mountains were
some ways away, and he would not be able to make such a long journey
that quickly. He was an adult 25 years previously when he moved with
Abram from Haran. His father, Haran, was apparently some 60 years
older than Abraham,[33] and so Lot may well have been quite an old man
by this time. Lot has no doubt that a severe judgment is about to come
and fears that he will be swallowed up by it.

**19:20 Look, here is a town near enough to run to, and it is small. Let
me flee to it—it is very small, isn't it? Then my life will be spared."**

Lot suggests to the angels that he be allowed to flee to a small town
nearby. Twice he emphasizes its smallness. Allowing it to remain
unharmed would not materially alter the effectiveness of the judgment
in rooting out the sins of Sodom. Unlike the mountains, it is near
enough for Lot to escape there and remain alive.

**19:21 He said to him, "Very well, I will grant this request too; I will
not overthrow the town you speak of. 19:22 But flee there quickly,
because I cannot do anything until you reach it." (That is why the town
was called Zoar.)**

Interestingly only one of the angels[34] replies. Lot's suggestion is
accepted. The town will be spared for the sake of Lot. The angel (or per-

---

[31]The English word "kindness," though followed by both NIV and NRSV
seems too weak for the Hebrew חֶסֶד (*ḥesed*) which refers to God's covenant loyalty and is the background to the New Testament's word ἀγάπη (*agapē*).

[32]The Hebrew word here is נֶפֶשׁ (*nephes*), often inaccurately translated by "soul."

[33]See the discussion of the birth order of Terah's sons at Genesis 11:31 above.

[34]Or are we to infer that God speaks here?

haps the LORD) urges Lot to flee there quickly. Since he has made the promise the judgment must wait until he has safely arrived in the town. The original name of the town is unknown. It came to be known as "Zoar" (צוֹעַר, ṣô'ar) which is linked by wordplay to the word "little" or "insignificant" (מִצְעָר, miṣ'ār) in verse 20.

The Destruction of Sodom and Gomorrah (19:23-26)

19:23 By the time Lot reached Zoar, the sun had risen over the land. 19:24 Then the LORD rained down burning sulfur on Sodom and Gomorrah—from the LORD out of the heavens.

The rapid pace of this narrative is indicated by the fact that the "coming of the dawn" (v. 15) had now given way to the actual rising of the sun. The entire series of events had taken only a few hours. Once Lot and his daughters had reached Zoar the judgment began. The word "rained" can be used of normal rainfall ((Job 38:26; Isa 5:6; Amos 4:7) but most often refers to God's judgment through rain, whether that be the Flood (Gen 7:4), hail (Exod 9:18), or burning sulfur (here and Ps 11:6). The connection with the Flood narrative is not accidental as we have noted throughout this narrative.

19:25 Thus he overthrew those cities and the entire plain, including all those living in the cities—and also the vegetation in the land.

The judgment, like the flood, affected the entirety of the physical system, including the cities, the land, the people and even the plants. Just as human wickedness brought on cosmic destruction in the time of the Flood, so too here human wickedness brings on comprehensive judgment that affects the entire environment and not just human beings. The only difference is that this judgment is localized, whereas the Flood was universal. It is as though God's strategy had changed. He promised to never again destroy the entire earth because of human wickedness. But what happens when human wickedness threatens to get out of control as it had at Sodom? God contains that wickedness by wiping it out in a severe and quick local judgment before it can spread to the rest of the world. The judgment on Sodom is a sort of miniflood as the pervasive intertextual echoing between this narrative and the Flood narrative suggests.

19:26 But Lot's wife looked back, and she became a pillar of salt.

Exactly what the angels had warned Lot not to do, Lot's wife does. She "looked back."[35] The movie version of this text overdramatizes as though some sort of miraculous transformation took place. It seems

---

[35]The same Hebrew verb occurs in verses 17 and 25 (נָבַט, nābaṭ).

more likely that Lot's unnamed wife was caught in the burning sulfur. Salt in the Old Testament is often a good thing,[36] but it can also serve as a sign of catastrophic destruction as in Judges 9:45 where salt is strewn over the destroyed city of Shechem as a sign of its total destruction.

Abraham Sees the Destruction of Sodom and Gomorrah (19:27-28)

19:27 Early the next morning Abraham got up and returned to the place where he had stood before the LORD.

The next day Abraham is anxious to see whether his intercession for Sodom had succeeded. The fact that he rises early shows his eagerness to find out what had happened. He returned to the place where he had met with the LORD and interceded for Sodom. The intercession had ended abruptly at ten righteous people. Had the angels found ten righteous in Sodom? What had happened to Lot and his family? Undoubtedly such questions weighed heavily on his mind.

19:28 He looked down toward Sodom and Gomorrah, toward all the land of the plain, and he saw dense smoke rising from the land, like smoke from a furnace.

In a moment full of pathos Abraham sees that his intercession had not saved Sodom and Gomorrah. Does he know of the deliverance of Lot? We are left to wonder. While the imagined audience knew of the descendants of Lot, Moab and Ammon, and that therefore Lot had been spared, there is no indication that Abraham ever met his nephew again. From the hills of Judah he could see the flat plain on the eastern side of the Dead Sea. The thick smoke which could indicate God's presence in a gracious or neutral way in this instance spoke of divine judgment to Abraham. And yet for the imagined readers it might be different. The phrase, "like the smoke of a kiln," occurs elsewhere only in the description of the LORD's appearance to Israel when they first arrive at Sinai (Exod 19:18). While God's judgment is severe it is so only for those who refuse him. The smoke like a kiln can signify either the severity of God's judgment by fire or the awesomeness of his majestic presence. Which it is depends upon peoples' response to him.

Summary Statement (19:29)

19:29 So when God destroyed the cities of the plain, he remembered Abraham, and he brought Lot out of the catastrophe that overthrew the cities where Lot had lived.

---

[36]Lev 2:13; Num 18:19; 2 Kgs 2:20-21; 2 Chr 13:5; Ezek 43:24.

The turning point in the Flood narrative comes in Genesis 8:1 when God remembers the righteous Noah. In this passage God is said to remember a righteous person yet again and, as in the case of Noah, he rescued a remnant from the total destruction. But things are different here. God[37] remembered Abraham, not Lot, and the result was that Lot was taken out from the midst of the destruction. For Abraham's sake, and not for Lot's own sake, Lot is spared. Noah preserves the future human family and his own family because of his righteousness. Lot cannot even save himself. He has to be taken out of the city by angels, and is saved through his association with Abraham.

3. The Final Result of the Lot Strategy (19:30-38)

From one angle it seems like such a small disobedience for Abraham to have allowed Lot to come with him when he left the other members of his father's house. After all, the narrator tells us that Lot came with him before Abram took him with him. Lot was not only willing to go, but he actually initiated it. On the other hand, Abram embraces Lot as his presumptive heir. The long-term result of the decision to take Lot along was the presence of two nations hostile to Abraham's descendants just across the Jordan, Moab, and Ammon. The tension between them and Israel continues even into the postexilic period when Nehemiah confronts an Ammonite named Tobiah (Nehemiah 13).

Lot's Daughters Commit Incest with Their Drunken Father (19:30-36)

19:30 Lot and his two daughters left Zoar and settled in the mountains, for he was afraid to stay in Zoar. He and his two daughters lived in a cave.

We do not know how long Lot and his two daughters stayed in Zoar. During the destruction of Sodom, Lot had told the angels that he was not able to flee to the mountains with so little time. He now takes what is left of his family and moves to the mountains, as the angels had originally suggested. The common view that the actions of Lot's daughters suggests that they thought the entire world had been destroyed and there were no other men available is belied by this verse. The small city of Zoar ("Smallville") had been spared the destruction of Sodom, and

---

[37]The use of "God" here rather than "the LORD" as in 19:27 would, in traditional source criticism, be evidence of a different source. But this seems implausible in the context and is more likely the result of deliberate variation.

Lot and his daughters had lived there for some time. Lot is afraid, for some unstated reason, to remain permanently in Zoar. It could be fear of bad influence on his daughters which the experience of Sodom had emphasized so forcefully. It could be that he feared another divine judgment. It could be that the people of Zoar were no more welcoming of him and his family than Sodom had been. In any case he moved to the mountains as the angels had originally suggested. They lived there in "the cave."[38] But this is a very different "cave" from the one at Sinai where Moses and Elijah received revelation of God's presence.[39]

19:31 One day the older daughter said to the younger, "Our father is old, and there is no man around here to lie with us, as is the custom all over the earth.

While some time may have passed between the move to the cave and the suggestion of Lot's unnamed older daughter, the narrator is unconcerned about such things. His two daughters were still of child-bearing age. The "older" daughter is actually described as the "first-born" (בְּכִירָה, bᵉkîrāh) while the "younger" is described as the "little" (צָעִיר, ṣāʿîr) daughter in order to continue the wordplay over the "little" town of Zoar. She comments that Lot is old, apparently too old to start over and accumulate enough wealth to provide a dowry. Furthermore, there is no man in that land[40] to "come upon" them. The NIV interprets this to mean "to lie with" them. For Lot's firstborn, having children is a high, perhaps the highest, priority. She bases her desire to have children on the fact that it is the "way" (דֶּרֶךְ, derek)[41] of the entire "land."[42] What she suggests is not the custom of the entire land and certainly not the custom of the entire earth. Her morality is based, not on the law of God, but upon what is commonly done by those around her. This is a shaky basis for making moral decisions, especially when one has grown up in Sodom. Certainly she could be mourning the loss of a fiancé. But to suggest that there was no man in the land at all is not plausible given the literary context. There probably were no men in the immediate environs of the cave, but they had just left Zoar. Further, the angels had announced destruction of only Sodom and its environs, not the entire land or the entire earth.

19:32 Let's get our father to drink wine and then lie with him and preserve our family line through our father."

---

[38]The Hebrew has the definite article.
[39]See the discussion in Kissling, *Reliable Characters*, ch. 3.
[40]The NIV's "around here" is periphrastic.
[41]The NIV has "custom."
[42]The NIV's "earth" is also perfectly plausible.

Where did they get the wine if there was not a single man in the land? The idea of their carrying wine on their way out of Sodom seems unlikely, although not impossible. Lot's firstborn daughter[43] suggests that her little sister collude with her to get their father drunk and then have sex with him in order to bear children through him, since allegedly there are no potential partners available. The relationship which she suggests is certainly incestuous both in modern terms and in biblical terms. The incest laws in Leviticus 18 and 20 do not specifically mention a man sleeping with his daughter.[44] But the fact that so many other more distant relationships are condemned is testimony that for Israel such a relationship can be assumed to be condemned. Or, perhaps it was understood to be covered by a "natural law" which made it illegal for all human beings, not just Israel. The parallels between this incident and the story of Ham and Noah are striking.[45] In both cases the patriarch gets drunk. In both cases a child takes advantage of the fact that the patriarch is drunk. In both cases the act committed is sexual in fact or at least in connotation.[46] In both cases the descendants of the patriarch's children are under a curse. In both cases the event happens after the patriarch's family has been saved from a divine destruction of the entire physical environment around them. In both cases the children of the patriarch seem to have brought the propensity to sin, which they experienced in a sexually violent world, with them through the judgment into the new life after the destruction.[47]

Lot's daughter's goal is to keep alive her father's seed. In a sense this seems somewhat noble. She wants to keep her father's name alive by

---

[43]The fact that Lot's daughters are not named is taken by some to be an indication of the patriarchal perspective of Genesis. An equally plausible interpretation would be that, given the embarrassing narrative, the lack of mention of their names is a way of discreetly protecting them and their descendants from unnecessary embarrassment.

[44]Leviticus 20:14 prohibits a man taking a wife and her mother. Lot took his daughters' mother as a wife and then unwittingly and under the influence of alcohol had sexual relations with his daughters.

[45]For parallels with the story of the concubine at Gibeah in Judges 19, see my unpublished paper, "Touching Evil: Yahweh's Changing Strategies," delivered at the Stone-Campbell Journal Conference, Cincinnati, OH, March 27, 2004, available from the author.

[46]See the discussion of Ham's looking upon the nakedness of Noah as a possible euphemism for sexual misconduct in Kissling, *Genesis Volume 1*, pp. 347-348.

[47]For this fact in the case of Noah's children see Genesis 6:5 and 8:21 and the discussion in ibid., p. 317.

ensuring that he has descendants. Her means of doing so, however, would remind the original and canonical audiences of the practices of the Canaanites which the laws in Leviticus so sternly warned them about. Lot's daughter shows the morality of Sodom. That morality anticipates the morality of Canaan at the time when Israel entered the Promised Land as an instrument of God's judgment on the Canaanites. The behavior is reminiscent of that of the generation of the Flood. Just as the Flood did not completely remove the tendency to sin from humanity (Gen 6:5 and 8:21), so taking Lot and his daughters out of Sodom did not completely remove the influence of the Sodomites. Remember they had lived as and had even intended to marry Sodomites.

19:33 That night they got their father to drink wine, and the older daughter went in and lay with him. He was not aware of it when she lay down or when she got up.

The little sister evidently agrees to the plan and together they succeeded in getting Lot drunk. He was so drunk that he was not even aware of having had sexual intercourse. The older sister, whose idea the plan was, went first. She succeeded, if you can call it that, in her plan. She would take personal responsibility for ensuring that Lot, the one-time presumptive heir of Abraham, would have descendants for the future. In addition to the immorality of it all, this shows the common tendency in the chosen family to take matters, which should have been left in the hands of the God who promised, into their own hands. The fact that Abraham allowed and/or encouraged Lot to come along with him to Canaan was the first example. Abraham could not have known, and may never have known, the moral horrors that would follow his decision to not fully obey the LORD's call to him.

19:34 The next day the older daughter said to the younger, "Last night I lay with my father. Let's get him to drink wine again tonight, and you go in and lie with him so we can preserve our family line through our father."

Perhaps one pregnancy attempt was not a secure enough strategy for Lot's older daughter. What if she did not get pregnant? What if she lost the baby? What if the baby was not a male? Lot's older daughter now asks her younger sister to commit the same heinous sin which she had committed the previous night. Lot cannot be cleared of responsibility either. He did not have to drink the wine. The Old Testament has ample teaching regarding the dangers of alcohol, much of it in the wisdom literature which is based more on common sense than on specific revelation. The justification for alluring their father into an incestuous relationship once again sounds noble and selfless. But it is no more convincing when repeated. It only reminds the reader of the human tendency to find justification for the most heinous things through appeal to the circumstances and to larger goals.

19:35 So they got their father to drink wine that night also, and the younger daughter went and lay with him. Again he was not aware of it when she lay down or when she got up.

Once again Lot falls for the ploy. He gets so incredibly drunk for the second night in a row that he is completely unaware of having had sexual relations. The text does not attempt to explain Lot's gullibility.

19:36 So both of Lot's daughters became pregnant by their father.

Strikingly, it only took one attempt for each daughter to become pregnant. The text never explains what conversations took place as it became obvious that Lot's daughters were pregnant. Did he find out? Did they lie and tell Lot that their children came from relationships with men in Sodom or Zoar? We are never told. What matters for the narrator is only the fact that Lot had made both of his daughters pregnant while drunk. Unlike Noah who awoke from his wine and knew what his youngest son had done, we are not told anything about what Lot knew then or later.

The Rival Nations Which Arise from Lot (19:37-38)

19:37 The older daughter had a son, and she named him Moab; he is the father of the Moabites of today.

The older daughter had a son and she, not Lot, gave him the name of Moab. The name may mean, "from father."[48] At the least the audience, fluent in Hebrew and its wordplays, would see the connection, even if it is not etymologically sustainable. The audience is assured that the Moabites with whom they are familiar are the same Moabites mentioned here. For the imagined audience, the Moabites, like the Edomites and the Ammonites, are off limits for the people of Israel (Deut 2:18-19). They are not permitted to conquer their land or to engage them in battle. The canonical audience would know the sad history that followed from this unpromising beginning. The Moabites and Ammonites were thorns in the side of the nation of Israel throughout its history. Even at the end of the history recorded in the postexilic literature the Moabites and the Ammonites are enemies of Israel (Neh 13:23). It is striking that Lot's daughters and not Lot himself gave names to his (grand)children. This may be a significant point in this case, even though women in Genesis often give names to children.

---

[48]"מוֹאָב," KB, p. 554: "explained [in LXX] as מֵאָב," i.e., "from [my] father."

19:38 The younger daughter also had a son, and she named him Ben-Ammi; he is the father of the Ammonites of today.

Just as the "little" sister followed her older sister into incestuous sin, she also had a son. She also names her son. The name "Ben-Ammi" means "son of my people" and may be a way of indicating the incestuous history behind his birth. If so, both of the sons of Lot through his daughters carry the memory of their origins through their names. The descendants of Ben-Ammi were the Ammonites with whom the imagined and canonical audiences were very familiar. The Ammonites settled to the north of the Moabites and by the time of Israel's entrance into the land were living further to the east, not immediately adjoining the Jordan. They too, like the Moabites, were a thorn in the side of Israel throughout their history until the last events recorded in the book of Nehemiah.

GENESIS 20

IV. THE PROMISE BEGINS TO FIND FULFILLMENT IN GOD'S WAY (20:1–25:18)

A. THE FAILURE OF ABRAHAM'S FAITH(FULNESS) SHOWS THAT THE PROMISE IS NOT ULTIMATELY DEPENDENT ON HIM (20:1-18)

This passage narrates a second incident when Abraham lies about Sarah, claiming she is his sister, not his wife. Along with a similar narrative about Isaac in chapter 26, these three narratives are used by many scholars as primary evidence of the use of conflicting sources in the constructing of the text of Genesis. Supposedly what we have here is a common oral tradition about a Patriarch lying about his wife being his sister to a foreign king. Each of three different sources then shaped the original story in their own distinctive way. But a later redactor brought them together into the present text of Genesis. However, this approach fails to read the stories in their narrative context. The three stories are not an example of a so-called "triplet" but three different stories which have very different messages. In the first, Abram evidently thinks that Lot is his heir and tries to protect the promise by preserving everyone's lives. In chapter 26, Isaac repeats the mistake of his father as part of the narrator's message about how the consequences of sin impact future generations. Chapter 20, however, has a very different message when read in its narrative context. In this text Sarah is already pregnant or would soon be pregnant with Isaac. Both Abraham and Sarah have been promised that within the year, nine months of which would be the period of the actual pregnancy, Sarah would have a son. The promise has been clarified — God would give Sarah a son by miraculous means — and Abraham has no reason to come up with some humanly contrived scheme to bring about the fulfillment of the promise. To lie yet again about Sarah's relationship to him is not just to repeat a sin. It is to place the promise in jeopardy by allowing the paternity of the child to be questioned. If Sarah goes into Abimelech's harem and has sexual relations with him, the identity of the father of Isaac would be in doubt. Abraham's faith simply fails. To know that the child will be born from Abraham's seed and out of Sarah's own body makes the lie not just another sin, but a major failure of Abraham's faith. In the previous narratives even if Abraham's actions were misguided attempts to help God fulfill his own promises, they nevertheless show Abraham's commitment to that promise. Here Abraham has no motive to pass Sarah off as his sister other than fear for his own life.

But what is the point of including such a story? I would suggest the following. By including this story, a story of the total failure of Abraham's faith, the narrator seeks to suggest to his or her readers that ultimately the failure of faith by the human partner in the promises of God will not stop the fulfillment of those promises. Abraham's faith may fail, but not God's promises.

1. Abraham Repeats the Lie about Sarah and Endangers the Promise (20:1-2)

20:1 Now Abraham moved on from there into the region of the Negev and lived between Kadesh and Shur. For a while he stayed in Gerar,

After the interlude of the story of Lot and his daughters in Genesis 19:30-38, the story of Abraham resumes. When last we heard about him, he had risen early in the morning and gone to the place where he had interceded with the LORD on behalf of Sodom. The rising smoke told him that his intercession had failed. At the time he had been living at Mamre, near Hebron. Now he moved further to the south to the very borders of the Promised Land. This time there is no famine driving him to Egypt. He stopped at the extreme southern and western border towns of ancient Palestine. Kadesh (Barnea) was the place from which the twelve spies had been sent. Shur was farther to the west and formed the southwestern border with Sinai and therefore Egypt which lay beyond it. We do not know what motivated the move but Abraham tends to get himself into trouble when he moves of his own accord without divine direction. He lives as a sojourner in Gerar, a city south of Gaza in what later came to be the Philistine coastal strip. Once again Abraham is a temporary resident (*gēr*) in a land that he has been promised, but over which he had no meaningful control. Both the imagined original audience and the canonical audience knew from recent and contemporary experience what it meant to live as sojourners in a land not their own.

20:2 and there Abraham said of his wife Sarah, "She is my sister." Then Abimelech king of Gerar sent for Sarah and took her.

After the move to Gerar Abraham again said of[1] his wife Sarah, "she is my sister." The narrator's descriptions are telling here. It is Abraham, not Abram. It is Sarah, not Sarai, whom, we are reminded is Abraham's wife, not his sister. If the pair is called Abraham and Sarah, then they have been explicitly promised that within a year Sarah was to have a son. This "laughable" idea was made into a promise by the LORD for whom nothing is too difficult. If Sarah is taken into the harem of a foreign king, the real paternity of the child that Sarah is already bearing will be in question. This time Abraham does not consult Sarah and ask her to lie for him as in Genesis 12:13. This time he cannot excuse himself with the rationale that the LORD had not been clear enough about exactly how the promise of innumerable descendants was to be achieved. Ishmael is not to be the heir. Sarah herself, barren though she has been for more than seven decades, is to have a son. The LORD could not have been clearer. To repeat the same mistake from 25 years previously and to put the promise at risk is difficult to fathom. This is perhaps the lowest point of the narrative of Abraham. It shows a failure of faith. Predictably Abimelech, the king of Gerar, sent for Sarah and took her. The shocking thing is that ordinarily in Hebrew, to "take" a woman is to marry her. It is unclear whether a marriage actually took place or whether she was merely taken into the harem in some less formal sense.

2. God Protects the Promised Child despite Abraham and Abimelech (20:3-7)

20:3 But God came to Abimelech in a dream one night and said to him, "You are as good as dead because of the woman you have taken; she is a married woman."

We are not told how long God waited until he revealed himself to Abimelech. The NIV's "one night" may suggest a longer time than is likely. God told Abimelech that he was a "dead one."[2] The reason was that the woman Abimelech had recently taken into his harem was married.[3] The imagined audience knew what God thought of ancient Near Eastern kings with harems (Deut 17:17).

---

[1]The Hebrew אֶל ('el) is confusing here. Ordinarily it would mean "to," i.e., that Abraham spoke to Sarah, rather than about her.

[2]The Hebrew has an adjectival participle. The NIV is periphrastic.

[3]The Hebrew for "married" (בְּעֻלַת בָּעַל, bᵉʿulath bāʿal) is literally "one lorded

20:4 Now Abimelech had not gone near her, so he said, "Lord, will you destroy an innocent nation?

The author is at pains to emphasize that though Abraham's foolish lie had once again placed the promise at risk, the LORD had ensured that the paternity of the child was not actually placed in danger.

Abimelech is not surprised at God speaking to him and addresses him as though he knows him ("my lord," אֲדֹנָי, 'ădōnāy). Abimelech intercedes with God in a way that has similarities to Abraham's intercession over Sodom in chapter 18. He asks, "Will you kill[4] a righteous nation?" Abraham had interceded for Sodom on the basis that the LORD could not sweep away the "righteous" with the wicked. Abimelech claims that his entire nation is "righteous."[5]

20:5 Did he not say to me, 'She is my sister,' and didn't she also say, 'He is my brother'? I have done this with a clear conscience and clean hands."

Abimelech responds to the Lord's warning by claiming that he had acted honorably without intending to commit the severe crime of adultery against Abraham. He acted on the (false) information given him by both Abraham and Sarah. Interestingly the narrator never tells us that Sarah had in fact also perpetuated the lie.

Although a resident of the land, Abimelech shows that at least some of the land's residents in the time of the patriarchs had moral principles equal to, if not superior to, the ancestors of Israel.[6] Abimelech claims that both his motives[7] and his actions (with "clean hands") were blame-

---

over by a lord." Did God accommodate his language to a Canaanite king who understood the word bā'al? Would the imagined audience notice this?

[4]The NRSV and NIV here have "destroy" but the more typical translation offered above keeps the sharpness of the original.

[5]The NRSV and NIV have "innocent" here. While this is undoubtedly the point Abimelech is making, the more literal "righteous" for צַדִּיק (ṣadîq) helps the modern reader see the later textual echo here.

[6]James E. Miller notes ["Sexual Offences in Genesis," *JSOT* 90 (2000): 46]: "It is significant that Abimelek, the Canaanite king, assumed that 'sister' was exclusive of 'wife', and that by declaring one Abraham was implicitly denying the other. Leviticus 18 and 20, which contain the incest laws, define Canaanites as practicers of incest and other sexual impropriety. Israelites are to be different from Canaanites by abstaining from incest, but Abraham, the father of the Israelite nation, surprises Abimelek, the Canaanite ruler, with his incest." This of course assumes that Abraham is telling the truth when he claims that Sarah is his half-sister, a doubtful proposition as we shall argue below.

[7]The NIV's "clear conscience" is more literally rendered "integrity of my heart."

less. He does not raise, of course, the issue of his simply taking Sarah into his harem without discussion or negotiation.

20:6 Then God said to him in the dream, "Yes, I know you did this with a clear conscience, and so I have kept you from sinning against me. That is why I did not let you touch her.

This verse informs us that the words which Abimelech addressed to God were evidently also part of the dream since God's response is once again in a dream. God confirms what Abimelech had claimed: his actions toward Sarah were done with a clear conscience and clean hands. Since this was so, God had kept Abimelech from sinning against him by not allowing him to sexually touch Sarah. Adultery is something that Abimelech was expected to know to be evil without direct revelation of the fact.[8]

20:7 Now return the man's wife, for he is a prophet, and he will pray for you and you will live. But if you do not return her, you may be sure that you and all yours will die."

Abimelech is directed to return Sarah to her husband. God also informs him that Abraham, as a prophet, will intercede for his life and his intercession will be accepted. Abraham will function the way Moses later did for Israel. Abimelech's very life is placed in the hands of a man who lied to him. God warns him that if he refused to obey God's command to return Sarah, he and his entire household would surely die. The Hebrew echoes the original command of God to the first man in Genesis 2:17. The words there, "You will surely die" are repeated here. Abimelech is placed in the situation of the first man with the freedom, like him, to accept or reject God's command, and also with a stern warning about the consequences of disobedience.

3. Abimelech Confronts Abraham over His Lie (20:8-13)

20:8 Early the next morning Abimelech summoned all his officials, and when he told them all that had happened, they were very much afraid.

The conversation between God and Abimelech took place during the night through a dream. Abimelech shows his willingness to obey by rising "early" the next morning. Abimelech took the dream seriously and warns all of his officials who might be tempted into inappropriate

---

[8]This is one of many texts in Genesis which imply that there is such a thing as "natural law." For the term see J.N.D. Anderson, "Law," *New Dictionary of Theology* (Downers Grove, IL: InterVarsity, 1988), pp. 377-378.

behavior toward Sarah. While Abraham claims later that he knew there to be no fear of God in Gerar, this text makes clear that precisely the opposite was in fact the case. The entire group had a great fear of God. The presence of such relatively righteous inhabitants of the land like Abimelech and Melchizedek helps explain why Abraham's possession of the land would have to wait until the iniquity of the "Amorites" with its consequent punishment would be full (Gen 15:16). Not all of the land's inhabitants were like the inhabitants of Sodom.

20:9 Then Abimelech called Abraham in and said, "What have you done to us? How have I wronged you that you have brought such great guilt upon me and my kingdom? You have done things to me that should not be done."

After discussing matters with his servants, Abimelech summoned Abraham to ask why he had lied to him and placed his kingdom in danger of divine judgment. Abimelech accuses Abraham of bringing great sin[9] upon him and his people — a great moral wrong. Abimelech asks rhetorically what evil he had done to Abraham to deserve this treatment from one of God's prophets. While the reader is not asked to approve of Abraham's lying which flows from an inexplicable failure of faith, Abimelech was not entirely innocent either. Like nearly all ancient kings Abimelech shows his power and virility through the harem, the multiplication of wives and concubines. Abimelech does not even pause to question the tradition of which he was a part, which treated women, especially foreign women, as sexual objects. His moral outrage, therefore, may be a little overdone given the position of power he had over Sarah and Abraham.

20:10 And Abimelech asked Abraham, "What was your reason for doing this?"

While the NIV's paraphrase of Abimelech's question is accurate, it loses some of the nuance of the Hebrew. Literally it reads, "What did you see that you did this thing?"

20:11 Abraham replied, "I said to myself, 'There is surely no fear of God in this place, and they will kill me because of my wife.'

Abraham's response is honest. He assumed, quite naturally, that a king in Canaan would have no fear of God. After all, the LORD had promised him that his descendants would one day possess the land of Canaan when the LORD's final judgment fell on them. Had not the recent destruction of Sodom indicated this? On the other hand, the only Canaanite king with whom Abraham had had direct contact up to

---

[9]Not great "guilt" as in the NIV but "sin" (חֲטָאָה, *ḥăṭā'āh*).

this point, other than Abimelech and the king of Sodom, was Melchizedek. Abraham was afraid that he would be killed because of the
desirability of his wife. While this fear is understandably human, it does
not excuse his lack of concern for Sarah. She was pregnant or soon to
be pregnant with the promised heir.

**20:12 Besides, she really is my sister, the daughter of my father
though not of my mother; and she became my wife.**

If Abraham had stopped there, things would have been better. In
this case he said too much. Faced with the embarrassing lack of faith
and his false assumptions (prejudices?) about Abimelech, Abraham
begins to rationalize his behavior. Commentators usually believe what
Abraham says. Abraham claims that Sarah is really his half-sister, shar-
ing a common father with Abraham, but having a different mother. The
narrator has already provided a genealogy of Abram in Genesis 11:27-
31. There is no mention there of what Abraham here alleges even
though that same text mentions that Abram's brother Nahor married
his own niece. The author of Genesis does not tell us that Sarah was
Abraham's half-sister. He only records Abraham claiming this when he
is caught in a lie. It seems unlikely that the readers are being invited to
believe Abraham at this point. Why then do so many readers accept
Abraham's word on this? This is a prime example of the simplistic, heroic reading of biblical characters which has plagued traditional readings.
The Bible is more subtle than that.[10] It displays even its heroes "warts
and all." The strategy of making up a story when you have been caught
lying is a common human failing from which the father of the faithful
is not immune.[11]

**20:13 And when God had me wander from my father's household, I
said to her, 'This is how you can show your love to me: Everywhere we
go, say of me, "He is my brother."'"**

Abraham uses the opportunity to refer to God's calling him from
Haran to leave his father's household, recorded in Genesis 12. This
explains his nomadic existence to Abimelech. Abraham claims that
when he left, he suggested that Sarah could show her loyalty[12] by always
claiming that Abraham was her brother. According to the narrator,
however, this strategy did not arise until Abraham first went to Egypt

---

[10]See Kissling, *Reliable Characters*.

[11]In the parallel story in Genesis 26, Abraham's son Isaac is clearly lying when
he claims Rebekah is his sister.

[12]The Hebrew word חֶסֶד (*ḥesed*) is better understood as "loyalty" than as
"love."

(Gen 12:11-12), and there is no indication that this was the typical strategy of Abraham and Sarah wherever they went. This does not prove that Abraham is lying in this verse also, as is apparently the case in verse 12. There are ways to harmonize what he says with what the author has said previously. But the reader must be careful here.

It is interesting that Abraham refers to the deity as "God," not as "the LORD" even though the narrator refers to the LORD giving the commission to leave his father's household in Genesis 12:1-3. This is probably an indication that Abraham did not actually know God by the name Yahweh and that cases in Genesis where the patriarchs are quoted as using that name are, strictly speaking, anachronistic. Since the author(s) of Exodus tell us that this is so, such uses of Yahweh in Genesis function as a sort of less direct form of a "dear reader" comment.[13]

4. Abimelech Blesses Abraham despite His Lie (20:14-16)

20:14 Then Abimelech brought sheep and cattle and male and female slaves and gave them to Abraham, and he returned Sarah his wife to him.

Just as Pharaoh had earlier given Abram many possessions in a sort of compensation for taking Sarai into his harem, so also Abimelech lavishes gifts on Abraham. The gifts include animals and servants. Most importantly, Sarah was returned. The parallel with chapter 12 where the Egyptian Pharaoh gave many valuable gifts to Abraham is striking. The narrator may be hinting at his or her perspective on Abraham's claim that she is his half-sister when Sarah is referred to as Abraham's wife, not his sister.

20:15 And Abimelech said, "My land is before you; live wherever you like."

Abimelech also offers Abraham the freedom to live anywhere that was "good [in Abraham's] eyes"[14] within Abimelech's kingdom. This seems to be the first offer of land which Abraham receives, but we will see that strings are attached to the offer.

20:16 To Sarah he said, "I am giving your brother a thousand shekels of silver. This is to cover the offense against you before all who are with you; you are completely vindicated."

---

[13]See the insightful discussion of this phenomenon in Herbert Chanan Brichto, *The Names of God: Poetic Readings in Biblical Beginnings* (New York: Oxford University Press, 1998), ch. 1.

[14]The NIV is periphrastic here.

Abimelech tells Sarah that the one thousand shekels of silver which he had given to Abraham would be "a covering of the eyes" to all who were with her. This phrase is difficult to interpret. The NIV may be correct to assume that the idiom hints that any embarrassment over the episode for which Sarah would drop her eyes is covered by the monetary reward. She can point to that money as proof that Abimelech was in the wrong in the situation and that he made restitution. Abimelech refers to Abraham as Sarah's "brother." The designation seems dripping with sarcasm. It is hard to know whether or not Abimelech is being portrayed as having believed Abraham's story about Sarah being his half-sister. In any case the relevant point in their transaction is that Sarah is Abraham's wife, not his sister.

5. Abraham, the Liar, Is Still the Intermediary for the Healing of Abimelech's Nation (20:17-18)

20:17 Then Abraham prayed to God, and God healed Abimelech, his wife and his slave girls so they could have children again,
    As readers we now discover that God had placed Abimelech under the curse of a physical malady. While Sarah was in his harem, no one would be able to bear children. God had told Abimelech that he and his household would die if he did not return Sarah. In addition to being a punishment for taking another man's wife, the affliction also shows God's providence. At least potentially[15] the paternity of Sarah's child would be protected. Turner helpfully notes,

> This is the first time we read of A. engaging in prayer . . . and perhaps even more significantly, the first time A. does anything for anyone which was not calculated to further his own ends in the fulfillment of the promise. . . . Was A.'s turning away from his own self-interest something for which Yahweh had been waiting for some time — in fact the condition for fulfilling the promise?[16]

While the text does not answer the question which it raises, Turner's suggestion reminds us that Abraham's faith grew through a process that required him to trust more and more.

20:18 for the LORD had closed up every womb in Abimelech's household because of Abraham's wife Sarah.

---

[15]Of course Sarah could have become pregnant by Abimelech and just not borne a child from him.

[16]Turner, *Announcements*, p. 87.

The LORD, unknown to the reader and perhaps to Abimelech, had closed up tight[17] every womb in Abimelech's household. This judgment is sent by God to protect Sarah and the promised child she was to bear. The narrator, unlike Abimelech in verse 16, again refers to Sarah as Abraham's wife, not his sister. This further supports the case that Abraham's story that Sarah was his half-sister was implausible.

---

[17]The Hebrew uses an emphatic construction here (qal infinitive absolute followed by the verb in the same stem) to emphasize the closing of the wombs among the women of Abimelech's house.

GENESIS 21

B. THE JOKE IS ON ABRAHAM AND SARAH: THE BIRTH OF ISAAC (21:1-7)

The idea that Abraham would have a son at 100 and that Sarah who had been barren her entire adult life would suddenly conceive and give birth to a son at the age of 90 was and is truly laughable. But through the wordplay on the name of Isaac ("He will laugh") the one who has the last laugh is the Lord. The great thing about this narrative is that Abraham and Sarah get the joke and remind themselves of God's hilarious graciousness every time they look at Isaac. Ultimately God began the process of fulfilling his promises in his way, not through human reasoning and human planning. Such reasoning, consciously or unconsciously, assumes limitations on God's power.

21:1 Now the Lord was gracious to Sarah as he had said, and the Lord did for Sarah what he had promised.

In Genesis 18:10 the Lord had promised that within the year he would return to Sarah and enable her to have a child. This verse shows the Lord's faithfulness to that promise. The NIV's "was gracious to" is a paraphrase that seems to miss the point. First the Lord "visited" (פָּקַד, *pāqad*) Sarah as he had said and then the Lord[1] did what he had promised. The Lord's faithfulness to his word even when the human participants in those promises fail him is a striking feature of this section of Genesis. Here the reader is reminded of this fact once again.

21:2 Sarah became pregnant and bore a son to Abraham in his old age, at the very time God had promised him.

---

[1] Daniel Boyarin, *A Radical Jew: Paul and the Politics of Identity* (Berkeley: University of California, 1994), p. 269, suggests the possibility that Paul (Gal 4:21-31) may have followed a Jewish reading in which Isaac's birth was entirely the work of God without Abraham. This seems inherently implausible given the very next verse. It is hard to imagine that the apostle Paul would know one without the other.

The NIV's "very time" is a Hebrew word (מוֹעֵד, *mô'ēd*) used of the appointed times of festivals and other significant events of revelation. At God's appointed times he does something special. The imagined audience might well make the connection with the special revelation that sometimes took place at the specially appointed times.

The switch from the LORD in verse 1 to "God" in verse 2 is the type of evidence that has been used to distinguish between the hypothetical sources J on the one hand and P or E on the other. But the usage may indicate no more than intentional variation. In fact the two verses repeat each other, a narrative example of the Hebrew penchant for parallelistic structure in prose as well as in poetry. God's faithfulness to his promise is emphasized yet again. This is remarkable given the failure of Abraham's faith that has just been recorded in chapter 20. This is yet another indication of God's grace. While human participation and obedience are necessary and expected, that flawed and fallible obedience is far too insecure a foundation for God's promises. God is faithful even when, perhaps especially when, we are unfaithful.

21:3 Abraham gave the name Isaac to the son Sarah bore him.

As God had commanded in chapter 17, Abraham gave the name Isaac ("He will laugh") to his son. The promise, which at first brought laughter from both Abraham and Sarah, brought a different type of laughter when the son was actually born. The Hebrew emphasizes the identity of Isaac by describing him as, "his son, the one born to him, whom Sarah bore to him, Isaac." This may prepare the reader for a similarly elaborate description of Isaac in 22:2, "Take your son, your only son, whom you love, Isaac." The ludicrous sounding promise that the 100-year-old Abraham and his long barren ninety-year-old wife Sarah would have a child gives way to the joyous laughter of celebration in the faithfulness of a God who does the implausible and the impossible. Every time the child's name is mentioned, the joke that God played on them would be recalled with great delight.

21:4 When his son Isaac was eight days old, Abraham circumcised him, as God commanded him.

Here Abraham's obedience is noted. The child at the vulnerable age of eight days is placed at risk by having an operation. But Abraham obeyed and did precisely what God commanded him to do in Genesis 17:9-13.

21:5 Abraham was a hundred years old when his son Isaac was born to him.

The reader is reminded of just how incredible the miracle was. Abraham had asked, "Will a son be born to a man a hundred years old? Will Sarah bear a child at the age of ninety?" (Gen 17:17). The answer is, "Yes, if God is behind it."

21:6 Sarah said, "God has brought me laughter, and everyone who hears about this will laugh with me."

The laughter of nonbelief (Gen 17:17; 18:12) is converted into the laughter of rejoicing (21:6). Sarah quite rightly acknowledges the source of her joy. God brought laughter to her after decades of frustration. She will tell others of God's marvelous joke on her. They will join in the celebration.

21:7 And she added, "Who would have said to Abraham that Sarah would nurse children? Yet I have borne him a son in his old age."

Sarah asks rhetorically, "Who would have predicted this?" Actually, God had predicted it. While Abraham had shown in the birth of Ishmael that he was capable of begetting children, Sarah's barrenness had long been confirmed. Perhaps every time Sarah nursed Isaac there was a little chuckle of joy and satisfaction.

Given the importance of Isaac's birth it is surprising that it occupies such a small space in the narrative. It soon becomes clear, however, that the narrator is much more interested in the relationship between Ishmael and Isaac. Despite Isaac's birth, Ishmael is still in the household. Whether or not Ishmael will be able to maintain his position as heir remains to be seen.

C. THE ENDGAME OF THE ISHMAEL STRATEGY: THE EXPULSION OF ISHMAEL (21:8-21)

Ultimately the scheme of Sarai to have Hagar bear a surrogate son for her comes from a failure to wait on God to fulfill his promises. The end result of that failure to wait is the conflict within the family which the birth of Ishmael caused and ultimately results in the expulsion of Hagar and Ishmael. The text is ambiguous as to whether Ishmael's descendants are destined to become enemies of Isaac's descendants or not. But Ishmael's expulsion does not mean that he is condemned to hell.[2] He also is under God's blessing. But his role in the working out of God's purposes is a minor one. This passage, along with the genealogy in 25:12-18, explains the ultimate long-term consequences of the scheme.

---

[2]While I would not want to endorse his entire project, Joel Kaminsky's recent work on election [*Yet I Loved Jacob: Reclaiming the Biblical Concept of Election* (Nashville: Abingdon, 2007), chs. 7-8] helpfully distinguishes between the nonelect and the antielect. Only the latter are under God's judgment. Ishmael's descendants fall under the "nonelect" category.

1. Sarah Demands the Expulsion of Ishmael and Hagar (21:8-11)

21:8 The child grew and was weaned, and on the day Isaac was weaned Abraham held a great feast.

Weaning in the ancient world took much longer than in the modern. Isaac was perhaps three or four years old when he was weaned.[3] Abraham marked the time with a great feast in celebration of the fact that the promised child had survived the risky early years of life.

21:9 But Sarah saw that the son whom Hagar the Egyptian had borne to Abraham was mocking,

While some English translations suggest that Ishmael was merely "playing" with Isaac (cf. NRSV), this seems unlikely given Sarah's reaction. The NIV gives the more plausible rendering, "mocking."[4] The word "mocking" is the same word, although in a different stem, as the word translated "laughing" in chapters 17 and 18. There it referred to the incredible promise of God to give Abraham and Sarah a baby to be named "He will laugh." Here the laughter is more cynical. It refers to Ishmael's mocking of Isaac. He refuses to even consider that God may use the infant Isaac as the primary channel of his blessing for all the nations.

The way in which the narrator refers to Ishmael is striking. His name is not used, and he is identified as "the son whom Hagar the Egyptian had born to Abraham." Hagar is not identified as Abraham's wife but merely the woman who bore him a son. Hagar is described as "the Egyptian." What is to be made of this rather odd description by the narrator? One possibility is that the narrator does not recognize Ishmael as a legitimate heir for Abraham and indicates this by referring to his Egyptian mother, who is pointedly not described as a wife or even a concubine of Abraham. The original audience had been brutally treated by the Egyptians in recent history. Perhaps the narrator is reminding them that they are not descended from Egyptians. Another possibility is that the narrator is implicitly showing Sarah's perspective on the matter without necessarily affirming it. The technique is known as "indirect discourse."[5]

---

[3]See Hannah's weaning of Samuel in 1 Samuel 1:22,23.

[4]Boyarin, *Radical Jew*, p. 270, notes that Paul's use of this narrative in his allegory in Galatians 4 shows that "Paul must have known of a tradition which reads מְצַחֵק as some form of persecution or harassment of Isaac by Ishmael."

[5]On free indirect discourse in the Bible see Adele Berlin, *Poetics and Interpretation of Biblical Narrative* (Sheffield: Almond, 1983), p. 98; Meir Sternberg, *The Poetics of Biblical Narrative* (Bloomington, IN: Indiana University Press, 1985), pp. 52-54.

21:10 and she said to Abraham, "Get rid of that slave woman and her son, for that slave woman's son will never share in the inheritance with my son Isaac."

Sarah commands Abraham to expel Hagar and Ishmael. The way she refers to them is instructive. She calls Hagar "that slave woman."[6] She is not referred to as either "my" (Sarah's) or "your" (Abraham's) slave woman, but "that" slave woman as though she had no prior relationship to Sarah or Abraham. When Hagar is first introduced to us she is called Sarai's "handmaid" (שִׁפְחָה, *šiphḥah*) rather than "slave woman" (אָמָה, *'āmāh*).[7] The difference hints at the contempt that Sarah now has for Hagar. Ishmael is not the son Sarah was to have through Hagar, nor Abraham's son, but "that slave woman's son." He is not to share the inheritance with Sarah's son Isaac.

A more literal rendering of Sarah's statement would read: "the son of this slave woman shall not be heir with my son Isaac." Laurence Turner helpfully notes that Sarah's statement indicates that even for Sarah, Ishmael will be an heir, just not an heir of the same status as Isaac.[8] The NIV misses this point through paraphrase.

21:11 The matter distressed Abraham greatly because it concerned his son.

The matter was very difficult for Abraham because in his judgment Ishmael was his son, not the son of "that slave woman." It is hard to know whether the phrase "his son" represents the narrator's point of view or by "indirect discourse" Abraham's point of view.[9] Is it the narrator or Abraham who regards Ishmael as Abraham's son, or both? In any case the narrator and Abraham differ in their perspective from that of Sarah.

2. The LORD Promises to Care for Hagar and Ishmael (21:12-13)

21:12 But God said to him, "Do not be so distressed about the boy and your maidservant. Listen to whatever Sarah tells you, because it is through Isaac that your offspring will be reckoned.

---

[6]While the NRSV is technically more accurate in translating the demonstrative pronouns as "this," the NIV's paraphrase "that" may be a better way of conveying in English the tone of Sarah's words.

[7]Another disparaging usage may occur when Rachel uses *'āmāh* versus Laban's and the narrator's *šiphḥāh* to describe Bilhah (Gen 29:29; 30:3).

[8]Turner, *Announcements of Plot*, p. 85.

[9]Sternberg, *Poetics*, pp. 52-54.

God speaks to Abraham, evidently while Abraham is pondering what Sarah wants him to do. He should not be distressed with the decision to expel Hagar and Ishmael. God calls Ishmael "the young man" or "the boy" (NIV). He is at least 13 years old at this point.[10] He is not called Abraham's son. God refers to Hagar as Abraham's slave woman. While this uses Sarah's term for Hagar, it does not adopt Sarah's distancing of Hagar by referring to her as "that slave woman." Hagar does belong to Abraham. She is not some isolated individual.

But God tells Abraham to obey Sarah's command. Abraham's descendants are to be counted from Isaac, not from Ishmael, and the separation of the two lines will clarify that point. As we will see, God does not lose his concern for Ishmael, but there is to be no confusion over who will be heir. Turner helpfully notes the irony: "It is ironic that in sending away Ishmael, A. must do 'whatever Sarah says' (21.12), just as he had once 'hearkened to the voice of Sarah' (16.2), in her suggestion which resulted in Ishmael's birth. The first suggestion he eagerly accepts; the second he resents."[11]

21:13 I will make the son of the maidservant into a nation also, because he is your offspring."

While Abraham is to expel Hagar and Ishmael, God immediately gives Abraham reassurance that Ishmael will also be blessed. In his grace, God promises to take the son of the slave woman and turn him into the father of a nation. This is reassuring for Hagar and Ishmael and also a part of the promise of many nations descending from Abraham. His son Ishmael will beget a nation as will Isaac.

3. Abraham Expels Hagar and Ishmael (21:14)

21:14 Early the next morning Abraham took some food and a skin of water and gave them to Hagar. He set them on her shoulders and then sent her off with the boy. She went on her way and wandered in the desert of Beersheba.

Abraham did not put off the decision no matter how difficult it was for him. He got up early in the morning just as he later does when the LORD commands him to sacrifice Isaac in chapter 22. The next morning he loaded Hagar with food and water and sent her away along with

---

[10]God may use the term "young man" as a way of putting Abraham's mind at ease. He is not a little child being cast out who cannot take care of himself.

[11]Turner, *Announcements of Plot*, p. 87.

Ishmael. The latter is referred to as "the child,"[12] perhaps to emphasize his vulnerability in this situation and the need for God's protection and care. Hagar wandered in the wilderness[13] south of Canaan near Beer-sheba, one of Canaan's traditional borders.

4. The LORD Protects and Provides for Hagar and Ishmael (21:15-21)

21:15 When the water in the skin was gone, she put the boy under one of the bushes.

Since Ishmael was at least thirteen during this incident, the translation "boy" is potentially misleading. Given the wilderness and its heat, when the water had run out there was nothing to be done but to wait for death. The NIV's "put" is more literally rendered "cast" as though Hagar was throwing away the child who had meant so much to her that she was willing to risk her mistress's wrath over him. Evidently Hagar had given up on the promises concerning her son in chapter 16.

21:16 Then she went off and sat down nearby, about a bowshot away, for she thought, "I cannot watch the boy die." And as she sat there nearby, she began to sob.

Hagar once again refers to Ishmael as a "boy" (*yeled*) while the narrator typically refers to him as the young man (*na'ar*). In desperation Hagar walks far enough away from Ishmael so that she cannot actually see him die. Her pain is indicated by her crying which the NIV nicely paraphrases as sobbing.

21:17 God heard the boy crying, and the angel of God called to Hagar from heaven and said to her, "What is the matter, Hagar? Do not be afraid; God has heard the boy crying as he lies there.

God now enters the situation. He hears[14] the voice of the young man Ishmael. The NIV assumes that Ishmael is crying also, although the Hebrew does not say this explicitly. The word for "cry" is actually not in the Hebrew text. Ishmael is referred to as a young man, not a "boy" as in the NIV.

Interestingly while God hears, it is the angel of God who acts. Though some would try to read this christologically, it seems more likely that

---

[12]The Hebrew here is יֶלֶד (*yeled*) rather than נַעַר (*na'ar*) as in v. 12.

[13]"Desert" may be too strong a word for the modern audience. This is not the Sahara but a wilderness where few people live.

[14]John Nugent pointed out to me the pun between Ishmael's name ("God hears") and the fact that in this passage God "heard" Ishmael crying.

this indicates the way God responds, by sending his messenger. But this messenger (or angel) is not just any messenger but specifically the angel of God. This is the only time in the Old Testament where the phrase "angel of God" is used. Typically it is "the angel of the LORD" as it was when he appeared to Hagar in chapter 16.

The angel asks rhetorically what the problem is. According to the angel there is no problem because God "heard the voice of" the young Ishmael. Apparently Ishmael has been calling out, presumably to God. The NIV again paraphrases by suggesting that he was "crying."[15] While this is possible, it has no explicit basis in the Hebrew text.

21:18 Lift the boy up and take him by the hand, for I will make him into a great nation."

Once again the translation "boy" gives the wrong impression. In the Hebrew Ishmael is described as a "young man" (*na'ar*). While the NIV's "take him by the hand" is a possible translation, the Hebrew וְהַחֲזִיקִי אֶת־יָדֵךְ (*wᵉhaḥăzîqî 'eth-yādēk*) could mean several things. I would tentatively favor translating it "make him strong with your hand." In any case, the promise to Ishmael is recalled. He will be made into a "great nation." While his descendants will not carry the line of promise, he is still under God's care and blessing. No matter what has happened between Sarah, Hagar, Ishmael, and Abraham, God's promise still stands.

21:19 Then God opened her eyes and she saw a well of water. So she went and filled the skin with water and gave the boy a drink.

It is not clear exactly what happens next. Was the well there and Hagar could not see it, or did the miracle consist in God providing water in the wilderness? In any case the original audience would be familiar with God's provision of water in that very wilderness in their recent national history. When it seemed that there was no hope of living, much less grandiose promises of becoming a great nation, God reminds Hagar of that promise and provides her and her son Ishmael with water. The meeting of that immediate need is a sort of down payment on the longer-term promise.

21:20 God was with the boy as he grew up. He lived in the desert and became an archer.

God's preservation of Ishmael did not merely occur when he was about to die of thirst in the desert. He continued to be with him. He grew up from a young man of thirteen to become an archer who lived in the desert. It is interesting that the Ishmaelites serve an important

---

[15]The Hebrew merely says that God had heard the voice of the young man, not that he was weeping.

role in the ongoing narrative. It was Ishmaelite traders who bought Joseph from his brothers and took him to Egypt. The descendants of Ishmael unwittingly facilitated God's plan of preserving the chosen nation alive by sending Joseph ahead of them to Egypt (Gen 45:5-8; 50:20).

21:21 While he was living in the Desert of Paran, his mother got a wife for him from Egypt.

Ishmael ended up living in the desert region south and west of Palestine in the north Sinai. Hagar, an Egyptian herself, saw to it that her son Ishmael got an Egyptian wife. That Hagar was able to do this in a patriarchal social system where fathers of the bride and the groom negotiated a bride price is noteworthy. It speaks of God's provision for her and perhaps hints at her own personal character. There is no mention of a future husband, and yet Hagar survives and thrives enough to enable Ishmael to have a wife.

D. A COVENANT WITH THE PEOPLE OF THE LAND (21:22-34)

The original and canonical audiences know the dangers of making covenants with the inhabitants of Canaan (Deut 7:2). But here, Abraham shows his own covenant loyalty in his dealings with Abimelech. The man whose descendants would be the channel of God's blessing to the rest of the world shows in his dealings with Abimelech the same covenant loyalty which God shows to Abraham. Abraham had been told in Genesis 15:16b that his descendants would have to wait for the fulfillment of the land promise until the iniquity of the Amorites had become full. That has not yet happened, and righteous Canaanites like Abimelech and Melchizedek demonstrate that the iniquity was not yet full.

1. Abimelech Recognizes God's Blessing of Abraham (21:22)

21:22 At that time Abimelech and Phicol the commander of his forces said to Abraham, "God is with you in everything you do.

When last we heard of Abimelech, Abraham was dwelling in Gerar near him, near the southwestern border of Canaan. Abimelech brings the "prince of his armies" to talk with Abraham. It may well be that there is some sort of implied threat of force in this. Abimelech did the speaking. He begins by acknowledging that God was with Abraham in everything he did. Evidently this refers to God's blessing and protection. Abimelech had experienced that at great personal cost quite recently in chapter 20. Here is human confirmation of what God had promised, "I will bless those who bless you and whoever curses you I will curse" (Gen 12:3a).

2. Abraham Commits to Deal Loyally with Abimelech (21:23-24)

21:23 Now swear to me here before God that you will not deal falsely with me or my children or my descendants. Show to me and the country where you are living as an alien the same kindness I have shown to you."

Abimelech now commands Abraham to give an oath to him by that very same God who has blessed him. The solemn promise which he expects is that Abraham would not deal falsely with either him or his offspring, whether currently alive or yet to be born. Abraham had dealt deceptively with him in claiming that Sarah was his sister, not his wife, so his fear was not without foundation. Abimelech claims that he had acted loyally toward Abraham. The NIV's "kindness" is perhaps too weak a translation for the Hebrew word חֶסֶד (ḥesed) which is used of God's faithfulness and loyalty throughout the Old Testament.[16] Abimelech asks that such loyalty be reciprocated to himself and his country. He reminds Abraham that the country is his as king and Abraham lives there as an alien sojourner. If they are to live peacefully together, events such as happened in chapter 20 where Abimelech and his extended family were brought under God's curse must not happen again. Abraham is an alien. The land is not his.

21:24 Abraham said, "I swear it."

Abraham quite readily accedes to Abimelech's demand. He solemnly swears to act loyally to Abimelech both then and in the future. In ordinary circumstances a king making such a demand would be coercive. The fact that Abimelech's military commander is present may hint at this. But Abraham's ensuing words indicate that he does not regard himself to be in such a subordinate position. The oath that he takes seems to be voluntary because he knows from recent personal experience, as does Abimelech, that God will protect him even as an alien.

The original imagined audience was warned against making treaties with the occupants of the land (Deut 7:1-5), something they did not keep in the case of the Gibeonites (Josh 9:1-21). How could the father of their nation enter into such a treaty? For them this indicates that the iniquity of Sodom had not yet spread to Canaan. The residents of the Promised Land were not yet ripe for God's judgment. There were godly

---

[16]See D.A. Baer and R.P. Gordon, "חֶסֶד," *NIDOTTE*, 2:211-218.

or at least nonhostile inhabitants at this point in time such as Melchizedek and Abimelech.

3. Conflict with Covenant Partners (21:25-26)

21:25 Then Abraham complained to Abimelech about a well of water that Abimelech's servants had seized.

While Abraham willingly pledged loyalty to Abimelech and his country, this did not mean that in Abraham's mind Abimelech had no reciprocal obligations. Abraham is not intimidated by Abimelech or his military commander. He rebukes[17] Abimelech because he also has obligations as a covenant partner. Abimelech's servants had seized a well of water from Abraham's herdsmen, something a loyal covenant partner would not do, especially one who had invited him to live where he pleased (Gen 20:15).

21:26 But Abimelech said, "I don't know who has done this. You did not tell me, and I heard about it only today."

Abimelech claims that he did not know who seized the well. Further, since Abraham had not previously told him about it, he only learned of it that very day. It is impossible to be certain whether Abimelech is telling the truth. Since Abraham finds it necessary to give a gift of seven ewe lambs to ensure rights to a (or is it "the") well he had dug, one must be careful in assuming that Abimelech is being entirely truthful. Conversely, he is a man who has demonstrated that he fears God. In either case Abraham makes it clear to Abimelech that it is not only Abraham whose integrity could be questioned.

4. A Ritual to Seal and Remember the Agreement (21:27-34)

21:27 So Abraham brought sheep and cattle and gave them to Abimelech, and the two men made a treaty.

While the covenant made between Abraham and Abimelech is two-sided ("bilateral"), only Abraham provides the animals used in the covenant formation ceremony. Sheep and cattle would be cut in two and the covenant parties would pass between them calling down upon themselves a curse should they violate the covenant.[18] Both sides have obli-

---

[17]The NIV's "complained to" for Hebrew יָכַח (*yākaḥ*) is in the hiphil which typically means "rebuke" or "correct."

[18]This presumes that the ceremony in Genesis 15 was common to covenants in Israel. Scholars often presume that the literal translation of the Hebrew for

gations in this covenant. Because this is a covenant between two human beings both sides have stated or implied obligations. This covenant is often regarded as the paradigm example of a bilateral covenant.[19] One problem with this view is that only Abraham provides the animals. If it were truly bilateral, one would expect Abimelech to have provided something to indicate his obligations in the covenant. In fact it may only be bilateral because Abraham has God on his side! He is a sojourning and wandering Bedouin with no historic claim to the land. His covenant partner is the king of that land who has an army to back up his claims. But Abraham has God, and Abimelech knows this from recent personal experience. He demands at least an oath from Abraham. Abraham is in no human position to contest this. But God is with him and so Abimelech's demand that Abraham make a solemn promise of loyalty to him turns into a bilateral covenant.

21:28 Abraham set apart seven ewe lambs from the flock, 21:29 and Abimelech asked Abraham, "What is the meaning of these seven ewe lambs you have set apart by themselves?"

In addition to the animals used in the formation of the covenant, Abraham designated seven other animals. These ewe lambs were proof that the well had been dug by Abraham and that he had water rights to the well. Just as Abimelech had given Abraham 1,000 pieces of silver as proof of Sarah's vindication (Gen 20:16),[20] here Abraham gives Abimelech seven ewe lambs as proof of his claim to the well's water rights. Abraham did this without prior negotiation, and so Abimelech questions the purpose of the extra lambs.

21:30 He replied, "Accept these seven lambs from my hand as a witness that I dug this well."

Abraham directs Abimelech to accept the seven ewe lambs as a witness that he had dug the well and therefore had rights to its water. Abraham takes the initiative based on Abimelech's claim that he had not authorized the seizure of the well. It is not absolutely certain that this is the same well to which Abraham referred in verse 25. Abraham

---

making a covenant ("to cut a covenant") is also an indication of this practice of dividing the animals, walking between the carcasses and calling down a curse upon themselves should they violate the provisions of the covenant.

[19]See the discussion and bibliography in Gordon J. McConville, "בְּרִית," *NIDOTTE*, pp. 747-755.

[20]The disproportion between the two gifts is noteworthy. Abimelech's 1,000 pieces of silver is twenty times the maximum bride price in the Torah (Deut 22:29). Seven ewe lambs does not compare in value.

uses the demonstrative pronoun "this" but does not even use the definite article for the first one. However, it seems most natural to assume that the same well is in view. Unfortunately the seven ewe lambs did not serve as an effective witness for very long. In the time of Isaac there was a continuing struggle over water rights to wells which Isaac's servants had dug in the land of Gerar (Gen 26:17-22). While it is not explicitly recorded, the ongoing narrative assumes that Abimelech accepted Abraham's witness and the water rights which they signified.[21]

21:31 So that place was called Beersheba, because the two men swore an oath there.

This is the first of two narratives which explain the origin of the place name "Beersheba." Here the name is explained by the fact that Abraham and Abimelech swore an oath there. The word Beersheba means "well of seven" or "well of [an] oath." Thus the reference is to the well, and by double entendre, to both the seven ewe lambs and the act of swearing. The Hebrew words for seven (שֶׁבַע, *šeba'*) and "to swear an oath" (שָׁבַע, *šāba'*) are similar in sound. Genesis 26:33, the other account of the origin of the name, explains that after Isaac's servants found water in the well at Beersheba he (Isaac) called it "*Sheba*'" (meaning "seven") resembling the word for oath in Hebrew.

Because of this, the city was named Beersheba up until the time of the audience. While in both cases the meaning of the name is the same, the later passage informs us that Isaac gave the place its name. This is a classic example of what the documentary hypothesis points to as a doublet, indicating that we have two different source documents relating and interpreting a common tradition in slightly different ways. Narratively speaking, it could be that Isaac is being portrayed as merely re-naming the place of the well Beersheba. He did this with other wells once controlled by Abraham which Isaac's servants re-dug (Gen 26:19). If so, hypothesizing a doublet is unnecessary.

21:32 After the treaty had been made at Beersheba, Abimelech and Phicol the commander of his forces returned to the land of the Philistines.

After the treaty had been completed, Abimelech and his general Phicol returned to their land. The verb "returned" is interesting given that Abraham was living in their land. How could they "return" to a land they were technically already in? One answer may be that in a certain sense Abraham now "owns" the land around Beersheba. He certainly

---

[21]Genesis 26:18 records that the Philistines did not refill the wells which were dug in Abraham's time until after his death.

"owns" the water rights to the well. If so, this is a sort of down payment on the promise of the land. Abraham later buys a grave for Sarah. Here he buys a well.

The author refers to the land of Abimelech as the land of the "Philistines." This is technically anachronistic since the Philistines did not enter Palestine until the beginning of the Iron Age, at roughly the same time as Israel's entrance into Canaan.[22] Abimelech ruled the land that in the experience of the audience was called the land of the Philistines. This is similar to the use of Dan in Genesis 14:14.

21:33 Abraham planted a tamarisk tree in Beersheba, and there he called upon the name of the LORD, the Eternal God.

Having obtained the water rights to a well and the more permanent sort of residence which such rights seem to imply, Abraham gives thanks to the LORD. The planting of a tree implies hope for a long sojourn, long enough to see the tree grow to a mature size. On other occasions Abraham had set up his tent near oak trees (Gen 12:6; 13:18; 18:1). The tree is a tamarisk, common in the desert region, south of Canaan.

Abraham worshiped by calling "upon the name of the LORD." Even the mere rights to water from a well which he had dug contains a germ of the promise of the land.

Abraham's worship referred to the LORD as the Eternal God, אֵל עֹלָם ('ēl 'ōlām). God's faithfulness is not just in the short term, but in the long term. The planting of the tree near a well, a symbol of ongoing life (Ps 1:3), indicates Abraham's confidence in that fact. That longevity is emphasized by the name used for the LORD: he is the eternal God.

21:34 And Abraham stayed in the land of the Philistines for a long time.

Abraham lived as a sojourner (וַיָּגָר, wayyāgār) in the land of the Philistines. He did not own the land and was not a member of the nation. But he sojourned there for a long time, an indication of the eventual fulfillment of the promise of the land. Abraham at least has a stable existence in the land and a peace treaty with the king of part of the land. The guarantee of water rights, so important for a herdsman like Abraham, is another indication that God's promise could be and was trusted by Abraham.

---

[22]See Lawrence A. Sinclair, "Philistines," *EBD*, pp. 1050-1051.

GENESIS 22

E. THE MATURING OF THE FAITH(FULNESS) OF ABRAHAM (22:1-19)

This famous passage, known as the Akedah[1] in Jewish tradition, is the highpoint of the Abrahamic narrative. While Abraham continues to appear in the ensuing chapters, this is the last time that God speaks with him, and in this passage we see the final securing of the promise and the flowering of Abraham's faith.

Separated from its wider cultural and biblical context the text has recently been read to endorse a monstrous God who demands child sacrifice, something to be abhorred by ethical people of any persuasion today.[2] But that is a facile and flawed reading of this text for at least three reasons.

First, it fails to take seriously the historical context. Other gods worshiped by those living around Abraham and perhaps even the gods which Abraham himself once worshiped sometimes required child sacrifice.[3] God asks Abraham to show the same commitment to him that those who worshiped false gods did to their gods.

Second, such readings fail to read this text within the context of the wider Abrahamic narrative where Abraham has repeatedly struggled with the tendency to use human schemes to see to it that the promise was fulfilled. This seems to have been the motivation for allowing Lot to go with him in chapter 12 as well as his embracing of Sarai's plan to have a surrogate son through Hagar in chapter 16. Abram had initially laughed at the suggestion that Sarah, renamed though she be, could bear a son at age 90 (Gen 17:17). But here Abraham has given up taking responsibility for God's promise. His son "He will laugh" (Isaac) came through

---

[1]Lit. "the binding" from the verb וַיַּעֲקֹד, *wayya'ăqōd*, "he bound" in v. 9.

[2]D.J.A. Clines, *What Does Eve Do to Help? and Other Readerly Questions to the Old Testament* (Sheffield: Sheffield, 1990) p. 50, calls it "the insane command to slaughter the promised son."

[3]Brian B. Schmidt, "Molech," *EDB*, pp. 912-914.

God's action. Abraham has come to the point where he recognizes that since it is God's promise, it is God's responsibility (and not his) to see to it that the promise is fulfilled. If God chooses to take back the son which He has provided, that is God's decision. Abraham has grown in trust to the point where he gives up all human pretensions to having the ability to do God's work for him and the responsibility to do it.

Third, such readings fail to recognize that the original and canonical audience had received the law which had prohibited the sacrifice of children to false gods in no uncertain terms (Lev 18.21; 20.2; Deut 18.10). The original audience knew that God had no intention of allowing a child, much less the long-awaited miraculously conceived promised son, to actually be sacrificed. The author tells them this in verse 1. The modern or postmodern reaction is a visceral one that makes no real effort to understand the text but sets the reader above it, judging its words by decontextualizing them.

1. Divine Testing of Abraham's Faith(fulness) (22:1-2)

22:1 Some time later God tested Abraham. He said to him, "Abraham!" "Here I am," he replied.
Because of the extraordinary nature of the test and the moral qualms which it would raise in the original and later audiences, the reader is informed first of all that what is to follow is only a test. God never intends that Abraham actually follow through with it. In some unknown way God speaks to Abraham by name. He responds readily, "Here I am." This is the first of three instances of this expression in the chapter (cf. vv. 7,11). In each case Abraham quite readily responds to a question. In this passage it is God's speech. Later it is Isaac's asking Abraham where the sacrificial animal is. Finally it is Abraham's response to the angel of the LORD telling him not to harm his son.

22:2 Then God said, "Take your son, your only son, Isaac, whom you love, and go to the region of Moriah. Sacrifice him there as a burnt offering on one of the mountains I will tell you about."
The instruction translated as an imperative "take!" in NIV is not a simple imperative, although it is difficult to find an elegant way to translate its exact nuance into English. It appends the Hebrew particle used when asking permission (נָא, *nā'*) to the imperative, which softens it a bit. It is as though God said to Abraham, "Would you please sacrifice your son."[4] The wording of this verse appears to be a deliberate echo[5]

---

[4]Moberly, *Bible, Theology, and Faith*, p. 78.
[5]For what follows see Turner, *Announcements of Plot*, pp. 87-88.

of the LORD's initial promise to Abram in Genesis 12:1-3. Abraham is commanded to take his son and "go." The Hebrew phrase underlying this (וְלֶךְ־לְךָ, wᵊlek-lᵊkā) was last used in Genesis 12:1. In some sense these two instances of this command begin and end the Abrahamic story. Crenshaw titles these two complimentary passages, "A Son Sacrifices His Father (Gen 12)" and "A Father Sacrifices His Beloved Son (Gen 22)."[6] Abraham gave up his past in leaving his father under divine command. In this text, in obeying another divine command, he gives up his potential future.

The elaborate description of Isaac slows the narrative down and focuses on just what it is that God asks Abraham to do. Isaac is first of all his son. He is not a servant or a relative but his son. Secondly, he is his only son. This may imply that Ishmael is no longer part of the picture. Conversely it could mean that Isaac is the only son of the promise. His name is Isaac (he will laugh). His name recalls the joyous celebration which Abraham and Sarah had at his birth. Long after merely human chances of having a child had faded, God had blessed them with Isaac. He made them laugh. And then Isaac is the son whom Abraham loved. With each additional description the depth of pain that Abraham was to face grows greater.

He is to go to the region of Moriah, near Jerusalem (2 Chr 3:1). He is to sacrifice his son, his only son, his Isaac, his beloved son, as a burnt offering on one of the mountains there. The audience descends from Isaac. If Abraham had been successful, they would never have lived. In some sense or other their very lives are at stake in this story.

Second Chronicles 3:1 informs us that Moriah was the mountain where Solomon built the temple. For the canonical reader Abraham's near sacrifice of Isaac pointed forward to the sacrificial system which the LORD later revealed to Israel. The sacrificial system in which Israel participated was thus in some sense a replacement, inadequate though it be, for the sacrifice of Isaac. Isaac was spared and with him all of his descendants. The sacrifices which were later offered at the Tabernacle and Temple were in some sense or other replacements for those who deserved to lose their very lives.

2. Abraham's Obedience (22:3-6a)

22:3 Early the next morning Abraham got up and saddled his donkey. He took with him two of his servants and his son Isaac. When he had

---

[6]James Crenshaw, "Journey into Oblivion: A Structural Analysis of Gn. 22:1-19," *Soundings* 58 (1975): 243-256, cited in Turner, *Announcements of Plot*, p. 87.

cut enough wood for the burnt offering, he set out for the place God had told him about.

Of all the days in his life that Abraham might have chosen to sleep in, this would be the one. Instead we are shocked that he got up early in the morning. The narrative pace slows to indicate the solemnity of the occasion. The detail gives us time to ponder and wonder just what was in Abraham's mind, in Isaac's mind, in the servants' minds. He saddles his donkey and we wonder what he is thinking. He calls the young men and then Isaac. Next[7] he cut the wood for the burnt offering. Finally he set out. We do not know exactly how old Isaac was in this narrative. The servants are referred to as "young men," as is Isaac (נַעַר, *na'ar*; cf. vv. 3,12). Ishmael was over 13 and Joseph over 17 when they were referred to as young men (Gen 21:12; 37:2; Exod 2:6).

22:4 On the third day Abraham looked up and saw the place in the distance.

On the third day of the journey from Beersheba Abraham, his son, and his servants were close enough to Moriah to see it in the distance. His young men were not to follow. Perhaps Abraham feared that they would try to stop him. Perhaps he knew that this was to be a private event between God and him.

22:5 He said to his servants, "Stay here with the donkey while I and the boy go over there. We will worship and then we will come back to you."

Abraham spoke to his "young men" (NIV "servants"), directing them to remain with the donkey that presumably had been carrying the wood and other supplies. The same word used to describe the young men is used of Isaac in this verse. This gives us some clue as to the age of Isaac. The Hebrew word *na'ar* has a flexible meaning spanning ages that we would more sharply differentiate. Shechem (Gen 37:2), who raped Dinah, is described with the term. But it can also, albeit rarely, refer to an infant (Moses).

Abraham tells his young men that he and Isaac are going to worship and that both of them will return. It is not clear what to make of this. Is Abraham hiding what he is about to do or expressing confidence that in some way or another God will bring back both he and Isaac?[8]

22:6a Abraham took the wood for the burnt offering and placed it on his son Isaac, and he himself carried the fire and the knife.

---

[7]The NIV seems to ignore the *waw*-consecutive here.

[8]Hebrews 11:19 seems to suggest this.

Once again the narrative slows down to give details which perhaps are designed to lead the reader to ponder the gravity of the situation. Instead of summarizing or allowing the reader to assume what exactly happened, we are given the details. The wood for the burnt offering is loaded from an animal onto Isaac, who is called "his son." This detail recalls the poignancy of the scene. The sacrificial victim is to carry the wood on which he would be sacrificed. Abraham carries the means for completing the sacrifice: the fire and the knife.

3. Isaac's Involvement in the Test (22:6b-8)

22:6b As the two of them went on together, 22:7 Isaac spoke up and said to his father Abraham, "Father?" "Yes, my son?" Abraham replied. "The fire and wood are here," Isaac said, "but where is the lamb for the burnt offering?"

Isaac now asks the obvious question which the young men were perhaps too reticent to ask. The pathos is increased by the way the narrator refers to Isaac and Abraham and the way they refer to each other. The narrator tells us that Isaac spoke to "his father." Isaac then actually used the word "father" in his speech to Abraham. Abraham responds with, "Here am I."[9] This is a narrative about a father and a beloved son, and the narrator is at pains to remind the reader of this fact. Isaac sees the fire and wood, but they have no animal. How will they get an animal? There is no indication that Abraham carried a bow with which to shoot one.

We do not know how old Isaac is. He is obviously old enough to carry the wood and to logically reason and ask reasonable questions. Is he old enough to resist being sacrificed? We do not know. It may be that the omission is a deliberate narrative device to lead the reader to ask the question and thus further engage in reflection on the situation.

22:8 Abraham answered, "God himself will provide the lamb for the burnt offering, my son." And the two of them went on together.

Abraham addresses Isaac once again as his "son." He tells him that "God will see to it, a lamb for the burnt offering." This evidently satisfies Isaac as they continue on without further conversation. The contemporary reader would like to know more about the personal dynamics involved. What was Abraham's tone of voice in these words? What was Isaac's nonverbal reaction? With the modern idealization of childhood we are desperate for answers. We are tempted to anachronism.

---

[9]The NIV paraphrases here and loses the connection with v. 1.

Our spoken or unspoken reaction can easily be, "This is child abuse of the most outrageous kind!" But this is the biblical world[10] and not our own, and such questions are not answered.

This poignant moment is highlighted by the repetition of the phrase "the two of them went on together" in verses 6b and 8. The conversation which is so packed with pathos is only a moment during the trip up the mountain. As soon as it is over, they resume the trip together. This may be a subtle hint that Isaac is aware of the situation at some level.

It is interesting that Abraham is quoted as saying "God"[11] will provide, while in verse 14 below Abraham calls the place "the LORD"[12] will provide. While this is technically anachronistic since the name of the LORD was apparently not revealed until the time of Moses, the audience would realize that the more generic name for God was actually manifested in a special revelation to Moses and Israel as the LORD.[13]

4. Abraham (and Isaac?) Pass the Test (22:9-11)

22:9 When they reached the place God had told him about, Abraham built an altar there and arranged the wood on it. He bound his son Isaac and laid him on the altar, on top of the wood.

As at other times in his life, Abraham builds an altar for worship and sacrifice. The narrative continues its slow pace by describing the details. Abraham arranged the wood on the altar. The next word "he bound" occurs only here in the Hebrew Bible. We had heard nothing of any rope before. We also do not know whether Isaac is strong enough to resist or whether he complies willingly. It could be argued either way. Perhaps the rope helped Isaac to comply by holding him down. The fact that Abraham binds Isaac argues against his complying with complete willingness,

---

[10]John Howard Yoder ["If Abraham Is Our Father," in *The Original Revolution* (Scottdale, PA: Herald Press, 1971), p. 102]: "Modern Western personalism had equipped us for a deep sentimental attachment of the father to the son; so that for a modern father to take the life of his son, in any state of mind except a drunken rage, is unthinkable. Thus we ask traditionally what it is supposed to tell us about the awfulness or the sovereignty or the paradoxical character of God that He would ask man to do something so contrary to his deepest nature and drives. But again we modernize. This kind of sentimental attachment of father to son, if it existed at all in the patriarchal age, can hardly have been viscerally as powerful as it is for us." My thanks to John Nugent for reminding me of this passage from Yoder.

[11]אֱלֹהִים (*'ĕlōhîm*) the generic word for "God."

[12]יהוה (*YHWH*) the name of Israel's God revealed to Moses in Exodus 3.

[13]Moberly, *Bible, Theology, and Faith*, p. 96.

although it is impossible to be certain. Isaac is placed upon the altar on the wood like a sacrificial animal. The narrative tension rises.

22:10 Then he reached out his hand and took the knife to slay his son.
The narrative reaches its summit as Abraham reaches for the knife to slay his son. For the imagined audience their very existence as a nation hangs in the balance. Should Abraham succeed in killing his son there would be no Israel. And yet amazingly all this is done in willing obedience to the command of God. God had given the son through miraculous means after several attempts by Abraham and Sarah to produce an heir by their own devices. Here Abraham gives up on such pretensions. The child is God's gift, and he is God's to take away. But the narrator indicates the pathos by describing Isaac not as "the young man" or "boy" but as "his son."

While imaginative depictions of this scene portray Abraham as having the knife raised, the text merely mentions that Abraham had the knife in his hand. The word used for knife in this passage (מַאֲכֶלֶת, *ma'ăkeleth*) is an unusual one, only used elsewhere in narrative of the cutting up of the concubine's body in Judges 19:29. The intertextual echo may be deliberate, but it seems more likely that the author of Judges is echoing Genesis rather than vice versa.

22:11 But the angel of the LORD called out to him from heaven, "Abraham! Abraham!" "Here I am," he replied.
The angel of the LORD once again speaks for God at a crucial moment. The repetition and the differences with the original commission to sacrifice Isaac are instructive (see chart below). In both passages the deity uses Abraham's name and Abraham responds "Here I am." But in the second message Abraham's name is used twice, it is the angel of the LORD rather than God who speaks, and the angel "called out from heaven" rather than merely spoke. This is probably a way of demonstrating the urgency of the second address. Clearly the angel of the LORD is God's spokesperson. He wanted there to be no mistake, and so he calls out and repeats Abraham's name. Abraham is ever-ready to respond to the divine word.

22:1	22:11
Some time later God tested Abraham. He said to him, "Abraham!" "Here I am," he replied.	But the angel of the LORD called out to him from heaven, "Abraham! Abraham!" "Here I am," he replied.

According to at least one Medieval Jewish tradition,[14] Abraham actu-

---

[14]Bruce Zuckerman in *Job the Silent* (New York: Oxford University Press, 1991),

ally did kill Isaac only to see him miraculously restored to life in front of
his own eyes. It is extremely unlikely that the narrator intended such a
meaning or that the original or canonical audience read it that way.

5. Isaac Is Spared through the LORD's Provision (22:12-14)

**22:12 "Do not lay a hand on the boy," he said. "Do not do anything to
him. Now I know that you fear God, because you have not withheld
from me your son, your only son."**
The angel of the LORD tells Abraham not to harm Isaac in any way.
He again uses the term "young man" (הַנַּעַר, *hanna'ar*)[15] to refer to him.
The angel speaks for God and even as though he were God. He tells
Abraham that now Abraham's fear of God is confirmed. This would seem
to imply that up until now there was some doubt about it. By Abraham's
willingness to give up the child that God had given him, we see the flowering and maturing of Abraham's faith. Abraham's actions demonstrate
that he has finally come to the realization that since it is God's promise,
it is also God's responsibility to fulfill that promise. He does not need
Abraham's help. Abraham did not try to hold back his son, his only son,
and that action demonstrated the flowering of his faith.

The phrase "Now I know" has elicited much discussion in recent
times because it seems to imply that there was something that God did
not know. It would seem to imply some limitation on God's absolute
foreknowledge. One must be cautious of building too much off of one
text. However, one way of explaining this text is the following: Abraham
did not actually fear God in the sense meant by the angel of the LORD
until he gave up his son Isaac. The meaning of the phrase "fear God" can

---

p. 16, notes the 12th-century poem of Rabbi Ephraim ben Jacob about the
Akedah:
> He [Abraham] made haste, he pinned him [Isaac] down with his knees
> He made his two arms strong.
>
> With steady hands he slaughtered him according to the rite,
> Full right was the slaughter
>
> Down upon him fell the resurrecting dew, and he revived.
> (The Father) seized him (then) to slaughter him once more.
> Scripture bear witness! Well grounded is the fact;
> And the Lord called Abraham, even a second time from heaven.

This attests to a theory of a resurrection of Isaac. Hebrews 11:19 informs us
that the hope of Isaac's resurrection enabled Abraham to obey the commandment to sacrifice Isaac.

[15]The NIV translates this as "boy."

often cause confusion for contemporary readers. In texts like this one, to "fear" God is not the emotion of terror which we experience when facing something threatening. Moberly helpfully points out the parallel passage in Exodus 20:20 where Moses explains that the Ten Commandments are given to test Israel so the fear of God would be on them and they would not sin by disobeying his commandments.[16] In other words, to fear God is to obey his commandments. Abraham has feared God by obeying his commandment, just as the nation which descended from Abraham would fear God by obeying the commandments given to them. It was only after Abraham's obedience to a challenging commandment that he could be called someone who feared God. The angel only knows that Abraham fears God when he becomes a fearer of God by offering up Isaac. He could not have known this before this time because Abraham had not yet become one who fears God in this sense.

The angel of the LORD says that Abraham had not withheld his son from "me," i.e., the angel of the LORD. This shows the closeness of the relationship between the angel of the LORD and God himself. While it is too much to read this as though the angel of the LORD is the preincarnate son of God, it is striking how the angel can speak as though he is God himself.

James 2:20-23 refers to this passage to demonstrate that Abraham's initial faith, attested in Genesis 15:6, was only fulfilled when he was willing to offer Isaac back to God as a sacrifice. The highpoint of the Abrahamic narrative, ironically, follows directly after chapter 20 which is the low point.

22:13 Abraham looked up and there in a thicket he saw a ram caught by its horns. He went over and took the ram and sacrificed it as a burnt offering instead of his son.

Abraham had assured Isaac that God would "see to" the providing of a lamb for the burnt offering. In the event God provided a ram, not a lamb. The ram's horns had somehow got entangled in a thicket and it was waiting there behind Abraham to be used as the sacrificial animal instead of his son. The sacrificial animal was to serve as a substitute for the actual sacrifice of the human person. The imagined audience would take note that their own very existence only came about as a result of God's grace. The sacrificial system in which they participated was founded upon the substitution of a ram for the human victim.

22:14 So Abraham called that place The LORD Will Provide. And to this day it is said, "On the mountain of the LORD it will be provided."

---

[16]Moberly, *Bible, Theology, and Faith*, pp. 80-84.

Abraham had assured Isaac that God would provide. When he does provide, he gives God praise by naming the place, "The LORD[17] will provide."

The narrator's explanatory comment, "On the mountain of the LORD it will be provided" seems to come from the time when Jerusalem had been established as the place of the temple. In the sacrificial system the LORD had provided for Israel a way to sustain and renew a relationship with him. By linking the sacrifice of a ram in place of Isaac to the Temple sacrifices there seems to be an indication that at least some of the Temple sacrifices were regarded as substitutionary. Animals were sacrificed as substitutes for human sacrifices. Abraham praised the LORD for providing a substitute sacrifice for the child given to him as part of the LORD's promises.

The verb translated "will provide" is more literally translated, "will be seen" and is a technical term in the niphal stem for God's appearance in times of special revelation.[18] The phrase "to this day" implies that the intended audience in their current experience knew of the statement about the mountain. Second Chronicles 3:1 informs us that the temple mount was in fact Mount Moriah. This could be a later explanatory gloss by a scribe who is informing the audience of how this event in the time of Abraham laid the foundation for what later happened there through the Temple sacrifices. There is no evidence that the Tabernacle, unlike the Temple, ever rested on a mountain.

The LORD is the focus of Abraham's statement. He saw to it that Abraham and Sarah had a son. He saw to it that a ram was caught in the thicket. He saw to it that this happened on the mountain where the Temple would later be built. As Christians we know that he saw to it that his son died on a cross for the sins of all humanity not far from this very mountain.

---

[17]Interestingly, while Abraham had referred to the deity by the generic word "God," in naming the place he uses the specific covenant name of God, the LORD (יהוה typically vocalized as *Yahweh*). Again this sort of variation in divine names is used as evidence of underlying sources in the composition of the Pentateuch. Typically when the actual name "LORD" occurs in the mouth of the Patriarchs scholars commonly assume that at the very least this is technically anachronistic since Exodus 6:2-3 ("God also said to Moses, "I am the LORD. I appeared to Abraham, to Isaac and to Jacob as God Almighty, but by my name the LORD I did not make myself known to them") seems to read most naturally as implying that the actual name was not revealed to them.

[18]Brevard S. Childs, *Biblical Theology of the Old and New Testaments* (Philadelphia: Fortress, 1992), p. 327.

6. The Promise Sealed and Reaffirmed (22:15-19)

22:15 The angel of the LORD called to Abraham from heaven a second time 22:16 and said, "I swear by myself, declares the LORD, that because you have done this and have not withheld your son, your only son, 22:17 I will surely bless you and make your descendants as numerous as the stars in the sky and as the sand on the seashore. Your descendants will take possession of the cities of their enemies, 22:18 and through your offspring all nations on earth will be blessed, because you have obeyed me."

Exactly why there is a pause between the two statements of the angel of the LORD to Abraham is not entirely clear. Perhaps the angel waited for Abraham to complete the offering of the ram on the altar. When Abraham had done so, he had completed his obedience. Once again the angel speaks as though he is the LORD himself. The LORD (through the angel) swears by himself because there is no one greater by whom he may swear.

Once again reference is made to Abraham's giving of his son, his only son. This time his action is tied to a reaffirmation of the promise. The very last recorded words of God to Abraham repeat the promise in an even more emphatic and perhaps less conditional form. God's promise to bless Abraham now becomes "surely bless."[19] The two images of the number of descendants (sand and stars) are combined for the first time, as though to emphasize a new certainty or comprehensiveness in the promise.

A new element is even added. God promises that Abraham's descendants will take possession of the "gates"[20] of their enemies. In the ancient world the gate of a city was not merely an entrance to it. At the city gate the elders met to hold court.[21] Those who controlled the gate controlled the legal system. The corrupt legal systems of the land of Canaan would be placed under the control of Abraham's descendants who would ideally use the legal system to protect the vulnerable. In other words the promise which has served as the thematic center of the entire Abrahamic narrative is now made more emphatic and expanded. The maturing of Abraham's faith has resulted in an even greater promise.

---

[19]The emphatic verbal construction, infinitive absolute followed by the same verb in the imperfect, is used here.

[20]The NIV's "cities" is based upon the fact that only cities have gates.

[21]Josh 20:4; Ruth 4:1,10,11; 2 Sam 15:2; Deut 16:18; 17:5; 21:19; 22:15,24; 25:7.

The final element of the reaffirmed promise is the implications of the promise for non-Abrahamic nations. All of them will "bless themselves"[22] through Abraham's descendants. This blessing for all nations will happen, the angel says, as a result and reward (עֵקֶב אֲשֶׁר, 'ēqeb 'ăšer) for Abraham's willingness to obey the ultimate commandment to give back to God the beloved son whom God had given him.

While systematic theologians often regard the covenant with Abraham as unconditional from the start, this is difficult to square with what the text of Genesis actually says. The promise may become unconditional, but only because of the obedience of Abraham. Would the covenant have become unconditional if Abraham's faith had not blossomed as it did? The text of Genesis does not address this question but there is no evidence to support such an interpretation.

22:19 Then Abraham returned to his servants, and they set off together for Beersheba. And Abraham stayed in Beersheba.

Having received a striking reaffirmation, expansion, and deepening of the promise, Abraham returns to his young men for the trip south to Beersheba. Strikingly Isaac is not mentioned as returning with them. It could be that we are to presume Isaac's presence. Hadn't Abraham promised his young men that he and Isaac ("we") would return? Another possibility is that Isaac did not return with Abraham at this time. Perhaps he was old enough to travel on his own. Like so many of the questions which we have about the interpersonal dynamics in this story, we receive no definitive answer.

What, if any, effect was there on the relationship between Abraham and Isaac? We are left to wonder about such things. Abraham travels with his young men back to Beersheba where he continues to live. The word "stayed" is usually translated "dwelled" (יָשַׁב, yāšab) and implies a more permanent form of residence than the word "sojourn" (גּוּר, gûr). With a newly secure, renewed, and expanded promise and with water rights and treaties with the local inhabitants, Abraham has come a long way from his original departure from Haran.

---

[22]The Hebrew is a hithpael form here which is ordinarily a reflexive. The NIV's passive, in keeping with its Calvinistic tendency, presumes that the original niphal in Genesis 12:3 should override the ordinary reflexive meaning of the hithpael. See the discussion of this matter above at Genesis 12:3.

F. POTENTIAL MARRIAGE PARTNERS
FOR ABRAHAM'S DESCENDANTS (22:20-24)

One of the great concerns for both the original and canonical audiences is that the nation which descended from Abraham would compromise its faithfulness to Yahweh through intermarriage with people who did not share the faith commitments of Israel (Deut 7:3-4). The question then naturally arises, how did/would the forefathers of the nation deal with this issue? Did they intermarry with the Canaanites when they lived in the Promised Land? This genealogical note anticipates the ideal solution to this problem. The patriarchs would send their sons back to the same extended family which Abraham had left behind when he originally came to Canaan. But this requires that there would be suitable marriage partners within that extended family. The multiplication of the family back in Paddan Aram where Haran was located makes such a solution possible. Rebekah, the future wife of Isaac, is specifically mentioned.

22:20 Some time later Abraham was told, "Milcah is also a mother; she has borne sons to your brother Nahor:
This text demonstrates that there was some form of continuing communication between Abraham and his extended family back in Haran. This may have been because Milcah also took a long time to conceive or communication between the two family groups was cut off for some time. Abraham has been in the Promised Land for at least 35 years (assuming that Isaac was at least 10 when he was nearly sacrificed at Moriah). We do not know how Abraham came to this knowledge. He was simply "told."

22:21 Uz the firstborn, Buz his brother, Kemuel (the father of Aram), 22:22 Kesed, Hazo, Pildash, Jidlaph and Bethuel."
There were eight sons born to Milcah in all. Uz is specifically mentioned as the firstborn because often genealogies were not given in the order of birth but in order of significance for the continuing narrative. This had probably been the case with Abram and Nahor's genealogy. Uz is the first mentioned descendant of Aram, a descendant of Shem in Genesis 10. The name also occurs in the genealogy of Esau (Gen 36:28) and as a place name in the book of Job (1:1). Buz, for some reason, is mentioned as Uz's brother in a list in which all eight are brothers. It may be that he was a twin of Uz. Buz is only elsewhere mentioned in Jeremiah 25:23 where he is one of the princes of Arabia along with Dedan and Tema. It is unclear whether the same Buz is meant. Kemuel is a name found elsewhere in the genealogies of Ephraim and Levi. His son

Aram may be named after the Aram in the genealogy of Shem who gave his name to the Arameans. Kesed, Hazo, Pildash, and Jidlaph are found only here.

Interestingly Bethuel is mentioned last. While he was not the first-born, he was not necessarily the youngest either. This may be a way of making a smooth transition to the next section where his daughter Rebekah will play an important role in the ensuing narrative.

22:23 Bethuel became the father of Rebekah. Milcah bore these eight sons to Abraham's brother Nahor.

Bethuel evidently was listed last among the sons of Nahor because he was the father of **Rebekah**, Isaac's wife. **Milcah**, the daughter of Abraham's and Nahor's long dead older brother Haran, was fertile. This ensured that there would be an extended family from which the patriarchs could find wives. Thus they would not be forced into marrying Canaanite women who did not share their commitment to God. Modern notions of incest must not be read back into this text.

22:24 His concubine, whose name was Reumah, also had sons: Tebah, Gaham, Tahash and Maacah.

Like Abraham, Nahor also had children through a concubine, **Reumah**. These four sons of the concubine, together with the eight born by his wife Milcah, produced twelve in all, parallel to the promised family of Ishmael and of Abraham's grandson Jacob. The latter also had eight sons by his "legitimate" wives and four by their concubines. The names of three of the four sons of **Reumah**, **Tebah**, **Gaham**, and **Tahash**, occur only in this passage. The last, **Maacah**, is given to both men and women and is a common name in the Old Testament.

GENESIS 23

G. THE DEATH AND BURIAL OF SARAH (23:1-20)

With the death of Sarah, Abraham lost his life's partner. She is also honored in her death as the matriarch of the nation of Israel. In terms of the plot of Genesis, Sarah's death makes it certain that only Isaac can be heir to the promise since Sarah will have no more children. Abraham could, and in fact did, have more. But the narrative of Sarah's death, or at least her burial, is tied to the promise in another way. While Abraham pays a high price for her grave, in this narrative he finally obtains permanent rights of ownership over a small piece of the Promised Land. This passage focuses all hope of fulfillment of the promise on Isaac, the only son of Sarah. This gives a sort of down payment on the promise to Abraham that his descendants will one day inherit the entire land of Canaan.

1. Sarah's Death (23:1-2)

23:1 Sarah lived to be a hundred and twenty-seven years old.
Since the promised child was to come from Sarah, her death makes it finally certain that Isaac is the only hope for the promise. Abraham has other sons through Keturah after Sarah's death, but only Isaac can be the promised heir. Sarah lived 37 years after the birth of Isaac and therefore saw him grow into a mature man, although he was not yet married when she died. Isaac married at age 40 which is extraordinarily late for an ancient Near Eastern man. The long life of Sarah shows God's blessing on her.

23:2 She died at Kiriath Arba (that is, Hebron) in the land of Canaan, and Abraham went to mourn for Sarah and to weep over her.
The arrangement at Beersheba with Abimelech evidently did not last since Abraham lived at Hebron when Sarah died. The old name for Hebron, Kiriath Arba, is given. The audience is reminded of the obvious, that Hebron was in the land of Canaan. The point may be to emphasize that Sarah, the matriarch of the nation, died in the Promised

Land, not outside of it. It is difficult to know just exactly what to infer from the fact that Abraham "went" to mourn over Sarah. Did he have to travel? Or is this just a way to slow the narrative down to show the importance of this event. The mourning was not merely something formal. He also wept over her. She was not merely a means to an end as she seemed to be earlier in the Abrahamic narrative.

2. Abraham Asks Permission to Buy a Grave (23:3-9)

23:3 Then Abraham rose from beside his dead wife and spoke to the Hittites. He said, 23:4 "I am an alien and a stranger among you. Sell me some property for a burial site here so I can bury my dead."

Abraham had evidently been with Sarah at her death, or at least he had spent some significant time sitting beside her dead body. He spoke to the Hittites who were the specific people occupying the area near Hebron. The Hittites mentioned here have no clear connection with the more famous Hittites of ancient Anatolia (Turkey). Here they control part of the hill country in what was later called the tribe of Judah. Abraham acknowledges that his residence is only temporary. He is an "alien" (גֵר, gēr) and a "sojourner" (תּוֹשָׁב, tôšāb), both terms implying transitory residence. With such a social status he has no inherited or other rights to the land. He therefore asks for the opportunity to buy a burial site that would become his permanent possession.

23:5 The Hittites replied to Abraham, 23:6 "Sir, listen to us. You are a mighty prince among us. Bury your dead in the choicest of our tombs. None of us will refuse you his tomb for burying your dead."

The Hittites respond readily to Abraham's request. Their address to Abraham shows deference and politeness. Whether it is to be understood as being applied a little too thickly is difficult for contemporary interpreters to determine. They address Abraham as "Lord" (אֲדֹנִי, 'ădōnî) and tell him that he is regarded as a "mighty prince"[1] among them. They offer Abraham the opportunity to use one of their tombs as the burial place for Sarah's body. They even give Abraham the right to choose the best tomb assuring him that no one would refuse his request.

It is difficult to determine whether this offer should be understood literally. Whether such a burial in a Hittite tomb would have been culturally acceptable to Abraham in this situation is also difficult to determine. The Hittites may well have known that accepting such an offer

---

[1]The Hebrew נְשִׂיא אֱלֹהִים (nᵉśî' 'ĕlōhîm) literally means "prince of God" or "the gods." It is often used, as here, of a powerful person or force.

would not be a serious option for Abraham. Conversely, they may not have understood why Abraham would have found it objectionable. The original and canonical readers, of course, were well aware of the problems associated with pagan burial customs for those who were called to be faithful to the LORD alone.[2]

23:7 Then Abraham rose and bowed down before the people of the land, the Hittites.

Abraham responds to their politeness. He bowed down before the people of the land, a sign of respect. Once again the original audience would have noted the contrast between these Hittites[3] in the time of Abraham and the later people with whom Israel had to deal when they entered the Promised Land (Deut 7:1; Josh 11:3).

23:8 He said to them, "If you are willing to let me bury my dead, then listen to me and intercede with Ephron son of Zohar on my behalf 23:9 so he will sell me the cave of Machpelah, which belongs to him and is at the end of his field. Ask him to sell it to me for the full price as a burial site among you."

While Abraham shows deference and respect for the Hittites in his response, he does not take their offer seriously. It may not have been intended to be taken literally. He asks not to use an already existing tomb, but for intercession with the owner of a particular tomb he would like to purchase. The word "intercede" is interesting. Does this imply that he may not be entirely willing or, is this a conventional ancient Near Eastern form of politeness? The owner is one Ephron son of Zohar. Abraham wants to buy the cave of Machpelah, which Ephron owned. The exact cave is specified by noting that it is at the end of his field. Abraham wants to buy it at its full purchase price and obtain full rights to it as his possession. The expressed willingness of the Hittites to help Abraham in his time of grief by offering a spot in one of their existing tombs becomes an opportunity for Abraham, the alien sojourner, to actually purchase a small piece of the Promised Land. The Hittites had said nothing about Abraham purchasing land from them.

---

[2]P.S. Johnson, "Life, Disease and Death," *DOTP*, p. 536: "Consultation of the dead is repeatedly and strictly forbidden and its practitioners were to be executed by stoning (Lev. 19:31; 20:6, 27; Deut. 18:11). This is one practice for which Canaan's inhabitants were condemned. Israel, by contrast, was to follow Yahweh's guidance (Deut. 18:14-15). There is growing extrabiblical evidence that among Israel's neighbors the dead were revered, consulted and appeased, and these practices were a constant temptation to Israel."

[3]The NIV translates the Heb. חֵת־בְּנֵי (*bᵊnê-ḥēth*) as "Hittites," although in almost all other texts the word for "Hittites" is הַחִתִּי (*haḥittî*).

3. Abraham Pays the High Price for the Grave (23:10-16)

23:10 Ephron the Hittite was sitting among his people and he replied to Abraham in the hearing of all the Hittites who had come to the gate of his city. 23:11 "No, my lord," he said. "Listen to me; I give you the field, and I give you the cave that is in it. I give it to you in the presence of my people. Bury your dead."

We now learn that Ephron was present during this conversation. It was held at the city gate where legal disputes and other matters of law were resolved in the ancient world. The narrator keeps reminding the readers that this was a negotiation with Hittites. Ephron is identified as a Hittite, and the readers are reminded that the conversation took place in the hearing of all the Hittites who were there that day. Ephron addresses Abraham respectfully as "my lord" as had the other Hittites. On the surface he offers to "give" Abraham the field attached to the cave along with the cave which Abraham requested. He seems to offer to "give" it to Abraham in a legal way, witnessed to by those Hittites who were present. Whether Ephron in fact is actually "giving" the land to Abraham without an expected and understood *quid pro quo* is hard to determine with certainty. This may be a polite way of offering to sell the cave, and he adds the field into the negotiation even though Abraham did not request it.

23:12 Again Abraham bowed down before the people of the land 23:13 and he said to Ephron in their hearing, "Listen to me, if you will. I will pay the price of the field. Accept it from me so I can bury my dead there."

Once again Abraham respectfully bows before the people of the land, emphasizing yet again his reverent attitude. His words are said publicly ("in their hearing") in order to ensure their legal standing. Abraham refuses the offer of the land as a gift, if in fact it was actually a gift. Abraham commits to paying the price of the field, which included the cave. He accepts Ephron's terms and includes the field in the purchase. Since the price has not been negotiated Abraham agrees to pay whatever price Ephron names. He asks only Ephron's commitment to sell it to him. Doing this publicly in a social situation in which written records were scarce may have been a way of ensuring the legal validity of the transaction.

23:14 Ephron answered Abraham, 23:15 "Listen to me, my lord; the land is worth four hundred shekels of silver, but what is that between me and you? Bury your dead."

Ephron responded publicly to Abraham as he desired, again using the respectful "my lord." The entire male population who was there that day could testify to the agreement. His price is 400 shekels of silver. Although Ephron pretends otherwise, the price is probably an exorbitant one. Israel's king Omri bought the hill of Samaria on which he built his capital for only 6,000 shekels (two talents; 1 Kgs 16.24). David purchased a threshing floor for 50 shekels (2 Sam 24:24), and Jeremiah purchased a field (admittedly during a siege) for seventeen shekels[4] (Jer 32:9). Ephron makes light of the price as though it is insignificant between two wealthy men like him and Abraham. The important thing is that Abraham buries his dead.[5] It is hard not to feel that, in rather subtle ways, Ephron is taking advantage of Abraham during his time of grief.

23:16 Abraham agreed to Ephron's terms and weighed out for him the price he had named in the hearing of the Hittites: four hundred shekels of silver, according to the weight current among the merchants.

Abraham does not dicker about the price, exorbitant though it may be. Abraham thus buys a portion of the Promised Land. God's blessings made it possible for Abraham to have the resources to make this purchase, and so in a sense we see the very beginnings of the fulfillment of the promise of the land. Abraham did not control much of the Promised Land in his own lifetime, and what he did control he had to purchase, but he does obtain a piece of the land! This purchase was done publicly in a publicly approved manner, emphasized by the reference to the weight then standard among the merchants. There is no disputing Abraham's right to the cave of Machpelah and its adjacent field.

4. Abraham Buries Sarah (23:17-20)

23:17 So Ephron's field in Machpelah near Mamre—both the field and the cave in it, and all the trees within the borders of the field—was deeded 23:18 to Abraham as his property in the presence of all the Hittites who had come to the gate of the city.

In order to hammer home the point yet once again the narrator clearly repeats the legal transaction. This time the location is specified as "near Mamre" the place where God had originally given the promise of a son to Abraham and Sarah. It included the field, the cave, and the

---

[4]If there was any significant erosion of the value of the shekel by inflation between the time of Abraham and the time of David or Jeremiah, this would only make the price more exorbitant.

[5]The Hebrew emphasizes "your dead" by placing it first in the clause, before the verb.

trees[6] within the field. All of this passed legally to Abraham as a purchased possession (NIV "property"). Once again the point is emphasized that this was no private transaction later subject to dispute; instead
it was publicly and legally authenticated in the presence of all those who
came to the courtroom of Hebron, the city gate. The elaborate and
expensive purchase shows the importance to Abraham of giving his
beloved wife a burial worthy of the mother of a great nation and of
kings. The promise of the land now has its down payment.

**23:19 Afterward Abraham buried his wife Sarah in the cave in the field
of Machpelah near Mamre (which is at Hebron) in the land of Canaan.**

With the transaction complete Abraham then buried Sarah there.
The repetitious description of the place reminds the reader yet again of
its significance. The wandering Bedouin now owns land in the Promised
Land. This property is said to be "in the land of Canaan." This rather
obvious point serves to emphasize the underlying significance. God had
promised the land of Canaan to Abraham. He had later informed him
that it would be another 400 years before his descendants would actually possess that land (Gen 15:16). In the meantime God had provided
a token and down payment on that future promise in the form of an
elaborate burial place for the matriarch of the nation. A small, but not
insignificant piece of the land promised to the descendants of Abraham
was now in Abraham's possession![7]

**23:20 So the field and the cave in it were deeded to Abraham by the
Hittites as a burial site.**

Just in case the reader has missed the oft-repeated point, it is
recorded yet again. Abraham now had legal possession of a burial site
by purchase from its original owners, the Hittites.

---

[6]Gary Hall reminded me, "Trees would have been identity marks, maybe even
boundary markers and were thus important to record as part of the transaction"
(personal communication with the author).

[7]The importance of this fact for the narrator and the original audience is
underscored by the elaborate, repetitive (in modern terms) descriptions of this
burial site in three other places in Genesis (35:16-21; 49:29-32; 50:13).

GENESIS 24

H. A WIFE FOR ISAAC (24:1-67)

This chapter, the longest in Genesis in English translations, tells in some detail the story of how Abraham solemnly entrusted his servant to return to the land of his relatives, from which the LORD had called him, to negotiate a suitable marriage partner for his son Isaac and to bring her back to Canaan (vv. 1-8). The servant accepts his commission, travels back to Aram, and there asks God for a specific sign of guidance to the woman he would have Isaac marry (vv. 9-14). The sign is given (vv. 15-28) and explained to Rebekah's family (vv. 29-49). Laban and Bethuel, Rebekah's brother and father confirm that the sign has indeed been fulfilled (vv. 50-51). The servant then joyfully negotiates the bride price and takes Rebekah back with him to meet Isaac (vv. 52-61). Finally Isaac and Rebekah meet, and Isaac seems to fall immediately in love with her and marries her (vv. 62-67).

Within the context of Genesis the narrative shows God's providence in seeing to it that the promise is fulfilled and not put in further danger. A wife for Isaac, the son of the promise, from among the Canaanites would risk a divided loyalty to that promise among the descendants of Abraham. Taking a wife from people who, however imperfectly, understand the calling of Abraham helps to ensure that the descendants of Abraham will be united in their desire to be used by God to be the channel of his blessing to all the nations. God's guidance in the situation ensures a future for the promise which he had originally made to Abram many years before. The next generation will be just as concerned as Abraham and Sarah were about the fulfillment of the promise.

1. Abraham Requires an Oath from His Servant to Find a Wife for Isaac from His Extended Family (24:1-9)

24:1 Abraham was now old and well advanced in years, and the LORD had blessed him in every way.

At the death of Sarah Abraham was 137 years of age. Some two or three years later he is described as "old and advanced in years." With his son Isaac, water rights in Beersheba, a fine family tomb, and the abundance of flocks and herds and other forms of wealth, Abraham had been blessed by God in all things. But one thing remained. His son must have a wife and he must not take the risk of a marriage to a Canaanite woman, who might lead Isaac away from focusing on God's promise.

24:2 He said to the chief servant in his household, the one in charge of all that he had, "Put your hand under my thigh.

Abraham spoke to his oldest (and presumably therefore his most trusted) servant in his house. Was this still Eliezer of Damascus as in Genesis 15:1? This servant was the ruler of all that Abraham owned. He asks him to make the symbolic action of a most personal and solemn promise. Putting the hand under the thigh is probably euphemistic for symbolically touching the private parts of Abraham.[1] The question is what was its significance? Perhaps Abraham's private parts are symbolic of his being head of a family. The entire family of which the servant is a part is dependent upon Abraham's generative capability, of which his genitals are the symbol. For the family to continue, his "only" son and heir must marry and have children. For the promise of God to find realization his son must remain faithful to the promise as his father had. Part of that faithfulness is dependent upon having a wife who would share in his desire to see the promise come to pass. Abraham asks[2] his servant to participate in this mission. He does not command him as the NIV's wording could suggest.

24:3 I want you to swear by the LORD, the God of heaven and the God of earth, that you will not get a wife for my son from the daughters of the Canaanites, among whom I am living,

Abraham makes his servant swear in the most solemn way that should Abraham die he would not allow Isaac to marry a Canaanite woman. Abraham is old enough now that he realizes he might not live to see Isaac marry. Isaac was 37 at the death of his mother Sarah, and this happens some time after that. Even at age 40, when Isaac actually married, he needed a father or a father figure to negotiate a marriage. Abraham asks for a commitment from his servant to serve in that capacity.

For contemporary readers the refusal to marry someone from a particular ethnic group may sound ethnocentric or even a bit racist. But race

---

[1]It is perhaps an unfortunate sign of the times in which we live that I find it necessary to make clear that this symbolic ritual in no way implies some form of homosexual relationship or attraction between Abraham and his servant.

[2]The Hebrew particle נָא ($n\bar{a}'$), the particle of entreaty, is used here but not represented in the NIV.

and ethnicity are not the issue. Many Canaanites were welcomed into the people of Israel when they adopted the faith of Israel. The imagined audience had recently received the Law which forbade, in the strictest of terms, intermarriage with the people of Canaan. This was not in any sense due to ethnic animosity but the simple fact that Israel would be tempted into idolatry and its associated practices through intermarriage.

Abraham refers to God in one of the most elaborate descriptions of him in the Bible. He is "the LORD, the God of heaven and the God of earth." The universal ruler had chosen a specific human family through whom to work out his extraordinary plan. But that family must remain faithful to the LORD if they are to be used in the way that he intended to use them. If Isaac is to be the lone heir through whom the promise of a great nation is to come, he must have a wife and children. If that nation is to see the fulfillment of God's promises, they must remain faithful.

24:4 but will go to my country and my own relatives and get a wife for my son Isaac." 24:5 The servant asked him, "What if the woman is unwilling to come back with me to this land? Shall I then take your son back to the country you came from?"

Abraham had been called to leave his "country" and his "people"[3] in Genesis 12:1. Here he asks his servant to return to his country and his people to get a wife for Isaac. While this could be interpreted as an act of disobedience on Abraham's part, the situation seems to have demanded it. Intermarriage with the Canaanites was a real spiritual danger for the patriarchs[4] as for the audience addressed by the narrative. This was also a danger for the canonical audience in the postexilic period (Ezra 9:1-4). While intermarriage with Abraham's extended family back in Haran was not without its problems, and his relatives certainly did not share Abraham's commitment to God alone, this seemed to be much better than the alternative of intermarrying with the polytheistic women of Canaan.

Even with Abraham approaching 140 years of age and Isaac approaching 40, Abraham still regards it as his responsibility to arrange a marriage for Isaac. The servant is quite willing to make the commitment, but he asks a quite understandable question. What if he is unable to convince a woman to return to Canaan with him? He suggests the possibility of taking Isaac back there, to the country from which Abraham had migrated at God's command some 65 years previously. The servant asks this as a question.

---

[3]The NIV uses the word "people" in Genesis 12:1 and "relatives" here for the same Hebrew word, מוֹלֶדֶת (môledeth), thus obscuring the connection between the two texts.

[4]Esau's marriages to Hittite women (Gen 26:34-35) show the danger.

24:6 "Make sure that you do not take my son back there," Abraham said. 24:7 "The LORD, the God of heaven, who brought me out of my father's household and my native land and who spoke to me and promised me on oath, saying, 'To your offspring I will give this land'— he will send his angel before you so that you can get a wife for my son from there.

Abraham immediately clarifies that Isaac is not to be taken back to Haran. The NIV's "make sure" is perhaps too weak for the Hebrew "Be on your guard!" (niphal of שָׁמַר, šāmar). This command is emphasized by its repetition at the end of Abraham's words in verse 8. Abraham knew that his own father had stopped halfway to the Promised Land. It would undoubtedly be a great temptation for Isaac to stay in Haran if he returned there to find a wife. Abraham wants to spare Isaac from this temptation.

Abraham recounts to his servant how God brought him out of his father's household and his people, and then promised him the land of Canaan for his descendants. God is described as "the LORD, the God of heaven" probably to emphasize his power to do what he had promised. Abraham reassures his servant that God's angel would travel in front of him preparing the way so that his mission would be successful. Abraham has no explicit word from God regarding this, but if God's promises are to be trusted and his warnings about Canaan are to be heeded, then he could also be trusted to be working in providing a suitable partner for his heir Isaac. As we have seen, the angel of God (or the LORD) is closely identified with God himself. For the angel to act is tantamount to God acting.

24:8 If the woman is unwilling to come back with you, then you will be released from this oath of mine. Only do not take my son back there."

Abraham realizes that since he does not have explicit directions regarding a wife for his son that it is potentially possible that his plan will not work out. He knows that he (and therefore his descendants) must be in Canaan, not back in Haran, if the promise of the land is to have any meaning. Isaac is not to move back to the place from which God had called Abraham to leave. The potential wife for Isaac, however, is not an automaton. Modern readers are tempted to assume that arranged marriages necessarily go against the will of the woman. While that may sometimes have been the case, examples like this show that the willingness of the female was often necessary for the arrangement to go forward. If a potential partner for Isaac was not willing to go back to Canaan with Abraham's servant, the servant would be absolved of his responsibility. In any case, Isaac was not to go back to Haran. By repeating this fact at the end of his speech to his servant, Abraham emphasizes its importance.

24:9 So the servant put his hand under the thigh of his master Abraham and swore an oath to him concerning this matter.

With his concerns addressed in a reasonable and reassuring fashion, Abraham's servant is now willing to make the solemn commitment which his master had asked of him. He places his hand under Abraham's thigh and swears an oath to go and find a wife for Isaac from Abraham's extended family back in Haran and not from the Canaanites.

2. The Servant Prays for a Sign of the Chosen Wife (24:10-14)

24:10 Then the servant took ten of his master's camels and left, taking with him all kinds of good things from his master. He set out for Aram Naharaim and made his way to the town of Nahor. 24:11 He had the camels kneel down near the well outside the town; it was toward evening, the time the women go out to draw water.

The material blessings with which God had blessed Abraham are shown in the lavish gifts which his servant is able to take as a bride price for Isaac's future wife. It took ten camels to carry it all. Camels were relatively rare during this era,[5] and the fact that Abraham had more than ten is a sign of God's material blessings to him. They were loaded with all of the good things with which God had blessed Abraham through his adventures in Canaan (and in Egypt!). Abraham may have been a wandering Bedouin with no place other than a grave plot to call his own, but God had also poured out his blessings on him at every turn.

The servant traveled to Aram Naharaim where Nahor then lived. The name means, "Aram of the two rivers" and is the area bounded by the Euphrates on the west and the Habur on the east.[6] While the town of Nahor could be another way of referring to Haran, it seems more likely that Nahor now lived in Naḥrima, mentioned in the El-Amarna texts.[7] When the servant arrived there, he made the camels kneel at a well outside the city. It was drawing toward evening when the cooler air made it a more pleasant time for the women of the city to come and draw water from the well.[8]

---

[5]See the discussion in K.A. Kitchen, *Reliability*, pp. 338-339.

[6]Gordon J. Wenham, *Genesis 16–50*, WBC (Waco: Word, 1994), p. 143.

[7]Ibid.

[8]The fact that the Samaritan woman at the well in John 4 was drawing water in the middle of the day is probably a sign of her being socially ostracized from other Samaritan women.

24:12 Then he prayed, "O LORD, God of my master Abraham, give me success today, and show kindness to my master Abraham. 24:13 See, I am standing beside this spring, and the daughters of the townspeople are coming out to draw water. 24:14 May it be that when I say to a girl, 'Please let down your jar that I may have a drink,' and she says, 'Drink, and I'll water your camels too'—let her be the one you have chosen for your servant Isaac. By this I will know that you have shown kindness to my master."

Having been reassured of God's guidance by Abraham, his servant prayed. He addresses God as "LORD, God of my master Abraham" because the basis of his appeal is God's loyalty (NIV's "kindness") to the promises he had made to Abraham. Twice he reminds God that Abraham is his "lord." He shows humility in not claiming any personal right to a hearing from God. The servant equates his experiencing success in his efforts today as an act of covenant loyalty to Abraham. He asks God to "make it happen" (hiphil of קָרָה, *qārāh*). He knows that his mission is a necessary part of the fulfillment of God's universal purpose through Abraham. If Isaac does not get a wife, there will be no descendants for Abraham to become a great nation. Biblical intercessory prayer is so different from what we often experience in the church. We are often tempted to ask God for what we personally want rather than asking him to use us in the fulfillment of what he wants.

The servant reminds God that he had taken his stand beside a spring. The fact that he describes it as a "spring" and not merely a well may be an instance of the narrator varying his language to retain interest, or it could be a hint that the servant hoped that this place would be the occasion of the springing to life of Abraham's potential descendants. The daughters of the men of the city were coming out to draw water. The servant asks that among these young women[9] there might be found a bride for Isaac. The servant asks for a sign of God's guidance. When he politely asks for a drink from one of the young women, the one whom God has chosen will gladly assent and offer to also do the time-consuming and perhaps physically draining chore of watering a herd of ten thirsty camels. This show of hospitality to a total stranger that goes well beyond the expectations of mere social politeness is an indication of something in the woman's character. The servant's master was generous in showing such hospitality. It would be appropriate for his future daughter-in-law to have the same character trait.

---

[9]NIV's "girl" for נַעֲרָה (*nāʿărāh*) could be misunderstood. Rebekah is a "young woman" not a little girl.

Typically Christians have pointed to Gideon's test of the fleece as the biblical language to describe a test in which a believer asks for God's specific guidance. But Gideon's test seems in its context to be a delaying tactic for someone who is reluctant to accept God's calling. It was actually a result of doubt not faith. It would be truer to the Bible to speak of asking for a cup of water with a herd of thirsty camels as a way of seeking specific forms of guidance. If the woman would pass this test, the servant would take this as a sign of God's continuing loyalty[10] to Abraham and his promises to him.

3. The Prayer Is Answered with Rebekah (24:15-28)

24:15 Before he had finished praying, Rebekah came out with her jar on her shoulder. She was the daughter of Bethuel son of Milcah, who was the wife of Abraham's brother Nahor.

God is here shown to be at work before a prayer is even worded to him. Isaiah 65:24 says similarly, "Before they call I will answer; while they are yet speaking I will hear." In anticipation of the prayer and because of the conversation between Abraham and the servant, God was already preparing Rebekah as a wife for Isaac. She was carrying a water jar on her shoulder.

The narrator gives the details of her genealogy in an interesting way. Rebekah is the daughter of the Bethuel who had been introduced in the genealogy in 22:21-23. Bethuel was the son of Milcah, the wife of Abraham's brother Nahor. For some reason the narrator does not say explicitly that Bethuel was also the son of Nahor, but only of Milcah, Nahor's wife and the niece of both Nahor and Abraham. The repetition underlines Rebekah's qualifications as a wife for Isaac.

24:16 The girl was very beautiful, a virgin; no man had ever lain with her. She went down to the spring, filled her jar and came up again.

Physical descriptions of biblical characters are rare and usually have some specific purpose. Rebekah's extraordinary beauty is reminiscent of Sarah's, and she will follow her deceased mother-in-law in being passed off to a king named Abimelech as Isaac's sister rather than his wife (Genesis 26). Her beauty may be mentioned to note the parallel between the two matriarchs and to prepare the reader for what is to happen. The word translated as "virgin" (בְּתוּלָה, bᵊthûlāh) does not by itself necessarily mean a literal sexually inexperienced girl, otherwise there would be no need to add, "no man had ever lain with her."

---

[10]The Hebrew word is חֶסֶד (ḥesed) here.

According to Wenham it means a woman of marriageable age.[11] The narrator uses this description to reassure the readers of the legitimacy of the father of Israel (Jacob) the forefather of the nation. The reader is drawn into the scene by the detail of Rebekah descending, filling her jar, and then ascending the stairs that led down to the spring.

24:17 The servant hurried to meet her and said, "Please give me a little water from your jar."

Sensing the LORD's leading, Abraham's servant hurried to take advantage of the opportunity. The hurrying of the servant reminds the reader of the hurrying which Abraham and his servant did in chapter 18 when he saw the divine visitors (18:2,6,7). One wonders whether the servant there is the same as the one here. He asks politely for a swallow of water from her jar.

24:18 "Drink, my lord," she said, and quickly lowered the jar to her hands and gave him a drink.

Rebekah responds respectfully to Abraham's servant, addressing him as "my lord." She then hurries (NIV "quickly") to grant hospitality to a stranger as Abraham and his servant had in chapter 18. She evidently holds the jar in her hands while the servant drinks. This was another sign to the servant (and the reader!) of the Lord's guidance in the situation. Rebekah's actions suggest admirable character traits that were previously found in Abraham and his servant.

24:19 After she had given him a drink, she said, "I'll draw water for your camels too, until they have finished drinking."

After giving a drink to a thirsty stranger, Rebekah offers not only to give some water to his ten camels but also to give them water until they were full. This sign of readiness to grant such lavish hospitality went beyond even what the servant had asked for as a sign of God's specific guidance in his prayer. Camels can drink up to 35 gallons of water at a time. To offer to draw as much as 350 gallons by walking up and down the steps to the well was an obvious sign of extraordinary hospitality.

24:20 So she quickly emptied her jar into the trough, ran back to the well to draw more water, and drew enough for all his camels.

Like Abraham in chapter 18, Rebekah hurried to complete her offer of hospitality, even running back to the well. She filled the watering trough enough times for each of the ten camels and presumably their riders too!

---

[11]G.J. Wenham, "Bethulah," *VT* 22 [1972]: 326-348. The assertion that had Isaiah intended a literal virgin in 7:14 rather than a young woman he would have used the word *bethûlah* rather than עַלְמָה (*'almāh*) is unsound.

24:21 Without saying a word, the man watched her closely to learn whether or not the LORD had made his journey successful.

Abraham's servant did not automatically conclude that Rebekah was the answer to his prayer even though she had fulfilled the servant's request of a sign from the LORD. He evidently knew that God was not bound to give a sign, and that a sign in and of itself was not adequate to confirm that the LORD was behind the fulfillment of the sign. He goes on to question Rebekah. It is not until he discovers that she is a relative of Abraham that he concludes that the LORD had in fact granted the sign. Here he merely watches her to see if she has the characteristics of a woman worthy to be the wife of the heir of God's promise. This warns us against simplistic understanding of "signs" of divine guidance. They can never be any more than one part of determining God's guidance, and faith must not be transferred from God to the sign that we request.

24:22 When the camels had finished drinking, the man took out a gold nose ring weighing a beka and two gold bracelets weighing ten shekels.

Rebekah had promised to draw water until the camels had finished drinking all that they wanted. This verse confirms that she was true to her word. Abraham's servant took some jewelry out of his satchel before he spoke to her. The value of the jewelry is noted by the fact that both the ring and the two bracelets were made of gold and by their weight. The ring weighed about a fifth of an ounce and the two bracelets four ounces each. As a potential "thank you" for a selfless act of hospitality they were truly extravagant. Rebekah had not been offered, nor had she expected any reward for her labor.

24:23 Then he asked, "Whose daughter are you? Please tell me, is there room in your father's house for us to spend the night?"

Undoubtedly Rebekah's clothing indicated that she still lived in her father's house. Other than prostitutes, unmarried women rarely lived alone in ancient Near Eastern cultures. Abraham's servant asks for the name of Rebekah's father and whether there would be a place for him and his men and their camels to spend the night.

24:24 She answered him, "I am the daughter of Bethuel, the son that Milcah bore to Nahor."

Rebekah answers the first question by identifying her father as Bethuel. The way that he is described by Rebekah is unusual in that Bethuel's mother is named first before his father. Typically one would not expect a man's mother to be mentioned unless it was somehow relevant to the specific situation. For the servant, her description clarifies that she is from the correct family and is, therefore, a potential partner for Isaac.

24:25 And she added, "We have plenty of straw and fodder, as well as room for you to spend the night."

Rebekah answers the second part of the servant's question. She reassures him that there is plenty of extra straw and fodder, even for ten camels, as well as places for him and his men to spend the night. This indicates that there is at least some level of prosperity in Abraham's extended family.

24:26 Then the man bowed down and worshiped the LORD, 24:27 saying, "Praise be to the LORD, the God of my master Abraham, who has not abandoned his kindness and faithfulness to my master. As for me, the LORD has led me on the journey to the house of my master's relatives."

Having received confirmation that the hospitable young woman was from Abraham's extended family, and having been reassured that he and his men would be gladly received as guests, Abraham's servant concludes that the LORD has, in fact, answered his prayer. The young woman who so generously offered to water a herd of camels was the woman God had chosen for Isaac. With the sign, the genealogical information, and the offer of hospitality all pointing in the same direction, then and only then, the servant concluded that God had been guiding him. In gratitude for this fact he bows down and worships the LORD. The faith of Abraham had spread to his servant, and we see evidence of this here.

The servant's prayer refers to "the God of my master Abraham." Does this indicate that for the servant, it is Abraham's God and not his own that he is thanking? If so, the servant knows the theological vocabulary that describes this God in a distinctive way. He refers to his "loyalty" (*ḥesed*)[12] and "faithfulness" (אֱמֶת, *'ĕmeth*), both terms which are among the most characteristic theological descriptions of God in the Old Testament.[13] The LORD had not forsaken these characteristics in his dealings with Abraham's desire to have a wife for Isaac who would not draw him away from worship and service of God alone. The servant also recognizes (for the first time?) that he personally has been guided throughout his long journey to the precise place where he was to go to arrange a marriage for Isaac. The LORD had "led" him on his "journey." The verb translated "led" is often used of God's guidance of Israel during the Exodus and wilderness periods.[14] The LORD did not begin lead-

---

[12]The NIV has "kindness."

[13]See, e.g., Brueggemann, *Theology of the Old Testament*, pp. 215-218, where he discusses the "credo" of adjectives, including *ḥesed* and *'ĕmeth* in Exodus 34:6-7.

[14]נָחָה (*nāḥāh*); Exod 13:17,21; 15:13; Deut 32:12; Neh 9:12,19.

ing his people at the time of the Exodus, however. He led Abraham and even his servant in very direct and specific ways. The servant has experienced for himself how God had guided him. God is no longer, if he ever was, merely the God of his master Abraham.

24:28 The girl ran and told her mother's household about these things.

For some reason when Rebekah runs and tells the news to her family, it is described as her mother's household,[15] and not as one might expect, her father's household. Certainly the servant assumed that he would be interacting with her father's house (24:23). We know from Genesis 24:50 that her father Bethuel is not dead. Is there the suggestion that somehow there is a division in the household between the mother's side and the father's side? Or perhaps Bethuel's age or mental capacity is such that he no longer leads the household. Once again, Rebekah is said to have run. She is just as eager to spread the news as she was to serve water to thirsty camels.

4. Abraham's Servant Explains the Lord's Guidance to Rebekah to Her Family (24:29-49)

24:29 Now Rebekah had a brother named Laban, and he hurried out to the man at the spring.

Strikingly it is Laban, Rebekah's brother, who first interacts with Abraham's servant and not her father Bethuel. Notice that Laban hurries out to the man. This may simply imply his enthusiasm for the demonstration of God's providence that the day's events are revealing. Conversely, it could be interpreted as Laban seeking to take charge of the situation or even as being motivated by greed. While Bethuel ultimately joins Laban in accepting the proposal that Rebekah become Isaac's wife (24:50), he otherwise disappears from the story. Significantly the gifts are given to Rebekah's unnamed mother and to Laban (24:53) and not her father Bethuel.

24:30 As soon as he had seen the nose ring, and the bracelets on his sister's arms, and had heard Rebekah tell what the man said to her, he went out to the man and found him standing by the camels near the spring.

Laban heard Rebekah's story and saw the lavish gifts that Abraham's servant had given her. Both of these things seem to have moti-

---

[15]The Samaritan Pentateuch here has father's household (rather than mother's) but this seems to be part of a harmonizing tendency; cf. Wenham, *Genesis*, p. 135.

vated Laban. It is interesting that the signs of material wealth are mentioned first. This may be the narrator's way of signaling to the reader that the potential material advantages of enhanced relationships with the émigré Abraham are of even greater importance than the story of God's guidance to Laban. Laban hurries out to meet the man both because of the potential material gain and because of his interest in his sister's recounting of God's guidance.

24:31 "Come, you who are blessed by the LORD," he said. "Why are you standing out here? I have prepared the house and a place for the camels."

Laban's greeting to Abraham's servant may be completely genuine or it may conceal a self-serving agenda. In either case he acknowledges that Abraham's servant has been blessed by the LORD.[16] Laban had seen the lavish gifts given to Rebekah and now had seen the ten camels full of gifts. Abraham's servant had truly been blessed by the LORD. Laban claims to have cleared the house in order to entertain Abraham's servant and his men and made a place for the camels to be cared for. Perhaps he left instruction with his household staff on the way out. Laban, whatever his motives, shows a similar sort of generosity as Rebekah.

24:32 So the man went to the house, and the camels were unloaded. Straw and fodder were brought for the camels, and water for him and his men to wash their feet.

Laban shows gracious hospitality in caring for the needs of the men and their camels. Water to wash one's feet was an expected part of hospitality in the ancient world.

24:33 Then food was set before him, but he said, "I will not eat until I have told you what I have to say." "Then tell us," Laban said.

Another expected part of ancient (and modern) hospitality is the offering and receiving of food. Abraham's servant is so urgent about his business that he refuses to take food before he has explained why he has come. While this might have the potential for being viewed as rude or ungracious, Laban assents.

24:34 So he said, "I am Abraham's servant.

The visitor begins by explaining who he is and what his role is in coming to Bethuel's home. He explains that he is Abraham's servant, expecting them to remember him from 65 years earlier. But this raises a question. Abraham was known as Abram when he left so long ago. God changed his name to Abraham later. How would Laban and his

---

[16]The use of the word "LORD" in Laban's mouth is anachronistic.

family have known that the Abram who had gone away had had his name changed to Abraham? It is possible that there was some form of continued communication between Canaan and Haran as we have seen in Genesis 22:20. Perhaps the name change had been previously communicated. Another possibility is that the similarity of the two names made recognition easier.

24:35 The LORD has blessed my master abundantly, and he has become wealthy. He has given him sheep and cattle, silver and gold, menservants and maidservants, and camels and donkeys.

Abraham's servant spoke of the material blessings that his master had received in accordance with the LORD's original promise while he still lived in Haran. Abraham had also become "great"[17] under the LORD's blessing. That wealth was expressed in livestock, precious metals, household servants, and pack animals. Laban had seen evidence of several of these in the short time he had known Abraham's servant.

24:36 My master's wife Sarah has borne him a son in her old age, and he has given him everything he owns.

The servant again uses the updated name of Sarah rather than Sarai, by which she was known when they originally left Haran for Canaan. Sarai was already 65 years old when they left and had been barren throughout her life. The servant recalls how Sarah finally had a son in her old age as another demonstration of God's blessing. He refers to the fact that Abraham had already given all his possessions to Isaac. The man that Rebekah would be marrying was, therefore, already quite wealthy. Apparently the inheritance had already been transferred to Isaac. This explains why the servant later refers to Isaac, rather than Abraham who is still alive, as his master (Gen 24:65). This information also suggests that Abraham is near death.

24:37 And my master made me swear an oath, and said, 'You must not get a wife for my son from the daughters of the Canaanites, in whose land I live, 24:38 but go to my father's family and to my own clan, and get a wife for my son.'

Abraham's servant explains that Abraham had made him swear an oath that he would not get a wife for Isaac from the women of Canaan, where he was living. That land had been promised to Abraham's descendants because it was falling under the judgment of God. But the promise had not yet been realized and the Canaanites remained in the land.

---

[17]The NIV's "wealthy" is a possible paraphrase of the Hebrew verb גָּדַל (*gādal*), although this obscures a possible connection to the promise in Genesis 12:2 where God promised to make his name "great."

Their influence, Abraham knew, would be damaging to Isaac, and so he insisted that his servant go back to his father's house and clan to get a wife for his son. The servant begins by quoting Abraham virtually word for word (v. 37). In verse 38, however, he begins to paraphrase. Abraham had referred to his "land" (אֶרֶץ, 'ereṣ) and his "kindred" (מוֹלַדְתִּי, môladtî), while the servant says "father's house" (בֵּית־אָבִי, bêth-'abî) and "clan" (מִשְׁפַּחְתִּי, mišpaḥtî).

24:39 "Then I asked my master, 'What if the woman will not come back with me'" 24:40 "He replied, 'The LORD, before whom I have walked, will send his angel with you and make your journey a success, so that you can get a wife for my son from my own clan and from my father's family.

Abraham's servant recalls expressing his concern to his master that the woman would not be willing to return with him. He then recounts his master's words when he commissioned him on his task. While Abraham does not say these exact words, the servant interprets them as, "The LORD, before whom I have walked." This echoes the command to Abram in Genesis 17:1 where the LORD commands him to "walk before me." According to the servant, Abraham had walked before the LORD in his presence as the LORD had commanded him to do.

When Abraham had originally commissioned the servant, he had referred to God as, "the LORD, the God of heaven, who brought me out of my father's household and my native land and who spoke to me and promised me on oath, saying, 'To your offspring I will give this land.'" For the servant to repeat these words could well be offensive to his hosts since they are those who had remained behind and did not follow God's call all the way to Canaan. He apparently paraphrases his master's words so as to not give offense.

Abraham's Actual Words (Gen 24:7)	The Servant's Version of Abraham's Words (Gen 24:40)
"The LORD, the God of heaven, who brought me out of my father's household and my native land and who spoke to me and promised me on oath, saying, 'To your offspring I will give this land'—he will send his angel before you so that you can get a wife for my son from there."	'The LORD, before whom I have walked, will send his angel with you and make your journey a success, so that you can get a wife for my son from my own clan and from my father's family.'

In the servant's version of Abraham's words he has him again refer to "clan" and "father's house." In so doing he adds weight to his earlier paraphrase in verse 38 by having Abraham use the exact terms he had earlier used. The purpose of this paraphrasing followed by exact repetition appears to be an attempt to emphasize the accuracy of the servant's version of the conversation so that there would be no distracting discussions about insignificant details.

24:41 Then, when you go to my clan, you will be released from my oath even if they refuse to give her to you—you will be released from my oath.'

The servant recalls that Abraham explicitly freed him from his obligation should the young woman not be willing to return with him. The repetition of the phrase, "released from my oath" may hint at the reason for this. If the servant remains under a solemn vow, Rebekah's family could use that fact to extract a higher bride price. By recalling Abraham's words releasing him from his oath and then repeating it, the servant makes it clear that he has already performed his duty.

24:42 "When I came to the spring today, I said, 'O LORD, God of my master Abraham, if you will, please grant success to the journey on which I have come. 24:43 See, I am standing beside this spring; if a maiden comes out to draw water and I say to her, "Please let me drink a little water from your jar," 24:44 and if she says to me, "Drink, and I'll draw water for your camels too," let her be the one the LORD has chosen for my master's son.'

Abraham's servant recounts to Laban his prayer earlier that day when he asked God for success. While the material differences between the original version and the version the servant tells to Laban are slight, they may not be without significance. In comparison with the original version the later version changes "girl" (נַעֲרָה, na'ărāh) to "maiden" (עַלְמָה, 'almāh). While the latter word does not necessarily demand virginity,[18] in this context it is certainly implied. The servant is assuming that Rebekah is, in fact, a virgin. The later account also refers to Rebekah as "the woman," which ensures that she is old enough to be married. The word translated "girl" is ambiguous. The servant also leaves out some of the rich theological vocabulary in the original prayer. He originally asked God to show "loyalty" to Abraham and said that the fulfillment of his requested sign would be a demonstration of that loyalty. This theologically loaded word (חֶסֶד, ḥesed) is omitted from his account to Laban. The servant may have feared that such theologically loaded language would have little effect on Laban. Originally the servant had referred to "your servant Isaac" while in his account to Laban it is "my master's

---

[18]John Walton, "**6596** 'alûmîm," NIDOTTE, 3:417-418.

son." It may be that the servant wants to emphasize that even though Abraham is frail, it is still a negotiation between the fathers of the prospective bride and groom, as was customary in that culture. While the servant clearly relays God's guidance in the matter to Laban, he also seems to be very careful in his wording in light of the delicate negotiation he is entering.

The Servant's Original Prayer	The Servant's Record of His Prayer
"O LORD, God of my master Abraham, please grant me success today and show loyalty to my master Abraham. [13]I am standing here by the spring of water, and the daughters of the townspeople are coming out to draw water. [14]Let the girl to whom I shall say, 'Please offer your jar that I may drink,' and who shall say, 'Drink, and I will water your camels'—let her be the one whom you have appointed for your servant Isaac. By this I shall know that you have shown loyalty to my master."	"O LORD, the God of my master Abraham, if now you will only make successful the way I am going! [43]I am standing here by the spring of water; let the virgin who comes out to draw, to whom I shall say, 'Please give me a little water from your jar to drink,' [44]and who will say to me, 'Drink, and I will draw for your camels also'—let her be the woman whom the LORD has appointed for my master's son."

24:45 "Before I finished praying in my heart, Rebekah came out, with her jar on her shoulder. She went down to the spring and drew water, and I said to her, 'Please give me a drink.' 24:46 "She quickly lowered her jar from her shoulder and said, 'Drink, and I'll water your camels too.' So I drank, and she watered the camels also.

Abraham's servant recounts how Rebekah turned out to confirm the sign for which he had just prayed. The servant informs Laban that Rebekah had come out before he had finished his silent prayer, in answer to that prayer. The narrator seems to imply that the servant's prayer was out loud, rather than silent. In the servant's version of the story, his prayer was "in his heart." It may be that the servant wanted to avoid any thought that Rebekah might have heard his prayer and taken advantage of the situation. The servant, unlike the narrator, does not comment on Rebekah's beauty as it would presumably be obvious to her family. He recounts how Rebekah's actions and their timing were confirmation of God's choice of a wife for Isaac. Rebekah's eagerness to be of service is highlighted by the word "quickly."

24:47 "I asked her, 'Whose daughter are you?' "She said, 'The daughter of Bethuel son of Nahor, whom Milcah bore to him.' "Then I put the ring in her nose and the bracelets on her arms, 24:48 and I bowed

**down and worshiped the LORD. I praised the LORD, the God of my
master Abraham, who had led me on the right road to get the granddaughter of my master's brother for his son.**

The servant did not mention that he had waited, watching Rebekah
to see if, in fact, she was chosen by the LORD. Having confirmed this for
himself, he wanted there to be no doubt about the conclusion and so
does not mention his waiting before coming to a conclusion. Seemingly,
immediately after this the servant asks whose daughter Rebekah was
and had it confirmed. Once again the servant does not mention key theological terms. In his actual prayer he uses the words "loyalty" and
"faithfulness." In his account of that prayer he speaks only of God's
leading. The servant may assume that these insights into God's character were not necessarily familiar to Laban and his family. The servant
refers to Rebekah as the granddaughter of his master's brother. This
emphasizes the kinship tie between Isaac and Rebekah and may be
designed to put Laban at ease with the potential marriage.[19]

**24:49 Now if you will show kindness and faithfulness to my master,
tell me; and if not, tell me, so I may know which way to turn."**

The servant now comes to the point of the discussion. Terms that
are central characteristics of God in the Bible are here used of human
beings. The servant asks that "loyalty" (*ḥesed*, NIV "kindness") and
"faithfulness" (אֱמֶת, *'ĕmeth*) be shown by Laban to Abraham. If Laban
and family were not willing to show such loyalty and faithfulness in
agreeing to Rebekah's marriage to Isaac, the servant would have completed his task and could return home. It may be that the servant's omitting of talk of loyalty and faithfulness until this point was part of a subtle, but deliberate strategy. Emphasis on God's loyalty and faithfulness
may have allowed Laban to conclude that mere mortals need not display
such characteristics. For Laban to refuse the marriage of Rebekah
would be, according to the servant, a breach of loyalty and faithfulness
to a family member.

5. Laban and Bethuel Confirm the Lord's Guidance (24:50-51)

**24:50 Laban and Bethuel answered, "This is from the LORD; we can
say nothing to you one way or the other.**

For the first time we learn that Bethuel had been present all along
even though only Laban had spoken up to this point. It may be he is too

---

[19]Modern western notions of incest must not be read back into this text in an
anachronistic fashion.

old and frail to function as the head of the family. In any case Laban
and Bethuel now answer together. Their response seems to mean that
since the matter has been guided by the LORD, they have no right to
resist the LORD's will.

**24:51 Here is Rebekah; take her and go, and let her become the wife
of your master's son, as the LORD has directed."**

They agree to the servant's request and grant permission for
Rebekah to be married to Abraham's son. They agree to this on the
assumption that the LORD has spoken regarding this matter. God had
guided his journey in finding Rebekah, in her fulfilling of the sign, and
now in the willingness of her family to allow her to be married to Isaac.

6. Abraham's Servant Praises the Lord for His Guidance (24:52)

**24:52 When Abraham's servant heard what they said, he bowed down
to the ground before the LORD.**

Once again Abraham's servant is quick to give thanks and worship for
the LORD's guidance and work in this situation. When Laban and Bethuel
agree to Rebekah's marriage, he bows to the LORD in worship and thanks-
giving. Abraham's servant, like his master, shows one of the surest signs of
a genuine relationship with the LORD, a ready thankfulness.

7. Gifts for the Bride and Her Family (24:53)

**24:53 Then the servant brought out gold and silver jewelry and arti-
cles of clothing and gave them to Rebekah; he also gave costly gifts to
her brother and to her mother.**

It is fascinating that there was no explicit agreement on the bride
price prior to Laban and Bethuel's agreement to the marriage. Perhaps
it was understood that the offer was conditioned on an acceptable bride
price being worked out. On the other hand Laban and Bethuel, having
seen the camels laden with expensive gifts may have concluded that the
bride price would be no obstacle. The servant's initial gifts and the ten
camels full of costly gifts no doubt reassured Laban of the ability of
Abraham to pay a generous bride price. Rebekah is given additional
gifts of gold and silver jewelry as well as expensive clothing. Costly gifts
are also given to Laban, Rebekah's brother, and her unnamed mother.
For some reason Bethuel is not said to have been given gifts. This is
another piece of evidence that he is somehow outside of the real picture
in terms of family matters. This may have been because of his age and

physical condition or because of the specific internal dynamics of the
family or both.

8. Rebekah Leaves with Her Family's Blessing (24:54-61)

**24:54 Then he and the men who were with him ate and drank and
spent the night there. When they got up the next morning, he said,
"Send me on my way to my master."**

Having resolved the issue for which he had come, the servant and
his men were now ready to enjoy the hospitality which Lot and his family offered. The next morning he was ready to return and asked to be
sent back to his master. When they actually arrive in Canaan, Isaac is
called his master (cf. v. 65). However, here Abraham seems to be intended. In the servant's judgment there was no time to be lost.

**24:55 But her brother and her mother replied, "Let the girl remain
with us ten days or so; then you may go."**

Once again Laban and his mother reply to the servant's request.
Bethuel is nowhere to be found. They attempt to stall Abraham's servant, requesting that Rebekah be allowed to remain there another ten
days or so. There may have been good reasons for this from their perspective. Everything had happened quite quickly and there was little
time for careful preparation for such momentous decisions. It is interesting that Laban and Rebekah's mother refer to her as the "girl" and
not as a woman or by her name. This might be a way to emphasize her
youth and vulnerability in contrast to what the servant had suggested.

**24:56 But he said to them, "Do not detain me, now that the LORD has
granted success to my journey. Send me on my way so I may go to my
master."**

The servant sees no reason to delay any further. He requests that
he be detained no longer. After all, hadn't the LORD granted him success on his mission?

**24:57 Then they said, "Let's call the girl and ask her about it." 24:58
So they called Rebekah and asked her, "Will you go with this man?"
"I will go," she said. 24:59 So they sent their sister Rebekah on her
way, along with her nurse and Abraham's servant and his men.**

For the first time Rebekah is explicitly brought into the discussion.
Laban and his mother are willing to let Rebekah go at such little notice
only if she is willing. Once again she is referred to rather impersonally
as "the girl." The fact that they would even consider Rebekah's opinion
on the matter shows that she is not viewed as a mere piece of property.

Pejorative contemporary readings of ancient arranged marriages say more about modern individualism than they do about ancient social realities. In the ancient world marriage was viewed much more holistically than it is today. It was a merger of two families, not just two individuals. The economic aspect of this merger sounds impersonal to modern ears, but was in fact a way of protecting the vulnerable in a patriarchal system. Subsistence agriculture was the economic reality for most families. There must be a way to ensure that women, who did not in ordinary circumstances inherit farmland from their parents, were cared for when they became an economic burden later in life.

The two families carefully negotiated a bride price. This performed two functions. It provided for the economic loss which the woman's family experienced when a young and healthy worker left the family. Secondly, from the bride price and, if necessary, from other resources, the woman was given a dowry. She took this dowry into the marriage and retained control over it. If she managed it well, it would be sufficient to care for her during her declining years. If she was divorced by her husband, the dowry went with her. Older women who had already been married often had difficulty in finding another husband. Without inheritance rights, such women had little access to the economic means to sustain themselves. The bride price and dowry system provided economic protection for them. This also created an economic disincentive for divorce. The groom's family had to pay the original bride price, which could be considerable. But the dowry, which was usually taken from the bride price, was controlled by the woman, even after marriage. Far from turning a woman into a piece of property, the bride price and dowry system was negotiated by mature adults who presumably had economic savvy, and was designed to protect the woman from being taken advantage of in a patriarchal system that could be cruel.

Rebekah, for her part, willingly consents to go with Abraham's servant immediately. She, along with her nurse,[20] departs with the servant and his men that very day. Once again the LORD's guidance of the situation is indicated by the ease with which the relevant issues are resolved so quickly and amicably. The system is patriarchal, but it had within it checks and balances on the power of men over women. The narrator here refers to Rebekah by her name (unlike Laban and her mother) and as "their sister." Perhaps there were other siblings present besides Laban. Alternatively the word "sister" may be used here in a more general sense of "female relative."

---

[20]Genesis 35:8 is the only other reference to Rebekah's nurse: "And Deborah, Rebekah's nurse, died, and she was buried under an oak below Bethel. So it was called Allon-bacuth" (NRSV).

24:60 And they blessed Rebekah and said to her, "Our sister, may you increase to thousands upon thousands; may your offspring possess the gates of their enemies."

Laban and family gave a blessing to Rebekah before she left for Canaan. It is interesting that God is not explicitly mentioned in the blessing. We have observed above that Abraham's servant had removed theological vocabulary from his account of the events to Laban and family. If this blessing is any indication, this may have been wise. God does not seem to explicitly enter into Laban's thinking here. In the blessing Rebekah is again referred to as "our sister." As noted above this may be imprecise, though intimate, language or may hint at the fact that there are other siblings. Rebekah's family wishes that she have many thousands of descendants and that her descendants would be powerful enough to overcome their enemies by coming to "possess their gates." In both of these wishes the promises to Abraham are echoed,[21] though in a more "secular" way in which God is not even explicitly mentioned.

24:61 Then Rebekah and her maids got ready and mounted their camels and went back with the man. So the servant took Rebekah and left.

Rebekah, having agreed to go and having received the blessing of her family, here actually departs. She took "young women" (NIV "maids") as well as her nurse and rode back on one of the camels she had volunteered to water the evening before. Like his master some 65 years before, Abraham's servant "went"[22] from Haran to Canaan.

9. Isaac Meets and Marries Rebekah (24:62-67)

24:62 Now Isaac had come from Beer Lahai Roi, for he was living in the Negev.

Instead of returning to Abraham who had commissioned him, the servant returns to Isaac. This is one piece of evidence for the theory that Abraham had already died by this time and that the remainder of the Abrahamic narrative is out of chronological sequence. In particular, his sons through his marriage to Keturah recorded in Genesis 25:1-6 would have already been born. But while it is true that the focus shifts to Isaac in this passage, there is no necessity of assuming that Abraham has died.

---

[21]For the increase in number of Abraham's descendants see Genesis 12:2,3; 15:5; 17:5; 18:18; 22:17; for possessing the gate(s) of one's enemies see Genesis 22:17.

[22]The verb which the NIV translates as "left" is literally "walk" or "go" (הָלַךְ, *hālak*). Although a very common verb, it may echo Genesis 12:1 here.

The narrative does not say so explicitly, and the overall narrative and chronological structure argues against inferring it. Nevertheless, it is striking that Isaac seems to be living by himself, and it is odd that Abraham is not mentioned if in fact he was still alive. Isaac had been living at "Beer Lahai Roi" a place which seems to mean, "well of the Living One who sees me." The reader recalls the wells over which Abraham and Abimelech had negotiated a treaty in chapter 20. The narrator explains that Isaac had been living in the Negev, the southern part of Judah in the deserted area near Kadesh Barnea. It may be that Isaac, at age 40, had been living apart from Abraham, thus necessitating the explanation by the narrator.

24:63 He went out to the field one evening to meditate, and as he looked up, he saw camels approaching.

The narrator may include these details to indicate that the LORD continued to guide Abraham's servant by noting yet another sign of God's serendipitous work in arranging a "chance" meeting between Rebekah and Isaac. With no thought of meeting his bride, Isaac wanders out into an apparently random field to meditate. The word translated "meditate" is a *hapax legomenon*. The ancient versions differ in their translation,[23] and the context is not specific enough to decide. The fact that Rebekah describes Isaac as "walking in the field to meet us" in verse 65 may suggest something more mundane than meditating. In any case, "by chance" he saw the camels coming toward him, which he surely must have recognized as his father's servant's caravan.

24:64 Rebekah also looked up and saw Isaac. She got down from her camel 24:65 and asked the servant, "Who is that man in the field coming to meet us?" "He is my master," the servant answered. So she took her veil and covered herself.

Rebekah then lifted up her eyes and saw Isaac. Her response is interesting. Literally Rebekah is said to have "fallen" (וַתִּפֹּל מֵעַל, *wattippōl mē'al*) from her camel. Even if it only means that she got off of her camel, she did so before she knew who Isaac was. Only after "falling" from the camel does she ask who the man was who was coming to meet them. This may be a Hebrew way of expressing "love at first sight" on the part of Rebekah. The servant tells Rebekah that the man approaching is his "master." From this, commentators often assume that Abraham has died, and that the servant knows this and now regards Isaac, not Abraham, as his "master." But this is surely going beyond what the text says. The servant told Laban that Abraham had already transferred his

---

[23]The Vulgate has "to meditate"; the LXX, "to gossip"; the Targum, "to pray."

possessions to Isaac (v. 39) and, this being the case, Isaac is quite rightly regarded as his master. This implies nothing about whether Abraham is dead or not.[24] In ancient culture we often assume that women were not ordinarily unveiled in public. Rebekah, however, had been traveling without her veil. When she realizes that her future husband is about to see her unveiled, she made sure to cover herself before he got any closer.

24:66 Then the servant told Isaac all he had done. 24:67 Isaac brought her into the tent of his mother Sarah, and he married Rebekah. So she became his wife, and he loved her; and Isaac was comforted after his mother's death.

When Isaac met the camel caravan, the servant[25] recounted all that he had done in finding a suitable wife for him. The narrative pace then suddenly picks up. Rebekah came to live in the tent of Isaac's mother Sarah. Some time later the wedding ceremony occurred. The arranged marriage did not turn out to be merely a marriage "of convenience." Instead the text explicitly says that Isaac "loved" Rebekah, arranged marriage or not. His love for her brought him comfort from the death of his mother. The future of the promise is made more secure as Isaac has married a woman who will not lead him away from God, one whom he also loves.

---

[24]The chronology of Abraham's life will be discussed in the commentary on 25:1.

[25]Interestingly, the servant is not identified as either Abraham's or Isaac's servant.

GENESIS 25

I. A FATHER OF MANY NATIONS (25:1-11)

And so we come to the end of the Abrahamic narrative. The heir has been born and the promise is now in his hands and, most importantly, in God's hands. Isaac has married a woman who shares his concern for the fulfillment of God's promise. In this section we find out about the later years of Abraham's life and how nations, other than those already mentioned in the earlier narrative, descended from him.

1. The Later Sons of Abraham (25:1-4,6)

25:1 Abraham took another wife, whose name was Keturah.

It is often argued by commentators that this passage is not in chronological sequence. Abraham was 100 years older than Isaac and died at 175. Isaac was 60 when Jacob and Esau were born. Abraham thus lived until the 15th birthday of his twin grandsons. This seems implausible to commentators since this is never mentioned. But silence is a shaky basis for evaluating historical plausibility. If the narrative is regarded as nonchronological, then the absence of mention of Abraham's marriage to Keturah[1] before Sarah's death is far more perplexing than the lack of mention of Abraham in the lives of his grandsons. Most events which happened in the lives of the patriarchs are not recorded since they were either unknown to the narrator or were irrelevant to his or her purposes.

This verse begins with a *waw*-consecutive, which is the ordinary way for Hebrew to indicate narrative sequence. For the *waw*-consecutive to

---

[1]Given the chronology of Genesis, Sarah died only three years before Isaac was married. If Abraham waited until after Sarah's death to marry Keturah, there is not enough time for the six sons (and perhaps unmentioned daughters) to be born before the marriage of Isaac in ch. 24. Therefore, if the events recorded here in ch. 25, happened before the events of ch. 24, the marriage to Keturah happened before the death of Sarah.

mean something else, there needs to be more evidence than silence about Abraham's role in the early years of Isaac and Rebekah's marriage. Assuming that this narrative is in chronological sequence makes the most sense overall (though see the discussion on v. 5 below).

Sometime after the death of Sarah, Abraham took another wife, Keturah. Keturah's name may be related to the Hebrew word for "incense" or "incense offering" (קְטוֹרָה, qᵉṭôrāh and קְטֹרֶת, qᵉṭōreth respectively). Her named descendants later participated in the spice trade from Arabia and lived in western Arabia.

25:2 She bore him Zimran, Jokshan, Medan, Midian, Ishbak and Shuah.

In Genesis 17:4-6 God promised that Abraham would father a multitude of nations and here is one part of the fulfillment of that promise. These nations lived on the edges of the Promised Land and were later involved in the spice trade. **Zimran, Jokshan, Medan, Ishbak**, and **Shuah** are mentioned only here and in the parallel genealogy in 1 Chronicles 1:32, which is evidently dependent on this text. **Shuah** might be associated with Shuḥu, a land on the Euphrates known from Assyrian sources and perhaps with the "Shuhites" from whom Job's friend Bildad came.[2] **Midian** is better known. The usual assumption is that these are the progenitors of Arabic tribes and that from Keturah's sons, like Hagar's son Ishmael, descended Bedouin tribes in the Arabian peninsula.

25:3 Jokshan was the father of Sheba and Dedan; the descendants of Dedan were the Asshurites, the Letushites and the Leummites.

Abraham and Keturah's son **Jokshan** fathered the Arabian tribal groups known as **Sheba and Dedan**. Two tribal groups also known as "Sheba" are mentioned in the table of the nations (Gen 10:7,28). The first of these is also associated with a Dedan and seems to refer to a set of northern Arabian tribal groups to the immediate south and west of Canaan.[3] These tribal groups may have merged at some point, thus explaining the alternate genealogy. The **"Asshurites"** are evidently not the well-known Assyrians with a capital city named Asshur but a desert tribe mentioned in Numbers 24:22,24 and Psalm 83:8. The **Letushites and Leummites** are otherwise unknown although they seem to have some relationship to each other.

25:4 The sons of Midian were Ephah, Epher, Hanoch, Abida and Eldaah. All these were descendants of Keturah.

---

[2]"Shuah," *EDB*, p. 1216.
[3]See the discussion in Kissling, *Genesis Volume 1*, p. 363.

The Midianites lived to the south of Canaan in what are, now, northwestern Arabia and the Sinai peninsula. **Ephah** is mentioned with **Midian** and Sheba as peoples who will use camels to bring gold and frankincense in Isaiah 60:6. **Epher** apparently means "young gazelle"[4] and may be identical with the two Appani mentioned in one of Assyrian king Ashurbanipal's account of his war against Arabia.[5] **Hanoch** is, in Hebrew, the same name as Enoch. **Abida** could mean, "the father knew [me]." An Arab tribe "Ibadidi" is mentioned in Assyrian records.[6] "**Eldaah**" may mean "God has called."[7] The original and canonical audiences presumably would have been familiar with these tribes from the trading that went through Palestine.

The verse ends with a summarizing statement to reinforce the point that the Midianite and other caravan traders with which Israel was familiar were distant cousins and should therefore be treated with respect. The Midianite traders were, of course, responsible for taking Joseph to Egypt and in this way helping to preserve the nation during a famine (Gen 37:36).

25:6 But while he was still living, he gave gifts to the sons of his concubines and sent them away from his son Isaac to the land of the east.

While the bulk of Abraham's inheritance was given to Isaac, Abraham did not send his other sons away in poverty. While they were the sons of his concubines, Hagar and Keturah, he still was concerned for their welfare as we have seen in the Ishmael episode in chapter 21. Abraham gave the sons of his concubines gifts **and sent them away** so that they would not be dependent upon Isaac. The Hebrew literally says that Abraham sent them "eastward to the land of the east." In the first volume of this commentary I noted the metaphorical significance of people traveling to the east from the time of Adam and Eve departing the garden. There it is an ominous sign of departing from the presence of God. It is difficult to determine whether something similar is happening here. In any case, in the history of Abraham's descendants, the descendants of Ishmael and Keturah's sons dwelled to the south and usually to the east of Canaan.

---

[4]Martin Noth, *Die israelitischen Personennamen in Rahmen der gemeinsemitischen Namengebung* (Stuttgart: Kohlhammer, 1928), p. 230.

[5]*ANET*, p. 299.

[6]Ibid., p. 286.

[7]KB, 1:51.

2. The Inheritance Goes to Isaac (25:5)

25:5 Abraham left everything he owned to Isaac.

If the *waw*-consecutive which begins this verse is taken in its typical sense, the transference of the inheritance to Isaac took place some time after Abraham's marriage to Keturah and the birth of her sons. If so, Abraham's servant's comment about Abraham having already given Isaac everything in Genesis 24:36 must not be understood in some legal or technical sense. The ancient practice of dividing the inheritance between one's heirs before death is also attested in the so-called parable of the prodigal son (Luke 15:11-13).

3. Abraham's Death and Burial by Isaac and Ishmael (25:7-11)

25:7 Altogether, Abraham lived a hundred and seventy-five years.

Abraham died at the age of 175. Ishmael would have been 88 and Isaac 75 at the time. The sons of Keturah would have been under 40. The author of Genesis gives a fairly complete and internally consistent chronology for the life of Abraham. At 75 he left Haran in answer to God's call to come to Canaan. After trying unsuccessfully to have children with Sarah, Abraham took Sarah's handmaiden Hagar as a secondary wife (concubine). Ishmael was born when Abraham was 87. At age 100 Isaac was born. Sarah died when Abraham was 147. Apparently sometime after this event Abraham took Keturah as a secondary wife and had six sons by her. Isaac was married three years after Sarah's death when Abraham was 140. His grandsons Jacob and Esau were born when he was 160. This seems to be the most natural way to read the Genesis narrative.

25:8 Then Abraham breathed his last and died at a good old age, an old man and full of years; and he was gathered to his people. 25:9 His sons Isaac and Ishmael buried him in the cave of Machpelah near Mamre, in the field of Ephron son of Zohar the Hittite, 25:10 the field Abraham had bought from the Hittites. There Abraham was buried with his wife Sarah.

Abraham expired (stopped breathing) and died at a good old age. He was old and satisfied.[8] God had promised him that a great nation would descend from him and from Sarah. When Abraham died, Isaac

---

[8]The NIV here translates the Hebrew שָׂבֵעַ (*šābēaʿ*) as "full of years." The word means "full" or "satisfied." There is nothing in the Hebrew that corresponds to "of years."

was married and had twin sons. The hope of a future nation descending from him was secure. His other sons would also make it possible for him to become the father of many nations. While he had been promised the land, God had made clear that the promise was only for the distant future. As a sort of down payment on the promise he had purchased and controlled for many years the cave of Machpelah. Sarah had been buried there 38 years previously and Abraham was still in control of it when he died. He had seen the LORD's protection and blessing throughout his life, even when his own responses showed a tendency to take God's matters into his own hands. At the end of his life, his life was long and full of God's blessings. He was completely satisfied.

The Hebrew idiom, "be gathered to one's people" may sound to Christians as though it implies a belief in the resurrection, but in fact this is questionable. The phrase only occurs in the Pentateuch in relation to the deaths of Abraham, Isaac, Ishmael, Moses, and Aaron. It may, however, refer to joining one's kinship group[9] in the afterlife, no matter how vaguely that afterlife is understood. Genesis 49:33; 50:13 demonstrate that this is something other than actual burial since Jacob was not finally buried for some months. Johnston[10] suggests that it is a stereotyped phrase originally derived from the practice of burial with the ancestors in a family grave even though this did not literally happen for Abraham, Moses, and Aaron. The fact that it only occurs in the Pentateuch may be an indication of the antiquity of the traditions found in the Pentateuch.

Interestingly Isaac and Ishmael are said to have buried Abraham. For some reason the sons of Keturah are not mentioned. This may have been because of pure geography, although the same could be said about Ishmael. More likely there is, by the time of Abraham's death, a social distance created between Isaac and the sons of Keturah who had been sent away. The fact that Ishmael did participate in the burial is striking. This implies at least civility between Isaac and Ishmael later in life if not, in fact, reconciliation. While Isaac is mentioned first, even though Ishmael was the older, they are both described as Abraham's "sons."

Abraham is buried in the cave that he had purchased at the time of Sarah's death for her burial. The details of that transaction are once again recalled. This may be because the narrator wants to reinforce the point that, though it was only a grave and an adjoining field, Abraham had obtained legitimate rights to a portion of the Promised Land long

---

[9]In Hebrew it reads "gathered to his peoples" in the plural.
[10]Philip S. Johnston, *Shades of Sheol: Death and Afterlife in the Old Testament* (Downers Grove, IL: InterVarsity, 2002), pp. 33-34.

before Israel went into Egypt. In death Abraham is joined once again to his beloved Sarah after 38 years without her.

25:11 After Abraham's death, God blessed his son Isaac, who then lived near Beer Lahai Roi.

The blessings from God which Abraham had received did not stop with his death. Isaac also experienced God's blessings. The promise originally made to Abraham is thus seen to continue through to future generations. Isaac settled[11] near **Beer Lahai Roi**, a well near Kadesh in the southern part of what was later to become Judah. Isaac had been living there when Rebekah was brought back to be his wife (Gen 24:62). The place's name probably means, "well of the Living One who sees me." The fact that Isaac lived there is used as evidence that Abraham had already died when Isaac married Rebekah and that this chapter is, therefore, out of chronological sequence. But we have already shown the internal coherence of the chronology of Abraham's life above. Further, Isaac was said to have been comforted by his marriage to Rebekah from his grief after his mother's death, not his father's (Gen 24:66). The narrative makes coherent sense as it is. This implies that Isaac returned to the place where he had been staying many years previously near the southern border of Canaan.

J. THE PROMISED BLESSING ON ISHMAEL FULFILLED (25:12-18)

While Ishmael was not the chosen son of Abraham through whom the promised was fulfilled, this does not at all imply that he was under God's curse. The Old Testament's concept of election is not the salvation for eternity of the elect and the eternal punishment of the damned. To be among the "nonelect" is not necessarily to be under God's condemnation. Instead election is about whom God chooses to use as the human channel for accomplishing his ultimate purpose to have a world under his blessing. There are major channels like Isaac and minor channels of that blessing like Ishmael. Here God shows that he was just as faithful to the promises concerning Ishmael which he had earlier made to Abraham when Hagar and Ishmael were sent away as he was faithful to the promises regarding Isaac.

25:12 This is the account of Abraham's son Ishmael, whom Sarah's maidservant, Hagar the Egyptian, bore to Abraham.

---

[11]The NIV's "then lived near" is interpretive and is not based on a literal reading of the Hebrew וַיֵּשֶׁב (wayyēšeb).

This short section on Ishmael begins with the standard introductory formula which is used to indicate new sections throughout Genesis: "This is the account of." Ishmael is not the son through whom the promise would be traced, and so it is significant that he (like Esau in ch. 36) is given a section of his own in the book. Even those not directly in the promised line of descent are nevertheless under a form of God's blessing merely by the fact that they are related to Abraham. Ishmael is described as "Abraham's son." This shows that his significance for the author stems from that fact. The explanatory "whom Sarah's maidservant, Hagar the Egyptian, bore to Abraham" is designed to remind the reader that while Ishmael is of importance and under God's blessing, he is the child of a scheme contrived by Sarai and Abram to do God's work for him in bringing about an heir from whom the promised nation would descend. God had rejected that scheme. Ishmael was not the promised heir.

Abraham was promised that Ishmael would father 12 princes and become a "great nation" (17:20). Hagar was told that he would live opposite his brothers (16:12). In this passage those promises are seen to be fulfilled. Ishmael is a sort of counterpromise character. He is blessed because he is Abraham's child. But his birth comes from a lack of patience and faith on the part of Abraham and Sarah.

25:13 These are the names of the sons of Ishmael, listed in the order of their birth: Nebaioth the firstborn of Ishmael, Kedar, Adbeel, Mibsam, 25:14 Mishma, Dumah, Massa, 25:15 Hadad, Tema, Jetur, Naphish and Kedemah.

Since Ishmael is not the promised child, his section consists mainly of genealogical material. The names of Ishmael's children are given in what probably is the order of their birth.[12] Since this is remarked upon, it seems to imply that ordinarily this was not the custom. It is only modern custom that assumes this in biblical genealogies. Ishmael has twelve sons listed. This forms a striking parallel with the twelve sons of Jacob which make up the nation of Israel. In a sense the descendants of Ishmael form a parallel nation to Israel.

Nebaioth may be the ancestor of the Arab tribe conquered by the Assyrian king Ashurbanipal in the seventh century B.C. and mentioned in Isaiah 60:7. It is unlikely that the later Nabateans are to be related to Nebaioth. Esau, in an attempt to appease his father's concerns over his previous marriages to Canaanite woman, married Nebaioth's sister

---

[12]Both NIV and NRSV assume that the Hebrew לְתוֹלְדֹתָם בִּשְׁמֹתָם (bišmōthām lᵉthôldōthām) "in their names, to their generations" means "in the order of their birth." Wenham suggests, "by their names and their clans."

(Gen 28:6-9). **Kedar** is here the progenitor of the Kedarites, a people mentioned frequently in the Bible and in Assyrian inscriptions from the eighth century B.C. onward. They were known to be seminomadic herdsmen in the desert east of Palestine.[13] **Adbeel** may be the progenitor of the North Arabian tribe, Idiba'ilu mentioned in the inscriptions of Assyrian king Tiglath-pileser III. If so, they were subdued by the Assyrian king and given the responsibility of the Egyptian frontier of the Neo-Assyrian empire. Only the canonical audience could have known about this, however.[14]

Mibsam has a name also borne by a Simeonite (1 Chr 4:25). His name means "balsam" according to Noth.[15] This would seem to imply some involvement with the spice trade which came from Arabia and through Palestine from ancient times. **Mishma** is found only here and in the dependent genealogy in 1 Chronicles 4:25 where they are brothers in Simeon's genealogy. Sarna[16] plausibly suggests that the two originally Ishmaelite clans were later absorbed into the nation of Israel through its southernmost tribe which bordered the grazing areas of the Ishmaelite herdsmen.

Dumah is only found elsewhere in the Bible as a nation somehow associated with the region of Edom in Isaiah 21:11. **Massa** is mentioned in the annals of Tiglath-Pileser III (744–727 B.C.) in association with Tema and other Arabian cities.[17] It is possible that a king of Massa is mentioned in Proverbs 31:1. **Hadad** is otherwise unattested. Three Edomite kings later bore his name (Gen 36:35-36; 39; 1 Kgs 11:14-22). This may have been due to the fact that Esau married an Ishmaelite woman, creating and sustaining continuing cultural contact. **Tema** is otherwise known as a city in northern Arabia (modern Teima). It was famous for its caravan trade (Job 6:16) and for the fact that Nabonidus, the last neo-Babylonian king, spent some ten years there while his son Belshazzar ruled Babylon in his stead.

Jetur is mentioned only here, in the parallel genealogy in 1 Chronicles 1:31, and as a tribal group against which the Transjordanian tribes waged war (1 Chr 5:19). Jetur is, presumably, the eponymous ancestor of the Ituraeans, a people located in southern Lebanon's Beqa' valley. **Naphish** is mentioned only here and twice in 1 Chronicles, once in a parallel genealogy (1:31) and once as a tribe against which the Trans-

---

[13]Sarna, *Genesis*, p. 175.
[14]Ibid.
[15]Noth, *Die israelitischen Personennamen*, p. 223.
[16]Sarna, *Genesis*, p. 175.
[17]*ANET*, p. 283.

jordanian tribes of Israel waged war (5:19). **Kedemah** probably means "easterners." They are mentioned only here and in the parallel genealogy in 1 Chronicles 1:31.

25:16 These were the sons of Ishmael, and these are the names of the twelve tribal rulers according to their settlements and camps.

This verse summarizes what has been listed in detail in verses 13-15. Perhaps this emphasizes that God's promise to Ishmael's mother and father had, in fact, come true. The imagined and canonical audiences would undoubtedly have been familiar with some, if not all, of the tribal groups mentioned, not least through their trading with Arabian caravaneers. The fact that there are twelve is no accident and is an echo of the promise to Abraham. His son Ishmael and his grandson Israel (Jacob) both had families with 12 sons in them and became the ancestors of prominent people groups. The author refers to the twelve sons as "princes" or "rulers," but makes clear that they initially ruled over settlements and camps, rather than nations with more elaborate social structures. The descendants of Ishmael lived Bedouin lifestyles.

25:17 Altogether, Ishmael lived a hundred and thirty-seven years. He breathed his last and died, and he was gathered to his people.

Ishmael also lived a good long life of 137 years. While not chosen to be the primary vessel of the line of Abraham, he lived under God's blessing nevertheless. His death is described like Abraham's. He expired and then died and was gathered to his people.[18]

25:18 His descendants settled in the area from Havilah to Shur, near the border of Egypt, as you go toward Asshur. And they lived in hostility toward all their brothers.

Ishmael's sons and their descendants settled in the area to the south and east of Canaan. **Havilah** is of uncertain location, although it is mentioned in relation to the River Pishon which flowed out of Eden in Genesis 2:11,12. If this is the same place and the audience is supposed to assume that the geography of creation still pertained, it would seem that they knew of the location of Havilah. It was somewhere in the environs of Canaan. **Shur** was southwest of Palestine on the eastern border of **Egypt**. The reference to the direction of **Asshur** is perplexing if it is assumed that this is the alternative name for Assyria as in the NRSV. More likely this is an area adjacent to Canaan. The NIV assumes that the Hebrew is implying something negative about Ishmael's descendants. Actually the Hebrew rendered literally says, "they fell before all their

---

[18]On the phrase, "gathered to his peoples," see the discussion above on Genesis 25:8.

brothers." It is difficult to know with certainty what the verb "fell" (וַיִּפֹּל,
nāphal) means here. But there is no reason to assume that it means
"lived in hostility toward" as in the NIV.

THE NARRATIVE OF ISAAC'S SONS: JACOB AND ESAU (25:19–37:1)

With a new introductory formula, "This is the account of Abraham's
son Isaac," we come to a new section of Genesis. But as in the previous
major[19] introductory formula in Genesis 11:27, the story which ensues is
not the story of the person named in the formula. In 11:27 Terah's story
becomes Abraham's story and in this section Isaac's story is largely the
story of Jacob and Esau. On the one hand the story is a story of struggle
between Jacob and Esau. On the other hand it is the story of Rebekah
and Isaac who foster the conflict between the twins from the earliest
days. The story ends with a form of reconciliation. There would appear
to be peace between Jacob and Esau who come together at the end of it
all to bury their father Isaac. But there are tensions. Jacob lives as a temporary sojourner in the Promised Land. Esau lives a more settled, permanent existence in Seir. But this is outside of the Promised Land.
When Jacob's descendants enter the Promised Land, the descendants of
Esau are already permanently established, their land immediately abutting Israel's land to the south. The ongoing tension between the two
nations continues throughout the Old Testament period.

The beginning point of the tensions in the narrative is the decision
of God. The descendants of Jacob, the younger brother, rather than
Esau, the firstborn, were chosen to continue the line of Abraham who
received God's promise in Genesis 12:1-3. Rebekah and Isaac, and their
favored sons, Jacob and Esau respectively, react very differently to this
revelation. Their differing and conflicting responses to the revelation
create the tensions which drive the narrative forward. Rebekah acts as
though she assumes that she must play an active role to ensure that the
promise with its blessing passes to Jacob. This is so even if it involves
duplicity. Isaac either is unaware of the revelation that the greater of the
two nations in Rebekah's womb will serve the lesser or he deliberately

---

[19]The introductory formula for Ishmael in Genesis 25:12 is a minor introductory formula parallel to the introductory formulae for Esau in Genesis 36:1 and
36:8.

ignores this fact. Rebekah's and Jacob's scheming and Isaac's indifference or ignorance result in a family with potentially violent hostility. Ultimately this leads to Jacob's forced exile for twenty years. But even in that exile in Paddan Aram the LORD blesses and protects Jacob. The end result is a large family of twelve sons and at least two daughters, the former lending their names to the twelve tribes of the nation of Israel. The exile also results in the transformation of Jacob into Israel and the transformation of Esau from someone intent on taking violent revenge on his younger brother into a person who grants forgiveness and reconciliation.

The Jacob/Esau narratives display a palistrophic structure as shown in the chart below. This has been known at least since the time of Fishbane and Fokkelmann.[20] My approach is an adaptation of theirs which regards the Jacob and Esau narratives as a complex unity. Each section is paired topically with another section in inverted order. The narrator thus invites the reader to focus on the similarities and differences between the paired passages. The structure also places emphasis on the middle section (29:30–30:24) where the birth of Jacob's children is narrated. The sons whose births are recorded in this section become the ancestors of the twelve tribes of Israel. The tensions which largely flow from the circumstances of their birth play themselves out in the Joseph narratives and in the tensions between the tribes from the time of their entry into the land under Joshua. Israel is a nation whose internal unity is at risk from the very beginning.

I. ISAAC'S STORY BECOMES THE STORY OF HIS SONS JACOB AND ESAU (25:19a)

25:19a This is the account of Abraham's son Isaac.

A new section is once again introduced with the formula: "This is the account of." In this case the account is that of Isaac, and yet Isaac is absent during most of it. The next section marker is not found until chapter 36 which concerns Esau. Isaac's story is, in fact, dominated by Jacob.[21]

---

[20]Michael Fishbane, "Composition and Structure in the Jacob Cycle (Gen 25:19–35:22)," *JTS* 26 (1975): 15-38; Jan P. Fokkelman, *Narrative Art in Genesis* (Amsterdam: van Gorcum, 1975).

[21]For a discussion of the "Toledoth" formulae in Genesis see Kissling, *Genesis Volume 1*, pp. 30-32. It should be noted that the previous formula was supposed

Another way in which Isaac's story is marginalized is the way the narrator refers to him in this passage as "Abraham's son." Isaac does not have a story of his own. He is either Abraham's son or the father of Jacob and Esau. His own role in the narrative is a relatively minor one.

II. FIRST STRUGGLES BETWEEN JACOB AND ESAU (25:19b-34)

The Jacob and Esau Narratives begin with the LORD granting their conception in answer to their father Isaac's prayer for his barren wife Rebekah. After trouble with the pregnancy Rebekah asked the LORD for guidance and was given a message which spoke of two nations being present in her womb and a somewhat cryptic message about the greater serving the lesser. The tension which this message seems to imply is lived out in Jacob and Esau's adult lives when Jacob takes advantage of Esau's hunger and lack of discipline over his physical urges to buy his birthright for some red stew.

This section with its depiction of tension between Jacob and Esau introduces the theme which is carried on throughout this section of Genesis. Within the palistrophic structure of the Jacob/Esau narratives this section forms a pair with the final section where the tensions receive a form of resolution in the personal reconciliation of Jacob and Esau.

Palistrophic Structure in the Jacob/Esau Narratives

A First Struggles between Jacob and Esau – 25:19b-34
  B Tensions with the Inhabitants of the Land over Women and Possessions – 26:1-33
    C Jacob Cheats Esau of His Blessing – 26:34–28:9
      D Jacob Meets God at Bethel as He Flees the Promised Land – 28:10-22
        E Jacob Arrives at Laban's House – 29:1-14
          F Laban Tricks Jacob into Marrying Leah as Well as Rachel – 29:15-29
            G Jacob's Children Are Born amid Tensions between His Wives – 29:30–30:24
          F' The LORD Blesses Jacob with Material Prosperity in Spite of Laban's Tricks – 30:25-43
        E' Jacob Flees from Laban Back to Canaan – 31:1-55

---

to concern Abram's father, Terah, but in fact was dominated by Abram. For an explanation of this see the discussion above at Genesis 11:27-32.

D' Jacob Meets God Back in the Promised Land — 32:1-32
C' Jacob Returns Esau's Blessing — 33:1-20
B' Tensions with the Inhabitants of the Land over Women and
    Possessions — 34:1-31
A' Final Partial Reconciliation of Jacob and Esau and Their Families —
    35:1–37:1

A. STRUGGLE BETWEEN JACOB AND ESAU AT BIRTH
(25:19-26)

25:19b Abraham became the father of Isaac, 25:20 and Isaac was forty years old when he married Rebekah daughter of Bethuel the Aramean from Paddan Aram and sister of Laban the Aramean.

The narrator rehearses some of the earlier events from the story of Abraham and Isaac. The Ishmael section (Gen 25:12-18) is somewhat of a necessary interruption in narrative terms. Abraham fathered Isaac (Genesis 21), but Isaac did not marry until he was a full 40 years of age (Genesis 24).

He married Rebekah who is described as the daughter and sister of Arameans. **Aram** is the biblical name for modern Syria. Their home is further described as **Paddan Aram**, a place obviously connected with the Arameans in some way. The point of this emphatic repetition of the **Aramean** origin of Rebekah is not immediately clear. Certainly Arameans are to be distinguished from Canaanites, and that may well be the implicit point. Isaac did not marry a Canaanite. The canonical audience in the postexilic period, as opposed to the imagined audience, would know of the later conflict with the Arameans in the history of Israel, but that does not seem to enter into the Genesis narrative.[22] Here the Arameans are not enemies but the people of Abraham's extended family. **Laban**, the brother of Rebekah, who will play such an important part in the life of Jacob, is explicitly mentioned. This prepares the reader for what is to come.

25:21 Isaac prayed to the LORD on behalf of his wife, because she was barren. The LORD answered his prayer, and his wife Rebekah became pregnant.

Like his mother Sarah, Isaac's wife **Rebekah was barren**. But **Isaac**, unlike his parents, did not attempt to solve this problem with his own resources. Isaac himself was a child of a miracle of the LORD. He had

---

[22]This is one piece of evidence that at least this section of Genesis comes from a very early time before the Arameans were enemies of Israel.

learned the lesson which took his father and mother so long to learn. **Isaac prayed to the LORD** because of his wife's barrenness, and the LORD **answered** with a "yes." Since Isaac is later portrayed as following his father Abraham's bad example in lying to a foreign king about his wife being his sister (Genesis 26), the reader must keep in mind his positive portrayal here.

25:22 The babies jostled each other within her, and she said, "Why is this happening to me?" So she went to inquire of the LORD.

The "sons"[23] crushed themselves (hithpael [reflexive] of רָצַץ, *rāṣaṣ*) within Rebekah's womb, and this led her to inquire of the LORD as to why. If the baby (she didn't yet know of the twins) was born in response to prayer, why would there be problems with him or her? Like Isaac, her question drove her to the appropriate response. She "sought" (דָּרַשׁ, *dāraš*) **the LORD.**

25:23 The LORD said to her, "Two nations are in your womb, and two peoples from within you will be separated; one people will be stronger than the other, and the older will serve the younger."

As was the case with Isaac when he prayed, the LORD responds to Rebekah's seeking him. In this case it is information that is given. The LORD told her that there were actually **two "nations"** (גּוֹיִם, *gōyyim*) pushing against each other in her womb. From these, two "peoples" (לְאֹם, *lǝ'ōm*) would be separated out with one **stronger** than the other and the "greater"[24] serving the "lesser" (צָעִיר, *ṣa'îr*). While the translations, including the NIV, typically assume that this refers to the older and **younger,** the Hebrew is, in fact, ambiguous.

In any case the LORD does not say that this will be true of the individuals but of the nations which will descend from them. What Paul says about this in Romans 9 is often misunderstood because of a failure to read the Old Testament carefully in context. Neither this passage, nor Malachi 1:2, which are both explicitly referred to in Romans 9, refers to Jacob and Esau as individuals but only as the ancestors of the nations Israel and Edom.

What may be more significant than what the prophecy actually says is the way that Rebekah interprets it. She then acts to try to ensure that her understanding of it actually comes to pass. Ironically, the ensuing narrative shows that Rebekah's effort to have Jacob served by Esau in their lifetimes is a failure. Esau does not serve Jacob.

---

[23] הַבָּנִים (*habānîm*) = "sons." NIV's "babies" is paraphrastic and may miss a subtle point.

[24] רַב (*rab*). The NIV's "older" is one interpretation of this general word.

25:24 When the time came for her to give birth, there were twin boys in her womb. 25:25 The first to come out was red, and his whole body was like a hairy garment; so they named him Esau.

The meaning of the prophecy begins to be clarified at the birth when Rebekah had **twin boys**. From each one a nation would descend. **Esau** beat his brother Jacob to birth by a few minutes. According to the traditional translation Esau was "**red**." But color terms in the Hebrew Bible are notoriously difficult to translate, and we don't know whether the color refers to his hair or his skin.[25] Athalya Brenner has noted that the word translated "red" includes everything from brown to yellow to pink.[26] The only other place that this word occurs is in describing David's handsomeness (1 Sam 16:12; 17:42). There does seem to be a wordplay, however, between this color (אַדְמוֹנִי, 'admônî) and Edom (אֱדֹם, 'ĕdôm), Esau's other name and the name for the nation which descended from him.

All of Esau's body was like a hairy cloak. It is not clear why Rebekah's firstborn was called Esau. It may be that there is wordplay between the word "hairy" (שֵׂעָר, śē'ār) and the word "Esau" (עֵשָׂו, 'ēśāw). However, this would be more convincing if it was wordplay with "Seir" (שֵׂעִיר, śē'îr), a region within Edom (Gen 32:3).

25:26 After this, his brother came out, with his hand grasping Esau's heel; so he was named Jacob. Isaac was sixty years old when Rebekah gave birth to them.

In the playful etymologies of Genesis Jacob's name (יַעֲקֹב, ya'ăqōb) means "heel grabber" because he came out just after Esau "grabbing his heel" (אֹחֶזֶת בַּעֲקֵב, 'ōḥezeth ba'ăqēb = "one grabbing the heel"). The event had significance for the author because it was paradigmatic of Jacob's future relationship with Esau. He grabbed[27] what was rightfully Esau's, whatever means were required.

The interest in the overall chronology of the patriarchal narratives is shown once again as Isaac's age at the birth of the twins is given. Isaac was 60 when they were born which means that he and Rebekah had been married for 20 years before they were blessed with children. The long years of waiting and praying had finally born fruit. We do not

---

[25]Wenham, *Genesis 16–50*, p. 176.

[26]Athalya Brenner, *Colour Terms in the Old Testament*, JSOTSupp 21 (Sheffield: JSOT Press, 1982), pp. 127-130.

[27]In Genesis 27:36 the verbal root of the word "heel" is used in the sense of "deceive." (הֲכִי קָרָא שְׁמוֹ יַעֲקֹב וַיַּעְקְבֵנִי זֶה פַעֲמַיִם) (hăkî qārā' šᵊmô ya'ăqōb wayya'qᵊbēnî zeh pha'ămayim) = "Is not he rightly called Heel Grabber for he grabbed at the heel these [two] times?"

know Rebekah's age when she married Isaac. She is described as a "young woman" (הַנַּעֲרָ, *hanna'ărā*; Gen 24:16) at the time and so was likely a decade or two younger than Isaac.

B. STRUGGLE OVER THE BIRTHRIGHT (25:27-34)

In this narrative the twins who struggled in the womb are now young men. But the prenatal struggle has not ended. Esau, the manly hunter of wild game, is shown to be dependent upon Jacob, the one who stayed at home and learned how to cook. Jacob the heel grabber grabs Esau's birthright at a vulnerable moment. Esau shows that he can be controlled by his physical urges, and Jacob shows that he will compete for the promise that he wants so desperately even if it means taking advantage of his vulnerable older brother.

25:27 The boys grew up, and Esau became a skillful hunter, a man of the open country, while Jacob was a quiet man, staying among the tents.

We now skip forward to Esau and Jacob as adults. The narrator shows no interest in the intervening years. **Esau** became a man knowledgeable about hunting game, a man of the field. **Jacob**, by contrast, was a "blameless"[28] man, who "dwelled in tents." The contrast is interesting. Presumably Esau also dwelled in tents when he wasn't out hunting. It is possible that the violence associated with hunting is being critiqued here. It seems to be so in the other case of a hunter in Genesis, Nimrod.[29] But an implicit critique of the violence of hunting is only a possibility. The parallel with Nimrod should not be overdone. If, however, a critique is present, the contrast between Jacob and Esau is twofold. First there is a contrast in character, Esau being associated with violence against animals and Jacob being "blameless." Second, there is a contrast between where they spent their time, Esau in the field, Jacob in tents. This information anticipates the two crucial events about to be narrated. In each incident Jacob takes advantage of his brother when he is out in the field. In each case the cooking of a meal by the one who stayed at home is used to his advantage.[30]

---

[28]The Hebrew תָּם (*tām*) is translated as "quiet" by both the NIV and NRSV, but in no other instance in the Hebrew Bible is such a meaning attested. The word is usually translated "blameless" or "innocent." It is used to describe Noah (Gen 6:9) and Job (1:1,8; 2:3; 8:20; 9:20-22), was required of Abraham (Gen 17:1), and is used of the "blameless" more generally (Ps 37:37; 64:5; Prov 29:10).

[29]See Kissling, *Genesis Volume 1*, pp. 365-366.

[30]My thanks to John Nugent for this insight. In a personal communication he

25:28 Isaac, who had a taste for wild game, loved Esau, but Rebekah loved Jacob.

The narrator straightforwardly announces the favoritism in the chosen family. **Isaac loved Esau** because the wild game which Esau hunted was "in his mouth" (צַיִד בְּפִיו, ṣayid bᵉpîw). No motivation is given for that fact that **Rebekah loved Jacob.** It could stem from her interpretation of the LORD's message to her in verse 23. While the LORD had decided that the greater of the children's descendants was to serve the lesser's descendants, Rebekah seems to translate this into favoritism for Jacob as an individual whom she interprets to be the lesser.

Even less certain is the case of Isaac. Did Isaac know of the LORD's message to Rebekah? Readers are not informed and can only speculate. The fact that Isaac's love for Esau has another basis than his future relationship to the promise to Abraham may hint at the fact that he does not know about the LORD's message to Rebekah. If he does know, his actions and words give no indication that he regards the future destiny of the nations which will descend from his two sons as in any sense his responsibility.

Isaac's lack of active involvement in attempting to see the promise come to fulfillment could be read as exhibiting a trusting attitude toward the sovereignty of God or as active opposition to it. In any case the favoritism which is shown by both Rebekah and Isaac to their respective favorites becomes a significant subtheme throughout the rest of Genesis. Isaac, however, cannot be admired for loving a son over his twin brother because he put wild game in his mouth through his hunting! While Isaac's favoritism, unlike Rebekah's, had a basis, that basis seems self-focused and even somewhat carnal.

25:29 Once when Jacob was cooking some stew, Esau came in from the open country, famished.

The situation of favoritism was not merely a part of Jacob and Esau's growing up years. In adulthood it was still operating. And then Esau had a bad day hunting. Jacob "stewed some stew."[31] Esau, a man of the field, came in from the field, faint and weary from hunger. The "grabber" had his opportunity.

25:30 He said to Jacob, "Quick, let me have some of that red stew! I'm famished!" (That is why he was also called Edom.)

---

also suggests that Rebekah may have intentionally kept Jacob at home where he would be safe and strategically placed to use any opportunity which might arise to his advantage.

[31]The Hebrew verb "to boil" (צִיד, ṣîd) is cognate to the noun for the boiled stew (נָזִיד, nāṣîd).

Esau begs[32] for "the red stuff, this red stuff" (מִן־הָאָדֹם הָאָדֹם הַזֶּה,
min-hā'ādōm hā'ādōm hazzeh). The narrator seems to imitate Esau's desperation in the way he words his plea to Jacob. The word translated
"red" is אָדֹם (*'ādōm*), while the word for Edom is אֱדוֹם (*'ĕdōm*). The
nation which descends from Esau is named for the fact that in desperation its forefather asked for "the red stuff, this red stuff." He ended up
becoming ancestor to a nation that might be called "Redland."

25:31 Jacob replied, "First sell me your birthright."
Jacob shows himself in this passage to be the grabber. He takes
advantage of Esau's need and lack of control in order to become the
firstborn. Ironically, if the prophecy did refer to the firstborn, Jacob is
placing himself in the place of the servant since the firstborn was to
serve the second born. In a sense he (temporarily) forfeits his eligibility
for the promise precisely by putting himself in the first position. It is no
accident that it is only after Jacob has been humbled by Laban and
before Esau that the promise is renewed (Gen 35:11-13).

It is not clear whether Jacob could realistically expect to collect on
his bargain since it was gained by coercion. But Jacob begins the pattern
of trying to force the prophecy to come true. He should have learned
the lesson from his grandparents Abraham and Sarah about what happens when humans try, by their own resources, to bring the promises of
God to fulfillment.

**25:32 "Look, I am about to die," Esau said. "What good is the birth-
right to me?"**
Esau shows that he is driven by his physical drives. Hunger, while
an extremely strong drive, can be controlled. In a household of the
affluence of Isaac was there no one nearby who could provide a meal
for Esau if he would but wait a few minutes? Delaying gratification is
one of the simplest lessons of wisdom that we learn as children. Unfortunately Esau is an adult and has not yet learned it. When our physical
drives control us, we reason the way Esau does, and we suffer the same
sorts of long-term consequences for our lack of short-term patience.

**25:33 But Jacob said, "Swear to me first." So he swore an oath to him,
selling his birthright to Jacob.**
Jacob demands that Esau take an oath first, thus forcing him into
an untenable position. If Esau breaks the oath or denies its existence,
he risks divine judgment. If he refuses to swear, he assumes he, the son
of a rich man, will drop dead of starvation! Esau, unable to see the real-

---

[32]There is no equivalent in the Hebrew to the NIV's "Quick!" Instead the verb
uses the particle of entreaty (נָא, *nā'*) with a hiphil imperative.

ity of the situation capitulates and sells his birthright to Jacob for a bowl of red stuff. He was unable to see the unreal picture to which his physical urges drove him.

25:34 Then Jacob gave Esau some bread and some lentil stew. He ate and drank, and then got up and left. So Esau despised his birthright.

Jacob gave Esau bread and lentil stew. Lentils are typically brown or brownish-red, not red. It may be this color which is being described when Esau himself is said to be "red."[33] Jacob added bread and drink to his "bargain." Esau acts as if nothing of significance has just happened. In a series of *waw*-consecutive verbs which are striking for their matter-of-fact-ness, Esau ate, drank, got up, left and . . . **despised his birthright.** It is as though the last of these was of no greater significance than enjoying a bowl of lentil soup!

---

[33]On the difficulty of translating color terms see Brenner, *Colour Terms.*

GENESIS 26

III. TENSIONS WITH THE INHABITANTS OF THE LAND OVER WOMEN AND POSSESSIONS (26:1-33)

This passage narrates the difficulties which Isaac and his family experienced with living in the land God promised to give them while they waited for the fulfillment of that promise. The problems they encounter are strikingly similar to the problems which Isaac's father Abraham had previously experienced. Isaac also used similar strategies to cope with those problems. Both fear for their own lives because of the desirability of their wives to the inhabitants of the land. Both address that fear with the lie that their respective wives are actually their sisters. Both ironically face famines in the Promised Land and a shortage of water and pasturage. In both cases these shortages cause tensions with the inhabitants of the land over scarce resources. We see Isaac struggling with the same issues in regard to God's promise as his father Abraham had struggled with and using some of the same inappropriate strategies. But in both narratives we see the promise of God to protect the chosen family in action. God blesses those who bless Abraham and his descendants and curses those who curse them, just as he had promised.

Within the structure of the Jacob/Esau narrative the problems Isaac encounters with regard to his wife Rebekah in the land of the Philistines are matched by the problems which Jacob later encounters in regard to his daughter Dinah in the land of the Shechemites (Genesis 34). So all three of the patriarchs, Abraham, Isaac, and Jacob, deal with the potential threat which female members of their families cause. Unfortunately none of the three's reaction to the threat is worthy of imitation.

Laurence Turner[1] helpfully compares and contrasts the three narratives:

> In chapter 12 Sarah was expendable because, as Abraham understood matters, she had no role to play in the fulfillment of the divine

---

[1]Laurence A. Turner, *Genesis*, Readings (Sheffield: Sheffield Academic, 2000), p. 112.

promise of nationhood. In chapter 20 likewise, she may be disposed of because although Abraham has now been told that she will have a child, he doubts that she ever will. But for Isaac, Rebekah has already fulfilled her role. She has given birth and the next generation is guaranteed. Having played her part she may now be set to one side. The Genesis narratives give us little hope for anything other than pragmatic patriarchal chauvinism from its male characters. Women are dispensable for all kinds of reasons.

While I see no reason to assume that in chapter 20 Abraham doubts Sarah will ever have a child, his point about "pragmatic patriarchal chauvinism" is on target. Isaac, like his father Abraham, is far from heroic in this narrative.

A. PROMISE REITERATED TO ISAAC IN ORDER TO GET HIM TO STAY IN THE LAND DURING A FAMINE (26:1-5)

26:1 Now there was a famine in the land—besides the earlier famine of Abraham's time—and Isaac went to Abimelech king of the Philistines in Gerar.

If this passage is intended to follow chronologically from the previous episode[2] this story occurs after the births of Jacob and Esau and after Esau sells his birthright to Jacob. The narrator makes an explicit connection to the story in Genesis 12:10-20 where Abraham, having only recently come to the Promised Land, experienced a famine there. That "first" famine had been more than 100 years earlier. Isaac, like his father Abraham, moved to the south, evidently intending to go to Egypt. The story then echoes Genesis 20:1-18, the second time that Abraham lies about Sarah being his sister. Isaac is retracing the steps of his father and is about to fall into the same sin that his father had fallen into twice previously.[3]

---

[2]וַיְהִי (way°hî) is ambiguous, but could indicate narrative sequence here.

[3]Rolf Rendtorff (*Canonical Hebrew Bible*, p. 23) comments: "Later, in connection with the famine Isaac experiences, at which point express reference is made back to the time of Abraham (26:1), the alert reader will see that Abraham should not have wandered off to Egypt but that God would have kept him alive if he had stayed in the land, as he did with Isaac (26:12)." But Rendtorff fails to notice that Isaac runs into the same difficulty and is guilty of the same lack of faith within the land. This also fails to relate this narrative to ch. 20 where Abraham, with Isaac in Sarah's womb, did not go to Egypt but repeated the same lie and thus put the promise in the same danger.

Isaac goes **to Abimelech, king of the Philistines**[4] **in Gerar**. The land that was later occupied by the Philistines was on the southern coastal strip, which would have been the natural path to take if one intended to go to Egypt to ride out the famine. One question is whether this Abimelech is the same one with whom Abraham interacted in chapters 20 and 21. If so, he would be more than 75 years older than he was then. One plausible alternative is to assume that this is some sort of throne name, like Pharaoh or Caesar. The Masoretic text may be hinting at this by putting an unnecessary and ungrammatical *dages forte* in the *mem* of Abimelech's name.[5]

26:2 The LORD appeared to Isaac and said, "Do not go down to Egypt; live in the land where I tell you to live.

The LORD, knowing Isaac's intention to go to Egypt, makes an appearance to him, warning him not to do so. Instead he is to live in the land that the LORD would instruct him to live in. This passage seems to echo for the original audience the prohibition of returning to Egypt (Deut 17:16). Abram had done this and placed the promise at risk (cf. Gen 12:10-20). Isaac was directed not to make the same mistake.

26:3 Stay in this land for a while, and I will be with you and will bless you. For to you and your descendants I will give all these lands and will confirm the oath I swore to your father Abraham.

The LORD commands Isaac to "sojourn" in the land where he was. The result of such obedience will be the transference of the promise of Abraham to Isaac. The NIV minimizes the connection between Isaac's obedience to the commandment and the consequence of that obedience by translating the conjunction as "and." A better translation would be "so that." This is consistent with the NIV's Calvinistic tendency in which human responsibility is often minimized. But the Hebrew construction[6] argues for a clear connection between obedience and receiving the blessing of the promise. If Isaac stays in the Promised Land, famine ridden though it be, God promises to be with him, to bless him, and to give "all these lands"[7] to him and his descendants. He also promises to confirm the oath sworn to Abraham, Isaac's father. Isaac need

---

[4]On the anachronistic nature of the description "Philistines" see the discussion on Genesis 21:32 above.

[5]See Wenham, *Genesis 16–50*, p. 183.

[6]A weak *waw* followed by imperfect which is dependent upon a preceding imperative has final force. Paul Joüon, *A Grammar of Biblical Hebrew, Part Three: Syntax*, trans. and rev. by T. Muraoka (Rome: Editrice Pontificio Istituto Biblico, 1991), p. 116b.

[7]The LXX here has "this land."

not fear a famine if God is with him. He will bless him even in the midst of the famine. Eventually his descendants will come to possess all the lands around him and the oath made to Abraham will be extended to Isaac. But Isaac must trust the LORD enough to remain in the land even during a famine.

26:4 I will make your descendants as numerous as the stars in the sky and will give them all these lands, and through your offspring all nations on earth will be blessed, 26:5 because Abraham obeyed me and kept my requirements, my commands, my decrees and my laws."

The LORD continues to reaffirm to Isaac the promise originally given to Abraham. His descendants would become as the stars in the sky, a promise previously given to Abraham (Gen 15:5; 22:17). He repeats the promise to give Isaac's descendants **all these lands** probably because right now, in its famine ridden state, it would not be so obvious what a blessing it would be. Isaac is tempted to leave the land, and here the LORD is inducing him to stay. The final element of the promise to Abraham is also repeated. All nations of the earth will bless themselves[8] through the offspring of Isaac. Abraham had received this promise in both its niphal ("be blessed," Gen 12:3) and hithpael ("bless themselves," Gen 22:18) forms. While theologically problematic for many evangelicals, verse 5 makes it very clear that these promises were available to be reconfirmed because Abraham was obedient.

The Protestant discussion of the relationship between God's grace and human response has been plagued by a failure to take such passages as this seriously. The promise is extended to Isaac because of Abraham's obedience to God's law. The words for law in this passage (מִצְוֹתַי חֻקּוֹתַי וְתוֹרֹתָי, *miṣwōthay ḥuqqôthay wᵊthôrōthāy*) are the specific words for particular laws. While the specific regulations of the law were not revealed until Sinai, Abraham obeys even some of the specifics of the law as later revealed. This is part of a pattern in the book of Genesis in which throughout the narrative the laws that are later given at Sinai are obeyed before they are specifically revealed. For example, at creation God obeys the Sabbath law (Gen 2:2b); Cain and Abel know of sacrifices and even of the doctrine of the firstborn/firstfruits (Gen 4:3-7). Noah is told to bring seven pairs of clean animals onto the ark before clean animals are defined (Gen 7:2,3). Abraham and Jacob tithe (Gen 14:20b; 28:22). Joseph recognizes adultery as a sin against God (Gen 39:9). Genesis 38:8

---

[8]The NIV here translates the hithpael as a passive, rather than a reflexive. See the discussion of the translation issue of the niphal and hithpael in the promises to Abraham at Genesis 12:3 above.

refers to the duty of levirate marriage which is codified in Deuteronomy 25:5-10.[9]

B. ISAAC LIES ABOUT REBEKAH BEING HIS SISTER (26:6-7)

26:6 So Isaac stayed in Gerar.

Buoyed by the LORD's promises, Isaac stayed in Gerar, rather than traveling on to Egypt as he had planned. His obedience in this instance showed his trust in God's promises when from a logical point of view it would have been "smarter" to go to Egypt where the Nile provided abundant water and was the natural place to go to ride out a famine in Canaan.[10]

26:7 When the men of that place asked him about his wife, he said, "She is my sister," because he was afraid to say, "She is my wife." He thought, "The men of this place might kill me on account of Rebekah, because she is beautiful."

When the men of Gerar asked about Rebekah, without consulting her, Isaac lied and said she was his sister. This is reminiscent of Abra(ha)m twice lying about Sarah (Gen 12:10-20; 20), although there are differences as well as similarities. In both narratives the patriarch and his wife are temporarily dwelling in a foreign land. In each case the beauty of the patriarch's wife is emphasized. In each case the patriarch is afraid for his own life because of the desirability of his wife.

But, the king of the foreign land where Isaac was temporarily dwelling showed no interest in Rebekah, unlike Sarai (Sarah). Isaac does not pre-plan the lie as did Abraham (Gen 12:11-13). And Isaac only lies about his wife when he is asked about her by the men of the place. In other words, Isaac repeats some of his father's mistakes but also shows some progress. While he too lies about his wife being his sister, he does not premeditate this nor does this result in his wife actually being taken into Abimelech's harem.

C. ABIMELECH CONFRONTS ISAAC OVER THE LIE (26:8-11)

26:8 When Isaac had been there a long time, Abimelech king of the Philistines looked down from a window and saw Isaac caressing his wife Rebekah.

---

[9]See James K. Bruckner, *Implied Law in the Abraham Narrative: A Literary and Theological Analysis*, JSOTSupp 335 (Sheffield: Sheffield Academic, 2001).

[10]The fact that later in Genesis Jacob was driven by desperation to go to Egypt during a prolonged famine is a different situation from the one Isaac faces here.

Isaac stayed for a long time in Gerar. Evidently throughout this time Isaac and presumably Rebekah had been pretending that they were brother and sister. The ruse was up when Abimelech saw Isaac playing with or caressing his wife Rebekah. The wordplay on Isaac's name ("He will laugh") is carried one step further. Here the "laughing"[11] which is going on is of a romantic or sexual type.

26:9 So Abimelech summoned Isaac and said, "She is really your wife! Why did you say, 'She is my sister'?" Isaac answered him, "Because I thought I might lose my life on account of her."

It would be interesting to know for certain if the Abimelech mentioned here is the same person mentioned in chapter 20. Or, if not the same person, did he know the story of how Isaac's father had also lied about his wife being his sister? Abimelech confronts Isaac with the evidence and asks why he would lie in this way. Isaac frankly expresses his assumption that the men of Abimelech's nation would gladly kill him in order to have Rebekah. Isaac's father, Abraham, had also unfairly assumed the immorality of Abimelech's people.

26:10 Then Abimelech said, "What is this you have done to us? One of the men might well have slept with your wife, and you would have brought guilt upon us."

Abimelech asks a very natural question. Why did you do this to us? By thinking that Rebekah was only Isaac's sister one of the men of Gerar might have slept with her and through that adultery brought guilt upon the entire people. The statement assumes that Abimelech regards adultery as wrong and a punishable offense. It also assumes that he does not regard sexual liaisons with unmarried women as being of equal seriousness. Abimelech seems oblivious to the desires of the woman. It is interesting to note that this Abimelech refers to what one of the men of Gerar might have been tempted to do. He does not say that he might have taken Rebekah as a sexual partner as the Abimelech of chapter 20 had done to Sarah. How Abimelech came to know that adultery was wrong is impossible to know with precision.

Certainly the Scriptures do assume at certain points that a partial but sufficient revelation was available to those who had not received special revelation like Israel had (e.g., Rom 1:19-20). This general revelation, or to be more precise, the interpretation of the general revelation that sinful human beings give to it, is never completely reliable.[12]

---

[11]The Hebrew word translated in NIV as "caressing" is צָחַק (ṣāḥaq), the verb from which Isaac's name derives.

[12]E.g., Abimelech regards adultery as a serious matter making his nation liable to judgment, but fornication seems a mere peccadillo to him.

Special revelation is needed. General revelation is, however, sufficient to hold men accountable.

26:11 So Abimelech gave orders to all the people: "Anyone who molests this man or his wife shall surely be put to death."

For this Abimelech as for his predecessors (if, in fact, they were different individuals), adultery was a capital offense. This was also the case in Israel's law (e.g., Lev 19:20-21 presumes this). Here we have a "pagan" king who somehow knows part of the (natural?) law of God. Both Isaac and Abraham before him assumed that the residents of the land which they had been promised had no moral scruples in regard to murder and wife-stealing from outsiders. Both of them were wrong in this assumption. The inhabitants of the land in the time of the patriarchs were not the inhabitants of the land at the time of Israel's entrance into the land. The iniquity of the Amorites was not yet full. They were not all like the men of Sodom. This may be a caution for the original and canonical audiences that they should not assume that all those who are outside the covenant are resistant to God and God's law. There are always Rahabs and Ruths and Tamars and Abimelechs among the nations.

D. ISAAC'S MATERIAL BLESSINGS RESULT IN PHILISTINE RESENTMENT AND HIS EXPULSION FROM GERAR (26:12-16)

26:12 Isaac planted crops in that land and the same year reaped a hundredfold, because the LORD blessed him.

Isaac acts as though he is a resident of the land, planting crops like a land owner. The potential fruitfulness of the land is indicated by the yield he received, one **hundredfold**. This came, however, under the LORD's blessing. The word "bless" echoes the promises to Abraham and shows that the promise has been transferred to the next generation.

26:13 The man became rich, and his wealth continued to grow until he became very wealthy. 26:14 He had so many flocks and herds and servants that the Philistines envied him.

Both the NIV and NRSV interpret the Hebrew root גדל (*gdl*) as "rich," "wealth," and "wealthy." While it is true that verse 14 goes on to enumerate various forms of wealth, the word literally means "become great" and is broader than mere riches. Regardless of the translation the point is that Isaac lived under God's blessing. Curiously the narrator refers to Isaac as "the man."[13] But ironically the signs of God's blessings

---

[13]One possible explanation for this is that it anticipates the way the phrases, "the man" and "the men" are used to denote Joseph and his brothers in the lat-

caused resentment among the Philistines. The increase in flocks and herds required water and pasturage, and they undoubtedly felt that Isaac's blessings came at their expense.

26:15 So all the wells that his father's servants had dug in the time of his father Abraham, the Philistines stopped up, filling them with earth.

The resentment over Isaac's blessings resulted in action. The Philistines knew that water was scarce and that it was essential for a man whose greatness, like Isaac's, was measured in flocks and herds. In order to frustrate him they filled up the wells which Abraham's servants had previously dug and had presumably been in the family for years. One wonders whether the wells included the well at Beersheba about which Abimelech and Abraham had made a treaty (Gen 21:22-34).

26:16 Then Abimelech said to Isaac, "Move away from us; you have become too powerful for us."

Just as Abimelech had visited Abraham in Genesis 21, in this passage this **Abimelech** also visits Isaac. Abimelech directs Isaac to **move away from** his people. The reason given is that Isaac had become either too "**powerful**" (NIV, NRSV) or too "numerous"; the Hebrew word can mean either. Interestingly this Abimelech did not bring his military commander with him as the Abimelech of chapter 21 had when he came to visit Abraham.

E. TENSION WITH THE PHILISTINES OVER WATER RIGHTS IN THE VALLEY OF GERAR (26:17-22)

26:17 So Isaac moved away from there and encamped in the Valley of Gerar and settled there.

Isaac realizes that the land is not yet his; it is only promised to his descendants. So, in order to avoid further conflict, Isaac moved away some distance to the river bed[14] **of Gerar**. Isaac set up semipermanent residence[15] there. On the one hand this would give his thirsty flocks a better chance at water. On the other hand river beds in Israel could become dangerous places when the early and latter rains came and sud-

---

ter part of the book (e.g., Gen 42:30). Another possibility is that this is an indication of a source used by the author.

[14]While the Hebrew נַחַל (*nāḥal*) can mean valley, it usually means the valley of a seasonal river or wadi. In light of the context of problems over water the translation "wadi" or "river bed" seems preferable.

[15]וַיֵּשֶׁב (*wayyēšeb*) implies more than temporary sojourn.

denly flooded the river bed. While this was not a long distance away (it was obviously near Gerar), it was evidently a place that Abimelech's people did not desire to live in.

26:18 Isaac reopened the wells that had been dug in the time of his father Abraham, which the Philistines had stopped up after Abraham died, and he gave them the same names his father had given them.

While Abraham and Abimelech had made a treaty over the water rights at Beersheba (Gen 21:22-33), there were evidently other wells in addition to that one. When Isaac moved some distance away from Gerar[16] he reopened those wells. The "**Philistines**" **had stopped** them **up after** Abraham's death perhaps to discourage Isaac from continuing to use them. They may have waited until after Abraham's death because of the treaty at Beersheba. Although that treaty was only explicitly about a single well, it may have carried an implicit understanding about other wells. Digging a well in the rocky soil of Palestine was a laborious, risky and expensive undertaking. To dig a successful one and then to lose rights to its precious water was a serious concern. When Isaac reopened those wells, he was careful to give them the same names which Abraham had given them originally. The name of one such well, Beersheba ("well of oath"), reminded everyone that Abraham had negotiated a treaty to ensure water rights to that well. Isaac had the same problems with Abimelech which Abraham had had with (an earlier?) Abimelech: his own safety because of his beautiful wife and water rights to wells that he had dug.

26:19 Isaac's servants dug in the valley and discovered a well of fresh water there.

In addition to reopening closed wells, Isaac's servants discovered a well of running water in the river bed of Gerar to which they had moved. Wells ordinarily collect water by seepage. This well had flowing[17] water, an unusual and priceless resource for herdsmen.

26:20 But the herdsmen of Gerar quarreled with Isaac's herdsmen and said, "The water is ours!" So he named the well Esek, because they disputed with him.

Isaac's problems were not solved merely by moving away from Gerar. When his servants found a fresh flowing spring of water, the

---

[16]I am assuming here that the *waw*-consecutive has its normal sense of narrative sequence. Wenham (*Genesis 16–50*, p. 192) argues that it is a flashback to the time before the expulsion.

[17]The NIV's "fresh water" is potentially confusing. The Hebrew has בְּאֵר מַיִם חַיִּים (*bə'ēr mayim ḥayyîm*), meaning "well of living water." The water is not merely fresh but flowing.

261

local herdsmen quarreled with Isaac over the rights to its water and
claimed it for themselves. Isaac **named the well Esek**[18] or "Dispute"
because of the dispute. Evidently Isaac did not try to negotiate with
Abimelech. His father had gone to the trouble of negotiating a treaty,
which was now being violated. Isaac evidently chose to abandon the well
to the herdsmen of Gerar.

**26:21 Then they dug another well, but they quarreled over that one
also; so he named it Sitnah.**

Isaac's servants then dug yet another well, and once again this started a quarrel with the herdsmen of Gerar. They must have been frustrated that these sojourners in their land had such "luck" in finding
water. This well was **named Sitnah** or "Opposition" (cf. NIV footnote).
It may be that the names indicate a growing frustration on the part of
Isaac. The difference in nuance between "Dispute" and "Opposition"
may hint at this. But Isaac does not regard the land as his own and
therefore does not consider that he has a right to defend the point no
matter how frustrating it must have been. His servants keep digging and
they keep finding water.

**26:22 He moved on from there and dug another well, and no one quar-
reled over it. He named it Rehoboth, saying, "Now the LORD has given
us room and we will flourish in the land."**

Isaac moved yet again in order to avoid strife. Once again a well was
dug, but this time there was no quarrel over it. He had finally moved far
enough away from Gerar that Abimelech's herdsmen were no longer
concerned about Isaac's flocks and their water supply. Isaac names this
well "Room Enough" or **Rehoboth** in Hebrew. Rehoboth may possibly
be near Wadi Ruheibeh/Nahal Shunra southwest of Beersheba.[19] He
explains the name by noting that the LORD, not Abimelech, had given
them a down payment on the promise of the land by giving them room
in it to live peaceably and to "be fruitful"[20] there.

---

[18]The Hebrew for "Esek" (עֵשֶׂק, *'ēseq*) is related to the Hebrew for "disputed"
(הִתְעַשְּׂקוּ, *hith'aśś°qû*).

[19]Laura B. Mazow, "Rehoboth," *EDB*, pp. 1116-1117.

[20]The NIV by paraphrasing the Hebrew וּפָרִינוּ (*ûpārînû*) as "flourish" loses the
connection with the creation mandate to "be fruitful." On the connection
between the creation narrative and the promises to the Patriarchs see the discussion above on Genesis 12:1-3.

F. THE PROMISE IS REITERATED IN BEERSHEBA (26:23-25)

26:23 From there he went up to Beersheba.

For some reason Isaac moved from Rehoboth to nearby **Beersheba**. The name means "Well of the Oath," and it was there that his father Abraham made a treaty or covenant with Abimelech. The treaty stipulated that, since Abraham's servants had dug the well, he had water rights there (Gen 21:22-33). That treaty had not lasted beyond the death of Abraham.

Isaac retraces the steps of his father geographically in this passage as he has done metaphorically throughout this chapter.

26:24 That night the LORD appeared to him and said, "I am the God of your father Abraham. Do not be afraid, for I am with you; I will bless you and will increase the number of your descendants for the sake of my servant Abraham."

The very night that Isaac moved to Beersheba, **the LORD appeared to him** again bringing much needed reassurance. The LORD tells Isaac that he is the God of his father Abraham. The point of this seems to be to emphasize that the promises which God had made to Abraham were still valid. The LORD told him not to be afraid after Isaac had just gotten through a period of quarreling over water rights in a land he neither owned nor to which he had any historic right. Just as the LORD had been with Isaac in calling upon him to ride out the famine in Canaan, so here the LORD promises his protective presence yet again. The reassurance echoes the promises to Abraham.

The LORD promises to "**bless**" him and increase the number of his descendants. He promises to do this for the sake of Abraham, who is called the LORD's servant. Abraham had referred to himself as God's servant in Genesis 18:3,5 but this is the only place in Genesis where the LORD referred to Abraham as "**my servant**." Isaac receives the renewal of the promises because of the faithfulness of Abraham.

26:25 Isaac built an altar there and called on the name of the LORD. There he pitched his tent, and there his servants dug a well.

In response to the LORD's gracious promises Isaac worshiped by building **an altar and** calling **on the name of the LORD**. This echoes the earlier action of his father Abraham in Genesis 12:7-8; 13:18. His tent was pitched there as a sign of something more than merely stopping temporarily. The decision to stay for the longer term is reinforced by that fact that his servants are successful in finding water through digging a well. The LORD has blessed Isaac abundantly in flocks and herds and his presence is seen in the ability of Isaac's servants to find water in dry soil for them.

G. ISAAC AND THE PHILISTINES RESOLVE CONFLICT BY EXCHANGING OATHS OF PEACE (26:26-33)

26:26 Meanwhile, Abimelech had come to him from Gerar, with Ahuzzath his personal adviser and Phicol the commander of his forces.

While Isaac's servants were discovering water, **Abimelech** followed Isaac to Beersheba. He was accompanied by **Ahuzzath** his chief herdsman,[21] and Phicol, his chief military officer. This episode is reminiscent of an earlier episode in the life of Abraham. While Abimelech does not bring his forces with him, only his commander, there seems to be an implied threat. The fact that he also brings Ahuzzath, if in fact he is his chief herdsmen, indicates the topic for discussion is water rights.

26:27 Isaac asked them, "Why have you come to me, since you were hostile to me and sent me away?"

Isaac asks a natural question of the men. Why would they seek him out when they expressed "hatred"[22] for him and had sent him away from Gerar only very recently? In phrasing it this way, Isaac makes clear that he is suspicious of the motives of Abimelech in coming to meet with him. He had been dealing with the hostility of Abimelech's herdsmen and assumed he had moved far enough away from them to be left in peace. The visit was not a welcome one for Isaac.

26:28 They answered, "We saw clearly that the LORD was with you; so we said, 'There ought to be a sworn agreement between us'—between us and you. Let us make a treaty with you

Abimelech and company answer Isaac's frank inquiry with straight talking of their own. The continued success of Isaac's servants at finding water and his growing prosperity had made it clear[23] to them that the LORD was with them.

The promise that the LORD had just made to Isaac is confirmed by the testimony of someone from another nation. This seems to suggest

---

[21]While the Hebrew מֵרֵעַ (*mērēa'*) usually means "friend," here the suggestion of Safren ["Ahuzzath and the Pact of Beer-Sheba," *ZAW* 101 (1989): 190-198] that it is related to an Akkadian term meaning "supervisor of the pastorages" fits the context better.

[22]The NIV's "you were hostile to me" is a good paraphrase, but it takes the edge off of Isaac's words. He uses the verb שָׂנֵא (*śānē'*), "hated," to describe their attitude toward him. The verb is not a perfect match for the English word "hate." Isaac may be exaggerating the point.

[23]They use the emphatic Hebrew construction, infinitive absolute followed by the perfect of the same verb, to indicate how clearly they had seen that the LORD was with Isaac.

that other nations are drawn to the people whom the LORD has chosen because they see the LORD's blessing on them. This seemingly innocuous statement is actually theologically loaded. The ultimate fulfillment of the universal portion of the promise to Abraham is being hinted at. Other nations see the LORD's blessings on the chosen nation and are drawn to the LORD. Because the LORD had so obviously been with Isaac, they want to make a covenant or treaty with him as the other Abimelech had made one with Isaac's father Abraham. The NIV nicely catches the subtlety of the Hebrew. The Gerarites speak both of an oath or "**sworn agreement**" and of a covenant or "**treaty**." They repeat the phrase "**between us**" in order to emphasize it. They do not demand a treaty, but plead for one.[24]

26:29 that you will do us no harm, just as we did not molest you but always treated you well and sent you away in peace. And now you are blessed by the LORD."

The substance of the requested treaty would be that Isaac would do Abimelech and his kingdom no "evil" (רָעָה, rāʻāh).[25] The basis for this request is the alleged way Abimelech had treated Isaac previously. Since Isaac had already claimed that Abimelech had "hated" him and sent him away, it would undoubtedly take some convincing argument to change Isaac's perspective. Abimelech claims that his people had not "struck"[26] Isaac and did only "good"[27] to him and that they had sent him away in peace. He ends his statement by saying in effect, "and now because of this you are blessed by the LORD!"

Certainly Isaac would have had difficulty in relating his current blessings to the fact that Abimelech had sent him away after conflict over wells that Isaac's men had dug! But Isaac is a man of peace, and so he does not contest the obvious fallacy in Abimelech's argument.

26:30 Isaac then made a feast for them, and they ate and drank. 26:31 Early the next morning the men swore an oath to each other. Then Isaac sent them on their way, and they left him in peace.

Instead of contesting Abimelech's somewhat skewed version of recent events, Isaac welcomes the opportunity to solemnly agree to

---

[24]The Hebrew reads, "Let there be, please (נָא, nāʼ, the particle of entreaty), an oath between us, between us and you."

[25]The word can mean "evil" in the moral sense, but more often refers to harmful things.

[26]The NIV paraphrases the Hebrew verb נָגַע (nāgāʻ), "to strike, touch" as "molest."

[27]The NIV's paraphrase of "did no harm" and "treated well" loses the sharpness of the antithesis between "evil" (rāʻāh) and "good" (טוֹב, ṭôb) in the Hebrew.

peace. In celebration Isaac holds a feast in which the fellowship of eating and drinking together would hopefully be a foretaste of peaceable relations in the future. The importance of the oath is shown by the fact that it was made early the next morning after a night of feasting. Isaac and Abimelech did not desire to sleep in on such an important occasion. The oath that was taken is said to be "a man to his brother" (אִישׁ לְאָחִיו, 'îš l'āḥîw), indicating the new relationship which the oath marked. Isaac and Abimelech no longer regarded each other as rivals, but as brothers. This time Isaac sent Abimelech and his men on their way, not the reverse. But this time it implies no hostility whatsoever. In fact they departed from him "in peace." The resolution of the conflict is a hint of God's ultimate purpose to choosing Abraham. It is God's desire and commitment that one day all nations will live in peace.

26:32 That day Isaac's servants came and told him about the well they had dug. They said, "We've found water!" 26:33 He called it Shibah, and to this day the name of the town has been Beersheba.

While the reader has already been informed of the (re)discovery of the well at **Beersheba**, Isaac is only informed after the peaceable resolution of the conflict over water rights and other matters had been sealed with an oath. The relief which the treaty must have brought to Isaac is made even sweeter by the discovery of yet another well in an arid land. With the treaty now sealed with an oath, there is no danger of losing the rights to the hard-earned water because of the jealousy of the Gerarites. Just as Isaac's servants had redug other wells which Abraham had originally discovered and named them with the names which Abraham had originally given them, the same thing seems to happen here.

The fact that we have two accounts of the naming of the Beersheba is pointed to in the traditional documentary hypothesis as a prime example of a "doublet" in which two sources (in this case E and J) modified, in different ways, an account of the naming of Beersheba.[28] But this ignores the context in which Isaac rediscovers and renames wells originally controlled by Abraham which the people of Gerar had filled in or expropriated. Isaac called this well **Shibah** meaning "Seven" or "Oath" in memory of the covenant that Abraham had made with the previous Abimelech in which the covenant sign was a gift of seven ewe lambs (Gen 21:22-31). The town nearby was still called "Beersheba" ("well of the oath") because of this. As the Isaac narrative ends, he is more secure in the promise than ever. His treaty ensuring peace with Abimelech and the wells over which he now has negotiated water suggest that his tenure in the land of the promise will be long and peaceful.

---

[28]Ephraim Speiser, *Genesis*, AB 1 (New York: Doubleday, 1964), p. 203.

IV. JACOB CHEATS ESAU OF HIS BLESSING
(26:34–28:9)

Having, theoretically at least, cheated Esau out of the rights to the first inheritance in Genesis 25:29-34, Jacob, encouraged by his mother Rebekah, also tricks Isaac his father into giving him the deathbed blessing intended for Esau. The consequences of Rebekah and Jacob's strategy, however, are not so easily manipulated.

The section begins (26:34-35) and ends (28:6-9) with narratives of Esau marrying women of whom both his parents disapprove and who do not share Isaac and Rebekah's commitment to God's promise. In between there is the ironic story of how the blind Isaac cannot see, either literally or metaphorically, what is really going on and so ends up blessing Jacob even though he intends to bless Esau.

The blessing which Jacob wins through trickery, however, turns out to be a rather pyrrhic victory. He runs away from Esau's anger penniless and must work for twenty years as a servant of his equally tricky uncle, Laban. Later he returns to the Promised Land with family and possessions galore only to give most of them away as a bribe to assuage the anger of the now affluent Esau. The blessing he supposedly won in this narrative is, in a sense, "returned" to Esau with interest in Genesis 33!

The section is structured in the following way. The section begins and ends with accounts of Esau's marriages, first to two Hittite women (Gen 26:34-35) and then to an Ishmaelite woman (28:6-9). These marriages outside of the chosen family are a problem for the original audience. In the structure of this section of Genesis, however, they prepare for Jacob being sent back to Haran to marry a woman from within the larger family (28:1-5). Jacob is thus contrasted with Esau in his choice of marriage partner. Chapter 27 begins with a fairly detailed account of how the blessing that Isaac intended to give to Esau ended up being given to Jacob instead (vv. 1-29). The latter part of the chapter concerns the discovery of the truth (vv. 30-33), Isaac's ambiguous message regarding Esau's destiny (vv. 34-40), and Rebekah's scheme to save Jacob from Esau's anger by sending him to Haran to find a life partner (vv. 41-46). Esau's marriage to Ishmael's daughter Mahalath (28:6-9) is an attempt to reverse the disappointment Isaac felt at his previous marriages.

A. ESAU'S MARRIAGE TO HITTITE WOMEN CAUSES CONCERN FOR ISAAC AND REBEKAH (26:34-35)

26:34 When Esau was forty years old, he married Judith daughter of Beeri the Hittite, and also Basemath daughter of Elon the Hittite. 26:35 They were a source of grief to Isaac and Rebekah.

The section regarding Isaac and Abimelech has served as a sort of interlude in the ongoing narrative. With these verses the thread is taken up again from chapter 25. For some reason Esau waits until he is **forty years old** before he marries. This would have been an extraordinarily late age in the Patriarchal era when marriages were typically arranged by parents soon after puberty. This may hint that Isaac and Rebekah have been intentionally postponing it because of the lack of suitable candidates who shared their commitment to the LORD and his promises. It may be that Esau, tired of waiting for his parents, took matters into his own hands. If so, it shows an impatience with the LORD's slowness to fulfill his promises or at least with Isaac and Rebekah's slowness to send back to their relatives for a suitable wife. This was how they had come together (ch. 24). Isaac, Esau's father, was also 40 years old when he married, and he had had the patience to wait for the right woman to be found.

Whether it implies impatience or not, Esau's choice was a poor one. To begin with he chose **Hittite** women who did not share the faith commitments of his family. The original and canonical readers of the Pentateuch would be conscious of the grave spiritual danger which such marriages presented as is made clear in the laws prohibiting such marriages (Deut 7:1-3). Secondly, he chose two wives, thus following the common cultural custom of polygamy. But Genesis advocates for an original monogamy[29] and views the multiplication of wives as problematic, even though it was commonly practiced in the ancient cultural environment of Israel. Thirdly, Esau evidently chose his own wives without consulting his parents.[30] Although contemporary western individualism balks at the idea of a forty-year-old man asking his parents to arrange a marriage for him, this very modern perspective should not be allowed to cloud our reading of Genesis.

Judith, the first of Esau's wives listed, is omitted in the more detailed genealogical information given in Genesis 36. Perhaps this was because she had no offspring. Her name seems to be connected with

---

[29]See Kissling, *Genesis Volume 1*, pp. 177-178.

[30]One wonders whether this text echoes the episode of the "sons of God" taking whatever "daughters of men" they chose in Genesis 6:1-4. For this as a possible interpretation of this difficult text see ibid., pp. 263-265.

the verb "to praise" (הָדָה, *hādāh*). The second of Esau's wives, **Basemath**, is here and in 28:9 described as the **daughter of Elon the Hittite**.[31] Her name is related to a Hebrew word for "fragrance."[32] While we are not told explicitly why, these wives of Esau were "bitterness of spirit"[33] for Isaac and Rebekah. Perhaps the above considerations are to be inferred, or there may have been personal animosity between them for other reasons. In any case, this narrative explains why Rebekah so easily convinced Isaac to send Jacob back to the extended family in Paddan Aram to get a wife (Gen 27:46–28:5).

---

[31]The variant data about Basemath in 36:3 will be discussed there.

[32]Sarna, *Genesis*, p. 189.

[33]The Hebrew מֹרַת רוּחַ (*mōrath rûaḥ*) has some level of ambiguity.

GENESIS 27

B. ISAAC PLANS TO GRANT THE BLESSING TO ESAU DESPITE THE REVELATION AND PREVIOUS ACTIONS OF ESAU (27:1-5a)

27:1 When Isaac was old and his eyes were so weak that he could no longer see, he called for Esau his older son and said to him, "My son." "Here I am," he answered.

If this passage is meant to follow chronologically from 26:34-35, Isaac would be 100 years old, given Esau's age in the previous passage. This would explain his physical condition and may be the reason we are given information about Esau's age. Because of Isaac's advanced age, his vision is seriously impaired. What Isaac "sees" in both the literal and metaphorical sense is essential to the ensuing plot, and the mention of it prepares the reader for the narrative which is to come. The reader does not know exactly what Isaac knows about the message given to Rebekah during her pregnancy when he calls for his oldest son. His wife Rebekah had struggled with the pregnancy 40 years previously and had been told by God that two nations were in her womb and that the older would serve the younger. As noted there, it is unclear whether this meant the individual sons or also the nations which descended from them. Also uncertain is whether the reader should assume that Isaac knew about this message from God, although it seems unlikely that Rebekah would have kept such an important matter from him. If Isaac does know, what he proposes to do in blessing Esau rather than Jacob indicates either that he understands the prophecy as only applying to the descendants of his sons or he is being portrayed as deliberately resisting the LORD's explicit will in the matter. The text does not seem to resolve this ambiguity and we are left wondering.

27:2 Isaac said, "I am now an old man and don't know the day of my death.

Isaac fears that he might die before he gives his blessing to his eldest son. Assuming the chronological arrangement of this section, the fear was irrational as he lived to the age of 180, another 80 years (Gen 35:28).

27:3 Now then, get your weapons—your quiver and bow—and go out to the open country to hunt some wild game for me. 27:4 Prepare me the kind of tasty food I like and bring it to me to eat, so that I may give you my blessing before I die."

Esau was a "skillful hunter, a man of the field" (Gen 25:27), and Isaac loved him over and above Jacob because he loved the game which his hunting made available (Gen 25:28). The NIV's "tasty food I like" could easily be translated, "the delicacies I love," which may suggest something more. It could be that Isaac is being portrayed as so driven by his cravings for delicious food that it causes him to actively, though perhaps unwittingly, work against God's purpose. If Isaac loved such game enough to favor Esau over Jacob, he may well have loved such game enough to bless Esau to get it. If Isaac knew of the prophecy and interpreted it individualistically, then he knew he was acting against God's stated intention that the older would serve the younger. But the narrative is illusive. We don't know exactly what Isaac knew about the prophecy if anything. And we don't know how he would have interpreted the prophecy if he did know.

27:5a Now Rebekah was listening as Isaac spoke to his son Esau.

Isaac evidently assumes that his conversation with Esau was private, but **Rebekah** was secretly **listening**. The narrator describes Esau as "his," i.e., Isaac's son, not "their," i.e., Isaac and Rebekah's son. This may be an instance of what is known as narrative "naming."[1] In some sense Isaac regards Esau as his son and Rebekah regards Jacob as her son, but not vice versa.

C. REBEKAH SCHEMES WITH JACOB
TO RECEIVE THE BLESSING (27:5b-17)

27:5b When Esau left for the open country to hunt game and bring it back, 27:6 Rebekah said to her son Jacob, "Look, I overheard your father say to your brother Esau, 27:7 'Bring me some game and prepare me some tasty food to eat, so that I may give you my blessing in the presence of the LORD before I die.'

---

[1]Adele Berlin, *Poetics and Interpretation of Biblical Narrative*, pp. 17-18. Close attention to exactly how the Hebrew narrator describes a person or how persons within the narrative describe themselves or other persons is often a vital clue to the perspective of the narrator. Hebrew narrators tend to give few explicit evaluations of characters and their actions, so such indicators are of great importance.

Once Esau has gone to hunt for game, **Rebekah** uses the opportunity to speak secretly with **Jacob**. He is described as **"her"** son, not "their" son because the narrator is indicating the extent of the favoritism of Isaac and Rebekah for their favorite sons. One of the techniques of Hebrew narrative is to show the narrator's perspective by subtle changes in the way characters in the narrative report the speech of others. Here Rebekah reports Isaac's conversation with Esau to Jacob. She paraphrases Isaac's words slightly.

Isaac's Original Words to Esau	Rebekah's Report of Isaac's Words
"Prepare for me delicacies which I love and bring them to me to eat so that my life will bless you before I die."	"Bring to me game and prepare delicacies for me to eat and I will bless before the LORD before I die."

Rebekah does not mention Isaac's love for Esau's delicacies. I am not sure of the significance, if any, of this omission. She adds something that Isaac did not say, and this does seem to have significance. In Rebekah's version Isaac promises to bless Esau "before the LORD." With this addition Rebekah draws attention to the solemn nature of what Isaac is about to do. It is not just his blessing — a wish from someone who will die and thereby lose any ability to see that the blessing comes to fruition — but a blessing "before the LORD." This is tantamount to a divine promise. To make such a promise and it have divine power behind it is a very different thing. By bringing this out explicitly to Jacob, Rebekah is, in effect, warning him. This must not be allowed to happen, or the blessing of Esau would have a divine imprimatur which cannot be reversed.

Whether Rebekah is correct in this assertion is another matter. There is no reason the LORD's initial message cannot be fulfilled even if Isaac gives his deathbed blessing to Esau rather than Jacob. Rebekah is portrayed as someone who chooses to take matters into her own hands rather than wait in faith for the LORD to fulfill His promises.

27:8 Now, my son, listen carefully and do what I tell you: 27:9 Go out to the flock and bring me two choice young goats, so I can prepare some tasty food for your father, just the way he likes it.

The NIV's periphrastic tendency softens verse 8 too much. The Hebrew literally reads, "And now, my son, obey my voice which I *command* you." For Rebekah the stakes are high and Jacob must obey her wishes even though he is 40 years old! Rebekah's use of "my son" may be a way of reminding Jacob of her authority over him. Just as Isaac told Esau to go and obtain an animal and prepare delicacies for him, so Rebekah commanded Jacob to do the same. But he could do it more quickly because his animal would come from the already gathered flock and not have to be hunted down like Esau's. Also Rebekah would do the cooking and she knew how to prepare delicacies which Isaac loved and might fool Isaac into thinking Esau had made it.

27:10 Then take it to your father to eat, so that he may give you his blessing before he dies."

Every person within the narrative world believes that the son who gets the blessing will in fact receive God's blessing even if the blessing is obtained through deceit. The deathbed blessing according to the human characters in the narrative contains within it the power to ensure its fulfillment. To Rebekah and Jacob the latter simply must receive the blessing before Isaac's death or Jacob will not be blessed, no matter what God has promised. Once again we see the tendency for human beings to think that the fulfillment of God's promises is somehow completely dependent on them, and they therefore throw ethics to the wind in order to obtain it. Abram and Isaac lied about their wives, and here Rebekah and Jacob use deceit, but the principle is the same. The narrator sees things differently, however, and expects his or her readers also to see this. Rebekah did not need to use deceit. She needed only to trust the promise which God had given her before the boys were born.

27:11 Jacob said to Rebekah his mother, "But my brother Esau is a hairy man, and I'm a man with smooth skin. 27:12 What if my father touches me? I would appear to be tricking him and would bring down a curse on myself rather than a blessing."

Jacob raises the natural concern that he will not easily fool his father into thinking that he is **Esau**. Esau was **a hairy man**, while Jacob was "**smooth**." The NIV, quite understandably, adds the word "**skin**" although it is not present in the Hebrew.

This is one of the occasions where a probable wordplay in Hebrew can be brought over into English. Jacob says simply that he is "smooth" (חָלָק, ḥālāq). This Hebrew word is capable of referring to "smooth" speech (Prov 26:28; Ps 12:3; Dan 11:32). Jacob is smooth all right, and this refers to more than his complexion. Jacob fears that Isaac will touch his skin and realize that Jacob is trying to trick him. The result would be a curse and not a blessing. Once again Jacob believes that Isaac's words of blessing and curse have a power independent of the motives of the one uttering them. Could not God overcome Isaac's curse, especially if that curse was in opposition to his will? Is a curse or a blessing from a patriarch tantamount to divine predestination?[2] While this might be

---

[2]See the discussion of this issue later in this commentary regarding Jacob's curse of Simeon and Levi in Genesis 49:5-7 below.

true in the minds of the human characters in the narrative, it does not seem to be the perspective of the narrator.

27:13 His mother said to him, "My son, let the curse fall on me. Just do what I say; go and get them for me."

Rebekah calms Jacob's fear by promising something she technically cannot guarantee: to take any potential curse on Jacob upon herself. If Isaac's curse is believed to have power independent of Isaac, it is not clear how Rebekah could transfer the curse to herself. In any case she directs Jacob to obey her despite his fears.

27:14 So he went and got them and brought them to his mother, and she prepared some tasty food, just the way his father liked it.

Jacob obeyed Rebekah and with the young goats which he had procured, she prepared a meal of delicacies which Isaac loved.

27:15 Then Rebekah took the best clothes of Esau her older son, which she had in the house, and put them on her younger son Jacob.

In this text we discover that Rebekah had a plan for ensuring that Jacob's deception would not be discovered. She had somehow obtained or retained Esau's finest garments and dressed Jacob with them. In the pre-washing-machine era the clothes retained Esau's distinctive smell and would be another element in the deception of Isaac.

The narrator describes Esau and Jacob as respectively Rebekah's older and younger sons. This echoes the promise which God had given Rebekah when forty years previously she had had difficulty with the twins before they were born. The LORD had told her then that the elder or greater would serve the younger or lesser. In this passage Rebekah seeks to make that divine promise come to fruition through deception.

27:16 She also covered his hands and the smooth part of his neck with the goatskins.

In addition to the clothing that bore Esau's body odor, Rebekah also used the goatskins from the goats which Jacob had procured as an element in the deception of Isaac. She covered the "smooth" Jacob's neck and hands with the goatskins so that, should Isaac, suspecting a ruse, touch Jacob's neck and hands, he would feel the hairy skin of Esau.

The ruse seems implausible at one level. No matter how hairy Esau may have been, it seems unlikely that his skin would resemble the skin of a goat unless Isaac's powers of perception had been seriously compromised by his age.

27:17 Then she handed to her son Jacob the tasty food and the bread she had made.

With the makeover of Jacob finished, Rebekah gave Jacob the delicacies she had prepared, along with some bread, and sent him to deceive his father.

D. ISAAC, THOUGH SUSPICIOUS,
GRANTS THE BLESSING TO JACOB (27:18-29)

27:18 He went to his father and said, "My father." "Yes, my son," he answered. "Who is it?"

The heavy use of the relational terms "father," "son," "mother," "older," "younger," etc., in this narrative is one of the ways the narrator continues to draw attention to the "announcement of plot"[3] given by the LORD to Rebekah in Genesis 25:23. Jacob addresses Isaac as "my father." Isaac reciprocates with "my son." But he is not sure which of his sons it is. He has not called for Jacob to come to him, and yet the voice of the one addressing him does not sound like Esau's. Rebekah is better at disguising Jacob than Jacob is at disguising himself. Throughout this section Isaac is suspicious, and yet when he checks for corroborating evidence he is all too easily fooled.

27:19 Jacob said to his father, "I am Esau your firstborn. I have done as you told me. Please sit up and eat some of my game so that you may give me your blessing."

Jacob begins the deception by describing himself as **Esau**, Isaac's **firstborn**. The use of "firstborn" recalls the promise of Genesis 25:23 yet again and Isaac's intention to go against that promise by blessing his firstborn. Jacob claims to have hunted the game and prepared the food. In fact he had done neither. He reminds Isaac that the purpose of the meal was so that he might receive his father's blessing. Jacob tells the story that Rebekah has told him to tell, and this begins to persuade Isaac against the evidence of his own ears that Esau stands before him.

27:20 Isaac asked his son, "How did you find it so quickly, my son?" "The LORD your God gave me success," he replied.

Isaac wonders how Esau could have hunted wild game, cooked it, and brought it to him so quickly. Jacob improvises by cloaking his actions in religious language. He claims that the LORD, Isaac's God had made it happen (הִקְרָה, *hiqrāh*).[4] In using this description for God Jacob implicitly claims that he is on a mission from the God of his father and is, therefore, doing God's will. Like Rebekah, Jacob brings the LORD into their scheme.

---

[3]For the term, see Turner, *Announcements of Plot*, p. 14. For Turner an "announcement of plot" is a key text which focuses the ensuing narrative around the question, "What will happen in relation to this text?" Examples are the promise to Abram in Genesis 12, and the dreams of Joseph in Genesis 37.

[4]The hiphil means something like "cause to happen." NIV paraphrases here.

27:21 Then Isaac said to Jacob, "Come near so I can touch you, my son, to know whether you really are my son Esau or not."

Isaac quite openly expresses some doubt about the identity of the one who claims to be **Esau**. He asks **Jacob**, dressed as and smelling like Esau, to come near so that he can touch his skin to confirm that it is the hairy Esau and not the smooth Jacob. Rebekah had cleverly anticipated what Isaac would do and had prepared Jacob for it.

27:22 Jacob went close to his father Isaac, who touched him and said, "The voice is the voice of Jacob, but the hands are the hands of Esau." 27:23 He did not recognize him, for his hands were hairy like those of his brother Esau; so he blessed him.

The narrator lets us in on Isaac's interior thoughts. He is fooled by the goatskins which may lead the reader to wonder about his mental discernment or his physical capacity. Goatskin is not easily confused with the skin of a hairy man. The NIV's translation "**hands**"[5] may be a little misleading in this instance. Perhaps the Hebrew should be translated "forearms" in this context.

27:24 "Are you really my son Esau?" he asked. "I am," he replied.

Isaac's suspicions from hearing Jacob's voice are not entirely put to rest by feeling his son's goatskin-covered forearms. He asks once again about the identity of his son. Jacob, once again lies. The chronology of this verse is confusing as verse 23 ended with "so he blessed him," something that apparently happened only after this conversation between Isaac and Jacob. Source critics use even little anomalies like this one to postulate different sources, but there are other explanations. Perhaps Isaac gave an initial blessing and then, seized with doubt, interrupted himself to confirm that he was actually blessing the correct son. The pause creates tension for the first-time reader[6] over whether Isaac will actually bless Jacob or not.

27:25 Then he said, "My son, bring me some of your game to eat, so that I may give you my blessing." Jacob brought it to him and he ate; and he brought some wine and he drank.

The Hebrew literally says, "Come near so that I may eat of my son's game so that my soul may bless you." The reversion to the third person (my son) is unnecessary and may be a way of reminding "Esau" (in reality **Jacob**) of the formality of the situation and of his favored status as Isaac's son. Jacob complies, giving Isaac the food Rebekah had prepared

---

[5] יָד (yād) usually does mean "hand" but can include the lower arm.

[6] For the insight which interpretation of a first-time reader's response produces, see Turner, *Genesis*, pp. 13-14.

and through his own initiative adding some wine. We hear nothing of the bread which Rebekah had prepared, although perhaps its presence is implicit. The wine, however, is Jacob's idea and may be an attempt to influence his father's already compromised mental clarity with alcohol.

27:26 Then his father Isaac said to him, "Come here, my son, and kiss me."

The narrator again reminds us of the relationship of Jacob and **Isaac** by unnecessarily referring to Isaac as his (Jacob's) father. Isaac asks for Jacob to **kiss** him, a typical sign of affection between parents and children in many cultures.

27:27 So he went to him and kissed him. When Isaac caught the smell of his clothes, he blessed him and said, "Ah, the smell of my son is like the smell of a field that the LORD has blessed.

The secondary motive for Isaac asking Jacob to kiss him now becomes clear. Unable to see, his sense of smell reassured him that it was Esau, despite the voice sounding like that of Jacob. Rebekah had anticipated this well by dressing Jacob in Esau's clothes. The outdoorsy Esau's clothing smelled like a fertile field, one the LORD had blessed with fruitfulness.

27:28 May God give you of heaven's dew and of earth's richness—an abundance of grain and new wine.

The blessing with which Isaac blesses Jacob implies the longer-term fulfillment of the promise of the land to Abraham's descendants. Only they will control land[7] on which **dew** will fall and which will grow grain and grapes. Intentionally or not, Isaac is trying to give to Esau's descendants the benefits of the promise of the land and in doing so is actively working against what God had revealed concerning those descendants in his message to Rebekah before the twins were born in Genesis 25:23-25. Unwittingly Isaac is actually cooperating with God's promise since it is actually Jacob's descendants whom he is blessing.

27:29 May nations serve you and peoples bow down to you. Be lord over your brothers, and may the sons of your mother bow down to you. May those who curse you be cursed and those who bless you be blessed."

The echoes of the language of the promise become explicit as Isaac continues in his blessing of Jacob, whom he thinks is Esau. Now he is explicitly going against God's revelation in his intention and yet unknowingly cooperating with it. The fulfillment of God's promises is

---

[7]Remember that Abram had been told that his descendants would have to wait 400 years to receive the land which God promised (Gen 15:13).

ultimately in God's hands, and here he works to reveal his purposes in spite of Isaac, even through the deception of Rebekah and Jacob.

Nations will be subordinate to the descendants of Jacob, and even among his brothers Jacob will be the lord. One wonders whether the plural "brothers" hints that there may have been other sons born to Isaac and Rebekah whose names have not been mentioned or whether this is a bit of poetic license. The blessing is apparently in Hebrew poetry with its "synonymous parallelism."

The blessing seems to point forward to the motif of brothers bowing down to other brothers in the Joseph narrative and is thus a narrative anticipation of what will come later in Genesis. Isaac ends with the hope or assurance that the descendants of Jacob will be protected by God in the same way (and with the same words) that the LORD had reassured Abram of his protection when he initially gave the promise in chapter 12. Those who curse the descendants of Jacob will receive God's curse. Conversely, those who bless his descendants will receive God's blessing. Isaac tries to carry the promise forward to the next generation of Abraham's descendants through his firstborn and favored son Esau, but in fact, does so for Jacob.

E. ISAAC AND ESAU DISCOVER JACOB'S TRICK (27:30-33)

27:30 After Isaac finished blessing him and Jacob had scarcely left his father's presence, his brother Esau came in from hunting.

Rebekah and Jacob's timing on their scheme was just good enough. Jacob left Isaac's presence immediately[8] before Esau returned from his hunt in the field. The unnecessary use of "Isaac,[9] his father" and "Esau, his brother" seems to be the narrator's way of emphasizing the relationship between Jacob, Isaac, and Esau. The trick which Jacob perpetuated was against his own father and his own brother and makes it even more questionable.

27:31 He too prepared some tasty food and brought it to his father. Then he said to him, "My father, sit up and eat some of my game, so that you may give me your blessing."

---

[8]The Hebrew uses the emphatic construction, infinitive absolute followed by the verb of the same root to emphasize how nearly the ruse had been to being discovered.

[9]The NIV omits Isaac's name, perhaps because it seems redundant in English. Perhaps so, but this misses the subtle way the narrator keeps reminding the reader of the enormity of the betrayal by recalling the relationships between the parties involved.

The Hebrew is more repetitive than the NIV here. Literally it reads, "And he, even he prepared delicacies and brought it to his father. Then he said to his father, 'Rise up my father and eat some of his son's game so that your life will bless me." Esau emphasizes his relationship to his father as [favored] son. The fact that Esau asked Isaac to "**sit up**" may indicate that Isaac was laying down on what is presumed to be his deathbed.

27:32 His father Isaac asked him, "Who are you?" "I am your son," he answered, "your firstborn, Esau."

Again the relationship of father and son is emphasized. This time the NIV catches it by a more literal translation. **Esau** uses the word "**firstborn**" evidently because status attaches to that position. But the word reminds the reader of the theme of reversal of ordinary status in the working out of God's promise. The "greater" will serve the "lesser" according to Genesis 25:23. Esau presumes that he is the "greater" because he is the older by a few minutes.

27:33 Isaac trembled violently and said, "Who was it, then, that hunted game and brought it to me? I ate it just before you came and I blessed him—and indeed he will be blessed!"

The NIV's "**trembled violently**," while accurate, loses something of the Hebrew's "Isaac trembled with a very great trembling." This comment about the emotional state of Isaac upon realizing how he and Esau had been fooled speaks volumes. Until now Isaac's resistance to the LORD's stated will that the descendants of the greater of his sons would serve those of the lesser can only be inferred. In this text it becomes plain how much Isaac had invested emotionally in his determination to bless Esau. The Hebrew narratives rarely comment explicitly upon the emotions of its human characters. Isaac asks the question to which the readers already know the answer, "Then who was it that I blessed?" He concludes that his blessing cannot be rescinded even though it was obtained through deceit. Jacob would indeed be blessed. Isaac almost seems to recognize the folly of his plan to bless Esau in contradiction to the LORD's word to Rebekah. He now concedes that the blessing will indeed come through Jacob and not his favored son Esau. Resistant though Isaac may have initially been to the reversal of the normal birth order, he now concedes the point.

F. ISAAC PREDICTS A FUTURE OF CONFLICT
FOR ESAU WITH JACOB (27:34-40)

27:34 When Esau heard his father's words, he burst out with a loud and bitter cry and said to his father, "Bless me—me too, my father!"

Just as Isaac's trembling at the thought of Jacob being blessed had been extreme, so is Esau's response to this news. He cried out with "an exceedingly **loud and bitter cry**."[10] Esau's anguished words show his pathos, "**Bless me**, even me, **my father!**" The words are desperate because Esau understands the enormity of what has happened. Perhaps, Esau suggests, there can be more than one blessed son!

27:35 But he said, "Your brother came deceitfully and took your blessing."

Isaac explains the problem from his point of view by describing Jacob to Esau as "your **brother**." For Isaac it does not matter that Jacob used deceit to get the **blessing**. However obtained, the blessing of Esau had been taken by Jacob and therefore could not be given to Esau. What has been done is done and there is no reversing it. It seems unlikely that the narrator shares Isaac's point of view as will be seen in the discussion of Jacob's deathbed blessing of his sons in chapter 49. Even patriarchal blessings are not divine predestination.

27:36 Esau said, "Isn't he rightly named Jacob ? He has deceived me these two times: He took my birthright, and now he's taken my blessing!" Then he asked, "Haven't you reserved any blessing for me?"

Esau plays on the name **Jacob** (יַעֲקֹב, ya'ăqōb) and the verb "**deceived**" (עָקַב, 'āqab). The grabber at Esau's heel at birth has grabbed the blessing. There is also wordplay between the Hebrew phrases "my birthright" (בְּכֹרָתִי, bᵉkōrāthî) and "**my blessing**? (בִּרְכָתִי, birkāthî). The fact that Isaac had not reserved any blessing for Esau as he hoped indicates that Isaac had no intention of blessing Jacob in any way and had reserved the entirety of his blessing and its presumed power for his oldest son. The fact that there is nothing left for Esau is a direct consequence of Isaac's favoritism to Esau.

27:37 Isaac answered Esau, "I have made him lord over you and have made all his relatives his servants, and I have sustained him with grain and new wine. So what can I possibly do for you, my son?"

Isaac rehearses the promise he had already given to Jacob and felt he could not rescind. The periphrastic tendency of the NIV clouds the issues in this verse. In the NIV Isaac says that Jacob had been made "lord" over **Esau**, but this translation is questionable. The terminology is different and one would not expect the Hebrew word גְּבִיר (gᵉbîr), translated by the NIV here as "lord," to be the natural opposite of "servant."[11]

---

[10]Literal rendering of the Hebrew וַיִּצְעַק צְעָקָה גְּדֹלָה וּמָרָה עַד־מְאֹד (wayyiṣ'aq ṣᵉ'āqāh gᵉdōlāh ûmārāh 'ad-mᵉ'od); cf. NRSV.

[11]Gᵉbîr means "mighty one" and often refers to great warriors in battle. Cf. Robin Wakely, "גבר," NIDOTTE, 1:810-814.

Further the use of "**relatives**" for the more literal "brothers" is another example. I suggested above that there may have been other brothers in Isaac and Rebekah's family. If so, there seems to be a difference between the relationship of Jacob and Esau on the one hand, and Jacob and the rest of his brothers, on the other. Jacob is to be Esau's *gᵊbîr*, but the rest of the brothers will be his servants.

In any case Jacob certainly is given the first position as the son with the blessing. Isaac regards the blessing as a zero sum game. Since Jacob had been given so much in terms of his position among Isaac's descendants and in the future possession of a Promised Land that is fertile, there is little left to give to Esau. What Isaac has said he has said, and there is no going back on it even though Esau is his beloved son.

27:38 Esau said to his father, "Do you have only one blessing, my father? Bless me too, my father!" Then Esau wept aloud.

Esau asks the quite understandable question, "Is there **only one blessing**?" Evidently the answer is in the nonresponse of Isaac. For Isaac there is only one blessing, and he has already given it away. Esau's tearful plea arouses pity for his situation and perplexity at Isaac's understanding of the blessing. Esau's weeping indicates just how important the blessing was to him, and not merely for selfish reasons. It is God's blessings as well as his father's blessing that he wants.

27:39 His father Isaac answered him, "Your dwelling will be away from the earth's richness, away from the dew of heaven above.

As the NIV understands it, Esau's descendants will not experience the land's (**earth's**) **richness** or the revivifying and life-giving **dew** from **heaven**. His descendants will thus live in a less fertile and more arid land than the descendants of Jacob. If understood in this way, Isaac's message to Esau is a sort of antiblessing. Esau will not receive the very things promised to Jacob in the blessing. The original and canonical audiences knew that Isaac had accurately anticipated the future. The Edomites, Esau's descendants, lived around the south end of the Dead Sea in an arid and relatively unfertile land.

But the Hebrew is not as unambiguous as the NIV and other translations seem to assume. Heard suggests rendering Isaac's statement, "Off of the bounty of the earth will be your dwelling and off of the dew of heaven above."[12] This translation retains the ambiguity of the Hebrew preposition מִן (*min*), which is used here either as a "privative" meaning "away from" or as a "partitive" meaning "a part of."[13] If the preposition is read in the par-

---

[12]Heard, *Dynamics of Diselection*, p. 112.

[13]The ESV helpfully provides a footnote giving, "and of" as an alternative translation for "and away from" in the main text.

titive sense, Isaac is promising Esau something positive. Like Ishmael's, Esau's destiny need not be read negatively. Isaac's words can be understood to imply a secondary blessing, but a blessing nevertheless.

27:40 You will live by the sword and you will serve your brother. But when you grow restless, you will throw his yoke from off your neck."

Without a fertile land from which to draw, Esau's descendants will live by raiding the possessions of others and in continual tension with them. They will be subordinated in some way to the descendants of Jacob, that is, they will "**serve**" them. The potentially positive part of Isaac's message for Esau is that his descendants will tire of servitude to the descendants of Jacob and they will then rebel against them and free themselves from that bondage. The canonical audience will see anticipated the times of Edom and Israel's history when the former asserted its independence from the latter.

G. REBEKAH SCHEMES TO SAVE JACOB FROM ESAU'S ANGER (27:41-46)

27:41 Esau held a grudge against Jacob because of the blessing his father had given him. He said to himself, "The days of mourning for my father are near; then I will kill my brother Jacob."

The rare Hebrew verb translated as "**held a grudge**"[14] in the NIV does seem to mean that in Genesis 50:15. In that passage Jacob's brothers fear that Joseph still holds onto a grudge against them. They assume he was only waiting for his father's death to turn on them. But in Genesis 49:23 it seems to refer to actual physical attack. If that is the meaning, then perhaps **Esau** actually beat up **Jacob** but without killing him. He would wait for his father's death to finish the job!

Esau had no way of knowing that Isaac would last another 80 years! This was not to be his final illness. The narrator gives us a rare example in Hebrew narrative of internal monologue by recording the internal words of Esau. His plan is to wait for Isaac to die and be mourned and then murder his own brother, Jacob.

27:42 When Rebekah was told what her older son Esau had said, she sent for her younger son Jacob and said to him, "Your brother Esau is consoling himself with the thought of killing you.

Somehow Esau's plans must have been verbalized because someone (a servant?) reported them to his mother Rebekah. Rebekah's "eyes and

---

[14]The verb שָׂטַם (śāṭam) is found only six times in the Old Testament, three of which are in Genesis.

ears" are everywhere in this narrative. The narrator yet again reminds us that Esau is the older and Jacob the younger of the twins. Rebekah told Jacob that Esau was assuaging his anger over what had happened by planning to kill him. Revenge is sweet and that sweetness was keeping Esau from acting immediately and bringing grief to his ailing father.

27:43 Now then, my son, do what I say: Flee at once to my brother Laban in Haran. 27:44 Stay with him for a while until your brother's fury subsides.

Rebekah again commands the 40-year-old Jacob to obey her. In order to avoid Esau's revenge he must return to Rebekah's family in Haran out of Esau's reach. There her brother Laban, who runs the household, would provide protection. Rebekah assumes that it will only take a few days[15] after the death of Isaac for his anger to subside. She, like Esau, assumes that Isaac's days are numbered.

27:45 When your brother is no longer angry with you and forgets what you did to him, I'll send word for you to come back from there. Why should I lose both of you in one day?"

Rebekah rightly assumes that eventually Esau's anger will subside and he will forget what Jacob had done to him in stealing his birthright and blessing. Interestingly she takes no responsibility for what has transpired. Was Rebekah's complicity in the scheme a secret? Rebekah promises to send for Jacob when Esau's anger is assuaged, a promise she never keeps. Jacob spends a full 20 years in Haran and only leaves when he has accumulated enough resources to live on his own.

Rebekah here shows her love for both Jacob and Esau, although admittedly she favors the former. If Esau murders Jacob out of revenge and then is killed or banished for murdering him, their mother Rebekah would lose both of them at the same time. Better to separate the estranged parties than to see their animosity boil over into violence.

27:46 Then Rebekah said to Isaac, "I'm disgusted with living because of these Hittite women. If Jacob takes a wife from among the women of this land, from Hittite women like these, my life will not be worth living."

Ever the schemer, Rebekah "handles" the blind and less than insightful Isaac. While Esau's marriage to **Hittite women** was initially a source of bitterness to Isaac and Rebekah (Gen 26:35), here Rebekah escalates the concern into mammoth proportions. Rebekah claims to abhor her life because of this fact. What would her life be if her favored son Jacob also took such a wife? This, of course, is another ruse to get

---

[15]Literal translation of Hebrew אֲחָדִים יָמִים (*yāmîm 'ăḥādîm*). NIV's periphrastic "for a while" obscures this.

Isaac to cooperate with her plans. Her feigned spirituality is too much to swallow. Intermarriage with the inhabitants of the land was a genuine spiritual danger for the patriarchal family and for both the original and canonical audiences of the Pentateuch, but the danger had not suddenly increased since Jacob had cheated Esau of his father's blessing.

GENESIS 28

H. ISAAC SENDS JACOB BACK TO REBEKAH'S FAMILY
TO MARRY (28:1-5)

28:1 So Isaac called for Jacob and blessed him and commanded him: "Do not marry a Canaanite woman.

Isaac calls **for Jacob** for the first time since he discovered the trick that had been played on him and Esau. The fact that he blesses him when he comes is probably meant to reassure him of their relationship despite the deception. Isaac commanded the still single Jacob **not to marry a "Canaanite" woman.** In Isaac's mind the local Hittite[1] women whom Esau had married would fall into the category of Canaanite.

28:2 Go at once to Paddan Aram, to the house of your mother's father Bethuel. Take a wife for yourself there, from among the daughters of Laban, your mother's brother.

We are not told exactly why Isaac did not send a servant to procure a wife for Jacob as his father Abraham had done in his own case. Isaac sends Jacob himself back to the extended family which Abram had left in obedience to God's command and promises. Abraham was wary of sending Isaac back there, but Isaac, for some reason, feels no such compunction. Both the NIV and NRSV interpret the Hebrew, "Arise! Go to Paddan Aram" as **"Go at once to Paddan Aram."**

To be technical, in returning to the extended household which Abram had originally left, Jacob would be reversing the LORD's original command to leave his father's house.

Isaac directs Jacob to the house of **Bethuel**, Rebekah's father, and specifically to one of the **daughters of Laban**, Rebekah's **brother**, for a potential wife. Evidently there was enough communication between the two families for Isaac to know that Laban had at least two daughters.

28:3 May God Almighty bless you and make you fruitful and increase your numbers until you become a community of peoples. 28:4 May he

---

[1]On the ambiguity of this term see P.E. Satterthwaite and D.W. Baker, "Nations of Canaan," *DOTP*, p. 602.

give you and your descendants the blessing given to Abraham, so that you may take possession of the land where you now live as an alien, the land God gave to Abraham."

Isaac takes the occasion of Jacob's send-off to bless him yet again, this time explicitly transferring to Jacob the original promise to Abraham which he had himself received. Isaac uses El Shaddai as the name for God, a phrase of uncertain meaning which the NIV renders "**God Almighty**."[2]

In his blessing Isaac uses the language of the creation mandate in Genesis 1:26-28 and the original promise to Abram in Genesis 12:1-7. Isaac calls down El Shaddai's creational blessing on Jacob so that, unlike his father and grandfather, he would be fruitful and increase in numbers until his descendants became a "congregation"[3] **of peoples**. Isaac blesses Jacob with the wish that El Shaddai would transfer the promise of Abraham to Jacob, specifically as it relates to the promise of the land. Since Jacob was about to leave the Promised Land to find a wife, his father's reassurance of the ultimate fulfillment of the promise of the land for his descendants must have been important to Jacob.

28:5 Then Isaac sent Jacob on his way, and he went to Paddan Aram, to Laban son of Bethuel the Aramean, the brother of Rebekah, who was the mother of Jacob and Esau.

Having blessed him yet again, **Isaac** sends **Jacob on his way**. He traveled **to Paddan Aram**, an alternative name for the region in which the city of Haran was found. He went **to Laban** whose familial connection to Rebekah is spelled out in monotonous detail. The importance of these family relationships is emphasized repeatedly in this section. Laban is described as the **son of Bethuel the Aramean**. Bethuel was Rebekah's father. Here he is described as the Aramean. The Arameans (or Syrians), the most notable nation to Israel's direct north, had a long history as both friend and foe of Israel of which the canonical audience would be all too aware. **Rebekah**, we are reminded, **was the mother of** both **Jacob and Esau.**

---

[2]According to Exodus 6:3, if taken at face value, El Shaddai, not Yahweh, was the actual name used by God when he appeared to Abraham, Isaac, and Jacob.

[3]The Hebrew word here, קָהָל (*qāhāl*) is used of the assembly or congregation of Israel gathered together. This is the Hebrew word which the LXX translated as ἐκκλησία (*ekklēsia*), usually rendered "church" or "assembly" in the New Testament.

I. ESAU MARRIES AN ISHMAELITE WOMAN ATTEMPTING TO PLEASE HIS PARENTS (28:6-9)

28:6 Now Esau learned that Isaac had blessed Jacob and had sent him to Paddan Aram to take a wife from there, and that when he blessed him he commanded him, "Do not marry a Canaanite woman," 28:7 and that Jacob had obeyed his father and mother and had gone to Paddan Aram. 28:8 Esau then realized how displeasing the Canaanite women were to his father Isaac; 28:9 so he went to Ishmael and married Mahalath, the sister of Nebaioth and daughter of Ishmael son of Abraham, in addition to the wives he already had.

Esau observed[4] Isaac's blessing of Jacob and sending to the ancestral homeland to be wed. In particular he noted Isaac's command to Jacob not to marry a Canaanite woman. Having observed Isaac's concern that Jacob not marry a Canaanite woman, it suddenly dawned on Esau what an evil[5] thing his marriages were in Isaac's eyes. It is not clear why it would have taken these events for Esau to realize this. Had Isaac and Rebekah not expressed their concerns when it happened? Esau had violated traditional procedure in taking wives by himself without his father playing the typical role of negotiator with the brides' parents. Perhaps this explains why Esau only later realized the problem his wives were for his family. But this may also be part of the portrayal of Esau as somewhat naïve or even dimwitted. He sells his birthright for a bowl of soup and is unaware until it is too late of Rebekah and Jacob's scheming.

Esau attempts to save the situation by taking another wife. If Isaac is unhappy with his Hittite wives, surely a marriage to a first cousin from the family of Isaac's half-brother Ishmael will please his father! Once again Esau does not ask Isaac's opinion nor request that he negotiate the financial terms. Once again he is naïve if he expects Isaac (and Rebekah) to approve of this marriage.

He married Mahalath,[6] who is called the sister of Ishmael's oldest son Nebaioth. This may be because Nebaioth was her full brother from the same mother and not just a half-brother. The canonical audience would undoubtedly know of the northern Arabian tribe descended from him.[7]

---

[4]The Hebrew reads literally, "And Esau saw that." The NIV seems to imply that someone else observed this and informed Esau.

[5]The Hebrew uses the word "evil" (רַע, *ra'*), while the NIV paraphrases here.

[6]She is called Basemath in Genesis 36:3. See further discussion there.

[7]Scholars no longer connect Nebaioth to the later Nabateans for "linguistic and historical reasons." Cf. W. Creighton Marlowe, "Nebaioth," *EDB*, p. 952.

V. JACOB MEETS GOD AT BETHEL ON HIS WAY FROM THE PROMISED LAND (28:10-22)

On the road to Haran, Jacob is without money or protection or family or blessing. The scheme to secure the blessing for Jacob had sent him away without it. Jacob is on the way to Haran to get a wife who would share Jacob's desire to see God's promises come to fruition. Jacob stops for the night at a place that later came to be called Bethel, "House of God." While there Jacob receives a dream of a staircase in which angels came from heaven to earth and back again indicating to Jacob that the LORD was sending his angels on missions to help Jacob. In the dream the LORD himself reiterates the promise originally given to Abraham and Isaac for Jacob, assuring him that no matter what his current circumstances the promise was still in place. Jacob awakes to express his wonder and to attempt to strike a bargain with God. He promises to return a tithe of whatever blessings God actually gave him while he was away from the Promised Land.

This narrative is paired in the palistrophic structure of the Jacob and Esau narratives with the narrative of the return of Jacob to the land 20 years later in Genesis 32:1-32 and with the narrative of his later return to Bethel in Genesis 35:6-15. God appears to him as he leaves the land and reappears to him when he returns to the land. He returns having learned lessons and with lessons still to learn, but God has never left him.

A. JACOB'S DREAM AT BETHEL (28:10-17)

28:10 Jacob left Beersheba and set out for Haran.
The narrative turns to focus again on **Jacob**, who leaves his parents and family at **Beersheba** for the long journey to the ancestral homeland. Here the homeland is referred to by the name of the city, **Haran**. Elsewhere it is termed Paddan Aram or Aram-naharaim, the area near the great bend in the Euphrates in northern Mesopotamia, in modern Syria. The fact that Haran is used may echo the original call of Abram from Haran in Genesis 12:1-3. If so, Jacob is returning to the very place from which his grandfather had been sent out.

28:11 When he reached a certain place, he stopped for the night because the sun had set. Taking one of the stones there, he put it under his head and lay down to sleep.
While still in the Promised Land, Jacob stops for the night. The importance of what is about to happen is indicated by the way the nar-

rative slows down and gives great detail. Jacob encountered a certain place. He lodged there for the night because the sun had set, and he didn't want to risk traveling in the dark. He took one of the stones of that place and put his head on it and went to sleep in that place. The word "**place**" is used three times, apparently to emphasize the importance of that very place. The NIV's paraphrastic tendency removes two of the mentions of the word for "place."

28:12 He had a dream in which he saw a stairway resting on the earth, with its top reaching to heaven, and the angels of God were ascending and descending on it.

At that place Jacob **had a dream in which he saw a stairway**[8] fixed to earth **with its top reaching** the heavens. The messengers or **angels of God were** using the stairway to travel down to earth or up to the heavens. Jacob is about to leave the Promised Land for an uncertain future. He is running away from the wrath of his brother Esau because he conspired with his mother to swindle him out of birthright and blessing. Jacob seems unable to trust in the LORD's timing. The LORD had promised that the older or greater would serve the younger or lesser. But the timing of that promise's fulfillment was to be left to the LORD. Neither the birthright nor the blessing means much to Jacob if he has to run away penniless to avoid his brother's revenge. The dream seems to be reminding Jacob that God's emissaries are busy at work in the Promised Land whether the heir apparent to that land is present or not.

In the wider narrative context this passage serves as a counterpoint to the Babel narrative (Gen 11:1-9). At Babel, humanity, in direct disobedience to God's commission to fill the earth, attempts to found an urban empire with a tower reaching to the heavens. In a striking bit of sarcasm the narrator informs us that Babel's great tower required that the LORD come down from his lofty heights to even be able to see it.[9] The man who will come to be called Israel is in a desperate situation. He brought this upon himself by his refusal to trust the LORD to fulfill the implicit promises that were made in the prebirth message to his mother Rebekah. Unlike the Babel narrative where humanity tries to reach heaven by their own efforts, Jacob sees that the connection between heaven and earth, though invisible, has certainly been already built. Humanity cannot climb a stairway to heaven of its own design. Instead we must accept in faith the fact that the stairway has already

---

[8]The traditional translation "ladder" is probably mistaken. While the word occurs only here in the Hebrew Bible, the cognate words in related Semitic languages refer to stairs; cf. KB, "סֻלָּם."

[9]On this passage see, Kissling, *Genesis Volume 1*, p. 383.

been built by God and is in constant use by his messengers. It is even possible that the stairs are reminiscent of the stairstep pyramidal shape of the Babylonian ziggurat.

28:13 There above it stood the LORD, and he said: "I am the LORD, the God of your father Abraham and the God of Isaac. I will give you and your descendants the land on which you are lying.

In Jacob's dream the LORD spoke to him words of reassurance as he was about to leave the Promised Land for what turned out to be 20 years. The LORD introduces himself as the "**God of Abraham**, [Jacob's] **father and the God of Isaac.**" The wording is curious. Isaac is literally Jacob's father; Abraham only his grandfather. But in this passage it is Abraham who is termed Jacob's "father." The Hebrew word, like the English often means something like "forefather." But why is Abraham alone singled out for this title? It may be that the LORD is reminding Jacob of the original recipient of the promise of the land. The favoritism of Isaac and Rebekah for their respective sons had muddied the water. Isaac had blessed Jacob only by being tricked into it. In this passage the LORD makes it clear that, Isaac's ambiguous blessing notwithstanding, he is guaranteeing that the promise of the land originally given to Abraham would go to Jacob's descendants and not someone else. To have the father's blessing was important in Jacob's eyes. Of far greater importance is the blessing of God. Up until this point, however, Jacob has not been focused on getting God's blessing, only his father's.

28:14 Your descendants will be like the dust of the earth, and you will spread out to the west and to the east, to the north and to the south. All peoples on earth will be blessed through you and your offspring.

Having reassured Jacob of the land promise, the LORD reiterates for Jacob the promise of a great nation. Its population will be uncountable like the particles of dust on the earth and Jacob's descendants will **spread out** in every direction. But there is more. The final element of the promise to Abraham also belongs to Jacob and his descendants. God's blessing on every "clan" (מִשְׁפָּחָה, *mišpāḥāh*) on earth will flow through Jacob (later named Israel) and his descendants. The promise of having the privilege of being the channel of God's universal blessing to the entirety of humanity will be Jacob's as it was Abraham's. The stem of the verb "to bless" here is niphal, which is typically passive in Hebrew. The NRSV, unlike the RSV, rightly translates it as a passive here as does the NIV. But even if the reflexive translation is preferred as in the NRSV margin, the point is fundamentally the same from a theological perspective. Jacob need not fear that his deceitfulness will result in the rescinding of God's promise to Rebekah. The line of promise will flow through Jacob's descendants, not Esau's, deserved or not.

28:15 I am with you and will watch over you wherever you go, and I will bring you back to this land. I will not leave you until I have done what I have promised you."

God also makes promises for Jacob personally, not just for his descendants. He promises his presence wherever he goes ("I will be **with you**") and promises to return him to the Promised Land. He reassures Jacob that he will never forsake him until his promises to Jacob have been fulfilled. Typically theologians call this divine providence. The reader is invited to understand that even the difficult and unfair things which Jacob is about to face happen under the providential care of the LORD.

28:16 When Jacob awoke from his sleep, he thought, "Surely the LORD is in this place, and I was not aware of it."

Upon waking from his dream **Jacob** realizes that what he had just experienced was not "just" a dream, but a divine revelation. Jacob comes to recognize that the LORD's very presence was in that place and he did not know it. This should have resulted in humility for Jacob. If the LORD is present even when we are not aware of it, we should be very careful how we conduct our lives in his presence. What Jacob thought was a rock pillow was a holy place. Jacob's use of the word "LORD" for God is anachronistic. He does not call the name of the place "House of the LORD" but "house of God." The name Yahweh had not been revealed to the patriarchs (Exod 6:3). The narrator is making the point that the God who revealed himself to Jacob was none other than the God who revealed his name as Yahweh to Moses.

28:17 He was afraid and said, "How awesome is this place! This is none other than the house of God; this is the gate of heaven."

Jacob comes to realize the implications of what he had just seen. He was afraid because he was standing in a fearsome[10] place. These stairs were the entrance gate to heaven, and he was standing in the very **house of God**. The original and canonical audiences knew of the Tabernacle/Temple and the fear that places of such extraordinary holiness produced. In many contemporary expressions of Christian faith this sort of reverent fear has been removed from our thoughts and therefore our experience of God.

---

[10]The NIV's paraphrase "awesome" loses the connection in the Hebrew between the verb "to be afraid" (יָרֵא, *yārē'*) and "fearsome" (niphal participle of *yārē'*).

B. JACOB'S VOW TO GOD IN EXCHANGE
FOR HIS PROTECTION AND BLESSING (28:18-22)

28:18 Early the next morning Jacob took the stone he had placed under his head and set it up as a pillar and poured oil on top of it. 28:19 He called that place Bethel, though the city used to be called Luz.

Jacob evidently awoke in the middle of the night only to realize that he had experienced a divine revelation. The next morning Jacob consecrated the place where he had received this revelation as a holy place. His stone pillow became a **"pillar"** (מַצֵּבָה, *maṣṣēbāh*). The original and canonical readers would find this quite striking, for such pillars were used in Canaanite worship and were strictly forbidden to Israel in the Torah (Exod 23:24; Lev 26:1). But Jacob does not do this in order to forsake his loyalty to monotheism. Instead he expresses his gratitude to God and recognizes the sanctity of what had just happened to him. The fact that this practice by Jacob implicitly receives the narrator's commendation indicates that the original readers knew that the Patriarchal period was very different from their own. It should not be judged by the later revealed standards of the Torah when such revelation was not available to the patriarchs.

By pouring oil on top of the stone which Jacob stood upright, he effectively anointed that place as a holy place. Because Jacob had come to understand that in some sense God had chosen to dwell there, he named the place Bethel, or "house of God." The audience would have been familiar with the city which grew up around this place. Its previous name had been Luz and presumably the original audience was familiar with that (Canaanite?) name. By renaming, the place comes to have a special significance in the working out of God's purposes for the descendants of Jacob as Bethlehem and Nazareth would for Christians.

Jacob says, "Surely the LORD (Yahweh) is in this place" (v. 16) but goes on to call the place Bethel, meaning "house of God" not "house of the LORD (Yahweh)." This again shows the Yahwistic perspective of the narrator and not the actual words spoken by Jacob.[11]

28:20 Then Jacob made a vow, saying, "If God will be with me and will watch over me on this journey I am taking and will give me food to eat and clothes to wear 28:21 so that I return safely to my father's house, then the LORD will be my God 28:22 and this stone that I have set up as a pillar will be God's house, and of all that you give me I will give you a tenth."

---

[11]Wenham, "The Religion of the Patriarchs," p. 181.

It is hard to know what to make of Jacob's vow. On the one hand Jacob does make a sort of commitment to God. On the other hand that commitment seems like bargaining. God must meet certain conditions and under those conditions, and only under those conditions, Jacob makes promises to the LORD.

Hasn't the dream convinced Jacob of the LORD's reality and power? Isn't the LORD already Jacob's God? Isn't Jacob diminishing God by saying that if certain conditions are met, Jacob would make the LORD "his" god? Notice Jacob does not say he will recognize that the LORD is the only God, just his god. Can God be bribed with tithes from what he has given to Jacob out of his grace? Jacob, whether he realizes it or not, is in no position to bargain with God. God, unlike Isaac and Esau, cannot be swindled or manipulated. It does not seem as though Jacob understands this very clearly at this point in his life.

God had already promised to be with Jacob. That promise came without conditions. Jacob turns the fulfillment of that promise into a condition of his being willing to serve God. His conditions are four. God must be with Jacob, guard his journey, provide him with food and clothing, and return him to his father's house in peace.[12] If God meets these conditions Jacob makes three promises: that the LORD would be his God, that the pillar he set up would be remembered as God's house, and that he would tithe[13] his possessions. God does not respond to Jacob's deal explicitly. However, the contrast between the gracious and seemingly conditionless promises of God and the bargaining of Jacob are a part of his portrayal. Jacob tries to manipulate everyone and everything in his life for his own ends, even God!

---

[12]The NIV is periphrastic here.

[13]On tithing as an example of the Patriarchs obeying the Torah before it was revealed in a sort of obedience to "natural law," see the discussion on Genesis 14:20 above.

EXCURSUS ON TRADITIONAL
HISTORICAL-CRITICAL APPROACHES:

GENESIS 28:10-22 AS REPRESENTATIVE EXEMPLAR TEXT

It is not one of the central purposes of this commentary to interact systematically with traditional historical-critical approaches. I have, however, made reference to such approaches from time to time. I thought it might be helpful to the reader if I interact with the approach as applied to one representative text, Genesis 28:10-22. For simplicity's sake I have chosen to use Steck's standard German guide to Old Testament historical-critical exegesis as a representative treatment.[14]

Steck takes the hypothetical student through the text in Hebrew to note what would seem to him to be tensions. He notices that the text makes no sense without a larger context; there must be a reason why Jacob is on a trip from Beersheba to Haran (v. 10). But for him the text presupposes that Jacob is going to Haran to flee from Esau's wrath, not to seek a wife. He never raises the possibility that both reasons are legitimate and that the trip had multiple purposes. As a result he assumes that Genesis 28 presupposes Genesis 27:41-45 but not Genesis 28:1-9. Thus two different reasons for the trip imply two different sources.

Steck sees a sort of artistic symmetrical structure in this narrative. This would ordinarily be a sign of unitary authorship. But Steck goes on to argue that this seeming symmetry hides a number of problems in the text as we have it.

Steck focuses on the fact that the place was called Bethel, where Jeroboam set up an altar with a bull-calf statue when the northern kingdom broke away from the south in c. 930 B.C. Steck reasons that Bethel would have no religious significance to anyone after the consolidation of worship in Jerusalem in the time of Josiah.[15] The focus on Bethel as a place of divine revelation implies for Steck that the source underlying at least part of this text was written prior to the time of Josiah. Only then would Bethel be important to the audience in religious terms. In terms of the traditional dating for the four Pentateuchal sources this would predate D and P.

Steck notes what he terms "changes" in the designation of God: YHWH in 28:13,16 but Elohim in 28:12,17,20,22. Jacob names the place

---

[14]Odil Hannes Steck, *Old Testament Exegesis: A Guide to the Methodology*, 2nd ed., trans. by James D. Nogalski (Atlanta: Scholars Press, 1998).

[15]2 Kings 17:28 informs us that a priesthood continued at Bethel after the destruction of the Northern Kingdom in 722 B.C. The altar at Bethel remained in use until Josiah destroyed it (2 Kgs 23:15).

Beth-el implying that he had seen El. El is either a shortened form of Elohim, the common Hebrew word for God, or the name of the head god of the Canaanite pantheon. Steck seems to opt for the latter, but gives no justification for such a decision. Even though Bethel is built off the word El for God, Jacob says, "Surely YHWH is in this place." Steck presumes that such variations in divine names indicate varying sources rather than a theological point by the narrator. The point of putting YHWH into the mouths of the patriarchs may be to indicate that the God who appeared to Abraham, Isaac, and Jacob is none other than the God who revealed himself to Moses under the name YHWH. Steck does not seriously consider this possibility.

Steck also notes that some parts of the narrative mention angels of God (v. 12) but others YHWH (v. 13). When Jacob wakes up, he does not mention the angels, but YHWH (v. 16) and God (v. 17). He does not consider that the dream may have included both an appearance of angels and of God or that the appearance of God was more significant for Jacob than the appearance of angels.[16] For Steck the fact that the stone is anointed with oil in verse 18 but this anointing is not mentioned in verse 22 indicates divergent sources. The fact that Jacob is said to be afraid after the theophany, rather than before it, also indicates textual disruption for Steck. This is evidently based on the assumption that such fear must always precede a theophany rather than follow it. Steck does mention the possibility that these pieces of evidence are peculiar only because of modern demands for a text's logic and consistency. He does not, however, seriously pursue this line of reasoning.

Steck sees a tension between 28:17 ("This is the house of God") and 28:22 ("This stone shall be God's house"). He reasons that one source assumes that the naming took place on Jacob's first visit to Bethel while the other source only promises a naming for the future. I fail to see why these two statements are in conflict with each other.

Steck is on firmer ground when he notes that there seem to be three times when Jacob names the place, twice naming it Bethel (28:19; 35:15) and once El-Bethel (35:7). He also notes that there seems to be confusion over exactly where the dream occurred. Was it a city or not (28:19)? Was the city, if it was a city, the same as Luz (28:19; Judg 1:23) or merely a nearby city (Josh 16:2)?

---

[16]Steck, *Exegesis*, p. 187: "[T]he appearance of YHWH speaking in 28:12-17 excludes the conceptualization of the heavenly ladder with messengers on the other hand. Either YHWH encounters Jacob directly or the encounter results indirectly through God's messengers at the gate of heaven."

With all of these observations in hand, Steck turns to the explanatory framework of historical-critical methods to attempt to explain the
text's tensions. He begins with traditional *source criticism*. Given that
the text has none of the stylistic features attributed to P, Steck sees this
text as a conflation of J and E. The following verses are attributed to E:
12,17,20,21a,22 because they contain Elohim and verses 11,16a, and 18
because verse 12 presupposes Jacob's sleeping and dream and they
mention sleeping. The blessing which Jacob receives in verse 13-16b is
regarded as J; verse 21b, "then the LORD shall be my God," seems to be
J, but Steck finds this hard to square with Genesis 4:26, which seems to
say on the surface that for J YHWH was worshiped from the time of
Seth. How could YHWH not already be Jacob's God if this were so? For
Steck E tends to dominate this passage with J being only fragmentary.
This is contrary to the usual pattern where E, if it exists as an independent source, tends to be fragmentary, with J being the dominant
early source. He notes that the more recent theories of Rendtorff and
Blum use a different model that does not rely on imagining the traditional sources but is built around the supposition of complexes of tradition. These complexes of tradition were added to over time and only
came into the Pentateuch in its later stages. The traditional sources, J,
E, D, and P never existed independently of each other.[17]

Steck next turns to *transmission history* bringing in the evidence
from Hosea 12:5,7 (Eng. 12:4,6). Steck suggests that Hosea's account of
Jacob may well be literarily independent of Genesis. If so, he hypothe-
sizes three independent written references to an incident which must,
therefore, go back to a common older tradition. If, however, the text-
critical problem in Hosea 12:5 is resolved by reading "with us" as "to
him," then Hosea has the same J-source tradition, as Steck identifies it
in Genesis 28. The question then arises whether J is an expansion of E
or an independent transmission of a common tradition?

Steck opts for the latter after a rather convoluted argument based
on *form criticism* of vow episodes. Since parallel instances of vows
(Jephthah, Samuel's mother, Absalom) do not presuppose a promise
taken up in a vow, the promise in 28:13-15 *could not* have been a part of
the original E narrative. Further J did not merely expand an existing E
since E could not have both a promise and a vow.

Steck goes on to speculate that originally there was a Canaanite
holy place at Bethel with an etiological story attached to it that the Jacob

---

[17]For current discussion of these issues, see Thomas B. Dozeman and Konrad
Schmid, eds. *A Farewell to the Yahwist? The Composition of the Pentateuch in Recent
European Interpretation* (Atlanta: Society of Biblical Literature, 2006).

group adopted for its own purposes, identifying El as their god. Only later was Jacob's name attached to the founding of the site when the Canaanite story was incorporated into the Jacob cycle.

While this is not the place to give a detailed response to Steck, a few observations about his presuppositions are in order. Steck reads what he perceives to be tensions in the text as contradictions that must by definition deny unity of authorship. Often these "tensions" are at best subtle differences. For example, it is a fact that in the dream Jacob saw angels and God, but only mentioned God when he woke up. But this is not a tension unless one is looking for it. Angels are messengers sent to do God's bidding. Why Steck assumes that a dream could not contain both is perplexing. That Jacob does not mention the angels when he awakes is easily explained. He focuses on the most significant person which he saw in the dream.

Steck assumes that the use of YHWH as the divine name indicates conflicting sources. Exodus 6:3 most naturally reads as implying that Abraham, Isaac, and Jacob did not know the name of YHWH. How then does it get into the mouth of Jacob in Genesis 28:16,21? Steck does not seriously consider that the readership of the Pentateuch would know that the narrator was being technically anachronistic. Jacob did not literally use the name YHWH because he did not know it. But the original readers, who did know the name YHWH, would understand the narrator's point in putting it into the mouth of Jacob. The same God who later revealed the name YHWH to Israel revealed himself to Jacob at Bethel.

Another problem with Steck's approach is a questionable level of confidence about the conclusions of previous source criticism, form criticism, and transmission history. For example, form criticism sometimes assumes that it can identify pure literary forms in the Hebrew Bible with a precision that goes beyond the limitations of our evidence. Just because three stories which mention vows do not have preceding promises from God does not mean that we can identify a pure vow form and use that to determine that the promise which precedes the vow in Genesis 28:13-15 must come from a different hand than the story of the vow! To give another example from source criticism, the very existence of E, the late dating of P and even the very existence of J have been under serious challenge for several decades now. Steck takes little account of this research.[18]

Steck also displays a sort of presupposition about authors and editors: authors are completely consistent when they narrate a story, but

---

[18]Steck shows no knowledge of the groundbreaking work of Whybray, *The Making of the Pentateuch*. For a recent update on the disappearing Yahwist, see Dozeman and Schmid, eds., *A Farewell to the Yahwist?*

editors are sloppy. Both parts of this presupposition must be doubted. Authors are not pedantically consistent. Just because Jacob set the stone up for a pillar **and** poured oil on it in 28:18 does not mean that Jacob must mention both the stone and the oil in the vow in 28:22. The lack of mention of the oil in Jacob's vow speech is no indication of a sloppy editor. Authors often display such variation and minor inconsistencies. But this is no secure basis for positing a conflicting source.

Equally problematic is the assumption that ancient Hebrew editors were so sloppy. Supposedly 3,000 years later Western Bible scholars, who have no access to Hebrew as a living language and thus no native intuition about style can separate out disparate sources down to the level of words and even individual phrases. There is no plausible explanation why authors of the original sources are supposed to be so consistent, but editors so sloppy.[19]

Steck also makes questionable historical judgments. For example he assumes that the "el" in the name Bethel is the chief Canaanite god El rather than an abbreviated form of the common Hebrew word for God, Elohim. Why this choice is made is never explained. Many thoroughly monotheistic names in the Hebrew Bible, both early and late use "el" as an abbreviation for Elohim, the word for the one God. The names of Dani*el*, Ezeki*el*, Ishma*el*, Isra*el*, *El*imelech, and *El*isha, show this practice throughout the period narrated in the Old Testament. Jacob, in the only text that we have, gave the place the name Bethel (v. 19), but interpreted that as meaning the house of Elohim (vv. 17,22), not the house of El.[20]

Steck's approach is representative of another problem in the use of source, form, and tradition criticism on the Hebrew Bible. One possible explanatory hypothesis is built upon another until a veritable superstructure of hypotheses emerges. But all of the hypotheses are vulnerable to the potential for error in the earlier hypotheses. By assuming that variations in the divine name indicate disparate authorship, the scholar then breaks the text into hypothetical sources. Added to this assumption is another that minor variations in detail indicate variant sources. Added to these assumptions is a theory about the development of Israel's religion from a polytheistic base. Eventually one has a theory of such complexity that one forgets just how many assumptions have been made along the way.

Steck does not use the tools of more recent developments in narrative analysis in his approach. Presumably he would regard such

---

[19]If contemporary interactions between authors and editors are any indication, it is often the editors who are more conscious of consistency than authors!

[20]The Hebrew has בֵּית אֱלֹהִים (*bêth 'ĕlōhîm*) in both verses 17 and 22.

approaches as simplistic harmonization. But the presumption that contemporary scholarship can answer complex historical-critical questions
with confidence with the available data and the available historical-critical set of approaches is untenable. The alternative is not a fundamen-
talist claim that Moses wrote the entire Pentateuch, even the report of
his death. We simply do not know the exact process by which the book
of Genesis came into its present form. The only source that we actually
know to exist, the text in its canonical form, must be interpreted. It is
difficult to see how Steck ever gets to the primary business of interpretation with his methodology.

In the book of Genesis we seem to have three accounts of Jacob giving a name to Bethel (Gen 28:19; 35:7; 35:15). However the three accounts came into the book of Genesis, someone thought that the three
accounts fit together. Is there a narrative approach that might help us
to understand this anomaly? In the first account Jacob gave a name to a
place that he immediately left for twenty years. No one was with him as
he ran away from Esau to Haran. There would be no reason for anyone
other than Jacob or God to know of the new name. In the second
account Jacob is back in the Promised Land twenty years later. God tells
him to go to the place that only God and Jacob know about and build
an altar there. Jacob does so. In the presence of his entire family he calls
the place El-Bethel ("God of the House of God") in memory of God's
appearance to him twenty years earlier. God had appeared to him at the
house of God when he most needed reassurance. There was initially no
revelation of God's presence; only Jacob memorializing his earlier experience for his family. Then Deborah, Rebekah's childhood nurse, died.
Apparently she had come to Canaan with Jacob when he left Laban.

Following her burial God appeared to Jacob. Now the entire family
witnessed the revelation, or at least Jacob's reaction to it. He replays the
event by setting up a stone as a pillar, and pouring oil on it, as he had
done earlier in chapter 28. Now his family participates in the experience
which he alone had with God twenty years earlier. While Steck might
argue that such a series of events is historically implausible, the story is
coherent in its present form. At God's command Jacob replays the
events of twenty years earlier in order to include his new family in them.
Steck's approach results in his missing the whole point of the account in
chapter 35. Instead he focuses on building speculation upon speculation
with no external controls. What is worse his approach misses the narrator's art and the theology behind it.[21] The desire to reconstruct the ear-

---

[21]Steck's attempt at application based on the conclusions reached through his use
of a quite convoluted process (pp. 201-202) is ambiguous and question-begging.

liest history of Israel through scientific methods is a noble pursuit. For that the historical-critical tradition must be commended. The critique of simplistic harmonizations and the attempt to understand texts in their original social locations is also a strength of this tradition. This must be continued if we are to progress in our understanding of Scripture. Whatever the limitations of the historical-critical approaches, the goals which led to their creation should not be abandoned.

GENESIS 29

VI. JACOB ARRIVES AT LABAN'S HOUSE (29:1-14a)

In this passage Jacob arrives in the home area of his mother Rebekah and providentially meets his future wife Rachel. He is then warmly received by Laban, Rachel's father. The warmth that initially greeted Jacob at his arrival does not, however, continue.

In the palistrophic structure of the Jacob and Esau narratives this section forms a pair with Jacob's departure from Laban in Genesis 31:2–32:1. The welcome he receives when he arrives is in stark contrast to the circumstances of his surreptitious departure.

29:1 Then Jacob continued on his journey and came to the land of the eastern peoples.

The Hebrew reads literally "Jacob lifted his feet and went to the land of the sons of the east." This is an odd way to say this. In fact this is the only construction of this verb with the noun "feet." This verse also has an unusual way to refer to the extended family of Jacob. Typically they live in Haran or Paddan Aram. Here the place is referred to as "the land of the sons of the east." The word "east" is an ideologically important word in the book of Genesis. Adam and Eve left the garden by going east. One leaves the presence of God when one goes east. Cain is banished to the east. It is in the east that the rebellion at Babel originated. Jacob goes into a form of banishment from the presence of God when he travels to Paddan Aram.[1]

29:2 There he saw a well in the field, with three flocks of sheep lying near it because the flocks were watered from that well. The stone over the mouth of the well was large. 29:3 When all the flocks were gathered there, the shepherds would roll the stone away from the well's mouth and water the sheep. Then they would return the stone to its place over the mouth of the well.

God guides Jacob to the correct place to find Laban's family and, unbeknownst to him, his beloved wife Rachel. The story begins at a well

---

[1]My thanks to John Nugent for reminding me of this.

where three flocks with their shepherds are waiting for the other shepherds to come and help them move the covering stone from the well.
Well water was undoubtedly scarce and the heavy cover prevented it
being easily stolen. The large stone covering the well could not be lifted in ordinary circumstances by the three shepherds.

**29:4 Jacob asked the shepherds, "My brothers, where are you from?"
"We're from Haran," they replied.**

Jacob addresses **the shepherds** as "**brothers**" no doubt to facilitate
a friendly atmosphere. They just happen to be from the city of **Haran**,
the residence of Laban and his daughters. God's providential care
which he had promised Jacob at Bethel is demonstrated yet again.

**29:5 He said to them, "Do you know Laban, Nahor's grandson?" "Yes,
we know him," they answered.**

Jacob asks if they know **Laban**. He refers to him as **Nahor's grandson**, not Bethuel's son. This elevation of Laban over his father Bethuel
is never explained in Genesis. It may have been Bethuel's poor health
or mental state. In any case Laban, Rebekah's brother, leads the household. His father, Bethuel does not. Being from the same relatively small
town the shepherds know Laban.

**29:6 Then Jacob asked them, "Is he well?" "Yes, he is," they said, "and
here comes his daughter Rachel with the sheep."**

Jacob asks the shepherds if Laban is in "peace." The Hebrew word
שָׁלוֹם (šālôm) means more than merely the absence of war. It includes
such ideas as well-being and health and enough material possessions to
be content. Laban is in "peace." Providentially **his daughter Rachel** was
bringing another of the flocks for the daily watering.

**29:7 "Look," he said, "the sun is still high; it is not time for the flocks
to be gathered. Water the sheep and take them back to pasture."**

For some unstated reason Jacob wants the shepherds to leave quickly. Perhaps he wanted to be alone to meet Laban's daughter. Certainly
the story reads like a tale of love at first sight. Jacob reasons that there
is still plenty of pasturage time for the sheep. If they watered them now,
they could return to the pasture and keep eating.

**29:8 "We can't," they replied, "until all the flocks are gathered and
the stone has been rolled away from the mouth of the well. Then we
will water the sheep."**

The shepherds reply that they were not able to water their sheep
until all of the flocks were **gathered**, presumably because the stone was
too heavy, and it required the other shepherds to help move it.

**29:9 While he was still talking with them, Rachel came with her
father's sheep, for she was a shepherdess.**

As Jacob was finishing his unsuccessful negotiation with the shepherds, Rachel arrived leading **her father's sheep**. The unusualness in that cultural situation of a woman functioning as a shepherd is explained by the narrator. She was by vocation **a shepherdess**.

29:10 When Jacob saw Rachel daughter of Laban, his mother's brother, and Laban's sheep, he went over and rolled the stone away from the mouth of the well and watered his uncle's sheep.

The humor in this verse is palpable. Ordinarily, it required more than three shepherds to lift the great stone which covered the well, but **when Jacob** sees **Rachel** for the first time, he is so struck by love that he can lift the stone himself! Contemporary western readers tend to be sidetracked by the issue of modern incest laws and the idea of Jacob falling in love with his first cousin. Such questions are simply not appropriate to an ancient Near Eastern text. Interestingly Jacob waters only **Laban's sheep**, not the sheep of the three other shepherds who were together unable to move the rock which Jacob has just moved.

The NIV periphrases what, in the Hebrew text, seems redundant to modern tastes. Three times Laban is called Jacob's mother's brother in the Hebrew. It may be that the narrator is hinting at the importance of this particular relationship for Jacob. It is the flock of his uncle that Jacob waters and the daughter of his uncle whom he desires for a wife. He had been sent to Laban by both his mother Rebekah (Gen 27:43) and his father Isaac (28:2).

29:11 Then Jacob kissed Rachel and began to weep aloud.

In ancient Near Eastern culture a kiss was not usually a romantic or sexual gesture, and certainly this kiss was not any more than is Laban's kiss of Jacob in verse 13 below. Jacob has just met a relative whom he had never seen. His weeping indicates the emotional nature of that meeting. Both the kiss and the weeping are signs of familial affection.

29:12 He had told Rachel that he was a relative of her father and a son of Rebekah. So she ran and told her father.

The NIV's past perfect "**had told**" for the Hebrew *waw*-consecutive construction is perplexing. A simple past tense — "told" — fits the context quite nicely. Jacob informs Rachel that he greeted her so warmly because he was a relative of her father whom he had never met. In fact Jacob was the **son of Rebekah**, Rachel's aunt. Rachel sees the significance of the news and urgently runs to inform her father.

29:13 As soon as Laban heard the news about Jacob, his sister's son, he hurried to meet him. He embraced him and kissed him and brought him to his home, and there Jacob told him all these things.

When **Laban heard the news about Jacob**, one of his nephews whom he had never met, he ran **to meet him**. He greeted him warmly by embracing and kissing him. He then brought him to his house. Jacob told him "**all these things**." The narrative is elusive here. Did he tell him about the tricking of Esau and Isaac? Did he tell him of his dream at Bethel? We are left to wonder.

29:14a Then Laban said to him, "You are my own flesh and blood."

Laban immediately recognizes the closeness of the familial relationship he has with Jacob. The use of "my bone and my flesh"[2] recalls Adam's statement upon seeing the woman created for him the first time. Jacob stayed with Laban an entire month, evidently working for him *gratis*.

VII. THE TRICKSTER BECOMES THE TRICKED: LABAN FOOLS JACOB INTO MARRYING LEAH AS WELL AS RACHEL (29:14b-29)

Jacob has arrived in Paddan Aram without resources for a bride price. Unfortunately he had fallen for Rachel, Laban's beautiful younger daughter. After a month Laban offers to pay Jacob a wage for the job he has been doing voluntarily for Laban. Given the opportunity to earn money toward Rachel's bride price, Jacob makes the mistake of revealing his feelings for Rachel. Starting from a weak bargaining position he agrees to a high[3] bride price. When he gladly serves seven years for Rachel, he finds himself being tricked into marrying a woman he does not love and serving yet another seven years for the woman he does love.

The blindness, both literal and metaphorical, which seems to strike Jacob reminds the reader of how Jacob had earlier taken advantage of his own father's blindness to steal the blessing away from Esau. Here the tables are turned. If the reader was surprised at just how blind and naïve Isaac could be, there is even more surprise at Jacob. Jacob woke up in the morning to find out that he had consummated a marriage with the wrong woman! This is a narrative that drips with irony. Jacob, a trickster from birth, is the victim of Laban's trickery.

---

[2]NIV periphrases here into an English idiom and loses the intertextual connection with Genesis 2:23.

[3]Walton et al. (*IVPBBCOT*, p. 62) suggest ten shekels of silver a year as an annual wage for a shepherd, yielding a bride price of 70 shekels. But Jacob is far more than a shepherd.

This text, however, does not just point the reader backwards to chapter 27. Within the larger palistrophic structure of the Jacob and Esau narrative this text looks forward to the narrative of Jacob using his own form of trickery on Laban to obtain flocks and herds and other possessions. Laban wins the initial battle, but in the end Jacob wins the war. He departs Laban's household a wealthy man despite his father-in-law's duplicity.

A. JACOB AGREES TO SERVE SEVEN YEARS FOR RACHEL (29:14b-20)

29:14b After Jacob had stayed with him for a whole month, 29:15 Laban said to him, "Just because you are a relative of mine, should you work for me for nothing? Tell me what your wages should be."

After a month of free labor Laban asks Jacob what his wages should be. After all, Laban reasons, he does not want to take advantage of the fact that Jacob is his "brother" or **relative**.[4] This, of course, did not stop Laban from using Jacob's free labor for a month. Although a subtle point, the reader sees the beginning of the tussle between two sneaky characters. Jacob is about to meet his match in Laban.[5]

29:16 Now Laban had two daughters; the name of the older was Leah, and the name of the younger was Rachel. 29:17 Leah had weak eyes, but Rachel was lovely in form, and beautiful.

Laban had two daughters as Rebekah had two sons. Laban, like Rebekah, manipulates the situation for the benefit of himself and his eldest daughter, **Leah**. In this he was like Isaac who attempted to manipulate the situation for the benefit of his eldest son Esau. Jacob and his mother had schemed to reverse his fortunes. He is about to taste a dose of his own medicine. Laban and Leah will make him the victim of another's scheming. Leah's eyes were "**weak**" (NIV text) or "delicate" (NIV footnote). By contrast Rachel was beautiful in both form and appearance.[6] In other words, no matter how one understands the Hebrew word translated "weak,"[7] Leah was not as beautiful, physically speaking,

---

[4]Heard (*Dynamics of Diselection*, pp. 147-151) gives a detailed account of the ambiguity of the Hebrew here. Laban's question in Hebrew could imply that he expects a "yes" or a "no."

[5]This is even more clear if the question is read as expecting a "no" answer and Laban only grudgingly offers to pay Jacob.

[6]The Hebrew has the word "beautiful" (יָפֶה, *yāpheh*) twice, i.e., beautiful of form (shape?) and appearance (sight).

[7]רַךְ (*rak*) could mean either "weak" or "delicate."

as Rachel. It is ironic that Leah's eyes are mentioned, especially if the word is to be understood as "weak." Jacob is about to have his own problem with seeing the weak-eyed Leah on his wedding night! It is not only Leah who is weak in the eyes!

29:18 Jacob was in love with Rachel and said, "I'll work for you seven years in return for your younger daughter Rachel."

The NIV translates the Hebrew *waw*-consecutive construction in a nonconsecutive way, "**Jacob was in love**" rather than the typical, "Then Jacob loved." It may be that after a month living in Laban's home and working *gratis* for him that he came to love Rachel in some new way. His offer of a bridal price of seven years' labor seems exorbitant to modern readers, but it must be understood within its historical context. The bridal price did not purchase the woman as though she were property. In a patriarchal society where subsistence agriculture or shepherding was the norm, the bridal price and its parallel dowry were designed to ensure the financial well being of women in a system where only males typically received an inheritance. The dowry consisted of money and possessions which the woman took into the marriage and controlled. Should her husband decide to divorce or abandon her, the dowry went back with her to provide for her continuing needs. Marriage was thus very expensive for the groom, especially if his bride was highly desirable like Rachel and commanded a high bridal price. The Torah fixed the maximum bride price at 50 shekels (Deut 22:29). According to Old Babylonian law casual laborers received 1.5 shekels per month.[8] At that rate[9] Jacob was offering 126 shekels. Jacob very carefully refers to **Rachel** as "**your** [Laban's] **younger daughter**" so there would be no confusion.

29:19 Laban said, "It's better that I give her to you than to some other man. Stay here with me."

Laban craftily shows no surprise at Jacob's exorbitant offer. Laban does not mention the financial advantage he was about to gain from Jacob. He merely remarks that a marriage with Jacob is preferable to some other person who is not related to his daughter. Laban does not refer to Rachel by name, referring to her only with pronouns. Is Laban already planning to fool Jacob into marrying Leah?[10] Or is he keeping his

---

[8]Wenham, *Genesis 16–50*, p. 235, quoting Driver and Miles.

[9]If anything, one would presume that Jacob would command more than this minimal wage from his uncle.

[10]For a younger sister to marry before her older sister could create a problem in that cultural situation. It could certainly bring shame on the older sister. It could even lead to her being viewed as an undesirable wife, an economically and socially tenuous situation.

options open?[11] In seven years someone may offer to marry Leah, weak eyes and all. If that happened, he would gladly give Rachel to Jacob.

29:20 So Jacob served seven years to get Rachel, but they seemed like only a few days to him because of his love for her.

The seven long years of serving Laban for Rachel's bride price did not diminish Jacob's love for her. In fact the seven years seemed like only a few days to him. The romantic tenor of this verse points to the blindness of such love — a blindness that will become only too literal when the marriage actually occurs.

B. LABAN TRICKS JACOB INTO MARRYING LEAH (29:21-25)

29:21 Then Jacob said to Laban, "Give me my wife. My time is completed, and I want to lie with her."

At the end of the seven years Jacob expects Laban to "**give**" him his wife because he has met his side of the agreement. He wants to consummate the marriage and move on in his life. Jacob refers to Rachel as "**my wife**" not by her name. This could be read as a reflection of the patriarchal system in which the wife is viewed more in terms of her function than in terms of who she was as a person. Conversely Jacob could be referring to Rachel as his wife as a way of claiming his rights to her. Rachel is no longer Laban's daughter, but is now, in Jacob's eyes, his wife.

29:22 So Laban brought together all the people of the place and gave a feast. 29:23 But when evening came, he took his daughter Leah and gave her to Jacob, and Jacob lay with her.

Laban pretends to meet Jacob's demand by hosting a marriage feast. He invites all the "men"[12] of the place. Laban waits until the evening when it was dark and Jacob's perceptions could have been clouded by the wine served at the celebration. The veils of ancient Near Eastern culture could have also played a part. But it seems improbable at best that a fully cognizant Jacob would have been fooled merely by the veils. Instead of Rachel as promised, Laban gave Leah to Jacob. He, unaware until the morning, consummated the marriage with the wrong woman. Like Isaac, whose diminished vision allowed him to be tricked into blessing the wrong son, Jacob's lack of vision, both literal and metaphorical, results in his marrying the wrong daughter.

---

[11]Wenham, *Genesis 16–50*, p. 235.

[12]The NIV periphrases here, although probably correctly, since it seems unlikely that only men would be invited to a marriage feast.

29:24 And Laban gave his servant girl Zilpah to his daughter as her maidservant.

In anticipation of the ensuing narrative the narrator informs us that during the wedding Laban gave his maidservant Zilpah to his daughter (Leah) to serve as her maidservant.[13] This prepares the reader for the use of her maidservant as a surrogate mother for Leah when the political infighting over who will bear Jacob sons begins. There is no indication of any concern on Laban's part for whether Zilpah wants to be given to Laban's daughter. As a servant girl she is regarded as not much more than property.

29:25 When morning came, there was Leah! So Jacob said to Laban, "What is this you have done to me? I served you for Rachel, didn't I? Why have you deceived me?"

When morning came, Jacob's ability to see, literally and metaphorically, was regained. He was shocked to find Leah in his marriage bed. The trickster was blind to the tricks of his father-in-law. Confronting Laban with his treachery, Jacob seeks to establish the original terms of the agreement. He had served for Rachel, not Leah. By asking this as a question Jacob seeks to elicit a (public?) admittance from Laban of his treachery. With no denial forthcoming Jacob asks why Laban had chosen to deceive him.

C. LABAN TRICKS JACOB INTO SERVING ANOTHER SEVEN YEARS FOR RACHEL (29:26-29)

29:26 Laban replied, "It is not our custom here to give the younger daughter in marriage before the older one.

Laban does not attempt to deny the deception. He explains that giving the younger daughter before the firstborn is simply not done in "this place." The rationale may or may not be true. Walton, Matthews, and Chavalas assert: "It is the practice of people of the ancient Near East, and still a tradition today in that area, for the oldest daughter to be married first." They seem to suggest that Hebrew culture is a shame, as opposed to a guilt, culture. In such cultures a younger sister could potentially shame a less desirable older sister by being married before her. Further, spinsters were a long-term drain on the resources of the ancient family.[14] But if this is "the practice" of people of the ancient

---

[13]The NIV translates the same Hebrew word first as "servant girl" and then as "maidservant" in this verse.

[14]Walton, et al., *IVPBBCOT*, p. 62.

Near East, Jacob, a man of the ancient Near East, does not seem to know about it! Such simplistic generalizations must be questioned. Heard has successfully questioned the presumption of commentators that Laban was a wealthy man.[15] Finances seem to be a significant part of his motivation. But since Jacob has already had sexual relations with Leah, he is in no position to argue the point. Whether there was such a custom or not, the deed was done. Jacob was related to Laban by family connection. But he had been Laban's servant and was without his own resources to dispute the point. Apparently he felt he must accept Laban's claim.

In reality Laban had a "plain Jane" daughter who, in the patriarchal context, would only be a drain on his resources. She was unlikely to attract a suitable partner with a suitable bride price on her own. In Laban's mind he had merely taken advantage of his "naïve" nephew and solved his potential problem. The cost of Leah's dowry, a servant girl, was undoubtedly a bargain from his point of view.

29:27 Finish this daughter's bridal week; then we will give you the younger one also, in return for another seven years of work."

Laban agrees to give Jacob his other daughter after the honeymoon with Leah was over; but only for another seven years of free labor. Interestingly in the Hebrew Laban refers to his two daughters only as "this one." He seems remarkably "objective" or even distant from them as individuals as though they were property in a business negotiation. In a patriarchal culture in a sense they were property. However, the narrator is much more personal in relating details in her or his own voice as compared to Laban. Also of interest is the complex way in which Laban explains that Rachel will require another seven years of free labor. The wording[16] may be a way of indicating Laban's discomfort with what he is doing to Jacob. Certainly Laban wants to be clear that another seven years are required. One wonders why he would think that Jacob would keep this bargain when it was imposed on him through treachery.

29:28 And Jacob did so. He finished the week with Leah, and then Laban gave him his daughter Rachel to be his wife.

Jacob, for some reason, agrees to Laban's deal. He completes the honeymoon week. Laban, finally true to his word, then gave him Rachel to be his wife. There is no mention of a bridal week or even a marriage celebration for Rachel. Perhaps another feast would be too awkward for

---

[15]Heard. *Dynamics of Diselection*, pp. 160-161.

[16]The Hebrew reads literally "for service which you will serve with me still — seven years — another."

Laban to explain to the guests who came to the first feast assuming it marked Rachel's marriage to Jacob. The narrator does not mention Leah's name (contra NIV) referring to her only as "this one." The narrator does, however, mention Rachel by name. We are never informed of how Leah and Rachel felt about all of this. They seem to be merely pawns in a game ruled by deceitful men.

29:29 Laban gave his servant girl Bilhah to his daughter Rachel as her maidservant.

As her dowry Laban gives Bilhah, his maidservant, as Rachel's maidservant.[17] At least there is some sort of equality for his daughters in this gesture. But for Laban, a woman, whether a daughter or a servant, is treated like a commodity in a business deal. The original readers would most likely have taken this for granted. They lived within a patriarchal system. Since we in the West do not live within such a system, we find the perspective of Laban shockingly insensitive.

VIII. JACOB'S FAMILY IS BORN AMID TENSIONS BETWEEN HIS WIVES (29:30–30:24)

In this section we read of the birth of the forefathers of the twelve tribes of the nation of Israel. The original and canonical audiences from the various tribes would undoubtedly see their own identity as tribes described in these stories of their ancestors' births. That identity included internal conflict between Jacob, his wives, and his children. That original conflict would be played out in the history of the internal tensions in the nation of Israel.

The twelve sons of Jacob are born to four different women; two primary wives and two secondary wives (concubines). Leah Jacob's first, but unloved, wife has four sons. Next Rachel's handmaiden Bilhah has two sons. This is followed by two sons born to Zilpah, Leah's handmaiden. Leah then has two more sons, for a total of six and a daughter. Finally Rachel has a son of her own with hopes of more sons to come. The internal family politics over who is Jacob's beloved and who will produce sons for him results in strategizing, bargaining, and even scheming.

When the tribes which descend from Jacob's sons enter the Promised Land, there are internal tensions from the very beginning. Eventually these tensions explode into a nation which is divided between

---

[17]The NIV once again translates the same Hebrew word first as "servant girl" and then as "maidservant" in this verse.

Judah, a son of Leah, in the south and the tribes of Joseph, a son of Rachel, in the north.

A. JACOB'S FAVORITISM FOR RACHEL (29:30)

29:30 Jacob lay with Rachel also, and he loved Rachel more than Leah. And he worked for Laban another seven years.

Jacob consummates his marriage with Rachel. His affections toward the two sisters are not changed by marriage. Jacob continued to love Rachel in comparison with Leah. This seems in some tension with verse 31 which states that the LORD saw that Jacob "hated" Leah and not merely loved her less. In any case, Jacob fulfills his part of Laban's deal and serves him, presumably faithfully, for another seven years. The narrator uses the same awkward construction that Laban had used in verse 27 in demanding another seven years uncompensated service. This repetition could be a means of confirming Jacob's precise meeting of the terms of Laban's conditions for his marriage to Rachel.

B. THE LORD'S FAVOR FOR LEAH
IN GRANTING HER FOUR SONS (29:31-35)

29:31 When the LORD saw that Leah was not loved, he opened her womb, but Rachel was barren.

After the bigamous marriages of Jacob had gone on for a while, the LORD recognized that Leah was "hated" (שָׂנֵא, śānē'). The NIV softens this to "not loved." Out of compassion for Leah's situation, a situation for which she was not responsible, the LORD enabled her to become pregnant while Rachel remained barren. The Old Testament does not suggest that every pregnancy and every case of infertility is the direct result of the LORD's action. But in this passage both Leah's fertility and Rachel's infertility are under the LORD's direct action or lack thereof.

29:32 Leah became pregnant and gave birth to a son. She named him Reuben, for she said, "It is because the LORD has seen my misery. Surely my husband will love me now."

As a result of the LORD "opening" Leah's womb, she became pregnant and gave birth to a son. She, not Jacob, named the boy Reuben. Reuben's name begins with the two Hebrew letters רְא as does the verb "to see" (רָאָה). It is as though Leah interprets the name as meaning "son of [God's] seeing." The "hated" and unwanted wife without sons to give to Jacob, found herself in a situation which she describes as "**misery**."

God has seen her misery and given her a son. Leah hopes that by giving Jacob sons while Rachel is barren, Jacob will begin to love her. The reader cannot but feel empathy for Leah's situation. But in thinking that she will win Jacob's love by bearing him children, she is sadly mistaken.

29:33 She conceived again, and when she gave birth to a son she said, "Because the LORD heard that I am not loved, he gave me this one too." So she named him Simeon.

While Rachel remains barren Leah has another son. She, not Jacob, **named him Simeon**. Simeon's name in Hebrew begins with the same three letters, שׁמע, as the Hebrew verb "to hear" (שָׁמַע, *šama'*). God[18] had heard that she was "hated"[19] and so gave her another son. She hopes that giving Jacob a second son will win his favor. It did not.

29:34 Again she conceived, and when she gave birth to a son she said, "Now at last my husband will become attached to me, because I have borne him three sons." So he was named Levi.

Leah conceives and bears yet a third son. Once again she hopes that this son will gain Jacob's love. The verb "**become attached to me**" (לָוָה, *lāwāh*) is associated by wordplay with her third son's name, **Levi** (לֵוִי, *lēwî*). In all three cases Leah deliberately names the son to echo by assonance (similarity of sound) a verb which expresses her wish that Jacob will somehow come to love her. This narrative is a sad one. The unfairness of her treatment by both her father and her husband is not her fault; but her attempts to change the situation by bearing him sons seem futile.

29:35 She conceived again, and when she gave birth to a son she said, "This time I will praise the LORD." So she named him Judah. Then she stopped having children.

Leah has a fourth son. This time there is no expression of hope that Jacob's attitude toward her will change. She chooses instead to praise God for the gift that her son was in and of himself. The wordplay this time is between the verb "**I will praise**" (אוֹדֶה, *'ôdeh*) and Judah's name (יְהוּדָה, *yəhûdāh*). Leah comes to realize that her sons were gifts even if they did not bring her the love she so desperately wanted from her husband. She finally understands that her four sons were gifts from the LORD and that should be enough. Perhaps it is no coincidence that it was at the birth of Judah that Leah came to this realization. The tribe which eventually assumed the place of leadership in the nation had a forefather whose birth brought forth trustful praise.

---

[18]The Hebrew LORD in vv. 32 and 33 is anachronistic.

[19]The NIV softens this to "not loved."

After bearing her fourth son Leah stops having children for the time being. God had opened her womb. Now that she understood the blessing of bearing children, the LORD evidently temporarily closed it again. But we should not conclude that Leah's aspirations for Jacob's love are completely over. Her remarks at the birth of Zebulun make clear that she never quite gives up on her strategy of winning Jacob's love through her ability to bear children.

GENESIS 30

C. RACHEL'S ENVY LEADS TO SURROGACY (30:1-8)

30:1 When Rachel saw that she was not bearing Jacob any children, she became jealous of her sister. So she said to Jacob, "Give me children, or I'll die!"

At a minimum Jacob has been married to Leah and Rachel for four years. During this time Rachel had born no sons to Jacob.[1] In a patriarchal world a woman's identity is often defined by the raising of children. Her value in the household is measured by her — not her husband's — ability to provide male heirs. Rachel quite understandably became jealous of her sister. She demands that Jacob give her "sons." If not, she is as a dead person.[2] One of the downsides of the patriarchal system into which Jacob, Rachel, and Leah have been born is the fact that without the ability to bear children, women often view themselves and are viewed by others as having little or no intrinsic worth.

30:2 Jacob became angry with her and said, "Am I in the place of God, who has kept you from having children?"

Jacob takes umbrage at Rachel's demand that he provide her with sons. Jacob assumes, quite naturally, that the problem is with Rachel's body and not his own. He had demonstrated his fertility by having children with Leah. Ultimately Jacob realizes, quite correctly according to the narrator, that God[3] has withheld from her "the fruit of the womb."[4]

30:3 Then she said, "Here is Bilhah, my maidservant. Sleep with her so that she can bear children for me and that through her I too can build a family."

Rachel, like Sarai before her, decides to use a female servant as a surrogate mother. Rachel uses a different Hebrew word than the narra-

---

[1]The Hebrew merely says that Rachel had not borne to Jacob. She asks specifically that Jacob would give her "sons" not "children" as NIV paraphrases it.

[2]The Hebrew uses a participle of מוּת (mûth), "to die."

[3]Notice that Jacob uses "God" not "LORD" in keeping with Exodus 6:3.

[4]The NIV periphrases here "kept you from having children."

tor used when describing Laban's gift of Bilhah to Rachel as a maidservant. It may be that Rachel uses a more "servile"[5] sort of word to describe her because she wants to make it very clear that any sons that come from the union are to be regarded as Rachel's, not Bilhah's. Bilhah is not to be regarded as a wife. The narrator explicitly disagrees with Rachel on this latter point. It is interesting and may be significant that Sarai says specifically that Hagar will be Abram's wife. In a parallel situation when Rachel wanted to have a child through Bilhah, she makes it very clear that any children born would be hers and not Bilhah's. Perhaps Rachel learned this lesson from the Hagar situation. Leah, by contrast, intentionally gives her handmaid to Jacob *as a wife* (Gen 30:9).

30:4 So she gave him her servant Bilhah as a wife. Jacob slept with her, 30:5 and she became pregnant and bore him a son.

Even though Rachel did not refer to Bilhah as Jacob's wife, the narrator says that Bilhah indeed became Jacob's wife. As noted above, the narrator uses a different, less disparaging, word for maidservant than Rachel had. Jacob, like his grandfather before, obeys his wife's directive and has a son through Bilhah.

30:6 Then Rachel said, "God has vindicated me; he has listened to my plea and given me a son." Because of this she named him Dan.

By using her position to assert her right to name the child, Rachel seems to be continuing with her claim that the child is hers, not Bilhah's. The narrator does not share Rachel's perspective on this issue. Ultimately Rachel loses this argument since **Dan** and Naphtali come to be regarded as the children of Bilhah, not Rachel. Like Leah, Rachel uses the occasion of naming her son to make a wordplay and a point in the battle with her sister for love and status in the family. The word "**vindicated**" (NIV) or more literally "judged" (NRSV) is the Hebrew verb דּין (*dîn*). The name Dan in Hebrew is דָּן (*dān*). The wordplay between them is interpreted by Rachel to mean that she has been *judged* by God as worthy to have a son.

30:7 Rachel's servant Bilhah conceived again and bore Jacob a second son.

Bilhah has a second son by Jacob. The narrator continues to describe Bilhah as Rachel's maidservant, a less pejorative Hebrew word than the one Rachel has used to describe her in verse 3. The narrator also says that Bilhah bore a son for Jacob, not for Rachel. These seem to be subtle indications that the narrator regards Bilhah as a full wife of

---

[5]Rachel uses אָמָה (*'āmāh*) versus Laban and the narrator's שִׁפְחָה (*šiphḥāh*). Genesis 21:10 may indicate a disparaging usage.

Jacob and not just as Rachel's servant who serves as a surrogate mother for Rachel's children.

30:8 Then Rachel said, "I have had a great struggle with my sister, and I have won." So she named him Naphtali.

Rachel, who regards the son whom Bilhah had borne to Jacob as her own son, takes the prerogative of naming him. Once again wordplay serves as a reminder of the battle between two sisters for the love of the same man. A more literal translation brings this out: "With Godlike wrestlings I have wrestled with my sister and I have prevailed." The Hebrew words for "wrestlings" and "wrestled" sound strikingly like the Hebrew name **Naphtali**.[6] Evidently it is not only Leah who thinks that Jacob's favor is to be won by bearing him sons. Jacob's love for Rachel is not enough if she does not also bear him sons. Such is the destiny of a woman, even the favorite, in a patriarchal system.

D. LEAH COPIES RACHEL'S SURROGACY (30:9-13)

30:9 When Leah saw that she had stopped having children, she took her maidservant Zilpah and gave her to Jacob as a wife.

Leah, seeing that she was no longer able to have children, copies Rachel's strategy by giving her maidservant **Zilpah** to Jacob so that Leah could give him more sons through her. Her plan, however, is subtly different from Rachel's. She intentionally gives Zilpah **to Jacob as a wife** without claiming that the children would be hers. Unlike Rachel, Leah does not use the more pejorative term for her maidservant.[7] It might seem that with the birth of Judah Leah had stopped struggling and had begun to trust God. But if that was so then her attitude soon reverted. When she sees that Rachel is able to have two children which she claims as her own through her maidservant, the contest is continued once again. The tensions between the tribes which arise later in the nation of Israel's history are sown in the dysfunctional conflict between Leah and Rachel as they seek to win or retain Jacob's love. Israel is a nation of tribes which trace their roots to the conflict between Rachel and Leah.

30:10 Leah's servant Zilpah bore Jacob a son. 30:11 Then Leah said, "What good fortune!" So she named him Gad.

Leah's strategy seems to work as Zilpah becomes pregnant and bears Jacob another son. But the history of this strategy in the case of

---

[6]"Wrestlings" (נַפְתּוּלִים, *nāphtûlîm*) and "I have wrestled" (נִפְתַּלְתִּי, *niphtaltî*) sound similar to Naphtali (נַפְתָּלִי, *naphtālî*).

[7]Leah uses the narrator's שִׁפְחָה (*šiphḥāh*) while Rachel uses אָמָה (*'āmāh*).

Hagar and Ishmael will caution even the first-time reader. Leah thinks that this birth is "good fortune" (גָּד, *gad*) and so names him "**Gad**" (גָּד, *gād*) another instance of wordplay at the birth of a son.

30:12 Leah's servant Zilpah bore Jacob a second son. 30:13 Then Leah said, "How happy I am! The women will call me happy." So she named him Asher.

Leah's maidservant Zilpah bore Jacob, not Leah, a second son. But Leah is given the prerogative, once again, of naming him. Moved by the blessedness which she feels, she names him **Asher**, whose name sounds like the Hebrew word for blessed.[8] It is interesting that Leah mentions that the "daughters," i.e., female family members, will call her blessed.[9]

E. LEAH BARGAINS WITH RACHEL TO BE ALLOWED TO BEAR JACOB TWO MORE SONS AND A DAUGHTER (30:14-21)

30:14 During wheat harvest, Reuben went out into the fields and found some mandrake plants, which he brought to his mother Leah. Rachel said to Leah, "Please give me some of your son's mandrakes."

The narrative jumps to some time later when Reuben is old enough to be out in the fields by himself. During the time of the winter **wheat harvest** (March or April) the mandrakes were ripe. According to Hamilton[10] mandrakes grow all over Israel: "There is no stalk, but large leaves fan out from the root at ground level. In the midst of these leaves appear violet flowers and yellow fruit. This fruit, which looks like a tomato, ripens in March and April, and emits a very distinct odor." The characters in the story evidently regard mandrakes as a fertility aid. The narrator, however, consistently attributes the sons born in this dysfunctional family to the grace of God, not a traditional aphrodisiac.[11] Rachel is evidently unsatisfied with producing children through her maidservant. She is desperate to have her own children. She therefore asks Leah for some of the mandrakes Reuben has gathered for his mother.

30:15 But she said to her, "Wasn't it enough that you took away my husband? Will you take my son's mandrakes too?" "Very well," Rachel said, "he can sleep with you tonight in return for your son's mandrakes."

---

[8]Blessed in Hebrew is אֹשֶׁר (*'ōšer*), while Asher's name is אָשֵׁר (*'āšēr*).

[9]The NIV's "happy" for *'ōšer* can be misleading in English. In Hebrew it is not an emotional state, but a status of being in God's favor and receiving the results of that favor. See Psalm 1:1.

[10]Victor P. Hamilton, *The Book of Genesis Chapters 18–50*, NICOT (Grand Rapids: Eerdmans, 1995), p. 274, quoting Moldenke.

[11]For mandrakes as an aphrodisiac, see S of S 7:13.

Rachel evidently had control of conjugal rights to Jacob. Leah accuses her of taking her husband away from her and then having the nerve to take away her son's access to fertility. By referring to Reuben as Leah's "son" both Rachel and Leah point to the conflict they are in. Leah wants Jacob's love which Rachel has; Rachel wants to give Jacob sons, something Leah has already done six times over! But for Rachel, Reuben is Leah's son, not Jacob's — or at least he is not primarily to be regarded in her mind as Jacob's truly legitimate son. Out of desperation and not waiting for God's timing, Rachel allows Leah to sleep with her own husband for one night in return for the power she presumes might be in the mandrakes. Rachel and Leah both have a long way to go before becoming the revered matriarchs of the nation of Israel.

30:16 So when Jacob came in from the fields that evening, Leah went out to meet him. "You must sleep with me," she said. "I have hired you with my son's mandrakes." So he slept with her that night.

Leah wastes no time, going out to meet Jacob as he returns from his work in the field that very evening. Leah gives Jacob no choice. He must sleep with her because she has purchased conjugal rights from Rachel with her (notice not "their") son's mandrakes. Jacob is entirely passive here. He is the one whose affection Leah and Rachel so desire along with the status of favored wife that comes with it. Rachel, not Jacob, controls conjugal access to him. Leah has purchased that access and Jacob has no option but to accede to the bargain Rachel has made. Rachel eventually sees that the mandrakes are useless as she doesn't have a child for at least two more years. Leah has two sons during that time!

30:17 God listened to Leah, and she became pregnant and bore Jacob a fifth son. 30:18 Then Leah said, "God has rewarded me for giving my maidservant to my husband." So she named him Issachar.

While Leah's prayer for a son is not explicitly mentioned, such a prayer is implicit. Her plea for another child (son), a fifth, was answered by God. Leah attributes this blessing to God giving her her "wages," which she "earned" by giving Zilpah, her maidservant to Jacob as another wife. In a way she views God as though he was Jacob. For Leah God, like Jacob, is reluctant to give his approval or love unless He gets something out of the bargain. One of the consequences of such extreme patriarchal societal structures is that human beings begin to view God as no more than a flawed patriarch.

The use of the word "wages" (שָׂכָר, *śākār*)[12] reminds the reader that

---

[12] The NIV paraphrases this phrase "rewarded me." Literally the Hebrew reads, "God gave [me] my wages."

Leah has just "purchased"[13] conjugal rights to Jacob from Rachel with Reuben's mandrakes. In naming her fifth son Leah makes a wordplay between the word "wages" (*śākār*) and the name **Issachar** (יִשָּׂשכָר, *yiśśākār*). But Leah does not relate the naming of Issachar to the rather humiliating fact that she must pay her rival Rachel in order to have sex with her own husband! Leah thinks, like Rachel, that she has God's approval for the scheme of giving her maidservant to Jacob as a secondary wife. She relates Issachar's naming to the wages she earned with God by giving up Zilpah.

The tensions and hierarchies created between the brothers and the tribes that descend from them by the fact that there are two primary wives and two secondary wives tell the reader another story. The scheming of Leah and Rachel sowed the seeds in Israel of the tribal tensions which are part and parcel of their experience as a nation. Jacob cooperated in the scheme even though he knew of the problems created for Abraham by taking Hagar as a secondary wife. There are the sons who are born first of all to Leah, there are the sons who are born to the maidservants Bilhah and Zilpah, there are the two sons born to Leah later, and finally there are the two sons born to the favored wife, Rachel. The tensions which arise from such a family structure are mapped into the "genetic code" of the descendants of the twelve sons. Jacob was raised in an environment of favoritism by his own parents, and that favoritism is Xeroxed into the dynamics of his own family.

30:19 Leah conceived again and bore Jacob a sixth son.

Evidently Jacob resumed at least sporadic conjugal relations with Leah at this time. She purchased a one-night privilege, but Jacob evidently overrode Rachel's objections and continued conjugal relations with Leah. From his point of view Leah was the only one who could produce sons for him from which he could build up a family that would one day become a great nation. So **Leah conceived** yet again **and bore a sixth son** of hers to Jacob.

30:20 Then Leah said, "God has presented me with a precious gift. This time my husband will treat me with honor, because I have borne him six sons." So she named him Zebulun.

As was the case with the birth of Judah, Leah views the birth of **Zebulun** as something for which to praise God. Zebulun is a gift from God. Leah's Hebrew has a wordplay that might be rendered in inelegant English as "**God has *presented* me with a** beautiful *present*."[14] The

---

[13]The Hebrew verb used in verse 16, שָׂכַר (*śākar*), is cognate with the noun "wages" (*śākār*) in verse 18.

[14]The Hebrew uses a verb, זָבַד (*zābad*), followed by a noun etymologically related to the verb, זֶבֶד (*zebed*), to make this point.

first-time reader might well think that Leah arrived at a certain level of maturity in her thinking at the birth of Judah. This text makes it clear that she was still (or resumed) trying to win Jacob's favor by giving him sons. Jacob, Leah hopes, will treat her with honor because she has given him what she thinks he wants. The wordplay this time is between the verb **"treat with honor"** (זָבַל, *zābal*)[15] and the name "Zebulun" (זְבֻלוּן, *zᵉbulûn*). This text has a sort of double etymological pun in that "presented," "present," "treat with honor," and the name "Zebulun" all contain the *zayin beth* (זִ) consonant combination in Hebrew.

30:21 Some time later she gave birth to a daughter and named her Dinah.

This verse does not tell us just when **Dinah**, Leah's daughter, was born; only that it was some time after the births of Leah's six sons. Jacob had other daughters besides Dinah whose names are not recorded here (Gen 46:7). Dinah is mentioned by name because this will be important in the ensuing story (ch. 34).

F. THE LORD BLESSES RACHEL WITH HER OWN SON, JOSEPH (30:22-24)

30:22 Then God remembered Rachel; he listened to her and opened her womb.

Sometime after the birth of Leah's sixth son Zebulun,[16] **God opened Rachel's womb** so that she was enabled to have a son. This is some years after Rachel had attempted to produce children through using mandrakes. Though Rachel rather superstitiously believed that the mandrakes contained the power of fertility, this verse makes clear that it was God, and not faith in old wives' tales about mandrakes, who brought about Rachel's fertility. She had been married to Jacob for at least ten years by this time, so the pregnancy was a welcome surprise. The human actors in this story consistently succumb to the temptation to take matters which belong in God's hands alone into their own hands. We face the same temptation as Christians.

30:23 She became pregnant and gave birth to a son and said, "God has taken away my disgrace."

---

[15]The wordplay is perhaps even more obvious with the exact form Leah uses: יִזְבְּלֵנִי (*yizbᵉlēnî*).

[16]It is not clear what the chronological relationship is between this verse and the birth of Dinah which is recorded outside of the series of sequential *waw*-consecutives which arrange the events in the narrative in time.

At long last the beloved wife of Jacob, Rachel, is enabled to become **pregnant**. What is more, **she gave birth to a son**, a potential heir. It is not as easy as it once was to relate to Rachel's words. Given the patriarchal context in which she lived, infertility was a major source of shame[17] and disgrace. In finally being enabled to have a son, Rachel thanked God for taking away that disgrace. She had tried to remove it herself through scheming with her maidservant and through folk remedies, but to no avail. Only God could remove her disgrace and enable her to have a son.

30:24 She named him Joseph, and said, "May the LORD add to me another son."

Rachel uses another wordplay in naming **Joseph**. In fact, this wordplay shows that Rachel is not satisfied with just a single son. She wants another one. Joseph's name (יוֹסֵף, *yôsēph*) and the verb "may he add" (יֹסֵף, *yōsēph*) are virtually identical in sound in Hebrew. There is also a wordplay with the verb translated "taken away" (אָסַף, *'āsaph*) in verse 23. It is interesting that the narrator uses the divine name "LORD" in recording Rachel's implicit plea. The irony is that in saying "yes" to that plea Rachel loses the opportunity to see her two sons grow to maturity. She dies giving birth to Benjamin, her second son.

IX. THE LORD BLESSES JACOB WITH MATERIAL PROSPERITY IN SPITE OF LABAN'S TRICKS (30:25-43)

When Jacob finished serving Laban for his two wives, Leah and Rachel, he had a large family but no means of providing for them. Laban realizes that he has himself been a beneficiary of the LORD's blessing of Jacob, and so he negotiates a financial arrangement to keep Jacob in his employ. They agree that all speckled and spotted sheep and goats would be Jacob's and all pure white or black or brown sheep or goats would be Laban's. But Laban tricked Jacob by removing all the speckled and spotted animals to another location before the agreement begins. Jacob thus starts without any animals of his own and must rely on the one-colored sheep and goats to produce speckled and spotted offspring. Jacob seems to have been tricked again.

However, the tables begin to turn against Laban in this passage. Jacob uses a breeding technique which he thinks produces speckled and spotted animals. He craftily uses the technique only on the strongest

---

[17]Hebrew culture was also more a shame-based than a guilt-based culture.

and healthiest animals, allowing the weak and sickly ones to bear young for Laban. His trickery works, and he gains remarkable wealth in only six years.

In the palistrophic structure of the Jacob and Esau narratives[18] this passage is linked to Genesis 29:15-30 where Laban tricks Jacob into marrying Leah as well as Rachel even though he loves only the latter. In this passage Jacob tricks Laban out of his wealth. The trickster Jacob emerges yet again and ultimately wins a battle of wits with Laban.

A. LABAN NEGOTIATES TO KEEP JACOB WORKING FOR HIM (30:25-34)

30:25 After Rachel gave birth to Joseph, Jacob said to Laban, "Send me on my way so I can go back to my own homeland.

Soon after Rachel finally produced a son for Jacob, the additional seven years Laban forced him to serve for Rachel was "coincidentally" up. It was time, Jacob felt, to return to his family in Canaan. Jacob evidently felt there had been sufficient time for Esau's anger to have assuaged. His relationship with his father-in-law hardly encouraged him to remain in his employment. It is interesting exactly how Jacob refers to the land of Canaan where his family lived as sojourners. Literally Jacob calls it his "place" and his "land."[19]

30:26 Give me my wives and children, for whom I have served you, and I will be on my way. You know how much work I've done for you."

It may seem strange to modern ears to hear that Jacob must be "given" his **wives and children** by Laban his father-in-law. On the one hand this seems to us moderns to treat people as though they were things. On the other hand, how could Jacob even think that his wives and children belonged to Laban rather than him? But Jacob, during the fourteen years in Laban's employment has had the status of a mere servant. When wives were given to servants and children resulted from the union, they "belonged" to the head of the household who "owned" the servant. For this reason Jacob demands that Laban "give," i.e., transfer, Jacob's wives and children to his responsibility as head of his own patriarchal household. The basis for this demand is Laban's knowledge of how Jacob had served faithfully and wholeheartedly for the agreed upon[20] fourteen years.

---

[18]See the discussion of this at Genesis 25:19b above.
[19]The NIV is periphrastic here.
[20]Actually these terms were imposed upon Jacob without negotiation!

30:27 But Laban said to him, "If I have found favor in your eyes, please stay. I have learned by divination that the LORD has blessed me because of you."

With Jacob having met his side of the agreement Laban is no longer the superior in this negotiation. He asks politely (**"if I have found favor in your eyes, please stay"**) realizing that Jacob has every right to take his family and leave. Laban claims that in practicing **"divination"** he has come to recognize that he has received the LORD's[21] blessing on account of Jacob's presence in his household. He, quite naturally, wants to remain under that divine blessing. The reader hears echoes of the promise to Abram. The LORD had promised to bless Abram and his descendants, to bless those who blessed them, and to pour out his blessings for the other nations through his descendants. Laban, a member of Jacob's extended family, has received blessings through Jacob.

As this narrative and other passages (e.g., Josh 24:2; Gen 31:30-35) make clear, Laban is no monotheist. But he is the ultimate pragmatist, and he has observed how Jacob's god[22] has blessed and protected him even though Laban had cheated him. It is interesting to consider whether the one true God has, in fact, spoken to Laban through his practice of divination.[23] Laban claims that this is so, but we have no confirmation or denial of the fact from the narrator.

30:28 He added, "Name your wages, and I will pay them."

Laban, realizing how valuable Jacob had become, offers Jacob to **name** his **wages** in order to remain as his hired servant. This seems a risky move for the crafty Laban; allowing the crafty Jacob to set his own wages. On the other hand Jacob is penniless and Laban thinks he holds the ultimate power in the relationship. The reader notes that the word "wages" comes up yet again, echoing the theme of buying and selling the rights of access to people in the immediately preceding narrative (Gen 30:14-16).

30:29 Jacob said to him, "You know how I have worked for you and how your livestock has fared under my care. 30:30 The little you had before I came has increased greatly, and the LORD has blessed you wherever I have been. But now, when may I do something for my own household?"

---

[21]The use of "LORD" is technically anachronistic in Laban's mouth (Exod 6:3). The narrator is showing that ultimately Yahweh (the LORD) was behind Laban's statement even though he was a polytheist who practiced divination and did not know the LORD.

[22]From Laban's perspective it must be Jacob's god, not his God!

[23]Although such practices are prohibited to Israel (Deut 18:10-12), the Old Testament does not deny that God can in some instances speak through such practices (e.g., 1 Samuel 28, the witch at Endor; Numbers 22–24, Balaam).

Jacob does not immediately answer Laban's question, instead reminding him of his effort and its results. Jacob claims that Laban knew how faithfully he had served him and how well his cattle had done under his care. He claims that Laban had very little when he began serving him. The fact that Rachel was his shepherdess may indicate the relative desperation of Laban in a patriarchal social system where women usually only performed such roles in desperate circumstances. The flocks had increased greatly and wherever "Jacob's feet touched down"[24] the LORD had blessed Laban. Laban was blessed because of Jacob, and this echoes the promise of blessing to Abraham and his descendants. Jacob reminds Laban, however, that he is penniless and needs to see to the needs of his now large household.

30:31 "What shall I give you?" he asked. "Don't give me anything," Jacob replied. "But if you will do this one thing for me, I will go on tending your flocks and watching over them: 30:32 Let me go through all your flocks today and remove from them every speckled or spotted sheep, every dark-colored lamb and every spotted or speckled goat. They will be my wages.

Laban does not dispute Jacob's argument about his faithful service and the LORD's blessing. Instead he asks what he could now "**give**" to Jacob. The word "give" seems a deliberate ploy by Laban to act as the generous benefactor to Jacob. Jacob disputes the appropriateness of the word "give." Jacob will earn whatever his wages will be. Jacob agrees to return to his shepherding responsibilities and guard Laban's flocks on one condition. His wages will be all the sheep and goats which are spotted or speckled and the dark lambs. This appears to be a most generous offer as sheep are mostly all white, goats mostly all black or brown.

30:33 And my honesty will testify for me in the future, whenever you check on the wages you have paid me. Any goat in my possession that is not speckled or spotted, or any lamb that is not dark-colored, will be considered stolen."

Jacob suggests a simple way to confirm his righteousness (NIV "**honesty**") in his business dealings. Laban can come at any time to examine the sheep that are separated off as Jacob's wages. **Any goat that is not speckled or spotted** and **any lamb that is not** completely **dark will be** regarded as **stolen** with the concomitant penalties.

30:34 "Agreed," said Laban. "Let it be as you have said."

Laban readily agrees to Jacob's conditions, but as we will see he has not finished with his scheming.

---

[24]Literal translation of Hebrew.

B. LABAN ATTEMPTS TO CHEAT JACOB OF HIS WAGES
(30:35-36)

30:35 That same day he removed all the male goats that were streaked or spotted, and all the speckled or spotted female goats (all that had white on them) and all the dark-colored lambs, and he placed them in the care of his sons. 30:36 Then he put a three-day journey between himself and Jacob, while Jacob continued to tend the rest of Laban's flocks.

While Laban verbally agrees to Jacob's plan, it is actually Laban, not Jacob, who removes the speckled and spotted goats and dark lambs from the rest of the flock. Laban thus removes (most of) the genetic potential for speckled and spotted lambs from the initial flocks with which Jacob is to begin. Jacob thus starts out with nothing. Any goats with spots or speckles or dark lambs will have to be produced from stock which was completely white or completely dark. In this passage we learn that Laban has unnamed sons who take the speckled and spotted goats and sheep and dark lambs a three-day journey away for pasturage so that they will not interbreed with the "pure" sheep, goats, and lambs. Laban has agreed to Jacob's terms, but he thinks he has foiled him yet again by greatly reducing the potential salary of Jacob.

C. JACOB TRICKS LABAN IN ORDER TO
INCREASE HIS OWN FLOCKS (30:37-43)

30:37 Jacob, however, took fresh-cut branches from poplar, almond and plane trees and made white stripes on them by peeling the bark and exposing the white inner wood of the branches. 30:38 Then he placed the peeled branches in all the watering troughs, so that they would be directly in front of the flocks when they came to drink. When the flocks were in heat and came to drink, 30:39 they mated in front of the branches. And they bore young that were streaked or speckled or spotted.

This is a difficult passage for us to understand. For one thing it seems as though Jacob's breeding strategy might be based on some superstition about a relationship between the color pattern which his sheep and goats see while mating and the color pattern of the resulting young which are born. That may well be what is in Jacob's mind.[25] The

---

[25]Although later Jacob gives the credit to God for his success in breeding animals (Gen 31:5-12). This does not explain why Jacob used the rods, and it may

narrator, however, is more reticent and merely affirms that, when the sheep and goats mated in front of the striped branches, the young ended up being streaked, speckled, or spotted. The narrator does not attempt to explain why Jacob did what he did and whether it had any effect on the young produced in mating that took place in front of the striped branches.

30:40 Jacob set apart the young of the flock by themselves, but made the rest face the streaked and dark-colored animals that belonged to Laban. Thus he made separate flocks for himself and did not put them with Laban's animals.

This verse is difficult to understand in Hebrew. I think it means that the lambs, which were born from Jacob's scheme having streaks, speckles, and spots were formed into a separate flock that Jacob took special care for since they were his wages. The animals that still belonged to Laban because they were pure white or dark were moved toward the streaked and dark-colored animals, which Laban had originally separated out of his flock and which Laban's sons kept a three-day journey away. In this way Jacob kept "his" flock separate from Laban's flock. The question of what happened when Jacob's flocks mated and produced pure white or pure "black" animals is not explicitly mentioned. One would assume that they were removed from Jacob's flock to Laban's. Otherwise Jacob could be accused of stealing.

30:41 Whenever the stronger females were in heat, Jacob would place the branches in the troughs in front of the animals so they would mate near the branches, 30:42 but if the animals were weak, he would not place them there. So the weak animals went to Laban and the strong ones to Jacob.

Jacob's observation or superstition that animals that mated in front of striped branches produced striped or spotted or speckled animals gave Jacob a huge business advantage in his dealings with Laban, an advantage which he put to good use. If mating in front of the rods produced animals which Jacob could claim as his wages, Jacob made sure that only the best and strongest animals mated there. Jacob did not want weak animals that would likely die or breed poorly. He selectively bred for strong animals that would be more likely to remain healthy and produce more offspring. Over time this meant that Laban's animals became weak and Jacob's strong. Jacob is ever the clever character. Here he starts to take advantage of his situation for his own benefit, to the detriment of his equally crafty father-in-law.

---

well be that in Jacob's mind there is a mixture of his own scheme and his faith in God.

30:43 In this way the man grew exceedingly prosperous and came to own large flocks, and maidservants and menservants, and camels and donkeys.

The consequence of this strategy in the long term meant that Jacob accumulated great wealth. That wealth is defined in terms of animals and the people needed to manage it. In the ancient Near East this meant there were male and female servants. Jacob left his home in Canaan penniless and after fourteen years of indentured servanthood to his father-in-law was still penniless. But in six short years he became notably wealthy. He even owned camels that could be used to trade goods at great distances. This happened, not because of Jacob's trickery but because of God's blessing.

GENESIS 31

X. JACOB FLEES FROM LABAN BACK TO CANAAN (31:1-55)

In this passage Jacob's relationship with Laban begins to break down as Jacob's wealth increases and Laban's decreases. The LORD instructs him to return to Canaan. He convinces his wives to agree to go even though it is against their father's wishes. He does this by claiming that Laban's treatment of him has been habitually unjust. He waits until Laban is three days distant on a trip and flees to Canaan. Even though Jacob has a three-day head start, Laban and his men chase Jacob down before he is able to cross the Jordan and enter the safety of Canaan. But the LORD who told Jacob to go warns Laban not to harm Jacob. Laban does, however, chastise Jacob and accuse him of stealing his household gods. This accusation was justified although Jacob was unaware of the fact. But Rachel tricks her tricky father by feigning illness and the household gods are never found. It is now Jacob's turn to chastise Laban. They settle their differences through the making of a covenant with a stone pillar and a pile of stones as a memorial.

This passage is paired in the palistrophic structure of the Jacob and Esau narratives with Genesis 29:1-14 which describes Jacob's initial arrival in Paddan Aram.[1] Jacob has come full circle. He went out empty and came back full — full of possessions and family. Even the trickery and duplicity of his father-in-law has not stopped the ultimate blessing of Jacob under God's watchful care.

A. LABAN AND HIS SONS TURN AGAINST JACOB (31:1-2)

31:1 Jacob heard that Laban's sons were saying, "Jacob has taken everything our father owned and has gained all this wealth from what belonged to our father."

---

[1]See the discussion of this at Genesis 25:19b above.

Jacob's wealth did not go unnoticed. Jacob heard that Laban's sons were grumbling about Jacob's success. As the heirs of Laban's wealth, which had become considerable while Jacob had served Laban for fourteen years, they saw their own inheritance slipping away. They accused Jacob of "taking" what rightfully belonged to their father and using their father's wealth as the capital from which he had gained his own wealth without benefiting their father. The situation could easily escalate into irresolvable conflict.

31:2 And Jacob noticed that Laban's attitude toward him was not what it had been.

It was not only Laban's sons who were dissatisfied with how the arrangement with Jacob was turning out. Jacob saw a change in Laban's face (פָּנֶה, *pāneh*), an indication of a change of **attitude**.

B. THE LORD COMMANDS JACOB TO RETURN TO CANAAN
(31:3)

31:3 Then the LORD said to Jacob, "Go back to the land of your fathers and to your relatives, and I will be with you."

In the face of potential hostility between Jacob on the one hand and Laban and his sons on the other, the LORD spoke to Jacob commanding him to return to Canaan. While the LORD does not specifically mention the problem of Esau's burning hostility toward him twenty years previously, he does promise to "be with" Jacob on the journey home and beyond. He also mentions Jacob returning to his **relatives**. It is interesting that the LORD refers to Canaan as **the land of your fathers**. Neither Abraham nor Isaac owned or controlled any of the land of Canaan with the exception of a grave. But the LORD had promised that Canaan would belong to the descendants of Abraham, and he had not given up on that promise.

C. JACOB CONVINCES RACHEL AND LEAH
TO AGREE TO LEAVE (31:4-16)

1. Jacob Explains the Problem with Laban (31:4-5)

31:4 So Jacob sent word to Rachel and Leah to come out to the fields where his flocks were. 31:5 He said to them, "I see that your father's attitude toward me is not what it was before, but the God of my father has been with me.

With both the degenerating situation and the LORD's explicit command to leave motivating him, Jacob calls for his wives **Rachel and Leah to come out to the fields** to discuss the situation. It is noteworthy that the narrator mentions Rachel, the loved wife, first. It is also noteworthy that neither Zilpah nor Bilhah are called. Jacob assumes that such a delicate matter should not be discussed at home where servants might overhear and warn Laban. Jacob is ever the crafty one.

Jacob tells his two primary wives of the change in their father's face (*pāneh*)[2] toward him.

2. Jacob Recounts How Laban Has Cheated Him (31:6-8)

31:6 You know that I've worked for your father with all my strength, 31:7 yet your father has cheated me by changing my wages ten times. However, God has not allowed him to harm me.

Jacob informs Rachel and Leah of what he claims they already know: he had done his duty and more. He had served[3] Laban with all of his strength.[4] But, Jacob reminds them, Laban had not reciprocated. In fact he had cheated him by changing his wages ten times. The first-time reader does not know what to make of Jacob's claim that Laban kept changing his wages. The narrator does not explicitly support it here, only reports Jacob's claim. This statement was made to Rachel and Leah who do not object to Jacob's claim in defense of their father. One might assume that they would know if Jacob's wages had been changed. Perhaps, then, the first-time reader is being led to trust Jacob's claim here. The fact that Laban does not dispute this assertion when Jacob makes it to him in verse 41 removes any initial doubt.

In any case, even though Laban tried to cheat Jacob (and succeeded at least once), Jacob has been protected by God.[5] No matter what Laban's intentions were, no evil had come against Jacob. One would like to take this statement of Jacob's maturing perspective on life at face value, but the reader knows to be cautious about the evaluation of the claims of "Jacob the Clever One." Of course God has been with Jacob,

---

[2]As in verse 2 above, the NIV has "attitude."

[3]In paraphrasing this as "worked for" the NIV loses the connection with Jacob being a servant of Laban's.

[4]The initial readers of the Pentateuch would likely see the connection between the loyalty which the LORD requires of Israel (Deut 6:5) and the loyalty which Jacob claims he has displayed toward Laban. In both cases it was "with all one's strength."

[5]Notice that Jacob uses the word "God" here, not "LORD."

protecting him as he had promised at Bethel (Gen 28:15). But Jacob still tries to manipulate situations through his own scheming. The reader is never quite sure when to trust or how much to trust Jacob. It is no accident that he is the forefather which gave the nation its name.

31:8 If he said, 'The speckled ones will be your wages,' then all the flocks gave birth to speckled young; and if he said, 'The streaked ones will be your wages,' then all the flocks bore streaked young.

Jacob claims that Laban changed his wages from **speckled** to **streaked** sheep and goats, but this seems inherently implausible. Laban had initially agreed that Jacob's wages would be all the speckled or spotted goats and sheep and all the dark-colored lambs. Laban had further agreed that Jacob's honesty could be confirmed or denied by the presence in Jacob's personal flocks of any all-white sheep or all-colored goats irrespective of whether they were speckled, streaked, or spotted. If Laban changed Jacob's wages so as to distinguish between speckled or streaked animals as Jacob claims, Laban would also lose the ability to verify Jacob's honesty. If the wages were speckled only and Laban found streaked ones, Jacob could argue that they came from the time when his wages were the opposite. It seems unlikely that Laban, who knew how to drive a hard bargain, would make such a bargain with Jacob. Jacob is exaggerating the degree to which Laban has cheated him.

Jacob's larger point, that God had watched over him even while his father-in-law cheated him, is something to which the reader can assent. By some "mysterious force," whatever the wages were, that was exactly what the mating of sheep and goats produced.

3. Jacob Recounts How God Has Blessed Him despite Laban (31:9-12)

31:9 So God has taken away your father's livestock and has given them to me.

Jacob acknowledges, striped branches in front of watering troughs notwithstanding, that it was God[6] who had brought him material blessings while in the employ of his crafty father-in-law. But while this must not be forgotten, the ambiguity of the characterization of Jacob and the way that he expresses God's blessings gives one pause. For Jacob it is a zero sum game. If his flocks are to increase, Laban's must decrease. The God who created a marvelously fruitful world is somehow limited in Jacob's mind. If he blesses one person he must of necessity curse another.

---

[6]Once again Jacob uses the word "God" not "LORD."

31:10 "In breeding season I once had a dream in which I looked up and saw that the male goats mating with the flock were streaked, speckled or spotted. 31:11 The angel of God said to me in the dream, 'Jacob.' I answered, 'Here I am.' 31:12 And he said, 'Look up and see that all the male goats mating with the flock are streaked, speckled or spotted, for I have seen all that Laban has been doing to you.

Jacob does not end his story there. He goes on to claim that during the breeding season he had a dream in which all of the male goats who mated were **streaked, speckled or spotted**. An angel of God then told him to notice this fact and explained that this has happened because of what Laban had been doing to Jacob. The angel, speaking for God, then tells Jacob that he is the "God of Bethel" the place where Jacob had anointed a pillar and made a vow about tithing to God as he was fleeing from Esau in Canaan. The angel told him to leave at once and return to his native land. The narrator does not record this dream at all. The reader is thus left to judge its veracity on other grounds. According to the narrator the LORD, not an angel of God,[7] told Jacob to go back to Canaan and promised to be with him. It is possible that the reader should assume that Jacob had such a dream and the narrator used Jacob's words to report it. But the overall characterization of Jacob makes this questionable. Jacob is trying to convince his wives to willingly and immediately leave their father and homeland. The claim that the remarkable breeding success which Jacob had was in fact divinely revealed in a dream to be directly from God is used by Jacob to buttress his account of how Laban had acted so deceitfully in his dealings with him.

What Jacob Said Had Happened	What Readers Know Actually Happened
31:10 "In breeding season I once had a dream in which I looked up and saw that the male goats mating with the flock were streaked, speckled or spotted. [11]The angel of God said to me in the dream, 'Jacob.' I answered, 'Here I am.' [12]And he said, 'Look up and see that all the male goats mating with the flock are streaked, speckled or spotted, for I have seen all that Laban has been doing to you. [13]I am	31:3 Then the LORD said to Jacob, "Go back to the land of your fathers and to your relatives, and I will be with you."

---

[7]We have noted that the use of "LORD" is probably anachronistic. It may be that "the angel of God" accurately reflects who actually spoke to Jacob in 30:3, and the narrator is simply using "LORD" to remind his readers that it was in fact Yahweh, the God of the exodus, who was speaking to Jacob.

| the God of Bethel, where you anointed a pillar and where you made a vow to me. Now leave this land at once and go back to your native land.'" | |

4. Jacob Recounts How God Commanded Him to Return to Bethel in Canaan (31:13)

31:13 I am the God of Bethel, where you anointed a pillar and where you made a vow to me. Now leave this land at once and go back to your native land.'"

The need to leave immediately is emphasized by a subtle addition of the phrase "**at once**" to the divine message. The reference to Jacob's experience at Bethel may imply that he must return to keep a vow there. Jacob's telling of this dream, if there was in fact a dream, seems too self-serving to be accepted without questions.

5. Rachel and Leah Agree to Leave (31:14-16)

31:14 Then Rachel and Leah replied, "Do we still have any share in the inheritance of our father's estate? 31:15 Does he not regard us as foreigners? Not only has he sold us, but he has used up what was paid for us. 31:16 Surely all the wealth that God took away from our father belongs to us and our children. So do whatever God has told you."

Rachel and Leah seem to believe Jacob's story. In any case, they adopt (or continue?) a negative attitude toward their father, Laban. As daughters they would not share in their father's estate which, in a patri-archal system, would be divided among his sons. But it is more than that. They think he regards them as no more than foreigners and not his flesh-and-blood daughters. Their evidence for this is that he had "sold" them to Jacob in exchange for his free labor. He did not give them dowries even approaching the value which he received from Jacob. The only known "gifts" were the maidservants Bilhah and Zilpah. The wealth that he gained from Jacob's free labor had already been spent for Laban's (in their view) selfish purposes. It was gone and they had no hope of ever seeing a proper dowry. Rachel and Leah see all too clearly the downside of the patriarchal system for women. They themselves are part of it. It does not even occur to them to ask Bilhah and Zilpah how they feel about what has happened. Rachel and Leah are persuaded also by Jacob's argument that God had taken away Laban's possessions. They now belong to Rachel and Leah and their sons.[8] The word "us" may be intentionally ambiguous. Do Rachel and Leah mean by "us," Jacob, Rachel, and Leah or just Rachel and Leah? Since in the context they complain about how Laban has deprived them and not Jacob of a proper inheritance through a dowry, it seems plausible to suggest that they interpret the events as applying to them and not Jacob. But the ambiguity may well be intended to let Jacob think he is included.

D. JACOB TRICKS LABAN BY LEAVING WHILE HE IS AWAY (31:17-21)

31:17 Then Jacob put his children and his wives on camels, 31:18 and he drove all his livestock ahead of him, along with all the goods he had accumulated in Paddan Aram, to go to his father Isaac in the land of Canaan.

Jacob persuaded his wives that it was time to leave because of the hostility and selfishness of their father. Jacob then loads his wives and his sons[9] onto the valuable camels which he has obtained while working for Laban. The livestock and goods which he had accumulated are driven or carried by animals. He leaves Paddan Aram to return to his father Isaac, who is still alive 20 years after Jacob deceived him on what was presumed to be his deathbed. The fact that the family evidently left directly from the fields shows the hurry which Jacob is in. He wants to escape from Laban's clutches as quickly as possible.

31:19 When Laban had gone to shear his sheep, Rachel stole her father's household gods. 31:20 Moreover, Jacob deceived Laban the Aramean by not telling him he was running away. 31:21 So he fled with all he had, and crossing the River, he headed for the hill country of Gilead.

This passage deals with two acts of deception that occurred in the process of Jacob leaving Laban for Canaan. First, when[10] they decided to leave, Laban was gone to shear his sheep. Rachel used the opportunity to slip into his home and steal the household gods. Rachel was still a poly-

---

[8]The NIV paraphrases Hebrew "sons" as "children" but this seems to miss the point. Rachel and Leah are just as much a part of a patriarchal system in which inheritances are passed from father to sons and not father to sons and daughters.

[9]The NIV paraphrases Hebrew "sons" as "children."

[10]This seems the most likely way to understand the Hebrew syntax (י plus noun plus perfect verb). Although it is theoretically possible that this happened some time earlier, it seems that Laban would have discovered it and searched for the household gods then.

theist at this time. She undoubtedly felt that Laban's frittering away of her inheritance more than justified taking the household gods. Such gods were regarded as useful for protecting the household. She was about to help Jacob establish a separate household in the distant land of Canaan.

Second, Jacob did not even tell Laban that he was leaving. The Hebrew relates these two events by using the same verb to describe them. Rachel "**stole**" (גָּנַב, *gānāb*) Laban's **household gods** and Jacob "stole the heart" (גָּנַב אֶת־לֵב, *gānāb 'eth-lēb*) of Laban by not telling him of his intentions. One may wonder, if Jacob was fleeing from Laban, why he could be expected to warn him of this fact? Perhaps Jacob is once again struggling with trusting the promise of God to be with him. The narrator's phrasing seems to imply that he should have faced Laban openly, trusting God to see to it that he and his family would be safely brought to the Promised Land.

The narrator refers to Laban as "the Aramean" for some reason.[11] It may be an echo of the beginning of the narrative of Jacob's stay in Paddan Aram which begins at 28:5 and ends here. Both refer to Laban as the Aramean,[12] and the geographical description may serve to delimit the boundaries of this section.

Jacob "**fled**" with everything he owned. He crossed the Euphrates[13] and set out in the direction of Gilead. Gilead was the region in modern Jordan bordering the Jordan River on the east between the Sea of Galilee in the north and the Dead Sea in the south. This was the typical route for travel to Canaan from the north in the ancient world. This part of greater Palestine was known for its abundant pasturage. With the flocks which Jacob now possessed this may have been one reason why he chose this route.

E. LABAN CHASES AFTER JACOB (31:22-23)

31:22 On the third day Laban was told that Jacob had fled. 31:23 Taking his relatives with him, he pursued Jacob for seven days and caught up with him in the hill country of Gilead.

---

[11]Note that even after 20 years Jacob is not an Aramean! The canonical audience may well recognize in Jacob's refusal to assimilate their own need to refuse to assimilate in Diaspora. My thanks to John Nugent for this insight.

[12]See also Genesis 25:20.

[13]In the Hebrew Bible "the river" unless otherwise defined is the Euphrates, the southern of the two great rivers in modern Iraq which defined ancient Mesopotamia ("the land between the two rivers").

Laban, who has been busy with sheep shearing, did not discover that Jacob was gone for three days. This may be because he was shearing sheep with the flocks watched over by his sons who had moved a three-day journey away (Gen 30:36). It would have taken his servants that long to make the journey to inform him of Jacob's departure. The verb used for that departure, "fled" was also used twenty years earlier when Rebekah warned Jacob of Esau's anger and told him to "flee" (בָּרַח, *bāraḥ*) to Laban (Gen 27:43). Jacob had "fled" there originally without the means even to pay a dowry to avoid the anger of his brother Esau. Now, twenty year later, and affluent, Jacob feels he must flee to avoid the anger of his father-in-law.

With a three-day head start Jacob is not overtaken by Laban until the tenth day of his journey, the seventh after Laban set out in hot pursuit. By that time Jacob had made it all the way to Gilead, but not yet to Canaan proper. Laban took plenty of backup in case the confrontation turned violent.[14]

F. GOD WARNS LABAN AGAINST HARMING JACOB (31:24)

31:24 Then God came to Laban the Aramean in a dream at night and said to him, "Be careful not to say anything to Jacob, either good or bad."

As Laban was about to overtake the fleeing Jacob, he stopped for one final night of rest. God warned Laban in a dream to guard himself from the consequences of saying anything to Jacob, good or evil. This would imply that somehow he, and not God, was in control of Jacob's destiny. Laban is again referred to as "the Aramean." This may signal the ending of the Laban narrative which began in 28:5 where he is described in the same fashion.

G. LABAN CONFRONTS JACOB ABOUT HIS TRICKERY (31:25-28)

31:25 Jacob had pitched his tent in the hill country of Gilead when Laban overtook him, and Laban and his relatives camped there too.

Jacob's location is mentioned because he was still in the Transjordan and not yet in the Promised Land where he would be safe. Laban

---

[14]The Hebrew reads "brothers" but this word (אָח, *'āḥ*) is often used more broadly of male kinsmen generally.

has his "relatives" or "brothers" with him and so things look a little threatening for Jacob and his family, even though God has warned Laban about what he might say to Jacob.

31:26 Then Laban said to Jacob, "What have you done? You've deceived me, and you've carried off my daughters like captives in war. 31:27 Why did you run off secretly and deceive me? Why didn't you tell me, so I could send you away with joy and singing to the music of tambourines and harps? 31:28 You didn't even let me kiss my grand-children and my daughters good-by. You have done a foolish thing.

Laban does not take God's words to him literally, for he does speak in an accusatory fashion to Jacob. He begins by asking Jacob exactly what he had done and why. He accuses Jacob of driving[15] his daughters away like captives of war. Laban accuses Jacob of running off secretly and thereby deceiving Laban. Furthermore Laban claims that if Jacob had merely told him, he would have thrown a joyous celebratory party. But Jacob and the reader are right to be suspicious of this claim. Laban also complains that he had no opportunity to kiss his (grand)sons[16] and his daughters good-by. Interestingly he places his grandsons before his daughters and this may be a subtle hint at the relative value he gives to his daughters. It is also interesting that Laban calls them "his" daughters and "his" sons and not Jacob's "wives" and Jacob's "sons."

H. LABAN REVEALS THAT GOD HAD WARNED HIM AGAINST HARMING JACOB (31:29)

31:29 I have the power to harm you; but last night the God of your father said to me, 'Be careful not to say anything to Jacob, either good or bad.'

Laban's claim is difficult in the Hebrew. Literally it reads, "There is to a power[17] of my hands to do evil to you." The NIV's translation seems the most likely. Laban's claim is qualified by the warning which he received the previous evening from the god[18] of Jacob's father. He

---

[15]This verb (נהג, *nāhag*) commonly refers to "driving" animals.

[16]Hebrew literally reads "my sons." One wonders whether Laban is using the word in a less precise sense or whether he feels that he has a claim on them since technically they were born while Jacob was his servant.

[17]אל (*'ēl*) could refer to strength or to a god whom he regards as empowering his hands.

[18]The small case "g" is more appropriate here (contra NIV) as Laban is a poly-theist who does not regard the god of Jacob's father as his own god, but power-ful nonetheless.

quotes with precision the statement which God had made to him (v. 24 above). In effect Laban does not have the power to do evil to Jacob, for if he did he would face the anger of Jacob's god. Laban's implied threat thus seems to be a bluff.

I. LABAN CONFRONTS JACOB OVER THE THEFT OF HOUSEHOLD GODS (31:30)

31:30 Now you have gone off because you longed to return to your father's house. But why did you steal my gods?"

Laban now interprets for Jacob why Jacob had left without saying goodbye. Laban uses the emphatic verbal construction[19] in describing both Jacob's leaving and his longing to return to his father's house. For Laban this longing to go home is understandable. But then he suddenly turns to accuse Jacob of stealing his gods. The household gods to which Laban refers were figurines which were believed to protect the family and ensure the fertility of crops and animals which were raised for food and for trade. Theft of such objects was a serious matter.

J. JACOB CLAIMS IGNORANCE OF RACHEL'S THEFT OF THE HOUSEHOLD GODS (31:31-32)

31:31 Jacob answered Laban, "I was afraid, because I thought you would take your daughters away from me by force. 31:32 But if you find anyone who has your gods, he shall not live. In the presence of our relatives, see for yourself whether there is anything of yours here with me; and if so, take it." Now Jacob did not know that Rachel had stolen the gods.

Perhaps buoyed by Laban's statement that God had spoken to him, Jacob matter-of-factly tells Laban why he ran away. He feared that Laban would rob him of Laban's daughters. Since Laban regarded them as still his daughters and not Jacob's wives, and since he came with his "brothers" to use force if necessary, Jacob's fear was a realistic one.

Jacob recognizes the seriousness of stealing Laban's household gods, and so he makes a rash oath.[20] Should any person be found with Laban's gods, he[21] is not to live. Jacob goes further and tells Laban that

---

[19]Infinite absolute followed by the verb of the same root. Cf. GKC, ¶ 113n, p. 342.

[20]For another example of a rash oath see Judges 11:29-40.

[21]Hebrew uses the masculine as its default gender for a person whether male

should he find anything which belonged to him in a public search, Laban was free to take it with him. Jacob, of course, does not know that he is risking the life of his beloved Rachel, who had secretly stolen the gods.

K. LABAN SEARCHES BUT FAILS TO FIND
THE HOUSEHOLD GODS (31:33-35)

31:33 So Laban went into Jacob's tent and into Leah's tent and into the tent of the two maidservants, but he found nothing. After he came out of Leah's tent, he entered Rachel's tent. 31:34 Now Rachel had taken the household gods and put them inside her camel's saddle and was sitting on them. Laban searched through everything in the tent but found nothing. 31:35 Rachel said to her father, "Don't be angry, my lord, that I cannot stand up in your presence; I'm having my period." So he searched but could not find the household gods.

Laban begins his search with Jacob's tent, whom he had directly accused of stealing the gods. We learn from this passage that Jacob slept alone in his own tent, while Rachel and Leah each had their own tents. The two maidservants, Bilhah and Zilpah also shared a tent. The dysfunctional relationship between Jacob and his primary and secondary wives is indicated by their sleeping arrangements. Somewhat surprisingly Rachel does not sleep in Jacob's tent, but in her own. After searching Jacob's tent, Laban next searches Leah's tent and the tent of the maidservants. The detail seems designed to heighten the suspense. When Laban finally comes to Rachel's tent, she alone remains in his mind as the potential thief. He evidently does not suspect the other servants of such a serious crime.

Laban's craftiness in business dealings evidently had its genetic effects as Rachel performs her own trick on him. Having hidden the teraphim[22] in the camel's saddle, Rachel sat on it! It is sometimes suggested, based on parallels from Nuzi that Rachel regarded the teraphim as connected to inheritance rights and that the terra cotta figures actually represented the dead ancestors of the home. On this hypothesis, in stealing them Rachel was trying to covertly claim inheritance rights of which, in her view, her father had unjustly deprived her. Rachel's ruse

---

or female. Here it is difficult to know whether Jacob is thinking only of male servants who might have stolen the gods without his knowledge or whether by "he" he means any person, male or female.

[22]The Hebrew narrator uses this more specific term for what are elsewhere referred to generically as "gods."

works as Laban carefully checks[23] throughout the tent and finds nothing, neither his gods nor anything else belonging to him.

Rachel pulls off the ruse by speaking with extra deference to her father. She humbly asks him not to be angry with her for not rising, addresses him as "my Lord," and explains why she cannot rise. The NIV paraphrases Rachel's "the way of women is on me" as "I'm having my period." While this is one plausible interpretation of Rachel's words and may well be correct, it could also mean that Rachel was claiming to be pregnant. Either excuse seems question begging. Surely a woman on her period or pregnant could get up and walk. But Laban does not even think to question Rachel and as a result misses out on finding his teraphim.

L. JACOB REBUKES LABAN FOR HIS ACCUSATIONS AND HIS TREATMENT OF HIM (31:36-43)

31:36 Jacob was angry and took Laban to task. "What is my crime?" he asked Laban. "What sin have I committed that you hunt me down? 31:37 Now that you have searched through all my goods, what have you found that belongs to your household? Put it here in front of your relatives and mine, and let them judge between the two of us. 31:38 "I have been with you for twenty years now. Your sheep and goats have not miscarried, nor have I eaten rams from your flocks. 31:39 I did not bring you animals torn by wild beasts; I bore the loss myself. And you demanded payment from me for whatever was stolen by day or night. 31:40 This was my situation: The heat consumed me in the daytime and the cold at night, and sleep fled from my eyes. 31:41 It was like this for the twenty years I was in your household. I worked for you fourteen years for your two daughters and six years for your flocks, and you changed my wages ten times. 31:42 If the God of my father, the God of Abraham and the Fear of Isaac, had not been with me, you would surely have sent me away empty-handed. But God has seen my hardship and the toil of my hands, and last night he rebuked you."

When Laban fails to find the teraphim, Jacob takes the opportunity to chastise Laban for his false accusations and for the long history of Laban's mistreatment of him. Jacob speaks angrily to Laban asking rhetorically what his transgression[24] or sin had been. He had done nothing that merited Laban hotly pursuing him as though he were an enemy

---

[23]The Hebrew verb translated "searched" (מָשַׁשׁ, māšaś) literally means to "feel."

[24]פֶּשַׁע (pešaʿ) is often translated "transgression." The NIV paraphrases this as "crime."

or a criminal. Jacob publicly challenges Laban to produce any evidence that Jacob or his family has stolen anything, much less his teraphim. With their mutual kinsmen present, Jacob asks for Laban publicly to produce the stolen items in the presence of witnesses and allow them to serve as judge and jury. With no response from Laban Jacob goes on to publicly remind Laban of his faithful and long service (20 years) to him. During that time Jacob had stolen nothing. In fact Jacob claims to be more than generous in bearing the cost of animals torn by wild beasts. He also endured Laban's demand that he pay for anything stolen. Under his care the flocks were healthy (they did not miscarry) and he did not eat animals from Laban's flock.

Jacob piles up his complaints, perhaps a little too thickly. He claims that the heat "ate" (אָכַל, 'ākal) him by day and the frost did the same at night. Sleep fled from his eyes, the conditions were so severe. This lasted for an intolerable 20 years during which Jacob "served" Laban. Not only that, Laban kept changing Jacob's wages. Since Laban does not dispute this assertion about changing wages 10 times in 6 years, the reader tends now to accept them at face value.

Jacob asserts that only God's providence had protected him from Laban's treachery. He refers to God as "the God of my father, the God of Abraham and the Fear of Isaac." For some reason the word father is singular even though Jacob refers to two of his "fathers," his grandfather Abraham and his father Isaac. It is hard to know what to make of the title "Fear of Isaac." Certainly it means that Isaac treated God with great respect. It is also appropriate in Jacob's speech to Laban. Laban has been warned by God, whom he has just referred to as "the God of your father" (Gen 31:29). Laban has good reason to fear this God. Jacob may be taking up Laban's terminology and using a traditional family title for God to remind Laban that the God who had warned him is to be feared.

In the traditional source-critical approach such passages indicate that originally the patriarchal traditions were developed independently and only at a far later time did redactors regard Abraham, Isaac, and Jacob as grandfather, father, and son. Each supposedly had his own "god," and only later tradition harmonized the gods into a single deity. In this passage the source-critical approach fails to appreciate how Jacob's description of the "God of my father" fits into the context of his conversation with Laban quite nicely.

31:43 Laban answered Jacob, "The women are my daughters, the children are my children, and the flocks are my flocks. All you see is mine. Yet what can I do today about these daughters of mine, or about the children they have borne?

Laban's response to Jacob's accusations is pointed, but he acknowledges that Jacob has the winning cards. Laban begins by claiming that the daughters[25] and their sons[26] are still his daughters and sons. They are not Jacob's wives or sons; in Laban's mind they still belong to him. Furthermore Laban claims that the flocks are also his. We must be careful about reading modern notions of ownership into the ancient world. When a servant took a wife and they had children, technically and legally the children and the wife belonged to the master, not the servant (Exod 21:4). But Laban's words show a disregard for the promises which he has made. Jacob was not Laban's servant in the technical sense. He was a sort of contract servant who had the right to leave. Laban's assertion is not unambiguously true and certainly implies that he is willing to go back on the commitments he has made to Jacob. The importance of God warning Laban is thus brought into focus. Laban can do nothing about Jacob unless he is willing to risk the wrath of the god who spoke to him. He regrets that he can do nothing about Jacob. Ultimately, Jacob outwits his wily father-in-law by allowing God to enter the situation. This is a hard lesson for Jacob (and for us!) to learn. He has not learned it once and for all, but at least there is a start. If God had not warned Laban, Jacob would have been in a very vulnerable position.

M. JACOB AND LABAN MAKE A COVENANT OF PEACE (31:44-54)

31:44 Come now, let's make a covenant, you and I, and let it serve as a witness between us."

Since Laban cannot use force against Jacob to deprive him of his wives and sons, Laban proposes that he and Jacob make a formal agreement. The biblical term for such binding formal agreements is "covenant." Such arrangements were usually public affairs with witnesses, rituals, and lasting means of remembering the covenant. Covenants in the Bible are typically between God and humanity. This passage, however, is one of several examples of human-to-human covenants. The covenant between Isaac and Abimelech regarding water rights and pasturage is another example in Genesis. The sign of the covenant, Laban proposes, would serve as a witness between Laban and Jacob and their families.

31:45 So Jacob took a stone and set it up as a pillar. 31:46 He said to his relatives, "Gather some stones." So they took stones and piled them in a heap, and they ate there by the heap.

---

[25]The NIV paraphrases "the women."
[26]The NIV has "children" for Hebrew "sons."

Jacob agrees to Laban's offer of a covenant by taking a stone and setting it up as a pillar. The pillar would serve as the covenant sign. Jacob
had done this earlier at Bethel when he was fleeing from Esau in chapter 28. This pillar thus sets off the narrative of Jacob's time with Laban
by a sort of inclusion. Jacob invites his "brothers," i.e., the male kinsmen
who have accompanied Laban, to participate in constructing the covenant
sign. By including them Jacob was attempting to ensure that they would
not just be witnesses to the covenant but partners to it. By adding a pile
of stones to the larger stone which Jacob had set up, they acknowledged
their participation in the forming of the covenant. The sealing of the
covenant through a covenant meal also indicates this.

31:47 Laban called it Jegar Sahadutha, and Jacob called it Galeed.
Laban, the Aramean, gave the pillar and heap of stones an Aramaic
name. **Jegar Sahadutha** means "heap of witness" in Aramaic. Jacob,
however, gave it the same name, but in Hebrew, the language of Canaan
to which he was returning. By giving it a Hebrew name Jacob reminds
everyone present and future generations that there is a difference
between the branch of the family which remained in Syria and the
branch which permanently migrated to Canaan.

**31:48 Laban said, "This heap is a witness between you and me today."
That is why it was called Galeed. 31:49 It was also called Mizpah,
because he said, "May the LORD keep watch between you and me when
we are away from each other. 31:50 If you mistreat my daughters or if
you take any wives besides my daughters, even though no one is with
us, remember that God is a witness between you and me."**
During the covenant formation ceremony Laban publicly clarifies
what the parties to the covenant are committing themselves to do and
not do. Laban refers to the "heap" (גַּל, *gāl*) as a "witness" (עֵד, *'ēd*).
When these two Hebrew words are combined, we get Galeed (גַּלְעֵד,
gal'ēd). The audience, whether "original" or canonical, would also be
familiar with another name for the site, "Mizpah."[27] The narrator informs the readers that Laban had originally used the verb צָפָה (*ṣāphāh*),
"to watch," when he solemnly spoke about the meaning and conditions
of the covenant. The place came to be called Mizpah because of this key
word *ṣāphāh* which Laban had used. Hebrew names for persons and
places often add an "m" sound to the verbal root. The association in
sound between Mizpah and *ṣāphāh* reflects this.

---

[27]This text is popularly known as the Mispah Benediction. In its context, however, it is a warning, not a blessing. My thanks to Gary Hall for reminding me of
this.

346

Laban asks for the LORD[28] to act as a sentry[29] guarding the safety of both Laban and Jacob and their families while they are separated from each other. The specific threat which Laban wants the LORD to guard against is not an external one. He specifically mentions Jacob's mistreatment of his daughters, either generally, or by taking other wives who will compete with Leah and Rachel for Jacob's affections and financial resources. Laban claims that since no man will be present in his absence to watch over his daughters' welfare, god[30] will do so.

31:51 Laban also said to Jacob, "Here is this heap, and here is this pillar I have set up between you and me. 31:52 This heap is a witness, and this pillar is a witness, that I will not go past this heap to your side to harm you and that you will not go past this heap and pillar to my side to harm me. 31:53 May the God of Abraham and the God of Nahor, the God of their father, judge between us." So Jacob took an oath in the name of the Fear of his father Isaac.

Laban now points to the covenant sign which Jacob and his kinsmen have erected. Laban claims that he had set up the heap of stones and the pillar; that Jacob actually set up the pile and the pillar is perhaps not relevant for Laban. He had taken the initiative in suggesting that the covenant be made. Laban had already declared the stones were a witness. In verse 52 he adds to their significance. They signify that each party solemnly promises to never cross the stones to the other party's side to inflict evil on them. Implicit is the fact that any travel to each others' lands will be for peaceful purposes only. So far as we know, there is never any further direct contact between the two branches of the family. Laban calls upon the god which both of their respective grandfathers, Abraham and Nahor, served and their mutual great-grandfather Terah served, as judge of the faithfulness of each party to the covenant. Laban is drawing upon the common religious tradition of the two sides of the family. This may perhaps be a hint that Laban knew that Terah's original move from Ur was initially intended to go all the way to Canaan (Gen 11:31). The part of the family that stayed behind in Haran, Laban implies, is just as legitimate a part of the family as the part which journeyed on to Canaan. That being so, the oath should be taken in the name of the common god who united the family that descended from Terah and his two sons, Abraham and Nahor.

---

[28]The use of "LORD" in Laban's mouth is anachronistic and indicates an implicit comment by the narrator that the God who spoke to Laban was in fact the LORD even though Laban did not know him by that name.

[29]The Hebrew verb *ṣāphāh* is often used of the work of the watchman or sentry.

[30]The NIV has "God," but this seems unlikely in Laban's mouth.

While Jacob swears an oath in joining the covenant, it is significant that he does not use the name of the god which Laban refers to in his speech. Jacob instead swears by the name of his father's God whom he refers to as the "Fear of Isaac." Jacob reminds Laban that the God whom he serves is to be feared above the gods that Laban served.

31:54 He offered a sacrifice there in the hill country and invited his relatives to a meal. After they had eaten, they spent the night there.

The NIV is not entirely clear who offered the sacrifice. The Hebrew text is explicit in mentioning Jacob as the offerer. There may be a hint of competition over who takes the initiative in the making of the covenant. Neither Laban nor Jacob trusts the other, and a covenant to ensure peace could well be a tricky negotiation in such circumstances. By providing the sacrificial meal[31] Jacob makes it clear that he is at least an equal partner to the covenant. Jacob invites his kinsmen who have accompanied Laban to participate in the meal that celebrated and sealed the covenant. It may be significant that Laban is not explicitly mentioned as participating in the meal. On the other hand the reader would perhaps assume that this is implicit. After a long day of negotiation which ended amicably with a covenant of peace between the antagonistic parties, Laban's group slept next to Jacob's before their departure the next day.

N. LABAN RETURNS HOME (31:55)

31:55 Early the next morning Laban kissed his grandchildren and his daughters and blessed them. Then he left and returned home.

Laban and his kinsmen rose early the next day to begin the journey back to Paddan Aram. So far as we know this was the last time he was to see his daughters and grandchildren. The Hebrew says that Laban "kissed his sons and his daughters." The NIV paraphrases this and reverses the order, but there may be some significance in the fact that what we would call grandsons are called "sons" and are kissed before Laban's daughters. The maidservants are apparently ignored. Whatever the strains that had arisen in the relationship, Laban shows his affection and respect for his daughters and grandsons by kissing them and blessing them prior to leaving them for his home.

---

[31]The Hebrew refers literally to "bread" but the point is the same.

GENESIS 32

XI. JACOB MEETS GOD
BACK IN THE PROMISED LAND (32:1-32)

In this chapter Jacob twice has an encounter with divine persons
(vv. 1,22-32) as he faces the daunting prospect of meeting his brother
Esau. The last time they were together, Esau was waiting for an opportunity to murder Jacob in revenge for his swindling him out of his
birthright and blessing. The two divine encounters prepare Jacob for his
meeting with Esau in different ways. In the first Jacob receives reassurance that God is present with him. In the second Jacob is crippled in a
wrestling match with a divine person, but succeeds in finagling a blessing out of him. The limp which Jacob takes away from that encounter
makes bowing before Esau a painful and difficult thing. Jacob the crip-
ple paints a pitiable picture when he finally limps up to meet Esau. No
longer able to manipulate the situation to his own advantage, Jacob
humbles himself before Esau and receives his forgiveness.

Jacob does not, however, merely rely on the reassurance which
these divine encounters gave him. He is still the old Jacob, grabbing and
striving with God and men. He attempts to prepare the ground for the
encounter with Esau by sending messengers and elaborate gifts ahead
of him. He also divides his family and flocks into two groups, hoping
that at least one of them will escape. And he also prays to remind God
of his promises. In all of these ways Jacob attempts to control the outcome of his meeting with Esau. He assumes Esau will still be seething
with anger over what he had done to him twenty years earlier.

In the palistrophic structure of the Jacob and Esau narratives this
passage is paired with the narrative of Jacob's encounter with God at
Bethel as he left the land to avoid Esau's wrath (Gen 28:10-22).[1] God or
his representatives appeared to Jacob both when he left and when he
returned to the Promised Land. In the time between these events the

---

[1]See the discussion above on Genesis 25:19b.

LORD had been with Jacob and protected and blessed him as he had promised he would (Gen 28:15). The canonical audience would undoubtedly see the Promised Land as the premiere place where God reveals himself to his people Israel. It is only when Jacob is back in the Promised Land that God reveals himself.

But there are differences between the divine revelation in chapter 28 and the revelations in chapter 32. In chapter 28 God's revelation was primarily intended to reassure Jacob. Even though his scheming to procure the birthright and blessing from Esau had had unintended negative consequences, the promise of God was still valid. Jacob would see God fulfill that promise. In chapter 32, however, the revelations are more complex.

A. ANGELS APPEAR TO JACOB (32:1-2)

32:1 Jacob also went on his way, and the angels of God met him. 32:2 When Jacob saw them, he said, "This is the camp of God!" So he named that place Mahanaim.

Having just survived a scare when Laban and his men chased down Jacob's family, Jacob receives divine confirmation that he is in the place God wants him to be. God's messengers meet him. God had just spoken to Laban warning him to leave Jacob alone, and now Jacob receives yet another confirmation of God's protective presence. While Jacob saw angels in a dream at Bethel when he originally left Canaan, in this passage he actually meets angels on his return twenty years later. God had promised to be with Jacob (Gen 28:15) and had been true to his word. Here he reminds him of his promise of protection as he faces the prospect of meeting Esau again. Jacob had once been at a place he called "house of God" (Bethel). In this passage he regards the place where he encountered the angels as the "camp of God." Once again there is a wordplay between "camp of God" and the place name "**Mahanaim**."[2] Jacob is coming closer to God as he geographically comes back to the Promised Land. Compared to Jacob's experience at Bethel in chapter 28, Jacob experiences God's presence more directly in this passage.

B. JACOB SENDS EMISSARIES TO APPEASE ESAU (32:3-5)

32:3 Jacob sent messengers ahead of him to his brother Esau in the land of Seir, the country of Edom.

---

[2]"Camp of God" is מַחֲנֵה אֱלֹהִים (maḥănēh 'ĕlōhîm) in Hebrew while Mahanaim is מַחֲנָיִם (maḥănāyim).

Interestingly Jacob does not attempt to sneak back into the Promised Land. He had fled twenty years earlier to avoid Esau's wrath. He now directly faces Esau's wrath by sending messengers to Esau and thus informing him of his return. God's messengers were sent to give Jacob reassurance of his presence. In this passage, Jacob also sends messengers.[3] We are not told how Jacob knows where Esau is. The narrator makes clear, however, that by this time Esau has separated from his parents and is living in the southern region of Seir, the place where Esau's descendants, the Edomites took up residence. Did communication take place with the home country while Jacob lived with Laban? Did the messengers go first to Isaac and only discover Esau's whereabouts through him? We are not told. Why was Esau living separately from his parents? Did his marriages with Canaanite women explode into outright conflict which necessitated separation? We are left to wonder. Where did Esau's possessions come from? Did Isaac and Rebekah give him an inheritance when he separated from them? Was this regarded as the birthright which Jacob swindled from Esau? We can only speculate, but the narrator invites the reader to wonder.

32:4 He instructed them: "This is what you are to say to my master Esau: 'Your servant Jacob says, I have been staying with Laban and have remained there till now. 32:5 I have cattle and donkeys, sheep and goats, menservants and maidservants. Now I am sending this message to my lord, that I may find favor in your eyes.'"

Jacob instructs his messengers to address Esau with great deference. They are to address him as though he is Jacob's lord and refer to Jacob as Esau's servant. They are to inform him that Esau's servant Jacob has attained great wealth measured in animals and servants of both genders. Jacob takes a risk in revealing such information. Esau was cheated out of the birthright and blessing. He might be tempted to take Jacob's possessions from him by force. Conversely, Jacob may be implicitly saying that he has no need of the birthright or any other form of material inheritance. God had protected him and blessed him even while he lived for 20 years as an alien[4] in a foreign land under the control of a treacherous father-in-law. It is hard to know what to make of Jacob here. Certainly there seems to be a touch of the manipulator in Jacob's strategy. The reassurance of God's protection does not mean that Jacob will not also use his persuasive rhetorical skills. And yet,

---

[3]The Hebrew word for "angels" and human "messengers" is the same (מַלְאָכִים, mal'ākîm).

[4]The NIV paraphrases "dwelled as a sojourner" (גּוּר, gûr) to simply "stay with."

Jacob initiates the meeting. Does he want reconciliation merely for his own peace of mind, or does he genuinely want to bring resolution to the cloud that hangs over his head? Is he trying to manipulate a gullible older brother or is he just using common sense?

The stated goal of the message that Jacob sends to Esau is to find favor in his[5] eyes. How would such a message do this? Certainly at least a part of what Jacob is doing is implicitly giving back the birthright of inheritance to Esau which Jacob had tricked him out of during a vulnerable moment (Gen 25:29-34).

C. ESAU'S COMING CAUSES JACOB TO FEAR (32:6-8)

32:6 When the messengers returned to Jacob, they said, "We went to your brother Esau, and now he is coming to meet you, and four hundred men are with him."

When Jacob's **messengers** return, they bring frightening news. They refer to Esau, not as Jacob's "lord" as he had instructed them when they went to Esau, but as Jacob's "**brother**." The messengers may not have been as concerned as Jacob was with being deferential or it may be that they are no longer addressing Esau and so the assumed deference is irrelevant. It is also possible that by referring to Esau as Jacob's brother they were seeking to soften their message with reassuring words. They went to deliver Jacob's message to Esau and presumably did so faithfully. They inform Jacob that Esau was **coming to meet** him with 400 men accompanying him. They do not explain why the men are with Esau.

32:7 In great fear and distress Jacob divided the people who were with him into two groups, and the flocks and herds and camels as well. 32:8 He thought, "If Esau comes and attacks one group, the group that is left may escape."

Jacob interprets the 400 men of Esau in the worst way. Rather than being a security force to protect Jacob as Esau may[6] have intended, Jacob interprets their presence as indicating Esau's intent to fulfill his vow to kill Jacob. One difficulty with this reading is that Esau had vowed to kill Jacob only after his father had died and been mourned. Since this had not yet happened, the reader might infer that Jacob is misreading Esau's intent. In any case fear is not always rational and Jacob is seized with

---

[5]Jacob again instructs his messengers to address Esau as though he were Jacob's lord.

[6]Another possible reading is that Esau came with hostile intent, but when he saw Jacob and his demeanor, he changed his intentions.

"**great fear and distress**." In a rare entrée into the internal conversation[7] of Jacob, we learn of Jacob's motivation. Jacob first of all acts to protect as much of his family and possessions as possible. By dividing both the people and animals into two groups, Jacob hopes that one group will escape if Esau[8] attacks the other. The word translated "**groups**" is actually the same word translated "camp" in verse 2 above (מַחֲנוֹת, *maḥănôt*). Jacob has forgotten that he is in the very camp of God at Mahanaim and so divides his household into two camps in an attempt to protect himself. How often we, like Jacob, fear enemies that do not, or would not exist if we would but wait on God in faith!

D. ESAU'S COMING LEADS JACOB TO PRAY (32:9-12)

32:9 Then Jacob prayed, "O God of my father Abraham, God of my father Isaac, O LORD, who said to me, 'Go back to your country and your relatives, and I will make you prosper,' 32:10 I am unworthy of all the kindness and faithfulness you have shown your servant. I had only my staff when I crossed this Jordan, but now I have become two groups. 32:11 Save me, I pray, from the hand of my brother Esau, for I am afraid he will come and attack me, and also the mothers with their children. 32:12 But you have said, 'I will surely make you prosper and will make your descendants like the sand of the sea, which cannot be counted.'"

It is interesting that Jacob turned to his own strategizing first, and then prayed. He is portrayed as continuing to struggle to trust God first and foremost. The structure of Jacob's prayer is:

> address to God (v. 9);
> statement of humility (v. 10);
> petition (v. 11a), and
> motivation for divine response (vv. 11b-12)[9]

Jacob begins his prayer by reminding God that he is the God of his forefathers "Abraham and Isaac" and not just his own God. He thus draws on the history of the relationship between God and his forbears as part of the basis for God to answer. Jacob refers back to Genesis 28:15,

---

[7]The Hebrew says, "Then Jacob said" evidently referring to internal conversation.

[8]Notice that in Jacob's own internal speech it is "Esau" not "my lord, Esau" or "my brother Esau."

[9]Samuel E. Balentine, *Prayer in the Hebrew Bible: The Drama of Divine-Human Dialogue*, OBT (Philadelphia: Fortress Press, 1993), p. 66.

"Know that I am with you and will keep you wherever you go, and will bring you back to this land; for I will not leave you until I have done what I have promised you" and Genesis 31:3, "Return to the land of your ancestors and to your kindred, and I will be with you." In Jacob's version the LORD had said, "I will do you good"[10] (vv. 9,12). He also changes the metaphor for the promise of numerous descendants from dust of the earth (Gen 28:14) to the sand of the seashore (v. 12).

Jacob may be feigning self-deprecation in verse 10.[11] Alternatively, the reader may infer that Jacob has come to a new appreciation of God's guidance and protection. Jacob had in fact left with only a staff, and he has returned with a large family, the basis for a great nation, and with numerous possessions. The two companies or camps to which Jacob refers are part of the preparations Jacob has made to meet Esau. In part the material blessings came from his scheming.[12] So Jacob *may not* be being portrayed as entirely sincere in his prayer; although this is merely a question the reader has, rather than a firm conclusion to which the narrator has led the reader.

When Jacob prays for God's deliverance,[13] he refers to Esau as his **"brother."** This may be a way of reminding God of the injustice of Esau's intended violence – one brother killing another. He also adds the killing of the mothers with the children as a potential consequence of Esau's anger. But Jacob fails to mention that the reader knows that Esau's anger primarily came from Jacob's own scheming. It seems as though Jacob uses an emotional appeal for God to protect the vulnerable (mothers, not women, and sons[14]) as a means of trying to manipulate God to protect him.

The final rationale that Jacob gives is the ultimate destiny of God's promise. If Esau kills Jacob, how will God's promise of innumerable descendants ever be fulfilled? His addition to God's words, "I will surely do you good" (vv. 9,12) with the use of the emphatic form seems to be another way Jacob amplifies the promise, and therefore God's obligation.

---

[10]Jacob uses the emphatic form (infinitive absolute followed by the same verb) here.

[11]So Balentine, *Prayer*, p. 68.

[12]Here Balentine (ibid.) is too definitive in attributing the material blessings to Jacob's trickery almost to the exclusion of God's blessings.

[13]NIV's paraphrastic "save" is better translated "deliver" (נָא הַצִּילֵנִי, *haṣṣîlēnî nā'*).

[14]One wonders whether "sons" (the NIV has "children") is being used generically or whether the fact that Jacob does not mention Dinah or any other unmentioned daughters is an indication of the importance he places on them. This could be a clue to what Simeon and Levi later see (Gen 34:31) as a callous attitude toward their sister Dinah.

Jacob receives no immediate response from God and so immediately sets about his own strategizing to ameliorate Esau's justified anger. This may be an indication to the reader that Jacob's prayer has already been answered. Esau has no intention to harm Jacob. But Jacob seems to assume in his ensuing actions that, since God had not explicitly answered his prayer, he must, in typical Jacob fashion, take matters into his own hands.

E. ESAU'S COMING LEADS JACOB TO ATTEMPT A BRIBE (32:13-21)

32:13 He spent the night there, and from what he had with him he selected a gift for his brother Esau: 32:14 two hundred female goats and twenty male goats, two hundred ewes and twenty rams, 32:15 thirty female camels with their young, forty cows and ten bulls, and twenty female donkeys and ten male donkeys.

Jacob readies himself for a confrontation with Esau; he does not run. He does, however, attempt to cleverly strategize about how to pacify Esau's anger. That night Jacob chose an extraordinarily extravagant gift for Esau. The narrator reminds the reader of the closeness of the relationship by referring to Esau as Jacob's "brother." There may be a wordplay between the word "camp" (מַחֲנֶה, *maḥănēh*) and the word "gift" (מִנְחָה, *minḥāh*).

The enormous gift consisted of large flocks of goats, sheep, cows, and donkeys with an ample number of males to serve for breeding purposes along with 30 female camels with their young.[15] There are no male camels for some reason. A large guilt produces a large gift from Jacob. One wonders whether this would rival or even surpass in value the birthright which Jacob had weaseled out of a famished Esau (Gen 25:29-34).

32:16 He put them in the care of his servants, each herd by itself, and said to his servants, "Go ahead of me, and keep some space between the herds." 32:17 He instructed the one in the lead: "When my brother Esau meets you and asks, 'To whom do you belong, and where are you going, and who owns all these animals in front of you?' 32:18 then you are to say, 'They belong to your servant Jacob. They are a gift sent to my lord Esau, and he is coming behind us.'" 32:19 He also instructed the second, the third and all the others who followed the herds:

---

[15]John Walton, *Genesis*, NIVAC (Grand Rapids: Zondervan, 2001), p. 605, notes that the gift is larger than some entire towns paid in tribute to foreign kings.

"You are to say the same thing to Esau when you meet him. 32:20 And be sure to say, 'Your servant Jacob is coming behind us.'" For he thought, "I will pacify him with these gifts I am sending on ahead; later, when I see him, perhaps he will receive me."

Jacob's strategy at this point may be to overwhelm Esau and his (mercenary?) men with herd after herd. This would remove the element of a surprise attack and perhaps wear down Esau's expected anger. Each part of the gift is divided into a separate flock. By the time Esau has endured and absorbed all of the flocks, perhaps he would be more amenable to receiving Jacob peacefully. Jacob protects himself and those closest to him by coming last in the train. Jacob instructs the servant responsible for the first flock to respond to Esau's question about who owned the flocks and what their purpose was with respectful deference. They are to be described as a gift, showing Jacob's generosity from a servant to his lord. While Jacob describes Esau as "my brother," in the actual conversation Jacob is the servant and Esau the lord. Jacob makes sure that each of his servants who led a flock said the same thing. He reminds them that they are to reassure Esau that "his servant Jacob is coming behind us" so Esau does not run after Jacob, but waits for him to arrive. Whatever Jacob's motives might have been originally, when he actually meets Esau, he is at the front of the procession, not hiding at the rear.

The readers are given another glimpse into Jacob's internal conversation. The narrator quotes what Jacob said (אָמַר, *'āmar*)[16] to himself. The word "face" (פָּנֶה, *pāneh*) occurs four times in the Hebrew of Jacob's internal conversation with himself. Jacob hopes to appease[17] Esau's face with the gift he was sending "before his face." After receiving this gift Jacob would "see his face" with the hope that perhaps[18] Esau would "lift up his face" to receive Jacob. Jacob does not yet know it, but he is about to see the *face* of God (32:30). The narrator thus seems to be pointing forward to the ensuing narrative. Jacob is concerned about his face and Esau's face; but things will be put in a different perspective when he sees God's face.

32:21 So Jacob's gifts went on ahead of him, but he himself spent the night in the camp.

The presents for Esau with the attendant strategy for ameliorating Esau are sent off to the south ahead of Jacob. Jacob, however, remained

---

[16]The NIV periphrases this to "he thought."

[17]The NIV has "pacify" for the Hebrew verb כָּפַר (*kāphar*), the verb often translated "to atone, make atonement."

[18]Jacob's uncertainty in this regard is indicated by the Hebrew word אוּלַי (*'ûlay*).

behind and lodged in the camp. Presumably this is the same camp where he had met the angels (messengers) and which he named "Mahanaim," saying "this is the camp of God." The same wordplay between the words "camp" and "gift" occurs again in the Hebrew (see Gen 32:2 above). This creates the setting for the ensuing narrative where Jacob wrestles with a man whom he concludes was divine.

F. JACOB WRESTLES WITH GOD AND IS CRIPPLED (32:22-32)

32:22 That night Jacob got up and took his two wives, his two maidservants and his eleven sons and crossed the ford of the Jabbok.

In this passage we hear of Jacob crossing the **Jabbok**. The Jabbok is a quick moving tributary of the Jordan which enters it in the Transjordan about 25 miles north of the Dead Sea. When Israel entered Canaan from Egypt, the Jabbok formed the northern border of the Transjordanian tribes. To cross the Jabbok to the south was, for the original readers, to enter the Promised Land. The geography of this section is not entirely clear. One possibility is that Jacob, already on the south side of the Jabbok, took his family and possessions to the north side where the river would protect them from any sudden attack by Esau's men. Another reading would have Jacob taking them over the river to the south with Jacob inexplicably returning to the north side. One question that arises is, why does Jacob wait until the night to do this? Was he trying to use the cover of darkness to fool Esau's spies? Wenham[19] suggests that Jacob's behavior is being portrayed as the erratic behavior of someone seized by fear. Although he reads the geography differently, this suggestion has plausibility.

It is interesting that Dinah, his daughter, and other unnamed daughters, are not mentioned. This may hint at the attitude which Jacob later seems to display toward her in chapter 34. Only Leah and Rachel are regarded as full wives, while Bilhah and Zilpah are referred to as Jacob's (not Rachel and Leah's) maidservants and not as his concubines or secondary wives.

32:23 After he had sent them across the stream, he sent over all his possessions.

Verse 23 informs us that Jacob did not actually stay with his family on the north side of the Jabbok but merely sent them and his remaining[20]

---

[19]Wenham, *Genesis 16–50*, p. 292.

[20]The Samaritan Pentateuch, LXX, and other versions read "all" his possessions, and this is reflected in the NIV.

possessions over the river.[21] One wonders what possessions exactly Jacob had left after the extravagant gift for Esau.

32:24 So Jacob was left alone, and a man wrestled with him till daybreak.

Jacob, left alone on the other side of the Jabbok, **wrestled** with a **"man"** who was **"with him"** until the rising of the dawn. This man obviously had divine power, and by this time Jacob was quite an old man.[22] Jacob ultimately concludes that this man was "God" or at least divine in nature. The Hebrew has a wordplay between the name of the river, Jabbok (יַבֹּק, *yabbōq*) and the verb "to wrestle" (אָבַק, *'ābaq*). It may well also echo the word Jacob (יַעֲקֹב, *yā'ăqōb*). Jacob holds his own for the entire night. It is not clear exactly when Jacob begins to realize that he is wrestling with more than a human being. The text is elusive as to the identity of the man. This has consequently created a fertile field for speculation.

32:25 When the man saw that he could not overpower him, he touched the socket of Jacob's hip so that his hip was wrenched as he wrestled with the man.

The man, whoever he was, realized that he did not prevail[23] against Jacob. The text does not say that he lacked the ability to overpower him; just that he did not overpower him. Jacob turned out to be a tenacious fighter. The fact that God or a divine emissary allows himself to be beaten by Jacob is a theologically profound notion. Kevin Walton aptly comments, "God works through an apparent position of weakness; on the face of it God has been defeated, but in this display of weakness, his plans not just for Jacob but for his descendants have moved closer to fulfillment."[24]

Using supernatural power the man touched Jacob's hip socket and dislocated his hip leaving him partially crippled.[25] Jacob's tendency to

---

[21]The Hebrew is admittedly difficult here. Literally translated it reads, "Then he took them; then he made them cross over the river; then he made what was his cross over."

[22]Kevin Walton [*Thou Traveller Unknown: The Presence and Absence of God in the Jacob Narrative*, Paternoster Biblical Monographs (Milton Keynes: Paternoster, 2003), p. 90], using the data of Joseph's age when he entered Egypt and other chronological information in Genesis, points out that Jacob was 97 years old at this point in time.

[23]The NIV's "could not overpower" actually conflates two separate meanings of the verb יָכֹל (*yākōl*), which can mean either "to be able" or "to prevail" but not both simultaneously.

[24]Walton, *Traveller*, p. 90.

[25]The Hebrew word for "thigh" (יָרֵךְ, *yārēk*), translated as "hip" in the NIV is

fight all comers results in his being crippled on the very morning when he must face his brother Esau. His persistence wrings a blessing out of his mysterious combatant, but it comes at a price. Jacob is both blessed and broken by this "magnificent defeat at the hands of God."[26] To be elected is a mixed bag for Jacob. It means great blessing, but also wounding.

Christians may well see here an anticipation of the end of the Bible's story. God accepted defeat of his son through human crucifixion. But the thought of that "defeat" has been the very thing that has brought countless people humbly seeking forgiveness. Jacob's victory in his wrestling match with God left him humbled and broken. But that very humility and brokenness prepares him to face Esau.

32:26 Then the man said, "Let me go, for it is daybreak." But Jacob replied, "I will not let you go unless you bless me."

It is not immediately clear just what daybreak has to do with Jacob's wrestling partner's desire to leave. It may be simply that the time for Jacob to confront Esau, his estranged brother, had come. The divine opponent must leave so that Jacob is ready to meet with Esau. Some commentators have speculated that in some "original" form of the story the assailant was a night spirit or a river demon that literally could not stand to be in the light. But this is to read more into the text than is present.[27] Kevin Walton suggests that underlying the statement is the fact that it would be dangerous for a human to see God in broad daylight. The divine man wants to protect Jacob from danger.[28]

---

euphemistic for penis in Exodus 1:5 and Judges 8:30. There may be an allusion euphemistically to the same thing in this passage. Geller ["Struggle at the Jabbok: The Uses of Enigma in a Biblical Narrative," *JNES* 14 (1982): 56]: "like that other sign of covenant, circumcision, [it] is a symbolic representation of the dialectic of positive and negative, blessing and curse. Like other cultic actions it stands on the dangerous frontier of holiness."

[26]F. Buechner, *The Magnificent Defeat* (San Francisco: Harper and Row, 1966), pp. 10-18.

[27]Claus Westermann [*Genesis 12–36*, Continental Commentary (Minneapolis: Fortress, 1995), p. 515]: "All exegetes agree that the basic narrative must be old. It bears animistic traits and is not to be dissociated from the region, the ford, the river. The danger of the ford is personified in the spirit or demon who does not want to let the traveler cross the river and attacks him so as to prevent him doing so." P. 517: "The attacker's request to let him go is prepared by and follows on v. 26a. It shows that the demon is one who is powerful only by night and loses his strength with the breaking of day."

[28]Kevin Walton, *Traveller*, p. 81: "In this case, the paradox would be that the very opponent who is fighting with Jacob is also concerned not to see him perish."

Whatever Jacob's faults, he wants to receive God's blessing, and for that he must be commended. Jacob with his mother Rebekah's help grabbed for the birthright and the blessing of his father. Here he wants a blessing from his divine opponent.[29]

32:27 The man asked him, "What is your name?" "Jacob," he answered. 32:28 Then the man said, "Your name will no longer be Jacob, but Israel, because you have struggled with God and with men and have overcome."

"**What is your name?**" is not a question that implies a lack of knowledge of Jacob's name but evidently refers to the meaning of the name. There is a contrast between the meaning of the new name, Israel ("God strives" or "he strives with God"), and the old name Jacob (trickster).[30] Jacob had been grabbing and tricking his way to God's blessing. That would no longer be true. The blessing which Jacob has wrestled out of the man is a new name. The name "Israel" means "God struggles," but as interpreted by Jacob's nocturnal opponent it refers to Jacob's struggle with God (and man) and the fact that he prevailed[31] in that struggle. Balentine helpfully addresses the significance of this narrative: "the new name is meant to embody a new character, a change from one who seeks to control to one who is controlled."[32] As he notes, this is followed up by Jacob changing his cowardly plans to send the bribes, wives, and children in front of him (Gen 32:13-21). Instead he himself went ahead of them at the risk of his life (Gen 33:3).

Of course the name Israel is not just Jacob's new name. It is the name of the nation which descended from Jacob. The original and canonical audiences would see their own identity in Jacob as he is transformed by this experience. The person Israel is God's struggle. The nation which descended from him is also God's struggle. The relationship between the covenant-and-promise-granting God and the nation receiving that covenant and those promises is not an easy one. God must wrestle with Israel as Israel wrestles with God.

---

[29]Balentine (*Prayer*, p. 70), suggests a parallel between the wrestling match and the earlier prayer of Jacob in 32:9-12: "In the one encounter he has tried to manipulate God with words, in the other he tries to muscle God with brute strength. . . . Isaac has been duped, but God is an opponent of a different caliber."

[30]See R.W.L. Moberly, *The Old Testament of the Old Testament*, OBT (Minneapolis: Fortress, 1992), p. 59. In Judges 13:17, when an unknown name is being asked for, the Hebrew interrogative מִי (*mî*), "who," is used rather than, as here, מָה (*māh*), "what," for an already known name.

[31]The Hebrew word used, יָכֹל (*yākōl*), is the same one used in verse 25 above.

[32]Balentine, *Prayer*, p. 71.

Significantly, unlike Abraham and Sarah, Jacob does not take up his new name but continues with the old one. This may imply that Jacob continues to struggle to become the person God has called him to be.

32:29 Jacob said, "Please tell me your name." But he replied, "Why do you ask my name?" Then he blessed him there.

The man had asked Jacob to say his name out loud. When he did, Jacob received a new name. Jacob, ever grabbing, wants the man to reciprocate. He wants to know his name. The man does not respond but asks why Jacob wants that knowledge. Perhaps Jacob thinks he will be able to control God or at least a divine emissary by a superstitious use of the name. Kevin Walton notes the difference between this passage where Jacob is denied knowledge of the divine name and Exodus 3:13-14 where God does not deny Moses knowledge of his name.[33] He contrasts the patriarchal era, where God reveals himself more directly to the patriarchs but without knowledge of his name Yahweh, and the Mosaic era where a new understanding of God's holiness makes direct revelation more threatening, but the name Yahweh is known. In any case the man does not respond by answering the question but by blessing Jacob.

32:30 So Jacob called the place Peniel, saying, "It is because I saw God face to face, and yet my life was spared."

While Jacob does not gain control over the divine emissary by learning his name, he does receive what he asked for, God's blessing. Evidently the man was now gone and Jacob realizes the significance of what has just happened. While it is true that human beings cannot see God without dying, in exceptional circumstances God can grant such experiences.[34] Jacob claims or realizes[35] that he had seen God face to face, and yet his life had been delivered from death. The name Jacob gives to the place, **Peniel**, means "face of God" and is a reminder to the nation of the extraordinary experience granted to Jacob at a time when he needed reassurance of God's protection as he was about to face Esau and his 400 men. If God delivered Jacob from the certain death that seeing God would ordinarily entail, he could be trusted to deliver him from any danger that Esau might pose.

32:31 The sun rose above him as he passed Peniel, and he was limping because of his hip.

---

[33]Walton, *Traveller*, p. 86.

[34]While this narrative relates only Jacob's claim to have seen God, Exodus 24:9-11 relates such an instance of God's exceptional grace at the founding of the Sinai covenant.

[35]The narrator does not say whether Jacob's interpretation of having seen God face to face is correct or not.

With the rising of the sun there was no more delaying the confrontation that Jacob feared his meeting with Esau would become. He had seen the face of God at Penuel[36] and was changed, but damaged by the experience. As he approached Esau, he would have no alternative but to show his vulnerability by limping up to him. He did not know it, but this may well have been part of God's strategy with Esau. If Esau saw Jacob's vulnerability, his anger might subside. In fact the reader never knows whether Esau had already forgiven Jacob or whether it was about to happen. In any case, it is in this state of vulnerability that God prepares Jacob for the meeting.

32:32 Therefore to this day the Israelites do not eat the tendon attached to the socket of the hip, because the socket of Jacob's hip was touched near the tendon.

The narrator makes clear that he writes at some historical distance from the events of Jacob's time. He writes for Israelites, now a nation come out of Egypt.[37] He explains for his audience an odd custom. In the ancient world the eating of meat was a somewhat rare occurrence for ordinary people, and so nothing was wasted. Even the tendon in the hip socket was valuable meat which would ordinarily be used for food. Because of Jacob's divinely caused injury, however, Israelites developed the custom of not eating the tendon in the hip. The injury which God caused Jacob came to be viewed as a holy thing which should be remembered. God's crippled nation should always remember that, although such divine crippling is painful and humbling, it is sometimes the necessary precursor to God's blessing. Sometimes we must be crippled in order to be healed. This was as true for the person Israel as it was for the nation named after him.

---

[36]The Hebrew place is known as Penuel (Judg 8:8-9; 1 Kgs 12:25) and is spelled this way in the Hebrew in this verse. The NIV harmonizes the spelling with Peniel in v. 30. The slight difference in spelling has been used to detect conflicting sources in the transmission history of the event. Wenham (*Genesis 16–50*, p. 297), however, plausibly suggests that the author has modified the spelling in v. 30 to make it sound more like "face of God." Such modifications are common in biblical etymologies.

[37]The debate in scholarship is not whether Genesis was written for Israel or not. It is part of the Pentateuch, a document that is clearly to be dated after Israel has left Egypt and entered the land. The debate is about how long after the entrance into the land is to be the assumed date of the original audience.

GENESIS 33

XII. JACOB RETURNS ESAU'S BLESSING (33:1-20)

The long-dreaded meeting with Esau is now upon Jacob. Crippled from the wrestling match with the divine person in 32:22-32, Jacob faces Esau that very morning. But the wrestling match has changed Jacob to a degree. His favoritism toward Rachel and secondarily Leah is shown by the order in which the family groups are placed; the maidservants and their sons face the potentially hostile Esau first, then Leah and her children, and finally Rachel and Joseph. But Jacob puts himself in front of them all. He indicates his humility by bowing repeatedly to Esau.

In the palistrophic structure of the Jacob and Esau narratives, this passage is paired with Genesis 26:34–28:9 where Jacob tricks Esau out of his birthright and blessing.[1] In this chapter, twenty years have passed. Jacob has become rich through the Lord's blessing. But in order to heal the rift caused by his actions twenty years earlier Jacob gives much of those riches back to Esau. The material possessions which Jacob has obtained while working for Laban are used to lavish Esau with an enormous gift designed to assuage Esau's wrath. In a sense the blessing which Jacob had earlier swindled out of Esau he now returns with interest. The means that Jacob used to obtain the birthright and blessing results in him giving much of his fortune away to his brother.

While their reconciliation is remarkable, Jacob has not entirely cast off his trickiness. When Esau suggests that he come and live with him, Jacob promises to meet him later, without any intention of actually doing so.

A. THE CRIPPLED JACOB MEETS ESAU (33:1-3)

33:1 Jacob looked up and there was Esau, coming with his four hundred men; so he divided the children among Leah, Rachel and the two

---

[1]See the discussion of this above at Genesis 25:19b.

maidservants. 33:2 He put the maidservants and their children in front, Leah and her children next, and Rachel and Joseph in the rear.

With the sun finally up and Jacob's encounter with the divine person finished, Esau arrived. Jacob saw him and had just enough time to arrange his wives and children into the pecking order of favoritism. The children[2] were put together with their respective mothers into four groups. The two maidservants, Bilhah and Zilpah, with their four sons and any unmentioned daughters, were placed in front where they were most likely to face danger. Next come Leah and her six sons and at least one daughter. Finally comes the favored wife, Rachel, with her only son Joseph. They are protected by being placed in the rear. While the experience at Peniel had an effect on Jacob, he demonstrates in this passage that the old tendency to cover his bets is still present. The favoritism which plays itself out in the later tensions between the brothers and the tribes which descend from them is displayed with shocking clarity. If forced to make choices, Jacob would rather have Rachel and Joseph spared and the other wives and sons and daughters die.

33:3 He himself went on ahead and bowed down to the ground seven times as he approached his brother.

Jacob at least shows enough courage to put himself in the front of his wives and children. He faces Esau and does not run from the situation. The name change to Israel "is meant to embody a new character, a change from one who seeks to control to one who is controlled."[3] This is followed up by Jacob changing his cowardly plans to send the bribes, wives, and children in front of him (Gen 32:13-21). Instead he himself went ahead of them at the risk of his life. The sevenfold bowing shows the manipulative part of Jacob's nature has not been driven out by the "draw" in his wrestling match with God. The picture of an old, limping Jacob who struggles in pain to bow seven times before his brother[4] is striking. Jacob presents himself as entirely vulnerable before Esau. The number seven is probably not accidental. One source helpfully notes: "To magnify the honor being given and the subservience of the person who bowed, this gesture could be repeated seven times. Some Egyptian texts from El Amarna (fourteenth century B.C.) portray vassals bowing seven times to Pharaoh."[5]

---

[2]Not "sons" here, but children (הַיְלָדִים, hayᵊlādîm).

[3]Balentine, *Prayer*, p. 71.

[4]The narrator, in describing Esau as Jacob's "brother," may be emphasizing the closeness which such a relationship should exhibit.

[5]Walton, et al., *IVPBBCOT*, p. 66. For a detailed treatment of the sources see *COS*, III:90, note 11.

B. ESAU ACCEPTS JACOB'S BLESSING (33:4-11)

33:4 But Esau ran to meet Jacob and embraced him; he threw his arms around his neck and kissed him. And they wept.

The reader does not know whether Jacob's strategies worked or whether they were unnecessary. When Esau saw his brother limping toward him, he ran to him. In an emotional greeting in which both of them wept, the conflict from twenty years before is seen to have melted away. Esau has forgiven Jacob. No matter the reason, this forgiveness must not be forgotten in our reading of Esau as a character. Whatever his faults might be, Esau has learned to forgive. In that forgiveness Jacob quite rightly saw the hand of God.

33:5 Then Esau looked up and saw the women and children. "Who are these with you?" he asked. Jacob answered, "They are the children God has graciously given your servant."

After greeting Jacob warmly, the groups of mothers with their children arrive. Esau asks who they are. Jacob refers only to the children, not to the wives. Jacob tells Esau that his children are a gift from God who had given them in his grace.[6] He refers to himself as Esau's "servant." Whatever God's oracle to Rebekah in Genesis 25:23 meant, Esau as an individual does not come to serve Jacob as an individual. If anything the opposite happens.[7] Jacob is grateful for Esau's acceptance of him, but he remains deferential. The tension between the "old Jacob" who grabbed everything possible and the "new Jacob" who had seen the face of God at Peniel is still present.

33:6 Then the maidservants and their children approached and bowed down. 33:7 Next, Leah and her children came and bowed down. Last of all came Joseph and Rachel, and they too bowed down.

Jacob's wives, maidservants, and their children come and deferentially bow before Esau as Jacob himself had done. Each of the groups approaches Esau and bows in the order which Jacob had set for them. The detail slows the narrative pace to highlight the moment. Not only Jacob, but also his wives and his descendants bow to Esau respectfully. Jacob takes no chances that Esau's anger will flair up again because of some perceived slight. In this situation Esau is the lord and Jacob and all of his family the respectful servants.

33:8 Esau asked, "What do you mean by all these droves I met?" "To find favor in your eyes, my lord," he said.

---

[6]The Hebrew verb is חָנַן (ḥānan), "to show grace or favor."

[7]See the discussion of Turner, *Announcements of Plot*, pp. 115-134.

Esau, having warmly greeted Jacob and having met his family, asks about the meaning of the herds[8] of animals which Esau had met as he traveled north to meet Jacob. Jacob, in an extraordinary moment of candor, tells Esau his real motivation. He, quite frankly, wanted to find favor in Esau's eyes through the gift of the animals. He again deferentially refers to Esau as his "lord." Jacob does not try to hide his motives or his intentions. This is quite unusual for Jacob and shows that the wrestling match with the divine man had a real effect on him.

33:9 But Esau said, "I already have plenty, my brother. Keep what you have for yourself."

Esau informs Jacob that the past twenty years have been good ones for him. His possessions had become great (רַב, *rab*) He addresses Jacob as "my brother" which seems to imply that Jacob's deferential treatment of him is not necessary. Esau does not view Jacob as his subordinate or his enemy, but his brother. Esau says that he does not want Jacob's gift. When Jacob insists, however, Esau accepts without further discussion. His initial refusal may just be politeness on Esau's part.

33:10 "No, please!" said Jacob. "If I have found favor in your eyes, accept this gift from me. For to see your face is like seeing the face of God, now that you have received me favorably. 33:11 Please accept the present that was brought to you, for God has been gracious to me and I have all I need." And because Jacob insisted, Esau accepted it.

Jacob immediately begs Esau to reconsider. Accepting Jacob's gift would reassure Jacob that he has found grace and forgiveness from Esau and that past animosities were truly over. Jacob had just literally[9] seen the face of God at Peniel. Seeing Esau's face was just as significant for Jacob. Jacob again uses deferential language in asking[10] Esau to accept the gift. Notably, however, he does not refer to Esau as his lord immediately after Esau had called Jacob his "brother."

In verse 11 Jacob again pleads with Esau to receive his gift, this time referring to it as his "blessing" (בְּרָכָה, *bᵊrākāh*). The echo of the earlier narrative in which Jacob has swindled Esau out of Isaac's blessing seems clear. Jacob, through this enormous gift is, in a symbolic sense, return-

---

[8]Esau uses the word translated "camp" (מַחֲנֶה, *maḥăneh*) in Genesis 33:2 instead of Jacob's word "herd" (עֵדֶר, *'ēder*). This may be an echo of Jacob's experience at Mahanaim, the "camp of God" in 33:1-2.

[9]Jacob is more certain about this than the narrator, who is reticent to identify exactly who Jacob's wrestling partner was.

[10]In the Hebrew Jacob twice uses the particle of entreaty (נָא, *nā'*) as though simple asking had given way to pleading.

ing the blessing to Esau. Jacob informs Esau that the gift will not impoverish him as God had been gracious and therefore he had everything he needed. Jacob went on to verbally persuade Esau to accept the gift. Because of God's blessing on Jacob, he could now return the blessing which was stolen from Esau and erase the slate. Whether Esau's initial refusals were mere politeness or not, in accepting the gift he was implicitly accepting the resolution of the conflict which Jacob offered.

C. JACOB AND ESAU LIVE IN PEACE, BUT SEPARATELY (33:12-20)

1. Jacob Gains Esau's Permission to Travel Separately (33:12-16)

33:12 Then Esau said, "Let us be on our way; I'll accompany you." 33:13 But Jacob said to him, "My lord knows that the children are tender and that I must care for the ewes and cows that are nursing their young. If they are driven hard just one day, all the animals will die. 33:14 So let my lord go on ahead of his servant, while I move along slowly at the pace of the droves before me and that of the children, until I come to my lord in Seir."

If it were not for this passage the reader would be quite tempted to believe the sincerity and humility of Jacob in trying to reconcile matters with his brother Esau. But these verses give one pause. Jacob reverts to the deferential language of "lord" and "servant." Jacob's overly polite refusal of Esau's offer to travel with him seems to hide his rather more self-serving agenda. Having pacified Esau through his gift, Jacob has no intention of establishing living arrangements that are too close to his brother, reconciled or not. So Jacob makes excuses for not traveling with Esau. The animals with newborn cannot be driven too hard for even a single day. Jacob exaggerates when he says a single day's hard driving would kill all the animals. He asks Esau, referred to yet again as Jacob's lord,[11] to pass on ahead of him. He disingenuously promises to follow at the pace of the animals and children until they arrive at Esau's home in Seir.

33:15 Esau said, "Then let me leave some of my men with you." "But why do that?" Jacob asked. "Just let me find favor in the eyes of my lord."

Walton's theory that Esau's men were mercenaries may falter on

---

[11]In this single verse alone there are three examples of the deferential language of "lord" and "servant."

this verse.[12] Esau refers to them as "the people who are with me,"[13] which may suggest that they are not mercenaries at all, but akin to Abram's 318 "trained" men in Genesis 14:12. They were in his permanent employ and used as a force only in an emergency. The expense of paying mercenary soldiers to walk slowly back to Seir with children and newborn animals makes it unlikely that Esau's men were actually professional soldiers.

Jacob asks why Esau has suggested this. He then makes a statement,[14] "I have found favor in the eyes of my lord." Jacob seems to be suggesting that if, in fact, he has found favor in the eyes of Esau, there is no need for him to check up on him by leaving his men to accompany them. Jacob seems to be playing on Esau's forgiveness. If the relationship has truly been restored, there is no reason to act in a suspicious or cautious way in regard to Jacob.

33:16 So that day Esau started on his way back to Seir.

As it turns out, Esau did have reason to be suspicious of Jacob's intentions. His gullibility or at least his inability to match wits with the crafty Jacob shows once again. Without further objections or questions, Esau leaves that very day to return home to Seir.[15] By leaving Jacob alone Esau allows him to avoid visiting him in the land that has become his own.

2. Jacob Remains in the Promised Land and Does Not Go to Seir (33:17-20)

33:17 Jacob, however, went to Succoth, where he built a place for himself and made shelters for his livestock. That is why the place is called Succoth.

Instead of following Esau back to his home in Seir, Jacob went north of the Jabbok and built a house and booths for his cattle. The word Succoth means "booths," and the settlement continued to carry the

---

[12]Walton, *Genesis*, p. 605.

[13]The NIV's "my men" takes only one of the possible meanings of this phrase. Walton seems to take another — i.e., to treat the phrase as more literalistic. In English "the people who are with me" does sound more like a description of mercenaries. I am not persuaded that this is so in Hebrew.

[14]The NIV interprets this as a question, although there is no interrogative pronoun in the Hebrew.

[15]Conversely, one could assume that Esau knew that Jacob really had no intention of coming to Seir and found that acceptable. Given the theme of Esau's gullibility, this seems less likely to me.

name which Jacob gave it at this time. It is the first house "owned" by
Jacob in or near the Promised Land. We do not know how long he stayed
at Succoth. Jacob had obtained some sort of resolution of the conflict
with Esau. He had a large family and ample possessions and even a semipermanent home in the Promised Land. Jacob, for the first time in his
life, is able to experience the joys of living under God's blessing.

The original audience would have also seen more in this narrative.
One of the festivals which God had given Israel to remember the experience of God's preservation when he brought them out of Egypt was Succoth or "Booths."[16] Succoth commemorated the fact that God endured
their rebellious spirit at Sinai and throughout their journey and yet preserved them alive in the wilderness. God had preserved them in the
wilderness while they lived in temporary shelters (Lev 23:39-43; Exod
23:16; 34:18; Deut 16:13-1). Jacob's building of booths for his cattle
would be read as an anticipation of that later festival. The man whose
name was Israel built booths. His descendants, the children of Israel also
built booths. For the nation this was out of necessity in the wilderness
period. But later on they built booths in obedience to God's command.
The man Israel prepares the way for the nation Israel. This is one piece
of a larger pattern in the book of Genesis in which the ancestors of the
nation of Israel obey the law (in part) before there is a law. This is a way
of reminding Israel of their heritage. The laws given to them at Sinai
were particular instances of more general patterns of the behavior expected of God's chosen people whatever the times or circumstances.

**33:18 After Jacob came from Paddan Aram, he arrived safely at the
city of Shechem in Canaan and camped within sight of the city. 33:19
For a hundred pieces of silver, he bought from the sons of Hamor, the
father of Shechem, the plot of ground where he pitched his tent. 33:20
There he set up an altar and called it El Elohe Israel.**

The narrative jumps forward to some later[17] time when Jacob actually crossed the Jordan and came to dwell in Canaan proper. This sort
of choppiness is contrary to contemporary literary tastes. In part, it
explains the tendency in historical criticism to assume that such choppiness indicates originally disparate sources. It seems highly questionable, however, that ancient readers would have reacted the same way.
Even more questionable is the presumption that modern western read-

---

[16]This is commonly known as the feast of Tabernacles, although that translation can be misleading.

[17]While the narrative does not specify exactly when the ensuing events happened, the information which Genesis supplies about chronology gives us a
rough idea. See Walton, *Genesis*, pp. 569-570.

ers can accurately make such stylistic judgments. The purpose of this section seems to be to prepare the reader for the narrative of the rape of Dinah which follows in chapter 34.[18] Jacob had had business dealings with Shechem's father Hamor before there was ever a problem with Shechem's rape of Dinah. The price which Jacob paid for the plot of ground may have given Hamor and the Shechemites reason to believe that Jacob was wealthy. Jacob's wealth was used to convince the people of Shechem to join Jacob's family by accepting circumcision.

Like his grandfather Abraham, Jacob builds an altar in the Promised Land as a sort of anticipation of their descendants' later possessing the land.

---

[18]Chapter and verse divisions in the Bible are not original and were added to the Latin Bible in the late Middle Ages by a British Bishop, Stephan Langdon.

GENESIS 34

XIII. TENSIONS WITH THE INHABITANTS OF THE LAND OVER WOMEN AND POSSESSIONS (34:1-31)

In this chapter Jacob has moved back to the Promised Land and has even purchased a place on which to pitch his tent. Tension with the inhabitants of the land arises when Shechem first rapes Jacob's daughter Dinah and then falls in love with her. Shechem and his father Hamor attempt to negotiate a marriage contract with Jacob and his sons. Jacob's sons, led by Simeon and Levi trick the inhabitants into accepting circumcision with the promise of joining Jacob's family and gaining access to his considerable wealth. When the Shechemites accept the offer, Simeon and Levi use the occasion to butcher the men of Shechem. The other sons join them in plundering the Shechemites. Jacob rebukes his sons sternly, but not for the moral outrage of using a solemn religious initiation ritual as an opportunity for murder. Instead Jacob is concerned that the Canaanites will gang up on him. The narrator, however, does not seem to share Jacob's perspective and gives the last words to Simeon and Levi. They rebuke Jacob for wanting to turn their sister into a prostitute.

In the palistrophic structure of the Jacob and Esau narratives this passage is paired with the narrative of Isaac lying to Abimelech about Rebekah being his sister (Gen 26:1-33).[1] Both passages speak of the tensions which the Patriarchs have with the inhabitants of the Promised Land over women and possessions. In this case the woman concerned is Jacob's daughter Dinah. In both texts the Patriarch is concerned about his own safety because the inhabitants are attracted to a key female figure in his family. In chapter 34 sexual relations actually occur. In both texts the Patriarch seems more concerned about himself than about what happens to the woman in his family. In both cases the inhabitants of Canaan seek available women and material goods which are controlled by the chosen family.

---

[1]See the discussion of this above at Genesis 25:19b.

A. SHECHEM RAPES DINAH AND
THEN FALLS IN LOVE WITH HER (34:1-3)

34:1 Now Dinah, the daughter Leah had borne to Jacob, went out to visit the women of the land.
The narrator carefully introduces **Dinah** in order to explain in part Jacob's attitude toward her. She was born to the wife who was imposed upon Jacob in a trick by her wily father Laban. He did not love Leah; in fact he hated her. As a result her children were not favored either. In Dinah's case this was compounded by the fact that she was a daughter who had no inheritance rights. Jacob almost does not regard her as his daughter so much as Leah's.

Dinah went out from the protection of her family to visit the daughters[2] of Shechem where Jacob had taken up residence. While this would seem to be a normal thing to do in our contemporary contexts, the story makes it plain that this was fraught with hidden danger. For the original and canonical audiences the violence and sexual immorality of the inhabitants of the land was a real temptation. In the case of an unaccompanied young woman, it was a danger for Israel. This in no way places the blame on Dinah for what happened. But it does serve as a warning of what could happen when Israel interacted too closely with the inhabitants of the land.

34:2 When Shechem son of Hamor the Hivite, the ruler of that area, saw her, he took her and violated her.
The rape[3] is emphasized by the use of three verbs. First Shechem saw her, then he took her, and then he violated her. The verb **"took"** (לָקַח, *lāqaḥ*)[4] is the verb normally used for marriage and by itself does not imply rape. But here it does indicate rape. The third verb "violated her" (עָנָה, *'ānāh*, "to afflict") makes this clear. There may be an echo of the temptation narrative in Genesis 3. There the man and the woman "saw" and "took" of the tree. The sexual violence that was displayed prior to the Flood, at Sodom and Gomorrah, and in the Canaan which Israel was about to enter, is displayed here. The path which eventually

---

[2]The NIV paraphrases as "women" here, and this may be misleading as Dinah's age is very young. See 34:4 below.

[3]For a thorough discussion of whether a rape is being described and affirmation of the traditional position, see Robin Perry, *Old Testament Story and Christian Ethics: The Rape of Dinah as a Case Study*, Paternoster Biblical Monographs (Milton Keynes: Paternoster, 2004), pp. 143-146.

[4]Notice how this verb shows up repeatedly in this narrative in verses 2,4,9,17, 21,25,26,28.

COLLEGE PRESS NIV COMMENTARY

led to the judgment of the Amorites (Gen 15:16) is being trod even in the time of Jacob. The fact that this is done by Shechem, the son of the ruler of the area and the man for whom the area was eventually named, shows the misuse of power by the mighty.

34:3 His heart was drawn to Dinah daughter of Jacob, and he loved the girl and spoke tenderly to her.

Ironically after raping Dinah, Shechem fell in love with her. Such is the fallenness and moral confusion often accompanying love and sex. Shechem's life "cleaved" to Dinah as was originally intended in the creation of marriage. The same verb (דָּבַק, *dābaq*) as found in Genesis 2:24 is used. He loved her and spoke "to her heart." There is, however, no indication that his feelings were reciprocated.

B. SHECHEM AND HIS FATHER HAMOR ATTEMPT TO NEGOTIATE SHECHEM'S MARRIAGE WITH DINAH (34:4-12)

34:4 And Shechem said to his father Hamor, "Get me this girl as my wife."

When Shechem's fickle feelings turned from lust to romantic love, he asked his father to follow the usual procedure and negotiate a marriage with Jacob for Dinah. While the vocabulary of arranged marriages sounds to modern ears as though the woman is treated as property ("bride price," "take a wife," etc.), in fact, the procedure was designed to protect the woman from being used and cast off for trivial reasons.

The narrator referred to Dinah in verse 3 as a "young woman" (נַעֲרָה, *nā'ărāh*) whereas Shechem refers to her as a "girl" (יַלְדָּה, *yāldāh*). What little evidence there is for the latter word implies a very young girl, perhaps not even of typical marriageable age.[5] But the nuanced meaning of a word used only 3 times in the Old Testament is difficult to discern. However, it is perhaps possible that the original audience would wonder whether Shechem was drawn to a little girl. If so, Shechem would be flouting a custom against taking advantage of a girl too young to have a voice in her own future.

34:5 When Jacob heard that his daughter Dinah had been defiled, his sons were in the fields with his livestock; so he kept quiet about it until they came home.

---

[5]Of the two other uses of this word in the Old Testament one refers to boys and girls playing together (Zech 8:5) and the other to boys and girls sold as child prostitutes (Joel 4:3).

Sternberg notices that Jacob *keeps still* (v. 5) when he hears of Dinah's situation.[6] It is his sons who have the appropriate anger. But to be fair to Jacob he initially maintains his silence while his sons were still in the field with the cattle. He is only silent until they come. It may well be that Jacob was outnumbered, or felt that he was, in the negotiations which were to follow. An outburst of anger may have gotten back to the Hivites. The narrator reminds us that Dinah was Jacob's "daughter." Even though Jacob seems, in the eyes of Simeon and Levi at least, to ignore this fact, the author emphasizes it. Jacob evidently heard about the rape before he actually talked with Hamor and Shechem. What he did not do was initiate any conversation with them. Sternberg compares and contrasts Jacob's reaction in this narrative to his reaction at Joseph's purported death.[7] But the situations are hardly parallel. Jacob presumed that Joseph was dead. A rape is a horrible thing, but it is not murder. While Sternberg is correct to note that Jacob never displays any anger over what has happened to Dinah, this verse should not be made to say more than it intends to.

34:6 Then Shechem's father Hamor went out to talk with Jacob. 34:7 Now Jacob's sons had come in from the fields as soon as they heard what had happened. They were filled with grief and fury, because Shechem had done a disgraceful thing in Israel by lying with Jacob's daughter—a thing that should not be done.

Hamor now goes out to negotiate a marriage between Dinah and Shechem. In the meantime Jacob's sons had returned from the fields. They also had been told what had happened to Dinah. Their immediate reaction was very different from Jacob's. They were heartbroken[8] and angry. To Jacob's sons Shechem had committed a heinous sexual sin. The canonical readers might think of Absalom's rape of Tamar or the moral degeneracy which arose in Israel during the period of the judges (Judges 17–21), itself reminiscent of Sodom and Gomorrah.[9] The narrator, apparently speaking from the sons' point of view, refers to Dinah as "Jacob's daughter" in order to emphasize the horror that Jacob

---

[6]Sternberg, *Poetics of Biblical Narrative*, p. 448.

[7]Sternberg notes that Leah was the unfavored wife, and Simeon and Levi, along with Reuben and Judah and Dinah were also her children. He says (*Poetics*, p. 462), "No wonder, then, that Jacob reacts so differently to the catastrophe that befalls Rachel's child" referring to news of Joseph's tragedy.

[8]עָצַב (*'āṣab*) in the hithpael is found elsewhere only in Genesis 6:6 of God's broken heart over humanity's violent evil before the flood.

[9]The same Hebrew word, נְבָלָה (*nebālāh*), occurs here and in Judges 19:23,24; 20:6,10; 2 Sam 13:12.

should have felt and expressed. Dinah was not just their full (or half) sister, but Jacob's daughter. The sort of behavior which Shechem committed came under the most severe form of divine judgment according to the Torah.

34:8 But Hamor said to them, "My son Shechem has his heart set on your daughter. Please give her to him as his wife.

It is interesting that Hamor does not admit to Shechem's crime. Does he know that Jacob has heard about it, or is he trying to cover it up? Hamor refers to Shechem as his son and to Dinah as their[10] daughter. He asks them, not just Jacob, to give her to Shechem as a wife. Hamor evidently realizes that her protectors are not (just) her father Jacob, but also her brothers, both half- and full. The negotiation is not just between the fathers of the bride and groom. Her brothers are also full participants in the negotiation.[11] This may be the narrator's way of emphasizing the concern of Dinah's brothers for her welfare and the relative lack of concern expressed by her actual father, Jacob.

34:9 Intermarry with us; give us your daughters and take our daughters for yourselves.

Hamor offers more than just a single marriage. He suggests a complete merger of the two clans. The daughters of the Shechemites will be taken as wives by Israelite men and the Shechemite men will take Israelite daughters as wives.[12] While the language of "give" and "take"[13] is offensive to modern ears, in fact this is the standard Hebrew terminology for marriage. While it is true that the women are not explicitly consulted as to their desires in the matter, in reality the matter was more complex. Fathers negotiated marriages on behalf of their sons and daughters. In particular the economic realities of vulnerable women in a patriarchal social system needed to be protected. Often the preferences of the son or daughter were consulted privately before the marriage took place. In this case Dinah is still in Shechem's home and

---

[10]The "your" in Hebrew is plural, which in the context must refer to Jacob and his sons. Hamor thus acknowledges that, in some sense, Dinah is both the daughter of Jacob and of her older brothers.

[11]For brothers as protectors of sisters see Eichler, "On Reading Genesis 12:10-20," pp. 23-37.

[12]The daughters of Jacob could be his literal daughters. Only Dinah and Serah (Gen. 46:17) are named.

[13]While too much should not be made of the fact, given that this is standard terminology, notice how often the word "take" is used in the narrative, vv. 2,4,9,17,21,25,26,28. It can mean "take by force," as in Shechem's rape of Dinah, or "gain by mutual agreement."

so cannot be consulted. This fact puts the supposed even-handed, even generous, offer of Hamor in a different light.

The original and canonical audiences would have seen a great danger in this offer. The Pentateuch strictly forbade any form of intermarriage because of the danger of apostasy which it posed (Deut 7:3-4). This danger was no theoretical one. Israelite men who took pagan women as wives were quickly drawn away from loyalty to Yahweh and into idolatry as the canonical audience knew well (1 Kgs 11:1-8; Ezra 9:1-14; Neh 13:23-37).

34:10 You can settle among us; the land is open to you. Live in it, trade in it, and acquire property in it."

The "deal" is sweetened further. Hamor offers the wandering family of Jacob permanent access to the land, including ownership with concomitant property rights. **The land is open** before them. They can dwell there permanently (שַׁב, *yāšab*), travel freely in it without harassment,[14] and even take permanent possession of it. But this means of taking possession of the land is a false one. Jacob is offered a stake in the Promised Land if he will but agree to have his family intermarry with the Canaanites. This would involve compromising their own faith traditions and merging them with those of the Hivites.

34:11 Then Shechem said to Dinah's father and brothers, "Let me find favor in your eyes, and I will give you whatever you ask. 34:12 Make the price for the bride and the gift I am to bring as great as you like, and I'll pay whatever you ask me. Only give me the girl as my wife."

Shechem then spoke to "her," i.e., Dinah's, **"father and brothers."** By wording it this way the narrator reminds his readers of the close familial relationship which (should have) obtained. Interestingly Shechem, like his father, addresses both Jacob and his sons, not just Jacob. Shechem speaks with formal humility seeking favor in their eyes. He offers, somewhat disingenuously, to give whatever bride price and marriage presents they would set. No matter what the price, Shechem promises to give it.

In speaking with Jacob and his sons Shechem refers to Dinah as a "young woman" (נַעֲרָה, *naʿarāh*) rather than a **"girl"** (the NIV has "girl") when he asked his father to negotiate a marriage. While this could be an insignificant variation, it is possible that by switching from "girl" to "young woman" when addressing Jacob's family, he is presenting Dinah as someone older than she actually was.

---

[14]The Hebrew verb used here, סָחַר (*sāḥar*), refers to freedom of movement, especially as it relates to economic activity. The participial form is used of traders.

C. JACOB'S SONS TRICK THE SHECHEMITES
INTO ACCEPTING CIRCUMCISION (34:13-24)

1. The Sons of Jacob Make Circumcision
the Condition of Intermarriage (34:13-17)

**34:13 Because their sister Dinah had been defiled, Jacob's sons
replied deceitfully as they spoke to Shechem and his father Hamor.
34:14 They said to them, "We can't do such a thing; we can't give our
sister to a man who is not circumcised. That would be a disgrace to
us. 34:15 We will give our consent to you on one condition only: that
you become like us by circumcising all your males. 34:16 Then we will
give you our daughters and take your daughters for ourselves. We'll
settle among you and become one people with you. 34:17 But if you
will not agree to be circumcised, we'll take our sister and go."**

Jacob's sons know that Dinah, their sister, had been raped by
Shechem. What is not known is whether Hamor and Shechem know
that they know this, since they have not mentioned it. The rape was
regarded by the brothers and by the narrator as a defiling act, one
which had serious consequences under the law (Lev 27:3; Deut 22:28-
29). Evidently they spoke to each other about this.[15] Curiously Jacob
does not speak even though, as Dinah's father, he would presumably
have the final say in any marriage arrangement. Dinah is once again
explicitly identified as the "sister" of Jacob's sons, who seem to show
more concern for her than the impassive Jacob.

The brothers claim that their real objection to the proposed marriage is the fact that Shechem and his people have not been circumcised. If Goldingay is correct to see in circumcision a symbolic warning
that sexual drives must be disciplined,[16] the ironies of this narrative are
manifold. Shechem's lack of sexual discipline is about to be remedied
through a painful operation on the very part of the anatomy which per-
petrated his crime. Further, we have not even heard whether Jacob's
sons had been circumcised at their birth in Paddan Aram. It also seems
ironic indeed for them to show such concern for the requirement of circumcision when their participation in idolatry had not yet been
removed. Both Rachel's theft of the household gods and the need for

---

[15]The Hebrew literally reads, "They said (דִּבֶּר, *dābar*) that he defiled their sister." This is an example of indirect discourse. The NIV and NRSV treat this as
the reason for their deceit, and while this is true, the paraphrase misses the fact
that they discussed this.

[16]Goldingay, "The Significance of Circumcision," pp. 3-18.

all of Jacob's household to put away foreign gods in Genesis 35:2 attest
to this. The hypocrisy and horrid form of evil behind their scheme is
shocking. A parallel would be forcing a person to be baptized in order
to marry into the family only to drown the person during the process of
baptism! The brothers have no intention of becoming one people with
the Hivites. Their only motive is revenge for the sexual crime of Shechem.
The fact that the punishment is to be meted out to the entire tribe is
another indication of the excessive anger of the brothers.

The brothers threaten that if the Hivites do not accept the circumcision of all males, the sons of Jacob would take[17] their "daughter"[18] and
go. There may be a veiled threat of force behind this last statement or
at least the bluff of such a threat. One must remember that Dinah is not
in their possession, and it is uncertain whether Jacob's household would
have enough adult men to overcome an entire town.[19]

2. Hamor and Shechem Convince the Shechemites
to Accept Circumcision (34:18-24)

**34:18 Their proposal seemed good to Hamor and his son Shechem.
34:19 The young man, who was the most honored of all his father's
household, lost no time in doing what they said, because he was
delighted with Jacob's daughter.**
The scheme works. Hamor and Shechem are taken in by the proposal of Jacob's sons. Shechem, who is described as a "**young man**" and
the most esteemed of his father's entire household, did not delay in carrying out the conditions set down for the marriage. His motivation was
his delight in Dinah, who is once again described by the narrator as
"**Jacob's daughter**." As strange as it might seem, Shechem seems to have
definite feelings for the girl which he had at first raped.

**34:20 So Hamor and his son Shechem went to the gate of their city to
speak to their fellow townsmen. 34:21 "These men are friendly toward
us," they said. "Let them live in our land and trade in it; the land has
plenty of room for them. We can marry their daughters and they can
marry ours. 34:22 But the men will consent to live with us as one people only on the condition that our males be circumcised, as they them-**

---

[17]The use of the verb "take" in relation to a woman is found once again as in
vv. 2,4,9,21 and 25.

[18]Not "sister" as in the NIV's paraphrase.

[19]One cannot presume that Jacob would have Abraham's 318 trained men
(Gen 14:14).

selves are. **34:23 Won't their livestock, their property and all their other animals become ours? So let us give our consent to them, and they will settle among us."**

In the ancient Near East courts met at the city gate. In this case the community must approve a proposal by two of its most prominent citizens, and quite naturally the decision was taken at the city gate. Hamor and Shechem said that Jacob's clan had peaceful[20] intentions. Since this was so, they should be allowed to dwell permanently in the land and to trade in it without harassment. According to Shechem and Hamor the land was spacious. Intermarriage was, for them, a quite reasonable suggestion. All of this positive reading of the situation is a preface to the more touchy issue. If such intermarriage was to take place, the community's men must submit themselves to circumcision in accordance with the custom of Jacob's family. They then add an inducement. The property of the affluent Jacob will effectively become theirs if they intermarry! The economic advantages of the situation override any consideration of the unpleasantness of having to submit to circumcision. By placing this inducement last, Hamor and Shechem support their argument rhetorically.

34:24 All the men who went out of the city gate agreed with Hamor and his son Shechem, and every male in the city was circumcised.

Sarna suggests that only adult males of military age were actually circumcised since they were the only ones eligible to marry Israelite women.[21] The basis for this is the fact that the phrase "all who went out of the city gate"[22] can refer[23] to going out to war, something only adult men did. The repetition of the phrase in the Hebrew would tend to support him. It is not simply every male, but some subgrouping, who were circumcised.

D. SIMEON AND LEVI LEAD JACOB'S SONS IN MURDERING THE SHECHEMITES AND TAKING THEIR WOMEN AND POSSESSIONS (34:25-29)

34:25 Three days later, while all of them were still in pain, two of Jacob's sons, Simeon and Levi, Dinah's brothers, took their swords and attacked the unsuspecting city, killing every male.

---

[20]The Hebrew adjective שָׁלֵם (šālēm) ordinarily means "peaceful" rather than "friendly."

[21]Sarna, *Genesis*, p. 237.

[22]The Hebrew phrase (כָּל־יֹצְאֵי שַׁעַר, kol-yōṣ'ê šā'ar) occurs twice in this verse. The NIV obscures this by paraphrasing the second occurrence as "every male in the city."

[23]Sarna (ibid.) suggests 2 Kgs 5:2 and Amos 5:3 as parallels.

On the third day[24] two of Dinah's (full) brothers, Simeon and Levi, killed every male in the unsuspecting village. Since all of the brothers participated in the deceit (v. 13), it is unclear why only Simeon and Levi participate in the murder[25] of the Shechemites. The narrator makes clear that part of the reason is that Dinah was their full sister. In murdering the Shechemites they were standing up for her. While only those men who went out of the city gates were circumcised, Simeon and Levi murdered every male, of whatever age or status. The horror of using circumcision as the means of murdering the males of an entire town is striking. This overrides any poetic justice[26] that readers may feel toward Shechem for raping Dinah. The narrator emphasizes the horror of their crime by describing the city as "**unsuspecting**" (בֶּטַח, beṭaḥ; cf. Judg 8:11; 18:7; Ezek 38:11; Zeph 2:15). The sacred symbol of covenant entry is turned into the means of personal, violent revenge.[27] However much we may sympathize with Simeon's and Levi's anger and are repulsed by Jacob's lack of it, this fact must not be forgotten.

34:26 They put Hamor and his son Shechem to the sword and took Dinah from Shechem's house and left.

The actual perpetrator of the crime and his (complicit?) father are also murdered. Sternberg notices that Dinah has been kept captive in Shechem's home during the entire dialog and negotiation process. In part this justifies what Simeon and Levi did since it is not just rape, but also kidnapping which is at issue. But why is this information kept from the reader until this point? The first-time reader gains a new sense of sympathy for Simeon and Levi. After all the only way, so they reasoned, to get Dinah back was to use trickery and violence. But this does not somehow justify what they have done. Even a first-time reader will remember the horror of reading that Jacob's sons used circumcision as a means of killing their enemies. The fact that after "taking"[28] Dinah from Shechem's house where she had been held captive they "went out"[29] echoes the *leitmotif* function of these two verbs in this narrative.

---

[24]The NIV's "three days later" is periphrastic and may be inaccurate.

[25]The Hebrew verb הָרַג (hārag) implies ruthless violence especially of a private nature and "kill" is too tame a translation.

[26]Sternberg, *Poetics*, p. 466: "Some poetic justice does attach to the discovery that Shechem's punishment started exactly where his sexual crime did."

[27]Note the parallel between this passage and the "hill [mountain] of foreskins" Josh 5:3; 1 Sam 18:25,27; 2 Sam 3:14.

[28]Notice once again how the word "*take*" (לָקַח, lāqāḥ) is used in the narrative: vv. 2,4,9,17,21,25,26,28.

[29]The Hebrew verb יָצָא (yāṣā') is used here and echoes "every man who *went out* of the gate."

34:27 The sons of Jacob came upon the dead bodies and looted the city where their sister had been defiled. **34:28** They seized their flocks and herds and donkeys and everything else of theirs in the city and out in the fields. **34:29** They carried off all their wealth and all their women and children, taking as plunder everything in the houses.

While Simeon and Levi did the actual murdering of the Shechemites, only[30] the rest of Jacob's sons, who had been in on the plot from the beginning, participated in the looting of the city where "their sister" had been defiled. The original audience would undoubtedly notice that simple justice was not motivating Jacob's sons here. If it had been, the sons of Jacob would have left the plunder alone as the LORD later asked Israel to do at Jericho (Josh 6:17-19). Instead this becomes an opportunity to make themselves even richer and more numerous. The women and children are "taken,"[31] evidently as captives along with their animals, crops, and household possessions.

E. JACOB AND SIMEON AND LEVI HAVE CONFLICT OVER WHAT HIS SONS HAVE DONE (34:30-31)

34:30 Then Jacob said to Simeon and Levi, "You have brought trouble on me by making me a stench to the Canaanites and Perizzites, the people living in this land. We are few in number, and if they join forces against me and attack me, I and my household will be destroyed."

Jacob, who has been silent throughout this narrative, finally breaks that silence. It should be remembered that Dinah, and her brothers Simeon and Levi, were all born to Jacob's despised wife, Leah. Jacob does not condemn the plundering in which all of his sons, presumably including Joseph, participated. Neither does he condemn the immoral use of the holy sign of circumcision as a means of gaining advantage in a lust for revenge. The slaughter seems only to be a problem for Jacob because it puts his personal safety at risk. His focus is on Simeon and Levi who actually carried out the murders. The use of pronouns in Jacob's accusation of them is striking. In the Hebrew this is even more

---

[30]Sternberg, *Poetics*, p. 472, "Simeon and Levi turn out to be the only ones who cling to anti-materialistic norms. . . . In their clean dissociation from the orgy of looting, they practice what the others only preach."

[31]Notice that the sons of Jacob end up "taking" the Shechemite women as wives or servants. Or is it merely that they raped them? (v. 29). While the former seems more likely, the use of "take" in Shechem's rape of Dinah gives the reader pause.

the case. Jacob claims that Simeon and Levi had "brought trouble" on
him and "made *[him]* into a stinking thing." Jacob claims that "I"[32] am
"few in number" and that the Canaanites and Perizzites who were living
nearby could well join forces against *him,* attack *him,* and destroy *him,*
along with *his* household. Sternberg comments, "In *verse 30* Jacob is concerned only about himself."[33]

**34:31 But they replied, "Should he have treated our sister like a pros-
titute?"**

Simeon and Levi are given the final word in this narrative. The NIV
is too periphrastic in this instance. The Hebrew does not say Simeon
and Levi "replied,"[34] only that they "said." Sternberg, quite plausibly,
suggests that they said this later to each other or to their brothers.[35] He
notes that the referent of the pronoun "he" is actually ambiguous. He
suggests that it was Jacob who treated their sister like a prostitute by
accepting money in exchange for the sexual favors of his daughter.
While this is debatable, the very ambiguity is provocative. From their
point of view it might not only be Shechem, but also her own father who
treated her like a prostitute.[36] It is noteworthy that Simeon and Levi
refer to Dinah as "our sister" not as "your" (i.e., Jacob's) daughter.[37] If
the words are addressed to Jacob, they seem to make the point that
Dinah is not properly esteemed by Jacob. Where is the natural anger
that a loving and protective father would have in such a situation? The
only anger Jacob expresses is directed toward his two sons, who quite
rightly speak of Dinah as "our sister." Jacob, on the other hand, never
refers to Dinah as "my daughter."

---

[32]While this is technically not grammatical in English, and may not be in
Hebrew, the Hebrew uses the first person singular, "I," not the plural. The NIV
changes this to "we" to make it grammatically palatable, but in so doing loses the
focus which Jacob has solely upon himself in this speech.

[33]Sternberg, *Poetics,* p. 474.

[34]Had this been intended, one would have expected the Hebrew verb עָנָה
(*'ānāh*) to be used.

[35]Sternberg, *Poetics,* p. 475.

[36]Ibid., p. 474: "He who twiddles his thumbs about the rape and deems the
gifts fair compensation is as guilty of making a whore of Dinah as the rapist and
the giver himself."

[37]Ibid., "[In verse 31 the use of] 'our sister' trembles with passion against the
father as well. The long-standing tensions created by favoritism and reflected in
the polar attitudes to the rape have thus far smoldered in the dynamics of the
kinship terms. As a result of the father's provocation, however, they burst into
flame. . . ."

GENESIS 35

XIV. FINAL RECONCILIATION OF JACOB AND ESAU AND THEIR FAMILIES (35:1–37:41)

The Jacob and Esau narratives began with tension between them, symbolized by Jacob grasping at Esau's heel even in the womb. In this final narrative we see the (partial) reconciliation of their tense relationship. The section begins with God sending Jacob back to Bethel to which he had originally fled from Esau so many years before. Jacob's change of name to Israel, first announced by the man in Genesis 32:28, is confirmed by God himself. God also reconfirms the fact that despite all that had happened, the promise of God to Abraham and Isaac would pass to Jacob. With the future of his descendants assured, Jacob unites with Esau to bury their father Isaac. Chapter 36 confirms that there are blessings for Esau too. In fact his elaborate double genealogy shows the remarkable way that God blesses the nonelect as well as the elect.[1] The overall effect of this section is to show that despite the problems that the human characters made and make for the promise, God was, and is, still at work to fulfill them. He can do this despite us or through us; but he will do it.

A. JACOB WITH HIS FAMILY RETURNS TO BETHEL TO BECOME ISRAEL (35:1-15)

1. God Commands Jacob to Return to Bethel (35:1)

35:1 Then God said to Jacob, "Go up to Bethel and settle there, and build an altar there to God, who appeared to you when you were fleeing from your brother Esau."

---

[1]For the distinction between elect, nonelect, and anti-elect see Kaminsky, *Yet I Have Loved Jacob*, chs. 7–8. Esau is "nonelect" but not "anti-elect" in Kaminsky's terms.

For whatever reason, God now[2] tells Jacob to move on from Shechem to Bethel. Jacob is told to "permanently dwell" (יָשַׁב, yāšab) there. This is not the same as taking permanent and everlasting possession which would require the gift of the land to Jacob. God had made clear to Abram that that would not happen for another 400 years (Gen 15:13). But Jacob is to have secure enough possession of the land at Bethel that he would be able to build an altar there and dwell there. Abram, when he first came into the land from Haran, had built an altar at Shechem and then Bethel. In retracing his grandfather's steps, Jacob received divine reassurance that God's promise to Abraham would in fact find fulfillment through him. God reminds Jacob that he had appeared to him at Bethel when he was fleeing from his brother Esau. That relationship had now been reconciled, although at great cost to Jacob, economically, physically, and in other ways. But through it all God had preserved Jacob alive and blessed him in many ways. Jacob had made a vow at Bethel to tithe and to make the LORD his God (Gen 28:21-22). That vow remained unfulfilled up to this point.

2. Jacob Prepares His Family to Return to Bethel (35:2-4)

35:2 So Jacob said to his household and to all who were with him, "Get rid of the foreign gods you have with you, and purify yourselves and change your clothes.

Jacob responded to God's command by first preparing his household for a direct encounter with God. Up to this time Jacob evidently had not insisted that his family demonstrate loyalty to the one and only God who had made promises to his grandfather and father. The polytheism that was a part of their way of life in Paddan Aram had continued. Here he tells them to get rid of their foreign gods which they had brought with them when they departed from Laban's household. They were also told to "**purify**" themselves and change their outer[3] clothing. Such a change of clothing at Sinai indicated symbolically the consecration or even "sanctification" of the nation prior to formally entering into a covenant with the LORD (Exod 19:10,14). The Hebrew word for "purify" (טָהֵר, ṭāhēr) is usually used in cultic contexts where ritual cleansing from "leprosy" or other defilements is indicated. The original and canonical audiences would see in this text an anticipation of the later laws of cleansing for the sake of ritual purity.

---

[2]The Hebrew waw-consecutive indicates narrative sequence.

[3]שִׂמְלָה (śimlāh), the outer garment also used as a blanket when sleeping.

35:3 Then come, let us go up to Bethel, where I will build an altar to God, who answered me in the day of my distress and who has been with me wherever I have gone."

The purification, both spiritually through the removal of foreign gods, and symbolically through ritual purification which included the changing of clothes, would prepare the chosen family for a trip to Bethel to worship. Jacob had seen a dream of stairs there with angels moving freely between earth and heaven (Gen 28:12). He had also received reassurance that, despite the failed attempt of Jacob and his mother Rebekah to procure the blessing by their own efforts and his consequent need to flee Esau's wrath, God would nevertheless see to it that Jacob received the land promised to Abraham (Gen 28:13). He would even be the channel of God's blessing to the world (Gen 28:14). Jacob had promised to return to Bethel and worship there if God would but protect him and enable him to return. Here Jacob intends to fulfill his promise, or at least part of it.[4] He intends to build an altar at Bethel as he did when he fled from Esau. Jacob shows his faith here, no matter how imperfectly formed it may be. He looks back on the last twenty years and confesses that God had indeed answered him during times of ("the day of") distress and had indeed been with him wherever Jacob had gone, as he had promised Jacob in Genesis 28:15. What had been at Bethel a dream was now a reality. Jacob shows his gratitude by acknowledging God's protecting providence.

35:4 So they gave Jacob all the foreign gods they had and the rings in their ears, and Jacob buried them under the oak at Shechem.

Whether out of obedience to the father of the family or out of genuine recognition of what God had done for Jacob while he was in Paddan Aram and in facing Esau, Jacob's family gave him their foreign gods as well as the earrings which were sometimes used to manufacture idols.[5] Since Rachel had taken a great risk in stealing her father Laban's household gods, this was no small or insignificant step. Jacob buries the remnants of his family's idolatry at Shechem, perhaps seeking to put the entire ordeal with the Shechemites behind him. The oak tree where he buried the idols and earrings may itself have been a place of idolatrous worship.[6]

---

[4]Jacob had also promised to tithe whatever God gave him (Gen 28:22). There is no indication that he ever fulfilled this promise.

[5]Exod 32:3,4; Judg 8:24-27. It may be that some earrings, in and of themselves, had idolatrous associations.

[6]Idol worship which took place at oak trees was condemned by Ezekiel (6:13) and Hosea (4:13).

3. God Protects Jacob's Family (35:5)

35:5 Then they set out, and the terror of God fell upon the towns all around them so that no one pursued them.

When Jacob's family left Shechem, none of the nearby towns attacked as might have been expected after the massacre of the inhabitants by Jacob's sons. The author makes it clear that the "terror of God" prevented them from pursuing Jacob's family. This would undoubtedly remind the readers of how the inhabitants of Canaan were filled with fear and dread when Israel first approached and then entered the land under Moses and Joshua.[7] Just as the LORD made other nations fear Israel as they entered the Promised Land, so God made the nations fear the original person Israel (Jacob) when he first returned to the Promised Land from Paddan Aram. For the original readers this fact would give reassurance of God's protection of them as they entered and began their life in Canaan.

4. Jacob Builds an Altar at Bethel (35:6-7)

35:6 Jacob and all the people with him came to Luz (that is, Bethel) in the land of Canaan. 35:7 There he built an altar, and he called the place El Bethel, because it was there that God revealed himself to him when he was fleeing from his brother.

In arriving at **Luz** (**Bethel**) Jacob has retraced his steps from twenty years earlier when he fled from Esau. The mention of "**all the people with him**" is reminiscent of his grandfather Abram's original departure from Haran (in Paddan Aram or nearby) when he took the people with him whom he had gotten in Haran (Gen 12:5). The narrator reminds the audience that Luz was the earlier name for what they now knew to be Bethel and that this city was in the land of Canaan. This seemingly pedantic remark makes a theological point. God had promised to bring Jacob back to the Promised Land at that very place. Bethel, named by Jacob ("house of God"), came to have great significance in the history of the nation. An obscure village where an exhausted and frightened Jacob had slept with stone pillows had become the house of God. Jacob's return there reminded the original audience of the Pentateuch that God's faithfulness had not ended with their forefather Jacob. Jacob's descendants, the contemporary nation of Israel, received the Promised Land.

---

[7]Deut 2:25; 11:25 (the LORD's promise); Josh 2:9 (Rahab's words).

As promised, Jacob built an altar at Bethel. Based on his experience recorded in chapter 28, Jacob had renamed Luz, the original Canaanite town, Bethel. Upon his return there 20 years later, he gave it a new name, "El-Bethel," meaning "God of the house of God." The new name did not stick, although the first one did. Israel came to regard the city of Bethel as an especially important place religiously. Jacob names the city after the God who was revealed[8] to him when he fled from Esau so many years previously. For Jacob, Bethel was not just the "house of God" but the place where he wanted to acknowledge and praise the God who lived in that place. God preserved his life from Esau's anger, protected him from Laban's trickery, and blessed him wherever he had gone. In renaming the city he had once named Bethel, El-Bethel, Jacob makes it clear to his family and to the readers that some sort of change has occurred. This God and his promises were to be the center of Jacob's life and the life of his family from now on. While Jacob does not, so far as we know, fulfill his earlier commitment at Bethel to tithe, he does reconnect himself and his family to the promises of God to Abraham.

5. God Blesses Jacob, Renaming Him Israel (35:8-13)

35:8 Now Deborah, Rebekah's nurse, died and was buried under the oak below Bethel. So it was named Allon Bacuth.

It is hard to know what exactly to make of this verse. Perhaps there was an unmentioned reunion with at least some of Jacob's family at Bethel when Rebekah's nurse, Deborah, was buried there. Another possibility is that Deborah had remained behind in Paddan Aram when Rebekah left to marry Isaac. She then left with Jacob many years later, perhaps anticipating a reunion with Rebekah. In any case, it is rare[9] for the name of a servant to be mentioned, and this undoubtedly implies her significance in the family. The oak under which Deborah was buried came to be called the "Oak of Weeping" (Allon Bacuth in Hebrew) because of the grief over her death.

35:9 After Jacob returned from Paddan Aram, God appeared to him again and blessed him.

The Hebrew has a *waw*-consecutive, the normal way to indicate narrative sequence. The mention of Paddan Aram yet again would seem to

---

[8]The Hebrew has a niphal here, which is usually to be rendered as a passive. The reflexive translation of the NIV and NRSV, "revealed himself," is also possible.

[9]Eliezer of Damascus, Abraham's servant mentioned in Genesis 15, is another example.

indicate that Jacob's arrival at Bethel, and not at Shechem or at the Jabbok in chapters 33 and 34, marks the ultimate end of his sojourn away from the Promised Land. Just as the LORD had appeared to him in a dream when he slept at Bethel on his way out of Canaan, here God appeared to him again. This time, however, the appearance was not in a dream but in some more direct fashion.[10] Once again God came with a blessing. This passage thus is deliberately paired with its counterpart in chapter 28. Together they form the beginning and end of Jacob's saga of bearing the consequences for playing God. Even though those consequences included being tricked and cheated and humbled, and finally handicapped, God had been faithful. His purposes would not be defeated by Rebekah and Jacob's scheming, nor by Isaac and Esau's resistance, nor by Laban's treachery. The promises, and the blessing which accompanies them and brings them to fruition, were still valid. In fact Jacob receives an even greater reassurance of this fact. What was once a dream has turned into a reality. The direct appearance of God to Jacob without a mediator turns the dream of Bethel into the reality of Jacob's return to Bethel.

35:10 God said to him, "Your name is Jacob, but you will no longer be called Jacob; your name will be Israel." So he named him Israel.

This text records the second time that a divine person has given Jacob the name Israel, the first being the unnamed divine assailant in Genesis 32:28. This fact has provided fodder for the documentary hypothesis. "Surely," so the reasoning goes, "Jacob did not receive the name Israel twice! There must have been an original oral tradition about the renaming of Jacob which was modified by the putative sources E and P."[11] But this fails to explain why a reputed later redactor would have left both texts in place. One possible explanation is that God is confirming for Jacob that what the divine emissary had promised at Peniel was in fact God's promise. Another possible explanation is that Peniel was outside of the Promised Land proper and only at Bethel is Jacob actually in the land. The point of the repetition would then be that he is Israel, whether in the land or out of it. For both the original audience which had lived recently in Egypt and the canonical audience which lived largely in the Diaspora, this would be especially meaningful. Their identity as the nation of Israel is secure whether they are in the land or not. Actually,

---

[10]Cf. v. 13, where "God went up from him at the place where he had talked with him."

[11]Notice that in both texts the deity is referred to as "God" (אֱלֹהִים, *'ĕlōhîm*), which according to the traditional Documentary Hypothesis was the word used in E and P before the Exodus.

as Wenham notes, by recording the giving of the name Israel, but not indicating its significance, the reader is presumed to know the previous story.[12] At Bethel Jacob finally arrives securely back in the land and God's reaffirmation of the angel's change of name in 32:28 ensures this.

35:11 And God said to him, "I am God Almighty; be fruitful and increase in number. A nation and a community of nations will come from you, and kings will come from your body. 35:12 The land I gave to Abraham and Isaac I also give to you, and I will give this land to your descendants after you."

God speaks again to Jacob, now called Israel, identifying himself as El Shaddai.[13] According to a literal reading of Exodus 6:3, this was the ordinary way in which God addressed the patriarchs. If, in fact, El Shaddai means or implies God's almighty power, the point would seem to be to emphasize yet again what Jacob had experienced about God. He had the power to protect him from any foe or harmful force. With Jacob now back at Bethel and thus securely in the Promised Land, God reiterates the promise he had made to Jacob in Genesis 28:13-15. That promise was an extension of the promises he had made to Abraham and Isaac, but it was also more. By beginning the patriarchal promise with the words "be fruitful and increase in number" the narrator clearly links the promises to the original creation commission in Genesis 1:26-28. While evangelical theology with its largely reformed roots tends to place redemption above creation, texts like this one[14] emphasize the point that the plan of redemption which begins with Abraham is an extension of God's original purpose in creating humanity. God's purpose in creation will be fulfilled through the descendants of Abraham, Isaac, and now Jacob.

Jacob is promised that not only will a nation descend from him but even a community of nations,[15] including even the leaders of those

---

[12]Wenham, *Genesis 16–50*, p. 325.

[13]NIV's "God Almighty."

[14]Another example of this is found in Exodus 1:7 where the multiplication of the descendants of Jacob in Egypt, a fulfillment of God's promise to make a great nation of Abraham, is described in terms which echo the creation commission in Genesis 1:26-28: "the Israelites were fruitful and prolific; they multiplied and grew exceedingly strong, so that the earth/land was filled with them." On this theme see Terence E. Fretheim, *God and World in the Old Testament: A Relational Theology of Creation* (Nashville: Abingdon, 2005).

[15]It is difficult to know what exactly to make of the promise of a community of nations springing from Jacob. The original audience might think of the people from many nations who joined them as they left Egypt (Exod 12:38) or the people of other nations who joined themselves to Israel when they first entered

nations, their kings. This promise was also made to Abraham (Gen 17:6) and Sarah (Gen 17:16). What God had promised to the persons who originally left Haran to come to the Promised Land has now been reaffirmed to Jacob when he returned from Haran (Paddan Aram).

But it is not only the promise of descendants that is reaffirmed. God also promised Jacob that he would be given the very same land which God had already given to Abraham and Isaac, his grandfather and father respectively. Of course the gift would only be realized in Jacob's descendants, the nation of Israel.

The timing of the reaffirmation of the promise to Jacob is no accident. Jacob had been exiled outside of the Promised Land for twenty years. That exile had occurred because he tried by his own efforts to make the promise come true. Laban had humbled him and he was humbled before Esau. It was only then that God moved forward with his promise to Jacob. The canonical audience would undoubtedly see their own exile in Babylon in the exile of Jacob in Paddan Aram. It was only after exile, when the nation of Israel had given up her pretensions to make their own way in the world that the nation as a whole begins to become truly faithful to the LORD alone. The process of exile had changed Jacob so that he was ready to receive the promise once again just as the process of exile had changed the nation of Israel so that she was ready to receive the promise once again.[16]

35:13 Then God went up from him at the place where he had talked with him.

After reaffirming for Jacob that he, through his descendants, would be heir to the Abrahamic promise including the promise of the land, God ascended from that place. In chapter 28 the angels were ascending and descending on the stairway between heaven and earth. God, not the angels, returns to heaven. But why are we told this? The revelation of God's direct presence, and not just in a dream which Jacob had while at Bethel the earlier time, indicates for Jacob and the readers a greater certainty to the promise. God himself had come down from heaven and spoken with Jacob. Interestingly the Hebrew makes it clear that this was a conversation. He spoke "with" Jacob and not just "to" Jacob. In chapter 28 Jacob had been afraid when he woke from his sleep and realized

---

the land (Rahab, the Gibeonites, etc.). The canonical audience might think of the many nations in which the people of Israel lived in Diaspora and/or the people of many nations who joined them through proselytism or other forms of assimilation.

[16]My thanks to John Nugent for suggesting that I give more emphasis to this point.

that the very place he was sleeping was the place of a divine revelation. It was the "very house of God" (Bethel) and the very "gate of heaven" (Gen 28:17). In this instance the revelation had been much more direct and yet Jacob showed no fear.

The Bible's theology of the revelation of God's direct presence is more complex and subtle than the quotation of a single half-verse, "No one has ever seen God" (John 1:18a), would suggest. While it is extremely unusual for a human being to see God and it is dangerous and presumptuous for a person to arrogantly walk into God's presence uninvited, there are specific rare occasions when this happens.[17] While in this instance one could say that God only talked with Jacob and had not appeared to him, this does not explain why God is said to have "gone up" from him after the conversation ended. In Genesis 17:22 the same construction[18] is used after an appearance of the LORD to Abraham.

6. Jacob Worships the God who Promises His Blessing (35:14-15)

35:14 Jacob set up a stone pillar at the place where God had talked with him, and he poured out a drink offering on it; he also poured oil on it.

Whatever the exact nature of the experience that Jacob had with God, it had a great impact on Jacob. He set up a stone pillar as a sort of altar. Upon the "altar" he poured out a liquid drink offering as well as oil. Usually libations consisted of wine[19] poured out over the altar as part of a larger sacrificial ritual. Oil as used in sacrificial rituals was from the first and best extraction of olive oil and was used in purification rites, as part of food offerings, and even with animal sacrifices.[20] By pouring wine and oil on the improvised altar Jacob indicated the sacredness of the experience. For the original and canonical readers the father of Israel (Jacob) anticipated the later sacrificial worship at the Tabernacle and Temple which his descendants (the nation of Israel) participated in under divine command.

---

[17]Exodus 24:10 says that Moses, Aaron, Nadab, Abihu, and the 70 elders of Israel "saw" (רָאָה, rā'āh, the normal Hebrew verb for "to see") the God of Israel. Verse 11 uses a different word (חָזָה, ḥāzāh) which implies a visionary experience.

[18]The verb עָלָה ('ōlāh) followed by the compound preposition מֵעַל, (mē'al). My thanks to Gary Hall for reminding me of this parallel.

[19]Psalm 16:4 refers to a drink offering of "blood" as part of a pagan ritual condemned by the Psalmist.

[20]James C. Moyer, "Oil, Ointment," EDB, p. 984.

35:15 Jacob called the place where God had talked with him Bethel.
After his act of worship Jacob called the place Bethel. This statement is perplexing for the contemporary reader. Had not Jacob already named this place Bethel in 28:19 and El-Bethel in 35:7? This is the third occurrence of Jacob naming this place! Further, God assumes that the place is already known as Bethel when he tells Jacob to settle there in 35:1. These sorts of texts are fodder for the documentary hypothesis. "Obviously," so the reasoning goes, "Jacob did not name the place three different times and by two different names. This must be the result of an original story which has been shaped in three different ways by the purported sources J, E, and P." But this judgment may be too hasty, despite its seeming plausibility. The passage is not just a "heap of blocks"[21] with no discernable structure. Wenham seems to suggest that, just as Jacob repeats other acts from the original experience at Bethel when he fled from Esau, here too he repeats the naming to reaffirm it in light of God's gracious reaffirmation of the promise to him.[22] This does not, however, explain 35:7 where the name El-Bethel is given. Certainly the fact that the name Bethel is given without explanation of its significance suggests that the reader is expected to know of the previous narrative in chapter 28. For the author the name Bethel is important, as we have three instances of Luz being named Bethel.

What significance might this have for the original and canonical audiences? I would suggest two possibilities. For the original audience Bethel, along with Ai, was one of the earliest cities Israel defeated when she first entered the land, preceded only by Jericho (Josh 8:1-29). Jacob's return to Bethel and the setting up of a place of worship there in a symbolic sense lays a claim on that place. For the canonical audience Bethel was the center which Jeroboam I used to set up a worship site as an alternative rival to the Temple in Jerusalem (1 Kgs 12:26-33). The syncretistic altar which Jeroboam set up there was designed to merge the worship of Yahweh who had brought Israel up out of Egypt with the worship of the fertility god(s) of Canaan, Baal. The latter was depicted as a bull or calf. By associating a calf with Yahweh, Jeroboam attempted to mix together the traditions of Yahweh and Baal. The canonical audience in the Diaspora would know that Israel's insistence on syncretizing their religious traditions resulted, after many prophetic warnings, in their dispersion in 722 B.C. For the audience Bethel was a place of religious renewal which rejected syncretism and polytheism before it was corrupted into being the center of that syncretism by Jeroboam. Bethel

---

[21]Gunkel, as cited by Westermann, *Genesis 12–36*, p. 549.
[22]Wenham, *Genesis 16–50*, p. 326.

was the house of the true God in Jacob's time long before its heritage
was twisted by the kings of the north into the center of Israel's unfaithfulness.

B. RACHEL DIES GIVING BIRTH TO
THE TWELFTH SON OF ISRAEL (35:16-21)

**35:16 Then they moved on from Bethel. While they were still some dis-
tance from Ephrath, Rachel began to give birth and had great difficulty. 35:17 And as she was having great difficulty in childbirth, the
midwife said to her, "Don't be afraid, for you have another son."
35:18 As she breathed her last—for she was dying—she named her son
Ben-Oni. But his father named him Benjamin.**

Just as Abram, when he first came into the Promised Land, moved
from the north to the middle to the south (Gen 12:1-9), so too does
Jacob when he returns from Paddan Aram. Bethel was in the middle of
Canaan, and in this passage Jacob and his family are traveling south to
where his father and grandfather had lived near Beersheba. Ephrath is
identified as another name for Bethlehem, the name more familiar to
the canonical and perhaps the original audience. For the canonical audience the mention of Bethlehem would remind them of the ancestral village of David. Jacob, the forefather of the nation of Israel was headed[23]
toward Bethlehem. In a sense, by intending to journey to Bethlehem,
Jacob was making a claim on that village for the later nation of Israel. A
good distance away, Rachel went into labor and had trouble.

While giving birth to a child is to this day a risky business even with
the latest medical technology, in the ancient world it was far more so.
Though precise statistics are impossible to provide, a high percentage
of babies died in childbirth. A significant percentage of mothers also
died. The midwife tried to reassure Rachel when her difficulty was at its
height by encouraging her that she had borne another[24] son.

As Rachel's life[25] was going, she named her son[26] Ben-oni meaning
"son of my trouble," evidently referring to her difficult labor and birth.

---

[23]Since the birth took place a "long distance" from Bethlehem, its mention
here implies that Jacob was headed toward it, but had not arrived, when Rachel
went into labor.

[24]The Hebrew phrase זֶה גַּם (*gam zeh*) has the sense "this also."

[25]The NIV has "breathed her last," and the NRSV has "as her soul was departing." In both cases the paraphrase of the Hebrew word נֶפֶשׁ (*nepheš*), which usually means "life" is unnecessary. The NRSV's "soul" risks the importing of a

Had the name remained, the child would be a constant reminder of the tragic nature of his existence. His birth caused his mother's death. Jacob may well have renamed him out of his own grief and out of concern that the child's very name would be a sort of curse on him. Instead Jacob names his youngest son, Benjamin, meaning "son of my right hand." The reference to "right hand" is ambiguous. The one who sits at the right hand of a powerful figure is the first in line to his power. But there is never indication that Benjamin is regarded as the firstborn or first in line to Jacob's inheritance. Alternatively "right hand" could be a reference to Rachel who gave birth to Benjamin. The problem in this case is that there is no known precedent[27] for a wife being referred to as the "right hand" of her husband, though her status as favored wife may warrant the metaphor.

35:19 So Rachel died and was buried on the way to Ephrath (that is, Bethlehem). 35:20 Over her tomb Jacob set up a pillar, and to this day that pillar marks Rachel's tomb.

Greek concept of the immortal soul into the Old Testament in an anachronistic way.

[26]Don C. Benjamin, "Israel's God: Mother and Midwife," *BTB* 19 (1989): 115-120, suggests the following:

> Some birth and resurrection stories in the Bible seem to assume that labor is protracted because the fetus is delaying its own birth. At that point, the midwife asks the mother to name the child. Then the midwife calls the fetus by name using the formula: "Lazarus, come forth (John 11:43-44)." Once the fetus hears its name, it stops struggling and is born. Biblical birth stories like those in Exodus 7:14-10:29; Joshua 5:13-6:27; Isaiah 26:10-27:13 assume the procedure of "calling the fetus" when they distinguish the name which the mother gives a child from the name which the father gives it. Since the father is seldom present during birth, the midwife may ask the mother to name her child during a protracted labor, and it is the mother's "temporary" name for the child which the midwife then uses to call the fetus. Later, when the child is adopted the father gives it an official name. In Genesis 35:16-20, for example, Rachel names her child "Labor Baby" (Hebrew: *ben-oni*), but Jacob renames it "My Baby" (Hebrew: *benjamin*).

Benjamin's theory does not seem to fit this narrative since the birth has presumably already happened or the midwife would not have known that the child was a boy.

[27]1 Kgs 2:19 does have a woman, King Solomon's mother Bathsheba, sit at his right hand. Psalm 45:9 does refer to a queen, and therefore a wife, as at the right hand of the king. Proverbs 3:16 depicts Lady Wisdom as possessing "long life" in her right hand.

Ephrath seems to be the same place as Ephrathah. If so, it was a town in the southern portion of the tribal territory of Benjamin[28] or the northern portion of Judah. The fact that Rachel was buried there, and not taken to the family tomb that Abraham had purchased near Hebron, may have been because of her sudden death. In any case her burial there, immediately after the birth of the son who later gave his name to the region in Israel, Benjamin, is not accidental. Once again a sort of historical claim to the territory is implied. Rachel, in her death, receives a down payment on the promise of the land. She died giving birth to Benjamin there, and centuries later Benjamin's descendants would take permanent possession of that very land. Canonical readers, if not the original audience, would see the providence of God in seeing an anticipation of the later significance of the city of Bethlehem. Bethlehem was the hometown of David and the place from which the prophet Micah had promised a new David would come (Micah 5:2). The memorial pillar which Jacob set up over Rachel's tomb was still present in the time of the original and/or canonical audience.

35:21 Israel moved on again and pitched his tent beyond Migdal Eder.

Jacob, who is designated by his new name as the eponymous ancestor of the nation of Israel, continues to follow the track of his grandfather Abraham in symbolically claiming ownership of the land. We are not certain of the exact location of Migdal-Eder.[29] In the context it seems to be somewhere along the road from Bethlehem to Beersheba. For some reason Jacob stopped his journey to his father in the south and took up a form of semipermanent residence[30] there.

---

[28]1 Sam 10:2; Jer 31:15 [assuming Ramah = er-Ram, a town five miles north of Jerusalem, cf. Josh 18:25]; Ruth 4:11; Micah 5:1. Josh 15:59, in a LXX addition, includes Ephrathah in a list of places near Bethlehem.

[29]Migdal-Eder would seem to mean "tower of the flock." Alternatively the word Eder could be a proper name and the phrase would mean, "the tower of Eder." Micah 4:8 has the same phrase and may be indicating a place in the environs of Jerusalem. Matthews notes: "Because of the association of nearby Bethlehem with the messianic figure in Mic. 5:1," Targum Micah 4.8 and Targum Pseudo-Jonathan at Gen 35:21, "identify Migdal Eder as the location for the appearance of the coming messiah." While the sources cited are later than the NT there is no inherent reason why a canonical reader, though not in this case the original reader, would not see some sort of messianic echo in this passage.

[30]שָׁכַן (šākan) implies a semipermanent form of residence, although still impermanent.

C. REUBEN, THE FIRSTBORN, DISQUALIFIES HIMSELF (35:22a)

35:22a While Israel was living in that region, Reuben went in and slept with his father's concubine Bilhah, and Israel heard of it.

It was during this period that Reuben, now a young man, had a sexual relationship with Jacob's concubine Bilhah. As Rachel's handmaiden, Bilhah was the last living memory of his beloved wife Rachel. De Hoop suggests that "Reuben's action might be construed as an attempt to seize power by seizing his father's harem."[31] He compares the similarities in language between Reuben's actions here and Absalom's in 2 Samuel 16:21. In both cases the person "went" to his "father's concubine(s)" and "Israel" would or did "hear" of it. Since Absalom is transparently starting a revolt against his father, it is possible to understand Reuben's actions in the same way. One problem with this suggestion is that Reuben only slept with one of Jacob's concubines, not his entire "harem." Jacob did not have a harem, unlike Absalom's father David.

Surprisingly Jacob does not immediately react in any way. He heard of the affair and remained silent about it until the time of the blessing of his sons in chapter 49.[32] Jacob was also silent at the news of Dinah's rape and later exploded at his sons, Simeon and Levi. For all three of these sons Jacob's initial silence was removed at his deathbed where he uttered curses on them rather than blessings (Gen 49:3-7).

D. JACOB'S FAMILY REHEARSED (35:22b-26)

35:22b Jacob had twelve sons: 35:23 The sons of Leah: Reuben the firstborn of Jacob, Simeon, Levi, Judah, Issachar and Zebulun. 35:24 The sons of Rachel: Joseph and Benjamin. 35:25 The sons of Rachel's maidservant Bilhah: Dan and Naphtali. 35:26 The sons of Leah's maidservant Zilpah: Gad and Asher. These were the sons of Jacob, who were born to him in Paddan Aram.

With the birth of Benjamin the original twelve tribes of Israel all now have the births of their forefathers recorded. With Reuben having sexual relations with one of his father's wives, the danger of generational

---

[31]Raymond de Hoop, *Genesis 49 in Its Literary and Historical Context* (Leiden: Brill, 1999), p. 512.

[32]1 Chronicles 5:1-2 points out what is implicit in Genesis. Because of Reuben's deed his birthright was transferred to the two sons of Joseph, Ephraim and Manasseh, who became the most prominent tribes in the north of the country.

confusion leads the narrator to summarize. This passage thus serves as a sort of summary of this section of the narrative in terms of the twelve sons of Jacob who gave their names to the twelve tribes of Israel.

The sons[33] are listed based on three principles in the following order (see the chart below). First of all they are grouped by their mothers, Leah, Rachel, Bilhah, and Zilpah. All of Leah's children are listed together even though only the first four were born in succession. Second, the children of the wives are listed before the children of the handmaids. Third, birth order of the sons determines the order in which the wives, on the one hand, and the concubines, on the other, are listed. Rachel was the beloved and favored wife of Jacob. His sons with her, Joseph and Benjamin, were Jacob's favorites. But in this list they are not named first. Leah, the unloved wife, has the honor of heading the first listing of the tribes of Israel. Birth order overrides Jacob's personal feelings in this passage.

Birth order	Mother	Gen 35:22b-36	Mother
1. Reuben	Leah	1. Reuben	Leah
2. Simeon	Leah	2. Simeon	Leah
3. Levi	Leah	3. Levi	Leah
4. Judah	Leah	4. Judah	Leah
5. Dan	Rachel's handmaid, Bilhah	9. Issachar	Leah
6. Naphtali	Rachel's handmaid, Bilhah	10. Zebulun	Leah
7. Gad	Leah's handmaid, Zilpah	11. Joseph	Rachel
8. Asher	Leah's handmaid, Zilpah	12. Benjamin	Rachel
9. Issachar	Leah	5. Dan	Rachel's handmaid, Bilhah
10. Zebulun	Leah	6. Naphtali	Rachel's handmaid, Bilhah
11. Joseph	Rachel	7. Gad	Leah's handmaid, Zilpah
12. Benjamin	Rachel	8. Asher	Leah's handmaid, Zilpah

The narrator does not show the same favoritism to Rachel and her children that Jacob does. The narrator does, however, reflect the patriarchal culture in which males ordinarily[34] were the only heirs and the fact that children of concubines did not have the same status as primary wives within the patriarchal family structure.

---

[33]Dinah and other unnamed daughters of Jacob are not mentioned as they did not found tribal groups in Israel.

[34]An exception is made in the case of a family which has only daughters; cf. the case of the daughters of Zelophehad in Numbers 27:1-11. The narrator should not be portrayed as being more patriarchal than he was.

Another interesting feature of the list is the fact that Reuben is specifically pointed out as the firstborn son of Jacob, not of Leah. Jacob was not the firstborn in his own family. With his mother Rebekah's help he tried to cheat his brother Esau out of the birthright and the blessing. But in his own family Jacob still regarded Reuben as the firstborn with all of the privileges and responsibilities which that implied. The reader has just been reminded of Reuben's affair with one of Jacob's (secondary) wives. The question arises thus for the first-time reader what the end result of these two facts will be. Will Reuben's status as firstborn override his sinfulness? The original and canonical readers, of course, know the answer. The tribe descended from Reuben was marginalized in the history of the nation because of his unfaithfulness.[35]

The listing of Jacob's sons ends with the perplexing comment that they were born to him in Paddan Aram. To be technical, Benjamin was not born until the family had returned to Canaan. This may be an example of the narrator using less than scientifically precise language or a subtle hint that the family is not really back in the Promised Land in an ideological sense until they have traveled all the way to its southern borders.[36] A less likely possibility is that since Benjamin was apparently conceived in Paddan Aram, he was regarded as being "born" there. This view seems to be based on the questionable basis of the discussion of the beginning of human life in the current debate over abortion in the western world.

E. JACOB AND ESAU TOGETHER BURY THEIR FATHER ISAAC (35:27-29)

35:27 Jacob came home to his father Isaac in Mamre, near Kiriath Arba (that is, Hebron), where Abraham and Isaac had stayed.

Jacob finally returns to the home from which he had fled more than 20 years previously. Surprisingly Isaac, his father whom he had tricked into blessing him then, was still alive. Isaac was living in Mamre near Kiriath Arba, the ancient name for the city familiar to the original and canonical audiences as Hebron. The narrator reminds us that in returning to Hebron, Jacob came to walk in the steps of his father and grand-

---

[35]The choice of the Reubenites to settle in the Transjordan and not settle with the rest of the tribes in Canaan only further marginalized the tribe (Num 32:1-37).

[36]A parallel may be found in the initial entrance of Abram into the land in Genesis 12:1-9 where he stopped at Shechem in the north, Bethel in the middle, and finally the Negev in the south, thus symbolically taking possession of it.

father who had also lived there. Just as all three received the promise, so all three have similar life experiences. Like Abraham and Isaac before them, Jacob too lived as a sojourner (גּוּר, *gûr*) in Mamre. He did not have permanent possession of it, only the promise that one day his descendants would have such possession.

35:28 Isaac lived a hundred and eighty years. 35:29 Then he breathed his last and died and was gathered to his people, old and full of years. And his sons Esau and Jacob buried him.

Under God's blessing Isaac lived to the great age of 180 years, long enough to see his many grandchildren. The significance of the passing of the generation from Isaac to Jacob is hinted at by the slowing of the pace of the narrative. Isaac's "breath failed," he **"died,"** and **"was gathered to his people."** He was not just old, but also **"full of years."** The repetitiveness slows the narrative down for the reader to absorb the significance of this event. Isaac was now dead. Esau had promised to wait for the death and mourning of his father before taking revenge. Would he do so now? No. In their father's death the reconciliation of Esau and Jacob is now complete. Notice that they are both described as Isaac's sons. Interestingly Esau is mentioned first. They both participated together as sons of their father in burying him. Death brought them together as life rarely did.

GENESIS 36

F. ESAU'S FAMILY REHEARSED (36:1-43)

1. The First Genealogy of Esau (36:1-8)

36:1 This is the account of Esau (that is, Edom).

This new section of Genesis begins with the introductory formula "this is the account of."[1] The last such section marker was in Genesis 26:19 where the account of Isaac was introduced. Most of Genesis 26:19–35:29 was about Jacob, the son of Isaac chosen to carry forward the promise. This section in chapter 36 is about Isaac's nonchosen son, Esau. Just as Abraham's story (under his father Terah's formula; cf. Gen 11:27) ended with a genealogy of his nonchosen son Ishmael (Gen 26:1-18), so also Jacob's story (under his father Isaac's formula; cf. Gen 26:19) ends with the genealogy of the nonchosen son, Esau.

The author reminds the reader that Esau's other name was Edom. Both the original and canonical audiences were familiar with Esau's descendants under the name of Edom. They had settled in the area south of the Dead Sea, and when Israel was traveling through their land to enter Canaan, the Edomites had offered firm resistance (Num 20:14-21). The canonical audience would be familiar with the long history of largely antagonistic relationships with the Edomites including their denunciation by such prophets as Obadiah.[2]

36:2 Esau took his wives from the women of Canaan: Adah daughter of Elon the Hittite, and Oholibamah daughter of Anah and grand-daughter of Zibeon the Hivite—36:3 also Basemath daughter of Ishmael and sister of Nebaioth.

---

[1] A more literalistic translation might be "these are the generations of." Such a translation, however, does not communicate the meaning of the phrase.

[2] Obad 1:1,8; Ps 137:7; Lam 4:21-22; Mal 1:2-3; 2 Sam 8:13-14; 1 Kgs 11:15-16; 2 Kgs 14:7; Amos 1:11-12.

The Two Versions of the Wives of Esau

Genesis 26:34-35; 28:9	Genesis 36:2-3
26:34 Judith daughter of Beeri the Hittite Basemath daughter of Elon the Hittite. 28:9 Mahalath, the sister of Nebaioth and daughter of Ishmael son of Abraham,	[2]Adah daughter of Elon the Hittite and Oholibamah daughter of Anah and granddaughter of Zibeon the Hivite— [3]also Basemath daughter of Ishmael and sister of Nebaioth.

In preparation for the genealogical material the author reiterates three of the wives of Esau, although the names differ from the earlier accounts. It is possible that these wives were additional to the wives mentioned in chapters 26 and 28. Another possibility is that they had alternative names (a common phenomenon in the ancient world when last names were lacking). However, the similarities as well as the differences between the two lists make this less plausible. In both lists one of the wives was a daughter of Elon the Hittite, but she has a different name, Basemath versus Adah. The name Basemath occurs in both lists, first as the daughter of Elon the Hittite and then as the daughter of Ishmael and sister of Ishmael's oldest son, Nebaioth. Both lists have Esau marrying a daughter of Ishmael and sister of Nebaioth, but they have different names, Mahalath and Basemath, respectively. One list has Esau marrying a daughter of each of two Hittites while the second list has one Hittite and one Hivite, father-in-law.

The first two wives listed, Adah and Oholibamah, were Canaanites, and if these are different names for the women mentioned in chapter 26, the marriages were the cause of great distress to Isaac and Rebekah (Gen 26:35). Adah means "jewel" and is also the name of one of Lamech's, the first bigamist, wives. Her father Elon's name means "oak tree." Such oak trees were often used as worship sites. Oholibamah evidently means "tent of the high place." If so, one of Esau's wives is associated by name with the entry of bigamy into the world and the other with idolatrous worship which took place on the high places.

Oholibamah is unusual in that her genealogy (according to the MT) includes her mother and grandfather, but not her father.[3] Her grandfa-

---

[3]The Hebrew text here reads "Oholibamah the daughter of Anah, the *daughter of* Zibeon." The SP, LXX, and Syriac, along with NRSV all read "son" instead of the second "daughter." But this seems to be more likely explained as textual harmonization with the original Hebrew being the more "difficult" and, therefore, more likely original reading. Another possibility is to retain the second use of daughter, but to assume it refers to Oholibamah and means "granddaughter" as in the NIV.

ther is said to be a "Hivite."[4] The specific identity of the Hivites is uncertain. The Shechemites and Gibeonites (Josh 9:1-7) were Hivites within the Promised Land, although usually they are described as living on the coastal region to the north of Israel (Josh 11:3 "under Mount Hermon"; Judg 3:3 "Mount Lebanon").

In Genesis 28:9 Basemath is called Mahalath.[5] She is referred to here and in 28:9 as the sister specifically of Nebaioth, Ishmael's firstborn son. This may be because both Basemath and Nebaioth were born of the same mother and were thus full siblings.

36:4 Adah bore Eliphaz to Esau, Basemath bore Reuel, 36:5 and Oholibamah bore Jeush, Jalam and Korah. These were the sons of Esau, who were born to him in Canaan.

These verses list the five sons of Esau born to his three wives while they still lived in the land of Canaan. Since Esau was already living in Seir when he met Jacob as he was returning to Canaan (Gen 33:14,16), evidently he had moved back to the Promised Land.[6] Eliphaz's name may mean "my God is fine gold."[7] One of Job's friends, a Temanite from what was or became Edom, bears this name. Eliphaz's descendants became a prominent tribe in Edom. Reuel's name is attested as an Israelite (Num 1:14; 1 Chr 9:8) and Midianite[8] name. The name means, "God/El is a friend" or "Friend of God/El." The later Edomites had syncretistic or polytheistic tendencies. These names, however, hint at some form of early religious faith in the descendants of Esau.

Jeush's name is attested several times in Israel (1 Chr 7:10; 8:39; 23:10; 2 Chr 11:19). It is also found in the Samaria Ostraca. The name could mean either "God helped" or "he is helping."[9] The meaning of Jalam's name is uncertain; it could mean the animal the "ibex," or it could be derived from a verb meaning "to be strong."[10] Korah's name means

---

[4]BHS suggests that הַחִוִּי (haḥiwwî), "the Hivite," be read הַחֹרִי (haḥōrî), "the Horite," in order to harmonize with v. 20. But there is no textual basis for this suggested emendation. It should be granted that it would be possible for an early scribe to make such a textual confusion.

[5]The Samaritan Pentateuch here and in vv. 4,10,13,17 reads Mahalat instead of Basemath. This seems to be a clear example of harmonization with Genesis 28:9 and is therefore not original.

[6]This may have happened when Isaac died or slightly before, Esau initially intending to live in Canaan with his brother Jacob.

[7]The Princeton Abridgment to BDB in Gramcord, *HALOT*, p. 920, suggests "fine gold" as the meaning for פָּז (paz).

[8]Moses' Midianite father-in-law bore this name, Exod 2:15; Num 10:29.

[9]Ernst Axel Knauf, "Yahweh," *VT* 34 (1984): 468.

[10]Ulrich Hübner, "Jalam," *ABD*, III:616.

"bald head" and is well attested in Hebrew and other Semitic languages. The original and canonical audiences would be familiar with a Levitical clan descending from Korah. He is most well known for leading a rebellion against Aaron's claims to the priesthood in Numbers 16.

36:6 Esau took his wives and sons and daughters and all the members of his household, as well as his livestock and all his other animals and all the goods he had acquired in Canaan, and moved to a land some distance from his brother Jacob. 36:7 Their possessions were too great for them to remain together; the land where they were staying could not support them both because of their livestock. 36:8 So Esau (that is, Edom) settled in the hill country of Seir.

The echo of the narrative of tension between Abram's and Lot's herdsmen in Genesis 12 in this narrative is striking. In this passage it is presumed that Esau was living alongside of Jacob in Canaan. Although this is never made explicit, Esau has apparently moved back to Canaan from Seir. This happened either when Jacob returned from Paddan-Aram or perhaps near the time of the death of their father, Isaac. Esau takes everything and everyone who belonged to him and moved away to the south to live in Seir. The narrator tells us that their possessions, in terms of livestock needing pasturage and water, were too great to be sustained by the land. This seems hard to square with other indications of the fertility of the land of Canaan. It could be that the specific area in the relatively arid southern portion of the country lacked enough free pasturage. God had blessed both Jacob and Esau with material wealth. That wealth was primarily measured and contained in flocks, herds, and the people who cared for them. Esau responded to this problem by moving out of the Promised Land altogether and thus removing himself geographically from the promise. It is also possible that the land had more than enough, but Esau's perception was that there was not enough. If so, we do not hear the narrator speaking in her or his own voice in verse 7. Although unmarked in obvious formal ways, actually the narrator may be representing the point of view of Esau[11] on the adequacy of the pasturage. Just as Lot moved outside of the Promised Land in chapter 12 and thus removed himself from the promise, so does Esau.

2. The Second Genealogy of Esau (36:9-43)

God's blessing of descendants for Esau is emphasized by the fact that he is given two genealogies, both of which begin with the

---

[11]This would seem to be an example of indirect discourse.

"*toledoth*"[12] formula which structures the book of Genesis. Esau, although nonelect, is given a blessing that goes beyond even that of Ishmael.

This second genealogy of Esau is divided into four sections. First, Esau's sons are listed again with the chiefs who descended from them (vv. 9-19). Second, the descendants of the Horite chief Seir are listed (vv. 20-39). They were the original inhabitants of the land of Edom and Seir's descendants intermarried with Esau's descendants. Third, kings of Edom before the development of Israel's monarchy are listed (vv. 31-39). Fourth, another list of chiefs of Edom is given (vv. 40-43).

The use of another section heading in this verse is perplexing as it concerns the descendants of Esau once again who have just been introduced in 36:1! The repetition of this introductory marker is thus taken by many scholars as an indication that some part or all of verses 9-43 is a later insertion which brings the genealogical information that was originally there up to date for a later audience. Such updating is not in principle different from referring to the name of the city to which Abram chased Lot's captors as Dan in Genesis 14:14. The fact that there is repetition of information in 36:1-8 for no apparent reason is another argument in favor of this suggestion. Yet another consideration is the fact that 37:1, "Jacob settled in the land of his father's sojourn, in the land of Canaan," follows naturally from 36:8, the account of Esau's settling in the hill country of Seir. Thus the section 36:1-8; 37:1 without the intervening 36:9-43 finishes off the account of the two sons of Isaac with one living in Canaan and one living in nearby Seir. Read in this fashion this section does indeed appear to be a later insertion.

However we must not be too hasty in coming to such a conclusion no matter what its seeming plausibility at first sight. Advocates of the older Documentary Hypothesis should be concerned about such a conclusion since genealogical materials with the formula "this is the account of" are typically assigned to the late Priestly source "P." But here the names of the wives differ from the names given in Genesis 26:34 and 28:9, passages typically assigned to P. Perhaps there are other reasons for this passage. We must also remember that what we refer to as genealogical material does not fit into modern conventions of a genealogy. Wilson's[13] groundbreaking work on Old Testament genealogies cautions us about imposing modern presuppositions about such material onto ancient name lists. What might seem contradictory to us did

---

[12]For the significance of this structural marker see Kissling, *Genesis Volume 1*, pp. 30-32.

[13]Robert R. Wilson, *Genealogy and History in the Biblical World*. (New Haven, CT: Yale University Press, 1977).

not seem contradictory to them. Often there was more than one accurate and reliable genealogy for the same person depending upon the social need being addressed. For official governmental roles there was one genealogy, for familial identity another. Both were regarded as legitimate in their particular spheres.

One possible explanation for the second section on Esau is that it differs from the first one in giving genealogical information for the descendants of Esau after the move from Canaan to Seir. The repetition of names from the first genealogy would then be explained by the fact that the children born in Canaan also moved to Seir with Esau. The new genealogy is given in light of that move.

Another consideration is that the existence of two genealogical sections implies a special form of blessing on Esau and his descendants. Even though he is not the chosen descendant, he is given the "special privilege" of having not merely one, but two genealogies in the book of Genesis.

Esau's Sons and the Chiefs Descended from Them (36:9-19)

This section describes Esau's sons through his primary wives (vv. 10-13) and secondary wife (v. 14) as well as the chiefs which descended from these three wives (vv. 15-18). It is structured in the following way:

> I. Introductory Formula v. 9
> II. Esau's Sons through His Primary Wives Adah and
>   Basemath v. 10
>   A. Esau's Grandsons through Eliphaz vv. 11-12
>   B. Esau's Grandsons through Reuel v. 13
> III. Esau's Sons through Oholibamah v. 14
> IV. Chiefs Descended from Esau vv. 15-19
>   A. Introductory Statement v. 15a
>   B. From Eliphaz v. 15b-16
>   1. List v. 15b-16a
>   2. Summary v. 16b
>   C. From Reuel v. 17
>   1. List v. 17a
>   2. Summary v. 17b
>   D. From Oholibamah v. 18
>   1. List v. 18a
>   2. Summary v. 18b
>   E. Summary Statement v. 19

36:9 This is the account of Esau the father of the Edomites in the hill country of Seir.

The NIV's paraphrase, "this is the account of" for the *toledoth* formula has the potential to confuse the English reader. This is the standard structural marker in the book of Genesis.[14] This is the second structural marker which concerns Esau (36:1), something unique in the book of Genesis. This shows the importance of Esau and his descendants to Israel. This time he is described as "the father of Edom[15] in the mountains of Seir." This prepares the reader for the fact that the emphasis will not be on Esau the person so much as on the nation which descended from Esau and eventually settled in the hilly land that was formerly called Seir.

36:10 These are the names of Esau's sons: Eliphaz, the son of Esau's wife Adah, and Reuel, the son of Esau's wife Basemath. 36:11 The sons of Eliphaz: Teman, Omar, Zepho, Gatam and Kenaz. 36:12 Esau's son Eliphaz also had a concubine named Timna, who bore him Amalek. These were grandsons of Esau's wife Adah. 36:13 The sons of Reuel: Nahath, Zerah, Shammah and Mizzah. These were grandsons of Esau's wife Basemath.

The repetition of information provided earlier in this section may indicate the use of a second source for the genealogical material regarding Esau. The sons of two of Esau's wives, Adah and Basemath, are listed and carefully distinguished from the sons of his third wife, Oholibamah, listed in verse 14. The separation between the first two wives, on the one hand, and the third, on the other, probably indicates the cultural prominence given to the first two wives. The two wives and their sons are listed in order in verse 10 and Esau's grandsons from each of the sons are listed in verses 11-13.

Eliphaz, the first-named son of Esau through his wife Adah had five sons named[16] through his legitimate wife or wives and a sixth through a concubine. The descendants of the son of the concubine, Amalek, became enemies of Israel and tried to slaughter them when they first came out of Egypt and were extremely vulnerable (Exod 17:8-16). The purpose of this parenthetical remark about Amalek coming from a secondary wife of Eliphaz may be to suggest that the Amalekites were not completely legitimate Edomites from the very beginning.[17] The fact that they, unlike the rest of the Edomites, attacked Israel sets them apart.

---

[14]On this structural marker see Kissling, *Genesis Volume 1*, pp. 30-32.

[15]The NIV uses "Edomites" for Hebrew's "Edom" in order to underscore the point that the descendants of the person, and not the person himself, are being emphasized.

[16]Verse 16 adds the name "Korah" to the list of Eliphaz's sons.

[17]Sarna, *Genesis*, p. 250.

Teman, the first-listed son of the first-listed son of Esau, is the epony-mous ancestor of the best known region in Edom. The name could be derived from the Hebrew root יָמַן (*ymn*) meaning "south." While it is speculated that Teman originally referred to the northern part of Edom,[18] it eventually included all of Edom (Jer 49:20; Amos 1:11-12).[19]

The identities of Omar, Zepho, and Gatam are unknown. The name Omar could mean something like "lamb" or could be derived from the common verb *'āmar* meaning "to speak." If the latter, it might mean something like "well-spoken" or "eloquent."[20] Zepho's name could be derived from either the word "pure, clear" or from a verb meaning "to behold." If the latter, the name might be a shortened form of a name meaning, "God's beholding."[21]

Kenaz is often assumed to be the eponymous ancestor of the Kenizzites, listed in Genesis 15:18 as one of the peoples whose land would be given over to Israel when the iniquity of the Amorites became full.[22] Here they are an Edomite subclan. Since the Edomites were not to be conquered, this identification is puzzling. It could be explained by some sort of later merger between the original Kenizzites and the Edomites whose territory abutted Israel's to the south and east. Alternatively it could be that there was no relationship between this Kenaz and the Kenizzites.

36:14 The sons of Esau's wife Oholibamah daughter of Anah and grand-daughter of Zibeon, whom she bore to Esau: Jeush, Jalam and Korah.

This verse repeats information already provided in verse five,[23] and this fact is used as evidence that this passage is a later insertion. But while this is possible, it presupposes a redactor who is rather clumsy. It also indicates our modern impatience with repetition. We moderns regard repetition as something unnecessary at best and as evidence of a tiresome focus on trivialities at worst. Modern Bible scholars would gen-erally prefer to hypothesize a composite text which has been rather awk-wardly redacted than become self-critical of our modern prejudices. In the ancient Semitic world from which Genesis arises, repetition is a means of emphasizing important things. In this case the repetition hon-ors the nonchosen line of Esau.

---

[18]Amos 1:12 places Teman in parallel with Bozrah, usually identified with modern Buṣeirah in the north of Edom.

[19]Cf. E.A. Knauf, "Teman," *ABD*, VI:347-348.

[20]Kenneth A. Matthews, *Genesis 11:27–50:26*, NAC (Nashville: Broadman & Holman, 2005), p. 650.

[21]Ulrich Hübner, "Zephon," *ABD*, VI:1080.

[22]Edwin C. Hostetter, "Kenaz," *EDB*, p. 763.

[23]See detailed comments at Genesis 36:5.

As noted above, the sons of Esau's wife from Seir, Oholibamah, are listed separately from the sons of his other two wives. This probably indicates the secondary social status of Oholibamah and her descendants in the nation of Edom. The NIV obscures the MT in order to harmonize this verse with verse 25 where Anah is obviously a man. The Hebrew reads literally, "Oholibamah, daughter of Anah, daughter of Zibeon." In other words Anah is Oholibamah's mother. The NIV takes the second "daughter" as "granddaughter" and applies it to Oholibamah, not Anah. This seems very unlikely. Probably there is a textual error in the MT, which should read בֵּן (ben, "son") rather than בַּת (bath, "daughter"). Jeush, Jalam, and Korah are discussed above at Genesis 36:5.

36:15 These were the chiefs among Esau's descendants: The sons of Eliphaz the firstborn of Esau: Chiefs Teman, Omar, Zepho, Kenaz, 36:16 Korah, Gatam and Amalek. These were the chiefs descended from Eliphaz in Edom; they were grandsons of Adah. 36:17 The sons of Esau's son Reuel: Chiefs Nahath, Zerah, Shammah and Mizzah. These were the chiefs descended from Reuel in Edom; they were grandsons of Esau's wife Basemath. 36:18 The sons of Esau's wife Oholibamah: Chiefs Jeush, Jalam and Korah. These were the chiefs descended from Esau's wife Oholibamah daughter of Anah. 36:19 These were the sons of Esau (that is, Edom), and these were their chiefs.

This list of "chiefs" (אַלּוּפֵי, 'allûphê) descended from Esau is nearly identical to the list of sons born to his three wives and their sons in verses 9-14. The only differences are found in the list of the sons of Eliphaz and in their order.

Verses 1-14	Verses 15-19
Eliphaz (Adah)	Eliphaz (Adah)
Teman,	Teman,
Omar,	Omar,
Zepho,	Zepho,
Gatam	Kenaz,
Kenaz,	*Korah*,
	Gatam
Amalek	Amalek
Reuel (Basemath)	Reuel (Basemath)
Nahath,	Nahath,
Zerah,	Zerah,
Shammah	Shammah
Mizzah	Mizzah
Jeush (Oholibamah)	Jeush (Oholibamah)
Jalam (Oholibamah)	Jalam (Oholibamah)
Korah (Oholibamah)	Korah (Oholibamah)

The name Korah shows up twice in the MT[24] of verses 15-19, once as a son of Eliphaz and once as a son of Esau through Oholibamah. While it might seem unlikely that two tribes would have the same name, they are not in the same genealogical relationship to Esau. Nevertheless, a copyist's error cannot be excluded. The two lists have different functions. The first list seems to represent the actual sons and grandsons of Esau while the second the political clans which descended from them.

The Descendants of Seir the Horite (36:20-30)

In this section we are introduced to the seven "sons"[25] of Seir and their descendants who became seven chiefs in Edom. The section is structured in the following way:

   I. Introduction to the seven descendants of Seir who
      became Horite chiefs vv. 20-21
   II. Chief no. 1 — Lotan's sons v. 22
   III. Chief no. 2 — Shobali's sons v. 23
   IV. Chief no. 3 — Zibeon's sons v. 24
   V. Chief no. 4 — Anah's children v. 25
   VI. Chief no. 5 — Dishon's sons v. 26
   VII. Chief no. 6 — Ezer's sons v. 27
   VIII. Chief no. 7 — Dishan's sons v. 28
   IX. Summary Statement vv. 29-30

These chiefs[26] ("leaders of a thousand") are to be distinguished from the Edomite chiefs listed in verses 15-19 in that they descended from the original inhabitants of the region of Seir, perhaps before Esau's migration there. Within the larger unit of 36:9-43 this passage shows the intertwining of the original population with the newer immigrant Edomite population. Timna, a sister of Lotan, became a concubine of Eliphaz, Esau's first son. Oholibamah (v. 25), the daughter of Anah, became the

---

[24] The SP omits this reference to Korah, although the LXX and Syriac have it. The SP is most likely harmonizing here. MT has the more difficult reading and is thus more likely to be genuine.

[25] More accurately "male descendants." Although it is impossible to be certain, it appears that at most five of the seven named "sons" are actually literal sons. Anah is the son of Zibeon and thus Seir's grandson (v. 25) and Dishon is Anah's son and thus Zibeon's grandson and Seir's great-grandson (v. 26). Hebrew genealogical conventions do not match modern conventions and must be understood on their own terms. All seven of these descendants of Seir became chiefs in the land of Seir.

[26] אַלּוּף ('allûph) is related etymologically to the word for one thousand, אֶלֶף ('eleph).

third listed wife of Esau. By such intermarriage Esau adopts the heritage of leadership of the descendants of Seir and, in a sense, becomes Seir when he takes over in Seir.

36:20 These were the sons of Seir the Horite, who were living in the region: Lotan, Shobal, Zibeon, Anah, 36:21 Dishon, Ezer and Dishan. These sons of Seir in Edom were Horite chiefs. 36:22 The sons of Lotan: Hori and Homam. Timna was Lotan's sister. 36:23 The sons of Shobal: Alvan, Manahath, Ebal, Shepho and Onam. 36:24 The sons of Zibeon: Aiah and Anah. This is the Anah who discovered the hot springs in the desert while he was grazing the donkeys of his father Zibeon. 36:25 The children of Anah: Dishon and Oholibamah daughter of Anah. 36:26 The sons of Dishon : Hemdan, Eshban, Ithran and Keran. 36:27 The sons of Ezer: Bilhan, Zaavan and Akan. 36:28 The sons of Dishan: Uz and Aran. 36:29 These were the Horite chiefs: Lotan, Shobal, Zibeon, Anah, 36:30 Dishon, Ezer and Dishan. These were the Horite chiefs, according to their divisions, in the land of Seir.

Lotan is otherwise unknown. Shobal is also the name of a Judahite and a descendant of Caleb (1 Chr 2:50,52; 4:1-2). This may be because the original tribal groups later joined the tribe of Judah. The name may be related to the Hebrew word for "ear of grain."[27] Zibeon[28] and Anah,[29] as Horites, are probably to be distinguished from the Zibeon and Anah in 36:2 who are Hivites.[30] Dishon,[31] Ezer and Dishan are otherwise unknown.

The sons of Lotan, the first listed son of Seir were Hori and Homam. Hori, whose name would suggest the Horites, is also the name of the father of the spy from the tribe of Simeon who spied out the Promised Land in the time of Moses (Num 13:5). Homam occurs elsewhere only in the genealogy based on this passage in 1 Chronicles 1:39. The mention of Lotan's sister, Timna, reminds the audience that there was intermarriage between the descendants of Seir and the descendants of Esau. Such intermarriage was the basis of a sort of royal pact designed to ensure that Esau's descendants would inherit leadership authority and status in their new land.

The sons of Shobal, Alvan, Manahath, Ebal, Shepho, and Onam are otherwise unknown, although the latter is also the name of a clan in Judah

---

[27]Matthews, *Genesis 11:27–50:26*, p. 653.

[28]According to Wenham (*Genesis 16–50*, p. 337), Zibeon's name seems to mean "hyena."

[29]Anah's name could be the name of a deity from Turkey (ibid.).

[30]Wenham, ibid., suggests the possibility of a textual error in v. 2, where Horites was accidentally miscopied as Hivites.

[31]The name refers to a type of antelope, perhaps the ibex. Cf. RSV.

(1 Chr 2:26,28). Ebal is also the name of the mountain opposite Mount Gerizim in the north where Israel pronounced blessings and curses.

In verse 24 an explanatory comment is given to distinguish this Anah from his uncle of the same name (v. 20) and presumably from the female mentioned in verse 2 who was the mother of Oholibamah.[32]

Verse 25 is perplexing in the Hebrew. Literally it reads, "These are the *sons* of Anah: Dishon and Oholibamah, daughter of Anah." One problem is that only one son is listed. Another is that a daughter may be listed as a son. The NIV harmonizes by translating "sons" as "children." It could be that the first Anah in verse 25 is a man and the second Anah is a woman, mentioned in verse 2 as Oholibamah's mother. Neither view is entirely satisfying. One is left to wonder. While Oholibamah is not a son and thus not normally mentioned in an ancient Near Eastern genealogy, she is mentioned here because she married Esau. That marriage cemented the alliance between the descendants of Seir and those of Esau.

Regarding the sons of Dishon, Hemdan is spelled Hemran in 1 Chronicles 1:41 due to *daleth/resh* (ד/ר) confusion. Eshban and Keran are otherwise unknown. Ithran is also the name of an Asherite (1 Chr 7:37). Of the sons of Ezer, Bilhan also is the name of a Benjamite (1 Chr 7:10), Zaavan is unknown, and Akan is spelled Jaakan in 1 Chronicles 1:42. The two sons of Dishan are Uz and Aran, the latter being otherwise unknown. Uz is also the name of an Aramaean tribe (Gen 10:23; 22:21) as well as the home of Job (1:10)

Kings of Edom (36:31-39)

36:31 These were the kings who reigned in Edom before any Israelite king reigned:
36:32 Bela son of Beor became king of Edom. His city was named Dinhabah.
36:33 When Bela died, Jobab son of Zerah from Bozrah succeeded him as king.
36:34 When Jobab died, Husham from the land of the Temanites succeeded him as king.
36:35 When Husham died, Hadad son of Bedad, who defeated Midian in the country of Moab, succeeded him as king. His city was named Avith.
36:36 When Hadad died, Samlah from Masrekah succeeded him as king.

---

[32]If, however, one follows the NIV in v. 2 and reads the second "daughter" as "granddaughter" then Anah is a man, as here.

36:37 When Samlah died, Shaul from Rehoboth on the river succeeded him as king.
36:38 When Shaul died, Baal-Hanan son of Acbor succeeded him as king.
36:39 When Baal-Hanan son of Acbor died, Hadad succeeded him as king. His city was named Pau, and his wife's name was Mehetabel daughter of Matred, the daughter of Me-Zahab.

One of the purposes of this chapter of Genesis is to show that God also blessed Esau, as he had done for Ishmael. Both had numerous descendants, even though neither of them was chosen to be the channel of God's promise. Just because someone was not chosen as the primary vehicle of God's plan did not mean that God had condemned them. Esau, like Ishmael, rose to a prominent position. An entire nation arose from Esau's descendants. The nonchosen one was also under God's blessing. In terms of developing into a nation, the descendants of Esau did so long before Israel did. They had at least nine kings before Israel had their first king. Being the chosen one meant living as slaves in Egypt for 400 years. During that time the descendants of Esau had developed into a significant nation in their own right. Having kings descend from the landless Abraham and Sarah was a part of God's blessing on them (Gen 17:16). The list of kings given here must also, in some sense, be seen as a sign of God's blessing on those who were not chosen.

But, while kingship can be a sign of God's blessing, the institution is also fraught with danger for God's people. Moses, in Deuteronomy 17:14-20 had warned the nation before even entering the Promised Land about kings "like the nations." The canonical audience would be especially cognizant of this as they were in Diaspora largely because of the failure of the kingship. Sadly the nation chosen by God wanted to be like the other nations in their leadership ideology. But that ideology had led them away from God, and permanent exile and dispersion had been the consequence. An unnamed king of Edom had, quite understandably from a purely political point of view, given Israel resistance when they wanted to cross through their land on the way to the Promised Land (Num 20:14-21).

There are signs in this listing of Edom's early kings that even for the descendants of Esau, the kingship was not an unmitigated blessing. None of the kings listed has his son succeed him. In each case the new king created a new line. This would seem to hint at a politically unstable situation in the ancient world.[33] There are also three different capi-

---

[33]Modern readers who have seen the overthrow of almost all monarchies in the last few centuries must avoid the temptation to read democracy into the

tal cities named, possibly another sign of political instability. Further, the kings come from at least four different places. Wenham[34] cautiously draws a parallel between the situations of Edom here and Israel prior to the monarchy in the chaotic era of the judges.

Early Kings of Edom

Name	Father	From	City Name	Other Information
Bela	Beor		Dinhabah	
Jobab	Zerah	Bozrah		
Husham		land of the Temanites		
Hadad[35]	Bedad		Avith	defeated Midian in the country of Moab
Samlah		Masrekah		
Shaul		Rehoboth on the river		
Baal-Hanan	Acbor			
Hadad			Pau	his wife's name was Mehetabel daughter of Matred, the daughter of Me-Zahab

Chiefs of Edom (36:40-43)

**36:40 These were the chiefs descended from Esau, by name, according to their clans and regions: Timna, Alvah, Jetheth,
36:41 Oholibamah, Elah, Pinon,
36:42 Kenaz, Teman, Mibzar,
36:43 Magdiel and Iram. These were the chiefs of Edom, according to their settlements in the land they occupied. This was Esau the father of the Edomites.**

This paragraph seems extraneous and unnecessary to the contemporary reader. We have already had sections of Edomite chiefs, Edomite

---

ancient world. In that world a succession of dynasties that last only a single generation implies a series of violent overthrows of the previous monarchy and the instability which such overthrows bring.

[34]Wenham, *Genesis 16–50*, pp. 339-340.

[35]The MT here reads "Hadar" but the SP, LXX, Syriac, Vulgate, and 1 Chr 1:50,51 read "Hadad." Perhaps the most easily confused letters in copying the MT's square script are the daleth (ד) and the resh (ר). This seems to be an obvious example of it.

kings, and chiefs of Seir in verses 9-39. Why is this material here? For some reason the names of the chiefs ("leaders of thousands") are different from those in verses 15-19. There is some overlap between the two lists. Teman and Kenaz occur in both lists. Oholibamah's name occurs in both lists, but in verse 18 she is a wife of Esau and mother of three of the chiefs, Jeush, Jalam, and Korah. Timna in verse 40 is the mother of Amalek in verse 16 according to verse 12. So, two chiefs in the land of Edom had names which were originally the names of women. It may be that the chiefs being described here are place names which are sometimes based upon the earliest tribal leaders and at other times based on other leaders. Most likely the two lists come from either different time periods in the history of Edom and/or from different social spheres. They remind the canonical (and perhaps also the original) audience that the descendants of Esau did become a significant nation. Whatever the conflicts which the descendants of Jacob had with the Edomites, the Edomites played a significant role in the history of the chosen nation. That fact should not be disregarded.

As Christians, of course, we know that Herod's father led the Edomites to adopt Judaism (and effectively reunited the divided family) in order for his son to gain the right to be recognized by the Romans as king of the Jews.

Comparing Two Lists of Edomite Chiefs

Vv. 15-19	Vv. 40-43
Teman,	Timna,
Omar,	Alvah,
Zepho,	Jetheth,
Kenaz,	Oholibamah,
Korah,	Elah,
Gatam and	Pinon,
Amalek.	Kenaz,
Nahath,	Teman,
Zerah,	Mibzar,
Shammah and	Magdiel and
Mizzah.	Iram. These were the chiefs of Edom,
Jeush,	according to their settlements in the
Jalam and	land they occupied. This was Esau the
Korah.	father of the Edomites.

G. JACOB CONTINUES LIFE IN THE LAND (37:1)

37:1 Jacob lived in the land where his father had stayed, the land of Canaan.

As noted above, this verse follows naturally from 36:8, indicating that while Esau moved out of the Promised Land, Jacob remained. The implicit consequence of this decision is that Jacob, unlike Esau, remains in a position to receive the blessings associated with the promise.

GENESIS 37

THE NARRATIVE OF JACOB'S SONS
(37:2–50:26)

While this section of Genesis is generally known as the Joseph Narrative, in fact the content is broader than that. The section includes chapter 38 about Judah and Tamar, and this should be taken into account in understanding the section in its entirety.[1] While Joseph is the most dominant and important character, the narrative as a whole is about the sons of Jacob as a group. The narrative reaches a sort of climax in chapter 49 when Jacob gives his final words to each of his sons before he dies. In a sense, the destinies of the twelve tribes of Israel seem to be set at that point, at least conditionally. That chapter makes clear that Joseph's descendants will be blessed abundantly (Gen 49:22-26). But surprisingly, it is Judah who is promised the role of leadership in the nation (Gen 49:10). The narrative begins with Joseph's first dream which is understood to mean that his brothers would bow down to him. In the end, however, Jacob says, "your father's sons shall bow down to you," about Judah, not Joseph (Gen 49:8). The dreams of Joseph, their interpretation, and their afterlife drive the plot of this section of Genesis. But as Laurence Turner first noted,[2] the dreams seem to announce a plot which does not find resolution in the way expected. Instead we have a sort of implicit two-pronged plot.

On the surface it is the story of Joseph. As Jacob's favorite, he is resented by his brothers. That resentment results in his initial humiliation as an imprisoned Hebrew slave in Egypt. Ultimately, however, he is elevated above his brothers, as second in command over all Egypt. He comes to forgive them and be reconciled to them. He even is able to see

---

[1]Traditionally in historical-critical approaches chapter 38 has been regarded as an insertion into the Joseph narrative. The Joseph Narrative is regarded as a sort of *novella* with a unified plot.

[2]See his seminal work, *Announcements of Plot in Genesis*, ch. 4.

God's hand in all the evil that was done to him. But somewhat surpris-ingly, in light of this plot, his descendants are not given the role of lead-ership within the nation which descends from Jacob's twelve sons.

The less obvious plot involves Judah, the fourth son of Jacob. His three older brothers disqualify themselves from the role of leader of the family. Initially Judah would also seem to disqualify himself. He is responsible for the enslavement of Joseph. He is less righteous than his Canaanite daughter-in-law, Tamar, who tricks Judah into fathering her two sons. In other words, Judah's story starts badly. But as the story of Jacob's sons progresses, Judah's characterization undergoes a transfor-mation. Judah becomes the leader of the sons who remained in Canaan. He convinces Jacob to allow them to return for more grain with Benjamin (43:3-14); something his older brother Reuben had been unable to do. Judah's speech influences Joseph to reveal himself to his brothers and start the process of reconciliation (44:18-34). When the family moves to Egypt, Judah is sent ahead to prepare a place to live in Goshen (46:28). Finally it is Judah who is given a blessing that goes beyond even that of Joseph, Jacob's favorite (49:8-12).

In a sense the two brothers rise to positions of prominence by very different routes. Joseph is his father's favorite. Though he experiences setbacks due to the duplicity of others, he is eventually exalted to an even higher position. Joseph is far from the perfect character he is por-trayed to be in Sunday school lessons. But he simply does not deserve the treatment he receives. He learns to forgive by seeing God's hand at work even in the evil done to him (45:5,7; 50:20). It is not surprising that his two sons are adopted as Jacob's own and that he receives an extensive blessing from his father (49:22-26).

Judah's journey to his father's blessing is circuitous in a different way. He suggests that Joseph be sold as a slave while Reuben is gone. He behaves reprehensibly toward his daughter-in-law Tamar and with-out sexual scruples. But as the narrative works itself out, a different side of Judah emerges as noted above. Judah climbs from a very low place of his own making to a position of prominence in the blessings of his father. In a sense his life is a demonstration of grace in God's dealing with sinful human beings and even of Jacob's grace, if grace be defined as meritless favor.

One thing that is typically ignored by traditional historical-critical scholarship is the implied historical or social context of Israel in which the narrative of chapters 37–50, including chapters 38 and 49, fits. Read as an entity, the narrative would fit best before the separation of the nation into the north and the south when the Joseph tribes dominated in the north and Judah in the South. Certainly the idea that this fits the postexilic situation where the north was largely gone and the Judean monarchy had been destroyed lacks coherence.[3]

For this section of Genesis the distinction I have been making between the meaning of Genesis for the original and canonical audiences is of particular importance. The original audience knew from their own experience the prominence of the tribe of Judah. Judah was given the first allotment in the Promised Land (Joshua 15), something the tribes of Joseph resented from the beginning (Josh 17:14-18). The first kings of the Monarchy came from Judah and the allied tribe Benjamin. The temple was built in the territory of Judah and Benjamin. For the canonical audience things are very different. Israel's experiment with Monarchy had turned out to be a disaster. The unfaithfulness of the kings of Judah led ultimately to the dissolution of the nation and permanent Diaspora. Most Jews never returned to the Promised Land. Even those who returned to Judah to rebuild the Temple during the Persian Empire knew that they were still enslaved (Ezra 9:8,9; Neh 9:36). The ruler's scepter that Jacob promised to the descendants of Judah (Gen 49:10) had turned out to be a mixed blessing. For the canonical audience the ascendency of Judah and Joseph did not last.

For Christians, however, the story is somewhat different. Israel's experiment with worldly kingship had been a painful rebuke to the nation. But the tribe of Judah still had the honor of giving birth to a king of a different sort. His name was Jesus, the lion in lamb's clothing from the tribe of Judah.

I. INTERNAL FAMILY TENSIONS RESULT IN JOSEPH'S ENSLAVEMENT IN EGYPT (37:2-36)

The Joseph that most Christians have learned about as children in Sunday school is not the Joseph of the Bible. Joseph is portrayed as being morally superior to his brothers. But that is not saying much. In this famous story Joseph is his father's favorite and Joseph uses that favoritism in an unwise way. The narrative begins with Joseph being something of a tattletale if not an outright slanderer of his brothers (v. 2). Joseph accepts and wears the outward symbol of his father's partiality, an elaborate coat, in a way that feeds his brothers' resentment of him. Joseph unwisely chooses to inform his brothers of his dreams which seem at face value to imply that he will rule over them and even

---

[3]Genesis 49 is to be contrasted in this regard with Deuteronomy 33, the blessing of Moses, where the tribe of Levi, not Judah, is given the greatest blessing.

over his parents. This causes further resentment. By the time Joseph is sent to check up on his brothers' shepherding work, the resentment has boiled over into hatred and the planning of a murder. Reuben and Judah, two of the older brothers, prevent this from happening. But the favoritism which Joseph has gladly embraced costs him dearly. He ends up as a foreign slave in Egypt, a place not typically hospitable to Semitic people, much less Semitic slaves. The brothers use Joseph's garment dipped in goat's blood to fool Jacob into mourning his favorite son in an ironic twist on how Jacob fooled his own father into giving him the blessing above his older brother Esau.

A. DEVELOPMENT OF INTERNAL FAMILY TENSIONS AMONG JACOB'S SONS (37:2-11)

1. The Origins of the Animosity of Joseph's Brothers toward Him (37:2-4)

37:2 This is the account of Jacob. Joseph, a young man of seventeen, was tending the flocks with his brothers, the sons of Bilhah and the sons of Zilpah, his father's wives, and he brought their father a bad report about them.

The text begins with the last instance of the structural marker which the author of Genesis uses to mark the sections of Genesis.[4] While most of the ensuing narrative is about Joseph, the section mentions only Jacob. Joseph is introduced as a young man of seventeen. Jacob, while undoubtedly quite affluent by nomadic standards, still owned nothing of the Promised Land. Jacob's sons are therefore involved in the business of nomadic shepherding. In this particular case **Joseph**, the next to youngest of Jacob's twelve, was shepherding with the four sons of the concubines. In terms of their position in the hierarchical structure of the patriarchal family the sons of the secondary wives were the least loved and most despised of the children of Jacob. They were also Joseph's immediately older brothers. The favorite son worked side by side with the despised sons.

The NIV's "**bad report**" may be too tame a translation which tends to whitewash what Joseph actually did. The Hebrew word translated "report" (דִּבָּה, *dibāh*) is used of false slander (Ps 31:14; Prov 10:18; 25:10). The word is used three times to describe the "bad report" about the Promised Land which the ten spies brought to Israel (Num 13:32;

---

[4]See the discussion in Kissling, *Genesis Volume 1*, pp. 32-33.

14:36,37). It may well be that Joseph's report was actually not true or only partially true. The phrase translated "bad report" could as easily be rendered "evil slander."

37:3 Now Israel loved Joseph more than any of his other sons, because he had been born to him in his old age; and he made a richly ornamented robe for him.

In this verse no attempt is made to hide the blatant favoritism of Jacob toward Joseph. Such favoritism is condemned, at least in terms of inheritance rights, in Deuteronomy 21:15-17:

> If a man has two wives, one of them loved and the other disliked, and if both the loved and the disliked have borne him sons, the first-born being the son of the one who is disliked, then on the day when he wills his possessions to his sons, he is not permitted to treat the son of the loved as the firstborn in preference to the son of the disliked, who is the firstborn. He must acknowledge as firstborn the son of the one who is disliked, giving him a double portion of all that he has; since he is the first issue of his virility, the right of the firstborn is his. (NRSV)

Jacob is portrayed as in violation of the Torah. While he cannot be held accountable for this since the Torah had not yet been revealed, the readers, who have received the Torah, are given a glimpse of why the LORD may have given such an instruction. The consequences of jealousy sown by the father's favoritism are the hatred of the other brothers toward Joseph and their decision to sell him into slavery.

The rationale given for Jacob's favoritism is interesting. Joseph was born **in his old age**. But Benjamin was born after Joseph and yet such favoritism is not made explicit in his case. There is strikingly no mention of Jacob's love or otherwise toward his daughters. Only two of them are actually named (Dinah and Serah [46:17]) and they play no significant role in the narrative since they will not found tribes in the nation or have inheritance rights under normal circumstances.

The NIV refers to Joseph's special garment as a **richly ornamented robe**. The traditional translation, the famous "coat of many colors" of Sunday school fame is unlikely to be an accurate translation of this difficult phrase. The popular translation is based upon the Greek (χιτῶνα ποικίλον, *chitōna poikilon*) which does mean "many colored tunic." The Hebrew phrase (כְּתֹנֶת פַּסִּים, *k³tōneth passîm*) is of uncertain meaning. The only other use of the phrase is in 2 Samuel 13:18, which describes the distinctive clothing of the virgin daughters of King David. *HALOT* suggests "tunic of the palm" and then speculates what that might mean. One possibility would be a garment whose sleeves went all the way to the palm. This could fit the virgin daughters of David who might dress modestly in view of their public lives. Others suggest a tunic with finely ornamented sleeves[5] or merely richly ornamented as in the NIV. These would fit the context of the daughters of David and explain how such a fine garment was a symbol for Joseph's brothers of the extent of their father's favoritism. Another possibility is that the garment would suggest royalty or high status.[6] If so, the garment would anticipate the high status that Joseph dreams of having over his brothers. Whatever the exact nature of the garment, this passage begins the *leitmotif* of Joseph's clothing in the Joseph narrative.

37:4 When his brothers saw that their father loved him more than any of them, they hated him and could not speak a kind word to him.

The narrator is careful to record the fact Jacob loved Joseph more than his brothers before he or she records the fact that the brothers perceived this to be so. Otherwise the reader might be tempted to think that this was only their perception. But the favoritism in this family is rather overt, and it breeds deep-seated animosity to the point of hatred. Their feelings of resentment were so intense that they **could not** even **speak** a peaceable word (לְשָׁלֹם, *l*šālōm) to Joseph.

2. Further Animosity Bred by Joseph's Dreams and Their Interpretation (37:5-11)

37:5 Joseph had a dream, and when he told it to his brothers, they hated him all the more.

Dreams in the Old Testament are usually not just the normal psychological reloading and replaying which they are understood to be in our post-Jungian world. In fact one might question whether the English word "dream" is the right choice for translation purposes. A dream in the Old Testament is virtually synonymous to a vision, potentially a divine revelation. Joseph cannot in any way be faulted for having this dream.[7] The fact that he told it to his brothers, however, is a choice that he made. With that choice Joseph bears its consequences. Surely Joseph could have anticipated their reaction. Their increased hatred is quite

---

[5]Sarna, *Genesis*, p. 255.

[6]Bruce K. Waltke, *Genesis: A Commentary* (Grand Rapids: Zondervan, 2001), p. 500.

[7]Even if one presumes that Joseph produced the dream because of egotistical ambition, the dream is by definition subconscious. Joseph can hardly be expected to control his subconscious.

predictable in a family with such overt favoritism. Joseph cannot be blamed for his father's favoritism. He can, however, be questioned for the way he conducts himself toward his brothers when he knows of their resentment of him.

37:6 He said to them, "Listen to this dream I had: 37:7 We were binding sheaves of grain out in the field when suddenly my sheaf rose and stood upright, while your sheaves gathered around mine and bowed down to it."

In Joseph's first dream he was with his brothers tying together **sheaves of grain** at harvest time. The dream seems to imply a setting in which they owned the land, had planted it, and now were reaping the harvest together. Since Jacob's family did not own land in Canaan and probably had no permanent control over fields in order to plant them, the dream seems to envision a situation in the future when the promise of the land has been fulfilled.

In the dream the sheaves of Joseph and his brothers are seemingly symbolic of their lives as individuals. Joseph's sheaf stands **upright** while those of his brothers **gather around** it and **bow down** in symbolic subjection to it. Whatever Joseph's intent in telling the dream, wisdom might have dictated that he keep this one to himself. If a dream has the potential to be a divine revelation, Joseph should have known how his brothers would have interpreted it and how seriously they would view the matter.

37:8 His brothers said to him, "Do you intend to reign over us? Will you actually rule us?" And they hated him all the more because of his dream and what he had said.

While the author never gives an interpretation of the dream, Joseph's brothers think the import of it is obvious. They also assume that the source of the dream is not some form of divine revelation about what is to be in the future, but something produced out of Joseph's inflated ego.

They ask Joseph two rhetorical questions. In each the emphatic form of the Hebrew verb in used.[8] The verb in the first question implies that Joseph would be king (מָלַךְ, *mālak*) and his brothers his servants. The second question uses a more general word for "**rule**" (מָשַׁל, *māšal*). The fact that they **hate** Joseph even **more** for **his dream** indicates that they think Joseph has produced the dream from his own ego. If they had regarded the dream as a divine revelation, they could not blame

---

[8]Infinitive construct followed the finite verb of the same root. In this case the finite verbs are both in the imperfect.

Joseph for having it. They also resent Joseph for having told them the dream. This was a choice that Joseph made. Our interpretive tradition has usually led us to defend Joseph as some type of Christ. But the Joseph portrayed in this text contributes to the animosity which Jacob's favoritism has sown in the family. Whether intended or not, Joseph gives undue emphasis to his own special position over against his brothers. This certainly does not excuse their behavior toward Joseph or in any way justify their actions. It does, however, make them understandable. This is a real family with real family tensions.

37:9 Then he had another dream, and he told it to his brothers. "Listen," he said, "I had another dream, and this time the sun and moon and eleven stars were bowing down to me."

Like the other sets of dreams in the Joseph narrative, this set consists of two dreams which seem to have similar points. Given the reaction to the original dream one has to wonder about Joseph's wisdom in relating the second dream to his brothers. It is interesting that he does not first tell the dream to his father Jacob. In this dream the key verb "to bow down" (שָׁחָה, šāḥah) occurs once again. But in addition to the representation of the eleven brothers (in this case through the figure of stars) there are also two other symbolical figures, the **sun** and the **moon**. Once again the dream is not interpreted by the narrator for the readers, here or anywhere else. The dream seems to be a repeat of the first dream, but with additional details this time.

The use of sun, moon, and stars as metaphors in the dream would likely create a different reaction in modern readers than in either the original or canonical audience. The heavenly bodies were worshiped as gods in virtually all ancient cultures other than Israel and by a significant percentage of people even within Israel at the popular level. The sun, moon, and stars were powerful gods. For them to bow down to Joseph indicates a supernatural status above even the sun and moon. In this dream, unlike the first one, it is to Joseph himself, and not to some symbolic representation of him, that the bowing down occurs.

37:10 When he told his father as well as his brothers, his father rebuked him and said, "What is this dream you had? Will your mother and I and your brothers actually come and bow down to the ground before you?"

Joseph recounted (סָפַר, sāphar; the NIV has "**told**") the dream a second time[9]; this time to both his **father** and **his brothers**. Jacob is

---

[9]Hebrew has a *waw*-consecutive which probably implies a second recounting *contra* NIV.

referred to as Joseph's "father." The content of the dream seems to undermine Jacob's position as Joseph's father. This produces a rebuke from Jacob. What sort of dream did Joseph really have? Was it a divine revelation, or was it a hidden desire to master even his own father? One point often lost on commentators[10] is the fact that at least as Jacob interprets the dream, it cannot possibly come true. If Jacob is the sun and Rachel is the moon, as seems to be the case, this dream cannot find fulfillment. Rachel died giving birth to Benjamin, the eleventh star in Joseph's dream (Gen 35:16-21).[11] She never bowed down to Joseph and since she has been dead for some time, it would seem to be impossible that she do so. Jacob may be highlighting this fact by mentioning her first. The list of those who, according to a natural interpretation of the dream, will come to bow down to Joseph are his mother (impossible), his father (highly unlikely), and his brothers (possible). In fact Jacob never bows down to Joseph; Joseph bows down to Jacob (Gen 48:12). The second dream, at least as Jacob quite reasonably interprets it, does not come true. This is yet another example of a plot thread in Genesis which surprises the reader and calls upon the reader to consider why this might be so. The brothers, of course, do come to bow down before Joseph, both unknowingly (Gen 43:26) and knowingly (Gen 50:18).

37:11 His brothers were jealous of him, but his father kept the matter in mind.

The end result of the dream episode was the burning jealousy[12] of the brothers. Jacob, however, guarded the conversation without passing judgment. Ironically the brothers, who react most emotionally against the dream, are the ones who end up fulfilling it, while Jacob, who does not, ends up not being part of the fulfillment.

---

[10]This was first pointed out to me by Laurence A. Turner. See his classic *Announcements of Plot*, ch. 4.

[11]The idea that Leah became Joseph's mother by adopting him (Sidney Greidanus, *Preaching Christ from Genesis: Foundations for Expository Sermons* [Grand Rapids: Eerdmans, 2007], p. 349) seems to be a harmonizing supposition without textual support. Even if Leah is regarded as Joseph's mother, there is no evidence that she ever bowed down to Joseph. She died before the family moved to Egypt (Gen 49:31).

[12]The verb קָנָא (*qāna'*) in the piel indicates a raging jealousy.

B. JOSEPH'S BROTHERS SELL HIM AS A SLAVE IN EGYPT (37:12-36)

1. Joseph's Brothers Plot to Kill Him When He Visits Them (37:12-20)

Joseph Sent to Report on the Welfare of His Brothers (37:12-14a)

37:12 Now his brothers had gone to graze their father's flocks near Shechem, 37:13 and Israel said to Joseph, "As you know, your brothers are grazing the flocks near Shechem. Come, I am going to send you to them." "Very well," he replied. 37:14a So he said to him, "Go and see if all is well with your brothers and with the flocks, and bring word back to me." Then he sent him off from the Valley of Hebron.

Sometime after the episode with Joseph's dreams his brothers were grazing **their flocks near Shechem**. This was the place where Dinah had been raped and Jacob's angry sons had killed the Shechemites. Since Jacob and his family were living in the south near Hebron at the time, they were a good distance[13] away from home and Jacob's direct supervision. This detail may have been included to remind the reader of the episode in chapter 34 when Jacob's sons used deception and violence. It may also echo the fact that the Dinah episode, like the one about to be narrated, happened in the context of Jacob's overt favoritism among his children.

The fact that Jacob's sons had gone all the way to Shechem to find pasturage may indicate that it was hard to find for those who were only temporary residents in the land, or it may have only been a shortage in the south where they lived. Matthews suggests the possibility that this is an "early indicator"[14] of the famine to come.

The narrator speaks of Jacob as **Israel** in this passage. This is common in this section of Genesis, and the variation may be simply for the sake of variety. Another possibility is that with the new name comes a new identity. When Jacob acts like the old Jacob, scheming and deceitful, he retains his old name. This is hard to square with the actual textual data, however, and it may be a collection of things is going on in the narrator's choice of name.

Why does the narrative slow down at this point? The amount of detail given to the simple act of Jacob sending Joseph to see how his brothers are doing indicates that something crucial is about to occur. The last time Joseph reported to Jacob on how (some of) his brothers were doing, it was

---

[13]Approximately 50 miles.
[14]Matthews, *Genesis 11:27–50:26*, p. 694.

a "bad" or "evil" report. Since that time the relationship between Joseph and his brothers had degenerated yet further. Jacob's transparent favoritism and Joseph's decision to tell his brothers his own dreams only made matters worse. In sending Joseph, Jacob may have realized that there was some risk involved. Joseph had been a bit of a tattletale before. His brothers' hatred of him could easily boil over into violence. This explains why the narrator slows the narrative pace down.[15]

Jacob begins by asking Joseph whether he knows[16] that his brothers are watching over the flocks at Shechem. He then asks Joseph to come to him so that he may be sent to his brothers. This requires a response from Joseph who says, like Isaiah, "Here I am."[17] The account has the suggestion of a formal commissioning for something of great importance.

Jacob tells Joseph to go and see about the peace of his brothers and the peace of the flock. The NIV and NRSV translate the Hebrew word (שָׁלוֹם, šālôm) by "well," but this obscures the connection between this verse (v. 14) and verse 4 where the brothers were not able to speak "peaceably" to Joseph. Jacob is sending Joseph to enquire about the peace of his brothers (and of his own flocks) when those brothers could not even speak in peace to Joseph. It may well be that the slowing of the narrative pace is designed to be a clue to the reader that Jacob is fully aware of the risk of putting Joseph into such a situation. Joseph is around seventeen, a young man in ancient culture, although there is no indication that he is yet married. The trip from Hebron to Shechem (and ultimately to Dothan) was a major responsibility given to a young man traveling alone to see his brothers who hate him.

Joseph Finds His Brothers at Dothan (37:14b-17)

37:14b When Joseph arrived at Shechem, 37:15 a man found him wandering around in the fields and asked him, "What are you looking for?" 37:16 He replied, "I'm looking for my brothers. Can you tell me where they are grazing their flocks?" 37:17 "They have moved on from here," the man answered. "I heard them say, 'Let's go to Dothan.'" So Joseph went after his brothers and found them near Dothan.

Joseph went to Shechem but was unable to find his brothers. Since Jacob's family would have only recently moved from Shechem, the place was undoubtedly familiar to Joseph. An unnamed man found Joseph wan-

---

[15]On the difference between "narration time" and "narrated time" and how Hebrew narrative uses the latter to give emphasis, see Shimon Bar-Efrat, *Narrative Art in the Bible*, JSOTS 70 (Sheffield: Almond, 1989), pp. 141-184.

[16]Or merely reminding him of what he does know.

[17]הִנֵּנִי (hinnēnî), literally, "behold me!"; cf. Isa 6:8. NIV is paraphrastic here.

dering like a lost sheep[18] and asked what he was seeking. For some unspecified reason the man knew who Joseph's brothers were and informed him that they had said they were going on **to Dothan**. Perhaps this man's knowledge came from the time that Jacob's family lived there and his sons killed the Shechemites. Dothan, if the site be correctly identified, was about 14 miles north of Shechem. The brothers had moved even farther away from their father, perhaps in search of adequate pasturage.

One has to ask why these details are included. What difference does it make that Joseph did not find his brothers at Shechem? Once again the narrative pace slows down as the event of Joseph's near murder and actual enslavement approach. It may be for this reason that the detail is given. In any case Joseph finds his brothers after a long journey and an equally long search.

Joseph's Brothers Plot to Kill Him (37:18-20)

37:18 But they saw him in the distance, and before he reached them, they plotted to kill him. 37:19 "Here comes that dreamer!" they said to each other. 37:20 "Come now, let's kill him and throw him into one of these cisterns and say that a ferocious animal devoured him. Then we'll see what comes of his dreams."

As Joseph was making his way to meet his brothers, **they saw him in the distance** and quickly **plotted to kill him**. They sarcastically referred to Joseph as "this lord of dreams" (בַּעַל הַחֲלֹמוֹת הַלָּזֶה, *ba'al hahǎlōmôth hallāzeh*). The cumulative effect of the open favoritism of Jacob and Joseph's interactions with them has born its fruit. Resentment unchecked is about to spill over into violence. Their plan is to murder Joseph and throw his body into a **cistern**, and tell Jacob that he was **devoured** by an "evil" **animal** (חַיָּה רָעָה, *ḥayyāh rā'āh*)[19]. They think that in so doing they will be able to falsify Joseph's dreams. In fact, as the ensuing narrative will show, they are actually assisting in the fulfillment of those resented dreams, or at least one of them. As Joseph later says, "You thought to do me evil; God thought of it for good" (Gen 50:20).

---

[18]תָּעָה (*tā'āh*) often refers to lost animals (Ps 119:176; Isa 53:6; Exod 23:4). Interestingly it also is used of "wandering" away from God (e.g., Ezek 44:10).

[19]The use of the word usually translated "evil" to describe an animal may be an allusion to the Garden of Eden narrative.

2. Reuben Tries to Save Joseph, but Judah Actually Does
(37:21-30,36)

Reuben Convinces His Brothers Not to Kill Joseph (Reuben Plans to Rescue Joseph) (37:21-22)

37:21 When Reuben heard this, he tried to rescue him from their hands. "Let's not take his life," he said. 37:22 "Don't shed any blood. Throw him into this cistern here in the desert, but don't lay a hand on him." Reuben said this to rescue him from them and take him back to his father.

We discover that the brothers are not all of one mind. **Reuben**, the firstborn, delivered him[20] **from their hands**. The means of deliverance which Reuben used were persuasive words. He begins by including himself in the plea. "Let *us* not take his life." He then shifts to the imperative, **"Don't shed blood."** The alternative would be to **throw him into a cistern in the desert**. The logic would seem to be that allowing the elements to take Joseph's life would somehow absolve them of some part of the responsibility for, and therefore the consequences of, murder. The narrator informs readers about Reuben's real motives, something relatively rare in Hebrew narrative. He did not have the authority or the power to stop them from taking their revenge on Joseph. His plan was to secretly rescue him and return him to his father.

Joseph's Brothers Cast Him into the Cistern (37:23-24)

37:23 So when Joseph came to his brothers, they stripped him of his robe—the richly ornamented robe he was wearing— 37:24 and they took him and threw him into the cistern. Now the cistern was empty; there was no water in it.

When Joseph finally arrived, we find out that he was wearing the special tunic that Jacob had given him. This seems to be rather formal attire for a meeting with shepherds in the field! It is probably indicative of Joseph's attitude. Unlike contemporary literature, physical description of biblical characters is minimal, and when it does occur, it is usually significant for the plot.[21] By wearing the garment which is the very embodiment of Jacob's favoritism, Joseph is rubbing his brothers' noses in it. This does not absolve them of responsibility for their violence and callousness. Joseph's lack of tact and good sense is, however, highlighted.

---

[20]The NIV's "tried to deliver" is conjecture. The Hebrew says straightforwardly "he delivered him."

[21]See Kissling, *Reliable Characters*, p. 19.

The narrator dwells on this point by the way the garment is described — "his tunic, his tunic of the palm" the same terminology used when Jacob gave the garment to him in verse 3.

After **stripping** Joseph of his tunic, his brothers **threw him into the cistern** as Reuben had suggested. Since the cistern was dry, there was no danger of Joseph drowning in it, undoubtedly a part of Reuben's plan. The narrator emphasizes this fact by the repetitive description of the cistern — it **was empty; there was no water in it.**

Judah Convinces His Brothers to Enslave Joseph Rather Than Kill Him (37:25-28)

37:25 As they sat down to eat their meal, they looked up and saw a caravan of Ishmaelites coming from Gilead. Their camels were loaded with spices, balm and myrrh, and they were on their way to take them down to Egypt.

The callousness of the brothers is shown by the fact that, immediately after throwing their own brother into a cistern, they sat down to enjoy a meal. God's timing is everything in the Joseph narrative. Having just decided to let Joseph die of exposure in the cistern, they "coincidentally" see a caravan of Ishmaelite traders crossing the Jordan from Gilead on their way to Egypt. "Coincidentally" Judah suggests the idea of selling Joseph as a slave to them. Canaan was at the center of trade in the ancient Near East. Goods from Arabia and Mesopotamia were most easily shipped to the Mediterranean and North Africa through Canaan.

Once again the seemingly unnecessary details of **camels, spices, balm, and myrrh** raise the question of why the narrative pace is slowed here. The allegorical tendencies of the church fathers read into this passage a parallel between Joseph being stripped of his robe and Christ being stripped of his robe.[22] They forgot that only the verse before records that Joseph wore the garment which showed his father's favoritism in order to remind his brothers of his status, something singularly un-Christlike.

For the original audience, this passage is the beginning of the explanation of why the descendants of Jacob ended up living in Egypt for such a long time. Joseph's enslavement in Egypt recalled Israel's own enslavement there. That enslavement was the result of the internal tensions among Jacob's sons. While God used these events in his provi-

---

[22]Mark Sheridan, ed., *Genesis 12–50*, Ancient Christian Commentary on Scripture (Downers Grove, IL: InterVarsity Press, 2002), pp. 237-238.

dence, the nation should learn the lesson that only by living by God's standards will the nation avoid slavery (and exile) and enjoy the benefits of the Promised Land.

37:26 Judah said to his brothers, "What will we gain if we kill our brother and cover up his blood?

For some unexplained reason Reuben is not present during this time. But in his hidden providence God was guiding the conversation. The hidden providence of God is a theme of the Joseph story. God is much less conspicuous in this section of Genesis than he has been previously.[23] This time **Judah** comes to the fore. His argumentation is not primarily ethical but pragmatic. He does not argue at first that it would be morally wrong to kill Joseph. Instead he says, **What will we gain** by killing him? The word translated "gain" (בֶּצַע, *beṣaʿ*)[24] is usually used of profit (often financial) by the abuse of others where those in power misuse their authority for their own benefit. Judah reminds his brothers that Joseph is **our brother**. Killing a brother would be especially heinous, and so the moral argument is hinted at. But Judah only slips in this consideration. The primary argument is pragmatic.

37:27 Come, let's sell him to the Ishmaelites and not lay our hands on him; after all, he is our brother, our own flesh and blood." His brothers agreed.

The "gain" that Judah alluded to is now clarified. If they would **sell** Joseph to the Ishmaelite traders who are passing by, they would at least gain financially. In this way they could avoid the moral culpability of violently laying their hands on Joseph. Judah ends with a moral argument, although it is a flawed ethnocentric one. It would be wrong to lay hands on "our brother, our flesh."[25] Judah does not even consider that it would be wrong to kill another human being. It is only wrong, according to Judah, when that human being shares their own flesh.

This tangled mess of an argument in which pragmatic consideration, money, and family solidarity are used as moral persuasion shows just where the incipient nation is. From the very first days as a family the internal seeds of their own destruction were sown in Israel. This text points this out to the original and canonical audiences. Judah's brothers agree with his (im)moral reasoning. The tribe from which king David

---

[23]I am grateful to Laurence Turner for reminding me of this.

[24]The word can be used more generally (Job 22:3; Ps 30:10; Mal 3:14). It is usually used of bribes (Exod 18:21; 1 Sam 8:3; Prov 15:27; Isa 33:15) or other forms of gain which the powerful achieve by illegitimate means.

[25]The NIV periphrases here.

descended was founded by the person who spared Joseph's life by convincing his brothers to sell him as a slave to traders who would sell him
to the Egyptians. Even the royal tribe is not exempt from the implicit
condemnation. Judah is only morally superior in relative terms.

**37:28 So when the Midianite merchants came by, his brothers pulled
Joseph up out of the cistern and sold him for twenty shekels of silver
to the Ishmaelites, who took him to Egypt.**

The brothers'[26] cruel treatment of Joseph may be hinted at by the
description. The Hebrew text reads literally "Then they dragged (מָשַׁךְ,
māšak) him, and then they lifted Joseph from the cistern." The price of
the sale was the going rate for slaves in the first half of the second millennium in the ancient Near East.[27] Later on the price rose to thirty
shekels of silver, the price paid for the betrayal of Jesus.

In this verse the traders are referred to as both **Midianite merchants**
and **Ishmaelites**. This is a commonly cited proof text for the use of (conflicting) sources in the composition of the Pentateuch. But in order for
such a conclusion to be drawn, one must imagine a redactor who is so
incompetent that he leaves in place from his sources a transparent contradiction within a single sentence. Another explanation which does not
require implausibly imagining an incompetent redactor must be sought.
One possibility is that the Hebrew phrase, "men of Midian [who were]
wandering traders,"[28] indicates where they were from and not their
genetic makeup. They were actually of Ishmaelite stock although they
hailed from the land of Midian. Another possibility is to note that the
two terms, Ishmaelite and Midianite overlap in their referents.[29]

Both descriptions would appear to be historically anachronistic.
Midian was the fourth son of Abraham's third wife Keturah (Gen 21:1)
while Ishmael was Abraham's first son through Hagar. As such Midian
and Ishmael were of the same generation as Jacob's father and his sons'
grandfather Isaac. There was no time for the nations of Midian and

---

[26]The NIV emphasizes the special heinousness of the crime by referring to the
nine sons of Jacob as Joseph's "brothers." They sold their own brother into slavery! The Hebrew has merely "they."

[27]Hoffmeier, *Israel in Egypt*, pp. 83-84, referring to Kitchen, "Twenty shekels
(Gen. 37:28) is the average price for slaves during the first half of the second millennium whereas in the second half of that millennium, owing to inflation, the
price was up to thirty shekels. By the first millennium, when many believe the
Genesis story originated, the price had risen to fifty or sixty shekels."

[28]The NIV paraphrases this as "Midianite merchants."

[29]Judges 8:24, referring to plunder from the battle with Midian, says, "It was
the custom of the Ishmaelites to wear gold earrings."

Ishmael to arise. More likely the author uses later terms with which the audience would be familiar. By the time of the writing and canonization of the Pentateuch the place called Midian in northwestern Arabia was well known and the ascription of "Ishmaelite" to traders was also well known.

Reuben Returns to See Joseph Gone (37:29-30)

37:29 When Reuben returned to the cistern and saw that Joseph was not there, he tore his clothes. 37:30 He went back to his brothers and said, "The boy isn't there! Where can I turn now?"

For some unexplained reason **Reuben** had been gone when Judah suggested selling Joseph as a slave. Upon his return he was shocked and grieved to find **that Joseph was not there**. He had intended to secretly free Joseph and take him back to his father's protection. Reuben expresses his horror by tearing his clothing, an ancient way of expressing extreme negative emotions such as grief and anger (1 Sam 4:12; 2 Sam 3:31; 13:31; Job 1:20). Clothing was expensive in the ancient world and tearing it showed just how deeply the person who did so had been impacted by the event.

Evidently the cistern was not in the immediate view of the brothers because Reuben has to go to them after discovering that Joseph was gone. Reuben refers to Joseph as a child (יֶלֶד, *yeled*).[30] The mournful words of Reuben are powerfully poetic in the original.[31] Already in trouble for his affair with Bilhah, now the firstborn son has failed to protect his young brother, his father's favorite at that! How will he explain it? Where can he even go, now that Joseph is gone?

3. The Brothers Fool Jacob into Assuming That Joseph Is Dead (37:31-35)

37:31 Then they got Joseph's robe, slaughtered a goat and dipped the robe in the blood.

The answer to Reuben's anguished cry is to cover up what they have done. The garment which was given to Joseph to show Jacob's special favor will now, in a delicious sort of irony for the other sons, be the means of proving his death. Reuben and the other brothers will be able

---

[30]Not the narrator's description of him as a "young man" (נַעַר, *na'ar*) of seventeen.

[31]Reuben's words, הַיֶּלֶד אֵינֶנּוּ וַאֲנִי אָנָה אֲנִי־בָא (*hayyeled 'ênennû wa'ănî 'ānāh 'ănî bā'*) repeat the "a" "î" and "nah" sounds in a poetic way.

to lie their way out of their responsibility by pretending to have found Joseph's garment. An animal is sacrificed from the flock so that its blood can be presented as Joseph's blood, implying a fatal fight with a wild animal.

37:32 They took the ornamented robe back to their father and said, "We found this. Examine it to see whether it is your son's robe."

The Hebrew may suggest that at first the brothers sent[32] the robe with long sleeves to Jacob and then[33] went to see him. Once again the narrator uses the long description of the robe to remind readers that this was the very robe given to Joseph to show Jacob's special love for him. Notice it is not described as "Joseph's robe" or "our brother's robe" but **"your son's robe."** The brothers unwittingly show their emotional distance from Joseph and Jacob. They let Jacob come to the conclusion.

37:33 He recognized it and said, "It is my son's robe! Some ferocious animal has devoured him. Joseph has surely been torn to pieces." 37:34 Then Jacob tore his clothes, put on sackcloth and mourned for his son many days. 37:35 All his sons and daughters came to comfort him, but he refused to be comforted. "No," he said, "in mourning will I go down to the grave to my son." So his father wept for him.

When Jacob looked at the robe he knew it was the very one he had given to his favorite son to demonstrate his favor. Jacob could only conclude[34] that an evil animal had eaten Joseph since his sons brought him only the robe and no part of his dead body. Jacob emphasizes the tragedy of the violent death which he presumes Joseph had experienced by using an emphatic construction[35] of the verb used to describe a lion (e.g., Deut 33:20; Ps 7:3; 17:12; 22:14; Jer 5:6) or a wolf (e.g., Gen 49:27) tearing apart its prey.

Jacob demonstrated his grief in customary ancient Near Eastern fashion by tearing his outer garment, putting on **sackcloth** and mourning for his son a long time. "His son" had died. The fact that he still had eleven other sons plus daughters was of no comfort.

---

[32]The Hebrew uses the verb שָׁלַח (šālaḥ) in the piel, usually meaning "to send off."

[33]The Hebrew has a *waw*-consecutive here.

[34]Sidney Greidanus, *Preaching Christ from Genesis*, p. 354, helpfully notes "Ironically, Jacob's sons seek to deceive their old father with their brother's robe and goat's blood, just as Jacob had earlier used his brother's garments and two little goats to deceive his blind father Isaac."

[35]Qal infinitive absolute followed by the perfect, both of the verb טָרַף (ṭāraph). The NIV uses the word "surely" to indicate this emphatic construction.

In grief, even after a long period of mourning, Jacob claimed that he would go down to Sheol, that is die, still **in mourning** for his son. The reader feels for Jacob's loss, but one wonders whether the extreme grief is somehow tied to the fact that Joseph was his favorite.

4. Joseph Ends Up as Potiphar's Servant (37:36)

37:36 Meanwhile, the Midianites sold Joseph in Egypt to Potiphar, one of Pharaoh's officials, the captain of the guard.

With Jacob still in grief over what he thinks is the death of Joseph, the narrator reminds the readers that Joseph's story will continue. **The Midianites sold Joseph** to the Egyptians, specifically **to Potiphar**, one of Pharaoh's eunuchs,[36] and captain of Pharaoh's select body guard. This of course gives Joseph a potential connection in high places. In retrospect we see in this the providential hand of God.

---

[36]The Hebrew סָרִיס (*sārîs*), as here, does not necessarily mean a literal eunuch. Potiphar is married, and there is no reason to assume that he had been literally castrated.

GENESIS 38

I. JUDAH'S STORY BEGINS BADLY (38:1-30)

With Joseph in Egyptian slavery, the narrative returns to the family in Canaan with the focus on Judah. Judah's story begins badly. Instead of remaining with his brothers and seeking to marry within the larger family, Judah follows his uncle Esau's example and marries a Canaanite woman. This leads to three sons, Er, Onan, and Shelah. Er marries Tamar and dies under the LORD's judgment for his evil. Onan, bound by ancient custom, is obligated to take Tamar as his wife, with the first son of their union counting as Er's heir, not his own. While Onan happily has sexual relations, he uses *coitus interruptus* to avoid impregnating Tamar. This brings the LORD's judgment on Onan who also dies. Judah then asks Tamar to remain as a widow, but in her father's house, while waiting for his youngest son Shelah to be old enough to marry her. This turns out to be a ploy as Shelah is never given to Tamar, and she is left without the right to marry and the means to live independently without marriage. Tamar, recognizing that by ancient custom Judah himself was obligated to take her if his sons could not, disguises herself as a prosti tute in order to entice Judah into meeting his obligation to take her in levirate marriage. The union results in a pregnancy which results in the birth of twin boys, the forefathers of the two major clans in the tribe of Judah. Judah does come to recognition that despite the means that Tamar used, she had been more righteous than he in the situation.

One of the primary purposes of levirate marriage was to protect women who would otherwise be left without any means of survival. It also ensured that the inheritance of sons who died unusually early would be preserved. Judah, instead of meeting his responsibility abandons Tamar, leaving her in an untenable situation. From this low point Judah, as a character in the narrative, undergoes a transformation into the leader of the brothers who receives Jacob's greatest blessing.

In traditional historical-critical approaches this chapter has been viewed as an interruption to the Joseph narrative, and therefore, secondary. This conclusion, however, fails to account for the many ways in which this chapter echoes the rest of the Joseph narrative and is echoed there. The same verb (יָרַד, *yārad*) is used of Joseph who was "forced to go down" to Egypt (39:1) and of Judah who voluntarily "went down" from his brothers (38:1). The same verbal construction (הַכֶּר־נָא, *hakker-na'*) is used of the brothers who ask Jacob to please identify Joseph's bloodied robe (37:32) and of Tamar who asks Judah to please identify Judah's personal items (38:25b). The same verb is used to confirm that they did identify the items requested. Jacob refused to be "consoled" at the death of Joseph (37:35) while Judah, by contrast, was "consoled" over the death of his wife (38:12).[1] Joseph's response to the temptation of a sexual liaison with a foreign woman is in marked contrast to Judah's. Joseph refuses to be seduced after repeated attempts by a superior while Judah initiates a relationship with a prostitute.[2] The presence of this story in Genesis argues strongly against the idea that the book is a postexilic fiction as is often presumed in historical-critical approaches. The Judean exiles would have no good reason to invent such a story about the forefather and many reasons to suppress it.[3]

A. JUDAH ABANDONS TAMAR (38:1-12)

1. Judah's Family through Marriage to a Canaanite Woman (38:1-5)

38:1 At that time, Judah left his brothers and went down to stay with a man of Adullam named Hirah.

The narrative has an indefinite chronological relationship (וַיְהִי בָּעֵת הַהִוא, *wayᵉhî bā'ēth hahiw'*)[4] to the narratives about Joseph in which it is embedded. It has been argued since the time of the Rabbis that if Genesis 46:12 is read in its normal sense, then Judah's grandsons/sons were born in the land of Canaan. If so, then there is not enough time for Judah to marry and raise two sons to adulthood and then unwittingly impregnate his daughter-in-law, Tamar before the move to Egypt.[5] Either the genealogy in chapter 46 is not counting only

---

[1]In both instances the Hebrew verb נָחַם (*nāḥām*) is used.

[2]The story of Joseph and Potiphar is designed as a foil to the story of Tamar's success in seducing Judah in chapter 38. Cf. A. Shinan and Y. Zakovitch, *The Story of Judah and Tamar* (Jerusalem: Magnes, 1992), pp. 220-222.

[3]My thanks to Gary Hall for reminding me of this.

[4]"It was at that time" is imprecise.

[5]Yairah Amit, *Reading Biblical Narratives: Literary Criticism and the Hebrew Bible*, trans. by Yael Lotan (Minneapolis: Fortress, 2001), p. 144.

those born in Canaan before the move to Egypt, or the events recorded in chapter 38 must be assumed to have happened earlier.

But this rests on questionable suppositions. Joseph was about seventeen when he was sold into slavery (37:2) and thirty when he began serving in Pharaoh's house (41:46). Including the seven plentiful years (41:47) and two years of famine (45:6) he was about 39 when his brothers visited him. This makes 22 or so years between the events of chapter 37 and the events of chapter 42. Considering that men often married quite young in the ancient world this is just enough time for Judah to marry, raise two sons to adulthood, be widowed, and have a baby with Tamar.

The readers are not informed of exactly why Judah chose at this particular time to live away from his brothers. Given the context of the sale of Joseph into slavery and the reaction of his oldest brother Reuben and his father Jacob to losing Joseph, those events may have influenced Judah's decision. The use of the verb "went down" (*yārad*) is interesting. This might imply going down in elevation from the central hill country where there was more open space for nomadic herdsmen to the plains nearer the Mediterranean where urban Canaanite civilization was more dominant. Adullam, the place where Judah settled, was on the so-called "Shephelah" and was eventually the westernmost fortified city in the tribe of Judah.

The verb behind the NIV's "**stay**" (נָטָה, *nāṭāh*, "to stretch out, to pitch a tent") is also interesting. While the verb is often used of "pitching" a tent (Gen 12:8; 26:25; 35:21), a tent is not mentioned in this text. It may be being used metaphorically of Judah stretching out culturally and religiously as well as literally stretching out the cloth of a tent. The original and canonical audiences were well aware of the dangers of associating too closely with Canaanite culture. This narrative serves as a warning of the problems which this can present and yet also a reminder that individual "Canaanites" may have as much or more potential for faithfulness as Israelites.

38:2 There Judah met the daughter of a Canaanite man named Shua. He married her and lay with her;

Judah follows the bad example of his uncle Esau in marrying outside the chosen family (Gen 24:3-4; 27:46–28:2). The danger for Israel of living so close culturally to the Canaanites was intermarriage and the ensuing loss of faithfulness to the LORD (Deut 7:3-4). Judah's story is an example of that danger. Judah "saw"[6] **the daughter of a Canaanite man** and took her and had sexual relations with her.

---

[6]The NIV paraphrases the Hebrew רָאָה (*rā'āh*), "to see," as "met."

The fact that the author uses "Canaanite" to describe the man indicates her or his point of view. The LXX has **Shua** as the name of the woman. The name means "Cry for help." The rapid pace of "saw," "took," and "went into" is a warning of how easily Israelite men could be attracted to Canaanite women by their physical lusts.[7] The fact that Judah's wife is not named may also reflect this. For him she is more an object of his sexual attraction than a person.

38:3 she became pregnant and gave birth to a son, who was named Er. 38:4 She conceived again and gave birth to a son and named him Onan. 38:5 She gave birth to still another son and named him Shelah. It was at Kezib that she gave birth to him.

The births of Judah's first three sons are recorded. For some unstated reason Judah named the first son, **Er**, while his wife named the second and third sons, **Onan** and **Shelah**. Shelah[8] was born **at Kezib**,[9] a town near Adullam from which his wife came. The Hebrew reads "*He* was at Kezib when she gave birth to him." This may indicate that Judah had moved away from his Canaanite father-in-law, Shua, perhaps leaving his wife behind to have her third child. According to Spina, Judah seems more and more removed with the birth of each successive son. For the first he is present and names him. For the second we assume he is present, but his wife names the son. For the third son, Judah may not even be present for the birth.[10]

The original audience might well notice the blessing of fertility on the forefather of one of the dominant tribes of the nation of Israel. Er's name means "watchful" while Onan's means "strong, vigorous." Shelah's name means, "drawn out" perhaps referring to his birth.[11]

---

[7]Frank Anthony Spina, *The Faith of the Outsider: Exclusion and Inclusion in the Biblical Story* (Grand Rapids: Eerdmans, 2005), p. 37: "[Judah's interactions] seem to have been casual as well, for there is not the slightest degree of anguish indicated in the narrative when Judah marries a Canaanite woman 'at first sight.' In the space of a single sentence (and only two verbs) Judah 'sees' and 'marries' a Canaanite woman as though the two actions are one."

[8]The LXX has all three sons born at Kezib.

[9]Evidently an alternative name for Achzib in Judah (Josh 15:44).

[10]Spina (*Faith of the Outsider*, pp. 40-41) makes much of the fact that, as he interprets the Hebrew, Judah was not present at the birth. For Spina this shows a calloused and misogynist attitude. Besides the fact that the NIV, while periphrastic, could be accurate in this reading, Spina seems to project modern attitudes about what defines a good father onto an ancient situation and then judges Judah for not meeting modern expectations. This seems anachronistic.

[11]Matthews, *Genesis 11:27–50:26*, p. 715.

2. Judah's First Two Sons Die under Divine Judgment
While Married to Tamar (38:6-10)

38:6 Judah got a wife for Er, his firstborn, and her name was Tamar. 38:7 But Er, Judah's firstborn, was wicked in the Lord's sight; so the LORD put him to death.

In rapid fashion Judah's son is old enough to marry. Judah took a wife named **Tamar** for his firstborn son. Tamar, whose name means "palm tree," may well have been a Canaanite woman. It is interesting to note that the normal terminology for marriage in Hebrew ("take a wife") is used of Judah arranging a marriage for his oldest son. Perhaps there was some form of force involved. In any case, **Er** was "evil" (רַע, *ra‘*) **in the LORD's**[12] **sight**. Because of this evil the LORD killed him. The author is not interested in exactly why this happened. The author's interest is in the fact that Er's death required Judah's next oldest son to step in for him and marry Tamar. The contemporary reader struggles with texts like this one. It is as though the creator of the universe does not have the right to determine who lives and who dies and when these things are to happen. God's longsuffering mercy throughout the scripture gives us ample reassurance that whatever the nature of Er's evil, the punishment was just. We sometimes bring to the scriptures a distorted view of human rights and see no reason not to enforce those standards on the God of the Bible. The Bible simply isn't interested in the exact nature of Er's evil.

For some reason the fact that Er was Judah's firstborn is of importance as it is not necessary for the plot, and it is mentioned twice. God often passes over the firstborn in Genesis. Sometimes because of the sinful choices they make (Cain, Reuben), and sometimes through no fault of their own.

38:8 Then Judah said to Onan, "Lie with your brother's wife and fulfill your duty to her as a brother-in-law to produce offspring for your brother." 38:9 But Onan knew that the offspring would not be his; so whenever he lay with his brother's wife, he spilled his semen on the ground to keep from producing offspring for his brother. 38:10 What he did was wicked in the Lord's sight; so he put him to death also.

In such a situation as referred to here the law in Deuteronomy 25:5-10 said the brother was to marry his brother's widow and the first male child born would be regarded as his brother's and inherit accordingly. But the law had not yet been given. We have yet another example of the

---

[12]The Hebrew has the tetragrammaton יהוה (*yahweh*) here, so the lack of capitalization in the NIV is perplexing.

patriarchs obeying the law before the law was given.[13] Somehow Judah knew of the law of levirate marriage before the LORD made it mandatory for Israel. Whether this came by a type of natural revelation or an actual but unmentioned revelation is uncertain. As noted below there is ancient Near Eastern precedent from non-Israelite law codes. The point for the audience would be that the laws revealed to Israel at Sinai and Moab were not new laws without precedent. They were known in part to the founding fathers of the nation before they even went to Egypt.

For some unstated reason Judah regards it as his duty to ensure that his oldest son has offspring. Unlike the law in Deuteronomy 25, there is no indication in the text that Onan could have refused. It may be Onan did not want to disregard his father and so capitulated even though he technically had the right to refuse. On the other hand, Onan took advantage of the situation on numerous occasions[14] for his own sexual pleasure.

Onan's strategy was subtle. By the use of *coitus interruptus* he was able to avoid giving a child to his brother. Far from being an implicit condemnation of birth control, this strategy was designed to avoid obedience to the law of God. That law was designed to protect the vulnerable, help ensure the economic stability of the extended family, and keep the memory of a deceased brother alive. Without children, in particular sons, to care for her, Tamar would be placed in a dangerous situation. In the ancient world widows often had no means of basic economic support without a husband. If Tamar married outside of the family, assuming that was an option available to her, the resources which Judah had given to Er for the bride price would be lost to the family. Further, Er's name would be completely lost as there would be no heir to carry his line forward.

It is not surprising to the original and canonical readers that Onan's refusal to perform his duty while pretending to do so, was a serious offense. His action is just as evil in the LORD's eyes as his brother Er's had been. The consequent divine judgment is also the same.

3. Judah Fails to Give Shelah to Tamar in Levirate Marriage (38:11-12)

38:11 Judah then said to his daughter-in-law Tamar, "Live as a widow in your father's house until my son Shelah grows up." For he thought,

---

[13]See the discussion of this theme at Genesis 26:5 above.

[14]וְהָיָה אִם־בָּא (*wᵊhāyāh 'im-bā'*) implies a frequent action (Waltke and O'Connor, *Biblical Hebrew Syntax*, p. 539). On the use of אִם (*'im*) to introduce a temporal clause see Numbers 21:9, GKC, 164d.

"He may die too, just like his brothers." So Tamar went to live in her father's house.

Evidently as Judah understood the legal principle, the next person who should keep alive the inheritance of his older brother(s) is Judah's third son Shelah. According to Judah, Shelah was not old enough to be an appropriate partner to Tamar. On this supposed basis Judah asked Tamar not to seek a quick resolution to her problem but to remain **a widow** and live **in [her] father's house** (and at his expense) until Shelah was old enough to consummate a levirate marriage with Tamar. Shelah was apparently not yet married.[15]

In an example of "interior monologue" the reader is given access to Judah's thoughts.[16] His real concern was not with the age and maturity of Shelah but with the fact that his one remaining son might suffer the same fate as his other sons who had married Tamar and ended up dying under the LORD's judgment. Tamar had been an "unlucky" wife, and Judah did not want to risk his own future posterity in order to conform to a law or custom of the times. This, of course, put Tamar in a quite vulnerable situation as she could not remarry someone else and had no husband or children to care for her should her father die.

38:12 After a long time Judah's wife, the daughter of Shua, died. When Judah had recovered from his grief, he went up to Timnah, to the men who were shearing his sheep, and his friend Hirah the Adullamite went with him.

The narrative skips forward to several (many?) years later. Shelah was by now of marriageable age and had not been given to Tamar. **Judah's wife . . . died.**[17] Judah grieved for his wife, but after a time it was back to the business of making a living by herding sheep. Judah, now a widower, traveled to **Timnah**, with his friend **Hirah**, for the annual sheep shearing. Timnah was in the northern part of what later became the tribe of Judah's territory and was originally given to the tribe of Dan. By the time the nation of Israel had come out of Egypt, it seems that the Philistines were already occupying the coastal strip near where Timnah was. It is not clear why Hirah's name comes up again unless it is to portray Judah as making and continuing friendships with Canaanites.

---

[15]We do not know whether Onan was already married when he took Tamar as a levirate wife. She may have been a second wife. But according to Judah, Shelah was not yet old enough to have a wife.

[16]While the Hebrew uses the verb אָמַר (*'āmar*) to refer to this, in these instances it evidently means that Judah "spoke to himself." On interior speech in Hebrew narrative, see Bar-Efrat, *Narrative Art*, pp. 53-64.

[17]It is interesting that she is unnamed. She is only known by the men in her life. She was the daughter of Shua and the wife of Judah.

B. TAMAR TRICKS JUDAH INTO IMPREGNATING HER
(38:13-26)

1. Tamar Tricks Judah into Sex with Her (38:13-18)

38:13 When Tamar was told, "Your father-in-law is on his way to Timnah to shear his sheep," 38:14 she took off her widow's clothes, covered herself with a veil to disguise herself, and then sat down at the entrance to Enaim, which is on the road to Timnah. For she saw that, though Shelah had now grown up, she had not been given to him as his wife.

The widowed Tamar now saw an opportunity to get out of the situation in which Judah had put her. Upon hearing of Judah's trip to Timnah for the sheep shearing, she disguised herself by changing out of **her widow's** garments and donning **a veil**. She made herself available to the recently widowed Judah at **Enaim on the road to Timnah**. The word Enaim literally means "opening of the eyes." The narrator seems to be hinting at the irony of Judah being blinded to the identity of the prostitute at a place named "Open Eyes." A further touch of irony is that Judah follows the path of his grandfather Isaac and father Jacob in being blinded as to the identity of a disguised person at a crucial point in his life's story.[18]

She waited at a crossroads, which may have signaled her intent to Judah. She did this because she realized that Judah had no intention of honoring his promise to give his son Shelah in levirate marriage to her. By now he was a young man and nothing had happened. Judah had asked her to live as a widow and now she tricks him when he is a widower.

Matthews points out that ancient Near Eastern law included the father-in-law in the line of levirate responsibility.[19] He refers to Middle Assyrian Law 33 and Hittite Law 193. The meaning of the first is ambiguous in the latest standard translation. But the second has been recently translated by Hoffner: "If a man has a wife, and the man dies, his brother shall take his widow as wife. (If the brother dies,) his father shall take her."[20] It may be that Tamar is tricking Judah into following a widespread ancient Near Eastern custom that he was refusing to obey to her detriment.

---

[18]One wonders whether Isaiah's comment about the nation as a blind servant (Isa 42:19) somehow echoes these three stories about Isaac, Jacob, and Judah.

[19]Matthews, *Genesis 11:27–50:26*, p. 707.

[20]*COS II*, p. 118. Hoffner dates these laws to the Old Hittite Kingdom (ca. 1650–1500 BC). They would, therefore be earlier than the Mosaic law but later than Hammurabi.

38:15 When Judah saw her, he thought she was a prostitute, for she had covered her face. 38:16 Not realizing that she was his daughter-in-law, he went over to her by the roadside and said, "Come now, let me sleep with you." "And what will you give me to sleep with you?" she asked.

Prostitutes did not typically cover their faces.[21] But Judah would have recognized her as **his daughter-in-law** if she had not covered her face.[22] That Tamar had to trick Judah into having intercourse with her indicates that for Judah such a relationship was a forbidden incestuous one. Miller argues that this is because of the intergenerational nature of the relationship, noting that other relationships in Genesis which we as modern people would regard as incestuous are passed over without any indication that they are inappropriate.[23]

But while Judah was opposed to incestuous relationships, he is portrayed as though he sees nothing wrong in consorting with a prostitute. The Hebrew text indicates this by using an unusual verb[24] to describe Judah approaching Tamar. We must always remind ourselves that Old Testament characters are not Christians and are not typically portrayed as being moral models for Christians or any other sort of reader.

Even more shocking for the imagined audience is the fact that Hirah, at least, assumes that she is a cult prostitute (cf. v. 21), something which Israel was to avoid. And yet the forefather of the most prominent tribe is portrayed as being guilty of having sexual relations with a woman who could be a (cult?) prostitute.[25] It is even possible that the spring sheep shearing would be an appropriate time for Judah to consort with a cult prostitute if he has begun to adopt the pagan beliefs of his friend Hirah.[26]

---

[21]Sarna (*Genesis*, p. 268) notes that Middle Assyrian laws required an unmarried cult prostitute never to be veiled, with a strict punishment for violation (cf. *ANET*, p. 183, paragraph 40). He also notes (p. 170) that in the same law code a veil, far from being the garb of a prostitute, was a sign of high social status. The difficulty with drawing such parallels is knowing whether the Middle Assyrian laws were typical practice in the ANE or particular to Assyria.

[22]The word "for" (כִּי, *kî*) here does not give the reason why Judah thought she was a prostitute, but the reason he did not recognize that she was not a prostitute.

[23]Miller, "Sexual Offences," pp. 43, 48.

[24]נָטָה (*nāṭāh*), the same verb used in 38:1 to speak of Judah stretching out his tent to stay with Hirah.

[25]While recent scholarship has questioned the existence of "sacred prostitution" in Canaan, J.M. Sprinkle ("Sexuality, Sexual Ethics," *DOTP*, p. 750) argues that such passages as 1 Kgs 14:23-24; 15:12; 2 Kgs 23:6-16 suggest that it cannot be ruled out altogether.

[26]See the discussion of cult prostitution below.

38:17 "I'll send you a young goat from my flock," he said. "Will you give me something as a pledge until you send it?" she asked. 38:18 He said, "What pledge should I give you?" "Your seal and its cord, and the staff in your hand," she answered. So he gave them to her and slept with her, and she became pregnant by him.

The negotiation over the price indicates that Judah did not bring (sufficient) money with him to the sheep shearing and that he had no prior plans to consort with a prostitute. The failure to discipline one's spontaneous sexual urges is regarded as extremely foolish behavior in the Old Testament (e.g., Proverbs 5–7), and here the forefather of Israel's royal tribe succumbs to it. The negotiated price, **a young goat**, could be used to produce other goats. Tamar acts wisely from her point of view. She needed tangible proof should she become pregnant that Judah was the father. She therefore demands an immediate **pledge**.

The pledge consisted of Judah's signet ring with its cord and his staff. Both of these items could be clearly identified as Judah's alone. The signet ring was used to make impressions in clay or wax and amounted to an authorized signature which was unique to every wealthy individual. The staff was a carved stick used as a walking stick or cane and as a means of protection from animals and other people. It would have a carved head that was distinctive to Judah.

2. Judah Fails to Find Prostitute to Pay Her and Recover Personal Items (38:19-23)

38:19 After she left, she took off her veil and put on her widow's clothes again.

Tamar's change of clothing from her prostitute's garb to her widow's clothes masked what she had done. This detail is not immediately relevant to the plot other than the fact that it explains why Hirah the Adullamite had trouble locating her. One reason the detail might be included is because of the *leitmotif* of (especially Joseph's) clothing in this section of Genesis. Once again it is the innocent, or at least more innocent, person whose clothing receives such emphasis.

38:20 Meanwhile Judah sent the young goat by his friend the Adullamite in order to get his pledge back from the woman, but he did not find her. 38:21 He asked the men who lived there, "Where is the shrine prostitute who was beside the road at Enaim?" "There hasn't been any shrine prostitute here," they said.

Some time later[27] Judah met his obligation, sending the promised

---

[27]The Hebrew's *waw*-consecutive seems to indicate temporal succession here as often, contra the NIV's "meanwhile."

young goat to the prostitute. Perhaps to avoid the personal embarrassment, he sent Hirah. He had been with Judah when he met the prostitute and would recognize her. Hirah is called "**the Adullamite.**" This may be the narrator's way of signaling how the chosen family's interaction with other nations does not always lead them closer to faith in the God who chose them. Judah was not a good moral example to the people of the nations in this instance.

When Hirah was not able to find the woman[28] on his own, he asked the men of the place about her whereabouts. He refers to her as a "**shrine prostitute**" (קְדֵשָׁה, $q^ed\bar{e}\check{s}\bar{a}h$). Hirah may be reflecting his ethnic background in this instance. She may have been an ordinary prostitute in Judah's eyes, but a cult prostitute in the eyes of Hirah and the men of the area. The local inhabitants had not seen a shrine prostitute there. This may have been because she was only trying to entice Judah and had slipped in and out unnoticed.[29]

There is a great debate over whether this is an appropriate translation for this Hebrew term and whether such a thing as temple or cult prostitutes even existed in Israel. The arguments in favor of their being cult or temple prostitutes are as follows. The Hebrew word ($q^ed\bar{e}\check{s}\bar{a}h$) used obviously refers to prostitution. The root of the word, (קדשׁ, $qd\check{s}$), refers to that which is "set apart" or "holy." Given that there is ancient evidence of *religious* functionaries being involved in sexual activities for money, it is argued that such pagan practices involved cult prostitution. The idea is that the gods were encouraged to make the land fertile through acts of "sympathetic magic." Religious worshipers paid for and performed sexual acts with cult prostitutes. This was supposed to encourage the gods and goddesses so worshiped to make the land fertile through their own sexual activity. The rain, in such a scenario, is the life-giving seed of the god(s) worshiped. A number of ancient Near Eastern texts link religion and sex. Herodotus, for example, informs us that every Babylonian woman had to prostitute herself once in her life, to a stranger within the temple of Ishtar.[30] Neo-Babylonian records from Uruk show that the temple hired out females as concubines for private citizens.[31] Old Testament texts such as Deuteronomy 23:17-18 and Hosea 4:14 are cited to demonstrate the existence of cult prostitutes.

---

[28]It is interesting that the narrator refers to Tamar as "the woman," not as "the prostitute" and definitely not "shrine prostitute" as Hirah describes her.

[29]Steve M. Hooks, *Sacred Prostitution in the Bible and the Ancient Near East*, Ph.D. Dissertation (Cincinnati: Hebrew Union College, 1985), p. 169.

[30]Herodotus, *Histories* 1.199.

[31]Karel van der Toorn, "Prostitution (Cultic)," *ABD*, V:512.

The question which has been raised by a number of scholars[32] is whether this Hebrew word for prostitution (*q⁾dēšāh*) refers to prostitution which was somehow also involved in Canaanite religious practice. It is asserted that unambiguous examples of ancient Near Eastern cult prostitution are either late and uncertain (Herodotus) or of questionable applicability. In particular there is little uncontested evidence that prostitution which involved religious personnel was linked to a fertility cult.

Deuteronomy 23:17-18, it is argued, needs to be interpreted more carefully than in the traditional scholarly understanding. The text reads as typically translated:

> None of the daughters of Israel shall be a temple prostitute; none of the sons of Israel shall be a temple prostitute. You shall not bring the fee of a prostitute or the wages of a male prostitute[33] into the house of the LORD your God in payment for any vow, for both of these are abhorrent to the LORD your God. (NRSV)

Those who dispute the majority opinion argue that the feminine Hebrew word (*q⁾dēšāh*) should be rendered "prostitute" while the etymologically related masculine (קָדֵשׁ, *qādēš*) should be understood as "pagan priest." Further the use of the Hebrew word "dog" (כֶּלֶב, *keleb*) might actually be literal rather than a euphemism for a male prostitute. The metaphorical use of this word to refer to a male prostitute is based upon a fourth-century B.C. inscription found at Kition which mentions temple personnel receiving stipends, and a dog is mentioned. The fact that the word "dog" is used of servants frequently in the ancient Near East leads to the assumption that "dog" in this instance refers to a temple servant.[34] But even if so, this does not necessarily mean that such a person was involved in cultic (homosexual) prostitution. The common assumption that *q⁾dēšāh* and *qādēš* are related in meaning because they are related by a common verbal root could be an example of the "etymological fallacy," the precarious idea that words must mean what their presumed roots mean.[35]

Hosea 4:13-14 is a part of a denunciation of idolatry. and it denounces the men of Israel who "go aside with whores, and sacrifice with temple prostitutes" (v. 14b). The traditional scholarly understanding of this text is that the prostitution referred to is part of baalistic wor-

---

[32]E.g., Hooks, *Sacred Prostitution*; M. Gruber, "Hebrew *q⁾dēšâh* and Her Canaanite and Akkadian Cognates," *UF* 18 (1986): 133-148.

[33]NRSV footnote, Hebrew, "a dog."

[34]Elaine Adler Goodfriend, "Prostitution (OT)," *ABD*, V:507-508.

[35]For a critique of the etymological fallacy see Donald A. Carson, *Exegetical Fallacies* (Grand Rapids: Baker, 1984), pp. 26-27.

ship. The joining of "sacrifice" and $q^ed\bar{e}\check{s}\bar{a}h$ seems to imply more than ordinary prostitution. Those who dispute this understanding argue that the prostitutes are normal prostitutes and the sexual excess referred to is not part of the ritual itself.[36]

Scholars should always be wary of going beyond the evidence and allowing a theory to drive the interpretation of the evidence. In this case, however, I think the interpretations of Deuteronomy 23 and Hosea 4 offered above strain credibility at certain points. The theory should be held with humility since we lack adequate evidence to put the matter beyond doubt. But it is hard to explain these (and other) texts without some form of religious prostitution being assumed.

38:22 So he went back to Judah and said, "I didn't find her. Besides, the men who lived there said, 'There hasn't been any shrine prostitute here.'" 38:23 Then Judah said, "Let her keep what she has, or we will become a laughingstock. After all, I did send her this young goat, but you didn't find her."

If Judah did not regard the woman he had had a sexual liaison with as a **shrine prostitute**, it is interesting that he does not correct Hirah when he refers to her that way.[37] In any case she was no longer there. Judah, perhaps ruing the foolishness of his actions, counsels Hirah to drop the matter. Paying for a new seal, cord, and stick was easier than succumbing to the humiliation of searching for a lost prostitute to pay an overdue bill for her services! Judah is no example for a nation that was supposed to be a light for the nations. It is to be noted that Judah is concerned that he would **become a laughingstock** to his Canaanite neighbors. This may well be a subtle indication of how far Judah has moved away from the faith traditions of his family.

3. Tamar Discovered to Be Pregnant, and Judah Discovers He Is the Father (38:24-26)

38:24 About three months later Judah was told, "Your daughter-in-law Tamar is guilty of prostitution, and as a result she is now pregnant." Judah said, "Bring her out and have her burned to death!"

Not only is Judah sexually immoral[38] and perhaps even religiously compromised by consorting with a cult prostitute; he is the worst sort

---

[36]Goodfriend, "Prostitution," p. 509.

[37]Another possibility is that Judah does not view the Hebrew $q^ed\bar{e}\check{s}\bar{a}h$ as anything other than a normal prostitute.

[38]The Hebrew words זְנוּנִים ($z^en\hat{u}n\hat{i}m$) and זָנָה ($z\bar{a}n\bar{a}h$) are used of sexual immorality more generally. The NIV's "prostitution" may be too specific.

of hypocrite. Judah is told that Tamar was guilty of sexual infidelity and had now become pregnant. Without even investigating the circumstances he orders that she be brought out in public and burned! He did this while he and his friend Hirah knew he had himself only recently consorted with a cult prostitute! This shows the worst sort of male chauvinism, abuse of power as head of the family, and personal hypocrisy as well as a double standard often exhibited by those in power. Ironically Judah is the person who gave his name to the tribe from which Israel's kings came! Election was no doctrine which encouraged personal, familial, or ethnic pride!

Judah has the power to order Tamar's execution as her father-in-law even though she has been living with her own father! It is also noteworthy that she is apparently condemned for being unfaithful to Shelah, to whom she is promised, while Judah tries to absolve himself of all responsibility for failing to give Shelah to her.

38:25 As she was being brought out, she sent a message to her father-in-law. "I am pregnant by the man who owns these," she said. And she added, "See if you recognize whose seal and cord and staff these are."

Tamar waited until the very last second to play her trump card. Evidently Judah was not even going to attend the execution. Tamar had to send **a message** to him. She, unlike Judah, showed concern for her father-in-law's dignity by not publically embarrassing him. Tamar's insight into Judah's nature is shown. She knew by intuition he would not deny that the seal with its cord and the staff were his. She also intuited that he would acknowledge his responsibility and act accordingly. The Hebrew phrase translated "**See**" (הַכֶּר־נָא, *hakker-nā'* = "Please take note") is also used when the brothers (including Judah) asked Jacob to identify Joseph's bloody robe (Gen 37:32-33).[39]

38:26 Judah recognized them and said, "She is more righteous than I, since I wouldn't give her to my son Shelah." And he did not sleep with her again.

To Judah's credit he acknowledged his sinfulness and Tamar's superior righteousness. He does not say that what she did was right, only that she had acted with more righteousness in the situation than he had. Evidently Judah took Tamar as his wife. But presumably because she was also his daughter-in-law and the relationship would be viewed as an incestuous one, Judah did not have any further intimate[40] relations with her.

---

[39]Greidanus, *Preaching Christ*, p. 374.

[40]The Hebrew uses the verb יָדַע (*yādā'*) euphemistically of sexual intercourse as in Genesis 4:1. Literally, "he did not know her."

C. TAMAR BEARS TWO SONS FOR JUDAH (38:27-30)

38:27 When the time came for her to give birth, there were twin boys in her womb. **38:28** As she was giving birth, one of them put out his hand; so the midwife took a scarlet thread and tied it on his wrist and said, "This one came out first." **38:29** But when he drew back his hand, his brother came out, and she said, "So this is how you have broken out!" And he was named Perez. **38:30** Then his brother, who had the scarlet thread on his wrist, came out and he was given the name Zerah.

This passage echoes Genesis 25:21-26 where Jacob and Esau struggle for supremacy while still in Rebekah's womb. In this narrative the progenitors of the two main clans of Judah are about to be born. They, too, seem to struggle for first place as did their later descendants. During the birth one of the twins' hands came out. The order of birth, in particular the order of birth of the first son, was of great importance. He was given a double portion of the inheritance (Deut 21:17) and called upon to lead the extended family in the future. In the case of twin boys who were born only minutes apart this could be quite disheartening for the loser in the birth race. In order to confirm who came out first the midwife tied a piece of **scarlet thread** around the hand. In the subsequent tussle for birth order the midwife was shocked to see that the other twin was actually born first. She says, "What? *You* have broken through?" The Hebrew verb for breaking through (פָּרַץ, *pāraṣ*) is often used of violent, forcible actions. In a wordplay on this event Judah named him **Perez** (פֶּרֶץ, *pāreṣ*). David descended from the clan of Perez (Ruth 4:18-22).

His brother, who had first extended his hand, but then passively followed his brother out of the womb, was named **Zerah**. No explanation is given of his name, although it comes from a root meaning "brightness" and may refer to the bright color of the scarlet string which had been tied onto his hand or wrist.[41]

Tamar is the first of four women in the Old Testament who end up being mentioned in Matthew's genealogy of Jesus. The others are Rahab, Ruth, and Bathsheba. Each of them is a foreigner.[42] Each of them had an irregular if not immoral marital union.[43] And all four of them end up in the line of David and through him in the line of Jesus the Messiah. A persistent, if minor, theme in the Old Testament is that God often uses people outside of his chosen nation for his purposes.

---

[41]Sarna, *Genesis*, p. 270.

[42]I presume that Bathsheba, whose name means, "daughter of Arabia" and whose husband, Uriah, was a Hittite, was not an Israelite.

[43]Besides Tamar, Rahab was a prostitute, and Bathsheba had an affair with David. Ruth visited Boaz at night at the threshing floor.

GENESIS 39

III. JOSEPH ENDS UP AS A SLAVE AND PRISONER IN EGYPT (39:1-23)

After the story of Judah the narrative takes up again the story of Joseph from chapter 37. Like Judah in chapter 38, Joseph is faced with sexual temptation from a non-Israelite woman. But unlike him, Joseph resists the temptation. Initially he pays a high price for his moral integrity. But Joseph is eventually elevated in every circumstance in which he finds himself. He is elevated from an ordinary slave to a slave in Potiphar's house. The success that the LORD gave him there resulted in Joseph being placed over Potiphar's entire house and possessions. After resisting Potiphar's wife's advances Joseph is put in prison. He is now a Hebrew slave in a prison, but at least it was a royal prison. Once again the LORD was with Joseph, and the success that he gave him resulted in his being trusted with the management of the prisoners, including Pharaoh's personal prisoners. The unjust and unfair things that had happened to Joseph since his enslavement by his brothers begins to form a pattern of God's providence. No matter how unjustly Joseph is treated, God sees to it that Joseph ends up in situations in which he will be elevated to a position of leadership.

A. JOSEPH'S INITIAL ELEVATION IN POTIPHAR'S HOUSE (39:1-6a)

39:1 Now Joseph had been taken down to Egypt. Potiphar, an Egyptian who was one of Pharaoh's officials, the captain of the guard, bought him from the Ishmaelites who had taken him there.

After the seeming interlude for the story of Judah and Tamar, the story of Joseph is resumed. In the history of the nation the dominant tribes politically and economically were Judah and the tribes descended from Joseph: Ephraim and Manasseh. The narrative of Jacob's sons which begins in 37:2 focuses on the progenitors of these tribes. **Joseph** was **taken** as a slave **to Egypt** by the Ishmaelites[1] who had purchased him from his brothers at Dothan. In the coincidence which speaks of divine providence, Joseph was purchased by a very important man in Egypt. His description is elaborate and indicates his importance for the narrator. His name, **Potiphar** is short for Potiphera, the name of Joseph's priestly father-in-law (Gen 41:45,50; 46:20). The longer form of the name means "he whom Re [the sun-god] has given." He was a "eunuch"[2] to Pharaoh and held an important office. The office could be translated "**captain of the guard**" and mean leader of Pharaoh's personal body guard or be translated "captain of the slaughterers" and perhaps mean either chief steward or chief executioner of Pharaoh's enemies.[3] In any case the person would have needed Pharaoh's complete trust. A chief steward could prevent or allow poisoning. The head of the bodyguard could prevent or allow assassination attempts. The chief executioner could kill Pharaoh's enemies or spare them.

39:2 The LORD was with Joseph and he prospered, and he lived in the house of his Egyptian master.

The tragic fracturing of Jacob's family which resulted in Joseph's being sold as a slave by his own brothers is not the end, but the beginning of the story. Through it all, **the LORD [is] with Joseph**. Though he was a slave, he nevertheless "**prospered.**" This verse alone should warn us about the danger of distorted theologies of prosperity which measure prosperity only or even primarily in monetary terms. Even though Joseph prospered as a slave, the narrator reminds us that he did so, not in his own house, but **in the house of his Egyptian master**. This is the reality of living in exile. Even when one prospers, there is always a sense that one is not at home and is ultimately in a quite vulnerable position. The original and canonical audiences both knew that ultimately the Egyptians would turn on the Jews.

39:3 When his master saw that the LORD was with him and that the LORD gave him success in everything he did, 39:4 Joseph found favor in his eyes and became his attendant. Potiphar put him in charge of his household, and he entrusted to his care everything he owned.

The way in which the LORD prospered Joseph was not lost on his master. It is significant that **his master** says that "**the LORD**" was **with**

---

[1] In Genesis 37:25,27,28 they are Ishmaelites as here. In 37:28,36 they are Midianites. See the discussion on 37:28.

[2] As here, סָרִיס (sārîs) does not always mean a literal eunuch.

[3] Walter E. Brown, "Potiphar," *EDB*, p. 1072.

Joseph. Potiphar knew of Joseph's god[4] and his dedication to him. Potiphar also knew that the LORD, and not some other god nor Joseph's "innate" abilities, had brought about this success. Obviously Joseph had been speaking of the LORD.[5] His life, especially in his "secular" pursuits as Potiphar's servant, was a living testimony to the LORD's power and blessing. This would not be lost on the original and especially the canonical audience in the Diaspora.

Because of the LORD's evident blessing of Joseph, **he found favor in [Potiphar's] eyes**. As a result Joseph became his personal **attendant** (שָׁרַת, *šārat*, "to attend, minister to"). Some time later,[6] after serving faithfully in that capacity, Joseph was given even greater responsibility. Joseph was placed over Potiphar's house and had responsibility for all that he owned. Given Potiphar's important position in Pharaoh's administration, this was undoubtedly a great responsibility. The canonical audience "stranded" in exile would learn the lesson. Presumably Joseph remained faithful despite the unfairness of the situation, and this brought about the LORD's blessing. Joseph is thus a model of how the exiled people of God should respond in situations in which they are outsiders and not in control.[7]

39:5 From the time he put him in charge of his household and of all that he owned, the LORD blessed the household of the Egyptian because of Joseph. The blessing of the LORD was on everything Potiphar had, both in the house and in the field. 39:6a So he left in Joseph's care everything he had; with Joseph in charge, he did not concern himself with anything except the food he ate.

The LORD had promised Abram, "I will bless those who bless you" (Gen 12:3). He did not say "I will bless everyone you come in contact with, because of you." In this instance the LORD did so anyway. While Potiphar was still Joseph's master, the fact that he gave Joseph such wide-ranging authority was a sort of blessing. Language about the LORD's blessing recalls the promise to Abraham and reminds the reader that the ultimate point of that promise was that Abraham's descendants were to be the channel of God's blessing to all nations.[8] In this

---

[4]For Potiphar, the issue would have been which god to respect, not whether only one God or many gods exist.

[5]I do not mean to imply that Joseph knew the name Yahweh.

[6]The *waw*-consecutive here may imply temporal succession.

[7]Cf. Jeremiah 29. My thanks to Gary Hall for this reference.

[8]The text also reminds us that the LORD had warned Abram that his descendants would be enslaved in a foreign land (Gen 15:13). My thanks to Laurence Turner for pointing this out.

passage we see a glimpse of that beginning to happen. The repetitive inverted or chiastic structure which the narrator uses to make this point serves to emphasize it all the more strongly.

A   From the time he put him in charge of his household[9] and of all that he owned,
   B   the LORD blessed the household of the Egyptian
      C   because of Joseph.
   B'   The blessing of the LORD
A'   was on everything Potiphar had, both in the house and in the field.

As a result of the LORD's blessing, Potiphar stopped even being concerned about his possessions which Joseph managed. His only concern was what he should eat. Joseph's obvious ability under the LORD's blessing earned him more and more trust and responsibility. Although a slave, he showed himself to be completely trustworthy.

B. JOSEPH FALSELY ACCUSED OF ADULTERY BY POTIPHAR'S WIFE (39:6b-19)

39:6b Now Joseph was well-built and handsome, 39:7 and after a while his master's wife took notice of Joseph and said, "Come to bed with me!"

The Bible rarely gives detailed physical descriptions of its human characters. When it does, it almost always has a significant role in the plot. In this case Joseph is said to be "beautiful of form and appearance."[10] This is significant because it helps to explain the attraction of Potiphar's wife to Joseph. When she looked at Joseph, she was so attracted to him that she asks him to sleep with her.

39:8 But he refused. "With me in charge," he told her, "my master does not concern himself with anything in the house; everything he owns he has entrusted to my care. 39:9 No one is greater in this house than I am. My master has withheld nothing from me except you, because you are his wife. How then could I do such a wicked thing and sin against God?" 39:10 And though she spoke to Joseph day after day, he refused to go to bed with her or even be with her.

Joseph, in contrast to Judah in the previous chapter, refuses his master's wife's advances. Joseph makes his point by twice referring to

---

[9]This structure is even more obvious in the Hebrew where the word "house" is paraphrased by the NIV as "household" here, and thus the connection with the end of the verse is lost.

[10]Literal translation of Hebrew יְפֵה־תֹאַר וִיפֵה מַרְאֶה (y°pēh-tō'ar wîpēh mar'eh).

Potiphar as his "**master**" (אֲדֹנִי *'ǎdōnî*). According to Joseph, and in this the narrator is in agreement, his master does not even know about the things in his house. He has developed such trust in Joseph that he has placed all of his possessions in Joseph's hands, trusting him to manage them well. To violate that trust by having an affair with his master's wife is something which Joseph is not prepared to do. It would not only show his untrustworthiness as a servant; more importantly, it also was a great evil and sinful in God's eyes.

Joseph did not believe that God had given up on him even though his very own brothers had sold him into slavery. His difficult circumstances came about by the violence and jealousy of his brothers. But this did not justify his taking advantage of his situation. The lesson for the original audience which struggled to stay away from the sexual immorality of Canaan would be obvious. Such temptations can be resisted, even when they are persistent. The lesson for the canonical audience would be to trust the LORD no matter where you are, even in the furthest recesses of Diaspora. Your faithful lifestyle will be rewarded in the end.

It is noteworthy that the temptation was not offered as a one-time impulse. Potiphar's wife **spoke to Joseph day after day**. He refused day after day and eventually **refused to . . . even be [near] her**. One senses either her desperation or her blatant sexual immorality. Whatever the origins of her behavior, Joseph shows his moral integrity by resisting the temptation each and every time.

39:11 One day he went into the house to attend to his duties, and none of the household servants was inside. 39:12 She caught him by his cloak and said, "Come to bed with me!" But he left his cloak in her hand and ran out of the house. 39:13 When she saw that he had left his cloak in her hand and had run out of the house, 39:14 she called her household servants. "Look," she said to them, "this Hebrew has been brought to us to make sport of us! He came in here to sleep with me, but I screamed. 39:15 When he heard me scream for help, he left his cloak beside me and ran out of the house." 39:16 She kept his cloak beside her until his master came home.

Joseph had been careful to avoid Potiphar's wife's sexual advances. But a servant is only able to avoid the lady of the house for so long. On one momentous day[11] for Joseph, and as it turns out for the people of Israel, Joseph happened to be in the house without other servants nearby. While this might be read as unwise, in fact Joseph ought not to be

---

[11]The narrator marks the significance of this day by saying, "And then it happened on this day" (וַיְהִי כְּהַיּוֹם הַזֶּה, *yayᵉhî kᵉhayyôm hazzeh*).

overly condemned for this. Taking advantage of the opportunity, Potiphar's wife violently seized[12] Joseph by his cloak and demanded once
again that he sleep with her. But then Joseph made an unwise decision
on the spur of the moment. Rather than struggle with her for his cloak
he maneuvered his body out of it and left her holding it while he fled
from the house. If he had stayed to struggle with it, even if it was torn,
Potiphar's wife would have a hard time explaining it. If he had been the
aggressor, why would his clothes be torn and not hers?

But she was quicker on her feet than Joseph on this occasion. She
saw that Joseph had fled leaving his garment in her hand. Frustrated by
Joseph's refusal of sexual advances, she saw an opportunity to punish
him instead. She called the servants of her house.[13] After they gathered,
she referred to Joseph pejoratively as a **"Hebrew** man." Her husband,
she implies, had brought him into the house to laugh[14] at her and the
other servants in the house. She appeals to their common ethnic identity which she shares with the other servants, but not with Joseph. She
may also implicitly be appealing to their resentment of Joseph's
advancement and elevation over the other servants. She claims Joseph
tried to force sex upon her and not the reverse. She claims that she had
screamed for help, but because she and Joseph were the only ones in
the house, no one heard her. Joseph supposedly reacted to the scream
by running out of the house, leaving his cloak behind. She claims the
cloak was left beside her, not in her hands as was actually the case.

The reader is astounded at first by the fact that no one does anything to Joseph after his master's wife has just accused him of attempting to rape her. Are they afraid of Joseph's authority? Or are they suspicious of Potiphar's wife's claim of attempted rape? The reader is left
to wonder. The theme of Joseph's clothing, however, arises yet again.
Once again when something happens to Joseph's clothing, he is about
to face trouble. In this case he could do nothing about it. Given that the
men of the house do not react to Potiphar's wife's claims, she keeps
Joseph's cloak as evidence against him when Potiphar returns. It is interesting that the narrator refers to Potiphar as Joseph's master and not as

---

[12]The word וַשׂרֶפ (*tāpaś*) is used of rape (Deut 22:28) and the capture of cities
and prisoners (1 Kgs 20:18; 2 Kgs 10:14; 16:9; 18:13; 25:6).

[13]The NIV's "her household servants" obscures the fact that the narrator
makes it plain that Joseph was living in *her* house. As such she has the upper
hand in all disputed matters.

[14]The echo of the theme of laughter in the Isaac and Ishmael stories is emphasized by the fact that Potiphar's wife uses the same verb, צָחַק (*ṣāḥaq*), here as
used there.

his wife's husband. This may be a subtle hint at the tension in the relationship between them.

39:17 Then she told him this story: "That Hebrew slave you brought us came to me to make sport of me. 39:18 But as soon as I screamed for help, he left his cloak beside me and ran out of the house." 39:19 When his master heard the story his wife told him, saying, "This is how your slave treated me," he burned with anger.

It is interesting what Potiphar's wife does and does not say to him when she accuses Joseph. She does not actually accuse Joseph of attempted rape or adultery but of mocking or laughing[15] at her. The ambiguity of this statement is interesting. Clearly she is at least accusing Joseph of attempted rape.[16] Why else would she scream for help? But she stops short of actually saying this.

She blames Potiphar for bringing "the **Hebrew slave**" into the situation. The xenophobia toward Hebrews which she shares with other Egyptians (Gen 43:32) is thus used to her advantage. She tells the story of how she, the supposed victim, ends up with the cloak of Joseph, the supposed victimizer. In her scenario Joseph had taken the cloak off, and when she **screamed**, left it "beside" her.

When Potiphar, referred to as Joseph's master,[17] heard the story, he was angry. His wife rather contemptuously said, "This is what *your slave* did to me." But the reader wonders at whom did Potiphar **burn with anger**? Was it Joseph or perhaps his wife or perhaps some combination? Joseph is not immediately executed or exonerated but put in prison. One must therefore wonder whether Potiphar completely believed his wife's story. It is possible that Joseph is put in prison to give Potiphar time to find out the truth. In the ancient world prisons were not places where one served out a sentence. They were merely holding places until a trial resulted in immediate acquittal or immediate punishment.

C. JOSEPH IMPRISONED, BUT ELEVATED (39:20-23)

39:20 Joseph's master took him and put him in prison, the place where the king's prisoners were confined. But while Joseph was there in the prison, 39:21 the LORD was with him; he showed him kindness

---

[15]The same verb (*ṣāḥaq*) as is used in verse 13 above.

[16]The Hebrew בָּא־אֵלַי (*bā'-'ēlay*), "came into me," would ordinarily be a euphemism for an actual sexual encounter. This fact creates ambiguity over whether she was or was not claiming that an actual rape had occurred.

[17]Notice Potiphar's wife is not Joseph's master also, only Potiphar.

and granted him favor in the eyes of the prison warden. **39:22 So the
warden put Joseph in charge of all those held in the prison, and he
was made responsible for all that was done there. 39:23 The warden
paid no attention to anything under Joseph's care, because the** LORD
was with Joseph and gave him success in whatever he did.

Rather than execute Joseph,[18] his master **put him in** a special
prison[19] where **the king's prisoners** were held. But even as a slave in a
foreign prison, Joseph was not beyond the reach of the LORD. Even
there he was with Joseph. He extended (נָטָה, *nāṭāh*, "to extend, stretch
out") his loyalty to Joseph and graciously gave **him favor** (חֵן, *ḥēn*, "favor,
grace") **in the eyes of the prison warden**.

Though Joseph came to the prison under a cloud of suspicion, he
nevertheless prospered once again. A prisoner himself, he was nevertheless placed **in charge of all** the other prisoners. Everything which was
done in that prison, Joseph did it.[20] Just like Potiphar, the warden came
to trust Joseph so implicitly that he no longer felt the need to manage
it himself. The fact that this included *everything* in the prison is given
special emphasis in the Hebrew (אֶת־כָּל־מְאוּמָה, *'eth-kol-mᵊ'ûmāh*, "all,
everything"). The narrator gives the same reason for the prison warden's trust in Joseph as he gave in the case of Potiphar. **The** LORD **was
with** Joseph and made whatever he did in the prison prosper.

Once again Joseph is held up as an example of how to handle the
awkward situations created by being exiles in a strange land. The LORD
is there, he is with his people, and he causes their work to prosper even
when it seems that the situation is impossible from a human point of
view.

---

[18]Rapists in Israel faced execution in the Torah (Deut 22:23-27). The fact that
Joseph was also a slave would presumably make his punishment even more
severe and make the fact that he was not executed all the more striking.
Conversely the audience could assume that the Egyptians were inappropriately
lax about such sexual crimes.

[19]בֵּית הַסֹּהַר (*bêth hassōhar*) "the house of roundness," a term perhaps suggesting a fortress. Potiphar was probably responsible for this special prison.

[20]Here the NRSV's more literal rendering comes closer to the original than the
NIV's paraphrase.

GENESIS 40

IV. JOSEPH INTERPRETS THE DREAMS OF PHARAOH'S CUPBEARER AND BAKER (40:1-23)

In this chapter we see Joseph no longer as the dreamer of two dreams but as the interpreter of two dreams. The two dreams are given opposite interpretations and have opposite fulfillments. In light of this the first-time reader wonders whether the two dreams of Joseph will have opposite or identical fulfillments and places the interpretation of Joseph's dreams in doubt. Given that the dreams are those of high officials in Pharaoh's court, there is the potential for the quick resolution of Joseph's difficult situation. But in fact, that resolution is put off indefinitely by a culpably forgetful cupbearer.

A. THE IMPRISONED JOSEPH COMES TO KNOW INFLUENTIAL PEOPLE IN THE COURT OF PHARAOH (40:1-3)

40:1 Some time later, the cupbearer and the baker of the king of Egypt offended their master, the king of Egypt. 40:2 Pharaoh was angry with his two officials, the chief cupbearer and the chief baker, 40:3 and put them in custody in the house of the captain of the guard, in the same prison where Joseph was confined.

We are not told how long Joseph spent in prison before the events which are recorded in this chapter unfolded. The Hebrew text merely states that it was "after these things." We do know that it was about 13 years between Joseph's original enslavement and his leaving prison to serve in Pharaoh's court (37:2; 41:46). We also know that the cupbearer waited two entire years before mentioning Joseph to Pharaoh (41:1). How much of the remaining 11 years were spent in prison and how much serving in Potiphar's house is not known.

The cupbearer[1] of the king of Egypt **and the baker** "sinned against"

---

[1]Literally "one who gives drink."

(חָטָא, ḥāṭā')[2] **their master, the king of Egypt**. Both of his "eunuchs"[3] made Pharaoh extremely angry.[4] Both of these positions required trustworthy persons who would resist palace intrigues and attempted *coups* through poisoning the Pharaoh. While we do not know what caused Pharaoh's anger, providentially they were imprisoned in the very prison which Potiphar, who was **captain of the guard**, oversaw; **the same prison where Joseph** had risen to a position of prominence! Joseph might be a slave and a prisoner, but he is associating with the most powerful people in Egyptian society.

B. JOSEPH GAINS AN OPPORTUNITY
TO HELP INFLUENTIAL COURT OFFICIALS (40:4-5)

40:4 The captain of the guard assigned them to Joseph, and he attended them. After they had been in custody for some time, 40:5 each of the two men—the cupbearer and the baker of the king of Egypt, who were being held in prison—had a dream the same night, and each dream had a meaning of its own.

The "**captain of the guard**" in verse 4 would be Potiphar,[5] not the warden. This would seem to imply that Potiphar still had some level of trust in Joseph even though his own wife had accused him of (attempted) rape. Joseph was imprisoned, not because Potiphar believed his wife's story, but for domestic, political expediency. Potiphar knew that these two eunuchs were in a very delicate and potentially dangerous situation. How he handled such prisoners would be very important to Pharaoh. To entrust Joseph with their care implies remarkable confidence in the young Hebrew.

Joseph served[6] them well, even as their imprisonment dragged on. Then on a single night the two men each **had a dream**. Unlike Joseph's

---

[2]Although we do not typically imagine that a human being can be sinned against, that is the word which is used here.

[3]NIV has "officials" here. In the ancient world one could be a "eunuch" (סָרִיס, *sārîs*) without being literally castrated.

[4]קָצַף (*qāṣaph*) is used of God's anger at Israel at Horeb, at the spy episode, at Meribah, etc. (Deut 1:34; 9:7-8,19) and refers to extreme forms of anger.

[5]"Captain of the guard" in Hebrew (שַׂר־הַטַּבָּחִים, *śar-haṭṭabāḥîm*) is used to describe Potiphar in 40:1. The "warden" in Hebrew is שַׂר בֵּית־הַסֹּהַר (*śar bêth-has-sōhar*).

[6]שָׁרַת (*śārath*) is used of Joshua serving Moses (Exod 24:13; 33:11; Josh 1:1), Elisha serving Elijah (1 Kgs 19:21), priests and Levites serving in the Temple (Exod 28:35,43 and often), as well as servants of various kings (1 Chr 17:19).

two dreams which seemed to be very similar, if not identical in meaning, these dreams had completely different meanings. The narrator
reminds the reader of the significance of this event by repeating the fact
that the two men were the cupbearer and baker, eunuchs for the king
of Egypt; the very ones being held in the prison which Potiphar oversaw
and which Joseph administrated.

This pair of dreams is the second of three pairs in the Joseph narrative and the reader is invited to read them intertextually (Genesis 41).
In each pair of dreams there are similarities, but also differences. In
each of the three pairs the second dream is either a warning of trouble
to come, or at least something that raises questions about its certain fulfillment. In each of the three pairs a sense of destiny (or at least seeming destiny) for the future is laid out. In each of the three pairs there is
some sense of God's revelation in the dream and/or its interpretation.

C. JOSEPH OFFERS PHARAOH'S OFFICIALS
ACCESS TO DIVINE GUIDANCE (40:6-8)

**40:6 When Joseph came to them the next morning, he saw that they
were dejected. 40:7 So he asked Pharaoh's officials who were in custody with him in his master's house, "Why are your faces so sad
today?" 40:8 "We both had dreams," they answered, "but there is no
one to interpret them." Then Joseph said to them, "Do not interpretations belong to God? Tell me your dreams."**

Joseph, who was ministering to the needs of Pharaoh's cupbearer
and baker, saw that they were upset and angered over their situation.
The word which the NIV translates as "dejected" might better be rendered angered.[7] Joseph asks why their faces were so "evil"[8] that day. It is
noteworthy that the narrator reminds the reader with the typical
Hebrew emphatic redundancy that the men were "Pharaoh's eunuchs"
and that they were with Joseph in "the prison of the house of his

---

[7]While one should not put too much weight on a word found only three times
in the Hebrew Bible, the other two instances of זָעַף (zā'aph – Prov 19:3; 2 Chr
26:19) describe situations in which a person who is in the wrong has angry
resentment toward those who point it out to him or the person he assumes to
be responsible for his difficult situation. This word choice could possibly suggest
the idea that the cupbearer and baker were in the wrong and had brought their
situations upon themselves.

[8]The NIV's "sad" is a possible translation for רַע (ra') but certainly a rare one,
and it eliminates the possible specific meanings the reader might give to a more
general word such as "evil" or "bad."

master" (literal translation of the Hebrew). This latter description is interesting as it seems to imply that the prison was somehow connected, whether literally or metaphorically, to the house of Potiphar. It could mean that the building was adjacent to Potiphar's house or that it was his personal prison.

The problem with the countenances of Pharaoh's eunuchs is that they had dreams which they believed were some form of divine revelation. But in prison, without the usual recourse to soothsayers and fortune-tellers, there was no one to help them with the interpretation of the dreams. Joseph remarks that God gives the interpretations of dreams.[9] Joseph reasons that since God controls the future, he controls what dreams can mean, whether or not they are divine revelation.

D. THE TWO DREAMS AND THEIR INTERPRETATION (40:9-19)

1. The Cupbearer's Dream (40:9-11)

40:9 So the chief cupbearer told Joseph his dream. He said to him, "In my dream I saw a vine in front of me, 40:10 and on the vine were three branches. As soon as it budded, it blossomed, and its clusters ripened into grapes. 40:11 Pharaoh's cup was in my hand, and I took the grapes, squeezed them into Pharaoh's cup and put the cup in his hand."

The chief of the cupbearers went first. His dream consisted of a vine which appeared before him with three branches. As it budded, its blossom shot up and its clusters of grapes ripened. This describes the quick maturation and ripening of the grapes. After the rapid ripening of the grapes the chief cupbearer mentions **"Pharaoh's cup"** three times.[10] The narration of the dream emphasizes the immediacy of the events described.

2. The Interpretation of the Cupbearer's Dream (40:12-13)

40:12 "This is what it means," Joseph said to him. "The three branches are three days. 40:13 Within three days Pharaoh will lift up your

---

[9]Laurence Turner pointed out to me in a private communication that Joseph's dreams in chapter 37 were not interpreted by God. Their interpretation by Joseph's brothers, Joseph, and Jacob are therefore not necessarily to be trusted.

[10]The NIV has only two of these uses of Pharaoh's cup, paraphrasing the third instance as "his cup" for stylistic reasons.

head and restore you to your position, and you will put Pharaoh's cup in his hand, just as you used to do when you were his cupbearer.

Although the readers are not told explicitly that Joseph interprets the dream through divine inspiration, this would seem to be implicit. He speaks confidently, "This is the interpretation of the dream." Rather surprisingly **the three branches** of the vine **are three days. Within three days** the dream will be fulfilled. Given the seriousness of the situation this is a very rapid fulfillment indeed.

That Pharaoh would "**lift up** [someone's] **head**" and that this would be a good thing is an unusual way to introduce the interpretation of the cupbearer's dream. It is probably used in this instance because the same phrase occurs in verse 19 in the interpretation of the parallel dream where the butler's head would be literally "lifted up" from him in an act of execution. The cupbearer is assured by Joseph that he would be returned to his position and would hand Pharaoh his cup, with Pharaoh trusting that he would never betray him and allow him to be poisoned by those seeking Pharaoh's power. Whatever distrust of him had resulted in his imprisonment, he would be restored to his customary[11] position. His head would be lifted up in an act of kindness.[12]

3. Joseph's Plea to the Cupbearer (40:14-15)

40:14 But when all goes well with you, remember me and show me kindness; mention me to Pharaoh and get me out of this prison. 40:15 For I was forcibly carried off from the land of the Hebrews, and even here I have done nothing to deserve being put in a dungeon."

With a favorable interpretation of the dream, Joseph asks a favor of the cupbearer. The precise relationship between the interpretation of the dream and the request that Joseph makes is ambiguous. The Hebrew phrase[13] which introduces verse 14 ("But" in NIV) can mean several different things. Of the possibilities attested elsewhere in the

---

[11]The NIV's "as you used to do" in Hebrew reads כַּמִּשְׁפָּט הָרִאשׁוֹן (kammišpāt hāri'šôn) "like the original custom."

[12]Wenham, *Genesis 16–50*, p. 383, points to 2 Kgs 25:27; Jer 52:31 as other passages using this phrase in the sense of "deal kindly with."

[13]כִּי אִם (kî 'im) elsewhere in the Pentateuch can mean "but" (Gen 15:4; 32:29; 35:10; Exod 12:9; Lev 21:14[?]; Num 10:30; 24:22; Deut 7:5; 12:5), "that" (Gen 47:18), "but only" (Num 26:33; Deut 12:14,18; 16:6), "unless" (Gen 32:27; 42:15; Exod 8:7; Lev 22:6), "except" (Gen 28:17; 39:6,9; Lev 24:2; Num 14:30; 26:65; 35:33), "but if" (Exod 9:2; 10:4; 22:22; 23:22; Deut 10:12[?]) and "if only" (Deut 11:22).

Pentateuch, the NIV's "but when" or "but if" fit this context well. If "but" (NIV's "**But when**") is used, Joseph is completely confident in asserting that the interpretation will, in fact, come to pass. If, however, the phrase is rendered "But if," Joseph is asking for the favor on the condition that his interpretation turns out to actually come from God and thus be found true.

Joseph asks the cupbearer to **remember** Joseph when things turn in his favor and show loyalty[14] to him. Joseph sees enough of the big picture to ask that the cupbearer **mention** him **to Pharaoh** so that Pharaoh would release him from "this [prison] house." Somehow Joseph knew that he was placed in the home of Potiphar with such close connections to Pharaoh and that this could well be the means of his gaining his freedom. Joseph is thus portrayed as being quite sensitive to God's working behind the scene in guiding the circumstances of his life no matter how unfair, irrational, and chaotic those circumstances might seem on the surface.

The basis for Joseph's request to the cupbearer other than the obvious tit-for-tat morality is the injustice of his situation. Given that the cupbearer undoubtedly regarded his own imprisonment as unjust — it was not his fault if someone else had plotted to poison Pharaoh — Joseph's appeal was designed to elicit sympathy from someone who had experienced a similar injustice. Joseph claims that he was violently stolen[15] from the "**land of the Hebrews**." In so describing the land of Canaan Joseph shows his faith in God's promise of the land to Abraham and his descendants. It may also be a way of claiming that he was a legitimate citizen of his land when he was stolen as a slave.

But the injustice did not end in the land of the Hebrews. In Egypt also he had been unjustly treated. He had done nothing to merit being placed in "the cistern." His description of the prison he was in as a "cistern" or "pit"[16] emphasizes the horror of the conditions there; but it also reminds the reader that this entire saga started when Joseph was thrown by his brothers into a cistern. Joseph had gone from one pit in Canaan to another in Egypt!

---

[14]חֶסֶד (ḥesed) is usually used of God's gracious faithfulness to his people. Here it has a more "secular" sense.

[15]The NIV's "forcibly carried off" gets at the idea. The Hebrew has the emphatic construction (infinitive absolute followed by the verb of the same root) of the verb גָּנַב (gānāb) "to steal."

[16]בּוֹר (bôr) can mean either "cistern" or "pit." The NIV's "dungeon" is an attempt to convey the nuance of the word, but it misses the intertextual wordplay.

4. The Baker's Dream (40:16-17)

40:16 When the chief baker saw that Joseph had given a favorable interpretation, he said to Joseph, "I too had a dream: On my head were three baskets of bread. 40:17 In the top basket were all kinds of baked goods for Pharaoh, but the birds were eating them out of the basket on my head."

The chief baker had waited until he had heard Joseph's interpretation of the cupbearer's dream before asking him to interpret his dream. This could be because he felt some part of the dream might have an ominous meaning. When he **saw that Joseph gave a favorable** (טוֹב, *ṭôb*) **interpretation** and perhaps noting the similarities between his dream and the cupbearer's, he related his dream.

In the baker's dream there were **three baskets** of "white."[17] The baskets were stacked upon his head and thus not protected from the birds. The baskets contained **baked goods** which were to be served to Pharaoh. Although they were designed to be eaten by Pharaoh, in fact birds ate[18] them instead. It may be that implicit in the dream is the fact of the baker's irresponsibility in allowing the birds to eat the Pharaoh's baked goods by stacking them and carrying them on his head. Pharaoh would not have been pleased with that.

5. The Interpretation of the Baker's Dream (40:18-19)

40:18 "This is what it means," Joseph said. "The three baskets are three days. 40:19 Within three days Pharaoh will lift off your head and hang you on a tree. And the birds will eat away your flesh."

Joseph wastes no time giving the interpretation of the baker's dream. Once again the number three stands for **three days**. Within that three-day period Pharaoh would also lift up his head as Joseph had said he would lift up the head of the cupbearer. Thus far the interpretations are quite similar.

But suddenly the interpretation takes a dramatic turn for the worse from the baker's point of view. Instead of lifting up his head in order to

---

[17] חֹרִי (*ḥōrî*) occurs only here, but is presumed to be derived from the root חוּר (*ḥor*) meaning, "to be white." The NIV assumes it means "white" bread. The NRSV assumes it means "white" cakes. Given that bleached white flour is a relatively modern phenomenon, the NRSV is to be preferred here, although this is far from certain. It could also mean that the baskets themselves were white in color.

[18] There is a wordplay in Hebrew between the description of the baked goods as Pharaoh's food (מַאֲכָל, *ma'ăkāl*) and the birds eating אֹכֵל (*'ōkēl*) them.

restore him to his position, Joseph says that Pharaoh will **hang**[19] him **on a tree**. The **birds** which ate Pharaoh's baked goods out of the basket in the dream are, in its interpretation, literal birds which **will eat** the baker's **flesh** while he hangs on the tree. Joseph, in a sort of model for truly speaking the words of God, does not shrink from telling the baker the difficult truth.

E. THE FULFILLMENT OF THE DREAMS (40:20-22)

40:20 Now the third day was Pharaoh's birthday, and he gave a feast for all his officials. He lifted up the heads of the chief cupbearer and the chief baker in the presence of his officials: 40:21 He restored the chief cupbearer to his position, so that he once again put the cup into Pharaoh's hand, 40:22 but he hanged the chief baker, just as Joseph had said to them in his interpretation.

The reader is now informed of the significance of the three days in the dreams of Pharaoh's chief cupbearer and chief baker; it was **Pharaoh's "birthday."**[20] As part of the celebrations Pharaoh hosted **a feast** or drinking party[21] for all of his servants. The invitation list for the party may have been chosen so that Pharaoh could make a statement to them about loyalty. As Joseph had interpreted the dreams, the heads of both the chief cupbearer and chief baker were lifted up. That this happened in the presence of all of Pharaoh's servants may hint at one of the underlying purposes of the feast.

And just as Joseph had said in his interpretation of the dreams, this lifting up of the head meant opposite things for the chief cupbearer and the chief baker. The outcome for the chief cupbearer is precisely as Joseph had said in his interpretation. He was **restored**[22] to his position (מַשְׁקֶה, mašqeh as in v. 13) so that he once again put (נָתַן, nāthan as in v. 13) the cup (כּוֹס, kôs as in v. 13) into Pharaoh's palm. This last item

---

[19]The verb תָּלָה (tālāh) does not necessarily mean hang by a rope on a gallows, although this is its meaning in several places in Esther (2:23; 5:14, et al.). It can refer to being hung up by one's hands (Lam 5:12) and may involve other forms of punishment.

[20]For the possibility that this day celebrated, not his actual birthday, but his "divine birth" at his accession to the throne, see the discussion in Hoffmeier, *Israel in Egypt*, pp. 90-91.

[21]מִשְׁתֶּה (mišteh) can mean either "feast" or "drinking party." The fact that it is the cupbearer who is the one who is restored may be hinted at by the choice of this particular word for feast with a possible meaning "drinking party."

[22]Hiphil of שׁוּב (šûb) as in verse 13.

uses a different vocabulary word than in verse 13 where the usual word for hand (יָד, *yād*) is used. This could be merely a variation of vocabulary to maintain interest or an indication that the chief cupbearer's new relationship with Pharaoh was even closer than the one before. The word "palm" over against the general word for "hand" might indicate this.[23]

The interpretation of the chief baker's dream turned out to be just as exact. He was hanged **just as Joseph had said** in his interpretation of the dream. The repetition of vocabulary in both cases reinforces the accuracy of Joseph's interpretations and confirms that they came from divine revelation.

F. THE CUPBEARER'S FAILURE TO REMEMBER JOSEPH (40:23)

40:23 The chief cupbearer, however, did not remember Joseph; he forgot him.

The immediate result for Joseph's personal situation, however, was not positive. By repetition the narrator reminds the reader of the stark unfairness of it all. Not only did the chief cupbearer not actively remember Joseph so as to do something to help him as he had requested; he actually forgot completely about Joseph. In neither case is this likely to be an accidental thing. In the Old Testament people are held accountable for what they (choose to) remember or forget.

---

[23]Another possibility, suggested to me by Laurence Turner in a private communication, is that the word "palm" echoes the garment given to Joseph by Jacob if the Hebrew description of that garment is taken to mean "tunic of the palm." One problem with this view is that different words for "palm" are used.

GENESIS 41

V. JOSEPH IS ELEVATED BY ACCURATELY INTERPRETING PHARAOH'S DREAMS (41:1-56)

If Joseph reached his lowest point personally in chapter 39, in this chapter he is rapidly elevated. In a short time he moves from the status of a Hebrew slave in an Egyptian prison to second in command over all Egypt. It was the narrating of his two dreams without a divinely given interpretation which started all of his troubles in chapter 37. Ironically in this chapter it is the divinely given interpretation of two dreams which results in his elevation. In this passage we see the hand of God in the circumstances in which Joseph was placed.

A. PHARAOH'S DREAMS (41:1-7)

1. Pharaoh's First Dream (41:1-4)

41:1 When two full years had passed, Pharaoh had a dream: He was standing by the Nile, 41:2 when out of the river there came up seven cows, sleek and fat, and they grazed among the reeds. 41:3 After them, seven other cows, ugly and gaunt, came up out of the Nile and stood beside those on the riverbank. 41:4 And the cows that were ugly and gaunt ate up the seven sleek, fat cows. Then Pharaoh woke up.

Joseph waited for a full two years to pass before anything happened because the cupbearer had forgotten about him. This time Pharaoh has a pair of dreams, just as Joseph himself had had earlier and in parallel with the pair of dreams which Pharaoh's cupbearer and baker had had two years earlier. In the dream Pharaoh was standing beside "the stream" which is assumed, quite plausibly, by the translations to be the Nile. In the dream **seven cows** came **out of the river** and fed among the rushes along the river. The cows were, like Joseph (39:6), beautiful of form.[1] They were also "fat of flesh" (וּבְרִיאֹת בָּשָׂר, *ûbʳrî'ōth bāsār*), a sign of a healthy cow.

---

[1]The cows are יְפוֹת מַרְאֶה (*yᵉpôth mar'eh*) while Joseph was וִיפֵה מַרְאֶה (*wîpēh mar'eh*).

The second half of the dream is just as striking[2] as the first. **Seven** more cows come up out of the stream. These seven, in utter contrast to the first group of seven, are "ugly of form" (רָעוֹת מַרְאֶה, *rā'ôth mar'eh*, literally "evil of form") and "thin of flesh" (וְדַקּוֹת בָּשָׂר, *w³daqqôth bāśār*), the exact opposite of the first group. Rather than feeding among the rushes these seven merely stand beside the first group, evidently unable to eat as the other cows are doing.

Instead of eating the rushes the second group of seven cows ate the other cows! The contrast between the two sets of cows is emphasized by repeating their description. Whether it was the horror of the dream or something else, Pharaoh awoke from his dream with the image of the seven thin, ugly cows having eaten up the fat, beautiful cows.

2. Pharaoh's Second Dream (41:5-7)

41:5 He fell asleep again and had a second dream: Seven heads of grain, healthy and good, were growing on a single stalk. 41:6 After them, seven other heads of grain sprouted—thin and scorched by the east wind. 41:7 The thin heads of grain swallowed up the seven healthy, full heads. Then Pharaoh woke up; it had been a dream.

Pharaoh fell back to sleep **and had a second dream**. Once again the reader is brought into the dream with "And behold!" This time the number **seven** is the number of **heads of grain** growing from **a single stalk**. The fertility of this picture is emphasized by the description of the heads as "fat" and "good." The use of the word "fat" to describe the grain echoes the first dream where the cattle are said to be "fat."

The second part of this second dream begins once again with "And behold!" **Seven** heads sprout up. But this time they are not "fat" and "good," but "**thin**" and "**scorched by [an] east wind**." The word "thin" echoes the "thin" cows of the first dream. In the ancient Near East winds usually came from the west and off of the Mediterranean Sea, often carrying moisture with them. But east winds come from the desert and are extremely dry, parching the crops. That is the imagery used in this passage. Contrary to what one might think, it was the **thin heads of grain** which **swallowed** the **seven** heads which were fat and full. With this troublesome image in his head **Pharaoh woke** once again and realized **it had been** another **dream**.

Modern readers must be careful of missing the point. It was not "just" a dream. Dreams were regarded in the ancient world as divine

---

[2] Both parts of the dream begin with "And behold!" (וְהִנֵּה, *w³hinnēh*).

revelation and interpreted dreams were one of the primary means of guidance for difficult decisions.[3] While the Old Testament is hesitant about the reliability of dreams,[4] one should not read that attitude into a non-Israelite like Pharaoh.

The double structure of Pharaoh's dreams invites comparison and contrast with the dreams of Joseph in chapter 37 and the cupbearer and baker in chapter 39.

B. PHARAOH SEEKS INTERPRETATION OF HIS DREAMS (41:8)

41:8 In the morning his mind was troubled, so he sent for all the magicians and wise men of Egypt. Pharaoh told them his dreams, but no one could interpret them for him.

The word translated "**magicians**" is an Egyptian loanword meaning "chief lector priest."[5] These individuals studied and transmitted ritual and magical texts which were used in the interpretation of dreams in the so-called "House of Life."[6] None of these magicians or any of the Egyptian wise men was able to offer an interpretation, or at least an interpretation which satisfied Pharaoh.[7] Pharaoh faced the same situation that the Babylonian king Nebuchadnezzar did in Daniel 2.[8]

C. THE CUPBEARER COMMENDS JOSEPH TO PHARAOH (41:9-13)

41:9 Then the chief cupbearer said to Pharaoh, "Today I am reminded of my shortcomings. 41:10 Pharaoh was once angry with his servants, and he imprisoned me and the chief baker in the house of the captain of the guard. 41:11 Each of us had a dream the same night, and each dream had a meaning of its own. 41:12 Now a young Hebrew

---

[3]J.H. Hunt, "Dreams," *DOTP*, pp. 197-201.

[4]Daniel L. Smith-Christopher, "Dreams," *EDB*, pp. 356-357. He cites Num 12:6-8; Jer 23:27,32; 29:8; Ps 73:20; 90:5; Deut 13:1-5. His chronological argument, however, is less convincing.

[5]Hoffmeier, *Israel in Egypt*, p. 88, argues that חַרְטֹם (*ḥarṭōm*) derives from Egyptian *ḥry-tp*, an abbreviation for *ḥry-tp ḥry-ḥb*, meaning "chief lector priest."

[6]Ibid.

[7]The Hebrew is ambiguous at this point, literally, "there was no interpreter of them for Pharaoh."

[8]Laurence Turner reminded me of this parallel.

was there with us, a servant of the captain of the guard. We told him our dreams, and he interpreted them for us, giving each man the interpretation of his dream. 41:13 And things turned out exactly as he interpreted them to us: I was restored to my position, and the other man was hanged."

The chief cupbearer, after a two-year silence, finally spoke up for Joseph. He begins by saying, "I have been forced[9] to remember my sins (אֶחְטָא, ḥăṭā'ay) today." The NIV softens the force of this by paraphrasing as "**I am reminded of my shortcomings**." This may be an instance where the reader would assume that the words would mean something more diplomatic ("shortcomings") to Pharaoh, but for the reader imply something stronger ("sins").

The chief cupbearer takes a risk in bringing up the time when Pharaoh had been extremely **angry**[10] **with his servants** the chief cupbearer and **the chief baker**. He reminds Pharaoh that he and the chief baker had been **imprisoned** in "**the house of the captain of the guard**," i.e., the prison which Potiphar oversaw. He relates the fact of the two dreams on **the same night**. The reader notes the similarities with Pharaoh's two dreams on the same night. The cupbearer also relates that each of the two dreams had its own "interpretation." While the NIV and NRSV translate this latter word as "meaning," a more natural translation would be "interpretation." This keeps the connection between the noun and the verb which is present in the Hebrew. Since there were two dreams on the same night and those two dreams had individual interpretations, the cupbearer (or the narrator) could be hinting this fact might be relevant to Pharaoh's dreams given that they both occurred on the same night.

After the introduction which explains the potential relevance of his suggestion, the cupbearer (finally) brings up Joseph. He is referred to as a "**young Hebrew**" and a slave **of the captain of the guard**. Pharaoh now knows that the person whom the cupbearer suggests as an interpreter of his dreams was young, a foreigner, a slave, and one who had so displeased his master that he had been imprisoned by him. This is a rather inauspicious introduction of Joseph to Pharaoh! Perhaps the cupbearer is protecting himself by giving all this information. Despite the rather substandard résumé from an Egyptian's point of view, this young Hebrew slave had been able to interpret both of the dreams and to give

---

[9]The verb "remember" is in the hiphil.

[10]קָצַף (qāṣaph) is used in situations of extreme anger when God or his representatives are about to bring down judgment on Israel (Exod 16:20; Lev 10:6,16; Num 16:22; 31:14; Deut 1:34; 9:7,8,19,22).

an accurate and different interpretation to each of them. His ability to interpret and to carefully distinguish between dreams which seemed so similar is thus highlighted for Pharaoh.

It happened, the cupbearer continues, that what this young Hebrew slave gave as the interpretation of each dream actually occurred. The cupbearer is careful not to bring Pharaoh too closely into the events that followed. In Hebrew[11] the person who restored the cupbearer and hanged the baker is an unidentified "he." He does not say, "You, Pharaoh, restored me and hanged him." The cupbearer, exercising the discretion which a servant who fears his master has, leaves it at that. Pharaoh must decide what to do with the information.

D. PHARAOH ASKS JOSEPH TO INTERPRET HIS DREAMS (41:14-16)

1. Pharaoh Quickly Sends for Joseph (41:14)

41:14 So Pharaoh sent for Joseph, and he was quickly brought from the dungeon. When he had shaved and changed his clothes, he came before Pharaoh.

Somewhat surprisingly given what Pharaoh has been told about Joseph, he sent for Joseph. Joseph had to hurry[12] to meet Pharaoh. The prison is once again, as in 40:15, described as a "cistern" or "pit"[13] echoing the incident when his brothers put Joseph into a cistern. Joseph's physical appearance and particularly his clothing are mentioned yet again. Throughout the Joseph narrative with the changing of Joseph's circumstances his clothing also changes. In this instance he shaves[14] and puts on new clothing as only appropriate for a visit to Pharaoh. After two long years of waiting, the opportunity arises and he must seize it quickly.

2. Pharaoh Explains the Problem and Joseph Promises God's Answer (41:15-16)

41:15 Pharaoh said to Joseph, "I had a dream, and no one can interpret it. But I have heard it said of you that when you hear a dream you

---

[11]The LXX maintains this by using infinitives without an explicit subject.

[12]Hiphil of רוּץ (rûṣ), "to run."

[13]בּוֹר (bôr) can mean either "cistern" or "pit." The NIV's "dungeon" is an attempt to convey the nuance of the word, but it misses the intertextual wordplay.

[14]This could mean either shaving his beard, or perhaps his entire head.

can interpret it." **41:16 "I cannot do it," Joseph replied to Pharaoh, "but God will give Pharaoh the answer he desires."**

The narrator wastes no time in getting to the point. Pharaoh tells Joseph of his dream and the fact that there is no interpreter (or interpretation) of it. Without explicitly identifying the cupbearer, Pharaoh tells Joseph what he had heard about him. "You listen to dreams to interpret them" he said. Joseph understands who he really is in the wider scheme of things. He bluntly explains, "Not me! God will announce Pharaoh's peace."[15] Joseph is careful to distinguish between any ability that he possesses and the fact that only God, who controls the future, can predict it. But Joseph also implies that the answer which God will give Pharaoh for his troublesome dream will not harm Pharaoh. Pharaoh can expect a peaceful response, one that will lead to Pharaoh's own peace.[16]

E. PHARAOH RECOUNTS HIS DREAMS TO JOSEPH (41:17-24)

41:17 Then Pharaoh said to Joseph, "In my dream I was standing on the bank of the Nile, 41:18 when out of the river there came up seven cows, fat and sleek, and they grazed among the reeds. 41:19 After them, seven other cows came up—scrawny and very ugly and lean. I had never seen such ugly cows in all the land of Egypt. 41:20 The lean, ugly cows ate up the seven fat cows that came up first. 41:21 But even after they ate them, no one could tell that they had done so; they looked just as ugly as before. Then I woke up. 41:22 "In my dreams I also saw seven heads of grain, full and good, growing on a single stalk. 41:23 After them, seven other heads sprouted—withered and thin and scorched by the east wind. 41:24 The thin heads of grain swallowed up the seven good heads. I told this to the magicians, but none could explain it to me."

While Pharaoh's recounting of his dream adds some color to the narrator's version and emphasizes his extreme revulsion at the sight of the "scrawny, very ugly and gaunt" cows, there seems to be no difference in substance. Pharaoh reliably conveys the context of his dream to Joseph. Pharaoh notes that after the scrawny cows had eaten up the fat cows they were unchanged in appearance. This would seem to imply that the scrawny cows would be victorious or would outlast the fat cows.

---

[15]The Hebrew has some ambiguity: אֱלֹהִים יַעֲנֶה אֶת־שְׁלוֹם פַּרְעֹה ('ĕlōhîm ya'ăneh 'eth-š'lôm par'ōh) could mean "God will respond to Pharaoh in peace" or "God will announce the peace of Pharaoh."

[16]The NIV and NRSV paraphrase and overinterpret here.

Narrator's Version	Pharaoh's Version
He was standing by the Nile,	[17]Then Pharaoh said to Joseph, "In my dream I was standing *on the bank of* the Nile,
[2]when out of the river there came up seven cows, sleek and fat, and they grazed among the reeds.	[18]when out of the river there came up seven cows, *fat and sleek*, and they grazed among the reeds.
[3]After them, seven other cows, ugly and gaunt, came up out of the Nile and stood beside those on the riverbank.	[19]After them, seven other cows came up—*scrawny and very ugly and lean. I had never seen such ugly cows in all the land of Egypt.*
[4]And the cows that were ugly and gaunt ate up the seven sleek, fat cows.	[20]The lean, ugly cows ate up the seven fat cows that came up first. [21]*But even after they ate them, no one could tell that they had done so; they looked just as ugly as before.*
Then Pharaoh woke up.	Then I woke up.

In the second dream the variation between Pharaoh's account and the narrator's is minimal. The narrator connects the two dreams more explicitly by speaking of both the cows and the **heads of grain** as "fat" (בְּרִיאֹות, *bᵉrî'ôth*), an adjective that would ordinarily only be used of cows, not heads of grain. Pharaoh emphasizes the negative features of the second set of heads of grain (as he did the second set of cows) by adding the adjective "**withered**" to the narrator's "**thin and scorched by the east wind**." But this may be a way of describing the emotional horror which Pharaoh must have felt. Pharaoh reminds Joseph that none of his "magicians" were able to explain the dreams to him.

Narrator's Version	Pharaoh's Version
[5]He fell asleep again and had a second dream: Seven heads of grain, fat and good, were growing on a single stalk. [6]After them, seven other heads of grain sprouted—thin and scorched by the east wind. [7]The thin heads of grain swallowed up the seven fat, full heads.	[22]"In my dreams I also saw seven heads of grain, full and good, growing on a single stalk. [23]After them, seven other heads sprouted—*withered* and thin and scorched by the east wind. [24]The thin heads of grain swallowed up the seven good heads.

F. JOSEPH INTERPRETS PHARAOH'S DREAMS (41:25-32)

41:25 Then Joseph said to Pharaoh, "The dreams of Pharaoh are one and the same. God has revealed to Pharaoh what he is about to do. 41:26 The seven good cows are seven years, and the seven good heads of grain are seven years; it is one and the same dream. 41:27 The seven lean, ugly cows that came up afterward are seven years, and so

are the seven worthless heads of grain scorched by the east wind: They are seven years of famine.

Joseph begins his interpretation by explaining that Pharaoh's two dreams are in reality one dream, told in two different ways or with two different symbol systems. Joseph had himself experienced a pair of dreams which seemed to mean similar things. But he had also interpreted the two dreams of Pharaoh's cupbearer and baker, and they had precisely opposite meanings, a good one for the cupbearer and an ominous, evil one for the baker. These dreams of Pharaoh, unlike the other sets of dreams, are most definitely of identical meaning. The noteworthy thing is "that which God is doing, he **has revealed to Pharaoh**." This fact is emphasized by the use of unusual syntax in the Hebrew in which the object clause ("that which God is doing") has been brought into first place before the subject and verb ("he has revealed"). The NIV and NRSV have interpreted the Hebrew participle as a future ("what God is about to do"), but this seems unnecessary. Joseph may be showing the urgency of the situation by using a construction which implies that God is already in the process of doing what he had revealed to Pharaoh in his dreams.

Joseph explains to Pharaoh that the "good" cows and heads of grain both represent **seven years** of good to come for his kingdom. They are the positive aspect of the dream and represent the same seven-year period. The two dreams tell the same story. That story begins with seven good years when cattle and crops will be healthy and fruitful. Likewise both the seven "thin and evil" cows and the seven "empty and east wind scorched" heads of grain **are seven years of famine**. Both the cows and the heads of grain stand for the same seven-year period of famine.

41:28 "It is just as I said to Pharaoh: God has shown Pharaoh what he is about to do. 41:29 Seven years of great abundance are coming throughout the land of Egypt, 41:30 but seven years of famine will follow them. Then all the abundance in Egypt will be forgotten, and the famine will ravage the land. 41:31 The abundance in the land will not be remembered, because the famine that follows it will be so severe.

Before fleshing out the rest of his interpretation of Pharaoh's dreams, Joseph reminds Pharaoh that God, through Joseph's interpretations, had enabled Pharaoh to see (hiphil of רָאָה, *rā'āh*) what he was doing. Joseph had said this at the beginning of his interpretation, and here he repeats it to ensure that Pharaoh understands that the interpretation comes from God, not from himself. He also repeatedly uses the word "behold!"[17] as though "showing" Pharaoh the meaning.

---

[17]Although the English translations usually leave it out, the Hebrew word הִנֵּה (*hinnēh*), "Behold!" is found in vv. 26 (twice),28,29.

Seven years of great abundance[18] of both flock and field will come upon the entire land of Egypt. This is the positive aspect, but it is deceiving. **Seven years of famine would** immediately **follow** the seven plentiful years. The famine will be so severe, Joseph warns, that the land of Egypt will forget the abundant years; **the famine will** exhaust or consume **the land**. As though to bring the point home even more forcefully, Joseph repeats himself. In verse 31 he says that the people of Egypt will "not even know" about the plentiful time because the following famine **will be so severe**. This is not news that one who feared for his own safety would want to deliver to a despotic Pharaoh. He might well kill the messenger for the content of the message. But Joseph does not flinch in describing the severity of the famine coming upon Egypt.

41:32 The reason the dream was given to Pharaoh in two forms is that the matter has been firmly decided by God, and God will do it soon.

Joseph now explains why the dream came in a repeated form. The repetition of the dream is God's way of emphasizing that the decision has been firmly made (נָכוֹן, nākôn), and there will be no talking him out of it. In fact God was already "hurrying to do it" (וּמְמַהֵר הָאֱלֹהִים לַעֲשֹׂתוֹ, ûmmahēr hā'ĕlōhîm la'ăśōtô). The two dreams were not two different revelations but the same revelation repeated to emphasize the certainty of their fulfillment.

G. JOSEPH MAKES A RECOMMENDATION ABOUT THE CERTAIN FUTURE (41:33-36)

41:33 "And now let Pharaoh look for a discerning and wise man and put him in charge of the land of Egypt. 41:34 Let Pharaoh appoint commissioners over the land to take a fifth of the harvest of Egypt during the seven years of abundance. 41:35 They should collect all the food of these good years that are coming and store up the grain under the authority of Pharaoh, to be kept in the cities for food. 41:36 This food should be held in reserve for the country, to be used during the seven years of famine that will come upon Egypt, so that the country may not be ruined by the famine."

While Joseph does not directly promote his own cause, he does seem to do so indirectly. The Hebrew is more ambiguous than the English translations. What Joseph says might be translated, "And now Pharaoh will see a man of discernment and wise." While the point might

---

[18]In Hebrew the words for "seven" (שֶׁבַע, šeba') and "abundance" (שָׂבָע, śābā') form a wordplay.

well be that Pharaoh should look for such a man, the imperative form is not used. Joseph could be hinting that Pharaoh will see such a man standing right in front of him! In the Hebrew there is a wordplay between the word for the certainty (נָכוֹן, *nākôn*) of God's decision to send seven years of plenty followed by seven years of famine, and the word for a discerning (נָבוֹן, *nābôn*) man. That *certainty* points to a *certain* sort of discerning man, Joseph! The discerning man whom Pharaoh will see should be placed over the entire land of Egypt. Pharaoh must act by appointing **commissioners** (literally, "appoint appointee," (וְיַפְקֵד פְּקִדִים, *w³yaphqēd p³qidîm*) over the land and enforce a twenty percent levy of the crops of the land of Egypt **during the seven years of** plenty. This would help to see the nation through the seven-year famine which would immediately ensue. The food of the coming good years should be gathered, and stored under Pharaoh's hand in the cities in order to be safely guarded[19] there.

The food so gathered would be like a savings deposit[20] or "rainy day fund" for the land for the seven years of famine which would definitely come on the land of Egypt. Joseph emphasizes the certainty of the seven years of famine through repetition. If food is stored up, the famine would not ruin the land of Egypt.

H. PHARAOH ACCEPTS JOSEPH'S RECOMMENDATION AND SELECTS JOSEPH TO CARRY IT OUT (41:37-45a)

41:37 The plan seemed good to Pharaoh and to all his officials. 41:38 So Pharaoh asked them, "Can we find anyone like this man, one in whom is the spirit of God?" 41:39 Then Pharaoh said to Joseph, "Since God has made all this known to you, there is no one so discerning and wise as you. 41:40 You shall be in charge of my palace, and all my people are to submit to your orders. Only with respect to the throne will I be greater than you." 41:41 So Pharaoh said to Joseph, "I hereby put you in charge of the whole land of Egypt." 41:42 Then Pharaoh took his signet ring from his finger and put it on Joseph's finger. He dressed him in robes of fine linen and put a gold chain around his neck. 41:43 He had him ride in a chariot as his second-in-command, and men shouted before him, "Make way !" Thus he

---

[19] שָׁמַר (*šāmar*) can mean either "to keep" or "to guard." I would suggest the latter meaning here.

[20] פִּקָּדוֹן (*piqqādôn*) is only found elsewhere in Leviticus 5:21,23 where it refers to something entrusted to a person for safekeeping.

put him in charge of the whole land of Egypt. 41:44 Then Pharaoh said to Joseph, "I am Pharaoh, but without your word no one will lift hand or foot in all Egypt." 41:45 Pharaoh gave Joseph the name Zaphenath-Paneah and gave him Asenath daughter of Potiphera, priest of On, to be his wife.

It is a truly remarkable sign of God's providential guidance of Joseph that Pharaoh and all his servants regard the interpretation of a young Hebrew slave as trustworthy enough to change the course of Egypt's policies! There is no dissent. No one warns Pharaoh of the risk of believing the interpretation of a young Hebrew slave. They are all convinced that Joseph has genuinely received divine revelation from a god who will not change his mind. With agreement over accepting Joseph's interpretation and policy recommendations in hand, Pharaoh suggests Joseph for the job of overseeing the collection and guarding of grain during the next seven years. He asks his servants, "Can a man like this one be found in whom is the spirit of the gods?" The NIV text has "God" in the text while the footnote suggests "gods" as an alternative. But the reading in the NIV's text seems historically anachronistic. While it is true that for a short time under Akhenaten (Amenhotep IV) Egypt worshiped only one God, this was an aberration which the following kings tried to erase from Egypt's historical record.[21] Pharaohs were almost uniformly polytheists, and Akhenaten is the exception who proves the rule. How Pharaoh came to discern that Joseph was empowered by the spirit of the gods is yet another example of God's providential guidance of the events of Joseph's life. The fact that God had told Abram in advance of the enslavement of his descendants in a foreign land (Gen 15:13) makes the reader aware that it is not just providential guidance for the benefit of Joseph personally, but for the sake of all the descendants of Joseph's father Israel.

Pharaoh consulted his servants, though, without a specific response from them being recorded. Pharaoh then tells Joseph that after[22] God had revealed everything regarding Pharaoh's dreams and their interpretations, the only reasonable choice for a **discerning and wise** man, such as Joseph had suggested, would be Joseph himself. In verse 40, Pharaoh proposes placing Joseph over his house and that all his people would show their submission[23] to Joseph. **Only** in regard **to the throne** itself would Pharaoh be greater than Joseph. Without waiting for a

---

[21]Kitchen, *Reliability*, pp. 328-333.

[22]The NIV and NRSV have "since" for אַחֲרֵי (*'āḥărê*).

[23]וְעַל־פִּיךָ יִשַּׁק כָּל־עַמִּי (*wᵊ'al-pîkā yiśśaq kol-'ammî*), literally, "all my people will kiss you upon your mouth" as a sign of submission.

response from Joseph, Pharaoh proceeds to formally place[24] Joseph over all the land of Egypt. The physical symbols of his new position are then publically given to Joseph to confirm Pharaoh's decision. This included taking his own personal **signet ring** (טַבַּעְתּוֹ, *ṭabba'tô*) **from** off of **his finger** and placing it **on Joseph's finger**, dressing him in garments made of byssus, the **fine** Egyptian **linen**, and placing a chain of gold on his neck. These tokens given in public would ensure obedience to Joseph as he managed the complex task of saving and storing twenty percent of the crops of Egypt for a predicted, though as yet unrealized, famine.

Joseph also was given the privilege of riding in the second of Pharaoh's chariots, the symbol of his status as the second in command. When he rode in the chariot, officials would direct the crowds to "bow the knee" (אַבְרֵךְ, *'abrēk*)[25] in order to symbolize his place of honor. In these ways Pharaoh showed Joseph the honor of being his second in command over all the land of Egypt.

The narrator continues his description of the honor bestowed upon Joseph by recording a statement that Pharaoh later[26] made to Joseph, "Apart from Joseph's permission, no one would be allowed to lift his hand or foot in the entire land of Egypt." The exaggeration is obvious, but the point is an emphatic one. Pharaoh also demonstrated Joseph's new status by giving him a new name, **Zaphenath-Paneah**, and a (new) wife, **Asenath**, the daughter of the undoubtedly prominent priest, Potiphera of On.[27] Joseph in a sense relives during his exile in Egypt Jacob's experience while "exiled" in Paddan-Aram. Both are placed in subordinate positions. Both receive wives from the person in authority. Both are intimately involved in two periods of seven years each.[28]

The echo with Joseph's former master Potiphar is unmistakable. Then Joseph was the slave and Potiphar the master. In that position Potiphar's unnamed wife was kept from Joseph. Now Joseph is the lord and Potiphera is the servant. He gladly gives (at Pharaoh's command), his named daughter, Asenath, to Joseph, as a wife. Imagine the oppor-

---

[24] רְאֵה נָתַתִּי אֹתְךָ עַל כָּל־אֶרֶץ מִצְרָיִם (*rᵉ'ēh nāthattî 'ōthkā 'al kol-'ereṣ miṣrāyim*), "See [let it be publically recognized] that I have placed you over all the land of Egypt."

[25] The NIV paraphrases this as "Make way!"

[26] The use of the *waw*-consecutive in verse 44 implies temporal sequence here, although it may only be later in the initial public ceremony described in vv. 41-43.

[27] On was near Goshen where the Israelites settled and was known for the worship of the Egyptian sun god, Ra. It was know as "Sun city." Cf. Sarna, *Genesis*, p. 288.

[28] Laurence Turner pointed these parallels out to me in a private communication.

tunities that Joseph would have missed had he consented to have an affair with Potiphar's wife! He would never have been in prison to interpret the cupbearer's dreams. Consequently he would never have been in a position to interpret Pharaoh's dreams! Joseph refused because it was wrong, but he could not have known the long-term positive consequences of remaining faithful to God and to Potiphar.

I. JOSEPH'S NEW STATUS (41:45b-46)

41:45b And Joseph went throughout the land of Egypt. 41:46 Joseph was thirty years old when he entered the service of Pharaoh king of Egypt. And Joseph went out from Pharaoh's presence and traveled throughout Egypt.

The repetitiousness of this section seems to serve to emphasize it. "Joseph went (out)" (וַיֵּצֵא, *wayyēṣē'*) begins the first and third lines, the word "Egypt" ends all three lines, while "the land of Egypt" ends the first and third lines.[29] In the center of this chiastic repetition Joseph's age is mentioned. The reader is let in on Joseph's patience. Sold as a slave at the age of seventeen, he is now **thirty years old**. For thirteen years he served as a slave or an imprisoned slave. At least the last two years, if not more, he was in the prison. During this entire time he evidently did not give up on his confidence that God was at work in his life. Now at age thirty he went throughout the land of Egypt; he stood in the very presence of Pharaoh and **went out** from there to serve in the entire land of Egypt. All of this happened because Pharaoh, for some unknown reason, trusted his ability to reveal God's intentions by the interpretation of dreams.

J. JOSEPH'S INTERPRETATION BEGINS TO BE FULFILLED (41:47-49)

41:47 During the seven years of abundance the land produced plentifully. 41:48 Joseph collected all the food produced in those seven years of abundance in Egypt and stored it in the cities. In each city he put the food grown in the fields surrounding it. 41:49 Joseph stored

---

[29]Notice the chiastic-like structure in the Hebrew:

וַיֵּצֵא יוֹסֵף עַל־אֶרֶץ מִצְרָיִם:

וְיוֹסֵף בֶּן־שְׁלֹשִׁים שָׁנָה בְּעָמְדוֹ לִפְנֵי פַּרְעֹה מֶלֶךְ־מִצְרָיִם

וַיֵּצֵא יוֹסֵף מִלִּפְנֵי פַּרְעֹה וַיַּעֲבֹר בְּכָל־אֶרֶץ מִצְרָיִם:

up huge quantities of grain, like the sand of the sea; it was so much
that he stopped keeping records because it was beyond measure.

As Joseph had promised, the land was indeed fruitful during the
seven years of plenty. They were harvesting grain by the fistful (לִקְמָצִים,
liqmāṣîm)! As Joseph had recommended, he gathered the (extra) **food**
during the **seven years** (of plenty) **and stored** that (extra) food in each
city near where it was grown. In this way there would be enough to survive the famine and it would be distributed throughout the country with
no need to transport it to outlying regions during a famine.

Joseph's storing up massive quantities of grain echoes the creation
narrative and particularly the Abrahamic promise. The earth's being fruitful is demonstrated during the seven years of plenty and thus echoes the
first chapter of Genesis. The grain is compared to the "**sand of the sea**"
and it could not be numbered, both allusions to the patriarchal promises.[30]
The grain was so plentiful that the counting systems failed!

K. JOSEPH'S AND ASENATH'S "FRUITFULNESS" DURING THE YEARS OF PLENTY (41:50-52)

**41:50 Before the years of famine came, two sons were born to Joseph
by Asenath daughter of Potiphera, priest of On. 41:51 Joseph named
his firstborn Manasseh and said, "It is because God has made me forget all my trouble and all my father's household." 41:52 The second
son he named Ephraim and said, "It is because God has made me
fruitful in the land of my suffering."**

While the land of Egypt was enjoying this extraordinary fruitfulness, Joseph and Asenath[31] were experiencing it within their own family. **Two sons were born** to them during the years of plenty. Joseph[32]
named them Manasseh and Ephraim respectively.

Like other times in Genesis, Joseph makes a wordplay in naming his
sons. **Manasseh** sounds like it is derived from the verb נָשָׁה (*nāšāh*),
meaning "to forget." By elevating Joseph in Egypt and giving him a fam-

---

[30]Gen 22:17; 32:13 for "sand of the sea"; Gen 15:5 for numberless descendants.

[31]In order to emphasize the extraordinary fact that Joseph, the follower of the
one true God, was married to a non-Hebrew from a family of clerics of a pagan
religion, Asenath is redundantly referred to here as "the daughter of Potiphera,
the priest of On."

[32]Unlike earlier instances in Genesis where the mother gave the name to the
child.

ily, God had helped him forget his troubles[33] and his family, his father's house. The troubles of slavery and of being forgotten in prison were gone, and now he had a family of his own.

Joseph also named his second son, **Ephraim**, by wordplay. Ephraim sounds like the verb פָּרָה (*pārāh*), "to be fruitful."[34] Joseph knows that ultimately it is God who provides creation with its capacity to be fruitful. The fruitfulness is also an allusion to the creation account (Gen 1:26-28) and less directly to the promises to Abraham.[35] Joseph refers to Egypt as "the land of my suffering." The word used for "suffering" (עָנְיִי, *'ānyî*) would remind the original audience of their suffering while slaves in Egypt.

L. THE FAMINE COMES AND BEGINS TO BITE (41:53-55)

41:53 The seven years of abundance in Egypt came to an end, 41:54 and the seven years of famine began, just as Joseph had said. There was famine in all the other lands, but in the whole land of Egypt there was food. 41:55 When all Egypt began to feel the famine, the people cried to Pharaoh for food. Then Pharaoh told all the Egyptians, "Go to Joseph and do what he tells you."

Just as Joseph had predicted, the **seven years of abundance** ended and the seven-year famine immediately ensued. All the other lands around Egypt were experiencing food shortages. However in all of Egypt there was sufficient bread[36] because of Joseph. He had recognized divine revelation regarding the future in Pharaoh's dreams and carefully planned to respond to that revelation. At least in the beginning years of the famine Egypt had been providentially protected. Only Egypt had had the foresight to prepare itself for such a famine. Events had shown that Joseph's words were indeed based on divine revelation and could be trusted.

Eventually even Egypt ran out of bread and the nation became hungry. They complained of this to Pharaoh, asking for bread. Pharaoh sent

---

[33]The word עָמָל (*'āmāl*) is often used in Job, Psalms, and Ecclesiastes of the toil and trouble of life in a fallen world.

[34]אֶפְרַיִם כִּי־הִפְרַנִי אֱלֹהִים בְּאֶרֶץ עָנְיִי (*'ephrāyim kî-hiphranî 'ĕlōhîm bᵉ'ereṣ 'ānyî*) has assonance between *'ephrāyim* and *hiphranî* and between *hiphranî* and *'ānyî*.

[35]Exodus 1:7 describes the multiplication of Israel while in Egypt, a part of the fulfillment of the promises to Abra(ha)m in terms of the creation account in Genesis 1:26-28.

[36]The NIV paraphrases לֶחֶם (*leḥem*) "bread" as the more general "food."

them to Joseph so he could tell them what to do. Pharaoh had trusted Joseph in the storing away of grain, and he trusted him now in the tricky business of the administration of its distribution during a severe famine.

M. JOSEPH'S PREPARATIONS BEGIN TO PAY OFF (41:56-57)

41:56 When the famine had spread over the whole country, Joseph opened the storehouses and sold grain to the Egyptians, for the famine was severe throughout Egypt. 41:57 And all the countries came to Egypt to buy grain from Joseph, because the famine was severe in all the world.

When the famine spread over the surface of the land of Egypt, **Joseph opened** up the grain storage facilities throughout[37] the country. And then[38] the famine worsened even more in Egypt. In this weakened condition the "entire earth" (וְכָל־הָאָרֶץ, $w^{\partial}kol\text{-}h\bar{a}\,'\bar{a}res$)[39] came to Egypt to purchase (bread) **from Joseph**. This was because[40] the famine had strengthened throughout the earth.

---

[37]The Hebrew emphasizes the opening *all* of the storage facilities just as the famine spread over *all* of the land of Egypt.

[38]The NIV assumes that the *waw*-consecutive here does not indicate temporal (or logical) sequence but the reason why Joseph had to open up the storehouses. This would be an unusual usage, to say the least, for the *waw*-consecutive. See Waltke and O'Connor, *Biblical Hebrew Syntax*, ch. 33.

[39]While this is probably hyperbolic, the point is none the less clear.

[40]Here Hebrew does use a particle, כִּי (*kî*), which commonly indicates the reason why something happened. In this case it explains why the entire earth came to Egypt to buy bread.

GENESIS 42

VI. THE FIRST TRIP TO EGYPT GOES BADLY
(42:1-38)

Joseph had spent thirteen long years first working as Potiphar's servant and then imprisoned because of a false accusation by Potiphar's wife. He had then spent another eight or so years storing grain and then selling it when the famine he had predicted struck. So far as we know he had made no attempt to contact his family back in Canaan. When his brothers arrive to buy grain and they don't recognize him, he uses the opportunity to play a sort of psychological game with them. In the process he seems to make his first dream come true in part. They do bow down to him and call him Lord. But where is the last and youngest brother? He falsely accuses them and unjustly imprisons them just as he had been unjustly imprisoned and falsely accused by them and by Potiphar. He imprisons all of them, planning to send only one back to retrieve Benjamin, his only full brother and the only brother he truly trusted. But he changes his mind after three days and decides to keep only one of them prisoner. He uses the situation to secretly get information from them about his family. However, he is emotionally touched by Reuben's words chastising them for selling Joseph into slavery so many years before. He therefore chooses Simeon, not Reuben, to remain in prison while the rest return home. He sends them on their way but secretly returns their silver. When they discover this, they take it as an ominous sign. When they tell the story to Jacob, he refuses to allow Benjamin to return despite Reuben's offer of two of his own sons as guarantees.

Within the broader context of the narrative this text heightens the tension as Joseph struggles to forgive and seeks to manipulate the situation to ensure that he is reunited with Benjamin, his only "real" brother.

A. JACOB INSTRUCTS JOSEPH'S BROTHERS TO BUY GRAIN IN EGYPT (42:1-2)

42:1 When Jacob learned that there was grain in Egypt, he said to his sons, "Why do you just keep looking at each other?" 42:2 He continued, "I have heard that there is grain in Egypt. Go down there and buy some for us, so that we may live and not die."

Since the famine had hit the entire known earth, Canaan, where Joseph's family lived, was also affected. This is the third time that a famine is mentioned as affecting the Promised Land in the book of Genesis.[1] The irony of this is tied up with the fact that God had told Abram that he would have to wait a long time for the fulfillment of the promise of the gift of the land. As a result the chosen family is tempted to go to Egypt when there is trouble in the Promised Land. This was the natural thing for inhabitants, even sojourners like Abraham, to do. Of course the readers, both original and canonical, know that Egypt is the place where they would end up being enslaved!

As the famine begins to bite, Jacob asks his ten sons why they sat around **looking at each other.** Jacob had come to know[2] that grain[3] was available for purchase in Egypt. In the Hebrew there is a sort of pun. Jacob "saw" that there was grain in Egypt, but his sons only "saw" each other.[4] Jacob tells them that he had "heard"[5] that **there was grain in Egypt.** Since it is, according to Jacob, a matter of life and death, he directs them to go down[6] to Egypt and buy grain there.

B. JACOB SENDS ONLY TEN OF JOSEPH'S BROTHERS TO EGYPT (42:3-5)

42:3 Then ten of Joseph's brothers went down to buy grain from Egypt. 42:4 But Jacob did not send Benjamin, Joseph's brother, with

---

[1]The others are during the time of Abram (Gen 12:10) and Isaac (Gen 26:1).

[2]The NIV's "learned" may be correct, but the Hebrew וַיַּרְא (wayyarʾ), "then he saw," may be hinting at some form of divine revelation.

[3]The KJV's "corn" is based on an older English usage in which "corn" meant "grain" more generally.

[4]In both cases the Hebrew verb רָאָה (rāʾāh) is used.

[5]Jacob may again be hinting at a divine revelation which he claims to have "heard." Undoubtedly the sons would have thought that he heard by rumor. This may well be the case, but the Hebrew leaves the reader wondering.

[6]The idiom of "going down" (יָרַד, yārad) to Egypt is a common one in the Pentateuch (Gen 12:10; 26:2; 37:25; 39:1; 43:15; 46:3,4; Num 20:15; Deut 10:22; 26:5).

the others, because he was afraid that harm might come to him. **42:5**
So Israel's sons were among those who went to buy grain, for the
famine was in the land of Canaan also.

The mission is clear. The sons are not to stay in Egypt, something
that had placed the promise at risk in the time of Jacob's grandfather
Abram. They are to go and **buy grain**[7] and return.

While Jacob evidently spoke to all of his sons, only **ten** of the eleven
actually **went** on the trip to Egypt. **Jacob did not send Benjamin**, the
only remaining (so far as he knew) son of his beloved wife Rachel. Of
course if Benjamin does not go and bow down to Joseph in Egypt even
the first dream will not find literal fulfillment! This is something that
Joseph seems to notice when they arrive without his brother Benjamin
(v. 9a below). Benjamin is described as "the brother of Joseph" as though
the other "brothers" were not in quite the same category in either Jacob's,
Joseph's, or the narrator's mind. Jacob does not send him because of his
fear that some permanent **harm**[8] **might come to him** as it had to Joseph.
Jacob had favored Joseph, and now he also favors Benjamin, the two
sons of Rachel, the wife he loved.

The narrator makes a summarizing comment that the sons of
"Israel"[9] (not Jacob) **were among** the many who came from Canaan **to
buy grain** in Egypt because of the severity of the famine in Canaan. The
presence of such West Semitic peoples in Egypt from ancient times is
well documented in the Egyptian archaeological materials.[10]

C. THE FIRST DREAM SEEMS TO FIND FULFILLMENT (42:6)

42:6 Now Joseph was the governor of the land, the one who sold grain
to all its people. So when Joseph's brothers arrived, they bowed down
to him with their faces to the ground.

The narrator provides a parenthetical comment which explains the

---

[7]The Hebrew has a sort of wordplay here. Jacob had commanded them to buy
(שָׁבַר, *šābar*) grain (שֶׁבֶר, *šeber*), but in fact they went down to buy (שָׁבַר, *šābar*)
grain (בַּר, *bar*). This may be simply the narrator's penchant for using variety to
make the narrative interesting.

[8]The Hebrew for the NIV's "harm" (אָסוֹן, *'āsôn*) is found only in this context
(Gen 42:4,38) and in the laws which discuss permanent harm coming to a pregnant woman or her unborn child (Exod 21:22,23).

[9]The exact reason the narrator here uses "Israel" instead of "Jacob" is perplexing. It may be that the national rather than individual move to Egypt is
receiving emphasis.

[10]Hoffmeier, *Israel in Egypt*, chs. 3, 4.

seeming coincidence of Joseph's brothers who had last seen him when they sold him into slavery meeting him on a grain buying trip to Egypt. Joseph is only described as the "**governor**" of Egypt. The word הַשַּׁלִּיט (*haššallîṭ*) is an unusual one and is found elsewhere only in three passages in Ecclesiastes (Eccl 7:19; 8:8; 10:5) where it seems to connote the strong and perhaps abusive use of power. This description of Joseph does not bode well for the brothers.

Joseph was the one who decided whether and to whom to sell grain among the hungry throngs coming from Canaan. Joseph's policy had put Egypt in an enviable position. But selling too much to outsiders would endanger his own nation's (Egypt!) preparations for seven long years of famine. He personally made the choices rather than allowing a surrogate to do so.

Given their desperate situation it is not surprising that the brothers bow down to Joseph **with their faces to the ground**. The reader is naturally reminded of how the Joseph narrative began with sheaves of grain representing the twelve sons of Jacob and the sheaves of Joseph's brothers bowing down to his sheaf. In this passage they come to buy from Joseph grain, the edible product related to sheaves and they bow down to him.

D. JOSEPH MISUSES HIS BROTHERS'
LACK OF RECOGNITION OF HIM (42:7-9)

42:7 As soon as Joseph saw his brothers, he recognized them, but he pretended to be a stranger and spoke harshly to them. "Where do you come from?" he asked. "From the land of Canaan," they replied, "to buy food." 42:8 Although Joseph recognized his brothers, they did not recognize him. 42:9 Then he remembered his dreams about them and said to them, "You are spies! You have come to see where our land is unprotected."

Just as Jacob "saw"[11] that there was grain in Egypt, Joseph "saw" his brothers. One might translate the ensuing sentence: "He recognized them, but Joseph did not give them recognition of him." This preserves the Hebrew wordplay between the verb נָכַר (*nākar*), which in different stems means "**recognized**"[12] and "**pretended to be a stranger**."[13] Joseph, sensing the moment, peppered them with hard questions. Joseph began

---

[11]This would seem to be an allusion back to verse 1 where Jacob similarly "saw" that there was grain in Egypt.

[12]In the hiphil; cf. BDB.

[13]In the hithpael; cf. BDB.

by asking their country of origin. They answered forthrightly explaining that they came **from . . . Canaan to buy food**.

In verse 8 the narrator repeats the information about Joseph's advantage of recognizing **his brothers** while remaining unrecognized in order to emphasize the point of how Joseph still had the upper hand. Verse 9a may reflect the fact that Joseph recognized that Benjamin was not present. Without his presence Joseph would have to depend upon the brothers who sold him into slavery in order to gain access to his only "real" brother. In addition, in an ironic twist, without Benjamin's presence, Joseph's dreams, particularly the second, could not be fulfilled, at least in a literal fashion. Joseph's actions in the ensuing narrative seem to be designed to reunite him with his "real" brother, Benjamin, and to have all of his family (including Benjamin?) come to bow down before him. He had tried to forget his father's house and the series of unfortunate events which led to his being sold into slavery; but the memories and the dream come back to him.

Joseph begins by accusing his brothers of being spies, coming to see the "nakedness of the land" (אֶת־עֶרְוַת הָאָרֶץ, *'eth-'erwath hā'āreṣ*). The NIV interprets this last phrase as meaning "**where our land is unprotected**," but this may be too specific. Wenham suggests "weakness" for a translation but then closes down the possibilities for interpretation to the merely military.[14] The weakness or "nakedness" could be related to their food supplies. Joseph accuses them of representing a coalition of Canaanite city-states who would seek to use the vulnerability caused by the famine to their political advantage. This is something the petty kingdoms of Canaan would desperately want to do because of Egyptian interference there from ancient times. This makes the accusation plausible and keeps Joseph from revealing his identity.

E. JOSEPH'S BROTHERS DEFEND THEMSELVES FROM HIS FALSE ACCUSATIONS (42:10-13)

42:10 "No, my lord," they answered. "Your servants have come to buy food. 42:11 We are all the sons of one man. Your servants are honest men, not spies." 42:12 "No!" he said to them. "You have come to see where our land is unprotected." 42:13 But they replied, "Your servants were twelve brothers, the sons of one man, who lives in the land of Canaan. The youngest is now with our father, and one is no more."

The subjection of his brothers is shown by the terminology they use

---

[14]Wenham, *Genesis 16–50*, pp. 401, 407.

to refer to Joseph ("**my lord**") and themselves ("**your [i.e., Joseph's] servants**"). They do not realize it, but in some sense the first dream of Joseph is coming true. They insist that they are **not spies** and that their only purpose in coming to Egypt is **to buy food**. They are telling the truth; they know this and Joseph's knows this; but they do not know that Joseph knows this!

By placing them in a defensive situation Joseph is able to draw information out of them. They tell him that they are all the **sons of one man**. Interestingly they do not claim to be "brothers" at first. This may be an indication of their consciousness of being half-brothers, their differing mothers conferring on them a status equal to the status of their mother in the eyes of their father.

The irony of Joseph's brothers, who sold him into slavery, telling the disguised Joseph that they are **honest men** is not lost on the reader. While what they have been saying is truthful, what they had been doing was not morally right, a meaning the word translated "honest" often has.[15] The "honesty" of Joseph's brothers continues as an issue in verses 19,31,33, and 34 below and thus is a sort of *leitmotif* in this passage. Their subjection to Joseph continues with their reference to themselves as Joseph's "servants" in verse 11. They repeat their claim that they are not spies in order to emphasize the point.

In verse 12 their defense continues, denying Joseph's accusation that they came to see the nakedness of the land. In verse 13 Joseph, by waiting, begins to draw even more information out of them. They mention that originally they were *twelve* "**brothers**." They yet again refer to themselves as Joseph's servants and explain that **the youngest** of the original twelve was back at home in Canaan with their father. Then they reveal something even more. One of the original twelve "brothers" does not exist[16] anymore! The irony is even greater with this revelation. In this text the brothers of Joseph tell Joseph who is standing in front of them that Joseph is no more!

F. JOSEPH OFFERS HIS BROTHERS A WAY
TO REFUTE HIS ACCUSATION (42:14-16)

42:14 Joseph said to them, "It is just as I told you: You are spies! **42:15** And this is how you will be tested: As surely as Pharaoh lives, you will

---

[15]כֵּן (*kēn*) is used of morally correct actions in, e.g., 2 Kgs 7:9; 17:9; Prov 11:19; Isa 16:6; Jer 8:6.

[16]וְהָאֶחָד אֵינֶנּוּ (*wᵉhā'eḥād 'ênennû*), literally, "and the one there is no existence of him."

not leave this place unless your youngest brother comes here. **42:16 Send one of your number to get your brother; the rest of you will be kept in prison, so that your words may be tested to see if you are telling the truth. If you are not, then as surely as Pharaoh lives, you are spies!"**

In verse 14 Joseph repeats his accusation (in a more emphatic form) that his brothers were actually spies, despite their denials. He proposes a test. If their story of their family is true, one brother will go back to get the youngest and bring him to Joseph. The other nine would remain **in prison** until that time. If the youngest was not brought back to Egypt, then the Egyptian governor would know that they were spies and presumably execute them.

Joseph conceals his identity to nice effect by twice swearing on the life of Pharaoh rather than by the name of God. In the first instance he swears by the life of Pharaoh that they would not get out of prison until and unless their youngest brother was brought back to Egypt. Joseph ends up changing his mind about this, so it is just as well that he did not take a solemn oath in God's name. The second oath in Pharaoh's name is dependent upon the first. If the youngest brother is not brought back to Egypt, the conclusion will be certain. The brothers will be convicted as spies.

In what Joseph may have thought would be a sweet sort of poetic justice, he commands them to be imprisoned while one of their number is sent as an emissary to bring the youngest brother back to Joseph. The brothers who had once imprisoned Joseph are imprisoned by Joseph. The reliability[17] of the brothers' words is at stake.

G. JOSEPH IMPRISONS, THEN FREES AND WARNS HIS BROTHERS (42:17-20)

42:17 And he put them all in custody for three days. 42:18 On the third day, Joseph said to them, "Do this and you will live, for I fear God: 42:19 If you are honest men, let one of your brothers stay here in prison, while the rest of you go and take grain back for your starving households. 42:20 But you must bring your youngest brother to me, so that your words may be verified and that you may not die." This they proceeded to do.

---

[17]דִּבְרֵיכֶם הָאֱמֶת (*dibrêkem ha'ĕmeth*) may imply that more than just the factual truthfulness of their words is at stake. The phrase could also mean "the trustworthiness of your actions."

Joseph receives no response from his brothers in regard to his demand that one of them return to Canaan to retrieve their youngest brother. He puts them into prison,[18] perhaps the very same prison where Joseph had been imprisoned. Three days later Joseph either had a change of heart or he thought that the three days was enough to make a point. He then spoke to them. He expresses a change of mind because of his "fear" of God.[19] The oaths that he had taken in Pharaoh's name could be superseded by his greater loyalty to God. It is not certain how the brothers would have understood what this mysterious Egyptian official was saying to them. The word translated "God" could as easily be translated "the gods," especially in the mouth of an official of polytheistic Egypt. Joseph may have been intending "God" but the brothers may have heard "gods." The reader is thereby drawn into the story. A monotheistic Joseph pretends to be an Egyptian who pretends to know something about the God of his brothers. But they may very well interpret what he says as a typical polytheistic statement because they expect an Egyptian official of Joseph's status to be polytheistic.

Joseph promises them that they will only be able to live under certain new conditions. It is not clear if Joseph intends to seem erratic to his brothers or not, but that must surely have been the effect. First he swears by the very life of Pharaoh, and then he goes against his oath, or at least changes the terms of it because he "fears the gods." This reversal of direction, or at least softening of his demands, occurs after only three days and without any words or actions on the part of the brothers. Joseph's brothers could prove that they were "**honest**"[20] **men**, as they had claimed, by leaving one of the brothers in prison as a guarantee **while the rest** took **grain** to their famine stricken **households**.

After returning home, the brothers were to bring their **youngest brother** back with them and thus confirm their words. Joseph then adds that if they did so they would not die. It is surprising that Joseph uses the plural[21] in this instance. After all he was only asking them to leave one of their brothers with him, and one might imagine that only his life

---

[18]The Hebrew word used, מִשְׁמָר (mišmār), is used of the prison where Joseph had been kept (Gen 40:3,4,7,10).

[19]The emphatic nature of this statement is emphasized by the Hebrew word order: אֶת־הָאֱלֹהִים אֲנִי יָרֵא ('eth-hā'ĕlōhîm 'ănî yārē'), direct object, subject pronoun, verb.

[20]The Hebrew term translated "honest," כֵּנִים (kēnîm), is only certainly used in this context. It is easily confused with the adverbial particle כֵּן (kēn) "thus, so"; cf. HALOT, p. 482: "[D]istinguishing I [כֵּנִים] from II [כֵּן] is often difficult."

[21]Hebrew has "you" in the plural in verses 18-20.

would be in danger. But Joseph knew that the severity and longevity of the seven-year famine would force them to come back again. If their youngest brother[22] was not with them, all of their lives would be at risk. Does Joseph here unwittingly tip his hand? How could he know that they would be forced to come back? If Joseph does slip up here, the brothers do not seem to catch on to it.

This time the brothers agree to the arrangement and do what Joseph asked. In this game of poker he had all of the cards.

H. JOSEPH'S BROTHERS UNKNOWINGLY ACKNOWLEDGE THEIR GUILT FOR THEIR TREATMENT OF JOSEPH (42:21-22)

42:21 They said to one another, "Surely we are being punished because of our brother. We saw how distressed he was when he pleaded with us for his life, but we would not listen; that's why this distress has come upon us." 42:22 Reuben replied, "Didn't I tell you not to sin against the boy? But you wouldn't listen! Now we must give an accounting for his blood."

Not knowing that Joseph, who had been disguising himself by speaking through an interpreter, would know what the brothers said to each other in Hebrew,[23] the brothers verbally acknowledge their guilt for what they had done to Joseph. The relationship of "brother" comes up in the Hebrew twice in this passage. The phrase "**to one another**" literally translated from the Hebrew is, "a man unto his brother." Thus the brothers spoke openly about the guilt which had come upon them because of their treatment of their "brother" Joseph. They had seen the distress of Joseph when he had pleaded for them to be gracious to him. They had not "heard" (וְלֹא שָׁמָעְנוּ, wᵉlōʾ šāmāʿnû) him then. Because of this a distress[24] to parallel his distress had come upon them.

Reuben, who had tried to save Joseph from them, refuses to share in their collective guilt. He had told them **not to sin**[25] **against** the lad.

---

[22]The Hebrew brings the object "youngest brother" into the first, and therefore emphatic, syntactical position.

[23]I presume that we are to assume they had adopted the language of Canaan by this time, even though they had been born in Paddan-Aram and might be thought to speak either Aramaic or a local dialect. Whatever the language was, Joseph knew it thoroughly.

[24]The NIV nicely shows the parallelism by using the word "distress" in both instances of צָרָה (ṣārāh).

[25]The Heb. אַל־תֶּחֶטְאוּ בַיֶּלֶד (ʾal-teḥeṭʾû bayyeled) demonstrates that one can "sin" against a person and not just against God, according to the text of Genesis.

Joseph, then aged seventeen is described by Reuben as a "lad" or "boy"[26] in order to emphasize the enormity of the crime. The favorite or not, spoiled and somewhat haughty or not, Joseph was only a lad. Just as the brothers would not listen to Joseph's cry for mercy, so, says Reuben, they would not listen to him, the oldest brother. Their crime, not Reuben's, had brought them to this situation. The consequences, however, included Reuben. Joseph's blood's [revenge] was being sought[27] now. The reader is reminded of Abel's blood crying out from the ground and of God's warning after the flood that those who violently kill will receive God's demand for accounting (Gen 9:5-6).[28]

Joseph, if he did not realize it before, now knows that Reuben had tried to save him. This may be the reason why Joseph passes over Reuben, the oldest, as his prisoner and opts for Simeon instead, the next one in line.

I. JOSEPH'S REACTION TO HIS BROTHERS' ADMISSION OF GUILT (42:23-24)

42:23 They did not realize that Joseph could understand them, since he was using an interpreter. 42:24 He turned away from them and began to weep, but then turned back and spoke to them again. He had Simeon taken from them and bound before their eyes.

The narrator reminds the readers that the brothers spoke so openly in front of him because **they did not realize that Joseph could** hear and **understand them**. The ruse of **using an interpreter** when none was needed had worked. Joseph's servants may or may not have understood what they said to each other. But Joseph was given a rare insight into the true character of his brothers.

It all proved to be too much for Joseph. Not wanting to give the game away by showing his true emotions, **he turned away from them**, removing himself at some distance. After composing himself he returned to speak **to them again**. We are not told what he said and especially how he said it. In any case, he chooses **Simeon**, the second oldest son of Leah and Jacob. As we have noted, this could well be because Joseph now understood that Reuben had honestly tried to protect him from the wrath of the other brothers. Reuben may then have been passed over as the prisoner because Joseph had learned of his innocence.

---

[26]יֶלֶד (*yeled*), implying a young child. The word "young man" (נַעַר, *na'ar*) is not used.

[27]נִדְרָשׁ (*nidrāš*), a niphal participle from דָּרַשׁ (*dāraš*).

[28]Wenham, *Genesis 16–50*, p. 408.

Another possibility is that Joseph saw some symbolism in choosing Simeon. Simeon, the second son of Leah, would be the ransom for Benjamin, the second son of Rachel.[29] Another consideration might be the violent nature which Simeon had displayed in the Dinah episode.[30] Whatever the reason or reasons, Joseph rather dramatically has Simeon **bound before** the very **eyes** of his brothers. This was the very thing that they had collectively done to Joseph more than twenty years before. The pathos of the moment is unmistakable. Joseph is not yet ready to grant forgiveness, no matter how emotionally traumatizing it was for him to withhold it.

J. JOSEPH SENDS NINE OF THE BROTHERS BACK TO CANAAN WITH GRAIN, PROVISIONS, AND A TRAP (42:25-26)

42:25 Joseph gave orders to fill their bags with grain, to put each man's silver back in his sack, and to give them provisions for their journey. After this was done for them, 42:26 they loaded their grain on their donkeys and left.

Joseph shows his authority in this passage. He commands and it is done. Their bags or vessels[31] were filled **with grain**, their **silver** was returned, and they were given additional **provisions for** the **journey**. With no bargaining chips at hand the brothers **loaded their grain on their donkeys and left** that place.

K. THE BROTHERS DISCOVER THE TRAP (42:27-28)

42:27 At the place where they stopped for the night one of them opened his sack to get feed for his donkey, and he saw his silver in the mouth of his sack. 42:28 "My silver has been returned," he said to his brothers. "Here it is in my sack." Their hearts sank and they turned to each other trembling and said, "What is this that God has done to us?"

When they stopped at the lodging place, one of the brothers **opened his sack**[32] to feed **his donkey** and **saw his silver**. Two different Hebrew

---

[29]Sternberg, *Poetics*, p. 291.

[30]Sarna, *Genesis*, p. 295.

[31]כְּלֵיהֶם (kᵊlêhem) is more general than "sacks" and can include all sorts of containers for various purposes. A sack is as good a guess as any.

[32]The variety of terms used to describe the containers for the grain is perplexing. שַׂק, (śaq) is used in 42:25,27a,35; אַמְתַּחַת (᾽amtaḥath) in vv. 42:27b,28a; 43:12,18,21, 22,23; 44:1,2,8,11,12). It may simply be a stylistic device using variety to retain interest. It is difficult to use this variation as an indication of changing sources, although this has been attempted. See Westermann, *Genesis 37–50*, pp. 111-112.

words for "sack" are used in verse 27. The first seems to be related to the English word "sack."[33] The second is only found in this context.[34]

The unnamed brother spoke to his brothers[35] about this. "My silver was put back in my sack, and moreover, Look! It's in my sack!" The hearts of the brothers "went out" when they saw the returned silver. They shook in fear as a man spoke to his "brother" saying, "**What is this [that] God has done to us?**" Literally the Hebrew says that they "shook out" the words themselves. They somehow knew that they were responsible to God for their callous casting off of Joseph. They could only imagine that God had turned them into thieves in the eyes of the second in command in Egypt in order to punish them for what they had done. For them God's retribution worked in the here and now. For some reason no one even thought to open the other bags.

L. THE NINE BROTHERS EXPLAIN TO JACOB WHY SIMEON DID NOT RETURN (42:29-34)

42:29 When they came to their father Jacob in the land of Canaan, they told him all that had happened to them. They said, 42:30 "The man who is lord over the land spoke harshly to us and treated us as though we were spying on the land. 42:31 But we said to him, 'We are honest men; we are not spies. 42:32 We were twelve brothers, sons of one father. One is no more, and the youngest is now with our father in Canaan.'

When the brothers arrive back in Canaan they tell Jacob almost everything. This time they do not hide what has happened to their missing brother Simeon. They describe Joseph as the "**lord over the land**" and quite accurately describe how he had spoken **harshly**[36] to them and accused them of being spies. They do not tell Jacob about how they used such deferential language with him, repeatedly referring to themselves as servant, and Joseph as "lord." This might be something assumed, or it

---

[33] שַׂק (śaq) is used of both "sacks" and of "sackcloth" worn by mourners (Gen 37:34).

[34] אַמְתַּחַת ('amtaḥath) may be related to Assyrian mataḥu and mean "pack." J. Greenfield, "The Etymology of אמתחת," ZAW 84 (1965): 90-92.

[35] The frequent use of the explicit "brother(s)" (18 times in ch. 42) in this narrative may be a way of emphasizing the point of the interfamilial tensions that had been a part of Israel's existence from its earliest days when it was not yet a nation, but merely an extended family.

[36] The brothers use the same words as the narrator does in verse 7: the verb דָּבַר (dābar) to describe the speaking with the adverb קָשֶׁה (qāšeh), "harshly."

could be a way of hiding the real dynamics of the discussions with Joseph so as to avoid excessive criticism. In any case they quite accurately tell Jacob that they claimed to be **"honest" men** and denied being spies and also that they were originally **twelve brothers** with one **no more and the youngest** still with his **father**. Jacob later criticized the brothers for giving away this vital piece of information when they should have been more circumspect with their language. They do not, however, try to tell tales to Jacob.

What They Actually Said to Joseph	What They Told Jacob They Said to Joseph
[10]"No, my lord," they answered. "Your servants have come to buy food. [11]We are all the sons of one man. Your servants are honest men, not spies." [12]"No!" he said to them. "You have come to see where our land is unprotected." [13]But they replied, "Your servants were twelve brothers, the sons of one man, who lives in the land of Canaan. The youngest is now with our father, and one is no more."	[31]But we said to him, 'We are honest men; we are not spies. [32]We were twelve brothers, sons of one father. One is no more, and the youngest is now with our father in Canaan.'

42:33 "Then the man who is lord over the land said to us, 'This is how I will know whether you are honest men: Leave one of your brothers here with me, and take food for your starving households and go. 42:34 But bring your youngest brother to me so I will know that you are not spies but honest men. Then I will give your brother back to you, and you can trade in the land.'"

The differences between what Joseph actually said and did and what the brothers tell Jacob he said and did are interesting. They neglect to mention that they were all held in prison for three days and that **"the man who is lord over the land"** changed courses. They also neglect to mention that Simeon would be kept in prison. More critically they neglect to mention that one of them had found his purchase price for the grain back in his sack on the way and would thus perhaps be facing the accusation of stealing upon their return. This ominous bit of news is withheld from Jacob.

They also add something which Joseph had not mentioned. They claim that Joseph had promised to return the brother kept with him and that they would then be free to trade in the land. Joseph had never mentioned this, and the brothers may be adding it as a further inducement to encourage Jacob to send Benjamin back with them. While the brothers do not materially misrepresent what Joseph had said, they narrate it in such a way as to increase the chances that Jacob would allow them to take Benjamin back to Egypt with them.

What Joseph Actually Said (42:18b-20a)	What the Brothers Claim Joseph Said
"Do this and you will live, for I fear God: [19]If you are honest men, let one of your brothers stay here in prison, while the rest of you go and take grain back for your starving households. [20]But you must bring your youngest brother to me, so that your words may be verified and that you may not die."	[33]"Then the man who is lord over the land said to us, 'This is how I will know whether you are honest men: Leave one of your brothers here with me, and take food for your starving households and go. [34]But bring your youngest brother to me so I will know that you are not spies but honest men. Then I will give your brother back to you, and you can trade in the land.'"

M. JACOB AND HIS SONS DISCOVER THE DEPTH OF THEIR PROBLEM (42:35)

42:35 As they were emptying their sacks, there in each man's sack was his pouch of silver! When they and their father saw the money pouches, they were frightened.

The conversation with Jacob evidently took place immediately upon their return before they had even unloaded their sacks with the precious cargo of food for a hungry household. Upon doing so, they along with their father Jacob saw the pouches of money in each of their sacks. The brothers had been afraid when one of the pouches was found along the way. Here their fright only increases, as does Jacob's.

N. REUBEN FAILS TO PERSUADE JACOB TO ALLOW THEM TO RETURN FOR SIMEON (42:36-38)

42:36 Their father Jacob said to them, "You have deprived me of my children. Joseph is no more and Simeon is no more, and now you want to take Benjamin. Everything is against me!" 42:37 Then Reuben said to his father, "You may put both of my sons to death if I do not bring him back to you. Entrust him to my care, and I will bring him back." 42:38 But Jacob said, "My son will not go down there with you; his brother is dead and he is the only one left. If harm comes to him on the journey you are taking, you will bring my gray head down to the grave in sorrow."

It is noteworthy that in this section the words "father" and "brother" recur repeatedly. It is not Jacob who speaks to them, but "**their father Jacob**." He complains that *they* had deprived him of children. The verb translated "deprived of children," שָׁכַל (*šākal*), is used of miscarriages due to natural causes (Gen 31:38; Exod 23:26; 2 Kgs 2:19,21; Job 21:10; Hos 9:14; Mal 3:11) but also especially of the violent killing of children (Gen 27:45; Lev 26:22; Deut 32:25; 1 Sam 15:33; Jer 15:7; Lam 1:20; Ezek 5:17; 14:15; 36:12,13,14; Hos 9:12). Interestingly Jacob blames his sons for the loss of Joseph as well as Simeon and the potential loss of Benjamin.

One wonders whether this reflects a lurking suspicion of his sons' explanation for Joseph's demise or whether he holds them accountable as his only brothers for not protecting him. Given what Jacob actually knows, his comment is irrational and could indicate his depression at what has happened within his own family. The sons cannot be blamed for what happened to Joseph so far as Jacob knows, and the imprisonment of Simeon is hardly something over which they had control.

In Jacob's mind Simeon is just as dead as Joseph. To send Benjamin back with them would be tantamount to a death sentence given the circumstances. Jacob's depression or extreme anxiety is not only indicated by his irrational blaming of his sons, but also by the final words of his statement in verse 36: "All things are against me."[37] Jacob is portrayed as thinking only of himself. He does not think of the bereavement of his sons for their brothers or their mothers for their sons. All of it has fallen on him.

Reuben, the firstborn, then addresses Jacob, who is once again referred to as "father" (v. 37). He offers Jacob the right to kill two of his own sons if he would take Benjamin back to Egypt and not return him safely to Jacob. It is an impulsive statement which cannot be taken literally. What good would it do Jacob to suffer the loss of yet another son, Benjamin, and compensate for it by killing two of his grandsons? Are the family's internal tensions so severe that such a thing could be seriously contemplated?

Jacob directly refuses Reuben's impulsive offer. Benjamin will not go down to Egypt with his other sons. The reason given once again surfaces the favoritism and internal tensions of the family. Jacob describes Benjamin as "**my son**" as though his brothers were not equally Jacob's sons. In Jacob's mind, since his full brother Joseph is dead, Benjamin is the only truly legitimate son left. The sons of Rachel, Joseph and Benjamin, are the only true sons in Jacob's mind. All the others lack legiti-

---

[37] עָלַי הָיוּ כֻלָּנָה (*'ālay hāyû kullānāh*), literally "upon me are all of these things."

macy in one form or another. If some harm should come to him on the way to Egypt, his grey head would go down in sorrow to the grave. In the Hebrew there is a sort of wordplay. Benjamin would not be "going down" to Egypt, because if he did and something bad happened to him, Jacob would "**go down**"[38] **to the grave in sorrow**. And so the brothers must wait.

---

[38]The verb יָרַד (*yārad*) is used in both instances.

GENESIS 43

VII. ON THE SECOND TRIP TO EGYPT JOSEPH REVEALS HIMSELF TO HIS BROTHERS (43:1–45:28)

In this section we see the turning point in the narrative of Jacob's sons. The resentment fueled by Jacob's favoritism resulted in the fracturing of the relationships between the brothers. Here Joseph overcomes his own understandable distrust and anger to offer reconciliation to his brothers. This does not come without emotional trauma (42:24; 43:30; 45:1). But ultimately what Joseph learns about his brothers, especially Reuben and Judah, when they do not realize that he is listening softens his heart and enables him to forgive.

After some time Jacob's family is again in desperate need of food. A return to Egypt is the only practical solution. Judah begins to come to the fore in this text as he, unlike Reuben, is able to convince Jacob to allow them to take Benjamin back with them to Egypt to buy grain. When they arrive in Egypt, Joseph invites them to a banquet at his own house at which they pretend to enjoy each others' company. Joseph then pretends to allow them to return to Canaan unscathed only to plant a "stolen" item in Benjamin's sack. This becomes the pretext for retaining Benjamin in Egypt. Judah's speech to "the man" Joseph, however, unmasks Joseph and the brothers reconcile. They return to inform an astonished Jacob that Joseph is still alive and plan a move to Egypt to ride out the famine.

A. THE BROTHERS RETURN TO EGYPT WITH BENJAMIN (43:1-14)

1. Judah Convinces Jacob to Allow Them to Return to Egypt with Benjamin (43:1-10)

43:1 Now the famine was still severe in the land. 43:2 So when they had eaten all the grain they had brought from Egypt, their father said to them, "Go back and buy us a little more food."

Jacob may have been hoping that the famine in the land of Canaan would let up. This would explain why the brothers did not press the point with him about taking Benjamin back with them to Egypt. In fact the famine did not get better but remained "heavy" (כָּבֵד, *kābēd*). Because of this they eventually ran out of the grain they had purchased on the previous trip to Egypt. Desperate for food to feed his hungry household Jacob, referred to in this passage as "**their father**," told them to return to Egypt and buy a "little" food. Perhaps Jacob is thinking that a small amount could be purchased without having to face the mysterious man who was lord over the land of Egypt.

43:3 But Judah said to him, "The man warned us solemnly, 'You will not see my face again unless your brother is with you.' 43:4 If you will send our brother along with us, we will go down and buy food for you. 43:5 But if you will not send him, we will not go down, because the man said to us, 'You will not see my face again unless your brother is with you.'"

This time **Judah** responds to Jacob. He says that "**the man**" was very clear. He uses the emphatic Hebrew construction[1] to make clear that the man was speaking with the utmost earnestness. That man controlled all sales of grain and other foods in Egypt and he was unequivocal. They would not be granted the necessary audience with the ruler of Egypt to buy food unless their youngest brother was with them to confirm their story.

Judah, speaking for the brothers, is very direct with his father. If Jacob would agree to send Benjamin with them, they would **go down** to Egypt to **buy food** for Jacob's household.[2] But if not, they refused to go down to Egypt without Benjamin. Judah emphasizes the point by repeating his opening statement from verse 3 to the letter in verse 5. They would not be granted the necessary audience with the ruler of Egypt to buy food **unless** their **youngest brother** was with them to confirm their story.

43:6 Israel asked, "Why did you bring this trouble on me by telling the man you had another brother?"

When Jacob responds to Judah the narrator describes him as "**Israel**." The connotations of this description might lead the audience to think more of Israel as the forefather of the nation than as the individual Jacob, although this is admittedly uncertain. The variation could

---

[1] הָעֵד הֵעִד (*hā'ēd hē'id*), hiphil infinitive absolute followed immediately by hiphil perfect 3ms of the same verb, עוּד (*'ûd*).

[2] In the Hebrew Judah is even more personal using the second person singular. They would be buying food for Jacob himself, not for themselves or their families, but for Jacob.

at certain points be simply for the sake of variety. But referring to Jacob as Israel also reminded the readers that while the stories are the stories of individuals, they are narrated because of their effect on the nation which later arose from those individuals.

Jacob accuses the brothers[3] of causing trouble or evil for him personally by giving away the information that they **had another brother** back at home. But surely Jacob is being unfair to his sons, and this would seem to be another example of the emotional blaming of others by a person upset at the circumstances in which he finds himself.

43:7 They replied, "The man questioned us closely about ourselves and our family. 'Is your father still living?' he asked us. 'Do you have another brother?' We simply answered his questions. How were we to know he would say, 'Bring your brother down here'?"

The accusation is against the brothers as a group, and so their defense of their actions is also as a group. They claim that **the man** closely **questioned** them about their family, asking unprompted whether their father was still alive and whether there were any other brothers. A comparison between what the brothers claim happened and what in fact happened makes it clear that the brothers were lying to Jacob. In fact, they, as Jacob suspected, offered the information about Jacob and Benjamin and without prompting. While it is true that they had no way to know that the man would require them to bring Benjamin back with them, Jacob is right to accuse them of giving important personal family information away that was now being used against them.

What the Brothers Told Jacob Happened	What Actually Happened
43:7 They replied, "The man questioned us closely about ourselves and our family. 'Is your father still living?' he asked us. 'Do you have another brother?' We simply answered his questions. How were we to know he would say, 'Bring your brother down here'?"	42:9 Then he . . . said to them, "You are spies! You have come to see where our land is unprotected." [10]"No, my lord," they answered. "Your servants have come to buy food. [11]We are all the sons of one man. Your servants are honest men, not spies." [12]"No!" he said to them. "You have come to see where our land is unprotected." [13]But they replied, "Your servants were twelve brothers, the sons of one man, who lives in the land of Canaan. The youngest is now with our father, and one is no more."

---

[3]In Hebrew the "you" is plural.

43:8 Then Judah said to Israel his father, "Send the boy along with me and we will go at once, so that we and you and our children may live and not die. 43:9 I myself will guarantee his safety; you can hold me personally responsible for him. If I do not bring him back to you and set him here before you, I will bear the blame before you all my life. 43:10 As it is, if we had not delayed, we could have gone and returned twice."

Judah once again speaks up, but this time he speaks personally and not on behalf of the brothers. **Judah** speaks to **"Israel, his father,"** a sign of national implications of what he is about to say. He asks Jacob to send Benjamin along with him. Benjamin is described as a "young man," the same terminology used to describe Joseph when at seventeen his brothers sold him into slavery in Egypt. This paints a rather ominous picture for what is about to occur. Judah argues that they must now arise and go and **live and not die**. The famine has evidently gotten to the place where their very lives were at stake. But it is not just Jacob's life or the lives of the brothers, but also the "little ones" (טַפֵּנוּ, *ṭappēnû*) who would die if they did not go. Judah also makes a promise to Jacob. Unlike Reuben who had previously offered the deaths of two of his sons, Judah offers himself. He promises himself personally in a pledge (אָנֹכִי אֶעֶרְבֶנּוּ, *ānōkî ʾeʿerbennû*) to Jacob. If Benjamin is not returned to Jacob, he will, for the rest of his life, be regarded as a sinner.[4] The canonical audience, if not the original, would know that when the nation split between the north led by the tribes of Joseph and the south led by the tribe of Judah, the tribe of Benjamin went with Judah, not Joseph. This is surprising given that Joseph and Benjamin shared Rachel as their mother and were Jacob's favorite sons. In this text we see Judah offering his life for Benjamin. The canonical audience might well see an anticipation of the later alliance between the tribes of Judah and Benjamin.

Judah says the delay caused by the internal argument[5] over whether to take Benjamin along would have allowed for two return trips by now. This is designed to put yet further pressure on Jacob to accede to their and Joseph's demand that Benjamin come along. In this text we begin to see the emergence of Judah as the *de facto* leader of the family. While in chapter 38 he had moved away from the family to live among the Canaanites, here he is back with his brothers and parents. He takes an assertive, leading role in negotiating with Jacob to take Benjamin along to Egypt. In the testament of Jacob in chapter 49 surprisingly Judah, not

---

[4]The English versions shy away from translating וְחָטָאתִי לְךָ (*wᵉḥāṭāʾthî lᵉkā*) with the word "sin," although that is the most common definition.

[5]The Hebrew uses the hithpael, הִתְמַהְמָהְנוּ (*hithmahmāhnû*), "we delayed ourselves."

Joseph, is given the leading role. This text narrates the beginning of the process whereby he becomes the family's leader, even though not Jacob's favorite.[6]

2. Jacob Sends Presents to the Man in Egypt (43:11-14)

43:11 Then their father Israel said to them, "If it must be, then do this: Put some of the best products of the land in your bags and take them down to the man as a gift—a little balm and a little honey, some spices and myrrh, some pistachio nuts and almonds. 43:12 Take double the amount of silver with you, for you must return the silver that was put back into the mouths of your sacks. Perhaps it was a mistake.

Jacob, again referred to as **Israel** and as the father of the brothers, finally accedes to Judah's conditions for a return trip to Egypt. They have reached the end, and the famine's effects have made the situation urgent. Jacob grants that "**it must be.**" But Jacob has experience in using gifts to placate a potentially hostile person who has the advantage in the situation. His lavish gifts to Esau may well have been a factor, in Jacob's mind at least, in their reconciliation. Jacob suggests that they make a gift of the most precious products which they have. Some undoubtedly had been grown in Canaan and others gained by trade with the caravans which passed through. The amounts are small, given the famine, but the list is striking.

The list has parallels with the list of the products of the Ishmaelite traders who bought Joseph as a slave from his brothers in 37:25. Both lists include **balm, spices, and myrrh.** The echo may be intended to remind the reader of the parallel. Joseph was taken as a slave to Egypt by people who also brought balm, spices, and myrrh. Joseph's brothers, who were responsible for enslaving him, now go to Egypt to face potential enslavement or worse and bring him balm, spices, and myrrh.

"Balm" (צֳרִי, *ṣārî*) is derived from a sort of sap obtained by making incisions in the bark of trees. Gilead, east of the Jordan, was famous for producing a medicinal variety (Jer 8:22; 46:11; 51:8), although it could also be used as a perfume. Suggested possible identifications "include storax, balsam and mastic, but none of these plants is indigenous to Palestine."[7] The word translated "spices" is not the typical generic Hebrew

---

[6]De Hoop, *Genesis 49*, pp. 568-574, goes too far in positing a pro-Joseph redactional strand that is overcome by a pro-Judah strand, but the surprising elevation of Judah over Joseph in Jacob's testament is a significant theological theme in Genesis. See below on Genesis 49.

[7]Rick R. Marrs, "Balm," *EDB*, p. 145.

word for spices,[8] but is identified as the *Astragalus tragacantha* plant.[9] It is sometimes translated "gum" and may have been used as a condiment.[10] Myrrh[11] was a plant product derived from the Burseraceae family. From ancient times it was used as incense, in medicine, and to drown out unpleasant odors. True myrrh comes only from Arabia and Somalia, but this text may be using the term more generically. In any case Jacob's family would have had easy access to buying myrrh from traveling caravans.

Three other products were part of Joseph's gift: **honey, pistachio nuts, and almonds**. Honey was a renowned product of Canaan, known as a land flowing with milk and honey (e.g., Deut 8:7-10). Honey was derived from bees[12] and was a sign of the fruitfulness of Canaan, available even in a time of famine. Given the extreme famine the gift should probably be viewed as luxurious.

In addition to the splendid gifts, Jacob also reminded his sons to attempt to return the money from the first sale of grain. According to them the money had mysteriously appeared in their sacks. It could be that Jacob is suspicious of his sons having stolen the original money. This may be hinted at by the word "perhaps." The mistake could be on the part of the Egyptian officials or on the part of the brothers. In any case, they should attempt to return what is not theirs. They also were to take along the money for the second portion of grain.

43:13 Take your brother also and go back to the man at once. 43:14 And may God Almighty grant you mercy before the man so that he will let your other brother and Benjamin come back with you. As for me, if I am bereaved, I am bereaved."

Jacob finally gets to the crucial point. Their "**brother**," Benjamin, is also to be taken.[13] After acceding to the demand he tells them to "arise and go."[14] Jacob closes by calling for God's blessing for the success of

---

[8]נְכֹאת (nᵉkō'th), not the generic בֶּשֶׂם (bāśām).

[9]Keith A. Burton, "Spices," *EDB*, p. 1247.

[10]Ibid.

[11]For what follows, Juris Zarins, "Myrrh," *EDB*, p. 930.

[12]The Talmudic suggestion that it was derived from dates may be based on a desire for an artificial consistency in Deuteronomy 8:7-10. Honey was derived from uncultivated land where wild bees thrived, not from keeping bees. Cf. Alan Ray Buescher, "Honey," *EDB*, p. 603.

[13]The emphatic nature of this conclusion is hinted at by the word order in Hebrew, וְאֶת־אֲחִיכֶם קָחוּ (we'eth-'ăḥîkem qāḥû), object clause first, followed by verb.

[14]The NIV attempts to capture the flavor of this by rendering, "Go back to the man *at once*" (my emphasis).

the journey. He uses the divine name El Shaddai, which the NIV renders "**God Almighty**," an apt title for God when asking him to override circumstances for the favor of his people. This was the characteristic way in which the Patriarchs, Abraham, Isaac, and Jacob referred to God (Exod 6:3) rather than Yahweh. Jacob hopes or affirms[15] that the Almighty God would give them **mercy before** "**the man**," the most powerful man in Egypt other than Pharaoh. God's mercy would, Jacob hopes, result in the man allowing their "other **brother**" (Simeon) as well as **Benjamin** to **come back** to their family. It is interesting that Jacob refers to Simeon as "your other brother," not "my son." By contrast he refers to Benjamin by name. The favoritism that so infects this family is still there even in the midst of this crisis. Significantly Jacob ends by speaking of himself, something he is wont to do throughout this narrative. This is not one of the more appealing features of Jacob as a character. If something happens and Benjamin and Simeon are lost, he will see his children taken from him. In a sort of disconsolate mourning Jacob sees only his own hurt and his own sad lot in life, "**If I am bereaved, I am bereaved.**"[16]

B. GUESS WHO'S COMING TO DINNER (43:15-34)

1. Joseph Prepares to Dine with His Brothers (43:15-17)

43:15 So the men took the gifts and double the amount of silver, and Benjamin also. They hurried down to Egypt and presented themselves to Joseph. 43:16 When Joseph saw Benjamin with them, he said to the steward of his house, "Take these men to my house, slaughter an animal and prepare dinner; they are to eat with me at noon." 43:17 The man did as Joseph told him and took the men to Joseph's house.

Interestingly the narrator describes the brothers as "**the men**." This may be to distinguish them from Benjamin who is described as a "youth" or "boy" (נַעַר, *na'ar*) in verse 8.[17] Another possibility is that this

---

[15]The Hebrew imperfect could be a simple future, "God Almighty will give" or a modal "May God Almighty give." In light of the context, where Jacob realizes he could be bereaved of both Simeon and Benjamin, if not all of his sons, the latter seems to be the sense here.

[16]While the NIV nicely captures the sense of this statement, in 42:36 they translate the same Hebrew verb (שָׁכָל, *šākal*) as "deprive me of children." This loses the connection between these two texts.

[17]Benjamin is at least 35 at this time as Joseph is about 39. All of the twelve sons of Jacob were born within a thirteen-year time span, and Joseph is the eleventh of twelve sons. This shows the flexibility of this Hebrew term.

description of the brothers as "the men" stands in contrast to the description of Joseph as "the man." They took everything that Jacob recommended ("**the gifts**" and **double . . . silver**) as well as **Benjamin**. They arose and went **down**[18] **to Egypt and presented themselves** to **Joseph**. The dramatic reuniting of Joseph and Benjamin, the two favored sons of the favored wife Rachel, is about to take place.

When Joseph saw his brother **Benjamin** with his ten half-brothers, he did not immediately react. Instead he seems to be carrying out a predetermined plan. He commanded the person over his house, (NIV's "steward") to bring "the men" to his house and there to prepare a feast.[19] Without explaining it to his steward he plans **to eat** with them **at noon**. These were not just any random bunch of west Semites coming to Egypt to buy food.

The Hebrew in verse 17 emphasizes two phrases, "the man"[20] in this context meaning the steward, and "the men" meaning the brothers of Joseph. It is striking that Joseph's steward, not Joseph himself, is referred to as "**the man**." In the immediately preceding section this phrase was used repeatedly for Joseph. Joseph is no longer the impersonal "man" that Jacob and his sons had discussed back in Canaan.

2. The Brothers Attempt to Return the Silver (43:18-23a)

43:18 Now the men were frightened when they were taken to his house. They thought, "We were brought here because of the silver that was put back into our sacks the first time. He wants to attack us and overpower us and seize us as slaves and take our donkeys."

The men, i.e., the brothers, were afraid **when they were** brought to Joseph's own **house**. They said, either internally or to each other[21] that this ominous seeming event was happening **because of the silver** which had been returned in their **sacks the first time**. Such special hospitality

---

[18]The NIV once again paraphrases "got up and went" as "hurried down to" Egypt.

[19]The NIV's "dinner" may be too tame a word, since the steward is commanded to slaughter an animal for the occasion.

[20]The NIV, perhaps to avoid unnecessary repetitiveness only uses "the man" once while the Hebrew has it twice. Literally the Hebrew reads, "The man did as Joseph had said to him. The man brought the men to [the] house of Joseph."

[21]An unusual, but not unheard of, use of אָמַר (*'āmar*) of internal, rather than external, speech. Cf. M. Niehoff, "Do Biblical Characters Talk to Themselves? Narrative Modes of Representing Inner Speech in Early Biblical Fiction," *JBL* 111 (1992): 577-595.

could not be genuine. Joseph, they thought, brought them there so that
he could assault them and fall upon them in order to take them as slaves
along with their donkeys. These thoughts are irrational[22] at several
points. If Joseph, the ruler of all Egypt, second only to Pharaoh, needed to enslave them, he could have done so publicly by using the pre-
tense of the (stolen) money. He did not need to do it privately in his
own house. Joseph further was not in need of more slaves or especially
donkeys. The words of the brothers instead seem to be designed to portray their panic in the situation and to thereby increase the narrative
tension in the story. The irony is that the brothers fear being enslaved
by this unknown Egyptian, who is actually Joseph, whom they had originally enslaved.

**43:19 So they went up to Joseph's steward and spoke to him at the
entrance to the house. 43:20 "Please, sir," they said, "we came down
here the first time to buy food. 43:21 But at the place where we
stopped for the night we opened our sacks and each of us found his
silver—the exact weight—in the mouth of his sack. So we have brought
it back with us. 43:22 We have also brought additional silver with us
to buy food. We don't know who put our silver in our sacks." 43:23a
"It's all right," he said. "Don't be afraid. Your God, the God of your
father, has given you treasure in your sacks; I received your silver."**

In a panic over their situation the brothers cautiously approached[23]
"the man who was over the house of Joseph." Once again the redundancy echoes Joseph being referred to as "the man" in the preceding
narrative. They talked with him **at the entrance to the house** either
because they had not yet gone in and were hesitant to do so or because
they wanted to speak privately and discreetly to Joseph's servant without raising the ire of Joseph. They begin with a "particle of entreaty,
craving permission to address a superior."[24] This particle always begins
a speech and is followed immediately by the word "lord." The subservience of the brothers to Joseph is emphasized by the fact that they
are so deferential to his steward.

They begin by reminding the steward that the first time they came
down to *buy* food. Perhaps this is to remind the steward that they did
not come down to steal it. They tell the steward that when they came to
the lodging place on the way home, they were surprised to see **the exact**

---

[22]On the irrational nature of such internal speech see Niehoff, "Biblical
Characters," pp. 584-585.

[23]In this context the use of וַיִּגְּשׁוּ (*wayyigg⁾šû*), "to approach, draw near," rather
than more common words implies a hesitancy by the brothers.

[24]See Princeton Abridged BDB #994 in Gramcord on this verse.

weight of silver with which they had purchased the food in each of their sacks.[25] They had personally returned, not wanting to be accused of stealing. They had brought **additional silver** to pay for the food this time. They claim not to know who put the silver in their sacks.

The steward reassures the brothers that they have nothing to fear. Using vocabulary of divine reassurance (Gen 15:1; 21:17; 26:24; 46:3; Num 21:34; Deut 20:3; Josh 11:6; Judg 6:23), he says, "Peace [be] to you. Do not be afraid." The steward then speaks of their "god(s) and the god(s) of [their] fathers." Most likely the Egyptian is not speaking as a strict monotheist in this case, and thus the word for the deity should not be capitalized in English. But in Hebrew the word *'ělōhîm* can mean either the one true God or, when used in polytheistic contexts, "gods" or "god." The reader hears this statement at two levels. On one level the steward is a polytheist. This does not require him to deny the existence of the god or gods worshiped by Jacob and his sons. But the monotheistic reader (and certainly the canonical reader) sees that the narrator might be speaking at another level. He puts "orthodox" monotheistic language into the mouth of a polytheistic Egyptian official to indicate that the God of Jacob and his sons had been at work.

The steward says that their god had put hidden treasure in their sacks and claims that he had received their money from the first transaction. The steward, of course, is lying. Or perhaps he is making an ironic wordplay on the ambiguity of the word *'ělōhîm*, which can sometimes refer to powerful human figures,[26] like Joseph, as well as deities.

3. The Brothers Prepare for the Dinner (43:23b-25)

43:23b Then he brought Simeon out to them. 43:24 The steward took the men into Joseph's house, gave them water to wash their feet and provided fodder for their donkeys. 43:25 They prepared their gifts for Joseph's arrival at noon, because they had heard that they were to eat there.

Simeon was then restored to his brothers. One can only imagine what must have been going through the minds of the brothers. The things that they were experiencing were simply too good to be true. Once again the Hebrew refers to "the man" meaning **the steward,** and

---

[25]Of course the brothers are fibbing since only one of them found the silver then (Gen 42:27). The rest found it when they got all the way back to Canaan with their father Jacob looking on (Gen 42:35).

[26]Possibilities of this usage include Psalm 82:1.

"the men" meaning the brothers. They were taken **into Joseph's house**, the person whom Jacob and his brothers had been referring to as "the man." Joseph's steward showed them typical ancient Near Eastern hospitality granted to guests by providing **them water to wash** with and feed **for their donkeys**. The brothers prepared the gifts which Jacob had sent along with them to curry favor with "the man."

Unbeknownst to them, the man they were preparing the gifts for was none other than Joseph. While he had spoken to his servants regarding the noon meal in the presence of his brothers, he had done so in Egyptian, not in Hebrew. As a result they were initially unaware as to why they were being taken to Joseph's own house to eat a meal with the most powerful man in Egypt save Pharaoh. They later heard about this and were thus able to make proper arrangements for the presentation of the gifts. By withholding this information Joseph is playing a sort of game. He wants to see how they react without their knowing that he and his servants are watching them all of the time. This might reveal their true character and whether they have changed in the years since they were together. The presentation of gifts is yet another indication of the subordinate status of the brothers. With Benjamin now there and Simeon restored to them, all eleven of the brothers are now in a subordinate position to Joseph as anticipated in his dreams in chapter 37.

4. Joseph Greets His Brothers and Benjamin (43:26-29)

43:26 When Joseph came home, they presented to him the gifts they had brought into the house, and they bowed down before him to the ground. 43:27 He asked them how they were, and then he said, "How is your aged father you told me about? Is he still living?" 43:28 They replied, "Your servant our father is still alive and well." And they bowed low to pay him honor.

The time has finally come. All of the brothers are gathered together and Joseph is there. In Joseph's own house[27] his brothers brought him gifts, and then **they bowed down before him to the ground** in fulfillment of Joseph's first dream.

Still playing the game, Joseph asked after their well-being.[28] He then asked after the well-being of their **aged father**, whom they had spoken

---

[27]The Hebrew emphasizes the word "house" (בַּיִת, *bayith*) by repetition, "Joseph came to the house and they gave him the gifts which were in their hands, [which they brought] to the house."

[28]וַיִּשְׁאַל לָהֶם לְשָׁלוֹם (*wayyiš'al lāhem lᵉšālôm*), "he asked after their peace." The word שָׁלוֹם (*šālôm*) means more than the English word "peace."

about to him on the previous trip. Joseph is concerned to see his father again before Jacob dies, and he wants to know whether he is still alive. He did this however without the brothers knowing what he was doing. He only used the information they had supplied to him and to them seems to be merely curious, or, more likely, testing them to make sure that their story was consistent. Joseph had grown up being Jacob's favorite, and the affection was obviously mutual. The brothers respond by describing Jacob as Joseph's servant. He is "our" father, but "your" servant, they say. They assure Joseph that Jacob **is still alive**. They then once again show their submissiveness to Joseph by bowing yet again. This time the Hebrew uses two different verbs[29] to emphasize the point of their bowing down. The NIV indicates this by translating, "bowed low to pay him honor." This emphasizes the point quite nicely. The brothers are not just going through an ancient Near Eastern formality. They are demonstrating their recognition of their subordinate status to the mysterious man from Egypt, who seems so personally interested in them.

43:29 As he looked about and saw his brother Benjamin, his own mother's son, he asked, "Is this your youngest brother, the one you told me about?" And he said, "God be gracious to you, my son."

Up till now Joseph has kept his composure and played the mind game he was playing with his brothers quite successfully. He had seen **Benjamin** before when he arrived but had quickly given orders to take them to his own house for a meal and had left. Now he had to meet Benjamin, his only "full, blood-brother," and keep up the ruse. Acting as though he had not yet noticed Benjamin, Joseph then "lifted up his eyes and saw"[30] him. The narrator describes him as "Benjamin his brother, the son of his mother" to emphasize the point. He and Benjamin were the only sons of the only wife whom Jacob genuinely loved.

Still maintaining his ruse, Joseph rhetorically asks the brothers whether this person was in fact their **youngest brother** of whom they had told him. Without waiting for an answer, Joseph spoke directly to Benjamin. Once again the powerful Egyptian man speaks of God, although the brothers do not know it. The word *'ĕlōhîm* for Joseph meant the one, true God. But for the brothers, who still think he is only a powerful Egyptian official, it must mean "gods." Joseph asks that **God** or "the gods" **be gracious** to Benjamin, using in Hebrew a theologically

---

[29] וַיִּקְּדוּ (*wayyiqqᵉdû*) "they paid homage" and וַיִּשְׁתַּחֲווּ (*wayyištaḥăwû*) "they bowed down."

[30] The narrator slows the pace of his narrative at this momentous point by going into detail: וַיִּשָּׂא עֵינָיו וַיַּרְא (*wayyiśśā' 'ênayw wayyar'*).

rich word, חָנַן (ḥānan). The brothers undoubtedly think that this is a polytheistic statement and is purely formal, not a theologically rich statement by a monotheist. Joseph refers to him affectionately as "**my son.**" The brothers do not realize what the readers know, that such affection is a sign of the man from Egypt's identity. To them it must have seemed as yet another perplexing sign of the strangeness of the situation. Why should the ruler of Egypt treat the youngest son of a Hebrew Bedouin with such apparent affection?

5. Joseph Hides His Emotions from His Brothers (43:30-31)

43:30 Deeply moved at the sight of his brother, Joseph hurried out and looked for a place to weep. He went into his private room and wept there. 43:31 After he had washed his face, he came out and, controlling himself, said, "Serve the food."

Even though Joseph had seen Benjamin previously, his feelings for his brother hit him suddenly. Unable to contain himself and not (yet?) wanting to reveal his identity to his brothers, **Joseph hurried out** and sought a place to weep privately. He found "the"[31] **private room**, perhaps his own bedroom or personal room, as a place to weep in private. The inner turmoil of the game he has been playing with his brothers has overcome him. If it were merely the issue of being reunited with Benjamin, he could have arrested him and had the others executed or sent away. The emotion seems to stem from the perceived need to continue disguising himself from his brothers.

Joseph **washed his face** to disguise his tears and came back to his brothers, all the while **controlling himself**. As though nothing had happened, he directed his servants to **serve the food**. While the game he is playing is emotionally traumatizing, he nevertheless plays it well.

6. The Dinner Takes Place under Odd Circumstances (43:32-34)

43:32 They served him by himself, the brothers by themselves, and the Egyptians who ate with him by themselves, because Egyptians could not eat with Hebrews, for that is detestable to Egyptians.

The eating arrangements are passing strange. Joseph, reverting to his role as ruler under Pharaoh of all Egypt, ate **by himself**. **The brothers** also ate **by themselves** because the Egyptians found it detestable to

---

[31]The NIV interprets the definite article as "his." The word for private room (הַחֶדְרָה, haḥadrāh) can mean bedroom or private inner chamber.

eat with Hebrews. One wonders whether the Egyptians would not eat even with Joseph, given that his Hebrew ancestry was known from the beginning of his association with Pharaoh's household (Gen 41:12). The original and canonical audiences were well aware that Hebrew culture, including their primary occupation, shepherding, and their sacrifices were abhorrent to the Egyptians (Gen 46:34; Exod 8:22). This created an unstable social situation in which they were distanced from Egyptian society into a sort of ghettolike existence. The trouble which this produced for the Hebrews (oppressive slavery) would await a Pharaoh who neither knew of nor respected Joseph. In this passage the beginnings of that trouble are subtly suggested.

43:33 The men had been seated before him in the order of their ages, from the firstborn to the youngest; and they looked at each other in astonishment. 43:34 When portions were served to them from Joseph's table, Benjamin's portion was five times as much as anyone else's. So they feasted and drank freely with him.

While the NIV's "**in the order of their ages**" is a possible interpretation, the NRSV is more literal in rendering, ". . . they were seated before him, the firstborn according to his birthright and the youngest according to his youth." Both versions assume that the verb "to sit"[32] is to be understood as a passive ("seated" by someone else) even though it occurs in the active. This helps to explain the astonishment that the men[33] experience. But read literally the Hebrew suggests that they sat down and not that they were seated by someone else. If so, the astonishment of the brothers must be from something other than the order of seating since they would know their birth orders. The exact cause of their astonishment is not stated. Perhaps it is merely the combination of odd things occurring.

Oddly, from their point of view, they are served **from Joseph's** own **table**. If Joseph is an Egyptian official, as they quite naturally presumed, why would he share food with them while the other Egyptians found it an abomination to eat with the Hebrews? Further, why would this powerful man show favoritism to **Benjamin** by giving him **five times as much** food as his brothers? Why was he so concerned about Benjamin? The game which Joseph is playing continues. It is somewhat surprising that, given the quite natural fears they had of this man, they would

---

[32]וַיֵּשְׁבוּ (*wayyēšbû*), a qal *waw*-consecutive.

[33]Notice it is once again "the men" rather than the brothers. This is yet another example of the contrast between Joseph who is described as "the man" and his brothers who are described as "the men" in this narrative.

drink and even become drunk (וַיִּשְׁכְּרוּ עִמּוֹ, *wayyišk³rû ʿimmō*)[34] with him. With the traditional idealized portraits of Joseph the translations want to somehow soften what is going on.

---

[34]The verb שָׁכַר (*šākar*) is stronger than the NIV's "drank freely" referring to Noah's drunkenness (Gen 9:21). All of the other uses of the verb likewise refer to drunkenness (S of S 5:1; Isa 29:9; 49:26; Jer 25:27; Lam 4:21; Nahum 3:11) with the possible exception of Haggai 1:6.

GENESIS 44

C. JOSEPH TRICKS HIS BROTHERS INTO RETURNING (44:1-13)

1. Joseph Lays Another Trap in His Brothers' Sacks (44:1-2)

44:1 Now Joseph gave these instructions to the steward of his house: "Fill the men's sacks with as much food as they can carry, and put each man's silver in the mouth of his sack. 44:2 Then put my cup, the silver one, in the mouth of the youngest one's sack, along with the silver for his grain." And he did as Joseph said.

Joseph continues to play his game leaving his brothers and first-time readers wondering exactly what is going on. After having gotten them drunk, he tells **the steward of his house** to fill the men's[1] sacks to the brim, **and put each man's silver in the mouth of the sack**. Joseph does not explain to him why.

Joseph then continues the game. His steward is commanded to put his cup, the silver cup, **in the mouth** of the sack of **the youngest one along with the silver for** purchasing the **grain**. The steward dutifully obeys. We are given no clue as to what the steward thinks about what is going on, intriguing though such information might be. In the Hebrew the phrase, "my cup the silver one" is placed in first position in order to give it emphasis. It is to be placed along with the silver money in the mouth of the sack of Benjamin so that it can be easily discovered when it comes time for Joseph's trick to be played out.

2. Joseph Springs the Trap and the Brothers Return to the City (44:3-13)

44:3 As morning dawned, the men were sent on their way with their donkeys. 44:4 They had not gone far from the city when Joseph said

---

[1] Notice that Joseph does not let even his steward know who these Hebrew men actually are.

to his steward, "Go after those men at once, and when you catch up with them, say to them, 'Why have you repaid good with evil? **44:5** Isn't this the cup my master drinks from and also uses for divination? This is a wicked thing you have done.'"

The Hebrew narrator draws the reader into the story. Literally the verse reads, "The morning light and the men were sent, they and their donkeys." The reader experiences seeing the morning light in his or her imagination. Once again the brothers are referred to as "**the men**" in contrast to Joseph who was viewed by them as "the man."

Joseph waits until shortly after they had left the city to instruct the steward of his house "to pursue after the men" (הָאֲנָשִׁים אַחֲרֵי רְדֹף, *rᵉdōph 'aḥărê hā'ănāšîm*). Once again the brothers are referred to as "the men." Upon overtaking them the steward is to ask, "Why did you return evil for good?" The accusation is quite broad. Joseph had treated them with great hospitality, inviting them to his own personal residence and giving them food from his own table. They had responded to such generosity by taking advantage of the situation and stealing from Joseph. And this was no petty theft. The steward was to claim that his lord drank from that very cup and even used it most certainly[2] **for divination**. In doing this the brothers had acted in an evil fashion, returning the goodness of Joseph's generosity by stealing a most precious possession. The question is often asked, how could Joseph be involved in divination? Wasn't this prohibited for God's people in both the Old and New Covenants? In fact, the narrator does not say that the steward's story is true, only that Joseph told him to tell the story in order to entrap his brothers. The brothers would be less likely to uncover Joseph's identity if they thought he was involved in the common ancient Near Eastern practice of divination. The law tells Jewish people to carefully avoid divination.[3] The suggestion that the mysterious man from Egypt was involved in divination would give the brothers an explanation for all the strange events that had unfolded before them in relationship to Joseph. Joseph is setting them up to believe his statement in verse 15 below.

44:6 When he caught up with them, he repeated these words to them. 44:7 But they said to him, "Why does my lord say such things? Far be it from your servants to do anything like that! 44:8 We even brought back to you from the land of Canaan the silver we found inside the mouths of our sacks. So why would we steal silver or gold from your

---

[2]The Hebrew uses the emphatic construction, infinitive absolute followed immediately by the imperfect of the same verb, here.

[3]The practice of divination is strictly forbidden for Israel in Leviticus 11:26 and Deuteronomy 18:10.

master's house? 44:9 If any of your servants is found to have it, he will die; and the rest of us will become my lord's slaves."

The steward, without an explanation as to exactly what Joseph was up to, nevertheless obeys and accuses the men of returning Joseph's good with the evil of stealing his divining cup. The initial response of the brothers is found in verses 7-9. They use deferential language in addressing Joseph's steward, addressing him as "lord" and referring to themselves as his "**servants**." Evidently one of the brothers spoke for the group, since the steward is addressed in the singular as "my" lord. The spokesman begins with a question worded deferentially and diplomatically, "**Why does my lord say such things?**" Surely the steward would agree that those who regard themselves as his servants would never do the sort of thing they had been accused of doing.

As evidence of their honesty they note the fact that they had attempted to return the silver used to purchase the first allotment of grain when they returned to Egypt. If they were honest enough to bring that money back all the way from Canaan, how, they ask, could they **steal silver or gold** from the house of the steward's lord (Joseph)?

The brothers are so certain of their innocence they call down a curse upon themselves. They continue with the deferential language, promising that the person who is found with the cup from among them, referred to as "your [i.e., the steward's] servants" **will die** and what is more the entire group of brothers would become his ("my lord") servants. The offer is a staggering one given what is about to happen. The statement echoes the dream of Joseph yet again. The very same brothers who enslaved Joseph could become slaves themselves.

44:10 "Very well, then," he said, "let it be as you say. Whoever is found to have it will become my slave; the rest of you will be free from blame."

The steward responds to the brothers as a group,[4] not to the individual spokesperson. He seems to take up the offer, but in doing so he softens it. Only the person who is found with the cup will become the steward's slave; **the rest** of them would **be free** of all guilt and responsibility. Somehow the steward knows that Joseph's primary concern is with the youngest of the brothers, not the entire group. Even though Joseph did not instruct his steward to negotiate with the brothers, his negotiation is in line with Joseph's intentions. He shows the characteristic of all good servants, the ability to anticipate his master's desires and intentions even when unspoken.

---

[4]"As you say" uses the plural in Hebrew.

44:11 Each of them quickly lowered his sack to the ground and opened it. 44:12 Then the steward proceeded to search, beginning with the oldest and ending with the youngest. And the cup was found in Benjamin's sack. 44:13 At this, they tore their clothes. Then they all loaded their donkeys and returned to the city.

The brothers are once again referred to as "men." Each "man" hurried and **lowered his sack to the ground** and each "man" **opened** his sack. Saying it this way rather than merely saying "they hurried and opened their sacks" allows the narrator to tie into the *leitmotif* of "the men" (i.e., the brothers) and "the man" (i.e., Joseph).[5] Describing Joseph as "the man" indicates his exalted status in relationship to his brothers who are merely, "the men." They hurry because they are so confident of their own honesty in this situation.

The steward searched thoroughly (וַיְחַפֵּשׂ, *wayᵉḥappēś*, piel of חָפַשׂ). Beginning with the oldest, he finished with the youngest (בַּגָּדוֹל הֵחֵל וּבַקָּטֹן כִּלָּה, *baggādôl hēḥēl ûbaqqāṭōn killāh*). **The cup was** thus **found** at the end of his search in the sack of Benjamin. One can only imagine how the growing confidence of the brothers as each of the first ten sacks searched did not contain the cup was dashed when it showed up **in Benjamin's sack**. How the steward knew the ages of the brothers must have been a mystery to them as it was at the meal. In this instance it is not mentioned as being noticed by the brothers.

The extreme grief over seeing the steward find Joseph's cup in Benjamin's sack, the youngest son whom they were to especially protect, is indicated by a typical Hebrew sign of mourning,[6] the tearing of the mantle. In this case the terminology is more specific than tearing the garments. The phrase[7] only occurs two other times in the Old Testament. In Joshua 7:6 Joshua did the same when Israel was defeated in battle because of the removal of God's protection over Achan's sin. Even more poignantly, in Genesis 37:34 Jacob "tore his mantle" when he inferred that Joseph was dead. The brothers act together in solidarity, this time not to enslave their second youngest brother, a brother they resented, but in grief over the possibility that their youngest brother would be enslaved.

---

[5]See Genesis 42:30; 43:3,5,6,7,11,13,14 for "the man" and 43:15,16,17,18,24,33; 44:3,4 for "the men."

[6]Num 14:6; Josh 7:6; Judg 11:35; 2 Sam 1:11; 13:19; 31; 1 Kgs 21:27; 2 Kgs 2:12; 5:7; 6:30; 19:1; 22:1.

[7]The verb קָרַע (*qāraʿ*), "to tear," followed by שִׂמְלָה (*śamlāh*), "mantle," as its object.

In grief each of them **loaded** their heavy sacks of grain upon **their donkeys and** voluntarily **returned to the city** to face the music. The eerie tones of that music had been in the background throughout this experience, but now it has blasted their eardrums with its ferocity.

D. THE BROTHERS RECONCILE (44:14–45:15)

1. Judah Offers Himself as a Substitute for Benjamin (44:14-17)

44:14 Joseph was still in the house when Judah and his brothers came in, and they threw themselves to the ground before him.

Judah is singled out as the representative of the brothers, thus "**Judah and his brothers**." Their solidarity as a group is subtly indicated by the fact that they are no longer anonymous men, but brothers. In some sense the entire "Joseph narrative" is more accurately designated "the narrative of Joseph and Judah's rise to prominence among their brothers."[8] Both Joseph and Judah will receive blessings from Jacob above and beyond what their brothers receive in Genesis 49. In this passage[9] we see Judah step to the fore. After coming to Joseph's house we discover that Joseph had remained there, undoubtedly to see the game which he had been playing with his brothers play itself out. The dreams of Joseph are echoed by the fact that upon seeing him his brothers fell on their faces **to the ground before him**. His dreams were coming true before his very eyes.

44:15 Joseph said to them, "What is this you have done? Don't you know that a man like me can find things out by divination?" 44:16 "What can we say to my lord?" Judah replied, "What can we say? How can we prove our innocence? God has uncovered your servants' guilt. We are now my lord's slaves—we ourselves and the one who was found to have the cup."

Upon their return Joseph confronts his brothers. He reminds them of how foolish they were to think that they could get away with stealing without Joseph finding out. He could most certainly[10] discover who stole from him **by divination**. The irony is that according to his steward Joseph used the silver cup which was stolen for divination. How could Joseph discover by divination who stole his divining cup when he no longer has the cup with which to practice divination! It seems to me to be more plausible to recognize that these claims are just part of the win-

---

[8]See de Hoop, *Genesis 49*, pp. 568-631.

[9]This was anticipated in Genesis 43:8.

[10]The Hebrew emphatic construction is used here yet again as in Genesis 44:5.

dow dressing for the psychological game Joseph is playing with his brothers.

Joseph refers to himself in this passage as **"a man like me"** and claims supernatural power to gain knowledge. The theme of "the man" which echoes as a *leitmotif* throughout this section of the Joseph narrative comes up yet again.[11] In this distressing situation it is Judah who takes the lead and addresses Joseph. He begins with honest frankness by asking the repetitive question, **"What can we say to my lord, what can we say?"**[12] Once again the deferential language ("my lord," "your servants") reminds the reader of Joseph's dreams. Judah continues by asking, "How can we justify ourselves?" He realizes that no explanation will prove satisfactory in this situation. He also recognizes the ultimate cause of their predicament. God has found out their iniquity and is so orchestrating events that the inevitable punishment which follows grievous sin has come upon them. The word translated "iniquity" (עָוֹן, *'āwōn*)[13] is not merely a synonym for sin but includes sin with its ensuing and inevitable consequences. Thus God is said to "visit the iniquity of the fathers onto their children for three and four generations." God does not visit "sin" onto future generations, but the consequences of sin do impact those who follow us. The older English word "iniquity" has this connotation, although it has largely been lost in contemporary English. Judah offers that all of the brothers become Joseph's slaves. The echo of Joseph's dreams comes up yet again. To reinforce the point he clarifies, "both we and the one in whose hand the stolen cup was found." Judah had personally guaranteed Benjamin's safe return to Joseph. Realizing that such a return was not likely to occur, Judah offers the entire group of brothers as servants just as they had offered to Joseph's steward on the road back to Canaan. Judah's confession of sin to Joseph, even though he does not know that it is Joseph, has a powerful affect on him.

44:17 But Joseph said, "Far be it from me to do such a thing! Only the man who was found to have the cup will become my slave. The rest of you, go back to your father in peace."

---

[11]See note 5 above.

[12]While Judah uses two different Hebrew verbs for "say" (אָמַר, *'āmar*, and דִּבֶּר, *dibbēr*, in the usual piel form) this seems to be a stylistic device, and the verbs carry no clear difference in meaning in this context.

[13]According to Koch citing *TLOT*, II:863ff. ("עָוֹן, *'āwōn*," *TDOT*, X:548-549) the root "expresses a 'dynamic holistic thought' that tries to conceive in a single sweep 'the various phases of a misdeed-consequence process (deed-consequence completion).'"

Joseph's words in response echo the words of the brothers when they are first accused by Joseph of stealing the cup, "**Far be it from me to do such a thing**" is similar to "Far be it from your servants to do anything like that!" the word addressed to the steward in verse 7.[14] Joseph's words are similar to his steward's in verse 10.[15] The punishment should fit the crime and in particular the criminal, not others who were not involved. The man in whose hand the cup had been found would become Joseph's servant. The striking correspondence between what the steward had said and what Joseph now says suggests that Joseph made sure that they would speak with one voice. The brothers would be free to go up to Canaan to their father in peace with only Benjamin staying in Joseph's custody.

2. Judah Pleads with Joseph for Benjamin (44:18-34)

Judah Explains the Situation with Benjamin and Jacob (44:18-29)

44:18 Then Judah went up to him and said: "Please, my lord, let your servant speak a word to my lord. Do not be angry with your servant, though you are equal to Pharaoh himself. 44:19 My lord asked his servants, 'Do you have a father or a brother?' 44:20 And we answered, 'We have an aged father, and there is a young son born to him in his old age. His brother is dead, and he is the only one of his mother's sons left, and his father loves him.' 44:21 "Then you said to your servants, 'Bring him down to me so I can see him for myself.' 44:22 And we said to my lord, 'The boy cannot leave his father; if he leaves him, his father will die.' 44:23 But you told your servants, 'Unless your youngest brother comes down with you, you will not see my face again.' 44:24 When we went back to your servant my father, we told him what my lord had said. 44:25 "Then our father said, 'Go back and buy a little more food.' 44:26 But we said, 'We cannot go down. Only if our youngest brother is with us will we go. We cannot see the man's face unless our youngest brother is with us.' 44:27 "Your servant my father said to us, 'You know that my wife bore me two sons. 44:28 One of them went away from me, and I said, "He has surely been torn to

---

[14]In v. 7 the brothers say, "חָלִילָה לַעֲבָדֶיךָ מֵעֲשׂוֹת כַּדָּבָר הַזֶּה" (*ḥālîlāh laʿăbādêkā mēʿăśôth kaddābār hazzeh*)" while here Joseph says, "חָלִילָה לִּי מֵעֲשׂוֹת זֹאת" (*ḥālîlāh lî mēʿăśôth zōʾth*)."

[15]In v. 10 the steward had said, "אֲשֶׁר יִמָּצֵא אִתּוֹ יִהְיֶה־לִּי עָבֶד" (*ʾăšer yimmāṣēʾ ʾittô yihyeh-lî ʿābed*)," while Joseph said, "אֲשֶׁר נִמְצָא הַגָּבִיעַ בְּיָדוֹ הוּא יִהְיֶה־לִּי עָבֶד" (*ʾăšer nimṣāʾ haggābîaʿ bᵉyodô hûʾ yihyeh-lî ʿābed*)."

pieces." And I have not seen him since. 44:29 If you take this one from me too and harm comes to him, you will bring my gray head down to the grave in misery.'

Judah's use of deferential language is obviously dictated by the circumstances. Joseph has all the power, and Judah and his brothers have none, the exact reverse of when the brothers sold Joseph into slavery. But there is more to it than that. The reader is reminded time and time again of Joseph's dream where the sheaves of the brothers bow down to Joseph's sheaf. Judah refers to Joseph as "my lord" five times (vv. 18[2×], 19,22,24), the brothers as "your" or "his" (i.e., Joseph's) "servants" five times (vv. 18[2×],19,21,23) and to Jacob as "your servant my father" twice (vv. 24,27).

Judah begins in verse 18 very gently so as not to risk causing offence. He uses two particles of entreaty (the particles are בִּי, *bî,* and נָא, *nā'*), refers to himself as Joseph's servant twice, and refers to Joseph as "my lord" twice. He asks Joseph **not** to **be angry** with him for presuming to speak to him. He recognizes that Joseph is like Pharaoh in the deference which he is entitled to by his high status. All of this is merely the introduction to what he has to say!

In verse 19 Judah begins by reminding Joseph of the question he had asked them when they came to Egypt for the first time to buy food. A comparison of the narrator's version of what was actually said to Joseph and what Judah says was said is instructive (see chart below). Joseph had asked whether they had a father or any other brothers. Ever so subtly Judah is applying the pressure on Joseph to convince him to change his mind. They had not brought the issue up, he claims, Joseph had. In fact, this is not actually true, and Judah is portrayed as massaging the past in a way that he thinks is more likely to illicit a sympathetic response from this mysterious lord of Egypt.

In the original version the brothers volunteered the information under the pressure of Joseph's accusation that they were spies. In Judah's version Joseph brought the matter up. Further Jacob is described by Judah as "aged" when in fact the brothers had never initially referred to Jacob's age. Judah says that the youngest son was born to his father in his old age, but this was not part of the original message. Judah claims that they had told Joseph that the brother who was dead and the youngest were the sons of the same mother and that the youngest is therefore the only one left of that mother. Finally Judah claims that they told Joseph of Jacob's special affection for the youngest son. None of this was actually said to Joseph. All of it is designed to elicit sympathy from Joseph. Their father was old and had lost the only other son of the favorite wife, leaving only the youngest, born in his old age, to be his special favorite. Perhaps Judah assumes that Joseph, who purportedly spoke with them only through a translator, would either not remember exactly what was said or would allow for the imprecision of translation.

What They Actually Had Said to Joseph	What Judah Says They Said to Joseph
42:13 But they replied, "Your servants were twelve brothers, the sons of one man, who lives in the land of Canaan. The youngest is now with our father, and one is no more."	44:20 'We have an aged father, and there is a young son born to him in his old age. His brother is dead, and he is the only one of his mother's sons left, and his father loves him.'

In verses 21-23 Judah continues his account of what had happened on the first trip. Once again he massages the details of what had actually transpired. Joseph spoke about bringing their youngest brother back with them twice (in 42:15 and 42:20). In neither case did Joseph say exactly what Judah claims he said. The brothers also did not say exactly what Judah claims they had said. The differences in the two accounts are instructive (see chart below). Joseph had never said to them, "**Bring him down to me so I can see him for myself**." He had simply said at first that they would not leave Egypt until the youngest brother came there to confirm their words. At first only one would be allowed to return to Egypt. Later Joseph changed his mind and imprisoned only Simeon. The brothers had never told Joseph, as Judah claims, that "**the boy cannot** forsake[16] **his father; if he** forsakes him **his father will die**." In fact the only death that Joseph referred to was the death of the brothers if they did not verify their story by bringing their youngest brother back with them to Egypt! Judah evidently does not want to remind Joseph that he had threatened them with death! Once again Judah massages the story to elicit the maximum amount of sympathy from Joseph. Surely the Egyptian official would not cause the death of their aged father by depriving him of the son he loves, would he?

What Actually Had Been Said	What Judah Claims Had Been Said
42:15 And this is how you will be tested: As surely as Pharaoh lives, you will not leave this place unless your youngest brother comes here. 42:20 But you must bring your youngest brother to me, so that your words may be verified and that you may not die."	44:21 "Then you said to your servants, 'Bring him down to me so I can see him for myself.' [22]And we said to my lord, 'The boy cannot leave his father; if he leaves him, his father will die.' [23]But you told your servants, 'Unless your youngest brother comes down with you, you will not see my face again.'

---

[16]The NIV's "leave" is too weak for עָזַב ('āzab).

In verse 24 Judah goes on to describe what happened when they got back to Canaan and related what had happened to their father. The deferential language continues as Judah refers to Jacob as "**your servant, my father**" even though the powerful Egyptian had never met Judah's father (so far as he knew). Judah claims that he told Jacob a true version of Joseph's words. He does not tell Joseph of Jacob's immediate rejection of the demand that Benjamin be brought to Egypt. Judah also did not relate how the brothers massaged their version of the events in little ways to take some of the sting out of Jacob's anger. In verse 25 Judah now refers to Jacob as "our," i.e., the brothers' father, rather than merely his own as in verse 24. After a time, Judah says, Jacob had told them to return and buy a little food in Egypt. But the brothers responded to him as one, "We are not able to go down [to Egypt]. If our brother, the **youngest, is with us then we will go** down. For we will not be able to even see the face of the man if our youngest brother is not with us."

In verse 27 Judah once again uses deferential language in referring to Jacob as "**your** [i.e., Joseph's] **servant my** [i.e., Judah's] **father.**" According to Judah Jacob had been very straightforward with his other sons. He had reminded them that the only woman whom he regarded as his wife (Rachel) had borne him only **two sons**. Leah was not really Jacob's wife even though she was the mother of his four oldest sons and six of the twelve total sons.[17] The narrator never records Jacob saying these words, although the sentiment behind them rings true to the narrative. Jacob's next words as Judah relates them are interesting. Jacob does not merely say that Joseph had been torn to pieces by wild beasts. Instead he says that one of his sons "**went away from me.**" He makes note that the conclusion he came to at the time, "**He has surely been torn to pieces,**" is just that, a conclusion. This may be a hint that Jacob had his own suspicions about the fate of Joseph. He only knows that Joseph went away and that he had not seen him again. We have seen subtle hints before that Jacob may have suspected foul play by his resentful older brothers for the demise of Joseph. This text is another, albeit subtle, hint. Jacob had then told his sons, according to Judah, what would happen if they took Benjamin back to Egypt and harm came to him.

Jacob's gray head would go down to the grave with the evil feelings (וְהוֹרַדְתֶּם אֶת־שֵׂיבָתִי בְּרָעָה שְׁאֹלָה, wᵉhōradtem 'eth-śêbāthî bᵉrā'āh šᵉ'ōlāh) of such a terrible event (v. 29). The narrator does record Jacob as saying something very similar to this in 42:38, although there the word "sorrow" (בְּיָגוֹן, bᵉyāgôn) is used rather than the more general word for "evil"

---

[17] As well as at least one daughter.

COLLEGE PRESS NIV COMMENTARY

as here. In light of the fact that Judah does use more exact terminology in verse 31 below, perhaps this should be regarded as an instance of minor variation in vocabulary for the sake of variety.

Judah Pleads with Joseph to Enslave Him, Not Benjamin (44:30-34)

44:30 "So now, if the boy is not with us when I go back to your servant my father and if my father, whose life is closely bound up with the boy's life, 44:31 sees that the boy isn't there, he will die. Your servants will bring the gray head of our father down to the grave in sorrow.

Judah comes to the conclusion of his plea to Joseph. He explains that, should the youth Benjamin not be with the brothers when they returned to Jacob, he would die immediately. Jacob's very life was tied up with the life of his only remaining son. If Benjamin was lost, his sons would "bring down [his] gray head to the grave in sorrow." Judah may be overstating the case to elicit sympathy from Joseph, but there is no question but that Jacob's heart would be broken beyond repair should he lose Benjamin after already having lost Rachel and Joseph.

Judah cloaks all of this in the most respectful and deferential language. Jacob is described as "your [i.e., Joseph's] servant, my [i.e., Judah's] father" in verse 30 and "your [i.e., Joseph's] servant, our [i.e., the brothers'] father" in verse 31. The reader is reminded of Joseph's dreams. Benjamin is twice described as "the youth," the very language used to describe Joseph when he was sold into slavery at the age of seventeen. Judah shows this deference while still calling on the emotional sympathy of Joseph. He has no idea that he is talking with Joseph and just what effect the familial language would have on him.

44:32 Your servant guaranteed the boy's safety to my father. I said, 'If I do not bring him back to you, I will bear the blame before you, my father, all my life!' 44:33 "Now then, please let your servant remain here as my lord's slave in place of the boy, and let the boy return with his brothers. 44:34 How can I go back to my father if the boy is not with me? No! Do not let me see the misery that would come upon my father."

Judah increases the emotional pressure on Joseph by mentioning that he had taken a solemn pledge guaranteeing the youth's safe return to his father. Under the conditions of that pledge, if Benjamin was not returned safely, Judah would bear the sin before his father all the remaining days of his life.[18]

---

[18]Interestingly Judah moves in and out of direct discourse here. He begins by quoting his words to his father, but then, in the middle of the quote he reverts to indirect discourse with the words "I will before my father." The NIV glosses

In verse 33 Judah finally makes his plea. He begs Joseph to let him remain as Joseph's servant instead of the youth (Benjamin), allowing him to go up to Canaan with his brothers. He continues the deferential language by referring to himself as Joseph's servant and Joseph as his lord. While this is undoubtedly a rhetorical strategy on the part of Judah, the reader hears yet again the echo of the dreams of Joseph.

Judah gives a final reason for his appeal in verse 34. How could he go up to Canaan to face his father if the youth, Benjamin, were not with him? He could not stand to look upon the evil state which he would find his father in if Benjamin was not returned. Judah, of course, had no way of knowing just how much his words would impact Joseph. He is merely appealing to his decency as a person who understands the relationship between a father and his sons.

---

over this by rendering וְחָטָאתִי לְאָבִי ($w^e h\bar{a}t\bar{a}'th\hat{\imath}\ l^e'\bar{a}b\hat{\imath}$) as "I will bear the blame before you, my father."

GENESIS 45

3. Joseph with Great Emotion Reveals and Reconciles Himself to His Brothers (45:1-15)

45:1 Then Joseph could no longer control himself before all his attendants, and he cried out, "Have everyone leave my presence!" So there was no one with Joseph when he made himself known to his brothers.

Unlike 43:31 where Joseph was still able to control himself,[1] in verse 1 he breaks down. The game playing had taken its emotional toll on him. Evidently Judah's words elicited such empathy in Joseph that he was no longer able to keep up the charade. The initial breakdown was in the presence of his attending servants, and so he called for all of them to leave him lest they witness what was about to happen. The narrator is careful to note that not a single person was with Joseph when he revealed himself to his brothers. Certainly this was a personal matter for Joseph and so he wanted privacy. But there is undoubtedly more to it. It could be that Joseph did not know what the reaction of the brothers would be. It could also be that they needed privacy to plan for the future of the family. The narrator uses Joseph's name and refers to his siblings as his "brothers," undoubtedly emphasizing that what was about to take place was the beginning of the process of familial reconciliation. Joseph is no longer "the man," and his brothers are no longer "the men."

45:2 And he wept so loudly that the Egyptians heard him, and Pharaoh's household heard about it.

Despite Joseph's best efforts to keep the interactions between his brothers and him private, his weeping was so forceful that **the Egyptians** who were around the house **heard** it. More importantly the household of Pharaoh heard about it. While they did not, evidently, at this point know exactly what was going on, they did know that something significant was happening, significant enough to make the highest official in Egypt under Pharaoh break into loud crying.

---

[1]Both passages use the rare Hebrew verb אָפַק (*'āppaq*) in the hithpael.

45:3 Joseph said to his brothers, "I am Joseph! Is my father still living?" But his brothers were not able to answer him, because they were terrified at his presence. 45:4 Then Joseph said to his brothers, "Come close to me." When they had done so, he said, "I am your brother Joseph, the one you sold into Egypt! 45:5 And now, do not be distressed and do not be angry with yourselves for selling me here, because it was to save lives that God sent me ahead of you.

Fighting through the tears Joseph finally told his brothers who he was. "**I am Joseph**" he said, adding an immediate question, "Is my father alive?" Apparently Joseph feared that Jacob may have already died, and that information was being withheld from him by his brothers. The question indicates that Joseph did not necessarily believe all of the story that Judah had been telling him.

The brothers were unable to answer, being terrified[2] at what they had just heard. Joseph, observing their shock and not wanting listening ears to overhear asks his brothers[3] to "please come near" (גְּשׁוּ־נָא, $g^e šû$-$nā$').[4] Still mute they complied and approached Joseph. With them closer he repeats the phrase that shocked them so, "I am Joseph." This time, however, he continues "your brother." This momentarily reassures them by reminding them of their common father. This is, however, immediately followed by "whom **you sold into Egypt**." This last clause would undoubtedly make his brothers' fears even greater, so it is followed immediately by the more reassuring verse 5. They had sold Joseph into Egypt and now were about to pay the consequences for their cruel treatment of Joseph. But in fact Joseph had come to see God's hand in all of it, even the evil choices they had made to sell their own brother into slavery. He no longer wanted to play games with his brothers, which achieved nothing. He had come to a form of forgiveness.

For Joseph **God** had **sent** him to Egypt before his family to preserve life. The narrator emphasizes the point by placing the last phrase ("to preserve life") in the emphatic first position. While the narrative does not comment on Joseph's contention, it does indicate, if Joseph is to be taken seriously and not ironically,[5] that Joseph has overcome his anger and desire for revenge. Rather than indicating an anachronistic belief in

---

[2]Wenham, *Genesis 16–50*, p. 416, suggests "dumbfounded."

[3]Notice that the narrator once again emphasizes the familial relationship by describing them as "brothers."

[4]By using the particle of entreaty, נָא ($nā$'), Joseph shows himself to be less forceful than if he had merely used an imperative.

[5]The brothers evidently don't completely believe that Joseph has forgiven them and see their choice to enslave him as part of God's work. In Genesis

divine predestination of all things, including evil, Joseph's words make more sense as affirming Paul's sentiment in Romans 8:28, "And we know that for those who love God all things work together for good" (ESV).

45:6 For two years now there has been famine in the land, and for the next five years there will not be plowing and reaping. 45:7 But God sent me ahead of you to preserve for you a remnant on earth and to save your lives by a great deliverance. 45:8 "So then, it was not you who sent me here, but God. He made me father to Pharaoh, lord of his entire household and ruler of all Egypt.

Joseph's brothers must not waste time in self-condemnation and second-guessing. They have more pressing issues with which to concern themselves; namely a severe and long-lasting famine. Joseph knows about the length of the famine through (the interpretation of Pharaoh's) dreams. The last time Joseph presented a dream to his brothers, they were resentful of the apparent meaning. But that dream and its interpretation had proven to be true.[6] Now they must trust Joseph's interpretation of Pharaoh's dream and act on it. The famine was to last seven years in total, which meant five more tough years; so tough in fact that there would be no plowing or harvesting! They must trust him and his interpretation or risk impoverishment and perhaps even starvation for their entire family.

Joseph reassures them that his interpretation of the future can be trusted by asserting that God had sent him before them to make **a remnant** of them on the earth[7] and keep them alive by a **great** act of **deliverance**. Joseph repeats the point yet again. God had been in control all along. The brothers had not sent Joseph to Egypt, God had. This removes the guilt they had in selling one of their own brothers into slavery and any grounds they might have for claiming credit for delivering the family from the famine. The responsibility and the praise go to God, not to them. Only God could have made a Hebrew slave into Pharaoh's fatherly advisor, lord over Pharaoh's entire household, and lord over all the land of Egypt.

45:9 Now hurry back to my father and say to him, 'This is what your son Joseph says: God has made me lord of all Egypt. Come down to

---

50:14-18 after the death of Jacob the brothers assume that Joseph would now take his revenge and make up a story in an attempt to assuage his anger.

[6]I refer here to the first dream, not the second dream.

[7]If we translate "on the earth," there is an echo of the universal aspect of the promise to Abraham. If we translate "in the land," there is perhaps an echo of the promise of the land of Canaan in the promise given to Abraham. In either case the promise to Abraham is subtly alluded to here.

me; don't delay. **45:10 You shall live in the region of Goshen and be near me—you, your children and grandchildren, your flocks and herds, and all you have. 45:11 I will provide for you there, because five years of famine are still to come. Otherwise you and your household and all who belong to you will become destitute.' 45:12 "You can see for yourselves, and so can my brother Benjamin, that it is really I who am speaking to you. 45:13 Tell my father about all the honor accorded me in Egypt and about everything you have seen. And bring my father down here quickly."**

The urgency in Joseph's words is shown by the fact that he tells his brothers to hurry to return to Jacob and by the fact that they were to tell Jacob not to delay. Joseph describes Jacob as "**my father**" as opposed to "our" father. While this may not be of any great significance, one wonders whether he is hinting at his special status with Jacob. The words that Joseph tells his brothers to deliver to Jacob are interesting for the way they begin. Literally the message is to begin, "Thus says" as though it was a prophetic pronouncement. But Joseph wants them to immediately identify him as Jacob's son. God has made Joseph, Jacob's son, **lord of all Egypt**. Even though he is Jacob's son, he can command his father to come down from Canaan to Egypt. He also uses the imperative when he says "**Don't delay**."[8] In a subtle, or perhaps not so subtle, way Joseph treats Jacob as a subordinate whom he summons.

Joseph does not offer Jacob the option of moving to Egypt. He informs him that he would **live in the land of Goshen**. Given the circumstances, this is perhaps understandable. It is interesting that Joseph matter-of-factly states that Jacob and his family will dwell specifically in Goshen even though he has not yet asked Pharaoh's permission. This may indicate Joseph's authority or his audacity or his cleverness or some combination of the three. It is also interesting how Joseph chooses to refer to his family. They are Jacob's sons (not Joseph's brothers) and Jacob's grandsons (not Joseph's nephews). Joseph also specifically tells Jacob to bring his **flocks and herds** and other possessions. Perhaps Joseph is anticipating what Pharaoh will say (v. 20) and wants to preempt it. Jacob will not be obligated to Pharaoh for all of his possessions while he lives in Egypt. He will bring his flocks and herds with him.

In verse 11 Joseph promises to **provide for** Jacob and his family in Goshen since the remaining **five years of famine** would not allow Jacob to care for them himself. In fact, Joseph uses the word "disinherit"

---

[8]The Hebrew might be rendered in English, "Don't [just] stand there!" (אַל־תַּעֲמֹד, 'al-ta'ǎmōd).

(שׁוֹרֵ֑שׁ, *tiwwārēš*)[9] of what will happen to them. The counterecho of the land promise is subtle but nevertheless present. Jacob will lose his inheritance, according to Joseph, if he does not move to Goshen to live out the famine. He must leave the land now in order for his descendants to inherit it later.

In verse 12 Joseph, having finished his instructions for what his brothers were to tell Jacob, turns to address them directly. Apparently they are still in some doubt about his identity or so it appears to Joseph. He reminds them that their own eyes are looking at him. He specifically points out Benjamin, whom he terms "his brother." Joseph shows his perspective here. Joseph regards Benjamin, in contradistinction to his half-brothers, as truly his brother. He reassures them that their eyes are not deceiving them; it is actually Joseph speaking.

In verse 13 Joseph commands his brothers to tell Jacob of all his "glory" in Egypt, thus reassuring him that he has the power and resources to take care of them in Egypt. Jacob's grandfather Abraham had visited Egypt in a position of powerlessness and endangered the promise in so doing. Jacob would not be likely to repeat that mistake unless he was reassured of Joseph's position. While Joseph is not rubbing it in, this would not ordinarily be something his older (resentful) brothers would like to do. To declare Joseph's glory to their father who had made his favoritism quite clear might be a hard pill to swallow. Joseph assumes that when Jacob hears of his glory, his brothers will be able to quickly convince him to come to Egypt.

45:14 Then he threw his arms around his brother Benjamin and wept, and Benjamin embraced him, weeping.

Joseph finally embraces his younger full brother Benjamin, the one he had schemed to get to Egypt. Benjamin, now convinced that it is, in fact, Joseph reciprocates. The long years of separation caused by his father's favoritism and his own (half-)brothers' deep-seated resentment are over.[10] The scene is a touching one of reconciliation and God's providence.

45:15 And he kissed all his brothers and wept over them. Afterward his brothers talked with him.

While being rejoined to his brother Benjamin is something expected, in this verse Joseph shows his forgiving spirit. Joseph **kissed** each

---

[9]Niphal from יָרַשׁ (*yāraš*), a common verb used to describe the inheritance of the Promised Land. The NIV's "become destitute" loses this echo.

[10]The need for Joseph to carefully negotiate with Pharaoh through members of his household to go to Canaan to bury his father (Gen 50:4-5) indicates that Joseph was not free to leave Egypt to visit his family even though he was ruler of all Egypt. He was still a slave.

one of the **brothers** who sold him into slavery. Eight of them had
intended to kill him! Joseph now kissed **and wept over them** as he
kissed them. The reconciliation is completed, at least from Joseph's
side, **when his brothers talked with** Joseph.[11] What a conversation that
must have been!

E. THE FAMILY PLANS TO MOVE TO EGYPT (45:16-28)

1. Pharaoh Hears and Invites Joseph's Family to Move to Egypt (45:16-20)

**45:16 When the news reached Pharaoh's palace that Joseph's brothers
had come, Pharaoh and all his officials were pleased. 45:17 Pharaoh
said to Joseph, "Tell your brothers, 'Do this: Load your animals and
return to the land of Canaan, 45:18 and bring your father and your
families back to me. I will give you the best of the land of Egypt and
you can enjoy the fat of the land.' 45:19 "You are also directed to tell
them, 'Do this: Take some carts from Egypt for your children and
your wives, and get your father and come. 45:20 Never mind about
your belongings, because the best of all Egypt will be yours.'"**

Pharaoh's house somehow heard[12] about Joseph's reconciliation
with his brothers. This could complicate matters for Joseph; but in fact,
this was viewed as good news at the palace. Joseph's leadership during
the famine and before had evidently inured him to the Egyptians. They
were glad to see Joseph reunited with his (estranged) brothers. Pharaoh
instructs Joseph to do what Joseph has already done, but he seems to be
even more generous. Joseph is to tell his brothers to **load** their **animals
and return to the land of Canaan and bring** their **father and** their **families
back** to Egypt. Pharaoh promises more than merely providing for
Joseph's family. He promises to give them the good portions of the land
so that they may eat from its abundance (literally "fat"). He also provides
them with the use of carts to carry their little children, wives and
their aged father Jacob.

In one area Pharaoh's directive differs significantly from what
Joseph had instructed his brothers to do. Pharaoh tells the brothers not
to be concerned about their "possessions" (NRSV) or "belongings"

---

[11]That the brothers remain distrustful of Joseph is clear from their attempt to
avoid the revenge they assumed he was planning after the death and burial of
Jacob (Gen 50:15-21).

[12]The Hebrew וְהַקֹּל (wᵉhaqqōl) typically means "sound" or "voice" but is used
here in the sense of "rumor" or "news."

(NIV). The Hebrew word is a quite general one.[13] In this passage it seems to be used more generally, as in the NIV. The material blessings of God to Abraham, Isaac, and Jacob, which had been substantial, are to be left in Canaan according to Pharaoh. He would provide them with the good things of the entire land of Egypt; what need would they have of their paltry possessions? But for Jacob and his family those possessions were part of the fulfillment of God's promises. They were not to be so easily abandoned.

2. The Sons Return to Canaan and Tell Jacob That Joseph Is Alive (45:21-28)

45:21 So the sons of Israel did this. Joseph gave them carts, as Pharaoh had commanded, and he also gave them provisions for their journey.

The brothers comply with Joseph's (and Pharaoh's[14]) directive to move the family to Egypt to ride out the famine. The narrator terms them **"the sons of Israel."** This is the typical phrase to describe the nation which later descended from them. This indicates to the readers that their actions are the actions of the incipient nation. Israel is moving to Egypt and the Pharaoh is paying the moving expenses! Joseph adopts Pharaoh's idea of sending carts to make the journey easier, taking the initiative of paying for their **provisions for** the **journey.**

45:22 To each of them he gave new clothing, but to Benjamin he gave three hundred shekels of silver and five sets of clothes.

This has to be one of the funniest verses in the Bible. Joseph is reconciled to his brothers, but he still favors Benjamin far and beyond the rest of them! There are half-brothers and Joseph has ten of them. But there is a brother and Joseph has only one. He, like his father Jacob, shows his favoritism by the giving of clothing and other material things. The *leitmotif* of Joseph's clothing is recalled once again. But this time Joseph is the provider of the clothing! The amount of money[15] given to Benjamin shows the power and wealth which Joseph has come to in Egypt. The fact that gifts are given to both Joseph's half-brothers and

---

[13]כְּלֵיכֶם (kᵊlêkem) could mean something as simple as cooking vessels to something as general as any type of personal possession.

[14]The narrator does not inform the reader whether Joseph told his brothers exactly what instructions Pharaoh had passed on to him. In any case they do not, apparently, tell Jacob about Pharaoh's instructions.

[15]Joseph was sold as a slave for only 20 shekels of silver. His gift to Benjamin was 15 times that amount!

Benjamin indicates that reconciliation has begun. The fact that Benjamin receives so much more indicates that the process of reconciliation is not yet finished.

45:23 And this is what he sent to his father: ten donkeys loaded with the best things of Egypt, and ten female donkeys loaded with grain and bread and other provisions for his journey.

In addition to the gifts given to the brothers Joseph sends a lavish set of gifts to Jacob in order to demonstrate the legitimacy of his brothers' story. The journey from Egypt to Canaan and back took perhaps fifteen to twenty days.[16] Ten donkey loads of provisions for the journey back were unnecessarily lavish enough. Another **ten donkeys** laden with the delicacies of Egypt would convince Jacob.

45:24 Then he sent his brothers away, and as they were leaving he said to them, "Don't quarrel on the way!"

After loading up the provisions, carts, and gifts, the brothers are sent back to get Jacob and his family. Joseph, sensitive to what his brothers must be going through, tells them not to "tremble" during the trip. The word could be referring to their fears that Joseph would still, somehow, seek revenge. Or it could refer to their "raging"[17] against each other in anger and blame over the past. The NIV's "**quarrel**" suggests the latter meaning in this instance. In either case Joseph is shown to be sensitive to their situation.

45:25 So they went up out of Egypt and came to their father Jacob in the land of Canaan. 45:26 They told him, "Joseph is still alive! In fact, he is ruler of all Egypt." Jacob was stunned; he did not believe them.

The brothers finally go back to Canaan as instructed to tell Jacob that Joseph is still alive. Jacob's reaction is to be **stunned**,[18] at first not trusting his sons' story. Why he did not trust them is unstated. Perhaps he had lingering suspicions about their earlier presenting Joseph's bloodstained coat as though they didn't know to whom it belonged. Perhaps he suspected that his patent favoritism had spawned in his sons a deceitful plot. Perhaps it is the sheer implausibility that Joseph would have risen to such a high position in the government of the world's dominant superpower. The reader is left to speculate.

---

[16]A longer trip than the one from Egypt to southern Canaan, that from Sinai to Kadesh Barnea, took about 11 days. See the discussion in Hoffmeier, *Ancient Israel in Sinai*, pp. 119-120.

[17]For the verb רָגַז (*rāgāz*) as "raging in anger against," see 2 Kgs 19:27,28 // Isa 37:28,29; Ps 4:5; Prov 29:9; Ezek 16:42.

[18]וַיָּפָג לִבּוֹ (*wayyāphāg libbô*) literally means "his heart was numb."

45:27 But when they told him everything Joseph had said to them, and when he saw the carts Joseph had sent to carry him back, the spirit of their father Jacob revived. 28 And Israel said, "I'm convinced! My son Joseph is still alive. I will go and see him before I die."

Joseph had anticipated Jacob's potential reaction well. He was convinced only after hearing the words that Joseph gave his brothers to convey to Jacob and after seeing the gift-laden **carts** that **Joseph had sent** along **to carry** Jacob back to Egypt. Jacob was at first stunned by the very idea of his beloved Joseph still being alive. When Jacob came to acceptance, his "spirit lived" (וַתְּחִי רוּחַ, *watᵊḥî rûaḥ*) once again. Jacob, again called Israel, expresses this by saying "Great."[19] He decides to go to Egypt to see his beloved son Joseph. Interestingly, he does not commit at this point to staying in Egypt.

The fact that Jacob mentions his impending death is to be noted. He probably thought he would not be there very long. Little did he realize that he would live for another seventeen years, all of them in Egypt (Gen 47:28).

---

[19] רַב (*rāb*), often an adjective meaning "great in number," is here used as an interjection.

GENESIS 46

VIII. ISRAEL MOVES TO EGYPT (46:1–47:27)

This section describes the move by Jacob and his family from Canaan to Goshen in Egypt. The detail that is given of what might seem a rather straightforward set of events indicates the event's significance for the larger narrative. When the man Jacob moves his family to Egypt to be reunited with his favorite son Joseph, it is not just a family that moves. It is the entire nation of Israel in embryonic form.

Jacob begins the journey by traveling to Beersheba in the extreme south of Canaan (46:1-4). Desiring divine reassurance about the move, he offers sacrifice there. The reassurance comes in the form of a night vision commanding him to go and promising to make him into a great nation while in Egypt. As God had earlier told Abram (15:1-16), living as sojourners outside the land of Canaan was a necessary precursor to the fulfillment of the promises.

The narrative of the arrival in Egypt (46:5-7) is immediately followed by a name list of those who moved to Egypt. By means of some ingenious mathematics there are 70 descendants of Israel counted (45:8-27). The traditional number of nations in the world was 70. Israel was called to be God's nation for the sake of all the other nations of the world. We see this beginning to happen in this narrative.

The actual meeting of Jacob and Joseph after more than 20 years apart is touching (46:28-30). Joseph then prepares his brothers and father to meet Pharaoh. His goal is to ensure that his father's family is given the freedom to live in Egypt. But due to Egyptian tension with Hebrew culture Joseph decides it would be best if they lived by themselves but under Pharaoh's protection and provision. The brothers and Jacob present themselves well before Pharaoh and are given the best of the land, the land of Goshen, in which to live. Jacob even blesses Pharaoh, hinting at the ultimate reason for the choosing of Abraham and his descendants. Abraham and his descendants receive God's blessing so that all the world might be blessed through them (Gen 12:3).

The final passage in this section explains how Joseph's wisdom in preparing for the famine is matched by his wisdom in the managing of the economy during the famine. Joseph blesses the farmers of Egypt and the region by allowing them to survive and continue farming. He blesses Pharaoh by gaining legal control of the land of Egypt and thus insuring a future income flow of twenty percent of the crops of Egypt's farmers.

A. THE JOURNEY TO EGYPT (46:1-27)

1. Journey to Beersheba (46:1-4)

46:1 So Israel set out with all that was his, and when he reached Beersheba, he offered sacrifices to the God of his father Isaac.

We don't know exactly where Jacob was located when his sons brought him news that Joseph was still alive. He took all of his possessions and all of his family[1] and went to **Beersheba**. The fact that Jacob's sons did not include Pharaoh's message to leave his belongings behind could explain this. The **sacrifices** which Jacob[2] **offered** at Beersheba may have been an attempt to receive explicit divine guidance as he took the risky step of moving his family to Egypt. It is interesting that Jacob offered his sacrifices specifically to **the God of his father Isaac**. Such divine titles mentioning one of the patriarchs have been used at least since the time of Alt as an indicator of divergent sources. According to Alt the three patriarchs originally worshiped different gods under different names.[3] The three deities were only combined and regarded as alternative names for the same god when the three independent patriarchal cycles were brought together into one fictional family relationship of grandfather (Abraham), father (Isaac), and son (Jacob). But there may be a more likely explanation. At this point Jacob may feel personally estranged from God or unworthy of a relationship. Or simply he wants explicit personal guidance that the move to Egypt is a continuation of what God had promised his grandfather and father.

---

[1]The Hebrew (וְכָל־אֲשֶׁר־לֹו, w^ekol-$'ăšer$-$lô$) is ambiguous as to whether "all that was his" refers to material possessions or includes family members and household servants.

[2]In the so-called Patriarchal period the head of the family served effectively as priest.

[3]Albrecht Alt, *Der Gott der Väter* (Stuttgart: Kohlhammer, 1929). In English, "The God of the Fathers," pp. 1-100, in *Essays on Old Testament History and Religion*, trans. by R.A. Wilson (Garden City, NY: Anchor Books, 1968).

Beersheba seems to be the final home of Isaac (Gen 37:14; 35:27) and was the last outpost before one entered the deserted wilderness which separated Egypt from Canaan. The risky decision to go to Egypt must be made with finality at Beersheba, after which there was no turning back. As Jacob was leaving the land in flight from his brother Esau at Bethel he also performed a worship ritual and received a divine revelation (Genesis 28).

46:2 And God spoke to Israel in a vision at night and said, "Jacob! Jacob!" "Here I am," he replied.

In response to the sacrifice that Jacob made, **God spoke to** him. The narrator refers to Jacob in this verse as Israel, reminding the reader yet again, that Jacob is the ancestor of the nation of which his readers were a part. God had spoken to Jacob at Bethel as he fled the Promised Land from the wrath of Esau in chapter 28. In this passage God speaks to Jacob as he is once again about to leave the Promised Land. Once again it happened at night.

In his speech God begins with a repetition of Jacob's name; he does not use the name Israel even though he had given him that name on two occasions (Gen 32:28; 35:10). It may be that God desires to speak to him personally rather than on the basis of his role as the founder of a family which will eventually turn into a nation. Jacob responds to God's call in the same way that Isaiah later did, **"Here I am."**

46:3 "I am God, the God of your father," he said. "Do not be afraid to go down to Egypt, for I will make you into a great nation there.

Jacob had offered sacrifices to the **God of [his] father** Isaac, and not directly to the god with whom he had a personal relationship. When God answers Jacob in the vision, he acknowledges this by identifying himself as the God of Jacob's father. Jacob needed reassurance that the move to Egypt was the correct one. God tells Jacob **not** to **be afraid to go . . . to Egypt** for in doing so he will further the fulfillment of the promise to Abraham. God had promised to **make** Abraham **into a great nation** (Gen 12:2). In this passage that promise is explicitly repeated to Jacob. God had also warned Abraham that the land promise would not be fulfilled until after a four-hundred-year stay by his descendants as sojourners and slaves in a foreign land (Gen 15:13). Abraham's own visit to Egypt had been fraught with danger from which God had protected him. The reader does not know if the narrator presumes that Jacob knows all of this or not. The readers both original and canonical do know that Egypt is the land alluded to in Genesis 15:13.

46:4 I will go down to Egypt with you, and I will surely bring you back again. And Joseph's own hand will close your eyes."

God promises to travel with Jacob to Egypt and gives him an emphatic[4] reassurance that he would bring him back to the Promised Land. Interestingly he will only come back as a corpse to be buried. This might seem strange to us. We might even be tempted to wonder whether God was faithful to this promise. But to be buried in the family grave was the sign in the ancient world of a life that ended well. God also promises that Jacob's favorite son, Joseph, will be there at his death to close his eyelids when he dies. This is a sign of great intimacy. Jacob would be reassured to know that despite all of the travails — losing Rachel and thinking he had lost Joseph and fearing that he had lost Benjamin too — at the end of it all God was faithful. Those whom he loved would be there at his death. Contemporary interpreters must be careful not to read anachronistically a doctrine of the resurrection into such passages.

2. Journey from Beersheba to Egypt (46:5-7)

46:5 Then Jacob left Beersheba, and Israel's sons took their father Jacob and their children and their wives in the carts that Pharaoh had sent to transport him.

Spurred by the assurance given by divine revelation, **Jacob left Beersheba** and in so doing left the permanently habitable part of the Promised Land to go to Egypt. His grandchildren and daughters-in-law joined the aged Jacob in riding **in the carts that Pharaoh had** provided. The fact that Jacob's secondary wives, Bilhah and Zilpah, are not mentioned may indicate that they had died sometime during the events recorded in the Joseph narrative.

46:6 They also took with them their livestock and the possessions they had acquired in Canaan, and Jacob and all his offspring went to Egypt.

Although Pharaoh had instructed Joseph to tell Jacob to leave his possessions behind, Jacob took all of them including the sheep and other animals. These were signs of God's blessing him while he lived in Canaan and would not readily be abandoned. Jacob, so far as we know, had not inherited them from Isaac, despite the deal he had made with his brother Esau and despite having received Isaac's blessing. Much of what he had obtained while in the service of Laban was given away as a

---

[4]While it is sometimes alleged by Hebrew grammarians that an infinitive absolute which *follows* a finite verb of the same root implies continuation, rather than the more common emphatic function when it precedes the finite verb, examples like this one argue against this distinction. See the discussion in Waltke and O'Connor, *Biblical Hebrew Syntax*, pp. 584-588.

bribe or gift to Esau. But God's blessing had, nevertheless, ultimately come to him. We see evidence of this here. We do not know if the brothers ever knew of Pharaoh's instruction to leave their possessions behind, or if they did know and chose not to tell Jacob. Or perhaps Jacob had heard them, but chose to ignore them. The fact that Jacob brought his sheep with him is significant for the ensuing narrative. The mention of "**offspring**" seems redundant given that Jacob's sons, grandchildren, and daughters-in-law are already mentioned in verse 5. But the word, once again, subtly echoes the promise to Abraham whom the LORD had promised to give "offspring" as numerous as the sand on the seashore and the stars in the heavens (Gen 13:16; 15:5; 22:16).

46:7 He took with him to Egypt his sons and grandsons and his daughters and granddaughters—all his offspring.

This verse serves as a sort of summary statement that reinforces the message of verses 1-6; Jacob took his entire family[5] to Egypt, no one stayed behind in Canaan. The use of the word "**offspring**" (זֶרַע, *zeraʿ*) once again echoes the promise of God to Abraham. The promised great nation is beginning to form. Jacob's large family forms the nucleus of the offspring which will one day number as the stars of the heavens. The mention of Jacob's daughters in the plural is interesting. Previously we have only read of Dinah. She had at least one sister as we are about to discover.

3. The Seventy Descendants of Jacob Who Go to Egypt (46:8-27)

This listing of the family that moved to Egypt is much more interesting than it at first appears. The narrator is determined to come up with 70 names. But this is done in a very unusual way. Two sons are listed as making the trip who actually died in Canaan. Conversely the wives of Jacob who died in Canaan are not counted! One son, Joseph, and his two sons didn't need to make the trip because they were already living in Egypt. One daughter, Dinah, who played an important part in the earlier narrative when she was defiled by Shechem, is not counted, even though she made the trip. Another daughter, Serah, who plays no part in the previous or later narrative is counted. The wives of Jacob's sons, at least four of whom are known to be Canaanites, are not counted, nor is Joseph's Egyptian wife. While only Joseph and his two sons are counted among the 70, the narrator perplexingly informs us that there were 66, not 67, who came to Egypt not counting Joseph and his two sons (v. 26)!

---

[5]The Hebrew emphasizes Jacob's grandsons, daughters, and granddaughters by placing them first in the sentence and placing the verb near the end.

While there could be a variety of approaches to understanding these perplexities, and perhaps some combination of those approaches is needed to explain all of them, one thing seems clear; for the narrator the number 70 is theologically significant. The most likely explanation for this is a sort of parallel between humanity as a whole and the nation of Israel as the potential new humanity. In Genesis 10 in the so-called "Table of the Nations" listing the descendants of Noah there are 70 nations listed. Noah functions as a sort of "New Adam" after the flood.[6] The number 70 is achieved by tracing some nations to the fifth generation while most others are traced to a single generation.[7] Likewise, when Israel goes into Egypt as recorded here, and when she comes out of Egypt[8] (Numbers 26), the number 70 is used in counting. In this instance it is arrived at by counting certain persons (and not counting other persons). Why is the number 70 so important symbolically and theologically that the author has to find it by counting in a way that seems artificial to us? The traditional 70 nations of the world are, in a symbolic sense, replaced by the 70 descendants of Israel (Jacob). What God had originally tried to accomplish through humankind as a whole in Genesis 1–11, since the time of Abraham, he was seeking to accomplish through a specific human nation. That nation was named after Abraham's grandson, Israel (Jacob). Israel, in a sense, is called to be the new humanity.

This theological point becomes even more obvious in the Masoretic text[9] of Deuteronomy 32:8. There Moses, about to die outside of the Promised Land, reminds the nation about to receive that Promised Land of the privileged position they had in God's plan: "When the Most High gave the nations their inheritance, when he divided all mankind, he set up boundaries for the peoples according to the number of the sons of Israel." While Moses is speaking poetically and not literally, the relationship between Israel and the nations is clearly affirmed; Israel with its 70 members (if you count them a certain way) is like the entire world of nations in miniature. What God wanted to do with humanity as a whole, he is now doing through a single chosen nation from that human family.

---

[6]On this see Kissling, *Genesis Volume 1*, pp. 322-326.

[7]See the discussion in ibid., pp. 355-358.

[8]The second census recorded in Numbers 26 seems to be based on the list here with the individuals mentioned now becoming clans in the tribal structure of Israel.

[9]One Qumran Manuscript (4QDeut^j) reads "sons of God" while LXX has "angels of God."

46:8 These are the names of the sons of Israel (Jacob and his descendants) who went to Egypt: Reuben the firstborn of Jacob. 46:9 The sons of Reuben: Hanoch, Pallu, Hezron and Carmi. 46:10 The sons of Simeon: Jemuel, Jamin, Ohad, Jakin, Zohar and Shaul the son of a Canaanite woman. 46:11 The sons of Levi: Gershon, Kohath and Merari. 46:12 The sons of Judah: Er, Onan, Shelah, Perez and Zerah (but Er and Onan had died in the land of Canaan). The sons of Perez: Hezron and Hamul. 46:13 The sons of Issachar: Tola, Puah, Jashub and Shimron. 46:14 The sons of Zebulun: Sered, Elon and Jahleel. 46:15 These were the sons Leah bore to Jacob in Paddan Aram, besides his daughter Dinah. These sons and daughters of his were thirty-three in all.

The narrator begins his list of Israel's descendants who went to Egypt with the children of Leah, the wife Jacob did not love. The narrator's perspective is thus in some tension with Jacob's own perspective. If Jacob were listing his descendants, Joseph and Benjamin might well come first!

In verse 8 we have an introduction to what is to follow. We are being given the names of the "**sons of Israel**." This phrase is used elsewhere to speak of the nation. The narrator makes it clear that the phrase "sons of Israel" in this passage means the individual Jacob and his "sons" or "descendants." **Reuben** is set apart from the rest of his brothers as **the firstborn** and the legally presumptive heir by being mentioned twice.

Reuben had four sons, **Hanoch, Pallu, Hezron, and Carmi**, who became the four clans of the tribe of Reuben. We are not told of their mothers, although we do know that Reuben had an affair with Jacob's concubine, Bilhah (Gen 35:22). Hanoch is only mentioned in this passage and as the progenitor of the clan by his name. Pallu, the second son of Reuben is only known elsewhere by the clan of his name which included Dathan and Abiram. They joined with Korah in rebelling against Moses and Aaron (Num 26:8-10). Hezron, the third son of Reuben, is only elsewhere mentioned in relation to the clan he founded (Num 26:6). He is to be distinguished from his great nephew of the same name, a grandson of Reuben's brother Judah (Gen 46:12; 1 Chr 2:5; 4:1). Carmi, the youngest son of Reuben, founded a clan named after him. His name is shared by Caleb's father.

Simeon, Jacob's second son, has six sons who founded tribal clans by their names. The name of the first, **Jemuel**, is spelled the same way in Exodus 6:15, but in Numbers 26:12[10] and 1 Chronicles 4:24 the name

---

[10]The Syriac here reads "Jemuel," but this is probably to be explained as scribal harmonization.

is "Nemuel." The tribal group name could have changed over time and this could explain the spelling in Chronicles. But this does not explain the difference between Numbers 26:12 and Exodus 6:15 unless one presumes differing sources here. Given that the LXX follows the Hebrew in this text and in Numbers, this is probably the result of an early copyist error. **Jamin**, the second son listed, is only mentioned elsewhere in relation to the clan he founded. The third son of Simeon, **Ohad** is not mentioned in the genealogies in Numbers 26 and 1 Chronicles 4. This is probably due to the fact that by the time of the entrance into the land the clan had completely disappeared. The Simeonites declined in population from 59,300 to 22,200[11] during the wilderness period, and so the total disappearance of one of the six clan groups is not surprising. **Jakin** (Jachin[12]), the fourth son, is otherwise known only from the clan which comes from him (Exod 6:15; Num 26:12). **Zohar**, the fifth son, founds the clan that is also known as "Zerah" (Exod 6:15; Num 26:12; 1 Chr 4:24). **Shaul**, the sixth son, is specifically identified as **the son of a Canaanite woman**. This may reflect the fact that the women of Shechem were taken captive after their men were slain in the incident with Dinah (Gen 34:29), an event where Simeon took a leading role. Simeon may have fathered a child with one of these captive women. In any case the marrying of a Canaanite woman, something strictly forbidden in the law (Deut 7:3), does not bode well for the tribe of Simeon.

The three sons of **Levi – Gershon, Kohath, and Merari –** would be well known to the original and canonical audiences as the three clans of the priestly tribe of Levi. Gershon[13] is the firstborn but the Gershonites are given relatively minor tasks compared to Kohath. Kohath was the clan of Moses and Aaron. Though listed as the second son of Levi, during the wilderness period the Kohathites were responsible for carrying the ark, table of showbread, lampstand, altars, and other sanctuary vessels. The fact that the descendants of Levi become the priestly tribe despite Jacob's seeming curse (Gen 49:5-7) is apparently explained by the fact that the Levites stand with Moses against the nation at the golden calf incident (Exod 32:25-29).

The sons of **Judah**, Jacob's fourth son through Leah, are listed next. **Er and Onan** are counted among the 70 coming into Egypt even though

---

[11]The decline is just as dramatic if one regards the Hebrew word אֶלֶף (*'eleph*) as meaning "clan" rather than "1,000." Cf. Jacob Milgrom, "Excursus 2," *Numbers*, JPSTC (Philadelphia: JPS, 1990), pp. 336-339.

[12]Jachin is called "Jarib" in 1 Chronicles 4:24. This may be an alternative name, the result of a name change of the clan, or a copyist error.

[13]In 1 Chronicles 6 the name is spelled "Gershom."

they **died** under divine judgment **in Canaan** for being wicked in the sight of the LORD (Gen 37:7,10). This fact shows that for the author arriving at the symbolic number 70 is more important than being numerically logical. **Shelah**, the third son of Judah, was withheld from Tamar, his older brothers' wife, for fear that he too would fall under divine judgment. As a result Tamar posed as a prostitute and had sexual relations with Judah. This resulted in the birth of the twins **Perez and Zerah**, sons who founded the two major clans of the tribe of Judah. Far from being "illegitimate" sons, they are straightforwardly presented as the foundation of (one of) the major tribe(s) in the nation of Israel. The book of Genesis shows no tendency to hide the weaknesses and "indiscretions" of its characters. This is probably because the biblical idea of election ("chosenness") is not what we tend to imagine it to be. Chosenness is not based upon the moral superiority of the chosen, but upon God's grace.

In order to get to 70 descendants some grandchildren will have to be included. In this instance it is Perez's (but not Zerah's!) two sons, **Hezron and Hamul**. Hezron gave birth to the clan from which David descended.

The descendants of Issachar and Zebulun are mentioned next because they were also sons of Leah, although they were born later after the four sons of the handmaids, Bilhah and Zilpah. **Issachar** has four sons mentioned, **Tola, Puah, Jashub, and Shimron**. Tola's descendants were heads of fathers' houses and warriors in David's time (1 Chr 7:1). A Tola, evidently named after this one, from the tribe of Issachar was one of Israel's judges (Judg 10:1). Puah[14] is the ancestor of the clan of "Punites" (1 Chr 7:1). Jashub[15] and Shimron are otherwise only known by the clans which descended from them. **Zebulun**'s three sons, **Sered, Elon, and Jahleel**, are otherwise known only from the clans that descended from them.

Verse 15 serves as a summary statement of the sons of **Leah**. Interestingly even though most of these descendants were grandsons and many were not technically born **in Paddan Aram**, they are still counted as such in order to arrive at the number 70 for the total. Also of note is the fact that **Dinah** and other unnamed daughters[16] of Jacob

---

[14]Hebrew has פֻּוָּה (*puwwāh*) here and in Numbers 26:23 while 1 Chronicles 7:1 has פּוּאָה (*pû'āh*), an understandable variation in spelling in Hebrew.

[15]The MT here, based on Codex B19, has יוֹב (*yôb*) but many other Hebrew manuscripts, the parallel passages (Num 26:24; 1 Chr 7:1), and the Samaritan Pentateuch read יָשִׁיב (*yāš[î]b*) or יָשׁוּב (*yāšûb*).

[16]Notice the plural here that the NIV, to its credit, retains.

are referred to in this passage, although they are not counted in the 33 male descendants of Leah listed.

46:16 The sons of Gad: Zephon, Haggi, Shuni, Ezbon, Eri, Arodi and Areli. 46:17 The sons of Asher: Imnah, Ishvah, Ishvi and Beriah. Their sister was Serah. The sons of Beriah: Heber and Malkiel. 46:18 These were the children born to Jacob by Zilpah, whom Laban had given to his daughter Leah—sixteen in all.

This section follows the list of descendants of Leah with the descendants of Leah's handmaiden, Zilpah. While Gad and Asher, Zilpah's sons, were born after Bilhah's sons (Gen 30:1-13) they are listed first because they are linked to Leah, the first, though unloved, wife of Jacob. The descendants of Gad and Asher, as the sons of the secondary wife who was the handmaiden of the unfavored first wife, would be regarded as lowest on the totem pole by Jacob. But the narrator lists a full sixteen descendants, including a sister, among the 70 counted descendants of Jacob who went down to Egypt.

Gad has seven listed sons who formed the basis of clans within the transjordanian tribe of Gad. The sons are otherwise unknown. There is some variation in spelling between the names listed and the clans which descended from them. The NIV's **Zephon** is actually spelled Ziphion, while the clan is known as the "Zephonites" (Num 26:15); **Ezbon**'s clan is eventually known as Ozni (Num 26:16); Arod is called **Arodi** (Num 26:17).

Asher has four sons, **Imnah, Ishvah, Ishvi, and Beriah**, and one daughter, **Serah**. All of the sons give birth to clans named after them except Ishvah, whose name does not appear in the census record of Israel in the wilderness (Num 26:44). Apparently the clan of Ishvah had died out by that time. Serah is the only daughter of Jacob besides Dinah who is actually named, although there may well have been many others who go unnamed (cf. v. 15 above). Two of Jacob's great-grandsons are counted among the 70 who go down to Egypt, **Beriah**'s sons **Heber and Malkiel**.

Verse 18, like verse 15 above, serves as a summary statement of the descendants of Leah through her handmaiden **Zilpah**. The total of 16 includes Gad and Asher (but not their wives), their 11 sons, 1 daughter, and 2 grandsons.

46:19 The sons of Jacob's wife Rachel: Joseph and Benjamin. 46:20 In Egypt, Manasseh and Ephraim were born to Joseph by Asenath daughter of Potiphera, priest of On. 46:21 The sons of Benjamin: Bela, Beker, Ashbel, Gera, Naaman, Ehi, Rosh, Muppim, Huppim and Ard. 46:22 These were the sons of Rachel who were born to Jacob—fourteen in all.

The descendants of the sons of Rachel are listed third, after the sons of Jacob's first wife, Leah, and even after the sons of Leah's hand-maiden and Jacob's secondary wife, Zilpah. The favoritism which Jacob had sown in his family is not shared by the narrator of Genesis.

Included among the 70 who "came into" Egypt are Joseph's sons, **Manasseh**, the firstborn, and **Ephraim**. Both of them were born in Egypt and so technically did not "come into" Egypt in the same way as the rest of the family. It is striking that Joseph's Egyptian wife, **Asenath**, the daughter of an Egyptian priest is specifically mentioned as the mother of Joseph's sons. This would have, no doubt, surprised the canonical audience if not the original audience.[17] Israel was strictly forbidden to marry outside of the nation for fear that such marriage alliances would result in the nation being led away from faithfulness to Yahweh alone (Deut 7:3). Joseph, not only married outside of the family, he married the daughter of a noteworthy Egyptian priest who led in rituals of worship to false gods! Joseph, of course, was placed in very difficult circumstances by his brothers' having sold him into slavery, and he was not under the later Mosaic law. His marriage was arranged for him by Pharaoh himself (Gen 41:45). The Bible does not hide such things, and this may be designed to remind the original audience that God is not only at work among his chosen people. There are many others who might initially be construed to be "outsiders" who are folded into the family. The mother of two of the largest tribes in the nation of Israel when it finally entered the Promised Land was the daughter of a pagan priest! This would seem to be a reminder that the ultimate purpose of God's choice of Abraham's descendants was to be a channel of his blessing to the entire world.

Benjamin, the youngest of Jacob's twelve sons, has ten sons himself! The textual problems in this list are complex because the genealogies of Benjamin in Numbers 26 and 1 Chronicles 7 and 8 list the names differently. Contemporary readers must remember that ancient Near Eastern texts do not use genealogies in the same way as their modern counterparts.[18] The Numbers account lacks **Beker** and **Gera**, perhaps because these sons of Benjamin never founded clans which lasted until the

---

[17]The canonical audience may even have been familiar with the traditions behind the Pseudepigraphal work Joseph and Asenath (1st century B.C.–2nd century A.D.). Joseph only married Asenath after her full conversion to the Jewish faith. Cf. C. Buchard, "Joseph and Asenath: A New Translation and Introduction," *Old Testament Pseudepigrapha*, vol. 2, ed. by James H. Charlesworth (New York: Doubleday, 1985), pp. 176-241.

[18]See the discussion in Kissling, *Genesis Volume 1*, pp. 247-249.

wilderness period, although Beker does show up in 1 Chronicles 7. **Naaman** and **Ard** are listed in Numbers as the sons of **Bela**, not Benjamin. This may be due to the fact that in the intervening time the clans of Naaman and Ard had joined the clan of Bela as subordinate clans. Many scholars believe that **Ehi** and **Rosh** were combined in the name Ahiram in Numbers 26:38. This clan is apparently the "Aharah" in 1 Chronicles 8:1. **Muppim** is otherwise known as Shephupham or Shuppim in the (textually) later genealogies. These sorts of changes in spelling, changes in relationship between tribes, and the possibility of copyists' errors are common in what we commonly (mis-)name biblical genealogies. Tribal groups disappear, reappear, and new groups sometimes newly appear in biblical genealogies. They are not to be considered scientific descriptions of biological descent.

The Genealogy of Benjamin in Israel's History

Genesis 46:21	Numbers 26:38-40	1 Chronicles 7:6-12	1 Chronicles 8:1-2
Bela	Bela	Bela	Bela
Beker		Beker	
Ashbel	Ashbel	Jediael	Ashbel
Gera			
Naaman	Naaman, son of Bela		
Ehi	Ahiram		Aharah
Rosh			Nohah
Muppim	Shephupham	Shuppim son of Ir	Rapha
Huppim	Hupham	Huppim son of Ir	
Ard	Ard, son of Bela		

Verse 22 serves as a summary statement of the descendants of **Rachel**'s sons. If Manasseh and Ephraim are counted, along with Joseph and Benjamin, there are 14 descendants of Rachel who came to Egypt among the total of 70.

46:23 The son of Dan: Hushim. 46:24 The sons of Naphtali: Jahziel, Guni, Jezer and Shillem. 46:25 These were the sons born to Jacob by Bilhah, whom Laban had given to his daughter Rachel—seven in all.

This paragraph lists the sons of Bilhah, the handmaiden of Rachel and one of Jacob's secondary wives. **Dan** has only one son listed, **Husham.**[19] **Naphtali**'s four sons, **Jahziel,**[20] **Guni, Jezer, and Shillem,**[21] are otherwise

---

[19]The clan that descended from Husham is spelled Shuham in Numbers 26:42.

[20]The NIV here transliterates the name as "Jahziel" rather than MT's "Jahzeel" in light of the spelling in 1 Chronicles 7:13.

[21]This name is spelled Shallum in 1 Chronicles 7:13.

only known through the clans which descended from them. Verse 25 serves as a summary statement of the descendants of **Bilhah**, Rachel's handmaiden and one of Jacob's two secondary wives. The number 7 contributes to the magic number of 70 total descendants of Jacob in Egypt.

46:26 All those who went to Egypt with Jacob—those who were his direct descendants, not counting his sons' wives—numbered sixty-six persons. 46:27 With the two sons who had been born to Joseph in Egypt, the members of Jacob's family, which went to Egypt, were seventy in all.

This paragraph serves as a summary statement of the entire section listing the family of Jacob in 46:8-25. But the way that the mathematics is done shows the symbolic importance of the number 70. The preceding genealogy is divided into four groups by their mothers: Leah (33), Zilpah (16), Rachel (14), and Bilhah (7). This adds up to 70 people. In verse 26, however, the number 66 is mentioned. This number does not count the wives of Jacob's sons, but neither did the original number. How then did the narrator arrive at the number 66? One possibility is to recognize that Er and Onan did not come down to Egypt because they died in Canaan and Manasseh and Ephraim were born in Egypt. This would mean 66 who did actually come down to Egypt from Canaan. But if these four are excluded, to arrive at 66, how can the number seventy be affirmed in verse 27 by including Joseph's two sons? The original 66 plus the two sons of Joseph would make 68, not seventy. One possibility is that the narrator now includes Dinah and Jacob himself. But neither of them is included in the original count of 70 derived by adding the number of descendants of each of the four wives of Jacob, but not Jacob himself or Dinah. In other words the narrator comes to the number 70 twice, but only by counting them in different ways! No matter how you count them, the number is 70, and that number matters for this narrator. It is not intended, evidently, to be a literal number but a symbolic number. The question then becomes, "symbolic of what?" Most likely the 70 descendants of Jacob correspond to the 70 nations mentioned as descending from Noah in Genesis 10. The 70 nations are not a comprehensive list of all the nations of the world, but the symbolic number for "all" the world. Jacob, the forefather of the nation Israel, is a sort of new humanity. The nation is chosen for the benefit of all the nations of the world. This is symbolized by having the entirety of the nation be counted as 70, one for each of the nations of the world. Needless to say, this is not how a contemporary author would make this point. But the point is a profound one even if the means used to affirm it leave us scratching our heads. The destiny of the entire world is tied up in this obscure little nation.

B. JOSEPH REUNITES WITH JACOB AND HIS BROTHERS
(46:28-30)

46:28 Now Jacob sent Judah ahead of him to Joseph to get directions to Goshen. When they arrived in the region of Goshen, 46:29 Joseph had his chariot made ready and went to Goshen to meet his father Israel. As soon as Joseph appeared before him, he threw his arms around his father and wept for a long time.

The meeting of **Jacob** with his long lost and presumed dead son Joseph is about to happen. **Judah** originally had the idea of selling **Joseph** into slavery in Egypt, thus separating his father from his favored son. There may well be some form of providential poetry in the fact that he must go ahead and arrange for the reuniting of the two. It is also probably significant that it is Judah, whom Jacob sends ahead, and not his firstborn Reuben or his other older brothers Simeon and Levi. Judah has begun the trajectory which results in his being given the role of leadership among the brothers. That trajectory culminates in Jacob's blessing in Genesis 49:8-12 where the ruler's staff is passed on to Judah and not his older brothers or even Jacob's favorite, Joseph.

Judah gets directions specifically to go **to Goshen**, the place that Joseph had promised they would live. After their arrival **Joseph** prepared **his chariot** and **went to meet** Jacob and his family there.

In one of the most poignant moments in the entire Bible, the reuniting of Jacob and Joseph, at first no words are spoken. Interestingly the narrator refers to Jacob as "Israel [Joseph's] father." Joseph appeared before Jacob, not vice versa, and he "fell upon Jacob's neck and wept upon his neck for a long time" (עוֹד עַל־צַוָּארָיו וַיֵּבְךְ עַל־צַוָּארָיו וַיִּפֹּל, *wayyipōl 'al-ṣawwā'rāyw wayyêbkᵊ 'al-ṣawwā'rāyw 'ôd*).

46:30 Israel said to Joseph, "Now I am ready to die, since I have seen for myself that you are still alive."

Once again the narrator refers to Jacob by his national name, **Israel**. Although what he speaks about is very personal, his own death, the narrator would remind readers that this person is the forefather of the entire nation of which they are members. When Joseph's brothers had presented their father with the bloodied garment of Joseph, Jacob had mourned that he would go down to the grave mourning Joseph (Gen 37:35). Now that he has actually **seen** Joseph **alive** again, he is ready to die in peace. Death in Genesis is regarded as the inevitable result of life in a broken world. But there is a big difference between death ending a life lived in sorrow and death which happens after a long, fruitful life with your family beside you. As the saying goes, "Parents should never bury their children." Jacob realizes that he doesn't need to die still mourning for his favorite son.

C. JOSEPH PREPARES HIS FAMILY TO MEET PHARAOH (46:31-34)

46:31 Then Joseph said to his brothers and to his father's household, "I will go up and speak to Pharaoh and will say to him, 'My brothers and my father's household, who were living in the land of Canaan, have come to me. 46:32 The men are shepherds; they tend livestock, and they have brought along their flocks and herds and everything they own.' 46:33 When Pharaoh calls you in and asks, 'What is your occupation?' 46:34 you should answer, 'Your servants have tended livestock from our boyhood on, just as our fathers did.' Then you will be allowed to settle in the region of Goshen, for all shepherds are detestable to the Egyptians."

After reuniting with his father and family, Joseph then strategizes with them to ensure that they end up being given the land of Goshen in which to live. Joseph knows Pharaoh well, or at least presumes that he does. Joseph intuits that when Pharaoh finds out that they are "detestable" (v. 34) shepherds, and they have brought their substantial flocks and herds with them, he will gladly allow them to live by themselves in the land of Goshen. In that way they would be separated from the palace and the rest of the Egyptian population.

Joseph proposes that he go and **speak to Pharaoh** first to prepare the way. He intends to tell Pharaoh that they have come, that they **are shepherds** and keep **livestock**, and that **they brought** all of their livestock and other possessions with them. He does not tell Pharaoh that he himself had told them, contrary to Pharaoh's wishes, to bring their livestock (45:10). Nor would he tell Pharaoh that he had already assured them that they would live in Goshen separated from Pharaoh and the other Egyptians.

Joseph proposes that when Pharaoh interviews them personally, they are to confirm Joseph's words that they are shepherds, thus ensuring that they remain **in Goshen**[22] and take up residence there. In fact, Joseph

---

[22]Hoffmeier, *Ancient Israel in Sinai*, p. 40: "During the Hellenistic period, the Septuagint translators of Genesis 46:34 added a note that the land of Goshen was 'of Arabia' (ἐν γῇ Γεσὲμ Ἀραβίας), showing that they understood that the northeastern delta where Goshen was situated was beside Arabia, which can only be Sinai." This may explain Paul's usage in Galatians 4 where Sinai is equated with Arabia.

would like them to claim (quite truthfully) that they had been tending livestock from their youth as had their fathers. This would make it more difficult for Pharaoh to imagine integrating them into court life.[23] The only
skills they had for generations were those despised by the Egyptians and
not congenial to full integration into court life. While we only have
Joseph's word for it that the Egyptians find shepherds so disgusting, this
probably reflects the urban Egyptian aversion to nomadic peoples, something they shared with all urban dwellers, ancient and modern.[24]

---

[23]Wenham's suggestion that Joseph's strategy is to absolve him of a potential
claim that he would nepotistically appoint his brothers to governmental positions fails to take account of Pharaoh's offer to provide for them (45:20).
Pharaoh offered to be nepotistic on Joseph's behalf.

[24]So Wenham, *Genesis 16–50*, p. 445.

GENESIS 47

D. THE FAMILY RECEIVES PHARAOH'S PERMISSION TO SETTLE IN GOSHEN (47:1-12)

1. Pharaoh Receives Joseph's Brothers (47:1-6)

47:1 Joseph went and told Pharaoh, "My father and brothers, with their flocks and herds and everything they own, have come from the land of Canaan and are now in Goshen." 47:2 He chose five of his brothers and presented them before Pharaoh. 47:3 Pharaoh asked the brothers, "What is your occupation?" "Your servants are shepherds," they replied to Pharaoh, "just as our fathers were." 47:4 They also said to him, "We have come to live here awhile, because the famine is severe in Canaan and your servants' flocks have no pasture. So now, please let your servants settle in Goshen." 47:5 Pharaoh said to Joseph, "Your father and your brothers have come to you, 47:6 and the land of Egypt is before you; settle your father and your brothers in the best part of the land. Let them live in Goshen. And if you know of any among them with special ability, put them in charge of my own livestock."

Joseph gets straight to the point when he meets **Pharaoh**. Not only did his **father and brothers** come, but also **their flocks and herds** and all their possessions came with them. While this is technically against what Pharaoh had suggested (45:20), Joseph gives him no opportunity to address the issue. They are already **in Goshen** waiting for Pharaoh's directive. In a single sentence Joseph has crafted the entire conversation toward his goal that his family be able to live under Pharaoh's protection in Goshen and with a relatively separate life and lifestyle. He manages to achieve this without ever telling Pharaoh that his family would rather remain separated from Egyptian culture.

Joseph took only **five** of the total[1] eleven **brothers** to present before Pharaoh. We are not told which brothers were chosen. As anticipated,

---

[1]The Hebrew phrase וּמִקְצֵה אֶחָיו (*ûmiqṣēh 'eḥāyw*; literally "from the end of his brothers") evidently means "from the totality of" as in Judges 18:2.

Pharaoh's first question concerns their **occupation**. Was Pharaoh testing Joseph's veracity at this point? If he was, Joseph had anticipated it and prepared his brothers for the question. They reply respectfully, referring to themselves as Pharaoh's **servants**. They answer as Joseph had suggested, saying that they and their fathers were shepherds.[2] They then go on to extemporize a bit. One wonders whether this might have made Joseph nervous. They tell Pharaoh that they only intend to temporarily live in Egypt (לָגוּר, *lāgûr*) and even that only because of the lack of pasturage in Canaan brought on by the severe **famine**. They then return to Joseph's "script" and ask, as servants, to be allowed to live specifically in the land of Goshen, undoubtedly because of its suitability for pasturage. Pharaoh, in his response, addresses **Joseph**, not the brothers. This could be the issue of translation or it could be that Pharaoh wants to make it clear to the brothers that any beneficence that they might receive from him comes only because they are Joseph's family. Pharaoh makes it clear to Joseph that **the land of Egypt** lies before him to choose **the best part of the land** for his **father and brothers** to live in. Since **Goshen**[3] was requested, Goshen it would be.

Pharaoh adds that if Joseph knows any of his shepherd brothers to have **special ability**, he is free to appoint them as chief over his **own livestock**. We are never informed that Joseph took Pharaoh up on his offer. Perhaps we should assume that he did. Joseph is clearly the key to his family surviving and thriving in Egypt.

2. Pharaoh Receives Jacob and His Blessing (47:7-10)

47:7 Then Joseph brought his father Jacob in and presented him before Pharaoh. After Jacob blessed Pharaoh, 47:8 Pharaoh asked him, "How old are you?" 47:9 And Jacob said to Pharaoh, "The years of my pilgrimage are a hundred and thirty. My years have been few and difficult, and they do not equal the years of the pilgrimage of my fathers." 47:10 Then Jacob blessed Pharaoh and went out from his presence.

---

[2]Although they do not emphasize the fact that they had been shepherds since their youth.

[3]Goshen is not attested as a place name in the Egyptian sources currently available. It was fertile enough for grazing and was on the eastern border of Egypt. Goshen is "generally identified with the area around Wadi Ṭumilât, a 56 km (35 mi) fertile strip of land connecting the eastern part of the Nile River Delta with Lake Timsah. It provides one of only two passages for traffic between Egypt and Sinai or Palestine to the east." Daniel C. Browning Jr., "Goshen," *EDB*, p. 521.

After settling the issue of where the family would live, Joseph then brings **Jacob in** to be **presented before Pharaoh**. But Jacob does not come seeking a favor from Pharaoh as his sons had. The fact that **Jacob blesse[s] Pharaoh** and not vice versa is significant. Jacob does not seek or need Pharaoh's blessing. Instead, though he is the king of the most powerful nation in the ancient Near East at this time, Jacob realizes that Pharaoh needs a blessing from him. The echo of the promise to Abraham that in his descendants all the nations of the earth would be blessed (Gen 12:3) must not be missed. The prime representative of a powerful nation receives a blessing through Abraham's grandson Jacob. This point is emphasized by its repetition in verse 10 which together with verse 7b form a sort of *inclusio* around the passage.

Interestingly after receiving a blessing from Jacob, Pharaoh's first question is about Jacob's age. Perhaps, as Sarna suggests, Pharaoh wants to know if Jacob had exceeded the Egyptian ideal lifespan of 110 years.[4] Jacob refers to his life as a "sojourn" (גּוּר, *gûr*), a temporary stay — but that temporary stay had been extraordinarily long, a full 130 years. Jacob describes those 130 years as "few" and "evil" or "troubled" (רַע, *ra'*). While he does not detail all the trouble or evil which he had seen in life for Pharaoh, Jacob does explain how he could regard a life of 130 as being a "few" years. His forefathers, Abraham (175 years, Gen 25:7) and Isaac (180 years; Gen 35:28) had "sojourned" much longer. Jacob may be using the word "sojourn" metaphorically, or he may be referring to the fact that neither he nor his forefathers had had permanent ownership of land or citizenship in a nation with the residence rights which such ownership or citizenship entails. But even a life that was relatively short by the standards of his ancestors and one full of trouble, is a sign of God's blessing to Pharaoh. While we are not told of Pharaoh's reaction to his encounter with Jacob, he must have been impressed by his longevity as well as by the fact that he had fathered a son as wise and capable as Joseph. Before **Jacob** left, he **blessed Pharaoh** a second time, bringing home the point to the readers that this was not just politeness but a hint of the fulfillment of Yahweh's promise that Abraham's descendants would be the channel of his blessing to all the nations of the world.

3. The Family Settles in Goshen (47:11-12)

47:11 So Joseph settled his father and his brothers in Egypt and gave them property in the best part of the land, the district of Rameses, as

---

[4]Sarna, *Genesis*, p. 320.

Pharaoh directed. 47:12 Joseph also provided his father and his brothers and all his father's household with food, according to the number of their children.

Joseph had promised to provide for his family during the famine (Gen 45:10). In this text, under Pharaoh's authority, he begins to do so. He **settled** them permanently **in Egypt**, even granting them **property** there. Ironically the first real inheritance of land other than an overpriced grave plot which the chosen family receives as its own is not in Canaan, but in Egypt. As promised, Jacob's family receives **the best part of the land.** But in this passage the land is no longer called Goshen, but by the updated name that the original and canonical audience would have known, **Rameses.** Rameses, as used in this passage, evidently refers to a district. The original audience would have known it as one of the cities which the later enslaved Israelites would be forced to build (Exod 1:11). It is also the name of a famous line of Egyptian Pharaohs. There were a number of places called Rameses in ancient Egypt. While initially Egyptologists identified Rameses as Tanis, and this is reflected in some older Bible atlases still in print, the later work of Hamza led to the current consensus that Qantir is the Rameses of the Bible.[5]

After settling his family Joseph did not leave them to their own resources but **provided** them **with** a **food** (לֶחֶם, *leḥem*)[6] allotment based on the number of mouths to feed. In normal circumstances this might not be such an extraordinary thing given Joseph's position and the power and wealth that it implied. But during a severe famine when there was no (extra) food, this showed extraordinary generosity and extraordinary influence at Pharaoh's court that would enable him to provide it.

E. JOSEPH BUYS THE LAND OF EGYPT FOR PHARAOH DURING THE FAMINE (47:13-26)

47:13 There was no food, however, in the whole region because the famine was severe; both Egypt and Canaan wasted away because of the famine. 47:14 Joseph collected all the money that was to be found in Egypt and Canaan in payment for the grain they were buying, and he brought it to Pharaoh's palace. 47:15 When the money of the people

---

[5]See the careful discussion of Hoffmeier, *Israel in Egypt*, pp. 117-119. He debunks the recent attempts of Redford and Lemche to cast doubt on this identification.

[6]"Bread" is often used of food in general.

of Egypt and Canaan was gone, all Egypt came to Joseph and said,
"Give us food. Why should we die before your eyes? Our money is
used up." **47:16** "Then bring your livestock," said Joseph. "I will sell
you food in exchange for your livestock, since your money is gone."
47:17 So they brought their livestock to Joseph, and he gave them food
in exchange for their horses, their sheep and goats, their cattle and
donkeys. And he brought them through that year with food in
exchange for all their livestock.

The severity of the famine is indicated by the statement that both
the land of Egypt and the land of Canaan "**wasted away**"[7] because of the
famine. God's providence in preparing the way before his chosen people, even through or despite the bitter jealousy and rivalry between the
brothers which resulted in Joseph being sold as a slave in Egypt, shines
brightly.

This passage shows how virtually all the land in Egypt came into the
permanent possession of Pharaoh in stages. First Joseph "gleaned"[8] all
the silver still left among the populace of Egypt and adjoining Canaan
in payment for the purchase of grain. Joseph ensures that the money
goes to the treasury of Pharaoh and is not frittered away by bureaucrats,
thus earning Pharaoh's trust and demonstrating his honesty. In the second stage the inhabitants of Egypt[9] come to Joseph begging for[10] food,
not grain. They are not thinking of planting and harvesting and thus
needing seed for next year's crop. They are only concerned about eating. They acknowledge that they no longer have the **money** to pay for
the food[11] they are requesting. Their only hope is that Joseph will have
compassion on them, not wanting them to die right in front of him.

Joseph's response shows his wisdom in protecting Pharaoh's interests and his concern to find a way to solve the concrete problems of a
populace on the verge of hunger. They had asked Joseph to "**give**" them

---

[7]The verb לההַ (*lhh*) is found only here although a related verb לאה (*l'h*) means
to tire or grow weary (cf. KB, pp. 512, 521).

[8]The verb used here, לָקַט (*lāqaṭ*), is used of gleaning fields for any leftover
grain after the harvest (Lev 19:9,10; 23:20; Ruth 2:2,3,7,8,15-19,23; Isa 17:5). The
Egyptians, having lived through some significant part of the famine, had only
minimal money in reserve, which Joseph gleaned from them.

[9]Interestingly only the inhabitants of Egypt sell their livestock even though the
famine had affected both Egypt and Canaan. Evidently those who lived in
Canaan found other ways of surviving the famine.

[10]Wenham (*Genesis 16–50*, p. 448) notes that the Hebrew verb (הָבָה, *hābāh*)
implies desperation in Genesis 30:1 and here.

[11]The Hebrew here has a wordplay, אָפֵס כָּסֶף (*'āphēs kāseph*), "the silver has
slidden away."

food; he asks them to "**give**"[12] him their cattle in exchange for food, since they have no silver to pay for it. Reluctantly or not, the Egyptians **brought** their cattle to Joseph. Animals were and are an important form of capital in an agricultural society. Whether they were actually physically exchanged for food to be cared for by Pharaoh's extensive herdsmen[13] or whether they were counted and their ownership transferred to Pharaoh but continued to be cared for by their original owners is unclear. In exchange for food, Joseph gained for Pharaoh **horses, sheep, goats, cattle, and donkeys**. The mention of horses is interesting as they were often used in warfare as especially valuable forms of transportation. Solomon, despite the warning in the law against future kings of Israel returning to Egypt to acquire horses (Deut 17:16), nevertheless did so (1 Kgs 10:28). But this giving up of their farm animals only got **them through that year**. While Joseph's actions sustained[14] them (v. 17), it only made Pharaoh more powerful and the people more economically dependent on him. Further, it was only a temporary measure.

47:18 When that year was over, they came to him the following year and said, "We cannot hide from our lord the fact that since our money is gone and our livestock belongs to you, there is nothing left for our lord except our bodies and our land. 47:19 Why should we perish before your eyes—we and our land as well? Buy us and our land in exchange for food, and we with our land will be in bondage to Pharaoh. Give us seed so that we may live and not die, and that the land may not become desolate." 47:20 So Joseph bought all the land in Egypt for Pharaoh. The Egyptians, one and all, sold their fields, because the famine was too severe for them. The land became Pharaoh's, 47:21 and Joseph reduced the people to servitude, from one end of Egypt to the other.

We are not told which year of the seven-year-long famine is being referred to here. At the end of the second year of the process of Egyptians needing Joseph to help them through the famine, they come to him for the third time. They have already spent their cash money and given over their **livestock** to Pharaoh. They acknowledge that they are out of money and out of livestock, something they acknowledge that Joseph already knew. They deferentially refer to Joseph twice as "**our**[15] **Lord.**"

---

[12]Both the Egyptians and Joseph use the verb יָהַב (*yāhab*).

[13]Wenham (*Genesis 16–50*, p. 446): "Rameses III is said to have employed 3,264 men, mostly foreigners, to take care of his herds."

[14]וַיְנַהֲלֵם (*wayᵊnahălēm*) is used of bringing people to a watering hole in a dry land (Ps 23:2; Isa 40:11; 49:10).

[15]The fact that in the Hebrew the suffixes are singular, literally "my" lord, may simply indicate that there was a single spokesperson for the group.

All they had left were their "corpses" and their land. The NIV translates the Hebrew word גְּוִיָּתֵנוּ (gᵉwîyāthēnû) as "**bodies**." While it can have that meaning, in this instance the more common meaning of "dead bodies" is probably intended. Having languished under the famine for some years their bodies were undoubtedly feeling the effects of the famine. The mention of their land is significant for what happens next.

They ask Joseph rhetorically, "Why should we and even our land die before your very eyes?" While this seems to contain some hyperbole, the situation is indeed dire. If they died, there would be no one to care for the land, and it would revert to untamed wilderness. They offer themselves, corpses though they be. Of equal importance from Joseph and Pharaoh's point of view, they exchange their land for food. They and their land, which takes on a sort of personality in the language they use to describe it, would become Pharaoh's servants. They ask specifically for seed with which to plant their land. With that seed they would be able to grow enough food to live on and the land would not become "desolate" for lack of human attention.

Joseph takes them up on their offer in part. He does not in this verse explicitly buy them, thus formally enslaving the entire population. But he does buy their land for Pharaoh. While the native Egyptians do not technically become Pharaoh's servants, they do become his tenant farmers. He comes to own the entire land of Egypt with the exception of the land controlled by the priests (v. 22). Joseph's wisdom in terms of Pharaoh's self-interest in storing up grain for a long famine was being demonstrated in the most remarkable way. He served Pharaoh's interests. Because Pharaoh had chosen to follow Joseph's divinely guided advice, Pharaoh came to own almost all of the land of Egypt. Ironically, however, by building up Pharaoh's power Joseph was laying the foundation for future Pharaohs to abuse that power by enslaving and brutally abusing the descendants of Jacob.

Historians wish that we had enough information about Egyptian society to know when Pharaoh came into personal ownership of the land of Egypt as this would help us in dating this text. But apparently we have too little knowledge to do anything more than speculate.[16] The end result of Joseph's anticipating the famine and helping the Egyptian population through it was that the land became Pharaoh's.

The Hebrew and Vulgate in verse 21 state that as part of the agreement the people were moved to cities (וְאֶת־הָעָם הֶעֱבִיר אֹתוֹ לֶעָרִים מִקְצֵה גְּבוּל־מִצְרַיִם וְעַד־קָצֵהוּ, wᵉ'eth-hā'ām he'ĕbîr 'ōthô le'ārîm miqṣēh gᵉbûl-miṣrayim wᵉ'ad-qāṣēhû) from one border of Egypt to the other. The NIV follows

---

[16]See the discussion in Wenham, *Genesis 16–50*, p. 448.

the Samaritan Pentateuch and the Greek.[17] I presume this is because it seems perplexing how the entire population could move into cities without abandoning the land, the very thing Joseph was trying to prevent. Perhaps the text indicates some form of communal living for the farmers of Egypt. In any case it seems a strange form of textual criticism to adopt a text that is more naturally explained as an attempt by later translators to resolve a difficulty by providing an explanation rather than a literal translation.

47:22 However, he did not buy the land of the priests, because they received a regular allotment from Pharaoh and had food enough from the allotment Pharaoh gave them. That is why they did not sell their land.

An exception to Pharaoh's buying up of the land of Egypt during a severe famine was the land owned by the priests of Egypt. **Because they received** an **allotment** of food or its cash equivalent[18] **from Pharaoh** from which they ate. The statement has a repetitive, chiastic structure:

A The land of the priests [Joseph] did not buy
  B For [there was] an allotment for the priests from Pharaoh.
    C And they ate their allotment
  B' Which Pharaoh gave to them.
A' Therefore they did not sell their land.

Ancient temples were often fairly major parts of ancient economies. As a consequence priests, of whatever god or gods, were officially sanctioned by the state. Many were economically and therefore in some senses politically independent of the monarchy. This text seems to explain why this was so in Egypt during the time of Israel's sojourn there.

47:23 Joseph said to the people, "Now that I have bought you and your land today for Pharaoh, here is seed for you so you can plant the ground. 47:24 But when the crop comes in, give a fifth of it to Pharaoh. The other four-fifths you may keep as seed for the fields and as food for yourselves and your households and your children." 47:25 "You have saved our lives," they said. "May we find favor in the eyes of our lord; we will be in bondage to Pharaoh." 47:26 So Joseph established it as a law concerning land in Egypt—still in force today—that a fifth of the produce belongs to Pharaoh. It was only the land of the priests that did not become Pharaoh's.

---

[17]See the footnote in the NIV.

[18]The Hebrew word חֹק (*ḥōq*) is often used of a law or statute. In this case it is used in the sense of "portion" or "allotted portion"; cf. KB, p. 346.

In this passage Joseph reminds the people of what they had agreed to do. He had that very day **bought** both them and their **land for Pharaoh**. This makes explicit what was only initially implicit in verse 20. Pharaoh owns the land and their labor. Out of his and Pharaoh's "generosity" Joseph sends them back to **plant** the very land that they once owned and that now belonged to Pharaoh. But instead of claiming all of the crop for the crown and feeding them from it, Joseph treats them more like tenant farmers. They were given seed to plant and the rent that they must pay Pharaoh was twenty percent of the crop. In future years they would have to provide their own seed. They are evidently not enslaved in the typical sense. Certainly the farmers could not have been happy to lose control over their land. But it was a severe famine and Joseph's plan was better than starvation. The generosity or otherwise of the rate of twenty percent is difficult to judge from this distance. Sarna[19] notes that the Old Babylonian king Hammurabi required fifty to sixty-seven percent of the crops of state-owned land. However, unlike here, this was after the deduction of expenses.

The Egyptians may or may not have regarded Joseph as being generous to them, but they were in no position to bargain. They acknowledge that Joseph had given them new life.[20] Their expression of gratitude[21] and their offer of, or acknowledgment of, their servant status to Pharaoh[22] seems strange to contemporary readers who are reflecting (consciously or not) on the sad mistakes of our own ancestors who engaged in the African slave trade,[23] but in the ancient world servitude such as the Egyptians experienced[24] was perhaps more like permanent employment as opposed to owning your own business. Most people were servants. Even so the famine had lowered their economic and social status.

---

[19]Sarna, *Genesis*, p. 322.

[20]הֶחֱיִתָנוּ (*heḥĕyithānû*), literally, "caused us to live."

[21]One could always argue that this was merely pro forma or even sarcastic. Although this would be impossible to prove, it is not easy to disprove.

[22]The statement "we will be in bondage to Pharaoh" could be an acknowledgment of a fact. Or it could be an offer to Joseph who has not been treating them like the servants they had previously agreed to become when Pharaoh purchased their "corpses" or bodies along with their land.

[23]I myself cannot forget the slave castle I once visited in Accra, Ghana, next to a missionary graveyard. At the castle white men abused and humiliated the slaves before sending them off. At the graveyard Methodist missionaries who gave their lives in missionary service for those Africans only to be stricken by malaria were memorialized. And these stood virtually next to each other!

[24]See Chirichigno, *Debt-Slavery in Israel and the Ancient Near East*.

The arrangement that Joseph made during the famine became a permanent "**law**,"[25] which was still in force in the days of the original audience. This would seem to be a useful piece of information that would allow the dating of this event. Unfortunately, however, we do not have enough information about economic relationships and taxation in ancient Egypt to do so.

The importance for the author of reminding the readers that the priests were exempt from this system of taxation is indicated by its repetition in verse 26. One can only speculate as to why it might be important. One possibility is that it hints at the importance of Israel keeping its own priesthood independent of the monarchy. When political leaders control the religion of a people, there is always the danger of the leaders using religion in service of their own interests. Israel's law ensured that only Levites could serve as priests. The history of the nation showed that only descendants of Benjamin or Judah served as kings. The two offices were kept strictly separate because of the danger of the kings corrupting the priests.

F. THE PROMISE PROGRESSES IN EGYPT (47:27)

47:27 Now the Israelites settled in Egypt in the region of Goshen. They acquired property there and were fruitful and increased greatly in number.

Raymond de Hoop[26] notes the parallel between this verse and 37:1[27] where Jacob dwelled permanently for the first time in the land of Canaan. The NIV interprets "Israel" as the people of Israel ("Israelites"), but there is good reason to leave the translation as "Israel" so that the reader must decide whether it is Israel the person or Israel the nation that is being referred to or both. Interestingly Jacob and his family acquired property in Goshen as though they were normal citizens of Egypt. The fact that they were described as being "**fruitful and increase**[ing] **greatly**" reminds the readers of the creation commission (Gen 1:26-28) as well as the promises of God to Abraham and his descendants.[28] The promise of a great nation is starting to look as though it could be fulfilled as God had promised.

---

[25]Here the word *ḥōq* is used in the typical sense of "law."

[26]De Hoop, *Genesis 49*, p. 325.

[27]Hebrew of 47:27a is: וַיֵּשֶׁב יִשְׂרָאֵל בְּאֶרֶץ מִצְרַיִם בְּאֶרֶץ גֹּשֶׁן (*wayyēšeb yiśrā'ēl bᵃ'ereṣ miṣrayim bᵃ'ereṣ gōšen*). Heb. of 37:1a is: וַיֵּשֶׁב יַעֲקֹב בְּאֶרֶץ מְגוּרֵי אָבִיו בְּאֶרֶץ כְּנָעַן (*wayyēšeb ya'ăqōb bᵃ'ereṣ mᵃgûrê 'abîw bᵃ'ereṣ kᵃnā'an*).

[28]The Hebrew verbs used here, רבה (*rbh*) and פרה (*prh*), are found together in Genesis 1:22,28; 8:17; 9:1,7; 17:20; 28:3; 35:11; 48:4.

IX. ISRAEL'S FINAL DAYS (47:28–49:32)

With the family securely settled in Egypt the narrator jumps ahead seventeen years to the last days of Jacob's life. With death facing him, Jacob calls his favorite son Joseph and gains his promise that his body will not be left in Egypt but taken to the family grave in Hebron. Sometime later Jacob's health takes a turn for the worse, prompting Joseph to take his two sons, Manasseh and Ephraim, to Jacob for his blessing. Jacob ends up adopting them as his own sons and blessing the younger, Ephraim, above his older brother Manasseh. Joseph, too, receives a personal inheritance (48:21-22).

All of this takes place before Jacob calls for all of his sons to come to his deathbed for his final words to them. This demonstrates the special place that Joseph and his sons had in Jacob's heart. Somewhat surprisingly, however, the blessing of leadership among the sons is given to Judah, not Joseph. In an allusion to the dreams of Joseph and perhaps as a rebuke of them Jacob says to Judah, "Your father's sons will bow down before you." Even though Jacob's blessing of Joseph is effusive, he is not given the role of leadership. The original and canonical audiences would understand this from their own experience. The tribe of Judah is given the first and prime inheritance in the Promised Land. The three tribal allotments of the descendants of Joseph do not satisfy them (Josh 17:14-18). The tensions that later resulted in the split of the kingdom between Judah in the south and the tribes of Joseph in the north are present from the beginning, from the time of the original family of Israel!

But the canonical audience would also know that there are exceptions to the principle that Jacob's words anticipate or even determine the future of the tribes that descend from Jacob's sons. The tribes of Simeon and Levi receive a curse, not a blessing from Jacob. But from the time when the nation came to Sinai on, the tribe of Levi, Moses' tribe, is given leadership of the nation in its relationship with God. After the exile and the disappearance of the monarchy it is the tribe of Levi, not the tribe of Judah, which maintains leadership in the nation.

After Jacob's final words to his sons he asks for their promise that he would be buried in Hebron. The structure of this section is thus palistrophic, a favorite technique of the narrator of Genesis.[29]

---

[29]Two examples of palistrophic structure in Genesis are the flood narrative (Kissling, *Genesis Volume 1*, pp. 272-273) and the Jacob narrative (see this commentary at Gen 25:19).

A Jacob Procures Joseph's Promise to Bury Him in the
   Promised Land 47:28-31
  B Jacob Adopts and Blesses Joseph's Sons, Ephraim and
    Manasseh 48:1-20
    C. Special Inheritance for Joseph 48:21-22
  B' Jacob Blesses His Twelve Sons 49:1-27
A' Jacob Procures Promise from His Twelve Sons to Bury Him
   in Canaan 49:28-32

The purpose of this structure would seem to be to emphasize the special inheritance for Joseph as his father's favorite. But this must be balanced by the consideration that 49:1-27 is the denouement of this section and of the book of Genesis as a whole.

A. JACOB PROCURES JOSEPH'S PROMISE TO BURY HIM IN THE PROMISED LAND (47:28-31)

47:28 Jacob lived in Egypt seventeen years, and the years of his life were a hundred and forty-seven. 47:29 When the time drew near for Israel to die, he called for his son Joseph and said to him, "If I have found favor in your eyes, put your hand under my thigh and promise that you will show me kindness and faithfulness. Do not bury me in Egypt, 47:30 but when I rest with my fathers, carry me out of Egypt and bury me where they are buried." "I will do as you say," he said.

Jacob lived the same number of years in Egypt after moving there as
Joseph had lived in Canaan before being moved to Egypt.[30] If Jacob died
at 147, seventeen years after moving to Egypt, Joseph would have been
about 56 at his death, since he was about 39 when Jacob moved to Egypt.
As the favored child of Jacob, even though he was the tenth son born to
him, Joseph is to play a special role in the working out of the promises.
In this he was like his grandfather Isaac. Both were not the firstborn sons
of their fathers, but were the firstborn sons of their fathers' legitimate
wives, Sarah and Rachel, respectively. In both cases there were tensions
between them and their older siblings Ishmael and Esau.

The length of Jacob's life given in verse 28 prepares the reader for
the events of his last days. Before he called for or addressed any of his

---

[30]While one must be cautious with the use of such numbers, L. Ruppert, *Die Josephserzählung der Genesis: Ein Beitrag zur Theologie der Pentateuchquellen*, Studien zum Alten und Neuen Testament (München: Kösel, 1965), pp. 178-179, notes that the factors of the ages of the deaths of the three Patriarchs all add up to 17. Abraham's 175 years = $5\times5\times7$; Isaac's 180 years = $6\times6\times5$; Jacob's 147 years = $7\times7\times3$. This serves to tie Joseph more closely to the patriarchs.

other sons, including Benjamin, Jacob calls for **Joseph**, his favorite, to come to his deathbed. Like the Egyptians who had hoped to find **favor in** Joseph's **eyes** in verse 25 above, so here Joseph's father hopes for the same. Jacob's actions are reminiscent of Abraham. Both asked a subordinate to place his **hand under** his **thigh** and make a solemn **promise**; in Abraham's case it was his chief servant; in Jacob's case it was Joseph. In both cases the patriarch was about to die.

Placing the hand under the thigh or groin is a custom the exact significance of which is lost to us. Perhaps the groin or the place near it symbolizes the procreative power or progeny of the person. Placing the hand there might have meant something like, "May my descendants which come out of my loins hold you responsible if you fail to keep your promise." Since this custom was used to exact a vow from Abraham's servant in Genesis 24, it may be that the custom indicates a form of subordination. If so, Joseph subordinates himself to his father.[31]

Jacob asks Joseph to act with loyalty and faithfulness toward him by ensuring that he not be buried in Egypt and thus outside of the Promised Land. In the ancient world being buried with one's fathers in the family grave was a key sign of a life that ended well as it should for those under God's blessing. For Jacob it was additionally a reminder to his family that they were the inheritors of the promises which he fought so hard to attain and retain. Those promises must not be forgotten. Egypt is not to become their permanent home. They belong in Canaan and Jacob's descendants must not forget that. Jacob's request to Joseph shows the original and canonical audience the importance that must be given to the promises of God to Abraham, Isaac, and Israel (Jacob). Joseph shows his devotion to his father by promising to do what his dying father had asked.

47:31 "Swear to me," he said. Then Joseph swore to him, and Israel worshiped as he leaned on the top of his staff.

Joseph, who is being treated as the firstborn son with special responsibilities as well as privileges, is asked to confirm his promise by solemnly swearing to it. He does so without any demurring or questioning.

The next clause is difficult to interpret and even to translate. After Joseph swore to his father, Israel "bowed down." This same word, שָׁחָה (šāḥāh), occurs in Joseph's dreams. The NIV closes the ambiguity by translating this word as **"worshiped."** Jacob obviously did not worship Joseph, but God. The question is why Joseph bowed down and espe-

---

[31]This was suggested to me by Laurence Turner.

cially to whom he did so. The Hebrew phrase rendered "**top of his staff**" could be translated in other ways. There is no "his" in the Hebrew, only the definite article, i.e., "the" staff. The word translated staff could as easily mean "bed" (הַמִּטָּה, *hammiṭṭāh*).[32] The word translated "**top**" could as easily mean "head" or "chief." The NRSV and NIV footnotes thus have Jacob bowing on the "head" of the "bed." Jacob could be bowing to the LORD in worship on the top of his staff or the head of his bed. Alternatively he could be bowing down out of respect for Joseph. De Hoop offers an interesting suggestion. The phrase could be translated, "bowed to the head of the tribe."[33] If so, Jacob bowed down to the person who was now "the head of the tribe," i.e., to Joseph. This view does have the advantage of seeing a clearer fulfillment of the second dream, where the sun, moon, and 11 stars bow down to Joseph, with Jacob being the sun, and the 11 brothers being the stars.

But this does not resolve the issue with Joseph's mother Rachel, representing the moon. She dies while giving birth to Benjamin, the eleventh star and never is said to bow down to Joseph. Further while de Hoop's translation is just possible, it seems unlikely and requires repointing of the MT without solid evidence. Also, if placing one's hand under another's thigh implies subordinate status, de Hoop's view is untenable.

Most likely Jacob expressed his gratitude to God rather than bowing to Joseph because he had Joseph back. He was even able to see Joseph's sons grow to young manhood before he died. But the possibility that Jacob is bowing down to Joseph must not be excluded as impossible.[34]

---

[32]This word or its exact homonym sometimes means "bed" (e.g., Gen 48:2; 49:33; Exod 7:28; 1 Sam 19:13,15,16; 28:23; 2 Sam 3:31).

[33]The Heb. root הַמִּטָּה (*hmṭh*)could be pointed הַמִּטָּה (*hammiṭṭāh*) meaning "the bed" or הַמַּטֶּה (*hamaṭṭēh*) and the phrase mean, as in Num 30:2; 1 Kgs 8:1,2; 2 Chr 5:2 "head of the tribe." See de Hoop, *Genesis 49*, pp. 329-330.

[34]De Hoop, *Genesis 49*, p. 324, criticizes Turner, *Announcements of Plot*, 1990, for not dealing with this text in more explicit detail when he claims that Jacob never bowed down to Joseph. But de Hoop's view has bigger problems as we have argued above.

GENESIS 48

B. JACOB ADOPTS AND BLESSES JOSEPH'S SONS, EPHRAIM AND MANASSEH (48:1-20)

48:1 Some time later Joseph was told, "Your father is ill." So he took his two sons Manasseh and Ephraim along with him.

We do not know how much time has passed between the previous scene and this one. It is of great significance that it is only Joseph who is told of his father's illness and that, at first, only he is present with **his two sons** at the bedside of his dying father. This illness is apparently very near the time of his death, and so this is no ordinary visit. The fact that neither Reuben nor any other of the brothers is invited shows that for Jacob, Joseph has a special role to play in his own life and in the lives of his continuing descendants. Joseph evidently knows this since he takes his sons along for one last meeting with Jacob before he dies. Joseph's two sons are listed in their birth order, **Manasseh**, then **Ephraim**, and this is the order in which Joseph views them.

48:2 When Jacob was told, "Your son Joseph has come to you," Israel rallied his strength and sat up on the bed.

No matter how weak Jacob had grown as he neared his own death, he was able to summon up the strength to talk with his (favorite) **son Joseph**. It is not entirely clear whether one should translate that Jacob "**sat up on his bed**" or "leaned on his staff." The Hebrew word מִטָּה (*miṭṭāh*) can mean either bed or staff. Rather inconsistently the NIV translates it as "bed" in this verse and in 47:31 as "staff."

48:3 Jacob said to Joseph, "God Almighty appeared to me at Luz in the land of Canaan, and there he blessed me 48:4 and said to me, 'I am going to make you fruitful and will increase your numbers. I will make you a community of peoples, and I will give this land as an everlasting possession to your descendants after you.'

Knowing his death is imminent, Jacob goes right to the point with Joseph. He begins by reminding him of the time that **God** had **appeared** to him and made promises to him as he was returning to Canaan from his twenty-year "exile" in Paddan Aram. Jacob may be implicitly making a point to Joseph that one day Jacob's descendants would get back to the land and begin to realize the fulfillments of those promises.

Jacob refers to God as El Shaddai, which the NIV, consistent with its Calvinistic tendency, interprets to mean "**God Almighty**." While this is the traditional rendering from the time of the KJV,[1] it is by no means certain and is really little more than a guess.[2] This is the name for God which the LORD, in Exodus 6:3, says the Patriarchs Abraham, Isaac, and Jacob, actually used.[3] Jacob refers to the place as **Luz**, not its more common, and for the audience current, name, Bethel. The similarities and differences between what God actually said to Jacob on that occasion and what Jacob reports him to have said are instructive.

God's Actual Words in Genesis 35:11-12	Jacob's Version in Genesis 48:4
"I am God Almighty; be fruitful and increase in number. A nation and a community of nations will come from you, and kings will come from your loins. [12]The land I gave to Abraham and Isaac I also give to you, and I will give this land to your descendants after you."	'I am going to make you fruitful and will increase your numbers. I will give you a community of peoples, and I will give this land as a lasting possession to your descendants after you.'

Notice the differences between what God actually said and what the dying Jacob reports him to have said. Jacob turns a command ("be fruitful and increase in number") into a promise of what God will do for Jacob ("**I am going to make you fruitful and increase your numbers**"). He turns a statement of fact ("a nation and a community of nations will come from you") into promises of what God will do ("**I will give you**

---

[1]This is probably based on the fact that the LXX sometimes translates El Shaddai as παντοκράτωρ (*pantokratōr*) and the Vulgate *omnipotens*.

[2]D.W. Baker, "God, Names of," *DOTP*, p. 361: "The compound *'ēl šadday* occurs six times in the Pentateuch (and one further time in Ezek. 10:5). The word *šadday* has been variously interpreted as 'strength' ('Almighty' in KJV, NIV, NRSV), 'mountains,' possibly relating to the mountain dwelling of the Canaanite El as well as other deities, or even 'God of the breasts,' based on the Hebrew *šad* or *šōd*. . . . Goddesses do supply nourishment for royalty and other gods in Ugaritic and Egyptian mythology, and a tie between Israel's God, nourishment and breasts is brought out by wordplay in Genesis 49:25."

[3]The fact that the Tetragrammaton, Yahweh, actually occurs in Genesis fairly often, even on the lips of the Patriarchs (e.g., 14:22; 15:2,8; 26:22; 27:20,27; 28:16), is one of the pillars of the source-critical approach to the authorship of Genesis. For alternative readings of this text in Exodus see Sarna, *Genesis*, pp. 31, 269.

[for] a community of peoples." Jacob omits entirely the statement
"kings will come from your loins" and subtly changes "a nation and a
community of nations," which would make Jacob's descendants a
"*nation*" (גּוֹי, *gôy*) like the other nations, into merely "a community of
peoples" (עַמִּים, *'ammîm*). It may well be that there is, in the final analysis,
not a lot of difference between being "a community of *nations*" and "a
community of *peoples*." Finally Jacob makes the **land** promise into a
"**lasting**"[4] promise.

The general tendency of these changes is to place more emphasis
upon God's promises and God's actions rather than upon human
involvement in those promises and the conditionality which such involvement entails. But why would Jacob do this? Why would he emphasize God's activity and responsibility for the promises and deemphasize
human involvement in those promises? Perhaps such emphasis on
God's action is designed to give reassurance to Joseph of the certainty
of the fulfillment of those promises, despite the untrustworthiness of
the recipients of the promises. Joseph knew of that lack of trustworthiness from difficult personal experience, having been sold into slavery by
Jacob's other sons. Perhaps this is a sign of Jacob's maturation. He no
longer thinks the promises are so dependent upon his own or his
descendants' grasping after them.

But why did the narrator give us this information? The conditionality or otherwise of God's promises is a great debate within and between
the Old Testament texts. An impressive list of texts can be given that
seem to affirm (at least at first reading) the unconditionality of promises, but an equally impressive list of texts can be assembled which implies
their conditionality.[5] For the canonical audience which was largely in
long-term Diaspora away from the land this was a real debate. Psalm 89,
for example, written in light of the exile, affirms in its first portion the
understanding that the promises (in this text specifically to David) were
unconditional (vv. 1-37, esp. vv. 30-37). But suddenly it turns from a
Psalm of praise into a Psalm of protest at the fact that Yahweh seems to

---

[4]The NIV here, as often, translates the Hebrew עוֹלָם (*'ôlām*) as "everlasting"
but this is a theological interpretation that expresses the Calvinistic tendency of
the translation rather than being an accurate construal of the Hebrew term,
which may or may not mean "everlasting" in the modern sense.

[5]See the discussion of this in John Goldingay, *Theological Diversity and the
Authority of the Old Testament* (Grand Rapids: Eerdmans, 1987). On p. 4 he anticipates his discussion: "God's commitment to Israel can be seen as unqualified
and permanent, made for the people's blessing as an end in itself; or it can be
seen as inherently conditional and always open to being terminated."

have abandoned them to permanent exile (vv. 38-51). "Lord, where is your steadfast love of old, which by your faithfulness you swore to David?" (Ps 89:49), the Psalmist asks. Evangelical Christians, schooled in popular-level theology designed to give reassurance to the insecure, look back on what Christ has done and conclude, of course it was unconditional from the beginning. But this is hardly a fair reading of Genesis or of the Old Testament where the issue is never clearly resolved.

48:5 "Now then, your two sons born to you in Egypt before I came to you here will be reckoned as mine; Ephraim and Manasseh will be mine, just as Reuben and Simeon are mine.

It is not entirely clear why Jacob turns to the topic of Joseph's children at this point. Perhaps this hints at the decline of his mental clarity as his death approaches, jumping from one topic to another without a clear connection between them. In this narrative Jacob effectively adopts Joseph's **two sons, Ephraim and Manasseh**, as his own sons. De Hoop takes this to imply that Joseph is somehow being diminished as he has no other recorded sons and Ephraim and Manasseh would now belong to Jacob, not to Joseph.[6] In fact in the history of the nation of Israel there is no tribe of Joseph, only Ephraim and the two halves of the tribe of Manasseh. Further the fact that Ephraim and Manasseh are compared to **Reuben and Simeon**, sons who were put aside by Jacob in his deathbed words (Gen 49:3-7) also implies, for de Hoop, a diminished role. But de Hoop fails to consider what I would deem as a more natural understanding of the situation. For Joseph's sons to be adopted by Jacob, he now receives a double, and as it turns out historically triple,[7] portion of Jacob's inheritance in Canaan. In the law the double portion was the portion given to the firstborn son (Deut 21:15-19). Joseph is given the place of the firstborn in the family. He is given the birthright.[8] It is true, as de Hoop notes, that Judah, not Joseph, is given the ruling position in both Jacob's deathbed "testament" and in having the kingship come from the Judean family of David. But that fact must not obscure the exalted position, which Joseph receives through Ephraim and Manasseh.

Notice that Ephraim is mentioned before Manasseh even though the latter is the firstborn son of Joseph.[9] This is a hint from Jacob that

---

[6]De Hoop, *Genesis 49*, pp. 363-364.

[7]In the allotting of the land of Canaan in the time of Moses and Joshua, Joseph receives one transjordanian tribal allotment (half of Manasseh) and two cisjordanian tribal allotments (one each for Ephraim and the other half of Manasseh).

[8]Gary E. Schnittjer, *The Torah Story* (Grand Rapids: Zondervan, 2006), p. 158.

[9]P.J. Williams, "The LXX of 1 Chronicles 5:1-2 as an Exposition of Genesis 48-49," *TB* 49 (1998): 370.

the order of birth will be reversed when he effectively adopts Ephraim and Manasseh as his own sons. In fact Ephraim and Manasseh will in a sense be his firstborn and second-born sons respectively. In chapter 49 Jacob will make clear that Reuben and Simeon will lose the rights of primogeniture because of their sinful actions; Reuben for his sexual liaison with Bilhah and Simeon (along with Levi) for his murder of the Shechemites while they healed from circumcision. This text may well anticipate that decision by Jacob concerning his two oldest sons.[10]

48:6 Any children born to you after them will be yours; in the territory they inherit they will be reckoned under the names of their brothers.

Since Jacob has adopted Manasseh and Ephraim as his own sons, to in a sense replace Reuben and Simeon, Joseph is left without any heirs of his own. Jacob addresses this problem by assuring Joseph that he would undoubtedly have other sons who could serve as his heirs. The NIV evidently understands the next sentence to mean that Joseph's later sons would be clans within the tribes of Ephraim and Manasseh. Of course time proved that Jacob was wrong in this assumption. Joseph would have no other sons. So near the end of his life Joseph adopted the children of Manasseh's son Machir as his own heirs (Gen 50:23). But this means that Joseph would not himself have great influence when the family settled in the Promised Land as Machir was given Gilead in the Transjordan. At times Gilead seems to function like an independent tribe, and this may be explained by these two texts (Gen 48:6; 50:23). Gilead was the place of Machir, the tribal group which formed the direct descendants of Joseph.

48:7 As I was returning from Paddan, to my sorrow Rachel died in the land of Canaan while we were still on the way, a little distance from Ephrath. So I buried her there beside the road to Ephrath" (that is, Bethlehem).

It is not entirely obvious why Jacob makes this statement to Joseph at this point. He had in verses 3-4 mentioned his encounter with God at Luz (Bethel) before turning to the issue of the inheritance of Joseph's sons in verses 5-6. In this text he reminds Joseph of the death of his own mother Rachel. While this follows on chronologically from verses 3-4, the death of Rachel immediately following the events at Bethel, this does not explain why Jacob even mentions it. This could be the narrator's way of describing Jacob's increasing lack of mental clarity as he faced death. On the other hand, remembering Rachel's death to

---

[10]On the tribe of Levi, the descendants of Jacob's third son, see the discussion below at Genesis 49:5-7.

Rachel's oldest son may be Jacob's way of preparing Joseph for his other parent's death. Conversely, Jacob may not be thinking about the impact on Joseph at all. Jacob remembers his beloved Rachel's death because he is facing his own death.

One thing that Jacob's words prepare the reader for is Jacob's stated desire in 49:31 to be buried in the family grave beside Leah, his "hated" wife and not Rachel, his beloved wife. He could not be buried next to Rachel because she died while the family was in transit. She was buried beside the road they were traveling on and not in the family grave.

The narrator[11] also informs the readers that **Ephrath**, where Rachel was buried, was none other than the hometown of King David, **Bethlehem**. There seems to be some sort of ironic providence going on in this text. The place where the beloved wife of the forefather of the nation of Israel, Jacob, died is the very place where the later beloved king of Israel, David, was born.

48:8 When Israel saw the sons of Joseph, he asked, "Who are these?"
48:9 "They are the sons God has given me here," Joseph said to his father. Then Israel said, "Bring them to me so I may bless them."

While Jacob had already referred to Joseph's two sons immediately above, apparently he either had not initially seen or noticed them, or had forgotten that they were there. His eyesight and perhaps also his attentiveness or his memory or a combination is being portrayed as failing as his general physical health fails. Seeing them (for the first time?[12]) he asks, **"Who are these?"** The statement could be merely rhetorical,[13] or it could be that Jacob either had never seen them before or didn't remember who they were.

Joseph's response, **"They are the sons whom God has given me** in this place," seems to indicate that Joseph has been able to count his blessings even while going through the traumatizing events of being enslaved and imprisoned and forgotten and, finally, exalted. Because Jacob, in his old age, shared the failing eyesight of his father Isaac he instructed Joseph to **bring** his two sons to him **so** that he could **bless**

---

[11]Or perhaps a later editor or copyist whose audience would no longer know that Ephrath was the earlier name for Bethlehem.

[12]The *waw*-consecutive which begins this verse would typically imply that Jacob only saw (or noticed) the boys after he had spoken to Joseph about adopting them as his own sons.

[13]Sarna, *Genesis*, p. 327, suggests here that this language is drawn from the legal adoptive process where the true identity of the candidate(s) for adoption are established by asking their father what their names are. He, however, cites no ancient evidence for this process.

them. The blessings which Jacob had received from the LORD would now be spoken and perhaps even formally transferred to the sons of his favorite son.

48:10 Now Israel's eyes were failing because of old age, and he could hardly see. So Joseph brought his sons close to him, and his father kissed them and embraced them.

The NIV seems to suggest that the dying Jacob[14] could still see, albeit poorly. This is consistent with verse 8 above. But the Hebrew is perplexing. Literally it reads, "the eyes of Israel were heavy from age. He was not able to see" (וְעֵינֵי יִשְׂרָאֵל כָּבְדוּ מִזֹּקֶן לֹא יוּכַל לִרְאוֹת, *wᵊʿênê yiśrāʾēl kābdû mizzōqen lōʾ yûkal lirʾôth*). While this might be a Hebrew way of describing limited sight,[15] the more natural way to read this is to assume total blindness. If so, this is in some tension with verse 8 where, if we assume the same scene is being described, Israel "saw" his grandsons. This could be explained then on source-critical grounds or by reading verses 8-9 as recording an earlier event of adoption.

In any case, the parallel between Jacob and his father Isaac is striking. Both are blind or nearly so as they get older. Both bless male descendants in light of the fact of their presumption that they were soon to die. Jacob knows that he had taken advantage of his father's lack of sight to deceive him. This event is naturally in the reader's mind as this text is absorbed. Like Isaac his father, Jacob, has the male descendants come near,[16] and like his father he kisses them (Gen 27:26-27). The Torah prohibited taking advantage of the blind (Lev 19:14; Deut 27:18).

48:11 Israel said to Joseph, "I never expected to see your face again, and now God has allowed me to see your children too."

While the NIV and other translations get the sense of this verse, a more literal rendering of the Hebrew is interesting: "To see your face I did not [dare] pray for; and behold God has allowed me to see [you] and even your descendants" (רְאֹה פָנֶיךָ לֹא פִלָּלְתִּי וְהִנֵּה הֶרְאָה אֹתִי אֱלֹהִים גַּם אֶת־זַרְעֶךָ, *rᵊʾōh phānêkā lōʾ phillāltî wᵊhinnēh herʾāh ʾōtî ʾĕlōhîm gam ʾeth-zarʿekā*).

---

[14]The narrator once again refers to Jacob as "Israel," perhaps reminding the readers that the events are significant for the future of the nation and not just for the literal family of Jacob.

[15]The usual Hebrew words for blind/ness are עִוֵּר (*ʿiwwēr*) and עָוַר (*ʿāwar*). Hector Avalos notes ("Blindness," *EDB*, p. 193): "Although modern societies and the Talmud recognize degrees of blindness, the usual Hebrew word for a blind person . . . seems to refer to total blindness (e.g., Deut 28:29)."

[16]The NIV assumes Joseph is the subject of the verb וַיַּגֵּשׁ אֹתָם (*wayyaggēš ʾōthām*) "he brought them near" but it could just as easily be Jacob who brought them near.

The word order and the vocabulary shows the abiding astonishment that Jacob had experienced at God's grace to him, the one who had struggled with God throughout his life. He had never prayed to see Joseph's face again because he had no expectation that the prayer could ever be answered! The sore that had never healed from his grief over losing Rachel and Joseph, the ones he truly loved, was now marvelously irrelevant.

48:12 Then Joseph removed them from Israel's knees and bowed down with his face to the ground.

In a poignant moment Joseph took his two sons, whom Jacob had adopted as his own, off of the knees of their (grand)father, and he solemnly **bowed down** to his father **with his face to the ground**. This verse confirms for us what we might have suspected; Manasseh and Ephraim were quite young at this point; young enough for both of them to sit on the lap of an ailing and dying grandfather. Joseph removes them from Jacob's knees so that it would be clear, just to whom it was that he was about to bow. Joseph's bowing to the ground is more than a *pro forma* act of respect. The second dream of Joseph when he was still a young man was interpreted to mean that his father, as well as his deceased mother and eleven brothers, would come and bow down to Joseph (Gen 37:10). Joseph had remembered that dream as well as the first one when the brothers first came to Egypt to buy grain (Gen 42:9). But in this text, the opposite of the second dream happens, at least in part. Instead of Jacob bowing down to Joseph, Joseph bows down to Jacob! Joseph no longer feels it necessary to scheme to make his dreams come true. And in fact, the second dream, at least as it was interpreted at the time, was never fulfilled.[17] Joseph, in a sense, concedes the point of Jacob's question, "Will your mother and I and your brothers actually bow down to the ground before you?" Whether that was a true interpretation of the dream or not, Joseph clearly did the opposite. He bowed down to Jacob.

48:13 And Joseph took both of them, Ephraim on his right toward Israel's left hand and Manasseh on his left toward Israel's right hand, and brought them close to him. 48:14 But Israel reached out his right hand and put it on Ephraim's head, though he was the younger, and

---

[17] I would hedge this statement because of the possibility, however slight, that Genesis 47:31, Jacob "bowed himself on his staff/bed," describes Jacob bowing to Joseph. This verse is the chief sticking point of Laurence Turner's otherwise brilliant suggestion about how the dreams of Joseph function as an announcement of plot in Genesis. See Turner, *Announcements of Plot in Genesis*, ch. 4.

crossing his arms, he put his left hand on Manasseh's head, even though Manasseh was the firstborn.

These verses describe a sort of jostling between Joseph and Jacob regarding whether the oldest son will receive the primary blessing from their adoptive father Jacob or not. The echoes of Jacob's own experience with his father Isaac are unmistakable. Joseph presumes that his firstborn son will receive the primary blessing and his other son a secondary blessing. Ancient custom and later even the law itself demanded as much (Deut 21:15-17). But one of the most distinctive ideas of Genesis (and of the entire Bible) is the theme of God choosing to use those whom the world would disregard as secondary while ironically making those whom the world would regard as primary, secondary. Even though Joseph was the eleventh of twelve sons he was still his father's favorite. But Joseph still expects that his oldest son, Manasseh, will receive the primary blessing, even though he himself was personally the object of his father's favor beyond his older brothers! Now it is true that Joseph is the oldest son of the only wife Jacob really loved, Rachel. Whatever his thinking on the subject, Joseph positions his young sons so that his dying father will put his **right hand**, symbolizing the primary position, on **Manasseh**, the oldest, and his **left hand**, symbolizing a subordinate position, on **Ephraim**, his younger son. But Jacob, ever the crafty one, sensing or seeing what has happened switches his hands so that Ephraim receives the right hand of blessing and Manasseh the left hand. Jacob, the younger twin, had pulled a similar sort of switch on his father Isaac at his deathbed blessing. He perpetuates that reversal of the system of honoring the oldest in the blessing of his adopted sons, Manasseh and Ephraim.

48:15 Then he blessed Joseph and said, "May the God before whom my fathers Abraham and Isaac walked, the God who has been my shepherd all my life to this day, 48:16 the Angel who has delivered me from all harm—may he bless these boys. May they be called by my name and the names of my fathers Abraham and Isaac, and may they increase greatly upon the earth."

Jacob begins his blessings by blessing Joseph through blessing Joseph's sons, Ephraim and Manasseh, whom he had just adopted as his own to take the place of Joseph. The God upon whom Jacob calls to bless Ephraim and Manasseh is vividly, if complexly described. First of all Abraham and Isaac walked around with this God. The use of the hithpael of the verb "to walk" echoes the Garden of Eden narrative where the LORD God is said to have "walked around" in the garden (Gen 3:8). In other words, this God enjoyed intimate fellowship with

Abraham and Isaac. But while Jacob does not say that God walked around with him, he also had experienced personally His presence. God had been his shepherd during all of his life, sustaining and protecting him. Further, either God himself is referred to as "**the Angel who** redeemed [Jacob] **from all** evil," or Jacob calls upon both God and the Angel to **bless** the **boys**.[18] The image of God as shepherd is not unique to Israel or to the God of the Bible but is applied to gods and kings commonly throughout the ancient Near East.[19] This image takes on special significance when we realize that Jacob and his entire family were themselves shepherds.

It is difficult to know whether the angel (messenger) who redeems, mentioned in verse 16, is another description for God or whether it is someone sent by God to help Jacob. While I would not want to make too much of this, the lack of the copula ("and") before the word "angel" argues against this being an angel sent by God. The parallelistic structure of the three descriptive clauses also argues against this.[20] The NIV seems to recognize this by capitalizing the word as though it were a divine epithet ("Angel"). Several times in the Old Testament the Angel of the LORD seems to be so closely related to God himself as to blur the distinction.[21] A אֵל (gō'ēl), "redeemer," in Ancient Israel was a relative who paid the debts for a person to free them from debt slavery as Boaz did for Ruth. When applied to God, as it is in this passage, it highlights the troubled circumstances and real and potential problems through which he had brought Jacob.

To ask for the God who walks in intimate fellowship with sinful human beings, who protects and guides like a shepherd protects and guides his sheep, and redeems from every form of evil, to bless Ephraim and Manasseh is a great blessing indeed.

De Hoop makes much of the fact that Joseph's boys are to be called by Jacob's name and the names of their great-great grandfather Abraham's name and their great-grandfather Isaac's name, but not by Joseph's name.[22] In this way Joseph is somehow diminished in this narrative. But

---

[18] הַנְּעָרִים (hannᵉ'ārîm) can be used of young people from young children as here, to Joseph at seventeen, or even young men up to thirty years of age.

[19] For kings as shepherds see Nahum 3:18. For the gods and kings of Mesopotamia and Egypt as shepherds in various periods, see Jack W. Vancil, "Sheep, Shepherd," *ABD*, V:1188-1189.

[20] Sarna, *Genesis*, p. 328.

[21] E.g., Gen 31:3,11,13; Exod 3:2,4. Cf. Sarna, *Genesis*, p. 328: "angels are often simply extensions of the divine personality."

[22] De Hoop, *Genesis 49*, p. 365.

this may be nothing more than the legal point that, as Jacob's adopted sons, the God of their fathers would be the God of Abraham, Isaac, and Jacob, but not Joseph.

The last clause of the blessing is interesting. The verb translated as "**increase greatly**" is only found in this passage (וְיִדְגּוּ, wᵊyidgû), but it seems to be related to nouns that mean "fish."[23] Jacob hopes that his adopted sons, Ephraim and Manasseh, will multiply like fish in the middle of the land. We might say, "May they multiply like swarms of minnows in the spring." The image links the promises of God to the creation account once again (Gen 1:20-22).

48:17 When Joseph saw his father placing his right hand on Ephraim's head he was displeased; so he took hold of his father's hand to move it from Ephraim's head to Manasseh's head. 48:18 Joseph said to him, "No, my father, this one is the firstborn; put your right hand on his head." 48:19 But his father refused and said, "I know, my son, I know. He too will become a people, and he too will become great. Nevertheless, his younger brother will be greater than he, and his descendants will become a group of nations."

Joseph saw Jacob crossing his hands and thus putting his right hand on the head of Ephraim. This did not just "displease" him (NIV) but was actually וַיֵּרַע בְּעֵינָיו (wayyēra‘ bᵊ‘ênāyw), "evil in his eyes"! His attempt to grab his father's right hand and move it to Manasseh's head, and his words to his father, may indicate that Joseph thought that his aged father had made a simple mistake.

Jacob refuses to allow his hand to be moved and to listen to Joseph. He emphasizes the point that this is no mistake by repeating the words, "**I know**." The fact that Ephraim, in Jacob's estimation, is to be given an exalted position among Jacob's sons does not mean that Manasseh will receive nothing. **He, too**, like the other nonelect in Genesis (e.g., Ishmael, Esau) will receive a great blessing. But it will not reach the level of Ephraim. Manasseh will spawn an entire people (עַם, ‘am),[24] and he and his descendants will become great, but his younger brother Ephraim will be greater. His seed will be "full(ness) of the nations" (וְזַרְעוֹ יִהְיֶה מְלֹא־הַגּוֹיִם, wᵊzar‘ô yihyeh mᵊlō'-haggôyim). This last clause is difficult to understand. Certainly the context would imply a contrast between Manasseh only spawning a people, while Ephraim by contrast would spawn something more involving (all?) the nations. It

---

[23]The related nouns are דָּג (dāg) and דָּגָה (dāgāh).

[24]This would seem to be more than just a clan or tribe. In the history of the nation of Israel, interestingly, Manasseh effectively divides into two populous tribes, one on each side of the Jordan.

could mean that his seed will incorporate into itself all the nations. Or it could mean "full of nations."[25] Sarna[26] suggests that Ephraim's seed would be plentiful enough to make nations. Whatever the exact meaning, this seems to be an allusion to the promise to Abraham (Gen 17:4-6) and Jacob himself (Gen 35:11). The Greek has εἰς πλῆθος ἐθνῶν (*eis plēthos ethnōn*), "for a multitude of nations," which is again somewhat ambiguous. Could it be an allusion to the role of Abraham's descendants, and in this case specifically Ephraim's, in being the channel of God's blessing to all the nations of the world? While one must be careful about reading back into Old Testament texts from the New Testament, this is certainly a possible understanding.

48:20 He blessed them that day and said, "In your name will Israel pronounce this blessing: 'May God make you like Ephraim and Manasseh.'" So he put Ephraim ahead of Manasseh.

This verse gives the summarizing blessing for the two sons. Interestingly, even though Jacob blessed "**them**," i.e., Ephraim and Manasseh, he uses the singular "you" in the actual blessing. This singular you could refer to Joseph who fathered both Ephraim and Manasseh, or it could be a so-called "distributive" where each of the individuals in the group receives the blessing.[27] Future generations of **Israel** will hold up **Ephraim and Manasseh** (in that order) as paradigms of God's blessing and will use their names in their own formulae of blessing.[28] The narrator reminds the reader that in placing Ephraim first in this formula for blessing, Jacob was once again reiterating his desire (prediction?) that Ephraim, the youngest, be put in the place of honor ahead of his older brother Manasseh.

C. A SPECIAL INHERITANCE FOR JOSEPH (48:21-22)

48:21 Then Israel said to Joseph, "I am about to die, but God will be with you and take you back to the land of your fathers. 48:22 And to you, as one who is over your brothers, I give the ridge of land I took from the Amorites with my sword and my bow."

Jacob, called Israel once again, realizes that his death is imminent. He wants to remind Joseph of the certainty of the fulfillment of God's prom-

---

[25] Wenham, *Genesis 16–50*, p. 454.

[26] Sarna, *Genesis*, p. 329.

[27] Ibid., p. 329, cites the priestly blessing in Numbers 6:21 "them" and Numbers 6:24-26 "you" singular as a parallel example of this.

[28] A similar construction occurs (although in a curse formula) in Jeremiah 29:22.

ises concerning the land and to reassure him that he too, not just his sons, will experience that blessing in a special way. Jacob seems to assume that, after he has died and the famine is over, Joseph would lead the family back to Canaan. Jacob, in light of God's promises and not present reality, describes Canaan as **"the land of your fathers."** Jacob, of course, turned out to be wrong about this. Joseph died in Egypt, and it took hundreds of years for the descendants of Israel to go back to Canaan.

Ephraim and Manasseh have both been granted remarkable blessings by Jacob. This surely would have brought great satisfaction to Joseph. But technically speaking, although he was the favored son, he had been up to this point left out of the blessings. Jacob remedies that anomaly by promising him territory which he claims to have personally taken from the Amorites with his own weapons.

The translation of verse 22 is challenging. As the MT is pointed, it reads literally, "And I give to you one shoulder over your brothers which I took from the Amorites with my sword and my bow." The word translated "shoulder" is interpreted by the NIV as a shoulder of land, i.e., a ridge. The NIV also interprets **"over your brothers"** as referring to Joseph himself rather than an extra "shoulder" (NRSV). Joseph, according to the NIV, is "one who is over [his] brothers."[29] If Joseph is granted an extra inheritance of land over and above what his brothers were to receive, this could be implying that Joseph is being given the "double portion" of the firstborn son (Deut 21:15-17).

The Hebrew word translated as **"ridge"** and pointed in the MT as the word "shoulder," (שְׁכֶם, šᵉkem), is spelled and pointed exactly as the proper noun, Shechem, referring to the person and the town named after him in Genesis 34. Jacob could just as easily be saying that he granted to Joseph the town of Shechem.[30] If so, his claim that he took it with his own sword and bow is a bit of bravado on Jacob's part. In fact, Simeon and Levi, not Jacob, killed the Shechemites. They and their brothers plundered the spoil only to be severely rebuked by Jacob. There is no narrative in Genesis that states or implies that Jacob himself

---

[29] The NIV takes the word "one" with what follows, i.e., "one (who is) above your brothers." This is, however, an unusual usage of the word "one" (אֶחָד, ʾḥd).

[30] SP reads אַחַת (ʾḥt) feminine rather than MT's אֶחָד (ʾḥd) masculine. City names in Hebrew, like Shechem, are typically feminine and SP is probably reading šekem, as the town Shechem rather than the word for "shoulder." The city of Shechem near Mount Gerizim was the sight of the later Samaritan temple which rivaled the temple in Jerusalem. On the tendency of SP to justify the existence and emphasize the importance of this temple and its location, see Emmanuel Tov, *Textual Criticism of the Hebrew Bible* (Minneapolis: Fortress, 1992), pp. 94-95.

won a battle against the Amorites or any other inhabitant of the land of Canaan.[31]

Interestingly Genesis 48:22 has Jacob promising Joseph, **"And to you, as one who is over your brothers I give the ridge of land I took from the Amorites with my sword and my bow."** The only episode recorded in Genesis that this might apply to is the slaughter of the Shechemites by Jacob's sons, led by Simeon and Levi, after the rape of Leah's daughter with Jacob, Dinah. Here Jacob claims that he was responsible for the victory, and yet in the next chapter he condemns Simeon and Levi for their anger in killing the Shechemites! This may alert the reader to the ambiguity of the patriarchal pronouncements (at least Jacob's). They express the will of the dying patriarch but also his prejudices.

---

[31]Sarna, *Genesis*, p. 330, seems to miss the possibility that Jacob is exaggerating instead hypothesizing a tradition in the life of Jacob not preserved in Scripture regarding a war with Shechem. While it is true that the city of Shechem does not need to be conquered in the book of Joshua and that Joseph was buried there (Josh 24:32), this is not sufficient reason to hypothesize a source for which there is no other evidence. If the source which is needed to prove a doubtful theory must be invented by the historian, there is no evidence for the theory at all.

GENESIS 49

D. JACOB'S FINAL WORDS TO HIS SONS (49:1-32)

1. Jacob Blesses His Twelve Sons (49:1-27)

While this section is technically not the center of this section of Genesis, it does play a crucial role in the broader meaning of Genesis. In some senses this passage is the culmination of the narrative of Genesis. Like its sister text in Deuteronomy 33 the text speaks of the future of each of the tribes of the nation of Israel in poetic form from the lips of a patriarch about to die. While the words spoken are not deterministic prophecy leaving the descendants of Jacob's sons to their inexorable fate, neither are Jacob's words irrelevant to the future of the tribes. They are rather to be understood as either a form of conditional prophecy or Jacob's prescient judgment of their future prospects based on his knowledge of them.

Given the internal family dynamics and recent history, several things are not surprising. The two sons of Jacob's beloved wife Rachel, Joseph and Benjamin, are given effusive blessings. The four sons of the concubines are blessed, but also seem to be marginalized. Reuben, Simeon, and Levi, the first three sons of Leah the hated wife imposed on Jacob are disqualified from leadership for their previous actions.[1] This leaves the mantle of firstborn to Judah who is given the ascendant position.

The narrator has given clues of Judah's ascendency. But this does not explain the surprise which Jacob has in store. Judah, not Joseph, will see his brothers bow down to him (v. 8). Judah, not Joseph, will have the ruler's scepter (v. 10). One is tempted to regard this as a type of revenge by Jacob for Joseph's presumed hubris in the second dream where he claims that the sun, moon, and eleven stars would bow down to him.

---

[1] Laurence Turner in a private communication notes, "Is it not ironic that Jacob, a character whose actions must surely have raised moral questions in the reader's mind more than for any other Genesis character, is the one who throughout this section passes moral judgment on others?"

Jacob interprets this to mean that Joseph's mother and father as well as his brothers would bow down to him. But this is to psychologize beyond the evidence. Nevertheless Judah is a surprising choice to be given the mantle of leadership within the family. This is especially the case given his inauspicious introduction to the narrative – he suggests selling Joseph into slavery and fathers two sons by his widowed daughter-in-law whom he confuses for a (cult) prostitute!

In order to understand this passage in the context of the Pentateuch, it must be read intertextually with what Moses says about the tribes that descend from Jacob's sons in Deuteronomy 33. In the comments below I will systematically compare and contrast Jacob's words and Moses' words, noting any insight that the intervening narrative (Exodus 1 through Deuteronomy 32) might provide for the differences.

Introduction (49:1-2)

49:1 Then Jacob called for his sons and said: "Gather around so I can tell you what will happen to you in days to come.

Having blessed Joseph and having adopted and blessed Joseph's sons Ephraim and Manasseh, Jacob calls for all of his other sons to come to his deathbed for what they and he presume will be his final words to them. Jacob claims that he will tell them what will happen to them "in the last days."[2] His deathbed words to each son are cloaked in a series of poetic aphorisms. While Jacob certainly uses language that the canonical audience at least would hear as implying some sort of prophecy, it is not at all clear that Jacob is predicting events through divine revelation that are predestined to happen. Fretheim helpfully comments:

> Prophecy would not be fully adequate to describe these materials. We understand them better as Jacob's judgment regarding the future of his son's lives on the basis of his thoroughgoing knowledge and evaluation of them. The past and present life of the son signals the way in which each future will be shaped. . . . The wisdom exhibited by Jacob . . . involves discerning how the future for each son grows out of past and present experience.[3]

---

[2] בְּאַחֲרִית הַיָּמִים (bᵊ'aḥărîth hayyāmîm) is almost a technical term in the prophets for the Eschaton (Num 24:14; Isa 2:2 // Micah 4:1; Jer 48:47; 49:39; Ezek 38:16; Dan 10:14; Hos 3:5). Here, in Jacob's mouth it may mean no more than "the future" as in the NIV. But in the larger canonical context the eschatological overtones of the phrase would be obvious to the canonical audience.

[3] Terence E. Fretheim, *Genesis*, NIB 1 (Nashville: Abingdon, 1994), p. 667.

49:2 "Assemble and listen, sons of Jacob; listen to your father Israel.

Jacob's words, which are delivered in poetry, are introduced in verse 2 with a standard Hebrew poetic line exhibiting so-called "synonymous parallelism" where the two lines of the couplet say essentially the same thing using synonymous words. The parallel structure is illustrated below with the implied words in brackets.

| **Assemble and listen,** | [to me] | **sons of Jacob;** |
| **Listen!** | [my sons] | **to your father Israel** |

The exact repetition of the word "listen" in the two lines emphasizes it. In Hebrew this word, וְשִׁמְעוּ (wᵉšimʻû), often means "to obey" someone and not just listen to them. If Jacob's words are not prophecies but words to ponder and obey, the conditional element in Jacob's statements about each of his sons is seen more clearly. In a sense Jacob is saying, "If nothing changes, this is what I foresee for the future of your descendants."[4] In the case of Simeon nothing much changed, and they ended up being scattered in Israel as Jacob anticipated. In the case of Levi, however, they ended up being scattered for a very different reason. The Levites, from whom the priests were drawn received no tribal allotment. Instead they were scattered throughout the other tribes in 48 Levitical cities. They were the religious leaders of all the other tribes and had the privileged status of serving as priests.

Jacob's Final Words to His Four Oldest Sons, the Sons of Leah (49:3-12)

The story of the first three sons of Jacob is the narrative culmination of the "pattern of disqualification"[5] that we have seen in the earlier narratives about Reuben, Simeon, and Levi. With those three "disqualified" from leading, Judah, the fourth son of Jacob, is given the role and responsibility of leading Jacob's descendants.

49:3 "Reuben, you are my firstborn, my might, the first sign of my strength, excelling in honor, excelling in power. 49:4 Turbulent as the waters, you will no longer excel, for you went up onto your father's bed, onto my couch and defiled it.

Jacob begins with his firstborn son **Reuben**. The reader must remember that Reuben, around the time of the death of Jacob's beloved wife Rachel, had had an affair with Bilhah, Rachel's handmaid and Jacob's secondary wife (Gen 35:22). At the time Jacob had said nothing. But Jacob here calls Reuben to account for his actions there. Jacob begins by pointing out the position that Reuben had in the family as the

---

[4]Subsequent history proved him right on this point.
[5]Schnittjer, *Torah Story*, p. 159.

firstborn. Reuben was born as Jacob's "power" and the "first [sign] of his manly vigor," a traditional phrase used to describe a firstborn son (וְרֵאשִׁית אוֹנִי, *wᵉrēʾšîth ʾônî*).[6] Reuben, because of his position and perhaps also because of his physical size, had an excess[7] of both honor and strength. These adjectives describe for Jacob what "could have been" for Reuben. This was his "destiny" from birth.

That destiny, however, Reuben unfortunately had spurned by his character and the actions that flowed from that character. Jacob describes Reuben with a word that means "reckless." When compared to water the word seems to mean "apt to boil over" or "easily stirred up to a froth." The NIV's **"turbulent"** nicely captures the second of these possibilities. In either case the simile suggests that Reuben's sexual or romantic urges are not under his control. This is indicative, for Jacob, of a character without appropriate moral constraints. The excess of honor and strength with which and for which he was born would not reach its natural course. Reuben, unless something dramatically changed in the lives of his descendants, would not have an excess of honor or power among the tribes of Israel.[8] The original and canonical audiences would know that the tribe of Reuben, after Israel had defeated the Amorite kings on the eastern side of the Jordan, jumped at the chance of obtaining good grazing land in the Transjordan. They thereby gave up any chance of an inheritance in the real Promised Land on the west side of the Jordan. This choice meant that they were separated from the rest of the nation and vulnerable to attack. In the long term the descendants of Reuben played no significant role in the development of the nation even though they were the descendants of Jacob's (Israel's) firstborn son. By the end of the wilderness period the destiny of the Reubenites is indicated by the rhetorical plea of Moses that "Reuben live and not die" (Deut 33:6). The remainder of Moses' statement is either an assertion of a reality ("even though his numbers are few," NRSV) or perhaps a further plea that the number of his descendants be few ("but let his men be few," ESV). In

---

[6]Cf. Deut 21:15; Ps 78:51; 108:36.

[7]יֶתֶר (*yether*) means "remainder" or "excess"; cf. KB.

[8]The MT of 1 Chronicles 5:1-2 (NRSV) reads: "The sons of Reuben the first-born of Israel. (He was the firstborn, but because he defiled his father's bed his birthright was given to the sons of Joseph son of Israel, so that he is not enrolled in the genealogy according to the birthright; though Judah became prominent among his brothers and a ruler came from him, yet the birthright belonged to Joseph)." Cf. Williams, "The LXX of 1 Chronicles 5:1-2," pp. 368-371. He notes that the LXX differs from MT here in the following way: 1) "he defiled" is "when he ascended"; 2) "was given" is "he gave"; 3) for first and third occurrences of "birthright" LXX gives "blessing"; 4) "sons of Joseph" is "his son, Joseph."

either case Reuben does not have a very promising future as a tribe, and nothing that happened during the time between Jacob's words and Moses' words changed that fact.

The fact was that Reuben's passion led him so strongly that he disregarded all social and moral taboos, and disregarded the shame that his actions would bring to his father for a single sexual encounter. The fact that he later tried to save Joseph from being enslaved did not, in Jacob's judgment, mitigate this. Jacob's anger at this is even more obvious if we follow the Hebrew and not, as the NIV and NRSV, the Greek and Syriac. Translated literally it reads, "You went up onto the couch of your father, then you defiled [it] – to my bed he went up!" According to the Hebrew Jacob begins the sentence by addressing Reuben in the second person ("You") directly but then switches to third person addressing the other sons or perhaps merely speaking rhetorically to himself.

49:5 "Simeon and Levi are brothers—their swords are weapons of violence. 49:6 Let me not enter their council, let me not join their assembly, for they have killed men in their anger and hamstrung oxen as they pleased. 49:7 Cursed be their anger, so fierce, and their fury, so cruel! I will scatter them in Jacob and disperse them in Israel.

Simeon and Levi are said to be "**brothers**." This is an unusual statement given that all the other ten sons of Jacob were also their brothers and Reuben, Judah, Issachar, and Zebulun were also their full brothers, all six having Leah as their mother. But surely the point is that they had joined together in the act of killing Shechem, Hamor, and the Shechemites while they were healing from circumcision – actions which Jacob denounced at the time in the strongest terms (Gen 34:30).

The translation of the next clause, "**their swords are weapons of violence**" is fraught with difficulty. The word מְכֵרֹתֵיהֶם ($m^{a}k\bar{e}r\bar{o}th\hat{e}hem$) translated "swords" is a *hapax legomenon* and the word translated "weapons"[9] is only one of many possible translations for the word. While I don't have a convincing alternative to the NIV and NRSV, it does seem rather trivial to say that a sword is a weapon of violence. What else would a sword be? Whatever the exact meaning, the violence of Simeon and Levi in killing the Shechemites while they were healing from circumcision is condemned. Their action is the old covenant equivalent of drowning someone as you baptize them.

In verse 6b Simeon and Levi are accused of hamstringing an ox.[10] There is no reference to literal violence against animals in the incident

---

[9] כְּלִי ($k^{a}l\hat{e}$) can mean "vessels," "utensils," "articles," etc. Cf. *DCH*, 4:420-424.

[10] The Hebrew here is singular, contrary to the NIV. The NIV also translates the singular "man" as "men."

with the Shechemites in Genesis 34. In fact 34:28-29 could be read to imply that they took their animals as spoils. If the men were killed, the women and children taken as plunder, what would be the point of hamstringing oxen? There would be no Shechemites around to use them! But that could be Jacob's point. Their senseless and wasteful cruelty against innocent and valuable animals shows that their violence was unjust and indiscriminate.[11]

On the other hand it may be that the word "ox" is singular because it is a metaphor for the prince Shechem. De Hoop, citing Miller's treatment of Ugaritic texts where bulls are metaphors for powerful leaders, comments:

> The quoted text illustrates clearly the metaphorical usage of the term "bull", which makes it possible to understand our text as a similar, metaphorical usage of the "bull" — terminology. "They hamstrung a bull" could be interpreted as "they hamstrung (=killed) a prince", which could form very well a reference to the narrated event in Genesis 34, that Simeon and Levi killed Shechem, the "bull/prince" after he was circumcised.[12]

Another possibility on similar reasoning is that verse 6 refers to the killing of Hamor the prince and the hamstringing of Jacob the ox, who was made vulnerable for the Canaanite and Perizzites by the killing of the Shechemites.[13] But in my judgment this view reads what seems to be a simple synonymous parallelism in a way that demands too much precision in poetic language.

In verse 7a Jacob calls down a curse on Simeon and Levi's rage as demonstrated by their actions against Shechem. Shechem was guilty of a single rape. Simeon and Levi were guilty of wholesale murder of the male members of an entire community. Shechem illegitimately took a single woman. Simeon and Levi illegitimately took all of their women and children.

In verse 7b Jacob announces a judgment against the descendants of Simeon and Levi. He claims that he himself will carry out that judgment (note, "*I will scatter them . . .*"). This may be simply an example of poet-

---

[11]Fretheim, *Genesis*, p. 665: "Simeon and Levi are the only sons considered together, no doubt because of the slaughter at Shechem (34:25-30). The poem includes strong language about them; they were murderous, violent, angry, arbitrary, cruel and harsh in their treatment of animals."

[12]De Hoop, *Genesis 49*, p. 101, citing P.D. Miller, "Animal Names as Designations in Ugaritic and Hebrew," *UF* 2 (1970): 177-186.

[13]C.M. Carmichael, "Some Sayings in Genesis 49," *JBL* 88 (1969): 435-444.

ic license, since Jacob will not be around to enforce the judgment. On
the other hand the sentence could be a claim by Jacob that his words
have divine power and sanction behind them.[14] But even if Jacob is
claiming divine authority for his words, this does not mean that they
carry some sort of predestining power. The outworking of this statement in the history of the tribes of Simeon and Levi is noteworthy for
its complexity. On the one hand both tribes were scattered among the
other tribes. The tribe of Simeon did not succeed in obtaining a separate territory of its own but was absorbed into the tribe of Judah's territory (Josh 19:9). The Levites were scattered throughout the other
tribes to serve as priests and teachers of the Torah. While there were
levitical cities within the other tribes, they had no area of their own. On
the other hand their long-term destinies as tribes were almost polar
opposites. The tribe of Simeon declined in population from 59 thousand and 300 men of 20 years of age and older at Sinai to 22 thousand
200 men after the 40 years in the wilderness. No explanation is given for
this dramatic decline. Eventually the Simeonites are absorbed into
Judah and disappear as a tribe. By contrast the Levites replace the firstborn sons as priests during the wilderness period and, though they have
no tribal territory to call their own, end up as the priests for the entire
nation. Their "destiny" as a tribe completely turns around during the
time the nation was in the wilderness.

A comparison of the deathbed statement of Jacob and the blessing
of Moses in regard to Simeon and Levi is instructive. Simeon is not even
mentioned in Deuteronomy 33 while Levi's curse by Jacob turns into an
elaborate blessing.

	Jacob in Genesis 49	Moses in Deuteronomy 33
Simeon	"Simeon and Levi are brothers— their swords are weapons of vio- lence. [6]Let me not enter their council, let me not join their assembly, for they have killed men in their anger and ham- strung oxen as they pleased. [7]Cursed be their anger, so fierce, and their fury, so cruel! I will scatter them in Jacob and dis- perse them in Israel.	NOT MENTIONED!!

[14]Fretheim, *Genesis*, p. 465: ". . . Jacob's repeated use of the first person reflects
a prophetic mode of discourse; strikingly Jacob himself (namely his word) serves
as the agent of judgment in v. 7."

| Levi | "Simeon and Levi are brothers— their swords are weapons of violence. ⁶Let me not enter their council, let me not join their assembly, for they have killed men in their anger and hamstrung oxen as they pleased. ⁷Cursed be their anger, so fierce, and their fury, so cruel! I will scatter them in Jacob and disperse them in Israel. | About Levi he said: "Your Thummim and Urim belong to the man you favored. You tested him at Massah; you contended with him at the waters of Meribah. ⁹He said of his father and mother, 'I have no regard for them.' He did not recognize his brothers or acknowledge his own children, but he watched over your word and guarded your covenant. ¹⁰He teaches your precepts to Jacob and your law to Israel. He offers incense before you and whole burnt offerings on your altar. ¹¹Bless all his skills, O LORD, and be pleased with the work of his hands. Smite the loins of those who rise up against him; strike his foes till they rise no more." |

The faithfulness of the descendants of Levi at the Golden Calf incident and elsewhere results in turning the words that seem to be a curse in Jacob's mouth into a blessing. Levi is scattered throughout the other tribes. But unlike Simeon they do not lose their identity. Instead the Levites became the leaders of worship and the teachers of Torah. Jacob's words are not a curse at all, but a sort of conditional prophecy.

49:8 "Judah, your brothers will praise you; your hand will be on the neck of your enemies; your father's sons will bow down to you. 49:9 You are a lion's cub, O Judah; you return from the prey, my son. Like a lion he crouches and lies down, like a lioness—who dares to rouse him? 49:10 The scepter will not depart from Judah, nor the ruler's staff from between his feet, until he comes to whom it belongs and the obedience of the nations is his.

With Reuben, and Simeon and Levi, having been passed over for any positive blessing, Jacob comes to the next son in line, **Judah**. While he was not his father's favorite, the preceding narrative has prepared us for what happens here. Judah's story began inauspiciously when he suggested that Joseph be sold as a slave for the Egyptian slave market (Genesis 37) and ended up fathering twin sons with his daughter-in-law Tamar, while she pretended to be a prostitute (Genesis 38). The contrast with Joseph in these early chapters could hardly be greater. But the portrayal of Judah begins to change when Judah takes the lead among the brothers in convincing Jacob to allow them to return with Benjamin

by offering himself as the guarantor of Benjamin's safety. He then medi-
ated with Joseph and led the way when the family came to Egypt. He
had emerged through these experiences as the leader of the brothers.

Jacob begins his message for Judah by telling him that his **brothers**
would **praise him** and **bow down** to him. He would also overcome his
enemies, symbolized by the metaphor of placing his hands on their
neck.[15] The fact that Jacob says that Judah's brothers would **bow down**
to him is striking in light of Joseph's dreams with which this section of
the book began. What Joseph thought was to be his role actually turned
out to be Judah's role, according to Jacob.[16]

In verse 9 Judah is compared to a lion in various phases of life and
various situations. He is first a young lion who goes up from having
eaten his prey. Then he is an adult male lion crouching down and
stretching out to rest. Finally he is a female lion that no one will dis-
turb.[17] The metaphor speaks of the strength and fearsomeness of Judah.

Jacob cedes leadership to Judah, and not his favored son Joseph, in
verse 10. Judah will have the scepter and the inscribed staff[18] as symbols
of the tribe's authority and leadership over the other tribes. This will
last until שִׁילֹה (šîlōh) comes, the Hebrew word in verse 10 which the
NIV periphrases as "**to whom it belongs**."[19] This word is extremely difficult to interpret with certainty.

The word could be a proper noun. If so, it could be a name of a
person or the name of a place. "Shiloh" could be the town of that name
where the Ark of the Covenant was once located before the building of
the Temple (Josh 18:1). But this rendering makes little sense with the
following phrase, "to it is the obedience of the peoples." Shiloh could
be the name of a person, but if so, there is no known person of that
name to whom Jacob's description would apply.

Another possibility is that the Hebrew word means "ruler." This
meaning could be arrived at by conjectural emendation of the Hebrew

---

[15]Tigay (*Deuteronomy*, p. 323) notes that both Jacob's and Moses' message for
Judah use wordplay between the name "Judah," the words for hands, and in
Genesis the word for "praise."

[16]Jacob originally had questioned Joseph's second dream, interpreting the sun,
moon, and stars to be Joseph's father, mother, and eleven brothers (Gen 37:10).
The narrator does not confirm or deny Jacob's interpretation.

[17]One difficulty with this reading is that the question is literally translated,
"Who will rouse him?" not "Who will rouse her?"

[18]Ironically Judah's staff had been the sign of his culpable guilt in the episode
with Tamar in Genesis 38.

[19]שִׁילֹה (šîlōh) is a famous *crux interpretum*.

text, but, as de Hoop points out,[20] none of the suggested emendations are supported by the early translations. The suggestion that the word is based on a supposed Akkadian word meaning "ruler" has been debunked by Moran who demonstrates that no such Akkadian word meaning ruler is attested.[21] The NIV adopts the most plausible explanation of the view that the word means "ruler." This view reads the text with the alternative reading of the Hebrew Qere[22] as well as the Samaritan Pentateuch, Targums Onkelos and Neophyti, and the LXX. In this view the Hebrew is read as meaning, "which [is] to him," i.e., "to whom it belongs." If this reading is followed the meaning would be that the tribe of Judah would maintain the ruler's scepter until the one to whom that scepter really belonged came. He would then take up the scepter from Judah. The meaning is thus clearly Messianic.

The problem is that there seem to be no examples of the phrase constructed in the way suggested with the meaning suggested. According to Moran it is "bad Hebrew" and more likely a product of later scribal misunderstanding than of the original author.[23]

Moran, followed by de Hoop, suggests retaining the consonantal text but revocalizing it to mean, "until tribute[24] is brought to him."[25] The **"obedience of the nations"** referred to in the very next line thus makes good sense. While less overtly messianic, this rendering seems to make the most sense and does not require emending the traditional text. No matter which of the last two mentioned views is adopted, the fact that the obedience of [the] peoples will be given to *šîlōh* links the person or thing being referred to, to the universal blessing of all nations for which Abraham was called ("in you all the nations of the earth shall be blessed").

49:11 He will tether his donkey to a vine, his colt to the choicest branch; he will wash his garments in wine, his robes in the blood of grapes. 49:12 His eyes will be darker than wine, his teeth whiter than milk.

Verses 11 and 12 seem to continue the description of a person who represents the tribe of Judah or will receive the scepter of leadership from the tribe of Judah. That person will live in circumstances of such

---

[20]De Hoop, *Genesis 49*, pp. 122-124.

[21]W.L. Moran, "Gen. 49.10 and Its Use in Ezek. 21.32," *Biblica* 39 (1959): 405-425.

[22]The *Qere* suggests שִׁילוֹ (*šîlô*) rather than the MT's שִׁילֹה (*šîlōh*). See *BHS*, p. 82, fn. 10[b].

[23]Moran, "Gen. 49.10," p. 410.

[24]Hebrew שַׁי (*šay*) means "tribute" in Isaiah 18:7; Ps 68:30; 76:12.

[25]Moran, "Gen. 49.10," pp. 412-414. De Hoop, with extensive additional arguments, *Genesis 49*, pp. 130-148.

abundant blessing that he could tie his donkey to a valuable vine and not worry about whether the donkey would destroy the plant. There are plenty more. The abundance of grapes would be such that the normally valuable products of grapes (wine) would be used as washing water. The picture is of extraordinary abundance. The original readers would perhaps be reminded of the description of Canaan as a land "flowing with milk and honey" (Lev 26:5; Isa 25:6; Joel 2:24; Amos 9:13). In verse 12 the person himself is described, once again in an idealized poetic way. "**His eyes will be darker than wine** and **his teeth whiter than milk**." The description of the eyes is interesting. The word which NIV translates "darker" (חַכְלִילִי, *ḥaklîlî*) is only found in this text and therefore determining its meaning is a challenge. The Greek has "amber" (χαροπός, *charopos*) probably thinking of the sparkling quality of the gem, rather than its typical yellowish color. It may be that the person is described as having eyes which "sparkle like wine." In any case this person is strikingly handsome. White teeth are a sign of health and youth. The metaphorical picture would have been even more striking for an ancient audience without modern dental care.

The canonical audience would see the fulfillment of this passage in the royal line of David, which came from the tribe of Judah. The New Testament sees the line of descent which led to Jesus the Messiah, the son of David. To him the obedience of the nations is due. The tribe of Judah was the ruling tribe, in reality or in hope, from the time of David.

The striking differences between this effusive blessing for Judah and Moses' blessing in Deuteronomy 33:7 must not be missed. Moses says of the tribe of Judah, "Hear, O LORD, the voice of Judah, and bring him to his people. With your hands contend for him, and be a help against his adversaries." While Moses' words do not contradict Jacob's and may well still presume the leadership of Judah, the emphasis is on the protection of Judah from adversaries rather than the honor of being given the ruler's staff.

Jacob's Final Words to the Later Sons of Leah (49:13-15)

Jacob now departs from strict birth order by completing his messages for the sons of Leah. Leah bore Jacob two additional sons after the four sons of the secondary wives had been born. Issachar was the ninth son of Jacob and the fifth of Leah while Zebulun was the tenth son of Jacob and the sixth of Leah. Interestingly Jacob blesses them out of their birth order, placing Zebulun ahead of Issachar.

The Later Sons of Leah: Issachar and Zebulun

Genesis 49	Deuteronomy 33
[13]*Zebulun* shall settle at the shore of the sea; he shall be a haven for ships, and his border shall be at Sidon. [14]*Issachar* is a strong donkey, lying down between the sheepfolds; [15]he saw that a resting place was good, and that the land was pleasant; so he bowed his shoulder to the burden, and became a slave at forced labor.	[18]And of *Zebulun* he said: Rejoice, Zebulun, in your going out; and *Issachar*, in your tents. [19]They call peoples to the mountain; there they offer the right sacrifices; for they suck the affluence of the seas and the hidden treasures of the sand.

The two tribes are paired together, probably because they were born in a deal between Leah and Rachel; Rachel getting the aphrodisiac mandrakes of Leah, and Leah getting the right to sleep with Jacob in return. They are later in life sons of Leah (along with Dinah). Although Issachar is the firstborn of the latter sons of Leah, he is mentioned after Zebulun in both the testament of Jacob and the blessing of Moses. The reversal of what might be the expected roles of older and younger is also clear from the wordings of their respective blessings. In both versions Issachar is the more passive, lying down and finding a resting place even at the cost of servitude (or is it merely hard work?[26]) in the testament, and remaining in tents in the blessing. By contrast Zebulun is to rejoice in his going out. The extension of Zebulun's borders to Sidon in the testament, even if it merely reflects Jacob's hope, also implies a more active future for Zebulun. In both accounts Zebulun is somehow related to the sea(s), even though the tribe does not end up bordering on the sea. Asher is on the coast and Naphtali is along the west side of Chinnereth (Galilee) with Zebulun between them.

In any case Issachar's "mixed blessing" from Jacob may be indicative of Jacob's attitude toward him. He was born as a result of Leah hiring Jacob for the night from Rachel in return for some of Reuben's aphrodisiac mandrakes. Zebulun, by contrast is conceived without such coercion.

Moses' blessing does not seem to carry the baggage of the unusual birth circumstances of Issachar as he and Zebulun together "call peoples

---

[26]Sailhamer, *Genesis* (p. 277), seems to read this more positively than most, who, like Sarna (*Genesis*, p. 340), take the words as referring to submitting to enforced labor, perhaps being "content to perform corvée labor for the local overlords in return for a quiet existence."

to the mountain,"[27] "offer righteous sacrifices," and "suck the affluence" that comes from controlling either the sea[28] itself or trade routes with access to it.[29] Moses' blessing amounts to a reversal of the virtual curse of Issachar by Jacob and a reaffirmation of the blessing of Zebulun.

49:13 "Zebulun will live by the seashore and become a haven for ships; his border will extend toward Sidon.

While Jacob anticipates that **Zebulun**'s descendants would enjoy the economic (sea trade, etc.) and other advantages of living by the coast, in the event things turned out differently for them. The original tribal area of Zebulun was landlocked in the northern part of the country, nestled between Asher to the west on the coast, Issachar and Naphtali to the east along the Sea of Galilee, Manasseh to the south and Asher, Naphtali, and eventually Dan, to the north. Josephus is aware of traditions that had Zebulun abutting both the Sea of Galilee on the east and the Mediterranean on the west.[30] But this is not the picture given in the book of Joshua (Josh 19:10-16). Once again, the hopes of Jacob do not seem to be immediately realized in the case of Zebulun and this may be another piece of evidence that Jacob's words are not to be regarded as prophetic in some sort of predestinarian sense. For whatever reason Zebulun was not given access to the sea and their territory did not stretch all the way to the northern coastal city of Sidon.

It may be that in time Zebulun's territory did eventually reach to the coast of the Mediterranean. The importance of access to the sea in secure harbors should not be minimized. The potential for access to such trade is one of the things that made Palestine such a prized pos-

---

[27]The mountain to which the two tribes call peoples is hard to pin down. Is it Mount Carmel on the Mediterranean or Mount Tabor or some other?

[28]Is this the Mediterranean or Chinnereth (Galilee) or perhaps both? Cf. Tigay, *Deuteronomy*, p. 330.

[29]Wright (*DOTP*, p. 912): Zebulun "is rich in terms of water resources, soil and building materials. . . . Perhaps more importantly, the tribal inheritance of Zebulun carried a number of important natural routes connecting the seacoast with points inland, including the Great Trunk Road running between Egypt and Mesopotamia. . . . [Several of Zebulun's cities] guarded strategic junctures on the main routes as witnessed by their appearance in Amarna texts 8, 224, 225 and 245 (cf. Josh 11:1)." He continues, "Zebulun's eventual control of the northwestern extremity of the Jezreel Valley and of the final bend of the *Via Maris* toward the Mediterranean is adequate to explain Jacob's words."

[30]*Ant.* 5.1.22: "The tribe of Zebulun's lot included the land which lay as far as the Lake of Genesareth [Sea of Galilee], and that which belonged to Carmel and the [Mediterranean] Sea." This occurs in his description of the original allotting of territory in the time of Joshua.

session for the great empires of the ancient world. De Hoop suggests that לְחוֹף יַמִּים (*lᵉḥôph yammîm*) "by the seashore" means an inward curving beach which in light of the later location of Zebulun would refer to the Gulf of Haifa.

49:14 "Issachar is a rawboned donkey lying down between two saddlebags. 49:15 When he sees how good is his resting place and how pleasant is his land, he will bend his shoulder to the burden and submit to forced labor.

Issachar is compared to a strong[31] donkey which, despite its strength, submits to servitude because of the pleasantness of its material surroundings. J.D. Heck notes,

> Most critical scholars think that Genesis 49:14-15 reflects a time when Issachar submitted to slave labor rather than do the hard work of subjugating the land. The oracle in Genesis 49:14-15 is generally considered one of derision of the freemen who had let themselves be enticed by the fertile plain and had thereby become humiliated as beasts of burden.[32]

Whether Jacob's words anticipate or reflect Issachar's future is a matter of perspective. Regardless, Issachar will allow himself to be "hired" just as his father Jacob was "hired" in order to conceive him. The desire for sexual pleasure which motivated Jacob to go along with Rachel and Leah's bargain will be matched by Issachar's desire for pleasurable circumstances. In both cases the person(s) submitted rather than battle against the difficulties which refusing to submit might create.[33] The Hebrew picturesquely depicts the submission to forced labor as a לְמַס־עֹבֵד (*lᵉmas-'ōbēd*) "melting into servitude."

Jacob's Final Words to the Sons of the Secondary Wives (49:16-21)

After offering his final words to the six sons of Leah, Jacob turns to the four sons of the handmaidens Bilhah and Zilpah. Dan and Naphtali, the sons of Rachel's handmaid Bilhah, were the fifth and sixth sons of Jacob. Gad and Asher, the sons of Leah's handmaid Zilpah, were the

---

[31]NIV's "rawboned" nicely interprets the Hebrew גֶּרֶם (*gārem*) meaning "bone" as a metaphor for strength.

[32]J.D. Heck, "Issachar," *DOTP*, p. 458.

[33]Turner, *Genesis*, p. 202: "Issachar had been conceived when his mother Leah had 'hired' Jacob for the night (30.18). Issachar's name (containing *Êkr*, "hire") had originally referred to the mode of his conception, telling us more about the father than the son. Here, however, the concept of 'hire' is transferred to the son who will become 'a slave at forced labour' (49.15)."

seventh and eighth sons of Jacob. Joseph, Jacob's favorite son, had a strained relationship with these four brothers, having given a slanderous or at least bad report about them to Jacob (Gen 37:2). But Jacob's words to them are surprisingly positive given their position in the family.[34] In the patriarchal family system sons of the secondary wives (concubines) had secondary status. Here they are placed after the later sons of Leah, Issachar, and Zebulun, even though they were born before them. In the pecking order of birth in the patriarchal family whether one's mother is a primary or secondary wife matters more than birth order.[35] Given the patriarchal family structure Jacob's final words for the future of the sons of the secondary wives are, as might be expected, brief, enigmatic, and tepid. In the history of the nation the four tribes ultimately[36] settle in the far north and in the Transjordan, far away from the locus of political and religious power in the center of the country.

Within the group of sons of the secondary wives Jacob plays with the birth order in minor ways. The secondary sons are blessed out of their birth order as the chart below indicates. Bilhah's sons, Dan and Naphtali are first and fourth in Jacob's blessing, while Zilpah's sons, Gad and Asher are second and third. This may be a subtle way of indicating the equal status of the four sons of the secondary wives. At their birth the sons of Bilhah were formally adopted by Jacob while the sons of Zilpah were not.[37] This would place the sons of Zilpah in the lowest place among the sons of Jacob. They were the unadopted sons of the concubine of the wife whom Jacob hated. By moving Zilpah's sons up in the order of the blessing Jacob may be partially restoring their status to a status nearly equal to the status of the other sons of a concubine.

---

[34]Mark McEntire (*The Blood of Abel: The Violent Plot in the Hebrew Bible* [Macon, GA: Mercer University Press, 1999], p. 33) observes: "In nine of the twelve descriptions of Jacob's sons violence forms a key component to the understanding of the son's (tribe's) identity (vv. 3c, 5b-7b, 8b, 15d, 17, 19, 23-24, and 27). Only three of the briefest descriptions (Zebulun, Asher, and Naphtali) contain no such reference. Is it significant that these non-violent tribes never achieve any degree of prominence in the biblical story of Israel?" Two of the three tribes he mentions are sons of the secondary wives.

[35]The fact that they are placed before the favorite sons of Jacob, Joseph and Benjamin, will be discussed below.

[36]Dan was initially granted an allotment in the middle of the country but ultimately abandoned it, moving to the far north (Josh 19:47).

[37]P.H. Wright. "Naphtali," *DOTP*, p. 587: "Bilhah's two sons were born 'on Rachel's knees' (Gen 30:3), a phrase signifying Jacob's formal recognition of their sonship through Rachel. Significantly, this phrase does not appear in connection with the birth of Zilpah's sons."

While that status is still quite low, there is a minor sort of compensation for the unfortunate fact of the circumstances of their births.

Birth order	Mother	Blessing Order	Mother
Dan – fifth	Bilhah's first	Dan – seventh	Bilhah's first
Naphtali – sixth	Bilhah's second	Gad – eighth	Zilpah's first
Gad – seventh	Zilpah's first	Asher – ninth	Zilpah's second
Asher – eighth	Zilpah's second	Naphtali – tenth	Bilhah's second

49:16 "Dan will provide justice for his people as one of the tribes of Israel. 49:17 Dan will be a serpent by the roadside, a viper along the path, that bites the horse's heels so that its rider tumbles backward. 49:18 "I look for your deliverance, O LORD.

Dan is born fifth of Jacob's sons by Rachel's handmaiden Bilhah. He is the first son mentioned after the six sons of Leah. Jacob begins his message about the descendants of Dan by wordplay between the Hebrew words for "Dan" (דָּן, *dān*) and "judge" (יָדִין, *yādîn*). The statement could mean either "act as a judge" in a legal sense or "provide justice" in a military sense as in the NIV. The only "judge" from the tribe of Dan was Samson, and he provided justice by defeating the Philistines militarily, not in a court. It is impossible to be certain whether verse 17 is to be viewed positively or negatively. **Dan** is to be a **serpent** biting at the heels of a horse that comes by, causing **its rider** to fall **backward**. Positively this could mean that Dan would cause the defeat of powerful enemies of the nation. The horse was a powerful military weapon in ancient warfare. The Torah directed that any future king of the nation trust in Yahweh for deliverance rather than rely on his own military strategy by accumulating horses (Deut 17:16).

Read negatively and intertextually it is hard to miss the allusion to the serpent biting at the heel of the seed of the woman in the curse on the serpent (Gen 3:15). But perhaps this uncertainty is deliberate. Whether the descendants of Dan defend the nation or are a tool of the serpent depends upon their future choices.

The same sort of ambiguity is also found in verse 18. Jacob seems to interrupt his deathbed message for his sons by a prayer. But Jacob's statement could be taken in more than one way. As Turner suggests,

> Is it a statement of quiet confidence in Yahweh? Or might it suggest, rather, a sense of frustration? Prior to this point only Judah has

received true commendation, with the emphasis decidedly toward the negative, or enigmatic. Thus Jacob's statement, "I wait for your salvation, O Lord", registers his awareness that his sons and the blessing he had fought for so hard himself, have brought more problems than actual blessing.[38]

If read as expressing frustration, Jacob's statement acknowledges that only the LORD can bring about a better future for Jacob's descendants.

Jacob's statement should be compared and contrasted with Moses' blessing as the nation of Israel is about to enter the Promised Land.

Genesis 49	Deuteronomy 33
[16]*Dan* shall judge his people as one of the tribes of Israel. [17]Dan shall be a snake by the roadside, a viper along the path, that bites the horse's heels so that its rider falls backward. [18]I wait for your salvation, O LORD.	[22]And of *Dan* he said: Dan is a lion's whelp that leaps forth from Bashan.

In both Jacob and Moses' testaments Dan is depicted as a crafty animal that clandestinely attacks its prey. The Dan of Deuteronomy 33 is the stronger animal. Dan's northern location is presumed in Moses' account[39] even though the tribe was given an original allotment in the south to the west of Benjamin and the northwest of Judah. The word "Laish" (לַיִשׁ, *layiš*) is the same as the word for "old lion" (*layiš*), and while Deuteronomy 33:22 uses a different word (אַרְיֵה, *'aryēh*), there may still be an echo. In either case, Dan's migration to the north sometime after the conquest is anticipated/reflected in Moses' testament.

The fact that Dan does not appear among the tribal list of the 144,000 sealed in Revelation 7:4-8 (Manasseh, the son of Joseph, takes his place even though Joseph is already included) may be another instance, in terms of Christian biblical theology, of a conditional element in whether a tribe has a future and what sort of future that might be.

49:19 "Gad will be attacked by a band of raiders, but he will attack them at their heels.

Gad is the seventh son of Jacob and the first by Leah's handmaiden Zilpah. As such he is one of two tribes on the lowest rung of the hier-

---

[38]Turner, *Genesis*, p. 203.

[39]The phrase "leaps forth from Bashan" refers to a transjordanian location that extends to the north of the sea of Chinnereth (Galilee) and next to the city of Laish, which Dan conquered when it moved from the south (Josh 19:47; Judg 18:27).

archical ladder in Jacob's family of twelve sons. Jacob's statement is full
of wordplay. A literal translation of the Hebrew would be, "A band of
raiders (גְּדוּד, gᵊdûd) will raid (יְגוּדֶנּוּ, yᵊgûdennû) Gad (גָּד, gād); but he will
raid (יָגֻד, yāgud) at the heel (עָקֵב, 'āqēb)." The word "heel" seems to play
on the name "Jacob" (יַעֲקֹב, ya'ăqōb). The statement is unclear in its
intent if it is to be regarded as a blessing. Jacob does not foresee victory for the descendants of Gad as much as a stalemate where each side
attacks and is attacked with no clear winner.

Jacob's commentary on Gad, like Dan, seems to echo the curse on
the serpent. The attack will be at the heel of his attackers. A comparison of the words of Jacob and Moses regarding Gad is instructive.

Genesis 49	Deuteronomy 33
[19]*Gad* shall be raided by raiders, but he shall raid at their heels.	[20]And of *Gad* he said: Blessed be the enlargement of Gad! Gad lives like a lion; he tears at arm and scalp. [21]He chose the best for himself, for there a commander's allotment was reserved; he came at the head of the people, he executed the justice of the LORD, and his ordinances for Israel.

There is a perplexing turnaround for Gad in the Blessing of Moses
which begs for a narratological explanation. Certainly Gad declines significantly in numbers during the wilderness period (45,650 to 40,500 a
loss of 5,150) so it is difficult to see the enlargement of Gad numerically. Perhaps the fact that Gad along with Reuben chose land in the Transjordan allows them to have more land than they would have had had
they settled in cisjordan. But that choice is ambiguous at best. Notice
that Moses at first regards the request to settle in the cisjordan as a repetition of the rebellion and un-faith of the twelve spies episode (Num
32:14,15). The choosing of "the best for himself" may allude to the selfishness of the choice of Reuben and Gad (Deut 33:21). The coming at
the "head of his people" (33:21) may allude to the "hurrying" or "van-
guard" which Reuben and Gad promise to be for the armies of Israel in
the cisjordanian conquest (Num 32:17). It is unclear whether Moses is
predicting that Gad will perform this function, or implicitly warning
them that they must do so. In any case, according to Moses Gad seems
to have a much more significant role in the nation than one would anticipate from his humble beginnings and from Jacob's words. This once
again indicates the conditionality of Jacob's words.

**49:20 "Asher's food will be rich; he will provide delicacies fit for a
king.**

Asher was the eighth son of Jacob and the fourth of the four sons of the secondary wives. As such he has the lowest status on the patriarchal family hierarchical ladder. Jacob's words for Asher are surprisingly positive unless one presumes that they contain an implicit rebuke for "inordinate luxury."[40] More likely they express Jacob's hope or anticipation that the descendants of Asher would receive material blessings, so much so that they would provide royal delicacies. Food would not be in scarce supply, but abundant ("fat," שְׁמֵנָה, šᵊmēnāh).

If anything Moses' blessing of the descendants of Asher is even more effusive. Not only will Asher's food be "rich," there will be so much extra oil that they could use it to dip their feet in it. Moses anticipates that Asher would be more blessed than his brother tribes who will regard the Asherites as their favorite. All of this for the tribe with the lowliest pedigree on the patriarchal family tree!

Genesis 49	Deuteronomy 33
[20]*Asher's* food shall be rich, and he shall provide royal delicacies.	[24]And of *Asher* he said: Most blessed of sons be Asher; may he be the favorite of his brothers, and may he dip his foot in oil. [25]Your bars are iron and bronze; and as your days, so is your strength.

49:21 "Naphtali is a doe set free that bears beautiful fawns.

Naphtali was the second son of Rachel's handmaid Bilhah and Jacob's sixth son. While it seems clear that Jacob's message for Naphtali is a positive one, the exact meaning of the Hebrew is far from clear. A literal rendering of the Hebrew would be: "Naphtali is a hind sent out, the giver of branches of loveliness." One potential problem with this rendering is that the "giver" is a masculine participle in Hebrew while the word for "doe" is feminine. But this could be an example of poetic playfulness with the gender of words. The difficulty is in finding the meaning. What does it mean for a deer (hind) to be sent out? The NIV and NRSV suggest that the doe is set free and as a result of that freedom gives **beautiful fawns**, which are described metaphorically as "branches." Another possibility is Wenham's suggestion that Naphtali was originally a doe that was set free, but later became domesticated and bore "fawns of the fold." Naphtali "exchanged her original freedom for a later more sedentary domesticated lifestyle."[41] Others, including

---

[40]Turner, *Genesis*, p. 203, suggests this as a possibility but suggests that the "exact connotations are elusive."

[41]Wenham, *Genesis 16–50*, p. 483, basing his translation "fawns of the fold" on Ugaritic and Akkadian parallels noted by Andersen.

the NRSV margin, translate the last phrase as "beautiful words." But this seems to hypothesize a complete change of subject. Moses' blessing for Naphtali is less ambiguous. In Deuteronomy Moses commands Naphtali to possess the sea (west?) and the south. The sea would seem to be either Chinnereth or a call to expand toward the Mediterranean. If we translate less literally it is merely a call to possess those portions of the land of Canaan to its south and west or perhaps the west and south edges of Chinnereth. The expansion of territory is an encouragement for Naphtali to fully possess their allotted land

Genesis 49	Deuteronomy 33
[21]*Naphtali* is a doe[42] let loose that bears lovely fawns.	[23]And of *Naphtali* he said: O Naphtali, sated with favor, full of the blessing of the LORD, possess the west and the south.

Jacob's Final Words to the Sons of Rachel (49:22-27)

The last of Jacob's sons to receive his parting words are his favorites, the sons of Rachel: Joseph and Benjamin. On the one hand they are the two youngest of the twelve sons. And so they wait until the end to receive Jacob's words. On the other hand they are the only sons of Rachel, the wife whom Jacob loved and whose sons he favored. In a sense there is a tension in Jacob's mind between the principle of the status of the older and the status of the favored. By waiting until the end to speak about them Jacob may be acknowledging their subordinate status in terms of birth order. But there may be another reason. By keeping his message for them until the end Jacob may be saving the best for last.

49:22 "Joseph is a fruitful vine, a fruitful vine near a spring, whose branches climb over a wall. 49:23 With bitterness archers attacked him; they shot at him with hostility. 49:24 But his bow remained steady, his strong arms stayed limber, because of the hand of the Mighty One of Jacob, because of the Shepherd, the Rock of Israel, 49:25 because of your father's God, who helps you, because of the Almighty, who blesses you with blessings of the heavens above, blessings of the deep that lies below, blessings of the breast and womb. 49:26 Your father's blessings are greater than the blessings of the ancient mountains, than the bounty of the age-old hills. Let all these rest on the head of Joseph, on the brow of the prince among his brothers.

---

[42]De Hoop, *Genesis 49*, p. 176, citing Gervitz, suggests that Hebrew אילה (*'ylh*) be pointed אֱיָלָה (*'ēlāh*) "sheep, ewe" and that "fawns" (אִמְרֵי, *'imrê*) be translated as "lambs."

Jacob begins with the oldest of the sons of his beloved Rachel, **Joseph**. Being the firstborn still has an influence on Jacob even though he was not himself the firstborn. In verse 22 Jacob begins by emphasizing the fruitfulness of Joseph's descendants. Twice Joseph is called "a son bearing fruit."[43] That fruit's continuance is emphasized by its location near a spring of water. The son bearing fruit has "daughters which march over a wall."[44] The NIV is probably correct to presume that this is a poetic way of describing the **branches** of a vine which **climb over a wall**.[45]

In verse 23 the tone suddenly changes. Joseph's descendants will be attacked by archers. Those archers would be violently bitter, and even after shooting they would still bear a grudge.[46] But Joseph is equal to the challenge. He shoots back at his enemies with a steady bow and limber arms aided by his God whose hands steady Joseph's. Whether this refers to the enemies of the descendants of Joseph in the longer-term future, or to the opposition which he experienced and would experience from his own brothers and others, or both is uncertain.

In verses 24-25 God is described is six ways. He is "**the Mighty One of Jacob**," "**the Shepherd**," "**the Rock of Israel**," Joseph's "**father's God**," "your Helper," and "**Shaddai**."[47] Jacob piles on the divine epithets as a way of reassuring Joseph and his descendants that whatever enemy might come their way, God would help them defeat their enemies.

Jacob goes on to describe the blessings that God will give the descendants of Joseph. Those blessings are not limited to protection

---

[43]The NIV paraphrases the Hebrew בֵּן פֹּרָת (bēn pōrāth). The masculine word ben is modified by a feminine participle porāt, evidently a playing with the gender as sometimes occurs in Hebrew poetry.

[44]Literalistic translation of בָּנוֹת צָעֲדָה עֲלֵי־שׁוּר (bānôth ṣāʿādāh ʿălê-šûr).

[45]Wenham (Genesis 16–50, pp. 455, 485) translates v. 22: "Joseph is a wild ass, a wild ass beside a spring, his wild colts beside the wall." The arguments are complicated and neither the traditional translation reflected in the NIV nor Wenham's alternative is without its problems.

[46]The NIV paraphrases the Heb. וַיְמָרֲרֻהוּ וָרֹבּוּ וַיִּשְׂטְמֻהוּ בַּעֲלֵי חִצִּים (waymārruhû wārōbbû wayyiṣṭᵊmuhû baʿălê ḥiṣṣîm). The Hebrew places all three verbs before the subject for emphasis.

[47]The NIV interprets שַׁדַּי (šadday) as "Almighty." D.W. Baker ("God, Name of," DOTP, p. 361) comments, "The word šadday has been variously interpreted as 'strength' ('Almighty' in KJV, NIV, NRSV), 'mountains,' possibly relating to the mountain dwelling of the Canaanite El as well as other deities, or even 'God of the breasts,' based on the Hebrew šad or šōd. . . . Goddesses do supply nourishment for royalty and other gods in Ugaritic and Egyptian mythology, and a tie between Israel's God, nourishment and breasts is brought out by wordplay in Genesis 49:25."

against enemies. They also include blessings of all nature, from the heavens above to the depths of the deep water; and nurture, the giving of children and their nursing at their mothers' breasts. Wenham[48] notes the alliteration in the Hebrew between the words "heaven" (שָׁמַיִם, šāmayim) and "breast" (שָׁדַיִם, šādayim), and "deep" (תְּהוֹם, tᵊhôm) and "womb" (רָחַם, rāḥam). Whether this applies to the male sphere of agriculture and the female sphere of bearing and raising children, as Wenham suggests, is less certain.

Verse 26a has Jacob claim that his blessings surpass previous blessings. The Hebrew is difficult and many translations including the NIV follow the Septuagint in reading a slightly different Hebrew text with the meaning "everlasting hills."[49] Jacob's blessings surpass the blessings of the ancient mountains or those of his ancestors, depending on whether one follows the MT or the LXX.[50]

In verse 26b Jacob says that these effusive blessings would be on Joseph's head. He calls Joseph a נְזִיר (nᵊzîr) **among his brothers**. The word almost always refers to the Nazirite, a person specially set apart under a vow to the LORD.[51] That is the most likely meaning for the original and canonical audiences who would have been familiar with Nazirite vows. His special place in the family and in Jacob's affection is thus affirmed.

The similarities between Jacob's Testament and Moses' Blessing are remarkable when it comes to Joseph. He receives the longest blessing by Jacob and Moses and has a leading role among his brothers/fellow tribes in each. Moses' blessing, when read intertextually, is largely a repetition and reaffirmation of Jacob's blessing.

The differences are also interesting. In Jacob's testament the deity is referred to as: "the mighty one of Jacob," "the shepherd," "the rock of Israel," "the God of your father," and "the Almighty." In Moses' blessing deity is referred to as "the LORD" and "the one who dwells in the bush." This makes sense given the revelation of "the LORD's" name to Moses and the experience of Moses with God at the burning bush. While both the testament and the blessing speak of blessings on the

---

[48]Wenham, *Genesis 16–50*, p. 487.

[49]The LXX's rendering, ὀρέων μονίμων (*horeōn monimōn*), "everlasting hills" implies an underlying Hebrew הַרְרֵי עַד (*harărê 'ad*) rather than the MT's הוֹרַי עַד- (*hôray 'ad-*), "my progenitors unto the. . . ." This is the reading of the NIV's footnote.

[50]See the discussion of Matthews, *Genesis 11:27–50:26*, pp. 908-909.

[51]Num 6:2,13,18,19,20,21; Judg 13:5,7; 16:17; Amos 2:11,12. The only case where the meaning "princes" is attested is Lam 4:7. Lev 25:5,11 uses the word of the "aftergrowth" which is especially set apart to the Lord.

"brow" of Joseph, Jacob describes him as one "set apart from his brothers" while Moses has him as the "prince" among his brothers.

But of perhaps even more significance is what is not said about Joseph. Although he is given a leading role, it is not the leading role in either the testament or the blessing. This is not what one might expect from the Joseph narrative and may indicate, as Turner has noted, that Jacob tries to ensure that Joseph's dreams do not find fulfillment by giving Judah the role of leadership. In the blessing of Moses Joseph once again comes in second, though this time to the tribe of Levi.

Genesis 49	Deuteronomy 33
²²*Joseph* is a fruitful vine, a fruitful vine near a spring, whose branches climb over a wall. ²³With bitterness archers attacked him; they shot at him with hostility. ²⁴But his bow remained steady, his strong arms stayed limber, because of the hand of the Mighty One of Jacob, because of the Shepherd, the Rock of Israel, ²⁵because of your father's God, who helps you, because of the Almighty, who blesses you with blessings of the *heavens above*, blessings of *the deep that lies below*, blessings of the breast and womb. ²⁶Your father's blessings are greater than the blessings of the *ancient mountains*, than the bounty of the *age-old hills*. Let all these rest on the *head of Joseph*, on the *brow of the prince among his brothers*.	¹³And of *Joseph* he said: Blessed by the LORD be his land, with the choice gifts of *heaven above*, and of *the deep that lies beneath*; ¹⁴with the choice fruits of the sun, and the rich yield of the months; ¹⁵with the finest produce of the *ancient mountains*, and the abundance of the *everlasting hills*; ¹⁶with the choice gifts of the earth and its fullness, and the favor of *the one who dwells in the bush*. Let these come on *the head of Joseph*, on the *brow of the prince among his brothers*. ¹⁷A firstborn bull-majesty is his! His horns are the horns of a wild ox; with them he gores the peoples, driving them to the ends of the earth; such are the myriads of Ephraim, such the thousands of Manasseh.

49:27 "Benjamin is a ravenous wolf; in the morning he devours the prey, in the evening he divides the plunder."

Benjamin is compared to **a wolf** that tears apart its prey. He then eats the prey and divides up the spoils throughout the day. The use of the word "spoils" indicates the military connotations of Jacob's words. Viewed positively the descendants of Benjamin can anticipate victory in battle. Viewed negatively they must fight in order to survive under pressure from their enemies.

Genesis 49	Deuteronomy 33
²⁷*Benjamin* is a ravenous wolf, in the morning devouring the prey, and at evening dividing the spoil."	¹²Of *Benjamin* he said: The beloved of the LORD rests in safety—the High God surrounds him all day long—the beloved rests between his shoulders.

Although Benjamin is, after Joseph, the favorite son of Jacob, ironically Jacob's final words to him do not unambiguously offer a blessing for Benjamin.[52] Moses' blessing is much clearer in this regard.

2. Jacob Procures Promise from His Twelve Sons to Bury Him in Canaan (49:28-32)

49:28 All these are the twelve tribes of Israel, and this is what their father said to them when he blessed them, giving each the blessing appropriate to him. 49:29 Then he gave them these instructions: "I am about to be gathered to my people. Bury me with my fathers in the cave in the field of Ephron the Hittite, 49:30 the cave in the field of Machpelah, near Mamre in Canaan, which Abraham bought as a burial place from Ephron the Hittite, along with the field. 49:31 There Abraham and his wife Sarah were buried, there Isaac and his wife Rebekah were buried, and there I buried Leah. 49:32 The field and the cave in it were bought from the Hittites."

The statements that Jacob made to his sons were not primarily for them as individuals, but for their descendants, the tribes of the nation of Israel. The words that Jacob spoke on his death bed are described as him "blessing" them with the **"blessing" appropriate to** each one. At first reading this seems perplexing. Certainly Reuben, Simeon, and Levi, do not, at least on the surface, seem to receive a blessing. Jacob's words seem closer to a curse. Similarly, although perhaps not as obviously, Jacob's words for Issachar, Dan, and Gad are ambiguous and are not anticipations of unmitigated blessing. Was it a blessing or a burden for the tribe of Judah to be given the responsibility of ruling a group of tribes who have internal rivalry in their DNA?

But perhaps we need to rethink the concept of blessing and what Jacob's words really are. If they are prophecies of the future in some sort of predestinarian sense, it is difficult to see how each of the sons has received a blessing. But if the words lay out for each of Jacob's sons and their descendants what their destiny might be if they do nothing to change it, they can easily be seen to be blessings. Jacob's words give encouragement or if needed, rebuke. But both encouragement and

---

[52]Turner, *Genesis*, p. 203: "The final blessing, that on Benjamin (49.27), continues the flow of short blessings which began with Zebulun's and which was interrupted by Joseph's. As with elements in the blessings on Dan (49.17) and Gad (49.19), it is not clear whether Benjamin's 'devouring' and 'dividing' as a wolf is intended to be positive or negative."

needed rebuke are blessings to those with ears open to hearing what God would say to them.[53]

Jacob describes his coming death as being **"gathered to [his] people."** While this might sound to modern ears that Jacob must have believed in some form of afterlife, this is unlikely. The language instead refers to dying a peaceful death and being buried in the family grave.[54] For Jacob it is very important that he be buried in the family grave that his grandfather Abraham had established in the land of Canaan. The exact location of that grave is given in great detail. Jacob wants there to be no misunderstanding. He had lived in Egypt for seventeen years. We do not know exactly how long it had been since the grave had last been used, for the burial of Leah; it could not have been more than fifty years or so but this was long enough for its location to be forgotten. The burial place was to be a **cave in** a **field** which originally belonged to **Ephron the Hittite.** The name of the cave with its field was **Machpelah** and was located **near** the city of **Mamre,** otherwise known as Hebron, in the south of the country. Finally, and perhaps most importantly, it was **in** the land of **Canaan,** the land which God had promised to eventually give to the descendants of Abraham, Isaac, and Jacob. That field and the cave in it had been publicly and legally purchased at the city gate of Mamre in the presence of the city's elders. Therefore, even though it had been many years before, it still legally belonged to the family of Abraham (see Gen 23:1-20).

This grave was important for at least two reasons. First, it was the family grave. Being buried with one's ancestors was a primary sign of a good and blessed life. Jacob was about to die at a good old age. Second, the grave was in the Promised Land. By insisting to both Joseph (Gen 47:29,30) and all of his sons (50:29) that he be buried there, he was emphasizing to them the importance of the promise and the continuing validity of it. The descendants of Abraham, Isaac, and Jacob would end up in the land where their forefathers were buried. The purchase of the cave of Machpelah was a sort of down payment on the promise of the land. Jacob, whatever his faults, was a man who believed in God's promises. For him, nothing was more important than participating in the fulfillment of those promises. He wanted to make sure that his sons understood this point and did what he could to ensure that his descendants would never give up hope of the fulfillment of the promises.

---

[53]Laurence Turner reminded me of the instance of Jonah, where negative words produced a positive result in the Ninevites.

[54]For a helpful discussion of how belief in life after death developed in the Old Testament, see Philip Johnston's *Shades of Sheol.*

The fact that this was a long-standing family grave is emphasized by Jacob. He notes that the three married couples who established the clan that had grown so much were all buried there: Abraham and Sarah, their son Isaac and Rebekah, and finally Leah and Jacob (he hoped). This grave, Jacob repeats in verse 32, was legally purchased from the Hittites, and therefore belonged to the family even though they were seminomadic when they lived in Canaan and had been in Egypt for seventeen years.

The fact that Jacob asks to be buried with Leah and not Rachel may be significant.[55] Jacob despised Leah during her lifetime. But in the end she was the Matriarch along with Sarah and Rebekah buried in the family grave. In some sense this shows Leah's rehabilitation in Jacob's eyes.

---

[55] I owe this suggestion to a TCM Institute student whose name I have forgotten.

GENESIS 50

X. JACOB'S DEATH, MOURNING, AND BURIAL (49:33–50:14)

The elaborate mourning for Jacob in Egypt and later in Canaan indicates his significance as the father of the second in command in Egypt. He dies with all of his sons present, although only Joseph is said to have shown the outward signs of grief. The embalming ("mummification") and prolonged mourning in Egypt (70 days of weeping) shows the status that he had in elite circles in Egypt. Jacob's sons keep their promise to bury him in Canaan. But Pharaoh ensures that the family does not use the opportunity of the burial to move back to Canaan. He sends a military escort with them and keeps their wives, children, and herds in Egypt to ensure their return. The man who gave his name to the future nation of Israel is given a state funeral by the Egyptian government.

49:33 When Jacob had finished giving instructions to his sons, he drew his feet up into the bed, breathed his last and was gathered to his people.

Evidently Jacob must have been sitting on the side of his bed as he addressed his sons with his final words. His words are referred to as **"instructions"** or even צַוָּה (ṣāwāh), "commandments." By using this terminology Jacob may be hinting that his words are not the settled destiny of his sons. However, if they want the future to be different, they must change things. As was noted above, the widely divergent ultimate results of the same words to Simeon and Levi demonstrate this. After finishing his "instructions" Jacob lay back in his bed, expired, and died. The phrase **"gathered to his people"** should not be overread as indicating a belief in life after death. More likely it is merely traditional terminology to describe a peaceful death after which one would be buried in the family grave after being mourned by that family.

50:1 Joseph threw himself upon his father and wept over him and kissed him.

While apparently Jacob died with all of his sons present, it is only Joseph who is explicitly mentioned as personally mourning. The favorite son of the father has just lost that father, and the normal signs of grief come flooding out. Joseph fell on Jacob's face[1] and **wept . . . and kissed him**. While weeping is a modern sign of grief that we share with the ancient audience, falling on the face of a corpse and kissing it may seem strange to some modern observers. But people in grief often touch and kiss the corpse at such times. This happens even in modern societies. What seems odd, or perhaps not so odd, is that only Joseph is said to have shown the typical signs of grief. The other brothers, including Benjamin, do nothing. While this is an argument from silence – just because nothing is narrated about them showing the signs of grief does not mean that we should assume that they experienced no grief – it is odd that only Joseph's expressions of sorrow are recorded.

50:2 Then Joseph directed the physicians in his service to embalm his father Israel. So the physicians embalmed him, 50:3 taking a full forty days, for that was the time required for embalming. And the Egyptians mourned for him seventy days.

As a high official in the Egyptian government Joseph had personal servants who were doctors. The death of the father of such a high official was not purely a private affair; something like a state funeral was needed. Therefore, instead of following family burial practices, Joseph has Jacob **embalmed** ("mummified") in the Egyptian fashion as befitted a prominent member of Egyptian society. Sarna[2] notes that Joseph did not have Jacob embalmed by professional mortuary priests. This was to avoid the connection with Egyptian religious beliefs ordinarily associated with mummification. This process, we are informed, took **a full forty days**.[3] The entire time of official mourning (lit., "weeping") was seventy days. Such a long[4] official period of mourning is evidence of the high esteem that Joseph enjoyed at Pharaoh's court. Jacob is given a royal burial.

---

[1]The NIV's "threw himself upon his father" is a paraphrase and may unintentionally give the wrong impression.

[2]Sarna, *Genesis*, p. 347.

[3]Mummification involved the removal of the internal organs and placing the body in embalming fluids. While we have no ancient descriptions of embalming, Sarna (*Genesis*, p. 347) notes, "Herodotus (*Histories* 2.86) reports that the body was placed in niter for 70 days. Diodorus of Sicily (Histories 1.91) describes a thirty day dressing of the corpse with oils and spices and seventy-two days of public mourning for a king."

[4]It is not clear whether the 70 days included the 40 days for embalming or followed them. Both Aaron (Num 20:29) and Moses (Deut 34:8) were mourned for thirty days. If the 70 days of Jacob's mourning included the embalming period, Jacob also was mourned for thirty days.

50:4 When the days of mourning had passed, Joseph said to Pharaoh's court, "If I have found favor in your eyes, speak to Pharaoh for me. Tell him, 50:5 'My father made me swear an oath and said, "I am about to die; bury me in the tomb I dug for myself in the land of Canaan." Now let me go up and bury my father; then I will return.'" 50:6 Pharaoh said, "Go up and bury your father, as he made you swear to do."

Joseph dutifully carried out the Egyptian mourning rituals to the end, but this was not the end of the matter. Joseph lived at the intersection of two worlds with two traditions. Having completed a rather elaborate Egyptian set of rituals, he desires to fulfill the wishes of his own father to be buried in the Promised Land. While he approaches the matter deferentially and not directly, he asks members of Pharaoh's house[5] to mediate his request with Pharaoh. Joseph evidently not only had a good reputation with Pharaoh, but also with those who were closest to him, the members of his own extended household. Joseph asks for the favor on the basis that he had already **found favor in** the **eyes** of Pharaoh's household.

Joseph bases his request on the fact that his **father** had **made** him **swear** to bury him in Canaan. What is new is that Joseph claims that Jacob desired to be buried in a tomb which he had himself cut out of rock. In Genesis 49:29-30 only the cave at Machpelah which Abraham, not Jacob, had purchased, is mentioned. While there is a source-critical explanation for the difference between these two texts, are there other plausible explanations?

One possibility is that Joseph wants to hide from Pharaoh the fact that his family had no traditional rights of ownership in Canaan, and the family therefore had to purchase even a grave in order to ensure intergenerational burial. Joseph presents the grave as something that Jacob dug himself, allowing the inference that this must have been on land which he owned. Another possibility is that Jacob did in fact cut a burial chamber for him (and perhaps Leah) within the cave of Machpelah.

Joseph asks for permission to go only on condition that he promises to **return** to Egypt. This undoubtedly would have been a concern of Pharaoh's who would not want to lose a highly valuable advisor. Joseph had accurately anticipated a prolonged famine and in preparing for it, brought the nation through it with the power of Pharaoh significantly strengthened. A purported visit to Canaan **to bury** Joseph's **father** must not, from Pharaoh's point of view, turn into a way of leaving Egypt. Pharaoh recognizes the importance of a solemn promise. On the basis of Joseph's solemn promise to bury his father in Canaan, he allows

---

[5]Not "court" as in the NIV.

Joseph to go. Pharaoh's reticence to allow Joseph to return to Canaan helps to explain why Joseph never sought to visit his family in Canaan before a famine forced them to come to Egypt.

50:7 So Joseph went up to bury his father. All Pharaoh's officials accompanied him—the dignitaries of his court and all the dignitaries of Egypt— 50:8 besides all the members of Joseph's household and his brothers and those belonging to his father's household. Only their children and their flocks and herds were left in Goshen.

When one considers that Egypt had just gone through a seventy-day period of official mourning for Jacob, the list of Egyptians who travel with Joseph to Canaan for the final interment of Jacob is quite striking. The elders and all the servants of Pharaoh's house, along with all the elders of Egypt[6] accompany him. The extraordinary regard that the Egyptian government and ruling elites had come to have for this former enslaved Hebrew criminal can only be marveled at. It is a sign of God's blessing on Joseph, his family, and on the nations through Joseph.

It is not only Egyptian high officials who attend the funeral. The entire **family** attends, whether of Joseph's house, his brothers' houses or even those in Jacob's own house.[7] What is of equal importance is who and what did not go to the funeral. The little **children** and **flocks and herds were left in Goshen**. If Joseph and his brothers had any thought of not returning, they would have to abandon their children and their possessions. Pharaoh made sure that Joseph would return to Egypt. He was simply too valuable to lose.

50:9 Chariots and horsemen also went up with him. It was a very large company.

With such an important group of people it was important to provide security for the trip into Canaan. Although Canaan would have been under Egyptian control at this time, the group was too important for Pharaoh to send them there without protection. Egypt was famous for its use of horses and chariots in its military battles. In the ancient world when most fighting was done by foot soldiers with little weaponry or armor, chariots with horses were a great military advantage. Pharaoh sent the best military guard with the best weaponry possible to protect Joseph, his

---

[6]The NIV paraphrases here.

[7]It is hard to know who exactly would not be in one of the twelve sons' houses that would be in Jacob's house. It could be daughters of Jacob, or his secondary wives, Zilpah and Bilhah. Perhaps even Ephraim and Manasseh, whom Jacob had adopted, would now be regarded as members of Jacob's, as opposed to one of his sons', house.

family, and the Egyptian officials with him. Once again the text emphasizes just how highly regarded Joseph was at the court of Pharaoh.

**50:10 When they reached the threshing floor of Atad, near the Jordan,
they lamented loudly and bitterly; and there Joseph observed a seven-
day period of mourning for his father. 50:11 When the Canaanites
who lived there saw the mourning at the threshing floor of Atad, they
said, "The Egyptians are holding a solemn ceremony of mourning."
That is why that place near the Jordan is called Abel Mizraim.**

This seemingly simple passage is full of interpretive difficulties.
Rather than going immediately to the cave of Machpelah near Hebron,
the funeral party stopped at **the threshing floor of "Atad."** This last
word could be a proper name, as in the NIV, or it could be the word
meaning "thorn." Its exact location is unknown and the descriptive
phrase orienting it in relationship to the Jordan River creates a series of
puzzles. The Hebrew phrase translated in the NIV as "near the Jordan"
(בְּעֵבֶר הַיַּרְדֵּן, *bᵉʿēber hayyardēn*) is usually to be translated as "beyond the
Jordan" from the perspective of the person speaking. This would mean
either west of the Jordan for someone speaking from the east or east of
the Jordan for someone speaking from within Canaan. It can also sometimes mean "in the Jordan valley."[8]

The question is what does it mean in this text? First of all, wherever
it was, Canaanites lived there. This makes the assumption that it means
a place in the Transjordan (i.e., east of the Jordan), where Canaanites
did not typically live, unlikely.

A location that is sometimes suggested is Beth 'Eglaim (Tell el-
'Ajjul) five miles southwest of Gaza on the Mediterranean coast. The
fact that it comes to have a name which includes the name of Egypt in
it (Mizraim) means it had a strong association with Egypt, something
that fits this location, but not as easily one near the Jordan where
Egyptian influence was not as strong. This view makes geographical
sense as it would be a stopover place on the way to Mamre (Hebron) in
the south of Canaan. Sarna[9] helpfully provides Egyptian background
information that would help to explain why they stopped there:

> The name Abel-mizraim suggests that the site had important
> Egyptian connections. It may well be . . . on the eastern Medi-
> terranean coast alongside the desert road that connected the Hyksos
> capital in the Nile Delta with Asia. Excavations have disclosed that

---

[8] B. Gemser, "Beeber Hajjardeb: In Jordan's Borderland," *VT* 2 (1952): 349-
355.

[9] Sarna, *Genesis*, pp. 348-349.

the town was an Egyptian stronghold. Just a little to the south, on the same highway, lies Deir el-Balah, where a large collection of Egyptian-style clay coffins have been found in a Late Bronze Age cemetery. The place was a burial ground for high-ranking Egyptians serving in Canaan and for Egyptianized Canaanite rulers and dignitaries. Such an association would explain why the cortege halted at Abel-mizraim for public homage to Jacob in his own country.

The problem with this view is that the twice-mentioned reference to its location "beyond" or "near" the Jordan makes little sense. The Jordan was the eastern border of Canaan, not its center. Such a location (on the extreme southwestern edge of Canaan) is not likely to have been described as "near the Jordan."

In my judgment the most likely location is somewhere west of the Jordan, but near it. This might suggest that this material actually came from the time when Israel was east of the Jordan at the end of the wilderness period,[10] although it need not do so. The difficulty with the view is that it leaves unexplained why a well-armed Egyptian funeral procession would travel around the south end of the Dead Sea in order to cross back over the Jordan into Canaan and from there travel south to Mamre (Hebron) on the west side of the Dead Sea. They could have more easily traveled directly to Mamre from the south rather than circle the entirety of the Dead Sea. It is striking that the party enters the Promised Land from approximately the same place that the nation of Israel later entered the Promised Land several centuries later. The original and canonical audiences are not likely to have missed this point. And this may be the point. In taking Jacob's (Israel's!) body to Canaan the funeral party anticipated the later route of the people of Israel as they entered the Promised Land. Theology, or perhaps better, divine providence guides geography.[11]

It is striking that after 70 days of official mourning in Egypt, the funeral procession had any tears left with which to "mourn with a very great and heavy mourning."[12] The extent of the mourning by the

---

[10]I cannot see how such a description would make much sense for a hypothe-sized audience in exile in Babylon.

[11]One is reminded of how Matthew, quoting Hosea 11:1 — a text about the nation of Israel — describes the early life of Jesus as including a trip out of Egypt into the Promised Land after the death of Herod because Jesus was the embodiment of the new or true Israel. Cf. Craig L. Blomberg, "Matthew," in *Commentary on the New Testament Use of the Old Testament*, ed. by G.K. Beale and D.A. Carson (Grand Rapids: Baker, 2007), pp. 7-8.

[12]A literal translation of the Hebrew.

Egyptians befits a king, but for Joseph and his family it was very personal. The seven-day mourning period in Canaan has ancient precedent,[13] but some of this could be based on this event.

The Canaanites, observing this large and well-armed Egyptian funeral procession and its elaborate mourning, commented on it. By a word-play between the word אֵבֶל (*'ēbel*) meaning "mourning" and the word אָבֵל (*'ābēl*) meaning "brook," they named the place **Abel-Mizraim**, "brook of Egypt." The author wants to make sure that the readers know that this was "near" or "beyond" the Jordan and so repeats this fact.

50:12 So Jacob's sons did as he had commanded them: 50:13 They carried him to the land of Canaan and buried him in the cave in the field of Machpelah, near Mamre, which Abraham had bought as a burial place from Ephron the Hittite, along with the field. 50:14 After burying his father, Joseph returned to Egypt, together with his brothers and all the others who had gone with him to bury his father.

The seven-day mourning ritual in or near Canaan at Abel-Mizraim was only a preliminary to the actual burial in the cave of the field of Machpelah. **Jacob's sons** obeyed his last wishes by burying him where he had directed them to bury him (Gen 49:29-32).[14] The narrator once again gives a very specific description of the cave's location and another reminder of how the Bedouin Abraham came to have the legal right to the property in which the tomb was located.

This is the fourth detailed description of the location of the grave and the means by which Abraham gained legal ownership of it (Gen 23:1-20; 25:9-11; 49:29-33) and is obviously of great importance to the author. The question is, "Why is it so important?" Certainly part of the answer comes in understanding the difference between ancient Near Eastern society and contemporary societies in their cultural approaches to mourning, burial practices, and the dead in general. Israel in common with most ancient cultures was extremely concerned about how the dead were treated. While Israel, unlike her neighbors, did not worship the dead, at least not in its official theology, one's present identity was very much tied up in where one came from and particularly who one came from. The nation of Israel was a people who began with the decision of

---

[13]1 Sam 31:13 for Saul; Job 2:13 for Job; the Epic of Gilgamesh. Sarna, *Genesis*, p. 349: "This is a well-established rule among Jews by the early second century B.C.E. (Ben Sira 22:12; cf. Jth. 16:24). Strict mourning for seven days . . . following the burial of a close relative has remained the Jewish practice."

[14]Wenham (*Genesis 16–50*, p. 489) suggests that only the sons actually entered Canaan proper and buried their father. As at the burial of Isaac there was reconciliation among the sons of Jacob at his burial.

a wandering Aramean to respond with faith and obedience to God's call to leave his family (Deut 26:5). He and they had no place to call their own for the first several hundred years of their existence. This grave had great significance. It was the down payment on God's promise that they belonged ultimately in Canaan. Israel must know about this grave and its location for it was the (only?) tangible link between their present existence in the land and the promises of God to the patriarchs to one day give the land to them. The readers are reminded that this grave was in **the land of Canaan**. It was specifically "**the cave** of **the field** of **Machpelah** which Abraham purchased." That field **Abraham bought** for a permanent possession of a grave (לַאֲחֻזַּת־קֶבֶר, la'ăḥuzzath-qeber) **from Ephron the Hittite** near Mamre. To the original audience the message was that they belonged in Canaan. After all, their forefathers had been buried there, and they knew the exact place of the grave!

The entire set of rituals for mourning Jacob was extraordinarily elaborate and long. But after it was all over **Joseph** and his brothers **returned to** life in **Egypt**. Abraham had been told that the promise of the land would have to wait for the completing of the iniquity of the residents of the land before it could be given as a divine gift to his descendants (Gen 15:13). On that occasion the family received warning that their sojourn outside of the land would be long and difficult, involving servitude. After burying their father, Joseph and his brothers went back to that strange land (Egypt) to face that future. They knew that one day their descendants would return to the very land where they had just buried their father. Whether they were conscious of this or not, the readers were conscious of it. That grave was the tangible evidence that going back to Egypt would one day be worth it.

XI. FINAL RECONCILIATION BETWEEN JOSEPH AND HIS BROTHERS (50:15-21)

With Jacob finally dead we discover that his brothers had never completely trusted Joseph's forgiveness. They feared that what they had done to him nearly 40 years previously[15] was unforgiveable. And so they make up a story. They send a messenger to Joseph claiming secret knowledge of some final words of Jacob to which Joseph had not been privy. Jacob had supposedly asked Joseph to forgive his brothers for enslaving him. The story is not very plausible. Why would Jacob say this

---

[15]Joseph was about 56 years old at this time; he was about seventeen when he was sold into slavery.

to them and not to Joseph? Joseph is not taken in by the story, but he is taken in by compassion for the guilt that they had been carrying for so long. His reassurances of his forgiveness and his continuing care for them bring the matter to its final resolution. Joseph is not in God's place as judge. Besides their intention in the matter and God's intention in allowing it were very different: the difference between evil and good.

50:15 When Joseph's brothers saw that their father was dead, they said, "What if Joseph holds a grudge against us and pays us back for all the wrongs we did to him?"

After the death and burial of their father Jacob, **Joseph's brothers** fear that they no longer have their father to protect them from any lingering resentment that Joseph might harbor toward them. Jacob is no longer there to keep the peace and Joseph now has the upper hand. The word which the NIV translates as "**grudge**" (יִשְׂטְמֵנוּ, *yiśṭᵊmēnû*) is used elsewhere of Esau's resentment of Jacob for cheating him out of the birthright and blessing (Gen 27:41). Interestingly, on that occasion Esau was waiting for the death and mourning of his father Isaac to pass and then planned to kill Jacob. Joseph's brothers assume that he has been waiting for the same thing. They are unable to believe that, given the heinous nature of their evil[16] deeds against him, it would even be possible for Joseph to have forgiven them. He should surely[17] **pay** them **back**. The power of guilt is such that it sometimes makes us incapable of believing that anyone could ever really forgive us.

50:16 So they sent word to Joseph, saying, "Your father left these instructions before he died: 50:17 'This is what you are to say to Joseph: I ask you to forgive your brothers the sins and the wrongs they committed in treating you so badly.' Now please forgive the sins of the servants of the God of your father." When their message came to him, Joseph wept.

The brothers, afraid that Joseph is about to unleash his pent-up fury on them, make up a story. Reticent to talk with Joseph directly they send Joseph notice of a message supposedly from Joseph's father. In that message from the grave, something like a modern will, Jacob is purported to ask Joseph to forgive the transgressions and sins of his brothers against him. Jacob acknowledges just how completely evil their actions had been. Based upon this (fictitious) message, the brothers then, in their own voice, beg (וְעַתָּה שָׂא נָא, *wᵊ'attāh śā' nā'*; "And now please forgive!") for

---

[16]The NIV translates הָרָעָה (*hārā'āh*) as "wrongs."

[17]The Hebrew uses the emphatic construction here, infinitive absolute followed by the verb of the same root.

forgiveness. They "pile it on" a bit by referring to themselves as "the servants of the God of your father," not as "your brothers."

Joseph sees through the transparent fiction of some message from his father for him after his death. He sees also the inability of his brothers to trust that he has in fact forgiven them. The fact that they would lie in such a transparent attempt to elicit mercy because they could not bring themselves to believe that Joseph had forgiven them saddens Joseph deeply, even to the point of weeping. In a family so fractured by favoritism, forgiveness, the acceptance of forgiveness, and the trust necessary to believe that forgiveness is possible are hard to obtain.

50:18 His brothers then came and threw themselves down before him. "We are your slaves," they said.

We are not told what Joseph's immediate reaction to his brothers' attempt to gain forgiveness was other than weeping. Perhaps he had no time to react in any other way. In any case, his brothers come and fall on their faces before Joseph. The reader cannot but think of the first dream. Although the word "bow down" is not used, their actions and words amount to the same thing. They offer themselves up as Joseph's slaves, hoping that this will save their lives.

50:19 But Joseph said to them, "Don't be afraid. Am I in the place of God? 50:20 You intended to harm me, but God intended it for good to accomplish what is now being done, the saving of many lives. 50:21 So then, don't be afraid. I will provide for you and your children." And he reassured them and spoke kindly to them.

Joseph tells them not to fear any retribution from him. All punishment for sin is the responsibility of God. He is not going to pretend that he is God. While he has not received the revelation of God's torah, Joseph knows that vengeance belongs to God alone (Deut 32:35). While that in itself is a comfort, the statement, if left by itself, does not necessarily indicate that Joseph has forgiven them. He could be saying nothing more than, "I am leaving it to God to punish you!" But Joseph goes further. Joseph sees God's providential hand, even in their evil intentions. According to Joseph the brothers were thinking to do evil to him, but God was thinking of the good that he could do. And what had God done? He had kept a great people alive.[18] The echo of the promise to Abraham is present even in the very last verses in Genesis. The descendants of Abraham are not yet a great nation, but they at least are a great people.

---

[18]The NIV's "the saving of many lives" is a weak paraphrase for לְהַחֲיֹת עַם־רָב (lᵉhaḥăyōth 'am-rāb). This misses the allusion to the promise that God would make Abraham a great and numerous nation.

In verse 21 Joseph goes even further. It is not only that Joseph could see God working in all of this, including even the decision to sell their own brother Joseph as a slave for the Egyptian slave market. He first reassured them by telling them not to be afraid. Then he himself committed himself to use his position and power to go on actively providing for their needs and the needs of their families as he had been doing for the last seventeen years. He then "comforted" them (וַיְנַחֵם, *waynaḥēm*) and "spoke to their hearts" (וַיְדַבֵּר עַל־לִבָּם, *waydabbēr 'al-libbām*). Joseph not only reassured them that he would not seek revenge; he actively cared for and expressed his commitment to care for his brothers in the future. He did not merely leave vengeance in the hands of God. He, for his part, actively forgave them. Joseph has come a long way from the boastful dreamer who thought to make his dreams come true by playing games with the minds of his brothers.

XII. FINAL DAYS OF JOSEPH (50:22-26)

The book of Genesis ends with a quick summary of the rest of Joseph's life. He lived to see the fourth generation of his descendants and to adopt his great-grandsons as his own personal heirs. Like his father Jacob, Joseph secures a promise from his relatives to carry his bones with them when they would later leave Egypt to return to the Promised Land. Joseph dies after a long and eventful life under God's blessing. He also dies still concerned about and believing in the promises of God.

50:22 Joseph stayed in Egypt, along with all his father's family. He lived a hundred and ten years 50:23 and saw the third generation of Ephraim's children. Also the children of Makir son of Manasseh were placed at birth on Joseph's knees.

While we are not told exactly why, this text makes clear that Joseph and the rest of his father's family remained in Egypt long after the famine was over. Certainly Pharaoh had made sure, by keeping their children and flocks in Egypt, that they would return after the burial of Jacob. But why they continued to live there is not explicitly explained. The word translated "**stayed**" (וַיֵּשֶׁב, *wayyēšeb*) in the NIV can imply permanent residence as in this passage. Jacob had anticipated that Joseph would move back to the Promised Land after the famine (Gen 48:21). But this does not happen. Perhaps the comfort and security of their life in Egypt is the explanation, although that is only one explanation.

Joseph lived another 70 years or so after reuniting with his family, attaining the Egyptian ideal[19] of 110[20] years. He **saw** the sons of **the third generation** of his youngest son Ephraim. This would seem to imply five generations, including Joseph, alive at the same time. This would make sense if Joseph lived to 110, a generation usually being about 20 years or so. In any case, the point would be that Joseph lived a good, long life, undoubtedly surviving and thriving through several changes of Egyptian Pharaohs. He lived under the blessing of God.

Since Joseph gave up his own two sons, Manasseh and Ephraim, so that Jacob could adopt them as his own (Gen 48:5) and since he had no other sons besides Manasseh and Ephraim, it seems that Joseph adopts the sons (not "children" as in the NIV) of Manasseh's son Machir, his great-grandsons, as his own. This seems to be the point of the Hebrew phrase "born at the knees of."[21] The clan that descended from Machir was given Gilead in the transjordanian tribe of Manasseh. But in the long run the Machirites were marginalized from influence in the nation because they were geographically cut off from the cisjordanian tribes. Joseph's main contribution to the future of the nation was not through his direct descendants. There was to be no tribe of Joseph. Instead the large and powerful tribes of Ephraim and Manasseh carried on Joseph's legacy.

50:24 Then Joseph said to his brothers, "I am about to die. But God will surely come to your aid and take you up out of this land to the land he promised on oath to Abraham, Isaac and Jacob."

At the end of his long and blessed life, Joseph spoke to **his** "**brothers.**" It is possible that this is to be taken literally and we are to assume that his brothers were actually going to outlive him. In my judgment a more likely possibility is that the word is being used of his family more broadly, of whatever generation. Joseph knows that he is dying, but he has not given up his faith in the promises of God. He reassures them that God would certainly[22] visit[23] them, bring them up from Egypt, and

---

[19]J. Vergote, *Joseph en Egypte* (Louvain: Publications universitaires, 1959), pp. 200-201.

[20]Matthews (*Genesis 11:27–50:26*, p. 931) notes the connection between the age at death of Joseph and Joshua, who actually centuries later interred Joseph's bones in Canaan (Josh 24:32).

[21]In Genesis 30:3 Rachel refers to the children of Bilhah that she would bear for her as "born at my knees." A similar sort of thing happens at the adoption of Manasseh and Ephraim by Jacob in Genesis 48. Cf. Job 3:12; Isa 66:12.

[22]The Hebrew uses the common emphatic construction of infinitive absolute followed by the verb of the same root.

[23]The NIV's "come to your aid" as a translation of פָּקַד (*pāqad*) is a periphrase that is overly interpretive.

give them **the land** that **he** had **promised to** give to **Abraham, Isaac, and Jacob**. Joseph knew that the only hope for Israel staying committed to the promise was if each generation taught the next generation about its importance. In this passage he teaches the next generation with his dying words.

50:25 And Joseph made the sons of Israel swear an oath and said, "God will surely come to your aid, and then you must carry my bones up from this place."

Joseph shows his own faith in God's promise of the land by making his family **swear an oath** to carry his bones up from Egypt to Canaan to be buried. He does not demand, as Jacob had, that he be immediately buried in Canaan. Perhaps the family had no hope of retaining control over the family grave while living in Egypt. But Joseph wanted to eventually be buried in the cave of Machpelah where Abraham, Sarah, Isaac, Rebekah, Leah, and finally Jacob had been buried. It had been over 60 years since Jacob's burial. Instead Joseph makes them swear that when God did indeed "visit"[24] them, as he surely would,[25] they would take his **bones up** with them and bury them in the Promised Land. This promise was remembered and fulfilled when Joseph's bones were interred at Shechem (Exod 13:19; Josh 24:32). Burial in the same place where one's family is buried was a sign of a blessed and fulfilled life. Despite all the trouble that Joseph experienced earlier in his life, at the end of it, he sees the blessings of God. He anticipates with a confident faith the fulfillment of God's promises, even if it will take a long time.

50:26 So Joseph died at the age of a hundred and ten. And after they embalmed him, he was placed in a coffin in Egypt.

After gaining a solemn promise that he would ultimately rest in the Promised Land, Joseph died in Egypt. The repetition of his age at death (110) shows the importance of that figure, probably the ideal age for the death of someone who had lived a long and blessed life. It is also possible that the canonical readers would recognize that even Joseph did not reach the ideal age of 120, that honor being kept for only Moses within the rest of the Pentateuch.[26] Joseph, as a high-ranking Egyptian official who had saved the nation during a prolonged famine, was given an Egyptian burial that honored him. He was **embalmed** ("mummified") in

---

[24]The identical construction is used here as in verse 24. The NIV once again periphrases this as "come to your aid."

[25]Once again the emphatic construction is used as in verse 24.

[26]See the discussion of "his days will be 120 years" on Genesis 6:3 in Kissling, *Genesis Volume 1.*

the Egyptian fashion and placed in a sarcophagus.[27] In this fashion his remains were preserved until they were taken with the Israelites when they left Egypt during the Exodus.

We come to the end of Genesis with faith in the promise firmly fixed but with the realization of it awaiting the future for fulfillment. Joseph's sarcophagus waits to be taken to its proper home in the Promised Land just as the nation waits for the same thing.

---

[27]The NIV's "coffin" is a paraphrase, which does not take account of Egyptian burial practices.

www.ingramcontent.com/pod-product-compliance
Lightning Source LLC
Chambersburg PA
CBHW060320100426
42812CB00003B/826